THE OXFORD HANDBOOK OF

LANGUAGE AND LAW

OXFORD HANDBOOKS IN LINGUISTICS

RECENTLY PUBLISHED

The Oxford Handbook of Language Evolution
Edited by Maggie Tallerman and Kathleen Gibson

The Oxford Handbook of Arabic Linguistics
Edited by Jonathan Owens

The Oxford Handbook of Corpus Phonology
Edited by Jacques Durand, Ulrike Gut, and Gjert Kristoffersen

The Oxford Handbook of Linguistic Fieldwork
Edited by Nicholas Thieberger

The Oxford Handbook of Derivational Morphology
Edited by Rochelle Lieber and Pavol Štekauer

The Oxford Handbook of Historical Phonology
Edited by Patrick Honeybone and Joseph Salmons

The Oxford Handbook of Linguistic Analysis
Second Edition
Edited by Bernd Heine and Heiko Narrog

The Oxford Handbook of The Word
Edited by John R. Taylor

The Oxford Handbook of Inflection
Edited by Matthew Baerman

The Oxford Handbook of Developmental Linguistics
Edited by Jeffrey Lidz, William Snyder, and Joe Pater

The Oxford Handbook of Lexicography
Edited by Philip Durkin

The Oxford Handbook of Names and Naming
Edited by Carole Hough

The Oxford Handbook of Information Structure
Edited by Caroline Féry and Shinichiro Ishihara

The Oxford Handbook of Modality and Mood
Edited by Jan Nuyts and Johan van der Auwera

The Oxford Handbook of Language and Law
Edited by Peter M. Tiersma and Lawrence M. Solan

For a complete list of Oxford Handbooks in Linguistics please see pp. 643–4

THE OXFORD HANDBOOK OF

LANGUAGE
AND LAW

Edited by

PETER M. TIERSMA

and

LAWRENCE M. SOLAN

OXFORD
UNIVERSITY PRESS

OXFORD
UNIVERSITY PRESS

Great Clarendon Street, Oxford, OX2 6DP,
United Kingdom

Oxford University Press is a department of the University of Oxford.
It furthers the University's objective of excellence in research, scholarship,
and education by publishing worldwide. Oxford is a registered trade mark of
Oxford University Press in the UK and in certain other countries

First published 2012
First published in paperback 2016

Published in the United States of America by Oxford University Press
198 Madison Avenue, New York, NY 10016, United States of America

British Library Cataloguing in Publication Data
Data available

Library of Congress Cataloging in Publication Data
Data available

ISBN 978-0-19-957212-0 (Hbk.)
ISBN 978-0-19-874496-2 (Pbk.)

ACKNOWLEDGMENTS

We would like to thank Loyola Law School for supporting this project via the Hon. William Matthew Byrne chair, and Brooklyn Law School for supporting the project through a Dean's Summer Research Stipend.

We also wish to express our appreciation to Loyola Law School graduate Laura Mismas and Brooklyn Law School student Elliott Siebers for research assistance.

Finally, the staff at Oxford University Press was very helpful throughout the editing process.

CONTENTS

PART III. MULTILINGUALISM AND TRANSLATION

PART IV. LANGUAGE RIGHTS

PART V. LANGUAGE AND CRIMINAL LAW

PART VI. COURTROOM DISCOURSE

PART VII. INTELLECTUAL PROPERTY

PART VIII. IDENTIFICATION OF AUTHORSHIP AND DECEPTION

PART IX. SPEAKER IDENTIFICATION

Preface to the Paperback Edition

In early 2012, Peter Tiersma and I wrote the Introduction to the original hardcover edition of the *Oxford Handbook of Language and Law*. At the time, Peter was combatting cancer. Sensitive to his fragile health, Oxford University Press published the book quickly—not an easy feat when it comes to producing such a large and complex volume. We were delighted with the publisher's excellent work, and celebrated the book's publication in the summer of that year. The *Handbook* contains many truly excellent articles by leading scholars in their fields. We were proud to have assembled a volume of such distinction. Perhaps other editors would have made different choices, and a multivolume set would have relieved us of the obligation to make as many decisions as we did. All in all, though, we believed this to be a very good book.

I write the preface to this paperback edition alone, which is a very painful experience, even though more than a year has passed since Peter passed away. Once again, though, I celebrate Oxford's support of these excellent contributions to the field. This is not a "Second Edition." There are no new pieces, and nothing has been deleted. Some articles are lightly edited and updated from the original 2012 publication. Other than that, the biggest difference between the two publications is the price, making these contributions more accessible to the people across disciplines who take an interest in the relationship between language and law.

Peter and I decided not to dedicate the original *Handbook*. Now, things have changed. Together, the contributors to this book dedicate this edition,

To the Memory of Peter Tiersma, 1952–2014

Lawrence M. Solan
Brooklyn New York
August 2015

Contributors

Mark Adler graduated in philosophy and then obtained a teaching certificate. He spent some thirty years in general practice as an English solicitor, adopting a "plain language" policy in the early 1980s. Since 1991 he has given seminars in the UK and overseas on plain legal writing. He has been chairman of Clarity and editor of its journal *Clarity*. He retired in 2007 but remains an active member of the plain language movement. Website: www.adler.demon.co.uk.

Janet Ainsworth is John D. Eshelman Professor at Seattle University School of Law. She writes for an interdisciplinary audience, applying research on language and communication to critique legal doctrines and case law in a variety of contexts, including criminal procedure, evidence law, employment law, and trial practice. A unifying theme to her work is its emphasis on exposing the influence of mistaken concepts of the nature of language in legal ideology and practice.

Cornelis J. W. Baaij is PhD researcher at the University of Amsterdam School of Law and founder of the Amsterdam Circle for Law and Language. His research concentrates on the methodological relations between law and language, within the fields of comparative law, legal interpretation, and legal translation studies. His particular point of interest is the impact of Europe's multilingualism on the possibilities of legal harmonization in the EU.

Michel Bastarache, C.C. was a judge of the Supreme Court of Canada from 1997 to 2008. He has also worked as a civil servant; a law professor and law dean; a businessman; a practicing lawyer; and a provincial appeal court judge. He has written extensively on language rights and other subjects of public law and is the editor and principal author of three books. Mr Bastarache is counsel to the law firm Heenan Blaikie.

Robert W. Bennett is the Nathaniel L. Nathanson Professor of Law at Northwestern Law School, where he also served as dean from 1985 to 1995. His most recent book, "Constitutional Originalism: A Debate" (Cornell University Press, 2011) engages issues of constitutional interpretation in a debate format, with Bennett and Larry Solum of Georgetown Law School exchanging principal essays and then responses.

Susan Berk-Seligson is Research Professor in the Department of Spanish and Portuguese of Vanderbilt University. Her research focuses on the experience of Spanish speakers in the U.S. criminal justice system, both in the courtroom and in pre-trial phases. Recent publications include *Coerced Confessions: The Discourse of*

Bilingual Police Interrogations (Mouton de Gruyter 2009) and the forthcoming third edition of *The Bilingual Courtroom: Court Interpreters in the Judicial Process* (University of Chicago Press 2016). She regularly serves as an expert in civil cases related to English-Only discriminatory workplace policies and in criminal cases involving capital crimes and other felonies.

Brian H. Bix is the Frederick W. Thomas Professor of Law and Philosophy at the University of Minnesota. He holds a JD from Harvard University and a D.Phil. from Oxford University. His publications include *Jurisprudence: Theory and Context* (5th edn, Sweet & Maxwell, 2009), *A Dictionary of Legal Theory* (Oxford, 2004), and *Law, Language, and Legal Determinacy* (Oxford, 1993).

Ronald R. Butters is Emeritus Professor of English and Cultural Anthropology and former chair of the Linguistics Program at Duke University, where he began teaching in 1967. He has served as president of the American Dialect Society, the Southeastern Conference on Linguistics, and the International Association of Forensic Linguists (2008–11), and he is a former co-editor of *The International Journal of Speech, Language, and the Law*. He consults frequently with American attorneys and has testified in forensic linguistic cases for over twenty years. His practical and scholarly interests include (1) ethical issues in forensic linguistic consulting, (2) statutes and contracts, (3) death-penalty appeals, (4) copyrights, (5) discourse analysis of linguistic evidence, (6) lexicography, and (7) linguistic and semiotic issues in trademark litigation.

Jasone Cenoz is Professor of Education at the University of the Basque Country. Her research focuses on multilingual education, bilingualism, and multilingualism. She is the editor (in collaboration with Ulrike Jessner) of the *International Journal of Multilingualism*. Her most recent books are *Towards Multilingual Education: Basque Educational Research in International Perspective* (Multilingual Matters) and *The Multiple Realities of Multilingualism* (edited in collaboration with Elka Todeva, Mouton de Gruyter).

Carole E. Chaski, PhD is the Executive Director of the Institute for Linguistic Evidence, the first non-profit research organization devoted to linguistic evidence and the CEO of ALIAS Technology LLC. Dr Chaski held a Visiting Research Fellowship (1995–98) at the US Department of Justice's National Institute of Justice, where she began the validation testing which has become an increasingly important aspect of forensic sciences since the Daubert ruling, and introduced the computational, pattern recognition paradigm to questioned document examination and forensic linguistics. Dr Chaski has served as an expert witness in Federal and State Courts in the USA, in Canada and in The Hague. Primarily a researcher and software developer, Dr Chaski consults with corporations, defense, and security on computational linguistic applications. Dr Chaski earned her doctorate and master's in linguistics at Brown University, her master's in psychology of reading at the University of Delaware and her bachelor's in English and Ancient Greek from Bryn Mawr College.

Malcolm Coulthard is Emeritus Professor of Forensic Linguistics at the University of Aston. He is probably still best known for his work on the analysis of spoken and written discourse, but since the late 1980s he has become increasingly involved with forensic applications of linguistics. He has written expert reports in over 200 cases and given evidence on author identification in the Courts of Appeal in London, as well as in lower courts in England, Germany, Hong Kong, and Northern Ireland. Recent publications include (with Alison Johnson) *An Introduction to Forensic Linguistics* (2007) and *A Handbook of Forensic Linguistics* (2010).

Deborah Davis, PhD is Professor of Psychology at the University of Nevada, Reno, and President of Sierra Trial and Opinion Consultants. She has worked as a jury consultant and as an expert witness on witness memory, coerced confessions, and sexual consent. She publishes frequently in these areas, including a 100-page review article on interrogations and a chapter on jury selection in the recent *Handbook of Forensic Psychology*, and chapters on sources of distortion in eyewitness memory and on memory for conversation in the recent *Handbook of Eyewitness Psychology*. Website: http://www.unr.edu/psych/faculty/davis.html.

Jan Engberg is Professor of Knowledge Communication at the Department of Business Communication, University of Aarhus, Denmark. His main areas of interest are the study of texts and genres, cognitive aspects of domain-specific discourse, and basic aspects of communication in domain-specific settings. The focus of his research is on communication and translation in the field of law. In this connection, he is co-chair of the section on LSP communication of the German Association for Applied Linguistics (GAL) and co-editor of the international journals *Hermes* and *Fachsprache*.

Paul Foulkes is Professor in the Department of Language and Linguistic Science at the University of York. His teaching and research interests include sociolinguistics, language variation and change, phonetics, phonology, and child language acquisition as well as forensic speech science. He is also a consultant analyst with J P French Associates, and has worked on over 200 speaker comparison cases.

Peter French is a Director of J P French Associates, the United Kingdom's longest established forensic laboratory specializing in the analysis of speech, audio, and language. He is Honorary Professor in the Department of Language and Linguistic Science at the University of York, where he teaches, undertakes, and supervises research in forensic speech science and sociophonetics. He is President of the International Association for Forensic Phonetics and Acoustics, a Fellow and UK Secretary of the International Society for Phonetic Science and a Fellow of the Institute of Acoustics. He has worked on over 5,000 cases being heard before courts up to and including the International Commission of Enquiry and International War Crimes Tribunal levels. He has appeared in court as an expert witness over 200 times.

Masahiro Fujita is a professor of social psychology at the Faculty of Sociology of Kansai University. He is one of the leading experts in psychology and law in Japan. He has been vigorously applying disciplines and methods in social psychology to decision-making processes in criminal proceedings.

Naomi E. S. Goldstein, PhD is Associate Professor of Psychology at Drexel University and a member of the faculty of the JD-PhD Program in Law and Psychology at Villanova Law School and Drexel University. Dr Goldstein specializes in forensic psychology, and her research examines juvenile suspects' capacities to waive Miranda rights and offer confessions during police interrogations. She also developed and is evaluating the efficacy of the Juvenile Justice Anger Management (JJAM) Treatment for Girls.

Durk Gorter is Ikerbasque research professor at the Faculty of Education of the University of the Basque Country in San Sebastian/Donostia, where he leads the Donostia Research group on Education and Multilingualism. He does work on European minority languages, linguistic landscapes, and multilingualism, in particular in educational settings. He has published numerous books and articles on those themes. From 1979 to 2007 he was a researcher in the sociology of language and head of the department of social sciences at the Fryske Akademy in Ljouwert/Leeuwarden, the Netherlands. He was also professor in the sociolinguistics of Frisian at the University of Amsterdam.

Maurizio Gotti is Professor of English Language and Translation and Director of the Research Centre on Specialized Languages (CERLIS) at the University of Bergamo. His main research areas are the features and origins of specialized discourse (*Robert Boyle and the Language of Science*, Guerini, 1996; *Specialized Discourse: Linguistic Features and Changing Conventions*, Peter Lang, 2003; *Investigating Specialized Discourse*, Peter Lang, 2011). He is a member of the editorial board of national and international journals, and edits the Linguistic Insights series for Peter Lang.

Risto Hiltunen is Professor of English at the University of Turku, Finland. His research interests include history of English, medieval and early modern English, the English language in legal settings, and discourse studies. He has recently published in the *Journal of Historical Pragmatics* and *Journal of Pragmatics*. He is one of the associate editors of *Records of the Salem Witch-Hunt* (Cambridge University Press, 2009).

Syûgo Hotta is a professor of language and law at Meiji University School of Law in Japan. His fields of interest extends from theoretical linguistics to language and law. Among the fields of language and law, he has been working on psycholinguistic aspects of trademarks and corpus-based analyses of lay participation in Japanese criminal courts.

Martha L. Komter has worked as assistant professor at the departments of Criminology and Sociology of Law at the Faculty of Law of the University of Amsterdam. She is currently senior researcher at the Department of Language and Communication of the Faculty of Arts of the Vrije Universiteit in Amsterdam. She has published widely on talk in various institutional settings: job interviews, courtroom interaction, and police interrogations.

Krzysztof Kredens received his MA in English Studies and PhD in English Linguistics from the University of Łódź (Poland). He is now a Lecturer in Applied Linguistics in the School of Languages and Social Sciences at Aston University (UK). His main academic interests are in socio-legal applications of linguistics including forensic linguistics, legal translation, and court and police interpreting. He is Deputy Director of Aston University's Centre for Forensic Linguistics and Secretary of the International Association of Forensic Linguists.

Richard A. Leo, PhD, JD, is a Professor at the University of San Francisco School of Law and a Fellow in the Institute of Legal Research at University of California Berkeley (Boalt Hall) School of Law. He is an expert on police interrogation practices, false confessions, *Miranda* requirements, and wrongful convictions. Professor Leo has published numerous books and articles on these subjects, regularly lectures on these subjects to criminal justice professionals across the country, and has consulted and/or testified as an expert witness in hundreds of cases. Dr Leo's 2008 book *Police Interrogation and American Justice* (Harvard University Press, 2008) has won several awards. In 2011 he received a Guggenheim fellowship. Website: http://www.usfca.edu/law/faculty/frames/FullTime.html.

As of 2016 **Karen McAuliffe** is a Reader in Law and Birmingham Fellow at the School of Law, Birmingham University. She holds a PhD and LLB from the Queen's University of Belfast and had also studied at l'Université Catholique de Louvain in Belgium and the Academy of European Public Law in Greece. Prior to entering academia she worked as a lawyer-linguist at the Court of Justice of the European Union in Luxembourg. Her main research interests lie in multilingual law production and the relationship between language, law, and translation in the EU legal order and she has published extensively in this area. She is currently working on a 5-year research project, funded by the European Research Council, on law and language at the European Court of Justice. Further details of that project and her other research can be found on her website at www.karenmcauliffe.com.

Marijke Malsch is a senior researcher at the Netherlands Institute for the Study of Crime and Law Enforcement (NSCR) in Amsterdam, the Netherlands. Malsch is also working as an honorary judge at the Appeals Court of Den Bosch and the District Court of Haarlem.

Nancy S. Marder is a Professor of Law and Director of the Justice John Paul Stevens Jury Center at Chicago-Kent College of Law. She is a graduate of Yale College, Cambridge University, and Yale Law School, where she was an articles editor of the *Yale Law Journal*. She then clerked for Justice John Paul Stevens at the US Supreme Court. She has written numerous articles and a book on the jury, and has presented her work at conferences in the USA and abroad.

Heikki E. S. Mattila is Doctor of Laws, Professor Emeritus of Legal Linguistics (University of Lapland, Finland), and Docent of Comparative Law (University of Helsinki). His research fields include comparative law and comparative legal linguistics, that is studies concerning different legal languages, especially legal Latin and legal French. He also researches general questions of legal language, for example, legal abbreviations. He recently published a general treatise on language(s) and law (in French and English): *Jurilinguistique comparée: langage du droit, latin et langues modernes* (Les Éditions Yvon Blais, 2012) and *Comparative Legal Linguistics: Language of Law, Latin, Modern Lingua Francas* (2nd edn). (Ashgate, 2013).

Liao Meizhen obtained his PhD in linguistics from the Chinese Academy of Social Sciences. He is a professor of linguistics and associate dean of the School of Foreign Languages, Central China Normal University. His academic interests include pragmatics, forensic linguistics, and metaphor. His representative publications include "Metaphor as a Textual Strategy in English" (*Text* 9, 2, 1999), "A Study of Interruption in Chinese Criminal Courtroom Discourse" (*Text & Talk* 29-2, 2009) and *A Study on Courtroom Questions, Responses and their Interaction* (Law Press, Beijing, 2003). Email: meizhenliao@sohu.com.

Sharon Messenheimer is a JD-PhD student in the law-psychology program at Drexel University and Villanova University School of Law. Her research interests include juveniles' comprehension of *Miranda* rights, forensic psychological assessment, and the relationship between police interrogation strategies and false confessions.

Janice Nadler is Research Professor at the American Bar Foundation, and Professor of Law at Northwestern University School of Law. She received a JD from the University of California at Berkeley, and a PhD in social psychology from the University of Illinois, Urbana-Champaign. Her scholarly interests lie at the intersection of law and psychology, and her research focuses on moral intuitions, compliance with the law, perceptions of injustice, negotiation, and dispute resolution.

Mami Hiraike Okawara is Professor and Dean of the University Library, Takasaki City University of Economics, Japan. Okawara is a public member of the Gunma Prefecture Local Labor Relations Commission and a mediator at Maebashi Family Court. She served as a research member of the plain courtroom language project of the Japan Federation of Bar Associations. She received her doctorate in linguistics at Sydney University. Her research interests include legal language analysis as well as author attribution analysis. She now serves as president of the Japan Association for Language and Law.

Tunde Olusola Opeibi, PhD, is Associate Professor in the Department of English, University of Lagos, Nigeria. He has been a Visiting Commonwealth Fellow at Westminster University, London, and Research Fellow of the Alexander Von Humboldt Foundation, Germany. His areas of research interest include discourse analysis, sociolinguistics, political communication, language and law, new media and civic engagement, and corpus linguistics. He is Nigeria's representative of Clarity (an international association promoting plain legal language). He has authored and co-edited full-length books and published several academic articles in journals in Nigeria and other parts of the world.

Peter L. Patrick is Professor of Sociolinguistics at the University of Essex, and a Member of the Essex Human Rights Centre. His research interests include language variation, Creole languages, applied sociolinguistics, language rights, and forensic linguistics. He was born in New York City and educated in Kingston, Georgia, and Pennsylvania. He is convenor, with Diane Eades, of the *Language & Asylum Research Group* (LARG) and a co-author of the 2004 *Guidelines for the use of language analysis … in refugee cases*.

Ralf Poscher is Professor of Public Law and Director of the Institute for Staatswissenschaft and Philosophy of Law, Dep. 2: Philosophy of Law at the Albert-Ludwigs University in Freiburg, Germany. He holds a PhD in Law and was awarded the post-doctorate degree "Habilitation" with the *venia legendi* for Public Law, History of Constitutional Law and Legal Philosophy, at the Humboldt-University Berlin. His writings include a wide range of topics in public law and jurisprudence. He has published books (in German) about the theory of fundamental rights and the concept of probability in police law and co-authored volumes in domestic and international public law. His most recent writings in English cover jurisprudential questions such as a critique of the principal theory of Robert Alexy, and the Hart–Dworkin debate. In 2007 he held a research fellowship at the University of Osaka, Japan and for the academic year 2007/08 was a Member of the Institute for Advanced Study in Princeton, USA. Together with Geert Keil (Philosophy, Humboldt-University Berlin) he coordinates the research group "Dealing Reasonably with Blurred Boundaries," funded by the Volkswagen Foundation.

Frances Rock is a Senior Lecturer in Language and Communication at Cardiff University, Wales, UK. Her research interests are in discourse analysis, interactional sociolinguistics, and literacies, drawing on broadly linguistic ethnographic methods. She is currently working on applications of language study to policing and other workplace and legal settings. Her research investigates both written and spoken language. She is an editor of the *International Journal of Speech, Language and the Law*.

Christina L. Riggs Romaine, MS is a PhD student in the clinical psychology program at Drexel University in Philadelphia, Pennsylvania. She is currently completing her clinical internship at the University of Massachusetts Medical School/Worcester State Hospital. Her research interests include *Miranda* comprehension and forensic assessment of juveniles, mental health treatment of offending and at-risk youth, and the effects of trauma on adolescents.

Susan Šarčević is Emeritus Professor of Legal German and Legal English and former head of the Department of Foreign Languages at the Faculty of Law of the University of Rijeka (Croatia). At the postgraduate level she taught Legal Translation, EU Institutions, and Translating EU Legislation at the University of Zagreb. Best known for her book *New Approach to Legal Translation*, she has published extensively on legal translation, legal lexicography, and multilingualism in the law. Her most recent publication (editor and author) is *Language and Culture in EU Law: Multidisciplinary Perspectives*. She has lectured worldwide on legal translation and is Research Professor at the Research Centre for Legal Translation of the China University of Political Science and Law in Beijing.

Sanford Schane is a Research Professor of Linguistics at the University of California, San Diego, where he continues to offer each year an undergraduate course, "Law and Language". He has worked with attorneys as a consultant and expert witness. He has published in law reviews and is the author of the book, *Language and the Law*.

Roger W. Shuy is Distinguished Research Professor of Linguistics, Emeritus, Georgetown University, where he taught graduate seminars in sociolinguistics and language and law. He has testified at trials in over 50 of the 500 criminal and civil cases he's worked on, and before the US Congress and International Criminal Tribunals. Since retiring in 1996, he has published ten books and a number of articles on the intersection of linguistics and law.

Tove Skutnabb-Kangas, emerita (University of Roskilde, Denmark and Åbo Akademi University, Finland), bilingual from birth in Finnish and Swedish, has written or edited around 50 monographs and over 400 articles and book chapters, in 46 languages, about minority education, multilingualism, linguistic human rights, linguistic genocide, the subtractive spread of English, and the relationship between biodiversity and linguistic diversity. She and her husband Robert Phillipson now live in Sweden, having spent 30 years on an ecological farm in Denmark. For publications, see www.Tove-Skutnabb-Kangas.org.

Lawrence M. Solan is the Don Forchelli Professor of Law and Director of the Center for the Study of Law, Language and Cognition at Brooklyn Law School. He holds a PhD in Linguistics from the University of Massachusetts and a JD from Harvard Law School. His writings address such issues as statutory and contractual interpretation, the attribution of responsibility and blame, and the role of the expert in the courts. His books include *The Language of Judges*, *Speaking of Crime* (with Peter Tiersma), and *The Language of Statutes: Laws and their Interpretation*, all published by the University of Chicago Press. Solan has been a visiting professor at the Yale Law School, and in the Psychology Department and Linguistics Program at Princeton University. Prior to joining the Brooklyn Law School faculty in 1996, he was a partner at a New York law firm.

Gail Stygall is professor of English Language at the University of Washington, Seattle. Her work focuses on legal discourse. Recent work has appeared in the *Routledge Handbook of Forensic Linguistics* (2010), the *International Journal of Speech, Language, and the Law* (2010), and the *Journal of English Linguistics* (2008). She is currently working on a book on complex documents—credit card agreements, mortgage disclosure agreements, pension and benefit plans, and EULAs and TOSAs online.

Peter M. Tiersma was the Hon. William Matthew Byrne Professor of Law at Loyola Law School in Los Angeles until his death in 2014. He received a PhD in linguistics from the University of California, San Diego, and a JD degree from the University of California, Berkeley. Tiersma wrote extensively on the relationship between language and law, including the books *Legal Language* (1999), *Speaking of Crime: The Language of Criminal Justice* (2005; with Lawrence Solan), and *Parchment, Paper, Pixels: Law and the Technologies of Communication* (2010). Website: www.languageandlaw.org.

J. D. Trout (PhD, Philosophy, Cornell University) is a professor of philosophy and psychology at Loyola University in Chicago. His books include *Measuring the Intentional World* (Oxford University Press, 1998), *Epistemology and the Psychology of Human Judgment* (with Michael Bishop; Oxford University Press, 2005), and *The Empathy Gap* (Viking/Penguin, 2009). His research has been supported by NSF, NEH, and Mellon grants, and his articles have appeared in *Philosophy of Science*, *Psychological Review*, *Law & Philosophy*, and *Speech Communication*.

David Woolls qualified and practiced as a chartered accountant until his early thirties, then read Theology and Philosophy at Oxford University before discovering both computing and linguistics. Since the late 1980s he has worked closely with universities, in particular Birmingham and Aston in the UK, developing a range of linguistic computer programs as tools to assist both forensic linguists and students. He is now CEO of CFL Software Limited, whose software programs are used by education, the music industry, and the legal profession, among others.

A. Daniel Yarmey received his PhD from the University of Western Ontario and is University Professor Emeritus at the University of Guelph, Guelph, Ontario, Canada. He conducts research on speaker identification, eyewitness memory and identification, and deception. His books and chapters include *The Psychology of Eyewitness Testimony* and *Understanding Police and Police Work: Psychosocial Issues*. He also works as an expert court witness in Canada and the USA.

Heather Zelle, MS is a JD-PhD student in the law-psychology program at Drexel University and Villanova University School of Law. Her research interests focus on the application of social science to the law, including *Miranda* comprehension, forensic psychological assessment, test development, and mental health treatment of offending and at-risk youth.

Abbreviations and Acronyms

ADHD	attention-deficit hyperactivity disorder
ASA	Advertising Standards Authority (UK)
CCT	Common Customs Tariff
CLS	critical legal studies
COE	Council of Europe
COI	Country of Origin Information
CORI	Country of Origin Research and Information
CRC	*Convention on the Rights of the Child*
CTARC	Communicated Threat Assessment Resource Corpus
DTF	decision tree forest
EBLUL	European Bureau for Lesser Used Languages
EC	European Commission
ECHR	European Court of Human Rights
ECJ	Court of Justice of the European Union/European Court of Justice
EEC	European Economic Community
EFTA	European Free Trade Area
ESL	English as a Second Language
EU	European Union
EULA	end-user license agreement
FBI	Federal Bureau of Investigation (USA)
HCNM	High Commissioner on National Minorities
HRs	human rights
IAFPA	International Association for Forensic Phonetics and Acoustics
ICANN	Internet Corporation for Assigned Names and Numbers
ICCPR	*International Covenant on Civil and Political Rights*
IPA	International Phonetic Alphabet
IPI	Illinois Pattern Jury Instructions
ITMs	indigenous/tribal peoples or minorities
LADO	Language Analysis for Determination of Origin
LD(F)A	linear discriminant function analysis
LEP	limited English proficiency
LHRs	Linguistic Human Rights
LNOG	Language and National Origin Group
LOTE	language other than English

LR	likelihood ratio
LR	logistic regression
LRs	linguistic/language rights
LWC	language of wider communication
MTM	mother-tongue-medium
NATO	North Atlantic Treaty Organisation
NENS	non-expert native speaker
NEP	no English proficiency
NGO	non-governmental organization
NS	native speaker
OCILA	Office of Country Information and Language Analysis (Netherlands)
OSCE	Organization for Security and Co-operation in Europe
POS	part of speech
RSD	Refugee Status Determination
RT	reaction time
UCAS	Universities and Colleges Admissions Service (UK)
UN	United Nations
UNCITRAL	United Nations Commission on International Trade Law
UNDRIP	*UN Declaration on the Rights of Indigenous Peoples*
UNHCR	UN High Commissioner for Refugees (known as the UN Refugee Agency)
UNIDROIT	International Institute for the Unification of Private Law
WTO	World Trade Organization

INTRODUCTION

LAWRENCE M. SOLAN
PETER M. TIERSMA

PAIRING language and law seems so natural. Even mentioning their relationship triggers one interesting question after another: What is it about legal language that sounds so different, even though it must be some dialect of natural language or we would not understand it at all? What linguistic features of laws and other legal documents make them susceptible to lawyerly manipulation, and is there a way to combat this practice? How does the language of police interaction with citizens, or interaction within the courtroom, reflect the power relationships that people experience when they enter those realms, whether voluntarily or otherwise? What happens when a society is comprised of people who speak different languages, but the legal system privileges just one of them? How well can nations with different legal systems practiced in different languages build multilingual, multinational institutions in which the players all understand their rights and obligations similarly? Can the explosion of learning about language and cognition be harnessed to produce reliable expert evidence in the courtroom on such matters as identifying people by the way they speak or write? If intellectual property consists of language, does that mean that a person or company can literally own a part of our linguistic heritage?

We elaborate on these questions briefly in this introduction and, of course, the following chapters of this state of the art *Handbook* address all of these matters. First, though, we wish to explore a foundational issue: What has happened over the past twenty-five years or so that has both enabled and triggered the wealth of learning that has begun to respond to these questions so fruitfully?

We believe that two entirely independent intellectual developments have triggered the advances that have recently been made in the study of language and law. One is the rise of interdisciplinary work in the study of law. The other is the tremendous foothold that linguistics has taken in the intellectual world.

The study of law has become comfortably interdisciplinary in the past thirty years. The major infiltrators were not the language sciences, but rather economics and sociology.

The study of law and economics, driven by the work of scholars such as Judge Richard Posner, has become a booming enterprise. Law and society research has also bloomed. As a consequence, it has become almost impossible to regard law as an autonomous discipline. And through economics, psychology entered the mainstream of legal thinking, in part through the work of such thinkers as Daniel Kahneman and Amos Tversky, whose pioneering research on cognitive biases and heuristics won Kahneman the Nobel Prize in economics after Tversky's death.

Other psychologists (and a few linguists, for that matter) were making inroads into the legal world by addressing such issues as juror comprehension and competence to stand trial. Over time, all of this interest in the contributions of other fields to the study of law has made legal thinkers more receptive to cross-disciplinary thought in general, and open to linguistic research in particular. In the 1990s, linguists were still offering arguments to justify their entry into the study of law and legal institutions. Such arguments are no longer necessary, at least not in the scholarly community.

Outside the academy, the reception has been more mixed. Nonetheless, in some areas, such as reforming jury instructions, policymakers in the United States have welcomed linguistic advice. Similarly, judges have not been afraid to cite the work of those engaged in the study of language and law to justify their decisions. In Britain, linguists have been participating actively in the rewriting of documents used to inform people of their rights in various legal settings. In the rest of Europe, where the civil law tradition dominates, translation theorists have become important in dealing with an increasingly multilingual legal order. There is growing interest in the study of language and law in China, and in Japan linguists have helped implement a new system of lay judges. Throughout the world, linguists have been welcomed into courtrooms as experts on such diverse issues as trademark law, speaker and author identification, and the meanings of statutes and contracts.

All of this activity is made possible because the study of language has grown exponentially since the middle of the twentieth century. Major universities throughout the world now have well-entrenched departments of linguistics, the members of which conduct research into every aspect of language. This is not the place to summarize this work, but we have identified a few basic—and for the most part uncontroversial—advances that serve, at least in general terms, as foundations for the growth in the study of language and law.

First, if the study of language has taught us anything over the past half century, it has taught us that while languages differ from each other, people are largely the same. We are born without any predisposition to learn any particular language. Rather, we come into the world equipped to learn whichever language(s) we are exposed to as children, which means that the languages themselves, while diverse, must somehow be sufficiently constrained in their structure, sound, and meaning to be accessible to whatever capacity we have to learn and use them. We take it that people who speak the same language have, by and large, acquired the same competence. It is this underlying assumption—generally affirmed by our experience in everyday interaction—that permits us to rely so heavily on language in our social institutions, including legal ones. If we all speak and understand our language more or less the same way, then we can put language to work in establishing societal rules of the road. A language-based rule of law assumes a base of language common to all.

Second, whatever we have in common with one another, we are all individuals. What we have learned about our native languages and their usage is personal to us. Our everyday working assumption that others speak, write, and understand language just the way we do is just that—an assumption. Differences among us may lead to misunderstanding, some of which goes unnoticed. And nuances in the linguistic habits of each of us as individuals may create the basis of distinguishing our speech and writing from the speech and writing of others, creating a tool for investigators. How individual our speech and writing are and how well we can draw inferences from linguistic differences are a matter of current research, and a significant amount of disagreement.

Third, however we may best characterize our individual knowledge of language, and however completely our knowledge of language is shared by others, language is without question a social phenomenon. And its use is instrumental: We can use language for all kinds of purposes. The language itself is robust enough for us to use it to describe a bucolic scene, or instrumentally: whether for egalitarian goals, to consolidate power in ourselves or others on whose behalf we act, or for a host of other purposes. Through language, we establish societal institutions, including legal ones. These institutions, like the languages through which they are created, differ from one another in salient ways, but also share a great deal of underlying structure. The more we know about the use of language in institutional settings, the better we can study particular institutions—legal ones in particular—and learn about their structure and the relationships among them.

Some of this learning has profound implications for how legal systems perform. Our understanding of the rule of law has at its core the notion that rules and norms can be expressed in language, and that therefore we can govern ourselves according to principles, rather than the personal preferences of individuals. This is the source of the maxim, "the rule of law, and not the rule of men," and it is crucially language-dependent.

Moreover, a great deal of research into the subsystems of language can be put to good use in the study of legal systems and institutions. Work in the areas of phonology and phonetics has taught us enough about sounds and sound systems of language to enable linguists to identify with some level of certainty whether an individual's voice and speech match those of a known individual, either using conventional methods of phonetics, or teaming up with engineers and computer scientists to develop algorithms that perform these tasks automatically. It has also taught us a great deal about which sounds are likely to be confused with one another, an important issue in the law of trademarks. Computational linguists have made impressive progress when it comes to authorship identification. Those trained in syntax and semantics, as well as psycholinguistics and the philosophy of language, have enabled us to better understand the sources of uncertainty in the meanings of laws, and the extent to which this can be remedied.

By the same token, the advent of corpus linguistics and the availability of large samples of language on computers has made it possible to compare questioned samples to reference sets, aiding in such tasks as the identification of authors, the meaning of terms used in a legal setting (an important issue in the interpretation of statutes and contracts), and in determining whether a trademark is legitimately novel. The methods of discourse analysis provide tools for analyzing interactions between citizens and the police, as well as courtroom interaction. Historical linguistics has uncovered facts that explain some of the peculiarities of legal language. And important progress in the study of pragmatics teaches us about the inferences that people ordinarily draw from acts of speech that can elucidate the complex interactions that occur when, for instance, people are forming a contract.

In short, legal thinkers have become open to contributions from scholars in other disciplines, including those who study language in all its components, at the same time that linguistics and related disciplines have blossomed into significant academic fields with impressive accomplishments. Scholars trained in law, those trained in language-related fields, including psychology, computer science, and the philosophy of language, and those trained in both (like the editors of this *Handbook*) have taken seriously the legal system's openness to new ideas by engaging in a broad program of interdisciplinary research.

This book contains some of the leading ideas that have arisen from this research. It is not encyclopedic. Rather, it is intended to capture the state of the art at the moment, and to reflect what we consider to be some of the most promising directions for continued research. Below are some of the topics covered in this volume. We do not summarize the articles individually, since they speak for themselves. Rather, we identify the issues that we believe can and should be addressed by the cross-disciplinary study of language and law.

UNDERSTANDING WHAT IS DIFFERENT
ABOUT LEGAL LANGUAGE

One way to investigate the nature of legal institutions is to compare how the institutions use language to how people ordinarily use language, and to draw inferences from the similarities and differences. To the extent that different legal systems make similar choices concerning language, we might conclude that the confluence reflects some inherent aspect of legal orders in general. To the extent that the choices differ, we can examine how they differ and what these differences tell us about the legal orders adopting the various approaches. And, of course, to the extent that legal language is nothing more than ordinary language, with the addition of its own technical vocabulary, we can come to understand how a legal order might expect people's conduct to conform to the language of legal documents as they are ordinarily understood.

This book begins with chapters that characterize aspects of legal language. We will see common threads, such as lawyers and judges clinging to expressions that derive from languages that the legal order no longer uses. In the Anglo-American context, this includes terminology in Latin, and terminology from Law French, a language used in the English court system well after people in Britain stopped using it in everyday discourse. The exploration reveals a number of regularities in the ways that legal language operates, suggesting that legal orders around the world attempt to harness linguistic regularities in an effort to make language both clear and definitive, two goals that sometimes work at cross-purposes.

INTERACTING WITH THE LEGAL SYSTEM

Most of the encounters that ordinary people have with the law are language events: interactions with lawyers and with the police, whether in the street, a car, or the courtroom. These are no ordinary experiences in the lives of most people, although they are in some ways structured to create the appearance that they consist of normal interactions. Fortunately, research by linguists, criminologists, psychologists, and legal scholars over the past two decades has exposed some of the underlying regularities in these experiences. Almost universally, they are explained by disparities in power permitting an authority to control the discourse in a manner that advantages the authority and disadvantages the other participant.

To take one important example, police have the right to stop motorists and to order them to produce required documentation. Yet they do not have the right to search a vehicle without probable cause. Nonetheless, police do search vehicles as a matter of routine, because motorists permit them to do so. Linguists and psychologists are beginning to explain the reasons for this dynamic. Part of it, no doubt, results from the fact that the same police officer who has ordered the driver to produce a driver's license and other documents is now requesting that same individual to permit a search of the vehicle, without specifying that the interaction has shifted from the obligatory to the optional. Moreover, the police often use the same speech acts to "request" consent as they do to give an order ("May I ...").

Once at the police station, efforts to assert one's rights become quite difficult, at least in the United States. Asserting one's right to remain silent by actually remaining silent may not be good enough. At least in some circumstances, one has to say that one does not want to speak. Asserting one's right to counsel is not a simple matter either. A person being questioned must state in clear terms that he is demanding a lawyer in order for the courts to recognize that he has asserted that right. All of this is in stark contrast to the linguistic benefit of the doubt given to police officers when they "request" that citizens allow a search.

Sometimes linguistic interactions can themselves constitute crimes, such as committing perjury by lying under oath, or hiring someone to commit a crime, or arranging for a bribe. Many of these interactions share a characteristic: on the surface they appear to be ordinary encounters between two individuals who are simply trying to communicate with one another. But a deeper look shows that quite a bit more is going on. Here, courts are usually perfectly reasonable in weighing the literal and the pragmatic in determining whether a crime has been committed.

Once in the courtroom, the roles of various actors become well-defined, with the structure of power clear to everyone involved. Depending on the legal system, the lawyer or the judge asks the questions; the witness answers and has little control over the experience. As much as legal systems appear to differ, especially between the adversarial and accusatorial systems that roughly distinguish between the United States and

Commonwealth countries on the one hand, and civil law countries on the other, court-room discourse is structured similarly enough to allow linguistic analysis to explain a great deal about who is in charge and who is not.

All of these interactions are well-studied, with new research filling in gaps and expanding our knowledge on a regular basis. This volume contains some excellent contributions to this area, both in criminal law and in courtroom discourse. We have intentionally invited contributions from different legal orders so that readers can themselves examine the similarities and differences among various legal systems with respect to many of the issues discussed above.

INTERPRETING LAWS

Laws are written to be followed. The very fact that there is some doubt about their interpretation means that something has gone wrong. For the most part, understanding and describing the linguistic issues that generate legal interpretive problems is a task for linguists, psychologists, and philosophers. With respect to the interpretation of statutes, the problems are largely conceptual. While all kinds of interpretive issues arise from time to time, the biggest problem is to decide whether statutory language should be construed broadly, within the outer boundaries of a word's set of meanings, or more narrowly, to include instances of ordinary usage. This, in turn, motivates a detailed exploration of the kinds of indeterminacy that arise in statutory cases, including vagueness, ambiguity, and the use of broad language that is not vague or ambiguous, but which is not sufficiently informative either.

Deciding what the legal system should do about the problems once they are identified is a legal matter, not a linguistic one. Moreover, interpretive problems arise not only with respect to statutes, but with respect to other authoritative legal documents, including constitutions and contracts. Each of these has its own set of issues, both linguistic and legal. For example, contract formation involves a complex set of interactive speech acts, which in turn feed into a set of interpretive principles. Whether or not one considers a constitution to be a kind of social contract, its formation occurs by virtue of an entirely different set of events, which in turn generate a different set of interpretive issues. In the chapters that follow, scholars from the fields of linguistics, philosophy, and law investigate these important issues.

LAW IN A MULTILINGUAL WORLD

Ten of the chapters—fully one quarter of this book—deal with issues that arise from the fact that we do not all speak the same language. They illustrate two different and, in many ways, conflicting aspects of the life of the law. First, we live in a time of unparalleled effort to create supranational legal systems that cut across legal cultures and national boundaries, and to harmonize the laws of individual legal systems so that cross-border transactions are not impeded by the fact that the participants do not communicate in the same language, and at times do not even share the same legal concepts. Thus, while the laws of most countries are written in a single language, the European Union currently enacts twenty-three equally authoritative versions of each law. Canada enacts two, and struggles further with the fact that Québec is a civil law province, while the federal government and other provinces share a common law orientation. And most countries in the world are parties to various treaties that obligate them to enact domestic legislation consistent with the terms of the treaty in an effort to create a fairly uniform set of legal rights and obligations, especially in the area of international commerce.

All of this creates a myriad of challenges, often engaging translation theorists, comparative law experts, and those trained in linguistics. Even within monolingual jurisdictions, interpreters and translators are needed in legal settings when one of the parties does not speak the language of the legal system, or when crucial evidence is presented in another language. We consider these efforts to make the world smaller to be among the most important aspects of the study of language and law today. And we consider it a wonderful tribute to our common human heritage that the efforts have not fallen apart to date. On the contrary, they have been quite successful. Several chapters in this *Handbook* help to explain why that is so.

At the same time, the world's linguistic diversity has a shadow side. Those who speak a minority language may not always enjoy the same rights and privileges as do the majority. In some instances, the problems appear complex, with even sympathetic societies having difficulty balancing the respect for linguistic and cultural diversity on the one hand, and the efficiency that comes from a standard vehicle of communication on the other. In other instances, the struggle to gain minority language rights is a symptom of the struggle of minorities to gain civil rights in general. That these problems arise in such seemingly diverse contexts around the world suggests that the struggle reflects a dark side of human nature. Scholars from very different legal and social cultures explore these issues here.

OWNING LANGUAGE

In an era characterized as the Information Age, those who have proprietary rights over the language used to convey the information surely have something of value. Intellectual property law is generally divided into patent law, copyright law, trademark law, and the law governing trade secrets. All of these protections include aspects of language, but copyright and trademarks are directly linguistic in nature. Plagiarism, while more an academic concept than a legal one, consists of using the language or ideas of another without attribution. Copyright, in contrast, protects language, but not the ideas that are expressed by the language. That is, a copyright creates a monopoly in the copyrighted language, unless an alleged infringer can legitimately claim to have independently written the same language. Trademark law actually gives businesses the right to exclude competitors from using the same or similar language, if doing so might cause confusion among products. Enforcing intellectual property rights is a powerful tool to use in a competitive market.

Not surprisingly, a host of linguistic issues arise in determining whether a trademark or copyright owner's rights have been violated, or whether a student or faculty member has committed plagiarism. For example, under what circumstances are individuals most likely to confuse one product with another when the names are not identical, but sound similar? This is a psycholinguistic matter with important legal consequences. To take another example, the strength of a trademark depends upon how much the name appears to be an ordinary description of the product. The more generic or descriptive the name, the weaker the trademark protection. Whether a trademark is descriptive of the product is certainly a question of language use. By comparing the trademark to a corpus of language in which the same expression appears, it is possible to determine how closely the trademark matches everyday speech.

By the same token, how close one expression must be to another for it to constitute either plagiarism or copyright infringement is a matter of legal policy. But the investigation of similarities and differences can be accomplished using linguistic tools. This book contains four chapters that deal with the detection of plagiarism, and trademark and copyright infringement.

Forensic linguistic identification

In the 1990s, the United States Supreme Court decided three cases that set standards for the admissibility of scientific evidence in court. These have become known as the *Daubert* trilogy, named after the first of the cases to be decided. Although the decisions apply only to federal courts within the United States, the *Daubert* regime has had worldwide influence over the discussion of what evidence should be admitted, and what evidence should not. Without doubt, the overriding issue is whether a forensic science should be adequately tested in the laboratory (or its equivalent) before it is admitted in court. The goal is to ensure that methods have been developed in a scientific manner, that the application of the methods to the case at hand follows the appropriate practice, and that the scientific community knows the rate of error—or to put it more positively, knows how likely the method is to produce an accurate result.

Linguistic identification has not been at the center of the controversy of forensic identification, but it has been making significant headway in two areas: speaker identification and authorship attribution. As for speaker identification, new algorithms are being developed and honed by computer scientists, while phoneticians who are trained in the area develop lists of features that they use in case analysis. More or less the same holds true in the realm of authorship identification, with some work relying on corpora that serve as a reference set with which to compare a questioned document's features. The work in both of these areas is proceeding at a rapid pace, with more and more promising results revealing themselves regularly. In this volume, we hope to have captured a sense of this progress.

These are not all of the ways in which language and law interact, and even within these topics our discussion is more schematic than encyclopedic. Nonetheless, we think that these themes address some of the most interesting issues that arise when the interactions of the fields are studied. Most importantly, we believe that all of the topics that we address are important ones, and of independent concern to the legal system. The starting point of all good interdisciplinary research is an important problem, the discussion of which will be enhanced by working across conventional disciplines. We have identified the problems addressed in this *Handbook*. The chapters, written by scholars well-versed in their specialties, do more than meet the goal of enhancing discussion. They demonstrate a state of the art that shows enormous progress in this interdisciplinary endeavor, pointing the way for future inquiry.

PART I

LEGAL LANGUAGE

CHAPTER 1

....

A HISTORY OF THE
LANGUAGES OF LAW

....

PETER M. TIERSMA

1.1 INTRODUCTION

....

ALL legal systems develop certain linguistic features that differ from those of ordinary language. Sometimes these practices differ only slightly, especially when a legal system is primarily oral or relatively young. At the other extreme, lawyers and judges may develop language that is entirely different from ordinary speech. Most modern legal regimes fall between these extremes. Typically, the legal profession uses language that contains a substantial amount of technical vocabulary and a number of distinct (often archaic) features. As a result, the speech, and to a greater extent, the texts produced by such legal systems may be difficult for the lay public to understand.

This chapter will explore the origins of the world's major legal languages. Of course, any language reflects the history of the people that speak it. The language of English law, for instance, was influenced by Anglo-Saxons, Danes, and Normans, all of whom settled in England at various times. Yet legal systems also have their own histories, which may not always mirror the histories of the nations in which they are located. Continental European legal language was heavily influenced by Roman law, even in countries that were never occupied by the Romans. In contrast, although England was ruled by Rome for several centuries, Roman law has had little influence there.

We will focus on the two most widely dispersed legal traditions around the world: the civil law system that arose in continental Europe, and the common law that developed in England. The civil law gradually spread not only throughout most of Europe, but also to former European colonies in Africa, Asia, and the Americas. Following similar routes, the common law stretches across much of the globe, from England to North America to African countries like Nigeria and finally to India, Pakistan, Australia, and Malaysia, which are all former British colonies. These countries adopted not just legal concepts derived from the common or civil law, but also much of the language used to express and apply those concepts.

We begin with the evolution of the language of the civil law. Next, we will turn our attention to the common law. The final major section will examine some of the world's remaining legal systems, which are often mixed systems that combine local elements with aspects of the civil or common law.

1.2 Language in the civil law tradition

1.2.1 The legacy of Roman law

The civil law that developed in western Europe is generally considered to be founded on Roman law. Unlike the situation with other civilizations, the law of Rome did not entirely disappear when its empire collapsed. Little remains of the legal systems of the ancient Egyptians, Mesopotamians, or Greeks. Roman law, on the other hand, has proved surprisingly durable.

Although certain aspects of the substance of Roman law have persisted into modern times, even more influential were its use of writing, procedural rules, and its method of categorizing and systematizing legal concepts and categories. Particularly important in developing these concepts was a class of men called *jurists* or *jurisconsults*. They were not lawyers in the modern sense. Rather, they were men of means who took it upon themselves to study the law and to offer legal opinions to litigants, magistrates, and judges. Much of what we know about Roman law derives from the written commentaries of the jurists, who were most active in the first three centuries AD.

In the course of the fourth century, the empire split into a western part (which included what is now Italy, Spain, France, and other parts of western Europe) and an eastern part, which became known as the Byzantine Empire or Byzantium (including the Balkan states and what are now the nations of Turkey, Lebanon, Israel, and Egypt, among others). The western empire and its legal system gradually declined, to be replaced by numerous small states that were largely governed by customary law, although "vulgarized" or "bastardized" vestiges of Roman law survived in certain areas (Merryman 1985:8).

In contrast, the Byzantine empire survived in some form or other for the next thousand years. The Byzantine rulers fancied themselves the successors to the original Roman emperors, none more so than Justinian, who reigned from 527 to 565. Justinian succeeded in capturing a fair amount of territory which had once been part of the western Roman empire, including parts of Italy. In order to re-establish the glory of Rome, he needed to revive its law. He also wanted to consolidate and improve it. He therefore charged a group of scholars to take available sources of Roman law (including the writings of the jurists) and to create a systematic body of law based upon them.

The result of Justinian's ambitions was the *Corpus Juris Civilis* (the "body of civil law"). It consisted of four separate works:

- the *Digest*, containing writings by the jurists;
- the *Code*, which contained various imperial enactments;
- the *Novels*, or Justinian's own enactments; and
- the *Institutes*, a type of textbook for students to learn the law.

The *Corpus Juris* was written mostly in Latin, the language of Roman law, even though the Byzantine language of administration was Greek. It remained the law of the Byzantines, but after they lost their possessions in Italy, was little known in the west (Merryman 1985:6–8; Robinson et al. 2000:1–3).

That situation began to change in northern Italy during the eleventh century, a time when economic activity and trade flourished, ultimately promoting the Renaissance. The population, especially in cities, grew rapidly. There was a need for a more sophisticated legal system.

Then, in the latter half of the eleventh century, a manuscript containing Justinian's *Corpus Juris Civilis* was discovered in a library in Pisa. Not far away, legal scholars in Bologna began to study Justinian's work and produced editions of it with their commentary (glosses) in the margins. These scholars and teachers came to be called *glossators*. Students flocked from all of Europe to the newly founded Bologna university to study Roman law. They returned to their native countries, where other universities were established and where Roman law was taught. Many places began to require that their judges have legal training, which generally meant being educated in the *Corpus Juris* (Merryman 1985:8–9; Robinson et al. 2000:42–58).

Civil law countries thus all share, to a greater or lesser extent, a common legal heritage that began in Rome, was systematized in Byzantium, was re-discovered and elaborated in northern Italy, and then spread throughout much of Europe. They also share some core legal concepts, as well as the language needed to refer to those concepts. That language is, for the most part, heavily influenced by the Latin terminology of the *Corpus Juris*. Due to this common heritage, European lawyers "speak the same conceptual language" (Mattila 2006:126, referring to the work of Rodolfo Sacco).

1.2.2 The influence of Latin

To the extent that European civil law lawyers speak the same conceptual language, they do so in large part because Latin at one time played such an important role in their professional lives. Whereas medieval English lawyers learned the law in Law French at the inns of court, the civil law was for many centuries taught at universities in Latin. This was true not just because of the legacy of Roman law, but also because Latin was the language of science and education throughout much of Europe.

In the legal sphere, Latin was long the predominant language of statutes and treaties. Although trials were generally conducted in local languages, the judgments were usually drawn up in Latin. Legal treatises were mostly written in Latin until a couple of centuries ago. Even today, the Catholic church employs Latin for legal purposes (Mattila 2006:128–36).

The use of Latin words and phrases has declined greatly during the past two or three centuries. Nonetheless, the civil law continues to use Latin to label certain key concepts, especially those that derive from Roman law. For instance, *causa*, *ex aequo et bono*, and *culpa in contrahendo* are still encountered in contract law, while *jus soli* and *jus sanguinis* remain important with respect to citizenship. Many other Latin terms have been nativized, especially in the Romance languages. *Delictum* may become *delict* or *delicto* or *delitto*. *Codex* is *code* in English and French, *codice* in Italian, and so forth. In other languages Latin terms tend to be translated into the vernacular, as when *codex* became *Gesetzbuch* in German and *wetboek* in Dutch (both meaning "law book").

Latin is thus far from dead. A study of modern Finnish legal language identified around 600 Latin expressions and maxims that were still in use. In eastern Europe the use of Latin has actually increased as nations have abandoned socialist law and seek to revive the civil law tradition (Mattila 2006:136–9).

Latin maxims or sayings about the law have been particularly durable. Illustrations include *pacta sunt servanda* (contacts must be carried out), *nulla poene sine lege* (no punishment without law), and *in dubio pro reo* (in case of doubt, favor the accused) (Mattila 2006:143). Such maxims may be difficult to translate accurately. And somehow they simply sound more erudite and authoritative in the original.

1.2.3 The *jus commune* and the survival of indigenous law

Although the *Corpus Juris* was highly influential, especially in areas such as contracts and torts, it did not provide rules or principles to govern all areas of life, even in regions where it was "received" as binding law. Canon law—the law developed by the Catholic church—applied to marriage and family. Customary and feudal law were important with respect to property and succession. And commerce was governed by what is called the *lex mercatoria* or *law merchant*. Together, these elements were known as the *jus commune*, or "common law," since it was common to much of Europe (Merryman 1985:9–13; Robinson et al. 2000:107–24). Despite the confusingly similar nomenclature, the common law of England (see Section 1.3) has a very different history and meaning.

For a while the *jus commune*, as taught in the universities, created a relatively unified European legal culture. Eventually, however, a rising sense of nationalism led to a greater emphasis on indigenous or customary law. It became increasingly common for local law to be applied in courts. There was also a growing tendency to write down these originally oral customs in the vernacular.

Of course, lawyers and judges trained in universities were steeped in Roman law, based on Justinian's *Corpus Juris* and the commentaries of the glossators and other scholars, virtually all of it in Latin. Thus, in what is now Germany, some states adopted or "received" Roman law virtually in its entirely. Others—Saxony is a good example—resisted wholesale adoption, in large part because of the influence of the *Sachsenspiegel*, a compilation of Saxon law that was composed in both Latin and the Germanic Saxon language. In France, the north became known as the *pays de coutumes* (the land of customary law) and the south as the *pays de droit écrit* (the land of written—mostly Roman—law). During the sixteenth century, most of the customs in northern France were codified, but law remained quite local, with varying mixtures of Roman and indigenous law, the latter differing from place to place. According to Voltaire, a traveler in France changed law as often as he changed horses (Robinson et al. 2000:188–212).

Although all civil law countries were influenced by Roman law to some extent, most have also retained a certain amount of customary law, with accompanying terminology. An illustration is Indonesia, which inherited the civil law system from the Dutch. Customary or *adat* law was generally respected by colonial officials and to some extent has remained in force following independence (Hooker 1978). In addition, Arabic legal terms are common in Indonesia, including *hukum*, which means "law" (Mattila 2006:115–17).

1.2.4 Codification

The eighteenth century, especially the latter half, was a time of political and intellectual turmoil in Europe. The Enlightenment encouraged a re-evaluation of the past and acceptance of new ideas for the future. A philosopher who proposed broad legal reform was the English lawyer, Jeremy Bentham. As noted, much of the law in continental Europe was customary, and the English common law could also be viewed as a type of customary law. Bentham was a proponent of legislation, and he therefore advocated converting customs into statutory law by means of *codification*. Customs would be written down and then enacted as statutes by the ruler or legislature. The statutes would be logically organized by subject matter and would be published in the form of a *code* that contained all of the law on a specified topic.

Bentham's proposal did not bear fruit in his own country, but it found favor on the continent, especially in France, which made Bentham an honorary citizen. Europe already had a fair amount of experience with codes, but those in the eighteenth and nineteenth centuries were revolutionary in a number of ways. An example is the Prussian *Landrecht*, inspired by Frederick the Great and promulgated in 1794. It aimed to state the law clearly and exhaustively, so that citizens could know what the law was, lawyers would become superfluous, and judges would be limited to applying the law rather than interpreting it. To be understandable to the citizenry, it had to be in German.

The somewhat later French Civil Code also strove to unify and reform French law while repealing all former law. The arrangement was similar to that of the *Institutes* of Justinian. Like the Prussian code, it aspired to be accessible to ordinary *citoyens*, but it avoided detailed rules and instead chose to state the law in relatively broad principles. In contrast to the over 17,000 articles of the *Landrecht*, the French civil code had somewhat more than 2,000. Although it originated in the French revolution, it was enacted largely though the efforts of Napoleon, which is why it is often called the *Code Napoléon* (Merryman 1985:26–30; 39).

The French Civil Code had a tremendous impact throughout continental Europe. Napoleon's conquests introduced it to Belgium, the Netherlands, Portugal, Spain, and parts of Italy and Germany, all of which were heavily influenced by it. Colonies of those nations, including much of Africa and Latin America, likewise used the code as a model (Robinson et al. 2000:247–76).

Codification took a somewhat different turn in Germany. The Prussian *Landrecht* was ultimately deemed a failure. Roman law and the French civil code were both influential. However, customary Germanic law also retained some importance. When Germany was unified in the nineteenth century, legal scholars drafted a new civil code that was based on Roman law, but incorporating native Germanic elements. Their efforts ultimately produced the *Bürgerliches Gesetzbuch*, or German Civil Code of 1896 (Merryman 1985:30–2). German jurisprudence was influential in other German-speaking areas, especially Austria, as well as the Nordic countries. And the *Bürgerliches Gesetzbuch* served as a model for codes in Japan, Brazil, and pre-revolutionary China, among others (Mattila 2006:180–1).

1.2.5 The influence of French

In Francophone countries it stands to reason that the language of law is largely French. In France itself, Latin was replaced by French for legal and administrative purposes starting in roughly the thirteenth century, although the language of ancient Rome continued to be used in certain areas, including university instruction in law, through the eighteenth century.

Even in European countries where it was not widely spoken, French had a heavy influence on law and government. It was the language of treaties and diplomacy during much of the eighteenth and nineteenth centuries. The widespread adoption of the *Code Napoléon* also promoted the use of French legal concepts and terminology. And the Napoleonic occupation of the Low Countries, the Iberian peninsula, and much of Italy greatly influenced the legal and governmental institutions in those places (Mattila 2006:187–201). For instance, the French high court (*Cour de Cassation*) was imitated in many of those countries, and as a result Belgium has a *Hof van Cassatie* and Italy has a *Corte de Cassazione*. In the Netherlands the high court bears the Dutch name *Hoge Raad*, but the process of bringing a case there is referred to as *cassatie*. In Spanish the process of appealing to the high court is called *casación*. All of these variants hark back to the French verb *casser*, meaning "break" or "quash," since the Court of Cassation quashes lower court judgments that it deems incorrect.

French law and its language have had great influence beyond Europe via its colonial empire. Many former colonies in sub-Saharan Africa use French for legal and governmental purposes because there may be dozens of indigenous languages, none of them widely spoken. In northern Africa, where Arabic is widespread, that language is gradually replacing French, although some degree of legal bilingualism remains common (Mattila 2006:212–16).

1.2.6 The triumph of the vernacular

We conclude our discussion of language in the civil law context by making a point that should be obvious, but which is nonetheless worth emphasizing. There has been a growing trend since the Middle Ages to express the law in languages that those subject to it can understand. In the thirteenth century, varieties of German were sometimes being used as legal languages (Mattila 2006:161). At around the same time, the Frisians and Icelanders were writing down their previously oral laws in the vernacular (Algra 2000; Tiersma 2010:137). The trend was intensified in the eighteenth and nineteenth centuries, when the Prussians, French, and others codified their laws using their national languages. Today, each civil law country has developed its own variety of legal language. Despite the great importance of Latin and French, modern legal languages are simply varieties of the national languages in question.

1.3 LANGUAGE AND THE COMMON LAW

The other major legal system in the word today is common law. It arose in England and by force of conquest was imposed on Wales and Ireland (Scotland retains to this day a type of civil law). Via the legacy of the British empire, the common law and English legal language currently hold sway in dozens of countries throughout the world.

1.3.1 Celts, Romans, Anglo-Saxons, and Danes

Although the British Isles have been inhabited for many thousands of years, the first people to have left historical traces are the Celts. Most of what we know about their legal system comes from Wales and Ireland. Although Welsh and Gaelic are still spoken in the British Isles, Celtic law and its language have largely disappeared.

Somewhat over 2,000 years ago, the Romans under Julius Caesar conquered what is now England. Roman law would surely have applied to its citizens who were living there. Yet it would have had limited influence on the lives of the Celtic population, and it seems to have disappeared after the Romans left the island in the fifth century to defend their disintegrating empire. The Romans did leave behind a linguistic legacy, but it consists mostly of place names and a few words of Latin origin, none of them particularly legal (Mellinkoff 1963:36–9).

The Roman retreat left a power vacuum of sorts, which the Angles, Saxons, and other Germanic warriors and settlers from the continent quickly exploited. They conquered most of the territory of what is now England. Their related languages eventually merged into one, which we now refer to as Anglo-Saxon, or Old English.

The Anglo-Saxons were not literate at the time and their law was entirely customary. Legal decisions were often made by a type of popular assembly, sometimes called *moots*. If someone injured or killed someone else, the victim or his clan were entitled to take revenge on the perpetrator, but in most cases he could save his head or hide by paying compensation. The amount depended on the severity of the injury and the status of the victim.

Oaths were often used to decide cases. The words of the oath were fixed and had to be recited verbatim, without stammering, or the person would lose his case. Other types of legal transactions, like wills and transfers of land, also relied on reciting exact verbal formulas. Use of these formulas, which often contained poetic devices as an aid to memory, indicated that the transaction was legally binding. Thus, "to have and to hold" was part of the formula used to transfer land. This alliterative phrase is still encountered in many deeds (Tiersma 1999:9–16). Interestingly, oaths retain a talismanic quality even today. After US Chief Justice Roberts made a verbal slip in administering the oath of office to President Obama in early 2009, he repeated the ceremony the next day to ensure that it was valid.[1]

Around the year 600, Christian missionaries arrived in England. In addition to religion, they brought with them (or re-introduced) literacy and the Latin language. Soon thereafter, the first written English laws appear. Several of the Anglo-Saxon kings issued codes of law, and some private legal transactions (wills and transfers of land) were also memorialized in writing. Many of these texts were drafted in Latin, but others were in Old English. They functioned primarily as records of customs or oral transactions (Tiersma 2010).

Vikings, mostly from what is now Denmark, raided the British Isles during much of the ninth and tenth centuries. Some of them later settled in England, especially in an area of northeastern England called the *Danelaw* (because it was governed by Danish law). The Scandinavians eventually merged with the Anglo-Saxon population, but their language left behind distinct traces in English. Most notable in the legal sphere are the words *gift, loan, sale, trust,* and the word *law* itself, originally meaning "that which is laid down" (Tiersma 1999:17).

By far the most significant invasion was yet to come, however. In 1066 William, Duke of Normandy, who claimed the English throne, crossed the channel and defeated the English defenders, an event now known as the Norman Conquest. English ceased to function as a written legal language, although it remained the spoken language of most ordinary people. The rulers of England were now men who spoke a type of French, and their written legal transactions were almost invariably in Latin.

By the end of the thirteenth century, statutes written in Latin started to become common. Royal courts were established and a class of professional lawyers emerged. French

---

[1] http://www.abajournal.com/news/article/did_roberts_oath_change_cause_obama_stumble/ (visited August 3, 2010).

was still spoken by the upper nobility at this time, so it stands to reason that oral proceedings in the royal courts would be in that language. Also, the language of written statutes shifted from Latin to French at around 1300, and remained so until it was replaced by English at the end of the fifteenth century.

Thus, at the time when the centralized English court system and the legal profession arose, French was the primary language in which the law was expressed. Of course, French has had a lasting impact on English in general, but this is even more so in the legal sphere. Words relating to courts and trials are almost entirely of French origin: *action, appeal, attorney, bailiff, bar, claim, complaint, counsel,* and *court* are but a few examples. Just about every area of the common law is full of French terminology, as attested by words for basic legal categories like *agreement, assault, easement, estate, felony, lease, license, misdemeanor, mortgage, property, slander, tort,* and *trespass.* French word order (noun+adjective) is apparent in terms like *attorney general, condition precedent, letters patent,* and *notary public.*

French was used as a legal language until roughly the seventeenth century, long after it ceased to be a spoken language in England. Reports of cases were in French for most of this period. This is important because the common law is based in large part on case law, or *precedent.* The legal principle that a judge uses to decide a case must generally be followed in later cases that present the same issue. These precedents can be found in case reports, and for hundreds of years those reports were written in French. Thus, many of the most important principles in the common law were first articulated in French. Moreover, almost all legal literature was written in that language.

Although English lawyers were not normally educated in Latin, they would nonetheless have had some knowledge of it. Maxims or sayings about the law were usually in Latin, as in *de minimis non curat lex* ("the law is not concerned with trifles"), *caveat emptor* ("let the buyer beware"), and *expressio unius est exclusio alterius* ("the expression of one thing is the exclusion of the other"). Writs (orders from the king or judge to a sheriff or lower court) were in Latin, and even today many retain Latin names, including the writs of *certiorari, habeas corpus,* and *mandamus.* Records of court cases were maintained in Latin until the early eighteenth century, which explains its widespread use for terminology found in case names (*versus, in personam, in rem, in propria persona,* etc.) (Tiersma 1999:19–34).

Although both Latin and French were and continue to be widely used in the civil law, as we discussed above, there is less overlap with the common law than one might expect. Some French terms used in English legal language, such as *agreement, crime, arrest,* and *misdemeanor,* are not used in French legal language or have a different meaning (Mattila 2006:231–2). Moreover, Mattila reports that, roughly speaking, only around one-fourth of the Latin terms and maxims in a sample of German legal dictionaries are found in dictionaries of legal English. This suggests that most of the Latin used by the civil and common law systems is unique to each (Mattila 2002). A study of Latinisms used in the United States and Spain reached a similar conclusion (Balteiro and Campos-Pardillos 2010).

1.3.2 The rise of English

The profession's continued use of French, long after it ceased to be a spoken language in England, was not always appreciated by the public. Critics suggested that lawyers wished to hide the law, thereby securing their monopoly on legal services. Lawyers responded that Law French (the distinctive dialect of French used by the English legal profession) was far more precise than English. Moreover, if the law were expressed in English, ordinary people might try to act as their own lawyers and, failing to properly understand the law, would "fall into destruction," in the words of Sir Edward Coke (Tiersma 1999:28–9).

As early as 1362, a statute—written in French!—required that all court pleading be in English, so that "every Man...may the better govern himself without offending of the Law." In 1650 Parliament, during the Commonwealth, passed another law requiring that all books of law be only in English. The statute was repealed when the monarchy was restored ten years later. By this time, however, Law French was moribund. Its use in legal proceedings, along with Latin, was finally abolished in 1731 (Tiersma 1999:35–6).

Documents previously written in French or Latin now had to be composed in English. Rather than translating them into idiomatic English, however, lawyers and clerks tended to favor a very literal, word-for-word, translation. Medieval deeds often began with the words *sciant omnes...*, which was translated as "know all men..." This phrase has been copied verbatim countless times since then. The criminal law concept of *malice afore-thought* is a direct translation of the Law French phrase *malice prepense*, preserving the French word order.

Moreover, many terms were not translated into English at all. These words and phrases were almost all technical terms that had acquired a specific legal meaning, making it difficult to find an exact English equivalent. Unlike those who developed the German legal system, which took great pains to "Germanize" foreign terms (Mattila 2006:169), English lawyers mostly incorporated French terms without change. Of course, the English language is renowned for borrowing foreign words, and French and Latin especially have been a major source for such borrowing. In the legal arena, some of these originally foreign words have entered ordinary speech, such as *court, judge, jury, plaintiff*, and *defendant*. Others, however, are completely unknown outside the profession (consider *tortfeasor* or *profit a prendre*), and their foreign origin makes it hard for people to even guess at their meaning.

In the last several decades a movement has thus arisen advocating for plain English (see Chapter 5). Proponents in essence argue that although all legal texts have officially been in the vernacular since 1731, the law is actually expressed in a type of English, often called *legalese*, that deviates in some important ways from ordinary language. Lawyers continue to hide the law, they suggest, but in place of Law French they now use obscure and convoluted English.

The legal system has not been impervious to these criticisms. Much anachronistic terminology has been replaced by more modern equivalents. The Law French term *cestui que trust* is being supplanted by the more common word *beneficiary*. The phrase *Cometh now plaintiff*, which was once used to introduce a pleading, has been modernized as *Comes now plaintiff* or simply *Plaintiff alleges as follows*. Most drafters are content nowadays to write *John Smith* in place of *the aforesaid John Smith*. Such changes have been especially common in consumer documents, including insurance policies and various types of disclosure forms.

There has also been a movement, which has met with some success, to make instructions to jurors more comprehensible (see Chapter 31). Still, the instructions of many jurisdictions are not exactly models of clarity, especially when it comes to the politically charged area of death penalty law. Part of the problem is that the language of instructions is often copied directly from statutes, which were never meant to be understood by jurors, but which judges resist translating into ordinary speech for fear of being reversed by a court of appeals (Tiersma 1999:211–40).

Thus, while there has been much improvement in the language of the law during the past decades, much remains to be accomplished.

1.3.3 Legal English around the world

Just as the civil law of Europe migrated to many parts of the world via colonialism, the common law and its language spread throughout the former British empire. Some of these countries are mostly English-speaking today, including Canada, the United States, Australia, and New Zealand. Others, like Pakistan, India, Nigeria, and Malaysia, have retained English legal language even though most of the population speaks indigenous languages for most purposes.

The American colonies rejected many things British when they won their independence. Yet they retained the common law system, including the notion of precedent. Despite reservations by some prominent Americans, most notably Thomas Jefferson, they also continued to use the legal language associated with that system. Thus modern English lawyers can understand American lawyers fairly well, and vice versa. Yet in some important respects the British and American legal systems have diverged, producing what are arguably differing dialects of legal English (Tiersma 1999:43–7). In contrast to the United States, countries such as Canada, Australia, and New Zealand broke away from the United Kingdom much later, and as a result their legal languages are closer to that of England.

In former British colonies where English is not widely spoken, it is common for lower court proceedings to be in native languages. Yet English is often used in the higher courts, as in India and Pakistan. The English used in these courts can be surprisingly conservative at times. Many former British colonies have high courts consisting of a chief justice and several *puisne* (associate or junior) judges.[2] *Puisne* comes from the Law French *puis* "after" and *ne* "born," and thus referred originally to a younger child (Baker 1990:177).

---

[2] See the constitution of Kenya, ch. IV, pt. 1, § 60.

As might be expected, the English used in higher courts is generally imbued with some local flavor. Thus, Indian courts take cognizance of customary law in some situations, which will generally be expressed in local languages. And Islamic law is applied to family matters of Indian Muslims, which leads to the use of much Arabic terminology in this area (Mattila 2006:248–9).

One would expect that in many of these countries, local languages will gradually replace English. To some extent this has started to happen in Malaysia, for instance, where high court judgments may currently be written not just in English, but also in *Bahasa Malaysia*. Of course, the same happened in England itself, where the local language (English) eventually supplanted Law French.

1.4 MIXED LEGAL SYSTEMS

In this section we consider what are sometimes called *mixed* legal systems. The term is often used in reference to jurisdictions that have aspects of both civil and common law. Scottish law could be cited as an illustration. Scotland is in many ways a civil law jurisdiction whose law was based on Roman law. Yet since the union with England, the British House of Lords has appellate jurisdiction over Scotland, and the common law has become increasingly influential (Robinson et al. 2000:228–48). The province of Quebec is likewise primarily a civil law jurisdiction, but once again subject to some common law influence because of Canadian federalism. The situation in Canada is interesting because its laws must be translated not just across languages, but across legal systems (see Chapter 11).

In a somewhat broader sense just about any legal system is "mixed"—subject to more than one set of influences and traditions. The *jus commune* mixed Roman law with canon, indigenous, and mercantile law. Many countries in Africa combine native customary law (almost invariably expressed in local languages) with the civil or common law (usually expressed in French, Portuguese, or English) (David and Brierley 1978:505–32).

China is an interesting case of what might be called a mixed system. There has long been a struggle between *li*, a Confucian approach that emphasizes social order, and *fa*, a legalist approach that emphasizes punishment (see Chapter 28). After the revolution of 1911, China adopted several codes patterned on the European civil law. During the subsequent Communist period, however, enacted law was largely supplanted by party directives. Litigation was discouraged, there were few lawyers, and judges often had no legal training (David and Brierley 1978:478–91). Without an established legal profession, a distinctive legal language would be unlikely to develop. As a result, the language of Chinese law is "very ordinary, almost banal and extraordinarily plain" (Cao 2004:vii).

Since the reforms of the late 1970s, however, China has begun to modernize its legal system. The country has adopted several codes that borrow from the civil and common law traditions, especially in the realm of commerce (Zhang 2006:11–13). It is therefore likely to develop a legal language that reflects these mixed influences.

1.5 THE GLOBALIZATION OF LEGAL LANGUAGE?

If legal systems are increasingly influencing each other, will legal language likewise be subject to globalization? One consequence of globalization on the law has been a growing need to translate from one legal language into another. Chapters 11–15 illustrate the challenges of doing so, especially across legal systems.

Another aspect of globalization is the creation of international alliances or confederations, such as the European Union. Curiously, as the nations of Europe create a common legal superstructure, they have discovered that despite their shared civil law tradition, it can be problematic to translate from one legal language into another. This is an important issue in the EU, which has around two dozen official languages (see Chapter 14; Gotti 2009). Vocabulary relating to new institutions or novel legal concepts usually does not present difficulties. For example, EU institutions and legal rules may be generally referred to by the French term *acquis communautaire* (used not only in French, but sometimes also in Dutch and English), by a direct translation (Italian *conquiste comunitarie* or *acquis comunitario*), or by a neologism (German *gemeinschaftlicher Besitzstand*) (Mattila 2006:120–1).

Yet in most cases EU law—for instance, directives of the Commission or decisions of the Court of Justice—is originally formulated in French or English and then translated into the other official languages using the existing legal terminology of those languages. As observed in Chapter 13, legal terms in one language cannot always be translated exactly into another. The meaning of *delict* in the civil law is not entirely the same as *tort* in the common law. Thus, a law or regulation, intended to be uniform throughout the EU, may acquire subtle differences in meaning via the process of translation.

One solution would be to have one official language, which could be used to draft a single authoritative version of all EU legal texts. Some have suggested that International English could carry out this function (Ferreri 2006). However, the EU seems firmly committed to the principle of multiple official languages, which inevitably requires translation.

A more likely approach is to build a corpus of common or uniform legal terminology with precise definitions that can be used in all national languages. At one time Latin terms fulfilled this function throughout much of Europe, but despite its historical importance, it is probably no longer a serious contender. Creating an entirely new vocabulary, on the analogy of invented languages like Esperanto, might also be a possibility, but it likewise seems improbable. Perhaps a more attractive notion is taking a certain number of legal terms from each EU language in order to create one common legal lexicon. Because of the great structural disparity of the major language families, this may also not be practical.

Using the vocabulary of an existing language may be the only feasible option. At one time French provided much legal terminology that could be used internationally, but today the most obvious choice is English. There is, in fact, a serious movement to create a common EU legal vocabulary using English as the basis, but it would have to be a type of international legal English that is not burdened by common law precendents.[3]

Whether the EU will embrace the use of international legal English, if only to standardize its legal terminology, is uncertain, as is the question of how widespread legal English will become in the rest of the world. In any event, predictions about the future go beyond the scope of this chapter, which is historical. No doubt a later edition of this *Handbook* will be able to answer these questions after the future has become history.[4]

---

[3] See http://www.juridicainternational.eu/the-launch-of-the-draft-common-frame-of-reference?id=10521. See also Von Bar et al. (2009); Pozzo and Jacometti (2006).

[4] I would like to thank Heikki Mattila of the University of Lapland and Barbara Pozzo of the University of Insubria for their assistance.

CHAPTER 2

....

LEGAL VOCABULARY

....

HEIKKI E. S. MATTILA

LEGAL language is based on ordinary language. Therefore, the grammar and most of the vocabulary of legal language are identical to those of ordinary language. On the other hand, legal language is one of the languages for special purposes, as a result of which it has certain characteristics which differ from ordinary language, for example, on the level of syntax and style. Legal language is characterized especially by the use of technical terms, the nature and number of which vary according to the branch of law. The present chapter[1] focuses on technical terms of the law from different angles, taking into account various legal cultures and linguistic zones.[2]

2.1 RELATION TO LEGAL CONCEPTS

....

To understand the fundamental nature of legal language, it is important to distinguish between a legal term and a legal concept. While the word *concept* refers to abstract figures created by the human mind, that is entities formed by features which are peculiar to

---

[1] The language of the article has been checked by Mr Michael Hurd of the University of Lapland and by Prof. Susan Šarčević of the University of Rijeka. Prof. Šarčević also revised the specialized terminology. In addition, Mr Kari Liiri, head of the Finnish division of the Translation Directorate of the Court of Justice of the European Union read the paragraphs related to the EU and made important suggestions. The author expresses his warmest thanks to these specialists.

[2] In many countries, lawyers and linguists have published treatises on legal language in which legal terminology is extensively discussed. In English, Mellinkoff (1963) is already a classic, supplemented by newer works such as Tiersma (1999) and Solan and Tiersma (2005). French legal vocabulary has been dealt with from the contemporary point of view by Sourioux and Lerat (1975) and later by Cornu (2005); historical aspects are taken into account in Gémar (1995). As for EU terminology, see notably Šarčević (2004). General treatises on language and history of language may also contain important information on legal terminology. An excellent example is Polenz (2013). Naturally, legal terms are widely examined in treatises of legal translation, such as Šarčević (1997) and Alcaraz Varó

a matter or thing, the word *term* designates the names of concepts, their external expression. Hence, a term may be defined as the linguistic expression of a concept belonging to the notional system of a specialized language.

2.1.1 Culture-specificity of legal concepts

Law does not exist in the physical world but has been created by human beings. As a product of history, all law is considerably culture-specific. Therefore, legal concepts often appear in only one legal system or some legal systems. In effect, the concepts of various legal systems always differ to a greater or lesser extent. The degree of this divergence depends on earlier interaction between the lawyers of the legal cultures in question. It is understandable that English and American legal terms correspond to a large degree: the United States was founded on colonies possessed by the British Crown, where English law was applied (though sometimes in a primitive way).

From a worldwide perspective, the most important practical differences are those between the conceptual systems of two major legal families, the common law and civil (Continental) law. Generally speaking, common law is applied in countries that have a British colonial past, while Continental Europe and Latin America are home to civil law countries. However, these two legal families have strongly influenced legal concepts throughout the world, including traditional religious and customary law. For historical reasons, the classifications and concepts of the common law and civil law differ, and therefore many Continental terms have no common law equivalent, just as many common law terms have no Continental equivalent, and similar terms with the same etymology may have different meanings (David and Brierley 1985).

However, there are also conceptual differences within major legal families, notably among civil law countries. As an example, one could mention the term *derecho foral*, a concept of Spanish law which can be explained by the fact that certain autonomous regions of Spain possess their own private law (civil law) system for reasons dating back to the times of the *Reconquista*. In these regions, the Spanish Civil Code is applied only subsidiarily. It is impossible to express the term *derecho foral* by a simple term in other legal languages since there is no identical corresponding concept of special private law in other legal systems. Therefore, one has to resort to an explanatory translation such as 'Spanish regional civil law' (Mattila 2008a:271–2).

and Hughes (2002). Moreover, legal terms are constantly the subject of research in national and international journals specialized in legal language or languages for special purposes, as well as in various collective works and conference publications (see the homepage of the *International Language and Law Association* at http://www.illa.org). For more references, see the bibliography in Mattila (2013).

Furthermore, it should be noted that a new pan-European legal system is gradually developing as a result of European integration: European Law, that is the law of the European Union (Communities, the EU). This law is intertwined with the national legal systems of the Member States of the Union. European Law partly has its own apparatus of legal concepts, expressed either by new legal terms or traditional terms used in a particular EU sense. These terms are often derived from legal French since French was the leading language of the European Communities till the middle of the 1990s. In other languages, these terms are expressed by various means, such as loan translations or naturalizations or direct French borrowings, for example *acte clair* and *acquis communautaire* (Peyró 1999:52–69).

Before the collapse of socialism, Socialist law was also counted among the major legal families (David and Brierley 1985). Because private ownership of the means of production was abolished after the October Revolution in Soviet Russia, later the Soviet Union, terms expressing this kind of ownership were no longer needed in legal Russian (e.g. terms designating various company forms). Simultaneously, new terms were introduced which had no counterparts in Western legal languages (such as *prodrazverstka*, 'the obligation to hand over foodstuffs'). In addition, certain areas of legal terminology were also reformed for reasons of principle even though the concepts were not really new. For instance, the term 'crime' (*prestuplenie*) was replaced by the term 'socially dangerous activity' (*sotsial'no opasnoe deistvie*) (Pigolkin 1990:10, 49–50). However, such radical neologisms were quickly abandoned and replaced by traditional Russian legal terms.

In contrast with Socialist law, religion-based law and traditional customary law are still widely applied outside Europe. These forms of law are often based on concepts that do not appear in modern Western law. For instance, the authors of treatises on Muslim Law use a large number of Islam-specific concepts which are expressed in treatises in Western languages by transliterated Arabic borrowings: *hiba, khula, mutwalli, nikah, quaraza-a Hasana, qiyas*, etc. (Verma 1988:index). The same applies to treatises on Hindu Law (see Mahmood 1986:index, and Mulla 1986:index).

The concepts of traditional customary law may also differ considerably from those used in modern law. For instance, traditional cultures may recognize special forms of marriage, like the one expressed by the Indonesian term *kawin bertandang* (Muhammad 1995:13–15). This form of marriage is recognized in the matrilineal customary law (*hukum adat*) of the Minangkabau people, according to which the husband remains a member of his mother's clan even after entering into marriage and continues to work with his mother and sisters in the mother's rice fields. From his wife's point of view, the husband is only a "visitor" (*pertandang*) who arrives in the evening and disappears the following morning and has no rights to her children or property. Naturally, there is no Western term to express this concept; a literal translation would be "visiting marriage" (*kawin* = "to marry", "marriage"; *bertandang* = "to visit"), but without further explanation this is meaningless to a Western lawyer.

2.1.2 Polysemy and synonymy

Legal terminology is characterized by polysemy.[3] This means that, even within a single legal culture, the same term may express several concepts depending on the context in which it is used. Extremely important in legal language, the phenomenon of polysemy constitutes the rule rather than an exception, a characteristic that applies to both nouns and verbs.

The frequency of polysemy can be explained by the fact that legal systems are in a constant state of change, and they also influence each other. For instance, the Latin expression *jus civile* has had several meanings over the centuries, which explains the polysemy of the English term *civil law*. In Antiquity, *jus civile* referred to the classical core of Roman law or to the law applied to Roman citizens. Later, this term was used in various senses. It referred, *inter alia*, to Roman law in general and, finally, to those legal rules which are applicable to relations between private individuals. Today, due to this development, the English term *civil law* refers to Continental (Romano-Germanic) law (as a major legal system essentially based on Roman law), as well as to the main part of private law in any country (Mattila 2013:142). Polysemy may sometimes be extremely misleading and cause misunderstandings in cross-border communication. For example, the term *supreme court* normally alludes to the highest jurisdiction in a State or region; however, in the State of New York "supreme court" is in reality an ordinary trial court.

The concepts expressed by one and the same legal term are often hierarchical or partly overlapping. A good example is the term *common law*, which today has three fundamental meanings: law based on the English legal tradition, case law created by courts in countries with an English legal tradition, and the case law developed by courts of law, as opposed to courts of equity.[4]

Nowadays, the European Union produces a great deal of polysemy. This is due to the fact that traditional legal terms often acquire specific Union law meanings (despite the tendency to create EU neologisms to avoid confusion with the legal terminology of the Member States). In the case of English, there are two reasons for EU-related polysemy. On the one hand, the main part of the legal system of the European Union originally comes from France; however, English has now displaced French as the leading language of the Union. This means that traditional terms of legal English are acquiring new meanings which are unique to the European Law of the Continental tradition (see Section 2.4.2).

The phenomenon of polysemy is reflected in legal interpretation (see Parts II and III of the present book).[5] The interpreter of a legal text must be able to attach the correct meaning to the polysemic terms appearing in it. He or she has to be aware of the fact that legal terms often have more meanings than those he or she already knows.

---

[3] Legal polysemy is discussed extensively in Cornu (2005). The discussion is based on legal French but is of wider interest.

[4] In addition, the term *common law* may refer to "the body of law to which no constitution or statute applies" (*Black's Law Dictionary*). See also, e.g. *The CCH Macquarie Dictionary of Law*.

[5] This is especially true in multilingual contexts such as the European Union. See Šarčević (2002).

Synonymy, which is the opposite of polysemy, occurs when several terms express one and the same concept. In non-Romance languages, a concept may often be expressed by a term of Latin origin as well as by a term of domestic origin. Due to the complicated history of the English language and law, synonymy is particularly frequent in legal English. This is manifested, *inter alia*, by a large number of binominal expressions (e.g. *acknowledge and confess, act and deed, will and testament*, etc.); trinominal expressions can be found as well (Tiersma 1999:61–5).

Synonymy is often partial. In spite of the problems it causes in legal language, this phenomenon also has advantages. Thanks to synonymy, potential lacunae in statutory provisions or contractual clauses may be avoided by enumerating a number of quasi-synonyms which, taken together, cover the semantic field in question. This method is frequently used, *inter alia*, by common law lawyers in the drafting of contracts (Beveridge 2002:65–9).

2.2 Relation to ordinary language and to other languages for special purposes

Legal language consists of a mixture of various elements: expressions of ordinary language used in their ordinary sense or in a technical sense, as well as expressions that can be used only as technical terms.

Legal texts usually contain a large number of words of ordinary language with precisely defined meanings which sometimes differ significantly from their ordinary meanings. This can be explained by the fact that legal messages are often addressed to a large number of people, even to all members of a society. Furthermore, legal messages frequently address problems in the everyday lives of citizens (marriage, birth, work, etc.). In branches of law *in statu nascendi*, the use of words of ordinary language in a technical legal sense is particularly widespread. This augments the risk of illusory understanding: a lay reader may think that he or she understands the meaning of a word which is familiar in appearance but in reality has a different meaning in legal language.

The difference between legal terms and words of ordinary language is relative and hard to define. According to one specialist, Gérard Cornu, legal terms may be defined on the basis of the notion of "legal-ness" or *juridicité*, as he puts it. In his opinion, it is possible to "recognise a native legal-ness in all that owes its existence to the Law, that is, on the one hand, all that the Law establishes (legal institutions), on the other hand all that can only be constituted in line with the Law (on this basis all legal acts the constitutive elements of which are defined by the Law can be included without any doubts)." Furthermore, the category of legal terms may also include words referring to legal facts in cases "where certain features of a phenomenon linked with legal effects correspond to conditions precisely defined by Law," such as *error* (Cornu 2007, *preface*; translation in Mattila 2006).

In addition, legal texts almost always include terms drawn from other professions (e.g. commerce, technology, land surveying, social work). To be able to fully understand such texts, the reader must possess knowledge of all the professions in question (Strouhal 1986:143), thus increasing the difficulty of the text. Some authors speak of an "accumulation of textual obscurity."

Besides legal terms and borrowings from other professions, the vocabulary of legal language includes words from the register of literary style. Legal authors use words of high written language. For instance, in legal English authors may speak of *misrecollection* rather than *forgetting* (Tiersma 1999:66). This upper-register language often includes Latin expressions of a cultural nature. In legal literature, one finds expressions such as *de facto* ("in fact," "in deed," "actually"), *in casu* ("in the present case," "in each particular case"), *ultima ratio* ("the final argument"), etc. When citing references, legal writers frequently use expressions such as *et al. (& al.) = et alii* ("and others"), *in fine* ("in the end"), *passim* ("here and there"), etc. Mattila (2013:180).

2.3 EXTERNAL FORM

A legal term may consist of a single word, a phrase, or a compound word. Such technical terms are frequently nouns; however, verbs and adjectives are also classified as terms. Generally speaking, legal language uses fewer verbs than ordinary language. This can probably be explained by the belief that nouns create an impression of greater objectivity than verbs. The impression of objectivity is considered to be especially important in cases of fact-stating. Adjectives are commonly transformed into nouns. The high percentage of nouns is one of the factors contributing to the obscurity of legal texts.

This obscurity is enhanced by the fact that legal texts often contain compound words or phrases. This is because the easiest way to coin a term to express a new legal concept is by using a compound word or phrase consisting of two or more words. The meaning conveyed by each word makes the term more transparent, enabling a person to immediately understand the content of the term. On the other hand, compound words and phrases are sometimes very awkward, such as the German term *Gesetzgebungsermächtigung* ("qualification with a view to legislating") or the French term *adjudication sur baisse de mise à prix* ("sale of immovable property by auction at a reduced starting price [due to lack of bids]").

There are also other reasons why legal terms are difficult to understand. First, many archaic words and phrases are still used—despite the growing popularity of plain language movements and efforts of language specialists in various countries to promote clarity.[6] These may be petrified expressions consisting of several words. For instance, until recently French courts of law used the phrase *Ouï (Oui) M. X en son rapport*

---

[6] However, there are many examples of creativity and innovation in legal language, such as the American terms *shrinkwrap* and *clickwrap* (Tiersma 2006a:31).

("Having heard Mr X's account"), which was hard to understand and therefore has been replaced today by the ordinary expression *Après avoir entendu le rapport de M. X* (Troisfontaines 1981:183). Second, legal terms often consist of words of foreign origin (notably Latin), thus making it more difficult to understand and remember (see Section 2.4.2). Direct Latin borrowings are also used as legal terms: *"habeas corpus* remains a writ"* (Kurzon 1987:237).

Legal abbreviations, particularly acronyms, may also be considered technical terms. Lawyers have used a great number of abbreviations since antiquity.[7] Although language specialists now emphasize the disadvantages of such usage, new bodies and institutions are constantly created in the world today, for example, in the European Union and in the United Nations, as a result of which more and more abbreviations are used in legal circles. There are various methods of creating legal abbreviations. Notably, it is very common to form initializations on the basis of the first letters of the words in a name or title: *BGB* (*Bürgerliches Gesetzbuch*, "German Civil Code"), *ZGB* (*Zivilgesetzbuch*, "Swiss Civil Code"), *NY UCC* (New York Uniform Commercial Code), *CC* (*Code civil*, "French Civil Code"), *CPP* (*Code de precédure pénale*, "French Code of Criminal Procedure"), etc. As a result, acronyms are becoming more and more frequent in legal texts. Abbreviations such as *Coreper* ("Comité des représentants permanents," "Committee of Permanent Representatives") in the EU and RICO ("The Racketeer Influenced and Corrupt Organizations Act") in the United States are pronounced like words and therefore fulfill the external characteristics of technical legal terms in this respect.

2.4 FORMATION

In principle, legal terms may be created in several ways. First, a word already existing in ordinary language (in the language in question) may acquire a specialized or enlarged meaning in legal contexts as a result of a more or less spontaneous linguistic evolution. Second, a term may be borrowed from a foreign legal language, and, third, a new term or neologism may be created. The following paragraphs focus on terminological interaction between legal cultures in the form of terminological borrowings and neologisms.[8]

2.4.1 Historical survey

For many centuries, Latin was the most important source of legal borrowings in Western legal languages. This can partly be explained by the general admiration for the cultural heritage of antiquity by later generations but primarily by the status of Roman and

[7] The history, present use, and techniques of legal abbreviations are discussed in Mattila (2008b:347–61; 2013:114–121).

[8] See, in more detail, Mattila (2009).

Canon Law in European legal history. Western lawyers mainly used Latin in their writings till the first centuries of modern times. As a result of centuries of language mixing, all legal languages in Europe contain a large number of Latin terms in the form of direct borrowings and naturalized words of Latin origin. Furthermore, numerous loan translations (calques) were produced and borrowed meanings were given to already existing words. For instance, a literal translation of *onus probandi* ("burden of proof") can be found in any European legal language Mattila (2013:162–173, 100).

After the Latin period, the dominant modern languages also spread their vocabulary to other legal languages. The expansion of powerful states, notably through colonialism, and the use of their languages in both general and legal contexts have greatly influenced subjugated legal cultures and their languages, both in Europe and on other continents. Some regional languages were also diffused in this way, such as Swedish in Finland.

In addition to compulsory means by the expansion of States, major languages have diffused their vocabulary into other languages by means of voluntary borrowing. The dominance of French legal culture and legal French in the eighteenth and nineteenth centuries, and especially the influence of the Code Napoléon, led to widespread borrowing of French legal terminology throughout Europe in the form of direct borrowings, naturalized words, calques, and borrowed meanings given to existing words. Since French was previously the leading *lingua franca* of diplomacy, the terminology of various languages in branches of law relating to international affairs still includes naturalized words of French origin and direct French borrowings *ordre public, renvoi*, etc. (Mattila 2013:159–60, 269–72). Similarly, the French Revolution contributed to the diffusion of French terms expressing the legal concepts of the new era. In many cases, these terms were borrowed by other languages as loan translations, such as *poder constituyendo* in legal Spanish (Martínez Bargueño 1992:13).

The international influence of legal German has clearly been more restricted. However, the golden period of German legal science at the end of the nineteenth century and the beginning of the twentieth century led to the adoption of many borrowings into the legal languages of Eastern Central Europe and Northern Europe. For the most part, these appeared in the form of loan translations, but also naturalizations of German origin, and even direct borrowings. Today, some direct borrowings, such as *Rechtsgeschäft*, are still used by academics in cross-border legal discussions in the central and northern parts of the continent (Mattila 2013:229–35).

2.4.2 Current tendencies

One still finds Latin borrowings in legal texts, particularly in legal scholarship. In certain countries they may also be found in legal instruments and documents (statutes, judgments, contracts, etc.). In fact, today Latin is used in some legal cultures even more than previously. For instance, an empirical study of American case law shows that certain Latin terms (*obiter dictum, ratio decidendi, sua sponte*, etc.) are now used more frequently in the decisions of higher courts in the United States than a few decades ago (Macleod

1997:248–51). In former socialist countries, ideological factors have recently resulted in an increased use of Latin in legal texts. In this way, lawyers from these countries emphasize that they belong to the old legal culture of Europe with roots in classical Roman law (Mattila 2013:173–86).

On the other hand, the presence of Latin in legal circles can also be explained by the fact that it still plays an important role in communication between lawyers in certain branches of law, especially those which are international in nature. According to an empirical study by our research group, key Latin terms of private international law appear dozens of times, some of them hundreds of times, in all standard conflicts treatises of any country.[9] The most common Latin term in private international law is *lex fori*, 'the law of the court' (Mattila 2005:83–8).

However, over the past few decades, many language specialists have stressed the disadvantages of the use of Latin expressions, particularly from the point of view of linguistic democracy. As a result, it can generally be said that today Latin expressions and maxims appear less frequently than earlier in legal and administrative texts. This is true in many countries. In Finland, for instance, our research group compared the use of Latin in legal literature in the 1950s and 1990s. In the 1950s, approximately 900 different Latin expressions and maxims were in use in Finland, whereas the number dropped to approximately 600 by the 1990s. In just a few decades, the use of Latin expressions had decreased by one third.

On the contrary, lexical borrowings from modern languages are increasing. This can be explained mainly by two powerful influences whose legal vocabulary is spreading on a global or regional scale: the United States of America and the European Union (founded on the basis of the European Communities by the Maastricht Treaty, which was concluded in 1991 and entered into force in 1993).

The legal culture of the United States and England, the common law, is considered to be very attractive in the world today. Therefore, the vehicle of this culture, legal English, exerts a strong influence on other legal languages, which is clearly manifested by the use of English borrowings in legal texts in other languages. Many of these borrowings have become established terms, such as *franchising* and *factoring*. As one might easily guess, the number of established and occasional English borrowings has greatly increased over the past few decades. In addition, numerous loan translations of English-language terms are found in various legal languages. A good example is *class action* (US) or *group action* (UK), which appear in legal French either in the form of direct calques (*action de classe* and *action de groupe*) or less faithful equivalents (*action populaire* and *action collective*) (Cornu 2007).

The officials of the European Union are constantly developing new administrative and judicial institutions in order to direct and implement European integration. It is

---

[9] It should be emphasized that this does not apply to all branches of law. A recent study of ours focused on all Latin words and sentences (established and occasional borrowings) appearing in leading treatises on the law of inheritance in certain countries. In the texts of a French and a Finnish treatise (both approximately 1,000 pages), one can find almost the same number of Latin words and sentences, about eighty different expressions and maxims; however, not a single one of them is identical! (Mattila 2008a:260–1).

important to avoid confusing the terms expressing such new institutions with terms already existing in the legal languages of some Member States but with a different meaning. Therefore, legal neologisms are frequently created. In fact, one may say that the European Union is the most important "factory" of legal and administrative neologisms in Western Europe. The terminological work of the Union is normally done in English and French, and new EU terms are created first in these languages. The neologisms created in these working languages then appear as lexical equivalents or borrowings in the other EU languages.

The terminological work of the European Union is challenging for several reasons. First, the Union is building a new type of legal system which has no direct historical model and which must be adapted to the national legal systems of the Member States. The need for neologisms is therefore great. Second, the administration of the Union is hugely complex with numerous parallel bodies, thus making it difficult to coordinate terminological work, a task which is aggravated by constant time pressures. Third, there are 23 official languages in the Union (as of 2009), some of which are structurally very different. Therefore, it is not easy to translate the neologisms created in English and French into all the other official languages.

Since French was the dominant language of the European Communities untill the middle of the 1990s, the legal English used in the Communities, and later in the Union, has been until recently a receiving language adopting many borrowings (*acquis communautaire, judge rapporteur*, etc.) from French (Harvey 2005:271–4). This is no longer the case because English has replaced French as the major working language of the Union institutions (except the European Court of Justice).

On the other hand, this evolution—the increased use of English in Continental legal contexts—makes it necessary to create English neologisms to express new EU institutions, as well as to consolidate English equivalents of terms designating old institutions and concepts in individual Continental countries, such as *court of cassation*, which has particular jurisdictional powers, and *compulsory portion* in the law of inheritance. At the same time, the conceptual content of many traditional common law terms tends to acquire a more Continental flavour when used to describe Romano-Germanic Law (e.g. the term *tort* in Continental contexts relating to non-contractual obligations).[10] The same applies when frequent Continental usage strengthens one of the established meanings of a traditional common law term, as in the case of the term *equity*, which is used in Continental legal literature in English only in the sense of "natural justice" (Beveridge 2002:71).

Due to this evolution, a new variant of legal English is being created which includes a number of terms which do not exist in common law English, along with a number of common law terms which are used with a more or less distinctive Continental meaning (Moréteau 1999:151–62; Ferreri 2006:44).

---

[10] Traditionally, the meanings of *tort* and comparable Continental terms correspond only roughly to each other. See, e.g., the entry *ilícito civil extracontractual* in Alcaraz Varó and Hughes (2007:844) where the authors add the word "approximatively" to the translation "tort".

2.5 LEGAL DICTIONARIES AND TERM BANKS

Traditionally, legal dictionaries (today increasingly in electronic form) constitute the key source for exact definitions of legal terms. The quantity and quality of these dictionaries vary greatly, as does their lexicographical structure. There are both fully alphabetical and partly systematic legal dictionaries. Quite often, they cover only one branch of law or are otherwise thematic. Special mention should be made of legal Latin dictionaries compiled in various linguistic zones.[11]

Legal dictionaries are frequently encyclopedic in nature, that is they contain not only legal definitions but also substantive information. The borderline between an encyclopedic dictionary and a legal encyclopedia in the proper sense is vague. An example of an exceptionally voluminous legal encyclopedic dictionary is the one compiled by Guillermo Cabanellas and Luis Alcalá-Zamora y Castillo (2003). Covering both Peninsular and South American legal Spanish, this dictionary consists of eight volumes containing more than 30,000 entries. Of course, there are many other sources of legal terminology, such as juridical treatises and official publications, which are usually useful in exceptional cases only.

The designations of various types of legal dictionaries vary in different linguistic zones. In German, a pure term dictionary is called a *Rechtswörterbuch* or *juristisches Wörterbuch*; an encyclopedic dictionary is often called a *Rechtslexikon*. In Romance languages, national variants of the Latin words *vocabularium* or *dictionarium* are used. In general, the former word (*vocabulaire*, *vocabulario*, etc.) refers to a pure term dictionary, and the latter (*dictionnaire*, *diccionario*, etc.) often, but not always, to an encyclopedic dictionary.

In the English linguistic zone, the most important source of legal terms is *Black's Law Dictionary*, which is still widely used and which has been completely updated by editor Bryan Garner, using modern lexicographic principles. Although published in the United States, this work contains a large number of classical terms from earlier periods of English law. However, there are other important dictionaries, including dictionaries of legal usage compiled by Garner (2011) and another one by David Mellinkoff (1992). Of course, there are new British law dictionaries as well. In the French linguistic zone, the dictionary edited by Gérard Cornu (2007) is worthy of special mention, as is the *Rechtswörterbuch* originally created by Cart Creifelds (2014) in the German linguistic zone.

Dictionaries with equivalents in two or more languages are useful not only for legal translation in the proper sense of the word, but also as a means of gaining a better understanding of the similarities and differences between corresponding terms in various

---

[11] In some linguistic zones, such as English and Spanish, Latin expressions are extensively included in general law dictionaries (*Black's Law Dictionary*, etc.). Legal Latin dictionaries with explanations in major languages are listed in Mattila (2013:199–201); those with explanations in some minor languages are listed in Mattila (2002).

languages. The number of bilingual (and multilingual) dictionaries in the field of law is enormous if one also takes into account minor languages and small glossaries. Robert Herbst's monumental dictionary (2002), which contains an extensive amount of phraseology, is a classic for major languages. The dictionary consists of three volumes, each with a different source language: English, French, and German. There are, of course, many other important works. On the basis of a broad comparison, the quality of legal dictionaries is said to vary greatly, sometimes to the point that it is risky to rely on them (Groot and Laer 2008). However, new means of improving their reliability are constantly being sought (Mac Aodha 2009).

Printed dictionaries are being increasingly replaced by electronic dictionaries and terminology banks, or simply "term banks." By far the largest is the new multilingual term bank of the European Union, IATE ("*Inter-Active Terminology for Europe*"), which is mainly intended for EU translation purposes but was opened to the public in 2007. Consequently, it can be used by anyone who needs equivalents in various EU languages or explanations of the meaning and use of terms in any EU language. The terms included in IATE cover all areas, but legal terms are widely represented among the entries. In addition to EU terminology in the proper sense, IATE includes a large number of classical and new terms in various branches of law in all languages of the EU Member States.

IATE was created by fusing the earlier term banks of key institutions of the EU into a single entity. It is "a centralised system for all European Union terminology resources with a single access point, demystifying jargon for all users within the European Union's Institutions and, in time, all EU citizens."[12] The institutions contributing to this term bank include the European Commission, the Council of the EU, the European Parliament, the Court of Auditors, the Economic and Social Committee, the Committee of the Regions, the Court of Justice, the Translation Centre for the Bodies of the EU, the European Investment Bank, and the European Central Bank.

In 2006, IATE contained some 1.4 million multilingual entries (concepts) and 7.7 million language-specific entries. It is understandable that such an enormous term bank, parts of which were compiled under great time pressure, is not homogenous from the point of view of quality and coverage. Many terms are still lacking in certain professional sectors, particularly in minor languages. Furthermore, the quality of equivalents and explanations varies. Therefore, use of the term bank requires common sense and critical thinking. Despite these shortcomings, IATE is an extremely valuable source of information on terminology for lawyers as well as translators.

---

[12] See http://ec.europa.eu/idabc/en/document/2294/565. The information in the text is based on the presentation of IATE on this homepage and on Rummel's PowerPoint slides (2005). See also Mattila (2007).

CHAPTER 3

THE GRAMMAR AND STRUCTURE OF LEGAL TEXTS

RISTO HILTUNEN

3.1 INTRODUCTION

THAT legal texts are generally considered difficult to read and understand stems from the law's societal functions of control and regulation. In order to provide a firm foundation for legal decision-making processes, which have to be systematic and just, the text of the law needs to be clear, explicit, and precise (Mellinkoff 1963). It is only to be expected that such strict conditions will impose equally strict requirements on the design of the language of legal texts (cf. Tiersma 1999:71, Gibbons 2003:36–73). Up to a point, such a design may involve stretching the capacities of the linguistic system well beyond the ordinary in order to meet the stringent demands on the proper form of the text. In the eyes of the public, the linguistic characteristics thus incorporated into the formulation of the law are frequently seen as an obstacle to understanding its content and as often leading to communicative failure wherever such texts are in focus. The fact that societies have specific professions especially designed to act as links between the public and the legal system itself suggests the potential risk of problems arising from the incompatibility of the routines of ordinary communication and those of the language of legal texts.

In this chapter, which addresses the language of legal texts with special reference to their grammatical and structural properties, the focus will be on written legal texts as materializations of the language of the legal code, a term that is here used to refer to the law as embraced in legal statutes (cf. Gibbons 1994:3; Kurzon 1994a). Although, strictly speaking, the term "code" may also refer to "a compilation not just of existing statutes, but also of much of the unwritten law on a subject, which is newly enacted as a complete system of law" (*Black's Law Dictionary*:250), statutes nevertheless constitute a focal point for examining the characteristics of legal texts, since they embody the functions of control and regulation of the law in a maximally clear, explicit, and precise wording. They can therefore be regarded as representing the law at its most prototypical. As far as legal language is concerned, the "code" that will provide the basis of the discussion and the source of examples below will be British Parliamentary acts. Although it will not be possible to deal with other kinds of legal texts in this chapter, it is hoped that the present account will also prove helpful for the grammatical and structural analysis of other kinds of legal texts, such as jury instructions (cf. Gibbons 2003:162–73), contracts (cf. Gibbons 2003:182–6; Trosborg 1997a, 1997b; Opitz 1983), and wills (cf. Finegan 1982).

While the approach followed here will foreground legal texts written in English, it may be assumed that the legal code will be characterized by analogous grammatical and structural properties in other European languages as well, subject to language-specific considerations of tradition, convention, and usage. The terms "language of the law", "statutory language", and "legislative language" will be used below as synonyms in referring to the language of legal texts.[1] Besides Parliamentary legislation, the other component of English law consists of common law (case law), that is "the body of law derived from juridical decisions, rather than from statutes or constitutions" (*Black's Law Dictionary*:270). This law, set out in juridical decisions, is recorded in law reports, which are used as an authority (or precedent) for reaching decisions in subsequent cases. Case law will not be further discussed in this chapter.

Another consideration relevant for the present purpose has to do with the time span to be covered. The law has to be revised and updated constantly to keep up with changes in society. In addition to revisions of content, this process also involves revising the language of the law. The following discussion will focus on the present day, but an additional purpose will be to illustrate how legal language has changed in terms of its grammatical and structural properties in the recent past of British parliamentary legislation. The discussion will focus on two dimensions of legal texts: their syntactic structure at the level of sentence and clause, and their functional characteristics at the level of discourse. As far as legal syntax is concerned, the discussion will essentially be based on the information provided in Gustafsson (1975), a classic study of the syntax of legal English, and the findings of Hiltunen (2001), a reappraisal of Gustafsson (1975) in the light of more recent material. The account of the functional organization of the relevant units in terms of the discourse structure of entire texts of Parliamentary acts, on the other hand, draws on the findings of Bhatia (1983). The emphasis will thus be on a "studies in legal language-as-object" approach, rather than on one of "studies in legal language-as-process" or "studies of legal language-as-instrument" (Stygall 1994:8, 12, 20).

---

[1] For further discussion of the linguistic terminology of legal texts, see Trosborg (1995) and Kurzon (1997).

3.2 SYNTACTIC STRUCTURES

One striking feature of legal language is the way in which words are combined into phrases, clauses, and sentences. Legal syntax is distinctly idiosyncratic in terms of both the structure and arrangement of the principal sentence elements. The sentence constitutes the basic syntactic unit, and is traditionally constructed as a self-contained, context-free entity. This is a basic starting-point for the drafting of legal texts, and its consequences for the language are pervasive (see Section 3.2.2). Such salient features as the length and complexity of sentences, the typical organization of clauses in complex patterns of parataxis (coordination) and hypotaxis (subordination), the preference for the passive voice over the active, the extensive use of nominalized verb forms, and the avoidance of grammatical ties across sentence boundaries, including pronominal anaphoric references (cf. Crystal and Davy 1969) may all be due, in one way or another, to the special status of the sentence, which is of overriding importance in the drafting of statutes. Some of these salient characteristics will be discussed below.

3.2.1 The sentence and its syntactic properties

3.2.1.1 *Sentence length*

Sentence-length is not only a distinctive feature of legal texts but also an interesting parameter of style. Gustafsson (1975:10–12) found the average sentence length for the *Courts Act 1971* to be 55.11 words (median 48.05 words), a figure considerably higher than for any other kind of prose for which comparative evidence was available. Comparing the result with those obtained for the genres of the 10 million word Brown Corpus, she found that the longest sentence in the Brown Corpus occurred in the genre of government documents, house organs, etc.: 25.49 words (median 21.78 words). The next genres in length were "learned and scientific writings" and "religion," with means 23.80 and 23.19 words, respectively (Gustafsson 1975:11).

As far as legal texts are concerned, in a brief survey of sentence length in British statutes over the 20-year period 1970–1990, Kurzon (1997:131) reported a consistent decline in sentence length from 92.50 (1970) and 45.06 (1980) to 37.06 (1990) words per sentence. Hiltunen (2001:56), on the other hand, found the average sentence length in the samples of the five statutes enacted in 2000 to be 45.05 words (median 37.60 words); in other words, since the 1970s sentences had become shorter by approximately ten words. While the figures may vary slightly depending on the content of the act in question and the size of the samples investigated, a trend towards shorter sentences is nevertheless apparent.

Although it is interesting to compare the figures for the different sets of data, sentence length is naturally a very crude yardstick for assessing the level of complexity in a text. In practice, short sentences may sometimes be equally, or more, difficult to comprehend than long ones. Of crucial importance is how sentences are constructed syntactically with regard to their information structure. Sentences where the linear flow of information is repeatedly interrupted are likely to be more difficult to process than those where such interruptions are removed by opting for alternative syntactic arrangements. However, due to the independent status of the sentence in statutory texts, alternative arrangements may not be available, and the result will often be a compromise between an ideal syntactic formulation and the desired information structure of a sentence.

Where linguistic resources fall short, other devices must be considered. One helpful practical solution to guide the reader through long sentences is to make use of a layout that graphically separates the hierarchical parts of the sentence into sections and subsections, for example, by means of indentation, itemized sequencing, adding keywords and short summaries in the margin, and the like. The following example from the *Electronic Communications Act* (2000 c. 7 (2) (2)) shows one way of organizing the text typographically (Hiltunen 2001:58):[2]

The arrangements must–

(a) allow for approval to be granted...;
(b) ensure that an approval is granted to a person...;
(c) provide for an approval granted to any person...;
(d) enable a person to whom the Secretary of State is proposing to grant...;
(e) make provision for the handling of complaints and disputes which–
   (i) are required by the conditions of an approved person's approval to be dealt with in accordance with...; but
   (ii) are not disposed by the application of that procedure;
(f) provide for the modification and withdrawal of approvals.

Later in the same act a sentence occurs with 382 words (8, 4).[3] However, this sentence is, in practice, no more difficult to understand than the above example, thanks to the way it is organized into an alphabetically itemized list of points. The relevance of sentence length as a criterion of complexity is thus once again called into question by such examples, for they show that layout devices may make the content of the sentence more readily accessible for the reader, while they simultaneously make allowances, if need be, for increasing the total length of the sentence considerably without risking comprehensibility.

Yet another point in considering the processing of long sentences is the fact that legislative texts are not in the first place intended to be read like more ordinary texts. They are written above all for professionals and for reference. The texts are likely to be consulted selectively, often with just one particular detail in mind. In this sense they are examples of encyclopedic text. They constitute works of reference, where information can be looked up, checked, and if necessary followed up in other acts, including those of other domains within the network of legislation.

---

[2] The British Parliamentary acts of 2000 to be cited below are available at: http://www.legislation. hmso.gov.uk/acts/acts2000/htm.

[3] This sentence, however, was outside the sample included in the study (Hiltunen 2001).

3.2.1.2 *The clausal structure of sentences*

Grammatically, sentences can be constructed in four different ways. They may be (a) simple sentences, consisting of only one main (or principal) clause; (b) compound sentences, consisting of two or more coordinate main clauses; (c) complex sentences, consisting of one main clause and one or more subordinate clauses; or (d) complex-compound sentences, consisting of two or more coordinate main clauses with one or more subordinated clauses (cf. Quirk et al. 1985:987–91). Considering the unconditional requirements of legal texts in terms of precision, avoidance of ambiguity, and detail of statements, it is to be expected that simple and compound sentences will be in a minority. In fact, the share of simple sentences is a little over 20 percent and that of compound sentences about 6 percent of the instances in the data of Gustafsson (1975) and Hiltunen (2001).

It is the complex sentence type that predominates in the texts. Complex sentences, consisting of a main clause with one or more (finite) subordinate clauses, constitute the most common sentence type in both the above sets of data.[4] In the 1975 material they constitute 73 percent of all sentences, as against 64 percent in the 2001 data. On the other hand, the syntactically most complicated type, the complex-compound sentence, makes up 25 percent of all instances in the 1975 material, but only 4 percent in the 2001 data. Thus, while the proportion of simple sentences has remained the same, the proportion of complex-compound sentences has been considerably reduced in favor of complex sentences. Similarly, in terms of the average number of (finite) subordinate clauses per main clause in syntactically complex sentences, the difference (2.86 vs. 2.52) also points to a decrease in level of complexity. Further research, however, is needed to establish more conclusively to what extent such differences may be regarded as indications of a permanent change in favor of less complicated sentences in legislative texts.

3.2.1.3 *Types of subordinate clauses*

As the core of syntactic complexity in legislative texts is to be found in hypotaxis (subordination) rather than parataxis (coordination), we also need to consider the type of subordinate clauses and their internal arrangement in sentences. The results of the two studies indicate that relative clauses make up about half of all instances of subordination, and adverbial clauses about a third. Among the rest, the most notable group consists of clauses introduced by the conjunction *that*. The last few decades do not seem to have witnessed any marked change in the language of British Parliamentary acts in the distribution of the types of subordinate clauses. The reason for this stability most probably lies in the functional properties of these clause types. Relative clauses, for instance, serve the important function of defining or qualifying a particular item in the preceding main clause, or its entire propositional content, while adverbial clauses provide a highly versatile way of expressing a variety of functions that are essential for the content of the law, such as conditions, purposes, reasons, concessions, and consequences. On the other

---

[4] The subordinate clauses in Gustafsson (1975) and in Hiltunen (2001) contain only finite clauses. However, in the analysis of Quirk et al. (1985:992–7), non-finite and verbless subordinate clauses may also be distinguished. This model was followed in Hiltunen (1984).

hand, the way in which qualifying relative clauses and adverbial clauses are organized in syntactic patterns of subordination within the sentence constitutes a significant characteristic of legal syntax (see Hiltunen 1984).

3.2.1.4 *The position of subordinate clauses in the legal sentence*

Subordinate clauses abound in legal texts. As observed by Bhatia (1983:34), in many cases several such elements "seem to compete for the relatively few positions available within and around the syntactic structure of the main provisionary clause."

Subordinate clauses may indeed occur in a variety of positions in the sentence, but for present purposes it is practical to consider them in terms of (a) sentence-initial (or left-branching) position; (b) sentence-medial (or nested) position; and (c) sentence-final (or right-branching) position. The following examples illustrate the three positional variations (with the main clause in italics):

(a) Left-branching

Where, on making his request for information, the applicant expresses a preference for communication by any one or more of the following means, namely:

(a) the provision to the applicant of a copy of the information in permanent form or in another form acceptable to the applicant,

(b) the provision to the applicant of a reasonable opportunity to inspect a record containing the information, and

(c) the provision to the applicant of a digest or summary of the information in permanent form or in another form acceptable to the applicant,

the public authority shall so far as reasonably practicable give effect to that preference. (*Freedom of Information Act* 2000 c. 36 (11)(1))

(b) Nested

In the case of any matter which is not one of the reserved matters within the meaning of the Scotland Act 1998 or in respect of which functions are, by virtue of section 63 of that Act, exercisable by the Scottish Ministers instead of by or concurrently with a Minister of the Crown, *this section and section 8 shall apply to Scotland subject to the following modifications—*(*Electronic Communications Act* 2000 c.7 (9)(7))

(c) Right-branching

Subsection (1) shall not prohibit the imposition by an order under section 8 of—

(a) *a requirement to deposit a key for electronic data with the intended recipient of electronic communications comprising data; or*

(b) *a requirement for arrangements to be made, in cases* where a key for data is not deposited with another person, which otherwise secures that the loss of a key, or its becoming unusable, does not have the effect that the information contained in a record kept in pursuance of any provision made by or under any enactment or subordinate legislation becomes inaccessible or incapable of being put into intelligible form. (*Electronic Communications Act* 2000 c. 7 (14)(4))

There are certain preferences for a particular type of clause to occur in a particular position in the sentence. For example, adverbial *if*-clauses specifying conditions and relative *where*-clauses describing cases (cf. (a) above) tend to be placed at the beginning of the sentence. Overall, the right-branching arrangement is, however, the most common. It is also likely to cause fewer processing problems for the reader than the other positions. On the other hand, sequences of right-branching clauses may also become rather complicated and difficult to understand, depending on how the clauses are arranged. Thus item *(b)* above (*a requirement for arrangements...*) contains two relative clauses in succession, introduced by *where* and *which*, the latter being followed by two clauses introduced by the conjunction *that.* The latter *that* clause in turn contains three participial insertions, introduced by *contained*, *kept*, and *made*, respectively, further complicating the syntax of the sentence.[5]

Nested (or "center-embedded") subordinate clauses are generally regarded as syntactically and perceptually problematic. Sentences involving only one clause in medial position do not usually give rise to any difficulties, but if multiple embeddings occur in this position they may put an extra strain on the processing capacity of the reader, as indicated by the text in (b) above. Multiple self-embedded constructions of the following type (Hiltunen 1984:117), however, are rare:

> *A person* who, when riding a cycle, not being a motor vehicle, on a road or other public place, is unfit to ride through drinks or drugs, *shall be guilty of an offence.* (*Road Traffic Act* 1972, c. 20 (19) (1))

A data-set of 373 sentences contained only six such instances.

A recent study (Karlsson 2007), reporting on the occurrence of multiple center-embeddings in a variety of computerized text corpora and other sources in several European languages, indicates that the maximal degree of (finite) center-embedding in written language is three and that recursive multiple clausal center-embedding is not a central design feature of language in use. In the case of legal texts, however, it is worth bearing in mind that in addition to embeddings in medial position, clausal insertions may also occur within both left- and right-branching sequences, increasing considerably the processing load of the propositional content of sentences. This is also borne out by the examples of left- and right-branching above.

Returning to the issue of change in legislative language over the last few decades, let us next consider the three patterns of organization of subordinate clauses in sentences. The findings reported in Hiltunen (1984, 2001) suggest an interesting development in this respect during the intervening decades.[6] The majority of subordinate clauses in both

---

[5] Such participial clauses, characteristically modifying an element in the main clause, constitute the bulk of non-finite clauses in legal texts. Grammatically, they are instances of so-called 'whiz-deletion', i.e. constructions where the relative pronoun and the finite form of the verb *to be* have been deleted (cf. Hiltunen 1984:110).

[6] The material in Hiltunen (1984) is from the British *Road Traffic Act* 1972, while that of Hiltunen (2001) is based on a selection of acts from 2000 (see Hiltunen 2001:55).

sets of data are found in sentence-final, right-branching position (59.7 percent in 1984, as against 77.7 percent in 2001). The figures also indicate a tangible increase in right-branching syntax in the later data. On the other hand, the proportion of left-branching syntax is fairly uniform in both sets of data (12.2 and 10.1 percent, respectively). In the case of the medial position, the figures indicate a decline of nested clausal insertions in the data from 26.3 to 10.1 percent; in other words, the proportion of nested clauses has lost ground by about half since the early 1970s in favor of right-branching ones. This change is likely to have resulted from an increasing awareness of the problems associated with the processing of medial insertions (Hiltunen 2001). Moreover, it probably originated from a public demand for simpler legal language, rather than from among the legal profession itself. It has to be borne in mind that a syntax which to a lay person may appear difficult to understand may to the professional be an aid for the quick processing of the subject matter. Legal professionals will have been trained to "read" the text according to principles that lay readers may not be aware of at all. From this perspective, syntactic characteristics such as those discussed above may be viewed as helpful devices, ensuring the syntactic consistency and the consequent perceptual predictability of legislative texts. Multiple sentence-medial embeddings may, however, be a borderline case in this regard, for they may hamper the reading and comprehension of the text for the lay and professional reader alike.

3.2.2 Other structural characteristics

As we have seen, the complexities of legal syntax are due to the communicative purposes of the law, coupled with the sentence as the basic syntactic unit of expression. The legal sentence may be broken down into its clausal elements by analyzing it in terms of parataxis (coordination) and hypotaxis (subordination), as suggested above. However, it also possible to view the sentence in terms of its constituents, especially the nominal elements. From this point of view, the sentence is essentially made up of nominal structures, which are frequently heavy and complex. Thus, in the sentence below the subject is a highly complex noun phrase, consisting of a long sequence of relative clauses that qualify the antecedent noun phrase (i.e. *the body*):

> *The body which, immediately before the coming into force of this subsection, was known as the Postal Services Commission and was designated in accordance with Article 22 of the Postal Services Directive as a national regulatory authority for the postal sector in the United Kingdom* is hereby abolished. (*Postal Services Act,* 2000 c. 26 (1)(4)).

Similarly, the object of the sentence may also be a noun phrase of considerable complexity. In the following example it is made up of a sequence of post-modifying relative clauses:

> The Secretary of State shall take *such steps as he considers appropriate for the purpose of bringing to the attention of the public the identity of any person who is a universal services provider for the purposes of this Act.* (*Postal Services Act,* 2000 c. 26 (2)(5))

The examples indicate that is also possible to view legal syntax in terms of the arrangement of nominal structures, contributing to the heavily nominal style of legal language. In addition to relative clauses, typically modifying subject and object noun phrases, the sentences also frequently contain prepositional phrases and/or adverbial clauses, which may be inserted in various places in the sentence. These further contribute to the discontinuous structure of the sentence (Gustafsson 1975:19–22; Swales and Bhatia 1983).[7]

The special nature of the legal sentence as a means of communication is also highly relevant to the process of drafting laws. The time-honored guidelines proposed by Coode (1845), for example, already relate the function of the essential elements to the syntactic arrangement of the legal sentence. According to Coode, the legal sentence consists of four elements: the legal subject, the legal action, the case to which the legal action is confined, and the conditions on the fulfillment of which the legal action becomes operative. The preferred order of these elements is the following:

(Case)	Where any Quaker refuses to pay any church rates,
(Condition)	if any church warden complains thereof,
(Subject)	one of the next Justices of the Peace,
(Action)	may summon such a Quaker.

As noted by Bhatia (1983:5), Coode's analysis is useful for its attention to the sentence structure and the arrangement of modifying clauses, although it may not apply to all legislative sentences, especially those with multiple and complex modifications.[8]

3.3 DISCOURSE

When we look at legal language above the level of the sentence, we are concerned with the level of discourse. It is characterized, for example, by the absence of pronoun references, not only within the sentence but also across sentence boundaries. On the other hand, discourse also refers to the use of language in terms of the context and the social and institutional practices to which it relates. Here it would appear at first sight that it might not be very relevant to the language of the legal code, bearing in mind that the sentence is a self-contained unit and that cohesive links between sentences, such as pronouns, tend to be avoided. This in turn results in the repetition of full noun and verb phrases as a preferred strategy, even at the expense of readability. In the example below, the noun phrase "an electronic signature" is repeated in three successive sentences.

---

[7] Gustafsson (1975) discusses nominalized verb forms and prepositions as a means of compressing a great amount of information into a sentence, while Swales and Bhatia (1983) deal with the ubiquitous complex prepositions, such as *in respect of, in accordance with, with a view into, in pursuance of,* etc., in terms of the syntactic environment of their occurrences and their discoursal functions.

[8] For further discussion of drafting manuals, see Kurzon (1985).

7. (1) In any legal proceedings—

    (a) *an electronic signature* incorporated into or logically associated with a particular electronic communication or particular electronic data, and...

  (2) For the purposes of this section *an electronic signature* is so much of anything in electronic form as—...

  (3) For the purposes of this section *an electronic signature* incorporated into or associated with a particular electronic communication or particular electronic data is certified by any person if that person (whether before or after the making of the communication) has made a statement confirming that—...

  (*Electronic Communications Act* 2000 c.7 (7)(1)(2)(3))

Ostensibly to minimize the risk of ambiguity, punctuation likewise tends to be kept to an absolute minimum. Such characteristics strongly indicate that the text is written and organized from the point of view of the writer, rather than the reader. From the writer's perspective the text may be admirably constructed, but from the reader's perspective it may be less satisfactory, especially if the reader is not a legal professional.

In spite of the status of the sentence as an independent unit in law, statutes should be seen as a form of institutional communication, with an interface with the world. This implies taking a more in-depth view of legal language, one which also involves a functional interpretation of the text in terms of its communicative context. An example of such an approach, with special reference to the organization of the multifarious qualifying clauses according to their communicative functions within the sentence, is Bhatia (1983). In his functional classification of legal qualifications, he distinguishes three categories: (1) preparatory, (2) operational, and (3) referential qualifications (Bhatia 1983:31).

Preparatory qualifications "describe cases" such as the following:

> *Where a secure tenant has claimed to exercise the right to buy and that right has been established*...the landlord shall...

They also include those that specify conditions:

> *If any person...fails to perform any duty imposed on him by this Schedule*...he shall be guilty...

They are usually placed at the beginning of the sentence.

Operational qualifications include those that specify 'legal means':

> The landlord...shall *by notice in writing served on the tenant*...extend...

Also included are those ascribing 'legal purpose':

> The Chief Land Registrar shall, *for the purpose of the registration of the title*, accept such a certificate...

Their syntactic position tends to be more variable.

Referential qualifications, finally, include qualifications assigning "textual authority," as in the example below:

Where a secure tenancy is a periodic tenancy and...there is a person qualified to succeed him, *the tenancy vests by virtue of this section in that person*...

"Textual mapping" is another illustration of such qualifications:

At the commencement of this section, every controlled tenancy shall cease to be a controlled tenancy...*except in the case mentioned in subsection (2) below.*

Such qualifications are typically placed at the end of the sentence.[9]

This type of functional analysis is also useful in illustrating the web-like nature of legislative texts. Although explicit cohesive ties between sentences are scarce, there is actually a dense web of explicit (legal) references to other parts and sections of the same act and to other acts bearing on the issue at hand. These are usually expressed by means of the title of the act in question (*Scotland Act 1998*) and the necessary referential identification (*subsections (1) and (2) of this section*), e.g.:

In the case of any matter which is not one of the reserved matters within the meaning of the *Scotland Act 1998* or in respect of which functions are, by virtue of *section 63 of that Act*, exercisable by the Scottish Ministers instead of by or concurrently with a Minister of the Crown, *this section* and *section 8* shall apply to Scotland subject to the following modifications—

(a) *subsections (1) and (2) of this section* are omitted;
(b) [...]

(*Electronic Communications Act* 2000 c. 7 (9)(7))

Such chains of references to other acts, sections, and subsections are not uncommon. Naturally, mastering such a technical aspect of the law requires training and expertise.

3.4 SPEECH-ACT THEORY

Another communicative approach to legislative language is one based on speech acts, for law inherently implies "doing things with words" (Kevelson 1982; Kurzon 1986). Not only can an entire statute be seen as a speech act with the illocutionary force of enactment, but many of the sentences within the statute may themselves have the status of speech acts. Legislative texts are rich in speech act phenomena, including both explicit performative verbs and illocutionary acts. The enacting formula of British Parliamentary acts is a good example of an explicit performative speech act, establishing the illocutionary force of the text to follow (cf. Trosborg 1997b:34).

Be it enacted by the Queen's most Excellent Majesty, by and with the advice and consent of the Lords Spiritual and Temporal, and Commons, in this present Parliament assembled, and by the authority of the same, as follows.

[9] Bhatia (1983:34, 48, 96).

The formula contains the performative verb *to enact*. It is here used in the passive form with an agent in the third person, but it may be paraphrased in the first person, which is the more typical form for a performative verb. The illocutionary forces most characteristic of statutory language include *permission* (commonly conveyed through *may*), *ordering* (*shall*), and *prohibition* (*shall not*) (cf. Kurzon 1986:9). Along with explicitly marked speech acts, it will be important for a lawyer to be able to detect any indirect illocutionary meanings in a text by being able to read between the lines.

3.5   CONCLUSION

The law has to be revised constantly so as to keep it up to date with social change. This need for revision, however, does not mean that the language of the law will automatically be updated at the same time. On the contrary: since the law is essentially a conservative institution, it follows that its language is relatively conservative as well. It is therefore not likely to change very quickly. In this chapter we have explored the structure of the legal sentence, together with some syntactic changes that have been in progress in legal English during the past few decades. For this purpose, Gustafsson's (1975) study of the frequencies of the basic syntactic parameters of legislative language was consulted as a point of comparison. Twenty-five years is a short time for syntactic changes to become apparent in speech, let alone in a written genre that is inherently conservative. The results nevertheless indicate that legal, statutory English usage is not immune to the pressure of social change. Among other changes, sentences have become shorter and there seem to be fewer subordinate clauses inserted in sentence-medial position. This would seem to indicate that the medial, nested position in the sentence, traditionally regarded as problematic for language processing, is giving way to other arrangements, in particular right-branching syntax. The two variables— sentence length and medial insertions—may also be interrelated. As the role of the more significant source of complexity is reduced, sentence length becomes even less of an issue. The effective utilization of layout devices further diminishes its relevance as a complexity factor.

Regarding the social motivation for the kind of changes described above, a possible answer may be sought in the "plain language" movement that propagates a simpler and more reader-friendly legal language. Such pleas have been voiced more intensively in some countries than others, but everywhere they have drawn public attention to features of "traditional" legal language as a source of complexity, even inaccessibility, for non-professionals. Such voices have undoubtedly also gained momentum in Europe as a result of the increasing exposure of the public to legal texts, for example, as a result of the transnational legislation of the European Union. The role of the internet in making publicly accessible legal materials, such as rules and regulations, should also be kept in mind.

Finally, the functional dimensions of some of the grammatical and structural properties of legal texts were considered in the light of the organization of legal qualifications. A functional analysis of this kind, together with the yield of pragmatics, especially in terms of speech acts and illocutionary meaning, considerably enhances and enriches the view of the nature of legal texts provided by more formal grammatical and structural considerations.

CHAPTER 4

....

TEXT AND GENRE

....

MAURIZIO GOTTI

4.1 INTRODUCTION

A number of features distinguish legal texts not only from those with general language but also from other specialized texts. The avoidance of the use of standard textual norms in favour of "deviant" options is not at all arbitrary, but derives from the main pragmatic principles typical of the legal field.

The most important of these principles concerns avoidance of ambiguity and precision of interpretation. This criterion also explains the high degree of conservatism typical of the law. Fear that new terms may lead to ambiguity favors the permanence of traditional linguistic traits, which are preserved even when they disappear from general language. Old formulae are preferred to newly-coined words because of their centuries-old history and highly codified, universally accepted interpretations. The reverence for tradition observed in legal language also reflects its close link with the ancient practice of using special formulae for oaths or appointments, for drafting edicts and statutes, for issuing laws, conferring honours or assigning property. In this context, formulaic language is used to ensure the action's validity.

Another consequence of this principle is the high level of redundancy which characterizes legal texts, generally due to the pleonastic use of lexical items. This involves a violation of the principle of conciseness (which is a distinctive feature of specialized discourse, cf. Gotti 2008), since the number of lexemes employed is far higher than necessary. For example, English legal drafters often employ two interchangeable terms for the same concept: e.g. *new and novel, false and untrue, made and signed, terms and conditions, able and willing*. There is a historical reason for this habit: each of these pairs often consists of a neo-Latin term coupled with an Anglo-Saxon parallel—a practice rooted in the age following the Norman Invasion, when England had two spoken languages: English (which accounts for the Anglo-Saxon term) and Norman French. The naming of concepts through both languages ensured comprehension by all sectors of the population. Apart from these historical considerations, legal English clearly retains to this day examples of redundancy. Although many legal texts could be redrafted in a more concise form, with no loss of meaning or increased ambiguity, compliance with tradition is stronger in legal discourse than is the search for conciseness. Although there are movements in many countries advocating the use of more ordinary language, most legal specialists continue to follow the practices codified by centuries of use.

4.2 TEXT

4.2.1 Textual complexity

One factor that characterizes legal texts is their great length and complexity. Written legal discourse is encoded by far longer sentences than those found in general language. For example, in Gustafsson's (1975) corpus of English legal texts, the average sentence length is around 55 words, twice as long as scientific texts and eight times longer than oral texts. The considerable sentence length of legal texts is due to the high number of items required to minimize ambiguity and misunderstandings. Each mention is supported by specifications that clarify its identity. For example, the noun phrase *this agreement* in example (4.1) is specified by 42 other words providing further information about its validity, the names of the parties involved, their legal address, the names assigned to them later in the contract and mention of the successors to the two signatories:

(4.1) This Agreement, effective as of the first day of April, 2003 between Dale Johnson Ryder Warren, an Association organized and existing under the laws of Switzerland ('Grantor'), its successors and assigns, and DJRW Johnson Ryder Simpson & C., its successors and assigns ('Member Firm')...(Gotti 2008:220)

Moreover, legal texts exhibit a high number of postmodifiers and relative clauses, in contrast to other kinds of specialized discourse, which instead prefer premodification. This phenomenon may also be explained by the need for maximum clarity typical of legal language—a need which contrasts with the high potential for ambiguity which is made possible by nominal attributes and other premodifiers. An example of this is the expression *Every person disposing of*, which allows two interpretations: *Every person who disposes of* and *Every person who has disposed of*.

Increased length often implies more complex relations between a noun and its postmodifiers. Such complexity is evident, for example, in the syntactic links within the noun phrase that serves as subject in the sentence reported in example (4.1):

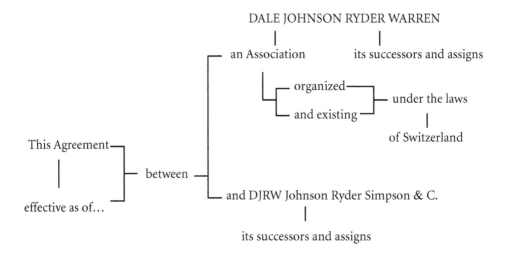

Similarly, the rare elimination of relative clauses and the frequent use of long postmodi-fiers leads to very long and syntactically complex sentences of this kind:

(4.2) The Tenant will … pay for all gas and electric light and power which shall be con-sumed or supplied on or to the Property during the tenancy and the amount of the water rate charged in respect of the Property during the tenancy and the amount of all charges made for the use of the telephone on the Property during the tenancy or a proper proportion of the rental or other recurring charges to be assessed according to the duration of the tenancy (Gotti 2008:218)

As can be seen, the considerable length of sentences in English legal writing is due to the rare occurrence of devices that in ordinary language would condense the surface length of a sentence, such as nominal attributes, premodification, main clauses reduced to sub-ordinates, omission of relative clauses, frequent use of non-finite rather than finite verbs, etc. If alongside such syntactic phenomena one also considers the cases of lexical redun-dancy discussed above, the greater length and complexity of sentences in English legal discourse becomes quite evident.

4.2.2 Anaphoric reference

Anaphoric reference is one of the most common devices deployed to increase textual cohe-sion (cf. Halliday and Hasan 1976). In conjunction with other referential phenomena, such as ellipsis, substitution, and lexical cohesion, it forms the textual framework which—combined with suitable cohesive devices—accounts for a text's constituent features. This phenomenon is familiar in common language but far less so in legal writing, where it is normally avoided in favor of lexical repetition. An illustration is the repetition of *The Member Firm, Grantor*, and *any (such) third party/parties* in the following paragraph:

(4.3) The Member Firm shall notify Grantor in writing, of any infringement, imitation, passing off or use of the Service Marks or any confusingly similar marks by any third party which comes to its attention. The Member Firm, as licensee, shall have the right to decide whether or not proceedings shall be brought by the Member Firm against any such third parties. In the event that it is decided that action should be taken against any such third party, the Member Firm may take such action in its own name. If the Member Firm chooses not to bring proceedings against any such third party, Grantor shall be entitled to bring proceedings in the name of the Member Firm and, in such event, the Member Firm agrees to cooperate fully with Grantor to whatever extent it is necessary or appropriate to prosecute such action. All legal costs shall be borne by the Member Firm and any damages awarded shall be equitably apportioned on the basis of damages suffered and costs incurred. (Gotti 2008:223)

Here, the repetition of such lexical items is far more acceptable than anaphoric reference through personal pronouns. This preference stems from the need for maximum clarity and avoidance of ambiguity, a typical trait of legal discourse mentioned earlier. In the following tenancy contract, for example, the repetition of *Landlord* in the possessive form, instead of the possessive pronoun *his/her*, seeks to avoid the anaphorical reference of *agents* to the word *Tenant* in subject position:

(4.4) [The Tenant will] Permit the Landlord or the Landlord's agents at reasonable hours in the daytime to enter the Property to view the state and condition thereof (Gotti 2008:218)

At times, however, there is excessive recourse to lexical repetition even in cases where the risk of ambiguity is very slight or nonexistent, as in the following example. The use of the postmodifier *of the Landlord* instead of the possessive adjective *his/her* is hardly justifiable, as it is obvious that the *other rights and remedies* mentioned cannot be attributed to a defaulting tenant:

(5) Provided that if the Rent or any instalment or part thereof shall be in arrear for at least fourteen days after the same shall have become due (whether legally demanded or not) or if there shall be a breach of any of the agreements by the Tenant the Landlord may re-enter on the Property and immediately thereupon the tenancy shall absolutely determine without prejudice to the other rights and remedies of the Landlord (Gotti 2008:219)

The need for maximum precision in legal language is confirmed by exophoric reference, with detailed specification of any contextual item mentioned in the sentence. An example of this is the unnatural effect, in everyday sentences containing vocative forms, of the interlocutor's surname when enquiring about his identity. Philips' (1987) corpus provides interesting instances of this use:

(4.6) JUDGE: Uh, Richard Reichenstein, (4 sec. pause) Is Richard Reichenstein your
       true name, sir?
   DEFENDANT: Yes, sir. (2 sec. pause)
   JUDGE: Ms. Miller, is your true name Elizabeth Miller?
   DEFENDANT: Yes, it is, your Honor. (2 sec. pause) (Philips 1987:88–9)

4.2.3 Textual mapping

The need for precision lies at the base of another relevant characteristic of legal texts: the
frequent references to parts of the text itself, specifying in the clearest way the textual
element being referred to. Note, for example, the frequent use of the 'textual-mapping'
(Bhatia 1987) adverbials *hereto*, *herein*, *hereof*, and *thereto* in the following sentence:

(4.7) Whereas, Johnson Ryder Archer & C., Johnson Ryder Chester & C., Dale Johnson
       Nelson & C., Dale Johnson Stokes & C., Grantor, Johnson Ryder International a
       partnership, and Dale Ryder Warren an association, have entered into the
       Component License Agreement, effective as of April 1, 2002 ('Component License
       Agreement'), a copy of which is attached hereto as Appendix B (without Appendices
       A and B attached thereto which are Appendix A hereto and a form of this Agreement)
       and made a part hereof as if fully recited herein and to which the Member Firm
       agrees to be fully bound as if originally a party thereto . . . (Gotti 2008:221)

These adverbials generally refer to a document or a part of it and specify its exact location or identification; in other cases they accompany past participles which otherwise
might be interpreted erroneously. Here are some examples:

(4.8) In section 21 thereof
       The hands of the parties hereto
       The day and year first above written
       By the license granted hereby
       Any regulations thereto
       Agreed by the parties hereto
       Fully recited herein (Gotti 2008:217–26)

4.2.4 Use of conjunctions

The same point may be made about the use of conjunctions. These items not only add
cohesion to texts but also have a pragmatic function, which clarifies the purpose of the
sentence that follows. For instance, after such expressions as *but*, *however*, *on the other
hand*, and so forth, one expects a sentence semantically opposed to the previous one,
with conjunctions like *as*, *since*, *for*, *because*, and others generally introducing a reason
or explanation. It is notable again that legal language strongly emphasizes the pragmatic
function of connectives by making meaning more transparent through inclusion in the

surface form of a lexeme denoting their illocutionary value. An instance of this may be seen in the following sentences, where the part in italics is often a more transparent paraphrase of common connectives:

(4.9) NOW, THEREFORE, *in consideration of* the premises and of the mutual covenants hereinafter set forth the parties agree as follows:

(4.10) The Member Firm agrees, both during and after the term of this Agreement, to cooperate fully and in good faith with Grantor and to execute such documents as Grantor reasonably requests *for the purpose of* securing and preserving Grantor's rights in and to the name 'Dale Johnson Ryder Warren' and to the service marks set forth in the attached Appendix A.

(4.11) *In the event that* it is decided that action should be taken against any such third party, the Member Firm may take such action in its own name. (Gotti 2008:221–3)

As the most common connectives may have several uses (and pragmatic values) despite their expressive conciseness, their place is often taken in legal texts by a longer but more pragmatically transparent paraphrase. The formulation of the text is subservient again to pragmatic requirements, as the need to ensure a single clear-cut interpretation prevails over text length.

4.2.5 Performative texts

One of the problems confronted by the analyst is how to profile certain speech acts within each part of a text, whether specialized or not. Language often serves different purposes, as the author employs the text to achieve various results simultaneously. Any attempt to assign a single illocutionary meaning to a text (or its separate parts) is therefore an unacceptable simplification. The range of speech acts based on Austin's (1962) and Searle's (1969) taxonomies is similar in specialized and non-specialized texts. However, there is one class (performatives) that occurs far more frequently in legal texts.

Language in the law is probably more performative than in any other field (cf. Kurzon 1986). Indeed, the mere statement of guilt or innocence pronounced by a judge makes the culprit guilty (or not guilty) of a crime, whether or not he actually committed it. Similarly, a court can declare legally 'deceased' a person who has been missing for a long time, even if that person may have moved to another country or changed his identity and therefore is not, physically speaking, dead. The importance of speech acts with a performative orientation—with a first-person pronoun and a conventional formula making the act legally valid—is confirmed by the following transcription of questioning in the courtroom, where the accused admits guilt (*I did it*) but only pleads guilty from a legal point of view at a later stage (*I plead guilty*):

(4.12) CLERK: Do you plead guilty or not guilty?
       DEFENDANT: Yes, I did it. I said I did it.
       CLERK: No. Do you plead guilty or not guilty?

DEFENDANT: Yes, I did it. I just want to get it over.

MAGISTRATE (to probation officer): Can you be of help here?

The probation officer goes over to the defendant and eventually goes out of court with her. Later in the morning the case is 'called on' again.

MAGISTRATE: Do you plead guilty or not guilty?

DEFENDANT: Yes, I did it.

MAGISTRATE: No, I'm asking you whether you plead guilty or not guilty. You must use either the words 'not guilty' or 'guilty'.

DEFENDANT: (Looking toward probation officer) She said, "Say guilty."

MAGISTRATE: No. You must say what you *want* to say.

DEFENDANT: Yes, I'll say what you like. I did it.

MAGISTRATE: No, you must use the language of the court. (To probation officer) Did she understand?

PROBATION OFFICER: Yes, she understood.

The probation officer once more approaches the dock, whispers to the woman and the word 'guilty' emerges. (Carlen 1976:110–11, quoted in Danet 1980:460–1)

4.2.6 Drafting conventions

Important elements of a particular legal system are its drafting tradition and stylistic conventions. These may differ in civil law and common law texts: the former are mainly characterized by generality, while the latter prefer particularity. Indeed, it is commonly asserted that civil law statutes are written in terms of principle, whereas common law regulations are written in detail as "the civil code draftsman is eager to be widely understood by the ordinary readership, whereas the common law draftsman seems to be more worried about not being misunderstood by the specialist community" (Bhatia 1993:137). This difference may also be observed in contracts: the common law rules typically give great authority to the wording of the document, while the civil law systems put more emphasis on the actual intent of the parties at the time when the agreement was entered into.

This stylistic difference derives from a basic conceptual differentiation underlying the two legal systems: in the civil law system the judiciary is entrusted with the task of construing, interpreting, and applying the general principles outlined in the civil code to specific real-life situations; this requirement therefore privileges stylistic choices such as generality and simplicity of expression. The common law system, instead, is based on the principle of precedence, by means of which the decisions taken by one judge become binding on all subsequent similar cases; this system therefore regards certainty of expression as the most valued quality in legal drafting. This conceptual differentiation is reflected in the drafters' stylistic choices: in common law legislation sentences are very long, consisting of three or more main clauses, each modified by many subordinate clauses; this remarkable sentence length is required by the great number of details to be inserted and the requirement that specifications should be precise and clear. Civil law sentences are shorter, with a less strict use of paragraphing; this makes the understanding of the sentences easier, but renders the reconstruction of the relationship between the various sentences more complex.

The same stylistic difference presents itself in contract drafting techniques:

> Parties with a Common Law background usually prefer long and detailed contracts, eager to mention and list expressly each and every contingency that could possibly become a subject of dispute under the agreement. This may be explained by their assumption and expectation that a contract can only be relied on to the extent it is expressly so worded. Parties with a Civil Law background, in contrast, find it often acceptable not to mention every detail because they expect that a court or an arbitral tribunal in interpreting the contract would not only look at the actual wording but also consider what the parties actually had intended to agree upon taking into account the circumstances surrounding the negotiations. (Borris 1994:84).

The adversarial nature of the common law system is probably also a factor, causing drafters to address ever more remote contingencies (Hill and King 2004).

4.2.7 Textual schematization

The different legal systems thus determine the adoption of different textual strategies on the drafter's part. For example, common law legislation is usually associated with a particular emphasis on explicit textual schematization (Driedger 1982). The different degree of textual schematization can be seen, for example, in the frequent use of alternative/complementary options with *or* in the following text, which is a UN document drafted in the common law style. Also, the way in which they are punctuated and set out emphasizes their function of making the provisions more semantically transparent:

(4.13) Grounds for refusing recognition *or* enforcement

   (1) Recognition *or* enforcement of an arbitral award, irrespective of the country in which it was made, may be refused only:
      (a) at the request of the party against whom it is invoked, if that party furnishes to the competent court where recognition *or* enforcement is sought proof that:
         (i) a party to the arbitration agreement referred to in article 7 was under some incapacity; *or* the said agreement is not valid under the law to which the parties have subjected it *or*, failing any indication thereon, under the law of the country where the award was made; *or*
         (ii) the party against whom the award is invoked was not given proper notice of the appointment of an arbitrator *or* of the arbitral proceedings *or* was otherwise unable to present his case; *or*
         (iii) the award deals with a dispute not contemplated by *or* not falling within the terms of the submission to arbitration, *or* it contains

decisions on matters beyond the scope of the submission to arbitration, provided that, if the decisions on matters submitted to arbitration can be separated from those not so submitted, that part of the award which contains decisions on matters submitted to arbitration may be recognized and enforced; *or*

(iv) the composition of the arbitral tribunal *or* the arbitral procedure was not in accordance with the agreement of the parties *or*, failing such agreement, was not in accordance with the law of the country where the arbitration took place; *or*

(v) the award has not yet become binding on the parties *or* has been set aside *or* suspended by a court of the country in which, *or* under the law of which, that award was made; *or*

(b) if the court finds that:

(i) the subject-matter of the dispute is not capable of settlement by arbitration under the law of this State; *or*

(ii) the recognition *or* enforcement of the award would be contrary to the public policy of this State. (UNICITRAL Model Law §36)

By arranging content schematically, the drafter can construct a denser, more cognitively demanding text such as the one cited above. The advantages of good paragraphing and the division of text into ordered sections and subsections are pointed out by Driedger (1982:78): "[It] provides a visual aid to comprehension by breaking up solid blocks of type; it delivers the sentence in packages, so to speak, making it easier for the mind to grasp the whole. It does visually what the reader would do mentally without it."

4.3 Genre

One of the phenomena that most distinguishes legal discourse is compliance with the norms governing the construction of its different text genres. There is usually a close link between the type of legal text and its structure, which in turn implies a number of correlations between the conceptual, rhetorical, and linguistic features that characterize the text itself. Genre not only provides a conventional framework but also affects all other textual features and constrains their conceptual and rhetorical development. With time, several text types have arisen—some derived from genres common in general language, others crafted specifically to meet the needs of specialists. Through training and professional engagements, specialists learn to follow given norms and patterns in each type of text. The conventional use of genres also produces certain expectations among readers, and whenever the rules are broken a text may be misunderstood or rejected.

Textual standardization occurs in all disciplinary fields but it is stronger in legal genres, particularly when a text is not free-standing but is an adaptation of an earlier text, incorporating all data reflecting the new conditions. This is the method followed for drafting legal contracts which, as they serve a range of recurring situations governed by specific norms, are often based on pre-printed forms with spaces for the parties' names and special clauses to meet individual requirements. Even when printed forms are avoided, the alternative is a checklist of textual provisions, from which the user can draw those required in a given situation.

4.3.1 Generic differentiation

Discourse analysts have discovered the importance of the genre concept for the understanding of discourse, not only to get a better understanding of the linguistic characteristics of texts, but also of the macrostructure of these texts, which appears to be organized according to genre expectations and conventions rooted in the socio-cultural context. For this reason, in recent years genre theory has looked more broadly at context, paying particular attention to a more comprehensive understanding of text/context interactions and focusing not simply on the form and content of genres, but more importantly on how genres are constructed, interpreted, used, and exploited in the achievement of specific goals in highly specialized contexts.

Indeed, any communicative situation combines several contextual factors, making it difficult to attribute a given linguistic peculiarity to a single originating factor. This awareness has led scholars to group together the contextual factors capable of identifying the parameters which distinguish different genres within a specialized language. Thus, for legal language, Danet (1980) adapted Joos's (1961) stylistic categories for degree of formality to the different modes of text production (distinguishing between WRITTEN and ORAL, with the former subdivided into COMPOSED and SPONTANEOUS). By this route she developed a sociolinguistic scheme for the genres of legal language (cf. Table 4.1), which characterizes each legal genre in terms of its style (frozen, formal, consultative, or casual).

As Table 4.1 shows, there are genres—for example wills, contracts and insurance policies—which combine highly formal traits with features typical of the written mode. Others, although written and formal (e.g. statutes, briefs, appellate opinions) exhibit a less frequent use of standard and repetitive clauses, on a par with that of witness examinations and motions, which belong to the oral mode. Even oral texts, however, may contain highly formal traits, as observed for example in verdicts, wedding vows, and oaths. These genres are highly codified and typically exhibit standardized, easily predictable sentences, often amounting to formulaic expressions. There are also less predictable genres, however, which allow for a greater degree of spontaneity and variation, both in content and expressiveness. They are usually oral and take on different levels of formality: higher in witness examinations or expert statements, lower in non-expert statements and client–lawyer conversation, right down to the informality of private conversation between lawyers.

Genres vary according to several factors, the main ones being the communicative purposes they aim to fulfill, the settings or contexts in which they are employed, the

Table 4.1 Danet's sociolinguistic scheme for legal genres

STYLE

Mode	Frozen	Formal	Consultative	Casual
Written	Documents: Insurance policies Contracts Landlord–tenant leases Wills	Statutes Briefs Appellate opinions		
Spoken–composed	Marriage ceremonies Indictments Witnesses' oaths Pattern instructions Verdicts	Lawyers' examinations of witnesses in trials and depositions Lawyers' arguments, motions in trials Expert witnesses' testimony	Lay witnesses' testimony	
Spoken–spontaneous			Lawyer–client interaction Bench conferences	Lobby conferences Lawyer–lawyer conversations

Source: Danet (1980:471).

communicative events or activities they are associated with, the professional relationships existing between the people taking part in such activities or events, and the background knowledge of each participant. For example, depending upon their communicative function and speaker's/writer's intention, legal genres differ as follows:

- legislative texts mainly have a regulative function as they impose obligations or confer rights;
- legal textbooks are essentially informative;
- counsel/witness exchanges have both an evaluative and an informative function;
- lawyers' arguments are principally meant to persuade and convince.

Legal genres also differ in the matter they cover. For instance, briefs and memoranda commonly focus on specific points, while statutes cover more extensive issues. Also, the difference between a statute and a contract depends on the degree of extension: while a statute has effects on the whole society, a contract only concerns the people or firms who are parties to the contract.

A generic categorization of legal documents is made by Tiersma (1999:139), who distinguishes them into two main categories: operative legal documents and expository documents. The former have a stronger legal power as they can create or modify legal relations. They have very formal and formulaic language (often expressing legal performatives) and follow a very rigid structure. Examples of operative legal documents are pleadings, petitions, orders, statutes, contracts, and wills. Expository documents, instead, delve into one or more points of law with a relatively objective tone. Their structure is less rigid and their language, although formal and specialized, is less formulaic. Examples of expository documents are judicial opinions, legal letters, and office memoranda.

Another generic categorization of legal documents (partly based on Trosborg's (1997b:20) model) distinguishes them into two main categories: primary and secondary. The former produce legal effects, while the main purpose of the latter is informative, explanatory, or pedagogic. Primary legal genres may further be distinguished into sources of law and legal documents. The former comprise legislation (statutes and delegated legislation), judicial precedent (judgments in law reports) and, where it exists, the Constitution; legal documents may be created by private individuals (such as articles of association, contracts, wills) or by institutions (such as arrest warrants, divorce decrees). Examples of secondary legal genres are law reviews, textbooks, and other works of legal reference.

Legal genres make use of specific discursive conventions which means they differ from other genres both in the legal field and in general language. For example, analyses of courtroom interactions during legal proceedings have shed light on the considerable divergences between the standard norms of verbal interaction and legal norms, especially in the case of cross-examinations of suspects and witnesses, which may be crucial to the outcome of the trial. The examining lawyer exploits all his linguistic skills to obtain admissions, substantiation, contradictions, and other evidence to prove his version of the facts.

4.3.2 Semantic conception and generic organization

The considerable codification of legal genres increases their semantic–conceptual coherence and transparency, as signalled by textual organization. The different semantic conceptions in legal genres—for example exemplification, temporal specification, causal links, concession, hypothesis, description, suggestion, conclusion, comparison (analogy/contrast), prediction, analysis, etc.—generally coincide with the pragmatic dimension of general language. In some cases, however, a given semantic–pragmatic realization may identify a certain legal genre. This happens in insurance contracts, where the hypothetical principle prevails and may be summarized as a prediction of the type: "If certain conditions are complied with (if the insured party pays the agreed premium at the right time) and if certain events take place (if the insured property is damaged or stolen, or if the insured person dies), a certain consequence will occur (the insured party will be compensated or his heirs will receive a given sum)." This logical-semantic pattern may be realized through a surface structure of the following kind (example from Crystal and Davy 1969):

(4.14)   If the Life Insured shall pay or cause to be paid to the Society or to the duly authorised Agent or Collector thereof every subsequent premium at the due date thereof the funds of the Society shall on the expiration of the term of years specified in the Schedule hereto or on the previous death of the Life Insured become and be liable to pay to him/ her or to his/ her personal representative or next-of-kin or assigns as the case may be the sum due and payable hereunder in accordance with the Table of Insurance printed hereon and the terms and conditions of the said Table (including any sum which may have accrued by way of reversionary bonus) subject to any authorised endorsement appearing hereon and to the production of this policy premium receipts and such other evidence of title as may be required

Also contracts structured around mutual, interlocking promises will often contain this pattern. Logical-semantic links of the hypothetical type are equally crucial in wills. Here the signatory's decisions are made dependent upon the occurrence of certain events: not only the testator's death but also other occurrences involving the life and death of heirs mentioned in the will, of the type: should X die before Y, if any of my children die before me, if X has no children, etc. In terms of linguistic realization, the prevalence of this logical-semantic function implies frequent recourse to hypothetical clauses. In his study of the language of wills, Finegan (1982) observed a far higher frequency of *if*-clauses compared to general texts. For instance, *if* occurs 25.71 times in every 100 sentences in wills, while it occurs only 4.20 times in standard American English (cf. Kučera and Francis 1967).

Elsewhere given semantic realizations may have no dominant role in the text but can take on greater pragmatic importance in certain genres. This is the case, for example, of the defining aspect in legal documents. Here it is customary to mark the first occurrence of a noun or phrase that recurs in the text with a defined term that can be used later on.

This term—generally introduced parenthetically or by expressions of the type *hereinafter called* or *in this agreement called* or simply *called*—is placed immediately after the first occurrence of the noun or its description. Often the conventional term for a given concept is capitalized, to show that it refers to a specific entity in a conventional manner. An example is found in the following passage:

(4.15)   WHEREAS, Grantor is the owner of the name 'Dale Johnson Ryder Warren' and certain service marks set forth in the attached Appendix A, and has been granted the right to sublicense derivatives thereof, that is, marks and names which use any one or more of the component names 'DALE', 'JOHNSON', 'RYDER' or 'WARREN' alone or in combination with other names or marks (which names and marks are referred to collectively as, 'Service Marks'). (Gotti 2008:220)

Having introduced the contracting parties and the object of the agreement by a suitable nomenclatory procedure, the rest of the document uses the term *Service Marks* to refer to the marks or names listed in (4.15).

4.3.3 Generic structure

Studies on legal genres have not only highlighted their different parts but also the contribution of each part to the overall pattern. A very popular model of genre analysis is the one devised by Swales (1990), which identifies the main parts of a genre as "moves" and their subparts as "steps." As example of the application of this model to the analysis of legal genres is Bhatia's (1993) explanation of the typical structure of a legal case report. The standard structure of this genre reflects the main stages in the interpretation of a case, and generally consists of the following four moves:

(1)   *Identifying the case*—Each case is identified and referred to in a consistent way so that it can be quoted and used as evidence in court, in law classes, in textbooks, in casebooks, and in other legal contexts.

(2)   *Establishing facts of the case*—This part informs the reader of the main facts of the case which are legally relevant for the judgment to be pronounced.

(3)   *Arguing the case*—This is the principal section of the genre and consists of several steps according to the nature and length of the legal case. The main steps are the following:

(a)   *Giving a history of the case*—Previous judges who have delivered judgments related to the case are mentioned together with their opinions and verdicts.

(b)   *Presenting arguments*—The arguments put forward by the present judge are illustrated here.

(c)   *Deriving "ratio decidendi"*—This step presents the principles of law derived by the judge for application to subsequent cases.

(4)   *Pronouncing judgment*—This last move is usually short and consists of a highly standardized formulaic statement reporting the judgment pronounced.

The moves and steps presented here are usually present in all judgments and can be considered the basic elements of the genre. However, more moves and steps may be present, depending on the complexity and length of the case being dealt with.

4.3.4 Intertextuality

Legal discourse is characterized by a high degree of intertextuality and interdiscursivity, particularly in such genres as legislation, judgments, cases, and textbooks. For example, a law case is basically a report based on the judgment of a particular judge deciding the outcome of a trial or an appeal. Records of such judgments are also used as precedents in future cases. They are also reported in textbooks and commented on in university lectures for teaching purposes. The interpretation of legal argumentation in previous law cases is considered an extremely relevant basis for the understanding of the legal principles in question. Furthermore, previous laws and regulations are commonly referred to when drafting new legislation, which must fit in consistently with the existing body of legal texts.

CHAPTER 5

....

THE PLAIN LANGUAGE
MOVEMENT

....

MARK ADLER

5.1 WHAT IS PLAIN LANGUAGE?

A discipline that might eventually become known as "plain language studies" is beginning to emerge through the collaboration of individual plain language proponents (whom I'll call plainers for short). Notably, in 2008 the two main international umbrella organizations (Clarity and PLAIN) and the Center for Plain Language in the United States set up a joint working group to develop what they hope will eventually become internationally recognized professional standards and accreditation.[1]

Meanwhile, unsurprisingly, there is no generally accepted definition of plain language, and until now it has been left to plainers to offer their own. Dr Neil James divides the many definitions into three categories:

> The most common definitions...define plain language by the "elements" that it works with. One of the best would be Joe Kimble's Plain English Charter, which is divided into sections covering 36 general, design, organisation, sentence and word elements.
>
> However, more recent definitions of plain language are becoming more general, focusing on the outcomes plain language produces:

---

[1] Known as the International Plain Language Working Group, it comprises two representatives of each of those organizations and six other members co-opted to represent between them all parts of the world. It is chaired by Dr Neil James of the Plain English Foundation <www.plainenglishfoundation.com> last accessed January 31, 2015. Since this chapter was written, the IPLWG's proposals and my critique were published at <www.clarity.shuttlepod.org/Resources/Documents/64_032111_04_final.pdf> and <www.adler.demon.co.uk/comment.htm> respectively, both accessed January 31, 2015.

A communication is in plain language if the people who are the audience for that communication can quickly and easily

- find what they need
- understand what they find
- act appropriately on that understanding.

At the other end of the spectrum, some practitioners define plain language by focusing narrowly on readability:

Plain Language is language that is easy to read by matching the reading skill of your audience. Plain language increases comprehension, retention, reading speed, and persistence. (James 2009a:35)

Dr Robert Eagleson has made the seemingly obvious point, frequently overlooked, that some text will inevitably be beyond the reach of non-specialists, not because of the language but because the ideas are inherently difficult:

An advanced text on cancer or a law about the ownership of shares...will remain complex. But the complexity will reside solely in the subject matter, and not be compounded by difficulty in language. For it is an error to assume...that difficulty in context must be matched by difficulty in language...complexity in subject matter does not call for complicated, convoluted language. (Eagleson 1987:45)

Bearing that in mind, I had privately suggested this definition, based on a well-known definition by Martin Cutts (1996:3):

'Plain language' means language and design that presents information to its intended readers in a way that allows them, with as little effort as the complexity of the subject permits, to understand the writer's meaning and to use the document.

Results-based definitions imply that plain language is not a dialect of the standard language but a relationship between the text and its audience. Text that will be plain for one audience will not be plain for another.

This is not the view of those outside the plain language world (including many lawyers), which is that plain language is simple language: primarily the use of short, familiar words in place of jargon, especially Latin. But that popular view over-simplifies the plain language movement and is becoming increasingly unrealistic as plainers extend the range of their studies and techniques.

That confusion has led me to doubt the wisdom of trying to define plain language in a way which is itself not plain (Adler 2013).

5.2 A VERY BRIEF HISTORY OF THE PLAIN LEGAL LANGUAGE MOVEMENT

Robust criticism of lawyers' language—sometimes from within the profession—dates back hundreds of years but has mostly been ignored.

Professor Heikki Mattila has documented a successful eighteenth-century plain language movement:

> The discussion on proper usage of legal language was very lively in the Prussia of the Age of Enlightenment..., as is clearly evident from the legislation of the time.... Care over proper usage of legal language radiated from German-speaking countries to other corners of Europe.... [In Russia, for example] new laws were to be drawn up in simple language, using words that everyone could understand, and concisely. Mattila (2006:96–7)

But these reforms did not survive the end of the Enlightenment, and the barnacles of legalese soon grew back, despite occasional criticism.

George Coode (an authority on legislative drafting) and A. J. G. Mackay (a Scottish sheriff) were notable nineteenth-century plainers (Coode 1845:67; Mackay 1887:326). Professor Reed Dickerson (1965) was teaching plain writing to his Indiana University law students in the 1940s, and published a book on the subject 20 years later. And Anthony Parker, an English solicitor, published plain precedents in the 1960s (Parker 1964, 1969). But Professor David Mellinkoff (1963), writing a detailed history and analysis of legal English, robustly criticized traditional language without suggesting that there was any movement to reform it.

However, by the 1970s various initiatives, encouraged by the belief that citizens should be able to understand their rights and obligations, had built up sufficient momentum to be identified as the beginning of the current movement. Plainer documents appeared from government and commerce in Canada, the United States, Australia, New Zealand, and England. In many of these countries the banking and insurance industries led the improvement of commercial documents, and parliamentary drafters began to apply plain language principles to legislation. At about the same time, Sweden and Finland began vetting their draft legislation to ensure that new acts were plainly written. President Jimmy Carter imposed plain language standards on the American civil service in 1978 and in the 1980s Margaret Thatcher made similar demands to improve British government forms (though both these initiatives were lost when they left office). Some jurisdictions passed legislation (written, strangely, in legalese) requiring plain language in consumer documents (Tiersma 1999:211–30).

The movement has since spread widely to other countries and languages. Japanese legal language has had particular problems arising from its use—in combination with two 48-symbol phonetically-based systems—of Chinese characters, "which have no phonetic relationship to spoken Japanese. Each character, which roughly speaking represents a word, must be memorized individually". The inevitable problems are exacerbated because many Chinese characters used in legal documents are unusual, the traditional legal-writing style has been Chinese (which does not fit Japanese syntax well), and there was no punctuation. But since the Second World War there has been gradual change, with the democratic constitution and parts of the legal code revised to make them more accessible to non-lawyers (Tiersma 1999:214–15).

Many judges have supported plain language, criticizing the obscurity of traditional drafting that has forced litigation about the meaning of legislation and of commercial documents. Lord Woolf, soon before he became Britain's most senior judge, was responsible for a dramatic revision of the civil court rules in plain language and he used them to discourage (though not abolish) verbose court papers.[2]

There is a strong wind in favor of plain language. There has been much change but progress is slow.

5.3 WHO IS INVOLVED IN THE MOVEMENT?

The plain language movement includes many plainers (practitioners and campaigners) worldwide. Law is only one aspect of the movement; some plainers promote plain medicine; others plain government, plain technical writing, plain finance, and plain scientific papers.

Some legal plainers are linguists, writers, editors, or legal translators. Some are practicing lawyers who write plainly for their clients; they might be private lawyers offering intelligible documents to the public, or government lawyers drafting plain legislation. Other plainers, whether or not they are lawyers, are one step removed from the public; they help lawyers redraft their standard documents and train them to write plainly for themselves; some are academics teaching the next generation of lawyers to communicate plainly.

There are several plain language voluntary organizations through which plainers meet and support each other. Notably, those interested in legal language have Clarity.[3] Clarity was formed by a British local government solicitor in 1983 for lawyers wanting to simplify legal English and it quickly became an international movement represented (though often sparsely) in some 50 countries, with more that 1,100 members at its peak. But it is now in decline, falling under the influence of non-lawyers and widening its focus from legal language to language (and design) generally. It is likely to merge with the Plain Language Association InterNational (PLAIN), a Canada-based but international non-profit company owned by fewer than 200 members and interested in plain language in all fields.[4] British Commonwealth lawyers interested specifically in legislation have the Commonwealth Association of Legislative Counsel,[5] although good drafting is only one of its concerns. American lawyers have Scribes, founded in 1953 to honor legal writers and encourage a "clear, succinct, and forceful style in legal writing".[6] Some plainers are active in more than one of these organizations but the evidence of networking websites like LinkedIn suggests that most plainers are not affiliated to any of them.

---

[2] <http://www.justice.gov.uk/courts/procedure-rules/civil/rules> last accessed January 31, 2015.
[3] <www.clarity-international.net> last accessed January 31, 2015.
[4] <www.plainlanguagenetwork.org> last accessed January 31, 2015.
[5] <www.opc.gov.au/calc> last accessed January 31, 2015.
[6] <www.scribes.org> last accessed January 31, 2015.

Over the last 30 years or so various institutes have been established to study and promote plain language, partly funding themselves with consultancy and training fees but in part relying on government or private sponsorship. Some have closed but others remain successful. Many small businesses now offer services similar to those offered by the institutes, typically including drafting, editing, training, the accreditation of documents, and the benefits of their research.

5.4 ADVANTAGES AND DISADVANTAGES OF PLAIN LEGAL LANGUAGE

5.4.1 Advantages

Various advantages for plain language over legalese have been identified:[7]

5.4.1.1 *It is more precise*

Traditional drafters often justify their style by asserting that complex ideas require complex language, and that what plainers criticize as verbosity is necessary to avoid ambiguity and achieve precision. But plainers and others have repeatedly shown by example that complex ideas *can* often be expressed much more plainly than in the traditional style. Moreover, plain revisions of traditional documents routinely expose and correct errors and ambiguities in the original texts. That legalese is *im*precise is predictable from the way it is constructed:

- Precedents are routinely used without being adapted to the individual circumstances (and often without being read).
- Material that in standard English would be spread over several sentences is accumulated in a single sentence, so that it is often unclear which words and phrases modify which others.
- The use of unnecessary extra words, non-standard word order, embedded clauses, and the absence of punctuation all exacerbate this problem.
- The use of abstract rather than concrete words masks the intended meaning.
- The misuse of passive verbs sometimes fails to disclose who is or should be acting.

5.4.1.2 *There are fewer errors*

As plain language almost invariably employs fewer words its use, given any particular rate of errors per 1,000 words, will tend to reduce the absolute number of errors. But beyond this, its use reduces the chance of mistake arising from the complexity of the

[7] See, for example, Mellinkoff (1963), Kimble (1994–5), Asprey (2003), Butt and Castle (2006), Adler (2007).

language, and it increases the chance that someone will spot any remaining errors before they do harm. It also avoids the risk that meaning will be inadvertently changed during "translation" between plain language and legalese.

5.4.1.3 *It is quicker and cheaper for everyone*

Lawyers typically charge hundreds of dollars an hour for encoding their plain language instructions in legalese and for translating legalese back into plain language for their clients. Plain language uses fewer lawyer-hours and reduces the waiting time for work to be done.

5.4.1.4 *It is more persuasive*

Most legal texts seek to persuade. A letter might seek to persuade an opponent to accept an argument or proposal or a client to accept advice. A pleading or witness statement should seek to persuade an opponent (or, failing that, the judge) that the client should win the case. A lawyer drafting a will, contract, regulation, or statute should hope to persuade those affected by it to accept the document and comply with the obligations it imposes.

But there can be no persuasion if the document is not read and understood.

5.4.1.5 *It is more democratic*

The New Zealand Law Commission summarized the need for plain legislation in this way:

> It is a fundamental precept of any legal system that the law must be accessible to the public. Ignorance of the law is no excuse because everyone is presumed to know the law. That presumption would be insupportable if the law were not available and accessible to all. The state also has an interest in the law's accessibility. It needs the law to be effective, and it cannot be if the public does not know what it is.... It seems once to have been supposed that law was the preserve of lawyers and Judges, and that legislation was drafted with them as the primary audience. It is now much better understood that Acts of Parliament (and regulations too) are consulted and used by a large number of people who are not lawyers and have no legal training.... Many other people refer to legislation in their jobs. (New Zealand Law Commission 2008: paras 1.1, 1.11, 1.12)

5.4.1.6 *It is pleasanter to use*

Some critics have complained that the plain English movement debases the language of Shakespeare. Plainers reply that while no legal language, traditional or plain, is likely to be confused with poetry in purpose or content, plain language is less tedious and usually more elegant than legalese.

5.4.2 Disadvantages

There has been virtually no attempt in the literature to rebut these arguments. However, in a rare recent exception Francis Bennion, a British authority on legislative drafting, argued that plain language is not always appropriate in legal documents (Bennion 2007).[8] His concern was that some legal texts (notably statutes) are designed to *be* the law rather than to explain it, and an explanation in plain language can come from other sources (notably "a competent lawyer"). Moreover, laypeople would not realize that their ignorance of the law might undermine their interpretation of documents that they thought they understood.

But is his distinction between *being* and *explaining* the law tenable, either logically or empirically? The text must explain the law to someone for it to be the law rather than gibberish. Moreover, before becoming the law the text must be enacted (and will often be amended) by the legislators, some of whom will have no professional qualifications. Further difficulties with Bennion's view are that:

- not all lawyers are competent;
- even competent lawyers (including appellate judges) have difficulty reading legalese;
- it is often impracticable (or financially impossible) for those affected by a legal document to obtain legal advice.

Bennion's complaint that plain language is a danger to the public seems to imply that legal documents should be deliberately made opaque. But that extreme view is not generally held.

5.5 ATTITUDES TO PLAIN LEGAL LANGUAGE

5.5.1 Non-lawyers

Non-lawyers almost invariably prefer plain language, often seeing legalese as a device by which lawyers cynically make themselves expensively indispensable (see, for instance, Adler 1991).

5.5.2 Judges

Many influential judges support the use of plain drafting (Adler 2007:21–5) but there has been little research. However, an investigation into American judges' attitudes in the 1980s (Kimble 2005:3) showed over 80 percent of judges polled attributing greater professionalism to plain language lawyers than to traditional drafters.

---

[8] For my answer see Adler (2008, 2013).

5.5.3 Practicing lawyers

Although most practicing lawyers still write legalese, many are aware of the need for change and some are effecting it. Thirty years ago lawyers generally accepted the orthodox view that traditional legalese is more precise than standard language and is necessary to reflect the complexity of the subject. They believed that plain language represents irresponsible over-simplification.

That view has since been discredited by extensive professional literature, but few practitioners have the time or inclination to study the theory or to improve their drafting skills. So the literature remains widely unread and the traditional view is still common. Lawyers are aware of pressure towards plain language from campaigners (in and out of the profession) and from those we might call the legislators (parliament, judges, and the lawyers' own professional bodies). But the pressure has not been intense and is more often resisted than not.

In 1992 I invited a selection of British lawyers to compare two traditional and two plain versions of a routine document and to complete a survey intended to test their knowledge of and attitudes to plain language (Adler 1993:29). The results (roughly summarized in Table 5.1) indicated:

- Almost everyone supported the use of plain English in the law (Table 5.1).
- Asked if they used plain English themselves, about half answered "yes" and most of the rest "maybe".
- But very few followed even basic guidelines like avoiding long sentences.

How these lawyers perceived the advantages and disadvantages of plain English is shown in Tables 5.2 and 5.3.

Table 5.1 Survey of British lawyers' knowledge and use of plain language

Question	Yes	Maybe	No
Do you support the use of plain English in the law?	45	10	1
Do you use plain English?	27	24	4
[Did the answers to questions about style indicate that the respondent followed the most basic guidelines for plain English?]	Not tested	16	40
Would you prefer one of the plain versions of the document over one of the traditional versions			
if you had to draft it?	32		22
if your opponent drafted it?	34		20
to explain to your client?	39		14

Total number of respondents = 76

Table 5.2 Perceived advantages of plain English

Does plain English have these qualities?	Yes	No	No reply
Easier for lay person to read	49	1	6
Quicker for lay person to read	47	0	9
Preferred by most clients	39	1	16
Easier for lawyer to read	38	1	17
More chance of seeing error reading	36	3	17
Generally more efficient	35	6	15
Quicker to write	32	9	15
Easier to take instructions	31	3	22
Cheaper	29	2	25
Easier to write	29	9	18
Less chance of error writing	21	12	23
Less likely to be interpreted perversely by judge	19	13	24
Probably preferred by judges	17	14	25
Legal effect more predictable	15	20	21

Total number of respondents = 56

Table 5.3 Perceived disadvantages of plain English

Reasons	Number so answering
Fear of error, ambiguity, or unpredictable effect	24
Belief that judges disapprove	14
Harder or slower to write (at least at first)	14
Dislike style; insufficient gravitas	8
Harder or slower to read	7
Unfamiliar, loss of tradition	6
Harder to take instructions	4
Contrary to expectation of other lawyers	3
Generally less efficient	3
More expensive	2
Legalese justifies fees	2
Restrained by employers	1
Disliked by clients	1

Total number of respondents = 56

5.6 Plain language drafting techniques

The range of techniques for plain drafting is much larger than is generally thought, and includes:

Planning

Consider:

what you want to say.
why you want to say it.
to whom you are saying it.
how to present it (including what extra information might be useful).

Organization

Organize the document coherently (that is, arranging the contents in a sensible order, clearly and logically divided into a hierarchy of sentences, paragraphs, and—where appropriate—chapters, parts, and so on).

Keep paragraphs short enough to keep readers in sight of the next break. If there is too much material on the subject of that paragraph, consider using sub-paragraphs or headings to maintain both consistency and brevity.

Begin paragraphs with a sentence that follows from the last paragraph and summarizes the current one.

Avoid sentences of more than 40 words and consecutive long sentences within that limit, aiming for an average between 15 and 25 words.

Move from the general to the particular.

Avoid irrelevant detail.

Keep subject, verb, and object close together, and generally in that order.

Keep like with like, so that all references to a particular thing or class of things are found together.

Design

Use blank space to:

make the page look appealing.
show the relationship between paragraphs, sub-paragraphs, and so on.
rest the eye.

Use color if it will help (for instance, to make the document attractive or to distinguish certain parts of the text) but remember that a reader might be color-blind and that someone might need to make monochrome copies).

Prefer plain to elaborate design to avoid distracting readers.

Choose fonts of suitable design and size, especially avoiding text too small for readers' comfort.

Embolden and italicize for headings and to a limited extent for emphasis (ensuring that no text looks more emphatic than a heading which applies to it).

Use the size and weight of the font in each heading to indicate the heading level.

Separate lists, so that instead of all the items forming a continuous paragraph, each item has its own indented sub-paragraph following grammatically, consistently, and without unnecessary repetition from the line that introduces the list.

Supplement or replace text with tables, graphs, flowcharts, pictures, algebraic formulas, and other graphics to help readers understand your message or to emphasize it.

Be consistent in design.

Language

Adopt as informal a tone as is appropriate in the circumstances (which include the readers' and writer's preferences and the relationship between them).

Prefer concrete to abstract language, and explain unfamiliar abstract ideas with examples.

Avoid:

language that will cause inappropriate offense,

misleading euphemism,

over-emphasis,

superfluous words,

long, archaic, or unfamiliar words where a short, modern, or familiar word is as appropriate,

nominalization,

clichés,

ambiguity,

vagueness.

Do not confuse readers by using different words for the same thing or by using a word in different senses.

Use active verbs unless there is good reason for the passive.

Express ideas positively rather than negatively where practicable.

Grammar

Write grammatically.

Punctuate normally.

Use capital letters only where standard language requires them (although some lawyers justify their use to flag defined terms.)

Avoid pointless obedience to unhelpful conventions that are not rules (like not starting a sentence with *and* or *but* and not ending a sentence with a preposition).

Style

Listen to the rhythm of your text in your mind's ear and edit to make your writing flow.

Editing

Read draft documents carefully, checking the use of these techniques as well as for clerical errors and the completeness and accuracy of content.

Re-read them as often as practicable.

Read as though you were the intended reader rather than the writer. If you are writing for different audiences read with the eye (or ear) of each.

As far as practicable, re-read the whole document after any change.

However carefully you have edited on screen, finish by checking the hard copy of any document that is to be printed.

If practicable, delegate some of this so that a fresh set of neural pathways will pick up mistakes to which you are blind.

Use computerized checks if they help, but don't trust them.

Testing

To the extent that it is practicable, test the otherwise finished document for comprehensibility: is the target audience likely to understand it in the way you intended and without undue difficulty?

The more sophisticated plainers benefit from studies in linguistics, physiology, psychology, and sociology, in particular to learn how the eye and brain function when we read, how the brain processes language, and how different people can differently interpret the same document. And they study rhetoric to make their writing more persuasive.

5.7 AN EXAMPLE OF TRADITIONAL WRITING MADE PLAIN

Here is a typical piece of legalese, chosen at random from an English lease, by which residential flats (apartments) were let in 2006 for 125 years for a premium of some £225,000 and a fictional (that is, non-existent) rent:

> If the whole or any part of the Rents[9] shall be unpaid for twenty one days after becoming due (whether formally demanded or not) or if there shall be a breach of any of the

---

[9] As detailed below, "Rents" (in the plural) were confusingly defined as the nominal "Rent" and the far-from-nominal management charges.

Tenant's covenants contained in this Lease the Landlord shall be entitled (in addition to any other right) at any time thereafter to re-enter the Premises or any part of it in the name of the whole and thereupon the Term shall absolutely determine but without prejudice to any right or remedy of the Landlord in respect of any breach of covenant or other term of this lease Provided that if the Tenant shall have served notice in writing on the Landlord at any time with the name and address of the Tenant's Lender on the property the Landlord shall not be entitled to exercise its right of entry herein until at least 21 days notice in writing has been given by the Landlord to the said Lender stating (i) details of unpaid rents and/or (ii) the nature of any breach of covenant on the part of the Tenant alleged by the Landlord and (iii) details of the Landlord's requirements for any such breach to be remedied insofar as the breach is capable of remedy

I have annotated the text to show how plainers would criticize it (with a few personal comments of my own), and I offer a plain redraft below.

Notes relating to the whole passage		
	Sentence length	
	This sentence has 210 words. It has been inflated by including in a single sentence what in normal English would be several sentences and by using more words than are necessary.	
	Punctuation	
	The difficulty of reading a long sentence has been unnecessarily increased by omitting the punctuation used in normal English.	
	Anomalously (but traditionally), there is some punctuation: in this case apostrophes and parentheses. But unusually, this text omits the extra spaces often used to indicate a missing period.	

Text	Commentary
If the whole or any part of the Rents	*If any rent* would do as well.
	The capital R is intended to indicate a defined term, but (1) word-initial capitals are used inconsistently for other purposes (and sometimes for no purpose) and (2) the indication is lost on non-lawyers.
	In this document, *Rents* were defined in clause 2 ("Definitions and Interpretation") as "The Rent the Estate Charge and the Building Service Charge". *Estate Charge* and *Building Service Charge* were separately defined in clause 2 but *Rent* was not. Confusingly, it was specified under clause 1 (*Particulars*) as "A peppercorn (if demanded)". Traditionally, the valueless peppercorn is included to provide an (unnecessary) contractual obligation by the tenant, but it is never demanded.
shall be	Despite the helpful convention that a word should not be used in different senses in a formal document, the archaic *shall* is traditionally used instead of the more natural *must* to denote obligation as well as to indicate the future tense. Here it means *is*.

(continues)

Continued

unpaid for twenty one days after becoming due	21 would be better in figures but if in words they should be hyphenated.
(whether formally demanded or not)	Words to this effect block a loophole but "(even if not formally demanded)" is neater.
or if there shall be a breach of any of the Tenant's covenants contained in this Lease	= "or if the tenant has broken any other covenant". Incidentally, *Tenant* is not a defined word so does not warrant a capital T. Following what is now common practice, the name of the original tenant was given with the other particulars (like the rent) in a form which looks like a definition but isn't. This use of *Tenant* refers not to that original tenant but to whoever holds the tenant's interest at the relevant time. *Covenant* has a technical meaning but it is unnecessary to specify it here; all obligations in a lease of this kind are covenants. But the drafter has nodded to the plain language movement by using *Landlord* (which is gender-neutral in British English) and *Tenant* instead of the traditional but user-unfriendly *Lessor* and *Lessee*.
the Landlord shall be entitled (in addition to any other right) at any time thereafter to	"the Landlord shall be entitled to" = "The landlord may". In fact, the landlord is by law usually *not* entitled to this remedy (see below). The clause is made less readable than it should be by the intrusion of two subordinate phrases between *entitled* and *to*.
re-enter the Premises or any part of it in the name of the whole	As soon as the landlord steps through the door he has entered the premises. The reference to "any part of it in the name of the whole" is superfluous verbiage (and *it* should be *them*). *Enter* (rather than *re-enter*) is sufficient. What difference does it make if the landlord has been there before? Could a tenant argue that a landlord who had not been there before (having bought the interest without inspecting the premises) cannot exercise this right?
and thereupon	*Thereupon* is archaic.
the Term shall absolutely determine	= "The lease will end".
but without prejudice to any right or remedy of the Landlord in respect of any breach of covenant or other term of this lease	= "but without affecting any of the landlord's rights which have already accrued", though this is of such doubtful use that I've omitted it from my redraft.
Provided that	This phrase has no technical meaning, being used variously for *but, if, and*, and the superfluous "And this document provides that". The capital P marks not a defined term but what should be a new sentence or paragraph.

(continues)

if the Tenant shall have served notice in writing on the Landlord	"Shall have served notice" = "has notified". The reference to serving notice suggests, but does not specify, some formality. It also leaves open an argument about whether service was effected by posting the document even if it did not arrive. "Has informed the landlord in writing" is a more natural form of words and blocks the loophole. "Has told" is even more natural but might just leave the argument open.
at any time	This phrase is redundant, being understood if no time is specified.
with the name and address of	*With* should be *of*. Otherwise, what is the content of the notice that the name and address accompanies?
the Tenant's Lender on the property	*On* is not the appropriate preposition, though a casual speaker might refer to "lending money on the property". It is unlikely that an unsecured lender would expect to benefit from this clause, so "the tenant's mortgagee" would be clearer and neater. Despite the capital L, neither *Lender* nor *Tenant's Lender* has been defined. "the…Lender" suggests that there could only be one lender (although there is a statutory rule that in leases "the singular includes the plural").
the Landlord shall not be entitled to exercise its right of entry	This is repetitive and inelegant.
herein	*Herein* is archaic and superfluous.
until at least 21 days notice in writing has been given by the Landlord	The active voice would be neater than the passive.
to the said Lender	*Said* is archaic and superfluous.
stating	*Giving* would be more natural.
(i)	Arabic numerals are easier to read and shorter.
details of unpaid rents and/or	*And/or* "has been clouding the law for more than one hundred years" (Mellinkoff 1963:306). I argued in Adler (2007:125) that the virgule "on its own means *and/or*, creating an infinite regress".[10] Here *or* is clearly an inappropriate alternative to *and*, as it seems to give the landlord a choice about which breaches the notice should specify. If landlords do choose (i) as an alternative to (ii), are they bound by (iii) or does that fall with (ii)? In any event, category (i) is superfluous, as failure to pay the rent is a breach of covenant covered by category (ii).
(ii) the nature of any breach of covenant on the part of	"On the part of" = "by".
the Tenant alleged by the Landlord	"Alleged by the Landlord" is superfluous.

(continues)

---

[10] See also Mellinkoff (1963:147).

Continued	
and (iii) details of the Landlord's requirements for any such breach to be remedied	"Details of the Landlord's requirements for any such breach to be remedied" = "how the breach is to be remedied".
insofar as the breach is capable of remedy	"Insofar as the breach is capable of remedy" = (in this context) "if the breach can be remedied". (The proviso is intended to extend to the mortgagee the protection given to the tenant by s.146 of the Law of Property Act 1925 (which uses *if* rather than *insofar as*).)

A plain language version of this clause might read (using small capitals to signal a defined term):

(A) The landlord may enter the FLAT, so ending this lease, if:

    (1) Any MANAGEMENT CHARGES are unpaid more than 21 days after they have become due (even if not formally demanded); or

    (2) The tenant has broken any other duty under this lease.

(B) (1) But if paragraph (B)(2) applies the landlord may not use this power until:

    (a) It has sent the lender written details of:

        (1) Any breach under paragraphs (A)(1) and (2); and

        (2) The landlord's reasonable requirements for correcting any remediable breach; and

    (b) 21 days have since passed without the breach having been remedied.

    (2) This paragraph applies to any lender:

    (a) For whose debt the FLAT is security; and

    (b) Whose name, address, and mortgage details the landlord has received.

This reduces the original 209-word sentence to the 90 words of paragraphs (A) and (B) (1), adding 35 words in paragraph (B)(2) to supply details missing from the original. A plainer might also want to add a note about the tenant's legal rights over-riding this remedy.[11]

5.8 CONCLUSION

Although some material is inevitably difficult to understand this does not justify legalese, for several reasons:

    1. Many of the faults which make legalese impenetrable can be cured by uncontroversial improvements in format and sentence structure without significant change of language.

[11] For a discussion of the difficulties involved, see Adler (2013).

2. Almost none of the impenetrable language adopted by the traditionalists is required by law.

3. The ideas expressed in legal documents (in contrast to those of theoretical science) will rarely, if ever, be so counter-intuitive as to be beyond the reach of clear explanation. And it is undesirable that they should be, as such complexity would make the obligations difficult to comply with and so defeat the purpose of the document. What difficulty there is (for instance in tax law) usually arises from complicated combinations of ideas which are individually comprehensible, and this difficulty can be avoided or substantially reduced by applying the techniques of plain language (including design) to set out the individual ideas and the relationship between them.[12]

---

[12] For an example of how an incomprehensible piece of legislation can be revised, see Adler (2010).

PART II

THE INTERPRETATION OF LEGAL TEXTS

CHAPTER 6

....

LINGUISTIC ISSUES IN STATUTORY INTERPRETATION

....

LAWRENCE M. SOLAN

6.1 INTRODUCTION

....

IN legal systems throughout the world, legislatures write laws and judges construe and apply them when a dispute arises over their interpretation. This chapter focuses on the nature of the language issues that cause the interpretive problems, and the ways that courts tend to address them. I will focus primarily on American law, in part because I know it better than the law of other legal systems, and in part because American judges, who operate in the common law tradition, generally justify their decisions in written opinions, creating a body of information about interpretive arguments and techniques that makes this legal system a good laboratory for investigating these issues.

As a preliminary matter, it must be acknowledged that American judges and scholars are not in accord about how statutes should be interpreted. Some, led by Supreme Court Justice Antonin Scalia, argue that the text should be given special consideration at the expense of ignoring the statute's purpose or certain extra-textual evidence of legislative intent (see Scalia 1997a; Manning 2003). Others would permit legislative intent and purpose to play a greater role in guiding decision makers. (Breyer 2005; Siegel 2009). Those disagreements will unfold as the chapter progresses. Nonetheless, it would be a mistake, I believe, to make too much of whatever disharmony ensues from these different approaches. Along with other scholars (Nelson 2005; Molot 2006), I believe that much of what is sometimes portrayed as categorical disagreement is more a matter of degree (Solan 2010). In reality, there are no American judges who would routinely ignore what a statute says in favor of divining what the legislature was interested in accomplishing based on extra-textual materials, and then base a ruling entirely on this analysis. By the same token, those dubbed "new textualists" (Eskridge 1990) most often attempt to apply interpretive rules of thumb for the purpose of ascertaining the legislature's goals while attempting to constrain the universe of evidence they consider in order to reduce the role of judicial discretion in the decision-making process. That is, textualists eschew some species of context, but are not anti-contextualist in principle.

Similarly, Continental legal systems, which are code-based and which approach interpretive issues from a somewhat different perspective, are faced with precisely the same problem: balancing the language, intent and broader goals of the legislation to produce an interpretation that is simultaneously as faithful as possible to all three considerations. Below, for example, is a provision of the Spanish Civil Code that deals with statutory interpretation:

> Norms are to be interpreted in accordance with the proper meaning of their words, in relation to the context, the historical and legislative background, and the social reality of the time in which they are to be applied, bearing in mind, fundamentally, the spirit and purpose of the former. (Art. 3.1).

In other words, Spanish judges are to pay attention to the language, as informed by the purpose of the statute and the intent of the legislature. The Code does not tell Spanish judges how to achieve the proper balance, but the considerations are clear.

This chapter will describe and illustrate some of the linguistic problems that make language inadequate to define rights and obligations without considering other values. In Section 6.2, I discuss linguistic indeterminacies of different sorts, including syntactic ambiguity, semantic ambiguity, ambiguity of reference and vagueness. Section 6.3 deals with laws whose meaning changes over time, creating a mismatch between the language and the goals of the enacting legislature. Section 6.4 discusses legislative errors—the legislature passes a law which, when applied literally in certain circumstances, tends to undermine the law's purpose rather than furthering it. Section 6.5 is a brief conclusion.

6.2 WHY WE NEED TO INTERPRET STATUTES: WHAT GOES WRONG

In an ideal world there would be no need to discuss statutory interpretation. To quote the early twentieth-century American Supreme Court Justice, Benjamin Cardozo, the goal should be to create "a code at once so flexible and so minute, as to create for every conceivable situation the just and fitting rule" (Cardozo 1921:143). However, as Cardozo lamented, "life is too complex" to make this aspiration a reality.

That being so, something must be breaking down in the communicative process that prevents laws from telling us with clarity what we must (or must not) do, and what will happen if we violate their prescriptions. In fact, a number of things break down, but the biggest problem is that events that result in legal disputes do not always match with clarity the meanings of the words in governing statutes. There are often borderline cases that do not clearly come within the intended meaning of the law, but they are not clearly outside the law either (Poscher, Chapter 9). When that happens, courts have no choice but to consider such questions as the intent of the legislature, the concerns that motivated the enactment of the statute, and occasionally, whether circumstances have changed substantially enough since the law's enactment to affect the way the law should be applied. In the remainder of this section, I will present examples of how syntactic ambiguity, semantic ambiguity, ambiguity of reference, and vagueness lead to interpretive problems that plague the courts.

6.2.1 Syntactic ambiguity

Surprisingly few cases involve questions that emanate from syntactic ambiguity (see Solan 2010). That is because most of the time the available readings are sufficiently different so that only one remains plausible in context. The classic example from Chomsky (1965:21), "Flying planes can be dangerous," has two distinct meanings, which result from two distinct, but available syntactic representations. Yet, in context, it will ordinarily be clear enough which of the possible meanings was intended.

Sometimes, however, syntactic ambiguity does matter in legal contexts. The most typical situation involves the scope of adverbs. *Liparota v United States*[1] is a good illustration. A statute made it illegal to buy or sell food stamps in the open market. Liporata bought some food stamps from an undercover agent at less than their face value. The statute read: "Whoever knowingly...acquires...[food stamps] in any manner not authorized by this chapter or the regulations...has committed a felony."[2] Liporata acknowledged that he knowingly acquired food stamps, but said that he did not know that it was illegal to buy them. The question, then, was whether "in any manner not authorized by this chapter or the regulations" comes within the scope of "knowingly." The statute is ambiguous in this respect. The adverb obligatorily modifies "acquires...food stamps," but only optionally modifies the "in any manner" phrase. The Supreme Court acknowledged the ambiguity, and applied the rule of lenity, an interpretive principle that resolves ambiguities in criminal statutes in favor of the defendant, since the accused was not on adequate notice that what he did was illegal.

6.2.2 Semantic ambiguity

Consider the 2001 decision of the United States Supreme Court in *Circuit City Stores, Inc. v Adams*.[3] An employee of Circuit City electronics stores sued for employment discrimination. Upon accepting the job, Adams had signed a contract in which it was agreed that all claims against Circuit City would be brought to arbitration. The Federal Arbitration Act calls for the enforcement of arbitration provisions in "a contract

---

[1] 471 U.S. 419 (1985).
[2] 7 U.S.C. § 2024(b)(1) (1985).
[3] 532 U.S. 105 (2001).

evidencing a transaction involving commerce to settle by arbitration a controversy thereafter arising from the whole or any part thereof...".[4] An exception to this rule, also stated within the statute, exempts from coverage "contracts of employment of seamen, railroad employees, or any other class of workers engaged in foreign or interstate commerce."[5] Adams wanted to sue in court, and not be subjected to arbitration. The issue before the Supreme Court was the extent of the exception.

By a five-to-four majority, the Supreme Court decided that Adams was required to arbitrate the discrimination claims, and that the exception did not apply. The majority reasoned that the statute applies to contracts "evidencing" commerce but that the exception applies only to employees "engaged in" commerce. This means that the exception should be construed more narrowly than the provision compelling the enforcement of the arbitration agreement. They further argued that the exception mentions only transportation workers, and that the expression, "or any other class of workers engaged in interstate commerce" should be understood in light of the examples contained in the statute itself.

The dissenters, in contrast, argued that the commerce requirement was inserted to make the statute constitutional. Under American constitutional law, Congress is permitted to legislate with respect to only those subject matters enumerated in the Constitution itself; foreign and interstate commerce is one such legitimate category of legislation. In 1925, when the law was enacted, only transportation workers were considered to be engaged in interstate commerce. That is no longer true, and it stands to reason that the enacting Congress intended the exception to protect all workers who wanted to sue their employees in court, as long as the worker is employed by a business engaged in interstate commerce.

Who is right? As a linguistic matter both understandings are plausible because the statute is semantically ambiguous. Perhaps Congress had in mind the particular categories of workers who were considered to be engaged in interstate commerce at the time they passed the law. But it is also plausible that Congress wished to exempt whatever workers it could exempt: namely, those workers engaged in interstate commerce, regardless of who in particular comes within that category. The question, in linguistic terms, is one of transparency. (See Anderson 2008 for other examples of this issue infecting the law.) On one reading, "seamen, railroad employees, or any other class of workers engaged in foreign or interstate commerce" can be looked at as shorthand for a list of those categories of workers that were considered to be engaged in foreign or interstate commerce at the time. This is a referential reading. It is the same as making reference to the members of the New York Yankees Baseball Club (or Real Madrid, for those who prefer a less American focus) as shorthand for those individuals who were members of the club at the time of the expression. On this reading, the statute would be read narrowly, since, as mentioned, the transportation workers mentioned in the text itself were the only ones who fit into this category at the time the statute was enacted.

---

[4] 9 U.S.C. § 2 (2010).
[5] 9 U.S.C. § 1 (2010).

But there is another reading, in which "any other class of workers..." acts as a variable: For any x, if x is a worker engaged in foreign or interstate commerce, then x comes within the scope of this exception. Thus, if an employee of an electronics store is considered to be engaged in interstate commerce at the time that the legal issue arises, then the exception should apply to that worker. Returning to our sports analogy, the expression "members of the New York Yankees Baseball Club" would apply to whoever happens to be a member at the time that the expression is relevant. Perhaps, for example, someone leaves something in his will to this group. The property would go to the members at the time of the person's death, under this reading.

Notably, the five most conservative justices constituted the majority and the four more liberal judges voted in dissent. Reading the opinions at face value, one would have to consider it a complete accident that the conservatives just happened to side with management, and the liberals with labor. The ambiguity licenses the judges to take the different positions they do. However, as Justice Breyer points out in his book, the majority position is only tenable if the judges ignore the purpose of the statute, and fail to consider the expression "any other class of workers..." as suggesting that the legislature intentionally left room for other classes of workers to be covered, or there would have been no need to add this catchall phrase (Breyer 2005). Thus, ambiguity can be used as an opportunity for judges to insert their own values into the law without violating the dictates of a statute, or it can trigger inquiry into the purpose of the law. American judges differ in their perspectives on purposive interpretation. European judges, trained in the teleological approach to statutory interpretation, are more uniformly committed to inquiring about the statute's purpose.

6.2.3 Ambiguity of reference

Ambiguity of reference generally occurs with pronouns. In *Bill thought he should be more productive*, the pronoun may refer to Bill, or it may refer to any male not mentioned in the sentence. Grammar limits reference to some extent. *He thought that Bill should be more productive* cannot be understood with *he* and *Bill* coreferring. Even here, context must clarify the intended referent, or communication will fail. Not many statutes contain ambiguity of reference that leads to interpretive difficulty, in part because the statutes do not contain many pronouns, and in part because the drafters tend to be careful enough to avoid the problem. However, such problems do arise occasionally.

Consider the United States Supreme Court case, *United States v Granderson*.[6] Granderson, who worked for the post office, was convicted of destruction of mail and sentenced to five years' probation. The maximum prison sentence under the federal Sentencing Guidelines would have been six months. While on probation, he was caught with illegal drugs. A statute states that in this situation: "the court shall revoke the

---

[6] 511 U.S. 39 (1994).

sentence of probation and sentence the defendant to not less than one-third of the original sentence."[7]

In order to sentence him to one-third of the original sentence, one must understand what "the original sentence" represents. The problem is that there was no original sentence other than the sentence of probation. In earlier times, American judges who sentenced a convicted person to probation would first sentence the individual to prison, and then announce that the court was suspending the prison sentence in favor of a period of probation. But judges do not do that anymore. Instead, they just sentence the individual to probation in the first instance. Therefore, the expression has no referent other than the sentence that was actually imposed.

The literal interpretation of the statute would require the judge to revoke the five-year period of probation and sentence Granderson, instead, to at least one-third of that sentence, which would be twenty months of probation. Of course, that makes no sense. No law would reduce a sentence for violating the terms of probation. Moreover, read literally, the statute would encourage multiple violations, which could soon reduce the sentence of probation to virtually no time at all. Sensibly, the Court recognized the problem and ordered that Granderson be sentenced to one third of the prison time that he would have had to serve had he not been sentenced to probation. That amounted to two months in prison.

6.2.4 Vagueness in word meaning

Without question, the most pervasive linguistic problem confronting statutory interpreters concerns what to do when an event occurs that could legitimately be described by the statutory word, but typically one would not use that word in those circumstances to describe the situation. Consider the following classic cases from American law. A nineteenth-century statute made it illegal to pay for the transportation to the United States of any person performing "labor" of any kind. Did a church's payment of transportation to bring a minister from England to New York violate the law?[8] In 1931, should an airplane have been considered a "vehicle" with respect to a statute that made it a crime to transport stolen vehicles across state lines?[9] Is trading a gun for cocaine "using a firearm" in a drug trafficking crime?[10] For that matter, is driving to a drug transaction with a gun in the rear of the car and the drugs in the front "carrying a firearm" for purposes of the same statute?[11] All of these cases require judgment about the goodness of fit between the statutory words (*labor, vehicle, use, carry*, in these examples) and events in the world.

---

[7] 18 U.S.C. § 3565(a) (1994).
[8] *Church of the Holy Trinity v United States*, 143 U.S. 457 (1982).
[9] *McBoyle v United States*, 283 U.S. 25 (1931).
[10] *Smith v United States*, 508 U.S. 223 (1993).
[11] *Muscarello v United States*, 524 U.S. 125 (1998).

Let us look at the earliest case, *Church of the Holy Trinity v United States*, which, although decided in 1892, is without question the most famous case in American legal history that addresses this issue. The statute made it a crime "in any manner whatsoever, to prepay the transportation ... of [an] alien ... to perform labor or service of any kind in the United States." The Supreme Court held unanimously that a New York church that paid the transportation from England of its new rector did not violate the law. In a famous passage, Justice Brewer wrote: "It is a familiar rule, that a thing may be within the letter of the statute and yet not within the statute, because not within its spirit, nor within the intention of its makers."[12] Brewer reasoned that the statute was intended to prevent the importation of physical laborers, not "brain toilers," to use his expression. He further found that a ruling to the contrary would trigger the "absurd result rule," which prohibits courts from applying a statute's language if the result of doing so would be absurd.

The case is sometimes seen as pitting against each other statutory language and legislative intent (Scalia 1997a). It is also sometimes discussed as a case in which legislative history was used as evidence of that intent, which in turn was used to trump the language of the statute. (See Vermeule 2006, Chomsky 2000 for differing views on this history.) Brewer had looked at the committee reports accompanying the statute's enactment and found that the legislature recognized that the language adopted was subject to the kind of strict interpretation at issue in this case, but did not intend for that interpretation to be given.

The case, however, illustrates another contrast in interpretive approach, which pervades many of the cases concerning word meaning. Brewer's famous observation about the letter and spirit of the statute did not put language in tension with extra-linguistic interpretation, but rather placed in tension two competing approaches to word meaning: a broad, definitional approach on the one hand, and an ordinary meaning, prototype approach on the other. For while we surely can call a minister's work "labor," we are more likely to use that word to speak of physical work, and that was no doubt even more the case in the late nineteenth century. In fact, many cases in which parties battle over the scope of word meaning can be characterized in just this way. One side argues that the events in dispute come within the definition of the statutory term, and they do. The other side agrees, but argues that in ordinary usage, a drafter is unlikely to have intended such a non-prototypical situation to come within the statute's domain, and this side is also right.

This difference in perspective mimics a debate over the nature of word meaning that has been taking place in the world of cognitive psychology for more than a quarter century. The classical view considers word meaning as a set of conditions, individually necessary, and together sufficient, which must obtain for it to be appropriate to use the word. A woman is an adult female human, a man an adult male human, and so on. This approach is attractive to the interpreters of legal documents. Laws themselves are written as definitions. Criminal statutes, for example, list the elements of crimes, each of which is necessary, and together are sufficient to determine whether a crime has been

[12] 143 U.S. at 458.

committed. It is attractive to analyze legal disputes by first determining whether the facts fit within the meanings of the statutory terms, and then ruling accordingly. This approach is embodied in the plain language rule of statutory interpretation: "Where [a statute's] language is plain and admits of no more than one meaning the duty of interpretation does not arise, and the rules which are to aid doubtful meanings need no discussion."[13]

American judges use this approach frequently. Consider *Small v United States*,[14] a case decided by the US Supreme Court in 2005. A statute made it illegal for a person who has been convicted "in any court" of a crime punishable for more than one year to possess a firearm. Small had been convicted of a crime in Japan, where he had served a three-year sentence. The issue was whether the statute refers only to American courts. The majority held that it did, since most statutes are not applied extraterritorially, and the word "any" is highly contextual in nature. But in dissent, Justice Thomas argued that the definition of "any" in the dictionary is broader than that, and that the statutory language was plain and should be applied as written: "The broad phrase 'any court' unambiguously includes all judicial bodies with jurisdiction to impose the requisite conviction—a conviction for a crime punishable by imprisonment for a term of more than a year."[15] This is a classic application of the plain language approach.

Beginning in the 1970s, this definitional view of word meaning became subject to challenge by psychologists, whose views resonate with Justice Brewer's approach to meaning in *Holy Trinity Church*. Most prominently, University of California at Berkeley psychologist Eleanor Rosch, in a series of experiments, demonstrated that people's knowledge of word meaning contains a great deal of information about the goodness of fit between a situation and a category (see Rosch 1975). We not only know what birds are, but we know that a robin is a good exemplar of a bird, an ostrich a poor one. We also know that concepts become fuzzy at the margins, so that category membership becomes uncertain. Widen a chair enough, and you have a love seat. But widen it too little to create a love seat, but too much to think it is a chair, and you can only shrug your shoulders or force the piece of furniture into one or the other categories, admitting that you are uncomfortable doing so.

This notion—that our knowledge of language contains information not only about whether we *can* categorize in a particular way, but also whether we *do* so categorize—is consistent not only with Justice Brewer's opinion in *Holy Trinity Church*, but more generally with the ordinary meaning rule in statutory interpretation, which judges often apply as an alternative to the plain meaning rule. Statements like the following are commonplace: "As in all cases [of statutory construction], we begin by analyzing the statutory language, 'assum[ing] that the ordinary meaning of that language accurately expresses the legislative purpose.'"[16]

---

[13] *Caminetti v United States*, 242 U.S. 470, 485 (1917).
[14] 544 U.S. 385 (2005).
[15] Ibid. at 397.
[16] *Hardt v Reliance Standard Life Ins. Co.*, 130 S. Ct. 2149, 2156 (2010) (internal citations omitted).

As for the psychologists of language, many now believe that both types of knowledge contribute to our knowledge of meaning. We take advantage of both defining features and typicality features in making categorial judgments in everyday life. (Murphy 2002). What role these different aspects of knowledge play in our conceptualization, however, remains a matter of debate. (See Armstrong et al. 1983; Connolly, et al. 2007 for discussion of limitations of the prototype approach.) For example, while most people would judge an ostrich to be a bad exemplar of a bird, when asked they know that an ostrich is indeed a member of the category "bird," and they do not think that this category is graded, but rather is discrete in nature. The legal consequence of this tension is that judges have the flexibility of focusing on one or the other of these aspects of word meaning to generate an interpretation that remains loyal to the language of a statute on the one hand, and consistent with their own values on the other.

6.3 WHEN MEANING CHANGES OVER TIME

I noted earlier that judges unavoidably refer to the intent of the legislature when resolving uncertainty in the meaning or application of a law to a situation that has arisen. But that is not the only extra-textual value that enters into the interpretive mix. When either legal or social circumstances have changed since a law's enactment, courts often will take these changes into account, sometimes having them trump the intent of the enacting legislature in favor of an interpretation that is more responsive to the present. The portion of the Spanish Civil Code quoted earlier in this chapter has this consideration built into it. Common law judges sometimes take such changes into account as well, although the matter is of some controversy. (For supporting scholarship, see Calabresi 1982; Eskridge 1994.)

Consider *Moskal v United States*,[17] a 1990 case decided by the United States Supreme Court. Moskal, who lived in Pennsylvania, had been turning back the odometers of used automobiles and then obtaining titles for the cars from Virginia through the mail. He would later sell the cars at inflated prices that reflected the mileage printed on the titles. The titles were genuine, the information contained in them, false. A statute makes it a crime to transport "any falsely made, forged, altered, or counterfeited securities"[18] across state lines. Automobile titles come within the definition of "securities" contained in the statute. The titles were surely not forged, altered, or counterfeited, so the question was whether they should be considered "falsely made." A majority of the Supreme Court justices accepted that interpretation, based largely on a compositional approach to interpreting the phrase: The titles were made to be false, and therefore were falsely made. Moreover, the overall purpose of the statute was to root out fraud, and Moskal's scheme was surely a fraud if it was anything.

---

[17] 498 U.S. 103 (1990).
[18] 18 U.S.C. § 2314 (2010).

That does not end the story, however. As Justice Scalia noted in dissent, at the time that the statute was enacted in 1939, "falsely made" was often used as a synonym of "forged." In fact, dictionaries from that era confirm this. Thus, it appears from the statute that it was intended to apply to documents that had been doctored in one way or another, but not to legitimate documents that contained misinformation. This interpretation would make the statutory language somewhat redundant, but it may well be what the legislature intended.

Let us assume that both the majority and dissenting opinions are correct: The best current reading of the statute is that it applies to documents containing false information, which is consistent with the broad purpose of the statute; and at the time of enactment, the legislators had in mind a narrower reading of the statute, namely, dealing with forgery and counterfeits. If this is the case, and I believe it is, then a conflict arises whether to give priority to the intention of the enacting legislature, or to the most natural reading of the statute today. In this instance, the Court chose the dynamic reading, which also happened to help law enforcement efforts.

6.4 LEGISLATIVE ERRORS

A very difficult issue presents itself when the legislature makes a mistake in legislation so that the language of the statute does not reflect the legislature's communicative intent. There are two ways in which this scenario typically manifests itself, and the difference between the two matters. (See Siegel 2001 for discussion.) Sometimes, the legislature makes what are called scrivener's errors. The legislature meant to use one word or syntactic structure, but used the wrong one and did not convey the meaning that it intended. The second creates more difficult problems for statutory interpreters, at least in the United States. Occasionally, the legislature simply writes a statute that cannot possibly accomplish what it set out to do because it got the facts wrong. When this happens, a judge who wishes to correct the error must correct not a simple error in wording, but an error in reasoning that led to the wording. Judges are more reluctant to do this. I illustrate both situations below.

6.4.1 The scrivener's error

When a lawyer attempts to bring a case as a class action, the court has to approve the application before the case may go forward on that basis. Congress has enacted the Class Action Fairness Act to define the conditions in which class actions may proceed in federal court, and those in which they should be litigated in state courts. The statute has a provision allowing for a rapid appeal of any such decision, but the statutory provision governing appeals contains an obvious mistake. It authorizes the court of appeals to decide the issue "if application is made to the court of appeals not less than 7 days after entry of the order."[19] This makes no sense. The legislative drafters meant to say "not more than 7 days after the entry of the order." As written, the statute says that once the aggrieved party waits a week, he can file an appeal any time after that forever. Just about all judges who have addressed the issue have been willing to correct this error, with one notable exception. Judge Jay Bybee of the United States Court of Appeals for the Ninth Circuit, quoting a 1917 case, argued that the plain language rule should apply.[20] The argument is that it should be up to the legislature to correct such errors, if, indeed they are errors.

Compare that case with *United States v Locke*.[21] A law requires those who are mining minerals on federal land to register with the Bureau of Land Management each year "prior to December 31."[22] The Locke family had a gravel mine on federal land in Nevada. A family member, knowing that a new registration requirement had been enacted, called the Bureau and was told that the papers had to be filed by the end of the year. An earlier version of a brochure issued by the government had made the same error, but it had been corrected by the time the Lockes had to file. Sure enough, the Lockes filed their documents on December 31. As a result, they lost their mining interest, because the statute says "prior to" December 31st, which means that they missed the statutory deadline by a day.

The lower court ruled in favor of the government, and the Supreme Court affirmed. Deadlines, the Court argued, are always arbitrary, so that there can be no serious argument that the purpose of the statute was to set one arbitrary date as opposed to another. The opinion generated an angry dissent, and some hostile scholarly literature (see Posner 1990:267–9). The outcome for the Lockes was not so bad, however. A footnote in the majority opinion suggests that the lower court re-examine the effect of the misinformation that the government had provided over the telephone. Although the government is typically not held responsible for such misinformation, this case, the Court suggested, might constitute an exception to the general rule.[23] As a result, negotiations ensued, and the government gave the Lockes back their mine.[24]

Legislative drafting errors of this kind pit against each other fidelity to the text as a value in its own right and fidelity to the communicative intent of the legislature. While it is, in principle, possible to argue that we can never really know what the legislature meant other than what it said, common sense tells us that the legislature made simple, human mistakes in both of these cases by miscommunicating its message. (See Boudreau et al. 2007 for discussion of a signal theory of communication that predicts such errors.) In these situations most, but not all, judges opt for correcting the error, rather than allowing an injustice to occur as part of an effort to discipline the legislature.

---

[19] 28 U.S.C. § 1453(c)(1).

[20] *Amalgamated Transit Union Local 1309 v Laidlaw Transit Servs.*, 448 F.3d 1092 (9th Cir. 2006) (Bybee, J., dissenting)(quoting *Caminetti v United States*, 242 U.S. 470, 485 (1917)). For critical discussion, See Siegel (2009).

[21] 471 U.S. 84 (1985).

[22] 28 U.S.C. § 2107(c) (2010).

[23] 471 U.S. at 90 n. 7.

[24] Telephone interview with attorney Harold Swafford, Esq., the lawyer who represented the Locke family, August 1996. For more detailed discussion, see Solan (1997: 241–2).

6.4.2 Getting it wrong

Far more difficult are cases in which the legislature wrote the wrong statute to accomplish its goal. It is one thing for a court to correct a typo, quite another to rewrite a statute based on a sense that the intended substance of a statute fails to accomplish the statute's purpose. *United States v Marshall*,[25] sometimes called "the LSD case," illustrates this problem. The case is famous in part because two well-known, generally conservative judges, Frank Easterbrook and Richard Posner, took opposite positions.

The case involved a statute setting penalties for selling various drugs, depending on the weight of the drug. It imposed a five-year prison sentence for selling more than one gram of a "mixture or substance containing a detectable amount of LSD,"[26] and additional time depending on the weight of the LSD sold. Marshall was sentenced to 20 years in prison for selling in excess of 10 grams of LSD. The LSD had been diffused into blotter paper, which could then be cut into squares and ingested, perhaps in a liquid. The problem with the statute is that the penalty depends in large part upon how much the carrier weighs. For example, one dose of LSD in a tall glass of orange juice could weigh enough to bring a defendant a hefty prison sentence. Moreover, as Posner's dissent points out, the same statute prescribes penalties for sale of "a mixture or substance containing a detectable amount" of other drugs: "[T]o have received a comparable sentence for selling heroin, Marshall would have had to sell ten kilograms, which would yield between one and two million doses."[27]

The problem with the statute is that the legislature that enacted it did not know that LSD is not manufactured and sold the same way that powdered narcotics, such as heroin and cocaine, are. A dose of LSD weighs almost nothing, and the carrier can be very heavy, and can be just about any ingestible medium, for that matter. Heroin and cocaine, in contrast, are typically cut with a white powder, such as powdered milk, which may vary in weight depending on the relative concentration of heroin to benign powder, but not nearly as dramatically as the weight of LSD embedded in a mixer may vary.

The court was faced with three choices. It could apply the statute as written, sentencing Marshall to a far greater prison term than he would have received had he sold an equal amount of heroin; it could apply the statute without regard to the carrier, on the theory that Congress simply made a mistake; or it could declare the literal application of the statute to this situation absurd, and therefore not applicable, under "the absurd result rule," discussed above. Easterbrook and another judge took the first option, which gave them a majority. Posner would have opted for the second, but did not prevail. The third was not considered, although it would have permitted the court to do justice in this particular case without concern about usurping the legislative function by rewriting the statute.

[25] 908 F.2d 1312 (7th Cir. 1990), *aff'd sub nom. Chapman v United States*, 500 U.S. 453 (1991).
[26] 21 U.S.C. § 841(b)(1)(A)(v)(2010).
[27] 908 F.2d at 1334 (Posner, J. dissenting).

6.5 CONCLUSION

This survey has attempted to provide examples of the kinds of problems that arise as a result of the imperfect match between the human language faculty on the one hand, and the goal of lawmaking on the other. The problems recur, but should not be seen as crippling. For every case in which problems of the kind described here occur, the law works smoothly and without controversy in many others. That is because, as we have seen, aspects of meaning that derive from the structure of language do not routinely lead to interpretive difficulty, and legislative errors that cause serious interpretive problems are not commonplace. Nonetheless, flexibility in our ability to place events and things into categories that we already use causes interpretive difficulties in borderline cases. In these circumstances, not only is the applicability of the law uncertain, but the approach to meaning is a matter of controversy in its own right. Moreover, the law permits a number of considerations to be taken into account in construing laws, but does not provide relative weights to these values. For these reasons, disputes over the meanings of laws will continue.

CHAPTER 7

CONTRACT FORMATION AS A SPEECH ACT

SANFORD SCHANE

7.1 INTRODUCTION

ACCORDING to conventional contract law, the formation of a valid agreement ordinarily involves an offer, an acceptance, and consideration. The former two elements typically take place through spoken or written language: An offeror proposes to do something in exchange for something of value to be given by an offeree. The latter may then accept the offer, reject it, or make a counteroffer. What is it that makes this particular verbal exchange so special, and how does it differ from other acts of speech that may also entail legal consequences, such as issuing a threat, offering a bribe, defaming someone, or perjuring oneself?[1] To answer this question I shall make use of *speech-act theory*, a linguistic approach to meaning advocated by two language philosophers, John Austin (1962) and John Searle (1969). Speech-act theory investigates how speakers interact through language and how the types of words used by them perform specific functions within the communicative process, such as reporting events, creating obligations, or bringing about new states of affairs. This theory offers a novel approach for accommodating the three traditional components of a contract. (See also Schane 1989, 2006; Tiersma 1986, 1992.)

The discussion begins with Austin's distinction between utterances that state facts or describe events and those that serve to perform the very acts that they denote. I then turn to Searle's theory of speech acts. There are five basic types of speech acts (called *illocutions*). It is the class of commissive illocutions—those where the speaker is committed to the

---

[1] In regard to some of the crimes involving the use of language, for threats see Shuy (1993: ch. 5), Solan and Tiersma (2005: ch. 10); for bribes see Shuy (1993: chs 2 & 3), Solan and Tiersma (2005: ch. 9); for defamation see Tiersma (1987); and for perjury, see Tiersma (1990), Shuy (1993: ch. 7), Solan and Tiersma (2005: ch. 11).

performance of a future act—that will be of most interest because this category includes promises, offers, and acceptances. I present Searle's requirements (called *felicity conditions*) that commissive illocutions must satisfy in order to be well-formed speech acts.

Traditional contract law maintains that every offer contains a promise of a future performance and it even equates the offer to a promise. The American Law Institute's *Restatement (Second) of the Law of Contracts* (1981) [referred to herein as "The Restatement"], a compendium of the principles underlying American contract law, states: "In the normal case of an offer of an exchange of promises, or in the case of an offer of a promise for an act, the offer itself is a promise..." (§24). Yet promise and offer are distinct kinds of commissive illocutions, because a promise encompasses a stronger mode of commitment than an offer. How then is an offer to be construed as a promise?

To reconcile this discrepancy one needs to examine some of the subtle differences among unconditional promises, conditional ones, and offers. A legal offer is equivalent to a particular type of promise—namely, a conditional promise that proposes an exchange. It is precisely this property that renders a legal offer different from an ordinary, everyday one. I propose a set of necessary criteria for a valid exchange, adapted from Searle's felicity conditions, that will explicate what can count as valuable consideration, the third element of the trio: offer, acceptance, consideration.

7.2 Speech-act theory

7.2.1 Austin: Constative versus performative utterances

The fact that speech can create specific acts may perhaps come as a surprise, for we tend to think of sentences merely as statements that describe events or situations that in principle should be verifiable: "The cat is on the mat," "It will rain tomorrow," "George bought my car." However, John Austin, a language philosopher, noted that speakers do not just utter true or false statements, but rather they may engage in the very acts designated by their words: (Austin 1971:13–22). A speaker who states, "I promise to repay the loan next month" is making a commitment to a future course of action; a minister who during a wedding ceremony says, "I now pronounce you husband and wife" creates the marital state; and if after the wedding ceremony I should remark to the groom, "I congratulate you on your marriage," I am obviously not informing him about his new marital status but rather I am engaging in the very act of congratulating. Austin referred to these kinds of utterances as *performative* because speakers perform the actions denoted by the verbs, whereas he called *constative* those statements that do describe events or states, such as "George bought my car."

Austin noted some interesting grammatical features of performative sentences (Austin 1962:53–66). The subject of such sentences is in the first person *I* or *we*, and the utterance is always directed to an expressed or an implied second person *you*. Moreover, its verb must be in the simple present tense. Observe the effect of a past-tense verb: A speaker who says, "I promised to repay the loan" or "I congratulated you on your marriage" is neither making a promise nor offering congratulations but rather is reporting a past act of promising or of congratulating. Hence, sentences with past-tense verbs will always be constative. As a further means for identifying performative utterances Austin proposed the *hereby* test: the word *hereby* may be inserted into a performative sentence but never into a constative one. Thus, one can say, "I hereby pronounce you husband and wife," but not "I hereby pronounced you husband and wife."

7.2.2 Searle: Types of speech acts

John Searle, also a language philosopher, first proposed the term speech act, a term that is particularly appropriate as it directly suggests that the performance of an act can come about through speech (Searle 1969). In fact, a speech act may be just as valid as a physical act. It may stand alone or occur along with a nonverbal act. Thus, one may propose to bet on the outcome of a sporting event by uttering the words, "I bet you that San Diego will beat Miami in next Sunday's football game," or by offering a hand shake, or even by performing both acts—the verbal and the physical—simultaneously.

According to Searle's theory, which I shall adopt for an analysis of contract formation, utterances are assigned to one of five possible speech acts or *illocutions*: assertive, commissive, directive, declaration, and expressive (Searle and Vanderveken 1985:179–216).

7.2.2.1 *Assertives*

It is the assertive speech act that most closely resembles Austin's constative utterance. The speaker asserts a proposition that represents a condition or a state of affairs that in principle could be true or false: "I *admit* that I failed to stop at the intersection," "I *claim* that the defendant was the person I saw leaving the bank." These two utterances represent *explicit* assertives as there is an overtly stated assertive verb (i.e *admit, claim*) preceding the propositional content of the assertion and it is the presence of this verb that leaves no doubt about the nature of the illocution being expressed. Other English verbs that function as explicit assertives include: *maintain, report, predict, inform, testify, confess, state, swear*. These various verbs differ from one another by the force or strength of the assertion. For example, to maintain is a stronger way of asserting than just to inform, and to swear about something is more forceful than merely to state it. However, it is generally more common and natural sounding for there to be no explicit illocutionary verb but instead for the type of speech act to be *implicit*: "I failed to stop at the intersection," "The defendant was the person I saw leaving the bank." In spite of the lack of any overt assertive verb, we still understand such utterances as assertives. The sentences previously cited as examples of Austin's constative category would also be instances of implicit assertives.

7.2.2.2 *Commissives*

In performing a commissive speech act a speaker commits himself or herself to perform or not to perform a future action: "I *offer* to sell you my car for $2500," "I *promise* not to drink when driving." Other verbs that function as commissives include: *vow, pledge, guarantee, swear.* (Some verbs belong to more than one illocutionary category. The verb *swear* is a commissive in "I swear to tell the truth," it is assertive in "I swear I deposited funds into our bank account yesterday afternoon."). Among the various commissive illocutions, a promise is the strongest mode of commitment that one can make. Here, too, it would be more usual for a commissive utterance to be expressed implicitly: "I will sell you my car for $2500," "I will not drink when driving." It is the commissive speech act that will be most relevant for contract formation.

7.2.2.3 *Directives*

In performing a directive speech act a speaker directs a hearer to perform or not to perform a future action: "I *order* you to pay the defendant $2000 as damages," "I *advise* you not to make a U-turn from this road." Other verbs that function as directives include: *ask, command, request, recommend, suggest.* Once again we find that directive utterances are frequently expressed implicitly: "You will pay the defendant $2000 as damages," "Don't make a U-turn from this road." Commissives and directives share a restriction: That which is to be performed or refrained from can take place only in the future. It is not possible, for example, to promise to do or to order someone else to do an act that has already taken place. However, there is no such tense restriction for assertives. Note the previous examples: "George bought my car" (past), "The cat is on the mat" (present), "It will rain tomorrow" (future).

7.2.2.4 *Declarations*

In performing a declaration a speaker brings about, as the very words are being spoken, the condition or the state of affairs enunciated in the proposition: "We, the jury, *find* the defendant to be not guilty," "I [umpire] *declare* that you [player] are out." A particularly spectacular declaration is reported in Genesis 1.3. "God said: *Let* there be light! And there was light." As these examples show, only certain individuals under special circumstances are authorized to make specific declarations. Other verbs that function as declarations include: *pronounce, name, bless, christen.* Declarations too may be expressed implicitly: "Not guilty!" "Out!" What is significant about declarations is that a situation or a state of affairs that did not exist previously comes into fruition at the very moment of speaking. For this reason, declarations can be made only in the present tense.

7.2.2.5 *Expressives*

In performing an expressive speech act a speaker expresses a feeling or an emotion about a proposition presumed to be true: "I *congratulate* you on your marriage," "We *are sorry* that you did not prevail in your law suit." Other verbs and verbal forms that function as expressives include: *thank, apologize, compliment, be happy, be angry, be surprised.*

Expressives have no implicit variants since their purpose is to inform the hearer about the precise nature of the emotion or the feeling that the speaker harbors in regard to what is stated. The verb of the presupposed proposition can appear in any of the three tenses. For example, I can be happy about something you did in the past, about something you are doing right now, or about something you will do in the future.

7.2.3 Searle: Felicity conditions

The *Restatement* defines a contract as "a promise or a set of promises for the breach of which the law gives a remedy, or the performance of which the law in some way recognizes as a duty." (§ 1).For a unilateral contract a promisor promises to do something in exchange for a promisee's performance: "I will pay you $200 if you paint the fence in my yard." For a bilateral agreement there is an exchange of promises: "I will drive you to the airport tomorrow morning if you will drive me there next week."

We have seen that a promise is a type of commissive speech act. Now just because someone has engaged in a speech act, it is not always without fault or *felicitous* (a term employed by Searle). For example, specific persons may be authorized to perform certain speech acts. This restriction is particularly apparent for declarations: only a member of the clergy or a justice of the peace may declare a marriage union, or just the umpire assigned to a particular game may call a player out. In addition, there are constraints on the speech act itself. Searle has provided an in-depth analysis of the speech act of promising and has proposed six conditions that this commissive illocution must satisfy in order to be fully valid or felicitous (Searle 1969:57–62). Two of them apply to the act of promising and the other four to what is being promised.

The *sincerity* and the *essential* conditions apply to the act of promising. The former establishes the promisor's good intention to carry out the promise and the latter requires that the promisee be aware of this commitment. Consider the application of these two conditions to the following promise: "I promise you that this afternoon I will deposit funds to your account." I am *sincere* provided that I indeed *intend* to deposit the funds this afternoon. If I have no intention of doing so, then I have violated the sincerity condition. Although I have indeed made a promise, it is not wholly felicitous. In addition, it is *essential* that you, the promisee, understand from my choice of words that I have made a promise and that I am committed to carry it through.

The law too expects that the participants to an agreement will deal with each other in good faith and that the promisee will be aware of the promisor's intention to contract. If at the time of making a promise one has no intention of carrying it through, then one may be subject to fraud. The requirement of acting in good faith is the legal correlate of the sincerity condition.

In traditional contract law one who returns a lost article but was unaware of an offer of an award is not entitled to the reward. The requirement of being aware of a promisor's intention to contract is the legal correlate of the essential condition.

The futurity, ability, benefit, and non-expectancy conditions apply to what is being promised. The *futurity* condition requires that the promised performance or forbearance is to take place in the future. In other words, I cannot promise to do something that I have already done. As noted previously, it is the very nature of commissive illocutions to require a speaker to engage in a future act. The *ability* condition stipulates that the promisor will have the necessary physical, mental, and/or financial means to carry out that which is promised. For example, I cannot promise to tutor you in French if I do not know the language. The *benefit* condition concerns the promisee. It presupposes that he or she will derive some benefit from what has been promised and furthermore is amenable to being the recipient of that benefit. Thus, if I promise to take you out to dinner tonight, I have reason to believe that you would like for me to do that. The *non-expectancy* condition stipulates that what I promise to do is not something that I would be expected to do in the ordinary course of events. It would be bizarre for me to promise to take you out to dinner tonight if we typically eat out every night or to promise to arrive at work on time if I have never been late in the past. These four conditions have corresponding legal correlates that will be relevant for evaluating the adequacy of consideration.

7.3 CONTRACT FORMATION

7.3.1 Promise versus offer

In its discussion of "offer" the *Restatement* refers to both unilateral and bilateral agreements by asserting that an offer "may propose the exchange of a promise for a performance or an exchange of promises," but it concludes the discussion by stating "*the offer itself is a promise*, revocable until accepted" (emphasis added). (Restatement §24). We are now faced with an apparently contradictory situation. Although both offers and promises are types of commissive illocutions, they are by no means on equal footing. To see how they differ one needs to distinguish between two kinds of speech acts—*autonomous* ones that go into effect immediately upon being uttered, and *cooperative* ones that first require a response from the addressee. (Hancher 1979). An example of an autonomous speech act would be the action of firing someone and of a cooperative one the making of a bet. Thus, if I as your employer, say to you, "You're fired," I have performed autocratically the act of discharging you. On the other hand, if I bet you $50 on the outcome of next Sunday's football game, then you must accept my proposal—by a handshake or by saying something like "You're on!", before the bet can take effect.

It is this distinction between autonomous and cooperative speech acts that differentiates *ordinary* promises from offers: A promise is an autonomous speech act; an offer is a cooperative one.[2] For example, if I *promise* to drive you to the airport tomorrow I become immediately obligated to do so—that is, no response is required from you in order for me to be obligated. Of course, subsequently you may choose to release me from that obligation, but that act is separate from the original commitment. On the other hand, if I *offer* to drive you to the airport I am obliged to do so only after you have accepted my offer. If you neither accept it nor reject it then I am free to change my mind and to retract it. Just as a bettor can call off a bet that is not taken up, an offeror can withdraw an offer that has not yet been accepted, but a promisor, acting in good faith, cannot renege on a promise.

This difference between a promise and an offer is also reflected in the speaker's assessment of the benefit to the addressee. In making a promise to drive you to the airport I have some reason to believe that you are in need of a ride and that you would be highly disposed to my taking you there. Because of this certainty I am able to commit myself to an immediate obligation. On the other hand, in making an offer I am less certain of your needing a ride, and if so, of my taking you there (as you may have already made previous arrangements). Because of this uncertainty, before obligating myself I will need to know whether you are amenable to my proposal.

Yet the *Restatement* has asserted that "the offer itself is a promise, *revocable until accepted*" (emphasis added). (Restatement, §24). In equating an offer to a promise has the *Restatement* failed to differentiate adequately between these two kinds of commissive speech acts and has it erred in affirming that a promise is revocable? It has not. But to understand how an offer can be construed as a *revocable promise* one needs to distinguish between *unconditional* and *conditional* promises. Unconditional promises place no restrictions on the performance nor do they require anything from the promisee: "I promise to take you shopping later today," "I'll drive you to the airport tomorrow." Conditional promises, on the other hand, require that some other event must (or must not) transpire before the promisor need perform: "I promise to take you shopping later today, if it doesn't rain," "I'll drive you to the airport tomorrow, if I can borrow my brother's car." The law refers to such happenings as *conditions precedent*. They may be fortuitous outside events (what the *Restatement* calls *aleatory*) or under various degrees of personal control.[3]

7.3.1.1 *Commitment versus obligation*

It is necessary to make an additional distinction between *commitment* and *obligation*. For an unconditional promise (e.g. "I promise to take you shopping later today"), at the moment of speaking I am both committed to keeping my promise and obligated to undertake the future performance. For a conditional promise (e.g. "I promise to

---

[2] Ordinary, everyday promises are autonomous speech acts, but legal promises are cooperative ones for (as I demonstrate shortly) they are equivalent to offers.

[3] "A party may make an aleatory promise, under which his duty to perform is conditional on the occurrence of a fortuitous event" *Restatement* §76.

take you shopping later today, if it doesn't rain"), at the moment of speaking I am still committed to keeping my promise but I will become obligated to undertake the performance only if the condition transpires. It is this difference between commitment and obligation that makes an offer more similar to a conditional promise than to an unconditional one. For an offer (e.g. "I offer to drive you to the airport tomorrow"), at the moment of speaking I am still committed to my proposal but I become obligated to the future performance only upon your acceptance. My offer is more or less equivalent to the following conditional promise: "I promise to drive you to the airport tomorrow, if you want me to drive you there." That is, I make an immediate commitment to a future act but am obligated to perform that act only if the conditional requirement occurs—namely, that you indicate a positive inclination toward my proposal.

Now in everyday dealings with family and friends one may feel morally bound to these kinds of unconditional or conditional promises and offers, but in the eye of the law they are *gratuitous*. In the event of a breach a promisee will generally have no recourse to a legal remedy. What then constitutes a legal promise, one that does protect the interests of a promisee? It is a conditional promise that contains a special kind of condition. In exchange for the promisor's promise it requires the promisee to perform (or to refrain from) an act or else to promise to perform (or to refrain from) an act of *benefit to the promisor*: "I will sell you my car, if you pay me $2500," "I will give you $5000 on your twenty-first birthday, if you promise to give up drinking and smoking until then."[4] A condition that proposes an exchange to be sure still functions as a condition precedent. Consider the immediately preceding examples: On your paying me $2500 (the condition precedent) I will hand over to you the title to my car; and by your giving me your promise to quit drinking and smoking, I am obligated to a future payment of $5000.

There is uncertainty associated with any kind of offer, because the offeror is not entirely sure whether the offeree desires what is being proposed (i.e. this uncertainty concerns the benefit for the offeree). For a legal offer—a promise that proposes an exchange, this uncertainty reflects not just the promisee's willingness to accept the promisor's future act but also the promisee's willingness to engage in the very performance that is requested of him or her. But now precisely because the promisor's obligation is contingent on the promisee's willingness to undertake his or her part of the bargain, the promisee needs to communicate that desire to the promisor either by performing the requested act or by promising to do so.

---

[4] A promisee's giving up of something or not acting in a certain manner can be of benefit to a promisor and can constitute a valid condition on an exchange. In *Hamer v Sidway*, 124 N.Y. 538 (1891), an uncle promised his nephew that if he would refrain from drinking and using tobacco until he became 21 years of age, the uncle would pay him $5000. The New York Court of Appeals held that the nephew's forbearance was sufficient to qualify as a legal detriment; as for the uncle, he benefitted from seeing his nephew refrain from activities that the uncle found unwholesome.

7.3.2 Acceptance

An offer can be accepted in one of two ways. For a unilateral offer, acceptance occurs when the offeree commences the performance requested by the offeror.[5] Suppose I have called up a handyman who does work for me and I leave the following message on his voice mail: "I will pay you $200 if you paint the fence in my yard." I arrive home later in the day and find him painting the fence. This act constitutes an acceptance of my offer. For a bilateral agreement acceptance takes place through an exchange of promises: "I will drive you to the airport tomorrow morning if you will drive me there next week." You accept my offer, not through the performance of an act, but through language—by replying "Okay" or "I accept" or with similar words.

Acceptance of a bilateral agreement, like offer, is a commissive speech act. By uttering, "I accept" or using equivalent words, an offeree becomes committed to the terms of the offer. Hence the felicity conditions governing commissive illocutions take effect here as well: The offeree *intends* to undertake the requested performance and it is *essential* to communicate effectively this commitment to the offeror. In addition, the offeree is to perform the requested act in the *future*, has reason to believe (because of the offer) that the offeror wants the act done and will *benefit* from it, has the necessary *ability* and competence to perform the act, and is *not expected* otherwise to do so.

Recall that the first two felicity conditions—the sincerity and the essential conditions—concern the act of promising or committing, whereas the remaining four—the futurity, the benefit, the ability, and the non-expectancy conditions—apply to the requested or promised act. For a bilateral agreement, where there is an exchange of promises, perforce all six felicity conditions apply to both parties. However, for a unilateral agreement, only the offeror has made a promise. Because the offeree has made no promise the sincerity and the essential conditions are not relevant here, but the four conditions governing the validity of the requested act will still be applicable.

7.3.3 Consideration

Many systems of law require that some other factor be present in order for a promise to become legally binding.[6] In the Anglo-American tradition that additional element is

---

[5] In classical contract law an offeree to a unilateral contract could accept the offer only by *completion* of the requested act. This had the undesirable consequence that an offeror could withdraw the offer at any time prior to completion thereby putting at a disadvantage an offeree that had already commenced performance. The modern view is that acceptance takes place on *commencement*, at which moment the offeror may no longer revoke. However, it is still the case that the offeror need perform his or her part of the bargain only after completion by the offeree. Tiersma (1992) has proposed that only a bilateral agreement contains an offer, whereas a unilateral one is based on promise and hence cannot be revoked. I argue in the text that a conditional promise that proposes an exchange is by its very structure equivalent to an offer. Therefore, I maintain that both bilateral and unilateral agreements contain offers.

[6] In Roman law a *nudum pactum*, a bare promise, was not enforceable. There had to be present some other *causae*, factors, to turn it into a *pactum vestitum*, a promise vested with the proper form (Corbin 1952:§§ 310, 302).

consideration. Although there is no simple definition, nonetheless various principles have evolved for characterizing consideration (Corbin 1952:164–7, §110). There must be: (i) an agreed exchange or a *bargain*; (ii) a *benefit* accrued by the promisor; (iii) a *detriment* incurred by the promisee; and (iv) a *quid pro quo* or a reciprocal performance. Foremost is the notion of an exchange or a bargain. The promisor offers a promise as an inducement for a performance or a return promise from the promisee. However, in order for that exchange to be valid, the promisor is to reap some benefit (other than the promisee's friendship) from the requested act, and the promisee, by expending some effort or funds in carrying out that act, will suffer a detriment. But in this situation benefit and detriment turn out to be reciprocal relations: The promisor, by making a promise to do something, will also bear a detriment, and the promisee, in obtaining the promise, will thereby derive a benefit; hence, there is a *quid pro quo*.

The presence of consideration supposedly indicates that the parties really do intend to have a legal agreement and it serves to differentiate promises with legal import from merely gratuitous ones. Consider these promises: "I will drive you to the airport tomorrow, if you pay me $25," "I will drive you to the airport tomorrow, if you can be at my house by 7 o'clock." In both cases the promisee has to do something in order for the promisor to become obligated. Yet not every condition imposed on a promisee will necessarily convert a promise into a legal offer.

For the first example it should be evident that there is adequate consideration, for by paying $25 the promisee is giving something of value desired by the promisor in exchange for the promise of a ride to the airport. For the second example the promisor is not bargaining for the promisee's showing up at the house, but rather the promisor (most likely because of an amicable relationship with the promisee) is willing to drive the latter to the airport without desiring anything of value in return so long as the promisee has some way of getting to the place from where the promisor will be leaving. This particular conditional promise is not too dissimilar from "I will drive you to the airport tomorrow, if it rains." In one case, the condition is under the control of the promisee ("if you can be at my house at 7 o'clock"); in the other case, it is aleatory or contingent on a fortuitous outside event ("if it rains"). Both situations exemplify a condition precedent on a gratuitous promise.

What is interesting about a condition on a promise proposing an exchange (e.g. "I will drive you to the airport tomorrow, if you pay me $25.") is that it simultaneously plays three essential roles: (i) It operates as a *condition precedent* on the promisor's promise. (ii) Because the occurrence of the condition is not fortuitous but under the control of the promisee the latter is free to accept or reject the terms, and it is this power entrusted to the promisee that has the potential to make this kind of promise a *legal offer*. (iii) Because the condition specifies the thing of value that the promisee must give in exchange for the promisor's promise, it stipulates the necessary *consideration* for a valid offer.

7.3.3.1 *The criteria for a valid exchange*

The speech-act felicity conditions serve to differentiate promises that are felicitous or well-formed from those that are defective in some way. I have established analogous constraints governing the requirements of a promisee's performance for the class of promises that propose exchanges. Furthermore, these joint requirements for both promisors and promisees have direct application for determining the adequacy of consideration in contract law. In order for there to be avalid exchange and hence an enforceable agreement, each of the parties must satisfy the following four criteria, an adaptation of Searle's felicity conditions.[7]

Criteria for a valid exchange:

(a) *Futurity condition:* Each party is to perform (or refrain from performing) a future act.

(b) *Benefit condition:* Each party sincerely regards the other party's performance as an exchange, and it is that sense that motivates entering into a bargain.

(c) *Ability condition:* Each party is able (physically, mentally, and/or financially) to perform the required act and will do something to further that performance.

(d) *Non-expectancy condition:* A party is not expected to do the act in the ordinary course of affairs.

Consider the following unilateral offer: "I will pay you $200 if you paint the fence in my yard." First let us apply the four criteria to what you, the promisee, must do: (a) The fence painting is to take place at a time future to my proposal—that is, you have not already painted the fence. (b) I want the fence painted and it is this desire that motivates me to propose a bargain. (c) You must know how to paint fences and you are physically able to do the job. (d) Given the normal course of events it is neither expected that you should paint my fence nor are you already obligated to do so.

The four criteria also characterize what I, the promisor, must do: (a) My payment of $200 is to take place at a time future to my proposal—that is, I have not already paid this amount for you to do the job. (b) I have reason to believe that you will benefit from the proposed exchange and that my payment is offered as motivation for you to accept my offer. (c) I have the financial means to pay you $200. (d) It is not expected that I should otherwise give you $200.

A violation of any of the four criteria will lead to insufficient consideration and hence invalid agreements. Consider the following examples of inadequate consideration, some of which are taken from the *Restatement*.[8]

7.3.3.1.1 Futurity condition: "Past" consideration

A promisor makes a promise in exchange for an act already performed.

> A gives emergency care to B's adult son while the son is sick and without funds far from home. B subsequently promises to reimburse A for his expenses. The promise is not binding. (based on *Restatement* §86, 1)[9]

---

[7] Searle (1969) deals exclusively with unconditional promises. I have modified the felicity conditions, thereby extending the analysis to legal promises (i.e. those that propose an exchange backed by consideration).

[8] Some of the examples presented here first appeared in Schane (1989).

[9] This example is based on the famous case of *Mills v Wyman* (3 Pick. 297, Mass. 1825) that involved a sick son cared for by strangers.

Here B promises to pay A for an act that A has already performed. Of course, had A communicated with B at the time the son fell ill, and had B at that time promised payment, A's subsequent caring for the son would have constituted valid consideration for B's promise.

7.3.3.1.2 Benefit condition: Sham consideration

A promisor makes a promise in exchange for a trifle or a ridiculously small sum of money.

> In consideration of one cent received, A promises to pay $600 in three yearly installments of $200 each. The one cent is merely nominal and is not consideration for A's promise. (based on *Restatement* §79, 5)

In general, the law does not look into the economic value of the consideration, and there are clearly contracts where the parties exchange things that do not have near equivalent monetary worth. For example, one may offer to sell an item at a price beneath its market value. If value is not at issue, then why should a cent not qualify as appropriate consideration? The benefit criterion stipulates that one truly desires what the other is to give. In this example it is highly unlikely that A is bargaining for B to pay one cent in exchange for A's payment of $600. On the other hand, if A has a gap in his coin collection, he indeed may want B to give him a certain rare penny in exchange for a promise to pay $600.

7.3.3.1.3 Benefit condition: Condition precedent on a gift

The desire aspect by itself in not a sufficient characterization of the benefit condition. The bargain element must also be present. One may indeed be sincere in wanting the other person to do something, but if that act is viewed only as a necessary condition precedent on receiving a favor or a gift, and not as something given as part of a bargain, there can be no consideration. Consider a previous example:

> I will drive you to the airport tomorrow, if you can be at my house by 7 o'clock.

Under normal circumstances, this utterance would be a gratuitous promise. I assume that you are able to find your way to my house, that the distance for you to travel there is reasonable, etc. I am not asking you to meet me there in exchange for my promise, but rather as a condition for you to enjoy the fruits of my generosity. My promise is motivated entirely out of my amicable desire to take you to the airport. I have no interest in your coming to my house at 7 o'clock other than for this purpose.

7.3.3.1.4 Ability condition: Fortuitous occurrence

The ability condition requires that the parties know how to do what they are to perform and are also physically, mentally, and/or financially able to do so. But there is another feature of this criterion. One must expend some effort in performing the act requested or alternatively be able to exercise some control over the outcome. Contrast the two following hypothetical examples, which are not from the *Restatement*:

> A has applied for admission to the Yale Law School complying with all their application requirements. B, his aunt, an alumna of Yale, says to him, "If you get admitted to Yale, I'll give you $5,000." Subsequently, A gains admission. A's acceptance by Yale is not consideration for B's promise. (Schane 2006:168)

A had applied to Yale before his aunt made her promise. Afterwards, he engaged in no act to further his admission to Yale. The decision for admission was completely out of his control. Essentially, it was a fortuitous event.

> A has applied for admission to several law schools. Both Harvard and Yale have accepted him. Now he needs to decide which law school to choose. B, his aunt, says, "If you go to Yale, I'll give you $5,000." A's subsequent choosing of Yale over Harvard is consideration for B's promise. (Schane 2006:168)

Here A had applied to Yale before his aunt made her promise, but he had also applied to Harvard. Once the aunt found out that her nephew had been admitted to both institutions, she offered him $5000 in exchange for his choosing Yale over Harvard. Because A had control over which law school he would eventually attend, his choice of Yale would constitute consideration for B's promise.

7.3.3.1.5 Non-expectancy condition: Preexisting Duty

A promisor makes a promise in exchange for an act that the other party is already committed to do.

> A offers a reward to whoever produces evidence leading to the arrest and conviction of the murderer of B. C produces such evidence in the performance of his duty as a police officer. C's performance is not consideration for A's promise. (Restatement §73,1)

C already had an obligation to apprehend felons as part of his contractual duties as a police officer. However, the consideration will become valid whenever the other person can perform the act outside of his current contractual duties or whenever he does more than he is currently obligated to do. For example:

> C's duties as a police officer are limited to crimes committed in a particular State, and while on vacation he gathers evidence as to a crime committed elsewhere. C's performance is consideration for the promise. (Restatement §73,2)

7.4 SUMMARY

Only a conditional promise that proposes an exchange is equivalent to the cooperative speech act of a legal offer. Other kinds of conditions function purely as conditions precedent and the promises associated with them are never commensurate with offers.

Searle's speech-act felicity requirements served to differentiate between promises that were felicitous or well-formed from those that were defective in some way.

Searle's original discussion of felicity conditions dealt with ordinary unconditional promises. It had little to say about conditional promises or about the kinds of promises relevant to the law. Because legal promises nonetheless are still promises it was imperative to incorporate a modified version of the felicity conditions into a speech-act analysis of contract formation. The resulting criteria for a valid exchange serve this function. It was my purpose here to show how these constraints are able to accommodate the special requirements of contract law.

Table 7.1 (adapted from Schane 2006:153) summarizes the relationship between the criteria for a valid exchange and their legal outcomes.

Table 7.1 Criteria for a valid exchange and their legal correlates

Failure to respect this condition:	Results in the following legal consequence:
1. Futurity condition Each party must perform (or refrain from performing) a **future act**	**Past consideration** A party has already performed the requested act; "past" consideration is no consideration
2. Benefit condition Each party **desires an act** to be performed by the other party and it is that desire that motivates entering into a bargain	**Sham consideration** A party is not "truly" bargaining for the act; absent a bargain there is only a gratuitous promise and no consideration
3. Ability condition Each party **is able** (physically, mentally and/or financially) to perform the act promised and must do something in furtherance of the performance	**Voidable contract** A party is deemed unable or unfit to perform the required act
4. Nonexpectancy condition It is **not obvious** that a party would do the act in the ordinary course of events	**Pre-existing duty** A party is already under a legal obligation to perform the act
5. Sincerity condition A promisor **intends** to do the act promised	**Fraud/Bad faith** A party has acted fraudulently or in bad faith and with intent to deceive
6. Essential condition Both parties know that a **commitment** exists between the promisor and the promisee	**No contract** An individual is unaware of a promisor's promise

CHAPTER 8

....

CONSTITUTIONAL
INTERPRETATION

....

ROBERT W. BENNETT

8.1 INTRODUCTION: ORIGINALISM AND LIVING CONSTITUTIONALISM

....

CONTEMPORARY debates about constitutional interpretation in the United States seem fixated on what is called "originalism," the view that, regardless of when some constitutional issue arises, guidance for resolving it is to be sought in "original" sources, those that accompanied the promulgation of the constitutional language in question. In the view of many self-styled "originalists," probing original sources is not simply a helpful tool in interpreting the document, but the *only* appropriate way—perhaps unless and until those original sources somehow come up empty. There are certainly disagreements among originalists, and we will return to a number of them, but in the different camps it is common to find an insistence that indeterminacy does not plague the enterprise, that those original sources can be mined at least with some regularity for objectively right answers to constitutional questions. Indeed, this seems to provide some of the appeal of originalism, for the apparent alternative is "living constitutionalism," in which a large dose of judicial discretion keeps constitutional interpretation in touch with a changing world. This is seen by originalists as relegating ill-defined responsibility to the doubtful authority of the judiciary. Originalists invoke the writtenness of the Constitution, the desirability of stability in the law, specific constitutional provision for amendments as signaling the acceptable mechanism for change, and the tenuous democratic credentials of life-tenured federal judges to depict originalism as the right approach to constitutional interpretation, and living constitutionalism as misbegotten.

Originalism, however, has been dogged by two interrelated sets of questions: (i) just what the approach means in practice; and (ii) whether in fact it comes up empty much more often than originalists acknowledge. Engaging those questions will, I think, expose the essential inevitability of a Constitution that is informed by an ongoing stream of contemporary insights and values. If this is so, originalism is simply incapable of providing the restraint that originalists claim for it. The resulting "living constitution" might theoretically be entrusted to non-judicial authority by eliminating or greatly scaling back judicial review in the name of the Constitution. There are, however, few proponents of a substantially diminished judicial review—in originalist camps or any other. The result is that, whether or not couched in originalist language, we are fated to have a judiciary-centered constitutionalism that is unavoidably a living one.

8.2 Tribulations of originalism

8.2.1 Constitutional language and original intention

We will return to qualify the point a bit, but there is relatively little controversy about the status of one "original" source, the language of the Constitution. (Monaghan 1981: 383–4). At the same time, it is broadly appreciated that language does not convey meaning all by itself, as anyone can attest who has found himself amidst speakers of a language in which he has been neither raised nor schooled (or, perhaps even more tellingly, has been lightly schooled). Language conveys meaning on account of social practice, understandings shared by speakers and writers, listeners and readers, about the significance to be ascribed to words, and phrases, and sentences. Social practice with regard to language may, however, be heavily dependent on context, and, even within fairly cohesive and enduring social groupings, may vary by degrees from one individual to another, and from one time to another. The response of originalists to this difficulty is historical inquiry to determine how the language was used "originally." This was—and often still is—characterized by many originalists as a search for the original "intention" with which the words were used, a characterization borrowed from the context of legislative interpretation. But that characterization brings to the surface a variety of difficulties.

8.2.2 The summing problem

Perhaps most obviously, the United States Constitution—like legislation—is the product of voting groups—in the case of the Constitution a multiplicity of them—while talk of "intention" is usually associated with mental states of individuals. Originalists who want to hark to intention must then confront what I call a "summing problem," how to amalgamate—or perhaps sidestep—the intentions of the individuals involved. One estimate puts the number of participants in the constitutional convention that formulated the (unamended) document, the continental congress that sent it on to the states, and then the various state ratifying conventions that adopted it, at about 2,000 (Rakove 1996:6). If the historical inquiry uncovered a high degree of commonality among those individuals about what their language was supposed to accomplish, that might provide the relevant original "intention." But the inquiry might instead uncover both differences among individuals and gaping holes in the evidence about the thinking of most of them. They may simply have had different things in mind, of course, but in addition, some may have been content with what they took to be major themes of the Constitution and then cast their votes for the entire document with little concern for any concrete implications of this provision or that.

The 2,000, moreover, participated in a variety of independent actions regarding the Constitution—formulating and recommending, transmitting to the states for their consideration, and then ratifying the document in 13 disparate state-centered gatherings. Even if amalgamation could be wrestled down for each separate action, a second order amalgamation problem for the different actions would be presented.

8.2.3 Degrees of generality of language

There are other problems. Constitutional language varies from the rather precise all the way to the very vague or general. The President is required, for instance, to be 35 years old, and each state is to have two Senators. But no state is to take life, liberty, or property without "due process of law."[1] It will often seem quite clear how the precise language is to be applied, even with little inquiry into the historical setting in which the language was crafted. So if California were to urge today that the disparities between its population and that of the least populous state (Wyoming) is so great that three or more California Senators are required, the language would seem clearly to foreclose that result. We might even imagine that if we were able to confront the original 2,000 constitutional actors with California's claim, there would be a consensus that the language was "meant" to foreclose it. In contrast, if we attempt to rely on the language, even as fleshed out by original social practice and shared usage, an inquiry about just what is in and what is out of a requirement of "due process" could be quite befuddling. To be sure, historical inquiry might uncover ample evidence of some due process requirements—a right to present evidence in defense of criminal charges, for instance—but not of many others, like a right of a criminal defendant to state-provided resources to support empirical research to bolster a claim of racial discrimination by a prosecutor's office in selecting a jury.

8.2.4 Degrees of generality of intentions

Even for an individual, moreover, the notion of intention is beset by complexities. It too can range from the precise to the general, with all sorts of nuance and gradations in between—for both precise and general language. And multiple intentions for a discrete

---

[1] U.S. Const., art. I, § 3, cl. 1; art. II, § 1, cl. 5; U.S. Const. amend. XIV, § 1.

bit of language can be harbored by a single individual at one time, posing the possibility of choosing among them. Someone could, for instance, vote for the 35-year age requirement for President fully intending firm adherence to that precise age, but do so for a mix of reasons, including providing a degree of confidence in the maturity of those who would hold the office. And one could vote for the Fourteenth Amendment's Equal Protection Clause, desiring to assure protection for the newly freed slaves, while ardently believing, for instance, that state laws requiring racial segregation in public schools do no offense to the equal protection ideal (Klarman 1991:252). An interpreter might then derive different guidance from original intention depending upon the aspect of intention from which it was sought.

8.2.5 Unforeseen problems

Yet another problem inheres in the nature of written laws, including constitutions. While adopted at one point in time, they often must be applied to problems that are generated by later events. Particularly with generally phrased language, and especially for laws like constitutions designed for the long run, those responsible for promulgating constitutional language may not have thought about some of the problems that over time the language seems to address. To be sure, even if there was no conscious consideration of a problem, there may have been implicit assumption just below the level of conscious attention. But as time goes by, a succession of questions may well arise as to which there was neither conscious consideration nor implicit assumption by those various actors who gave us the constitutional language.

Thus, technological change may frame problems that were not foreseen. The First Amendment, for instance, protects "freedom of speech…[and] of the press," but is understandably silent about electronic means of communicating, such as radio signaling, to say nothing of email and texting (Scalia 1997b:37–8).[2] But social, political, and economic change may also intrude. The original Constitution, for instance, provided for selection of (those two) United States Senators by state legislatures,[3] but nothing was said about the voting rules for that selection. It was not long before bicameral state legislatures sometimes found themselves divided along cameral lines between two (or more) candidates, with no guidance from constitutional language about whether each house got one vote, or perhaps each legislator got one vote in a combined count, and in either case whether a plurality or majority of the relevant collectivity was required. Perhaps that problem was foreseen by some of the gang of 2,000, and if so there may have been assumptions about its resolution. But perhaps not.

It may, for instance, have been broadly assumed among the 2,000 that worthy senatorial candidates would be few, and that serious discussion of the merits of each would routinely lead to a consensus in the relatively confined community of a state

---

[2] See U.S. Const., amend. I.
[3] U.S. Const., art. I, § 3, cl. 1.

legislature. At the time the Constitution was adopted, many participants were actually quite disdainful of political parties, and there likely was something approaching a consensus that parties neither would nor should play any substantial role in serious governmental decisions, surely including the choice of United States Senators (Hofstadter 1969:viii). But the assumption about the role political parties would in fact play proved quite wrong, and the emergence of fierce political partisanship may have contributed to the senatorial selection difficulties that emerged (Bennett 2003:58–60).

An even clearer example of a problem that was likely not foreseen is that of the "faithless" presidential elector. The president (and vice-president) are formally chosen by presidential electors in separate meetings in the various states held on the same day about 40 days after what Americans think of as presidential "election day." The total number of electors is constitutionally allocated among the states, and each state legislature is given authority to determine the "manner" of selection of the state's quotient.[4] It seems clear that this approach to presidential selection contemplated a highly discretionary process in which electors would engage in serious debate and discussion at those disparate meetings about who would make the best president. For if debate, discussion, and then discretion-laden decision-making was not the presumed norm, there would seem to have been little point in creating the office of presidential elector in the first place.

But the emergence of political parties bedeviled that process as well. States gravitated to popular election as the "manner" for choosing electors, and parties nominated candidates for president and vice-president and also for the office of elector in each state. A norm of party loyalty then loomed large, so that electors were expected to, and routinely did, vote for the candidates of their party. But not always, and the occasional maverick among electors came over time to be thought of as "faithless," because he broke faith with a commitment that was increasingly taken for granted.

There has also been a sea change over the years more generally in attitudes toward popular election with a broadly distributed franchise, not only as the "manner" for choosing electors, but in a variety of other public decision-making contexts as well. The movement has often been advanced by constitutional amendment. Thus, United States Senators were originally chosen by state legislatures, but the Seventeenth Amendment now requires popular election. Originally state by state designation of eligible voters almost universally limited the franchise to adult men, and usually included property qualifications as well. Now on account of the Nineteenth and Twenty-Sixth Amendments, women have won the right to vote, as have those 18 years or older. Amendments have also forbidden states from denying the right to vote on account of race, and from imposing poll taxes.[5] And states have more generally done away with property or wealth requirements for voting. In addition many states now use popular election for the state judiciary. More than a few also have active systems of

---

[4] See U.S. Const., art. II, §1, cls. 2, 4.
[5] U.S. Const. amends. XV, XXIV.

"direct democracy" in which legislation or (state) constitutional amendments can be adopted by popular vote.

Given this history, if we were somehow able to interrogate our 2,000 constitutional actors about the appropriateness of faithless elector voting at the turn of the twenty-first century, they would likely confess to having had neither conscious thought nor unconscious assumption about the question, embedded as it is in an entirely different world of presidential politics and more broadly of the role of popular elections in public decision making.

8.2.6 Intervening decisions: Precedent and constitutional amendment

Originalism has also had to grapple with two additional problems, analogies to which are found in the statutory context. The first is how to deal with precedent, prior judicial decisions that come to be seen as erroneous by originalist lights. Particularly when originalists see their approach as probing some "objective" constitutional truth, they tend to resist deference to prior decisions (usually by courts manned to one degree or another by different judges) that they now believe missed the mark. But this risks instability in constitutional law, putting it in some tension with the notion that originalism is an important bulwark of stability. Not surprisingly then originalists have been sharply divided about the nature and extent of deference owed to precedent.

The second problem is how to mesh constitutional amendments with the preexisting text. There are variations on the theme. One is akin to the problem of "erroneous" precedent. Above and beyond what it says explicitly, an amendment may be predicated on assumptions about constitutional law that are seen as misguided by originalist lights. Under those conditions should an amendment be taken to have adopted the prior error, bestowing solid originalist credentials on it? And if so, just how far can the new meaning generated by amendment be allowed to reach?

Again the intrusion of political parties into the electoral college process provides a nice illustration of the difficulties. The coordination that political parties brought to the process caused problems with the constitutional scheme for choosing the nation's chief executive officers. The process was aimed at the choice of both a president and vice-president, but under the original scheme, there were not to be two separate votes as there are today, but instead a single integrated process, in which electors met separately in each state and cast two votes, undifferentiated between the two offices. The state meetings were to be held simultaneously, with the clear assumption that each would proceed independently of the others.

The candidate with the largest number of electoral votes became president, if he commanded a total at least equal to a majority of the number of "appointed" electors. The vice-presidency then went to the candidate with the highest number of electoral votes after the president had been chosen, whether or not that "runner-up" commanded an electoral college majority.[6] This presented the possibility that there would be a presidential tie between two candidates (or even three[7]), each of whom commanded the required majority, in which case the presidential selection was to be made in the House of Representatives from among those tied candidates. But it was assumed that such a scenario would be rare. It might well be that no candidate would achieve the required majority (in which case the selection also went to the House), but it seems to have been assumed that ties between candidates with the required majority would come about only through uncanny accident (Bennett 2006:74–94). And with the vice-presidency going to the candidate with the highest number of votes after the president had been chosen, no vice-presidential backup procedure was necessary unless there was a tie in that count, in which (presumably rare) case the vice-presidential choice was assigned to the senate.

The election of 1800 brought home the voting problem that political party coordination had wrought for this process. We can call the two parties that had emerged at the time "Federalists" and "Republicans." If political parties dominated the process, and party designated electors faithfully cast their two votes for the party's presidential and vice-presidential candidates, the result could well be a presidential tie between two candidates each of whom commanded the requisite majority of appointed electors. In the 1800 election, the Federalists foresaw the problem, and had one of their electors break ranks, so that John Adams, their candidate for President, had one more electoral vote than Charles Cotesworth Pinckney, the Federalist choice for vice president. But the Republicans won, and all their electors cast their two votes faithfully—for the presidential candidate Thomas Jefferson and the vice-presidential candidate Aaron Burr. The result was a tie, though through a very different sort of dynamic than was originally foreseen. When Burr did not gracefully step aside, the presidential selection was relegated to the House backup procedure. In the House procedure each state had one vote (as is still the case today, should the procedure prove necessary), and the Republicans did not command a majority of delegations—again a piece of the puzzle that was produced by the rapid emergence of political parties, with members of the House counting political party loyalty as very important. It took 36 votes to produce the Jefferson presidency that the Republicans had had in mind from the outset (Bennett 2006:22–3).

The Twelfth Amendment was adopted in response to this fiasco. By requiring "distinct ballots" at the electoral college meetings, the Amendment separated the votes for president and vice-president. With the vice-presidential choice separated in this way, the Amendment inserted a majority requirement for that office, and retained the senate as the seat of vice-presidential selection if the electoral college process proved indecisive for that office. But while this was clearly a response to the tie problem that political party coordination had produced, a reluctance to own up to the role political parties were

---

[6] See U.S. Const., art. II, § 1, cl. 3.

[7] If there were five electors, for instance, a minimum of three votes would be necessary for the required majority, but there would be a total of ten votes, comfortably accommodating three candidates with three votes each.

playing in the process—and in American political politics more generally—was still evident. The Amendment makes no mention whatsoever of parties.

So how are originalists to think of the relevance of the Twelfth Amendment for contemporary constitutional questions that keep arising about the role of parties—like how much control the state might exercise over political party processes for choosing their candidates,[8] or the nature and extent of free speech rights to which parties might be entitled under the First Amendment?[9] If the "meaning" of words in the text is required to change the constitutional status of political parties, perhaps the original disdain for them must be heeded, despite the "intention" behind the Twelfth Amendment. To this day, the Constitution contains no explicit language dealing with a role for political parties. But if instead a degree of approval of, or at least acquiescence in, a political role for parties is ascribed to a Twelfth Amendment "intention," how far does that approval or acquiescence reach?

The First Amendment, of course, came before the Twelfth, so how does originalism come to grips with the reach of the silent acceptance of political parties in the Twelfth for rights under the First? Actually the problem is even more tangled, for First Amendment restrictions are assumed to be applicable to the states on account of incorporation into the Fourteenth Amendment.[10] So is an originalist to view First and Fourteenth Amendment free speech protections for parties as congruent or different, and in one or both cases in or out of some shadow silently cast by the Twelfth?

8.3 A NEW ORIGINALISM

In response to problems like these, a new wave of originalists has abandoned the notion of original "intention" as the key to interpreting the Constitution, urging instead that the quest is for original "meaning." It is the constitutional language that is adopted, they argue, not what any actors thought or intended. We have seen, of course, that "meaning" may depend on context, and the only appropriate context for this group of originalists is the original one.

But this serves more to shroud than to solve the problems we have discussed under the rubric of "intention." For even the notion of "original meaning" itself has no clear meaning, except as associated with some person or persons—real or imagined. If the actual persons involved may have attached different and complex "meanings" to the words used, and in many cases may not have foreseen the kinds of problems that in fact emerge, the originalist must either accede to one or another of those "intentions" or find some alternative to them to be assigned to some fathomer of meaning.

---

[8] See, e.g., *Terry v Adams*, 345 U.S. 461 (1953).
[9] See, e.g., *Randall v Sorrell*, 548 U.S. 230 (2006).
[10] See *Near v Minnesota*, 283 U.S. 697, 707 (1931).

Original meaning enthusiasts largely slough over these problems. They tend to depict the inquiry as an "objective" one. Here is the characterization of one set of originalists about how to conceive of the inquiry into "meaning":

> The [original unamended] Constitution means what a reasonable person in 1787 would have understood it to mean after considering all relevant evidence and arguments. Under this approach, original meaning represents hypothetical mental states of a legally constructed person. (Lawson and Seidman 2006:7)

While this imports a "constructive" person into the picture, by itself that character does not dispel any difficulties. For this originalist construct does not tell us anything about the characteristics of the eighteenth-century "reasonable" person, or how to judge the "relevance" for him of "evidence and arguments." If the real persons involved may have attached different "meanings" to the words used, or had complex amalgamations of meanings, those differences and complexities are presumably due to some combination of different upbringings, psychologies, and external influences that shaped their thinking processes as they considered and voted on the language. It may even be a function of stylistic differences, of differential familiarities with specialized vocabularies, or of different degrees of facility in the use of language—including degrees of meticulousness and precision, on the one hand, or casualness, or even carelessness, on the other. An interpreter fully informed about those differences would presumably have to choose among those influences, and characterizing the choices in terms of "relevance" does not tell us how to make the choices.

8.4 ORIGINALIST GUIDANCE FOR CONSTITUTIONAL DECISION MAKING

8.4.1 The possibility of guidance from history

These problems do not mean that originalism comes up completely empty as a vehicle for constraint on judicial choice. Some contemporary problem that becomes the subject of litigation may seem quite congruent with an "original" problem for which there was an original consensus solution. If after delving into the historical record, for instance, an originalist interpreter is confident that the ability of a criminal defendant to present relevant evidence in his defense was required by "due process," an attempt today to cut off that ability might seem to present a problem indistinguishable from what was unearthed in the historical record. Originalist constraint could be found in that probing of history.

Any such conclusion will, however, require judgment. It is sometimes urged, for instance, that elector faithlessness cannot be forbidden by state law, because elector discretion was originally intended. But as we have seen, elector discretion in the first presidential election and elector discretion in the twenty-first century are embedded in political settings that are quite different. For that reason, they do not pose the "same" issue at all. Today's setting—and hence today's "issue"—was likely not even imagined by any original participants. If they were fully informed about today's issue, there is no reason to think that they would believe they had solved it back then. Using the word "discretion" to characterize each of the two issues may shroud the differences, but it does not make them the same.

In the search for stability or certainty, originalists often seem to slight the required judgment, insisting that original applications and today's problems are the "same" simply because they can be described in common terms. But that is just a matter of the language chosen to describe issues. It should hardly be surprising if technological and other societal changes over a 200-year period have so transformed some problem that it poses a different normative question today than did an issue back then to which today's issue bears some surface resemblance. If the issues are described in words that convey the respective contexts in which they originally were and then later are embedded, differences become easy to appreciate.

Even recognizing the differences does not mean that the history provides no help, only that the help provided requires normative evaluation—"judgment" as it is known for the world of judging. The judge must apply his or her own scheme of values in deciding whether there are normative differences between historical problems and present ones, and then what any normative differences that are identified counsel in solution of the problem under adjudication. The result is not the formulaic answers originalists sometimes depict, but the guidance that application of values can provide.

It should be noted that the recent gravitation by originalists to original "meaning" instead of original "intention" has brought with it some embarrassment even for this possibility for guidance. For some original meaning enthusiasts do not think that the "meaning" of general language can extend to mere "applications," no matter how fervently insisted upon originally. The school segregation example illustrates the dilemma. Even if we assume a clear historical record that those involved in formulating and enacting the Equal Protection Clause believed that state required school segregation would not violate the equal protection guarantee (or that it would), those who adopt this stance would resist finding that conclusion as part of the "meaning" of equal protection. They would write off the clearest historical record about attitudes toward segregated schools as "mere" applications of the general constitutional language, not relevant to its "meaning" (See, e.g., Balkin 2007:488). Whether or not they found relevant normative differences between historical applications and present ones, this faction of "original meaning" originalists would find the history of modest relevance at best.

8.4.2 The possibility of guidance from language

A second source of originalist guidance is relatively precise constitutional language. But here too there are complications. We have seen that language meaning is often influenced by the context in which the language is found, and context can cast doubt on

apparent clarity. The context can be social or historical, and we will return to those possibilities, but it can also be linguistic. Article I of the Constitution provides, for instance,
that:

> every...vote to which the concurrence of the Senate and House of Representatives
> may be necessary (except on a question of adjournment) shall be presented to the
> President...[for his approval or veto and if] disapproved...shall be [to take effect]
> repassed by two thirds of the Senate and House of Representatives.

The use of the word "every" seems all inclusive in requiring presentment to the president, and the mention of one and only one exception for adjournment reinforces that
impression. But Article V provides a constitutional amendment procedure which starts
with proposal by "two thirds of both Houses," and includes neither explicit cross reference to Article I nor independent language about presentment to the president for veto
or approval.

Given this larger context, Article V has been broadly understood not to require presentment.[11] Particularly given the multiplicity of persons involved, it could well be that
there was no discoverable intention to provide for presentment of proposed amendments, despite the sweeping language of Article I. Or perhaps the appropriate "context"
for interpreting "every" in this Article I provision is "ordinary" Article I votes. And one
might derive some comfort in reaching this conclusion from the fact that the two-thirds
vote required in Article I to override the president's veto is the same vote that would
already have been secured in the proposal of an amendment. In these ways context will
occasionally provide an opening for stretching the surface meaning of rather precise
language.

A second embarrassment in giving precise language its seemingly clear meaning is
akin to the normative differences problem in deriving guidance from historical applications of general language. The march of history may make a seemingly clear application
quite awkward, or even perverse. Article IV, for instance, allows the admission of new
states to the union, but provides that "no new state shall be formed or erected within the
jurisdiction of any other state...without the consent of the legislatures of the states concerned." When Virginia announced its secession from the union in the wake of Abraham
Lincoln's election as president, however, and a breakaway portion of the state applied for
admission to the union as "West Virginia," the stance of the new president and of the
Congress was that Virginia remained a part of the union. But they also took the position
that the state's consent to admission of West Virginia was not required—or rather that a
"legal fiction" would be employed to find the required "consent" in the approval of a rival
Virginia government set up in a portion of the state basically coterminous with the
would-be West Virginia. As a result of this action, what was once Virginia now has four
Senators rather than the seemingly mandated constitutional "two" (Kesavan and Paulsen
2002:293–301).

---

[11] See *Hollingsworth v Virginia*, 3 U.S. (3 Dall.) 378, 381 (1798).

In the statutory context, the courts have long recognized an exception to the literal reach of language if it would produce an "absurd result," and many originalists have imported this "exception" into constitutional interpretation. Indeed originalists who embrace the "original meaning" variant sometimes take liberties with the literal reach of constitutional language even when avoiding "absurdity" does not seem quite right as a characterization of the justification. In an example we glimpsed earlier, for instance, Justice Scalia, who styles himself an original meaning originalist, concludes that larger social purposes behind the First Amendment's speech and press protections justify extension of that solicitude to vehicles of expression beyond speech and press. The limited language, he tells us, stands as a sort of "synecdoche" for the whole (Scalia 1997b: 43–4).

The most appealing justification for avoiding the literal reach of language in this way is to hypothesize an ongoing "intender" who would not have countenanced "absurd" or even quite awkward results. There is much to be said for a safety valve of this sort, but recognizing it does qualify the constraint that even precise language can bring.

8.4.3 The possibility of guidance from precedent

And finally it should be noted that for originalists who allow deference to precedent into the decision-making mix, additional interpretive constraint is available. Like original expected applications, prior judicial decisions can provide fixed points and justificatory rationales with which new problems can be compared and analyzed. Just as with historical applications, new problems may be judged to exhibit no substantial normative differences from problems presented by precedents. And even when normative differences are discerned and acknowledged, they can be evaluated. But just as with guidance from history, precedent cannot typically be applied without allowing normative evaluation into the decision-making mix.

8.5 CONCLUSION: A REALISTIC VIEW OF CONSTITUTIONAL DECISION MAKING

The constraining possibilities surveyed in Section 8.4 will typically fall far short of dictating answers to cases under adjudication. Particularly when the constitutional language is generally phrased, judges will usually have to employ their own complex of values in the solution of problems. In this sense, originalism can provide no escape from a "living Constitution." Indeed surveying the landscape of orginalism's insights and limitations, the conclusion seems inescapable that constitutional interpretation is much more art than science. The attempt by some originalists to depict the process as objective, as akin to factual inquiry, egregiously oversimplifies a reality in which judgment, nuance, and even occasional inconsistency will characterize the most conscientious decision-making.

In this regard, it is important to appreciate that constitutional interpretation by courts is not the kind of abstract enterprise that originalists seem to have in mind. Courts interpret the Constitution as part of a process of dispute resolution, in which the contours of the dispute will often be defined by an evidentiary record or factual allegations of a highly particularized nature. The process makes the judges acutely aware of some consequences of their decision, and it might be expected that they would frequently be influenced by their senses of those consequences. The question of West Virginia's admission to the union never reached court, for instance, but if it had (and had overcome hurdles to justiciability), it would be quite surprising if the judges charged with determining whether Virginia had consented would, could, or should, have ignored the implications of their decision for the looming clash between northern and southern states over the future of the union.

It is, however, important not to provide a caricature of the "values" that judges employ. They might well include views about substantive issues of public policy—like whether Virginia's secession was acceptable, or whether gay marriage is a good idea or a bad one—but views about public policy hardly exhaust the values that judges bring to the process. On account of training and acculturation, for instance, virtually all judges harbor views about the task of judging—like the deference due to legislative (or administrative) value judgments or fact finding, the proper sway of the "case" or "controversy" requirement and other limitations on justiciability, the role of precedent, and whether judicial opinions should focus narrowly on the facts of a case, or broadly on implications for other problems that can be perceived down the road.

The role of value complexity is nicely illustrated in the judicial stance of Justices Scalia and Thomas in engaging issues of the constitutional status of "direct democracy" at the state level. Scalia and Thomas are the two current Supreme Court Justices who unabashedly identify themselves as originalists (See, e.g., Scalia, 1997b:37–8). At least initially, that might have led them to entertain doubts about direct democracy, for we have glimpsed the rampant original constitutional refusal to embrace popular voting with a broadly distributed franchise in structuring the operations of government. And at the state level, the Constitution is often understood to give voice to that doubt through the "guarantee clause," which enjoins "the United States" to "guarantee to every state...a Republican form of government."[12] Rather than probing and applying those original sentiments, Scalia and Thomas argue instead for deference to direct democratic decision-making on account of its "democratic" credentials.[13]

---

[12] U.S. Const., art. IV, § 4.
[13] See *Romer v Evans*, 517 U.S. 620, 636, 646-47 (Scalia, J., dissenting, with an opinion that Justice Thomas joined) (1996); *U.S. Term Limits, Inc. v Thornton*, 514 U.S. 779, 845, 883 (1995) (Thomas, J., dissenting, with an opinion that Justice Scalia joined).

It is, of course, doubtful that historical inquiry would have solved contemporary questions about direct democracy, embedded as they are in a vastly changed context of governmental decision-making. Indeed, as we have seen, that context has been shaped in part by constitutional amendments. What is significant, however, is that originalist judges were so drawn to contemporary values about "democracy" that they did not even probe the historical question.

In its attempt to claim objectivity for its approach to interpretation, originalism can actually point to an honored precedent. Constitutional review by courts in the United States is usually traced to the 1803 decision of the national Supreme Court in *Marbury v Madison*[14] In *Marbury,* Chief Justice John Marshall argued that the Constitution was "law," indeed the most supreme of written "law," and as such must be dealt with by courts in any clash with less paramount law, like federal statutes (or state law of one form or another). In justifying judicial enforcement of constitutional dictates, however, Marshall deployed three examples where a statute seemed clearly to violate a constitutional prohibition.[15] Fully in charge of the language used to characterize the issues presented by his three examples, Marshall essentially made them constitutional violations by definition. Real constitutional questions that arise in real cases, in contrast, generally cannot meet that standard, for at least a couple of reasons. First, any real world interpretational problems where the result is seemingly obvious will seldom get to court, because, aside from possible delay, the party in jeopardy will usually have nothing to gain. Second, that same party will be able to wade in on the articulation of the issue posed, and will, of course, steer far clear of unconstitutionality by definition. As generations of constitutional law students have learned, the constitutional question actually posed in *Marbury* was not at all like Marshall's three examples. He held that a federal statute was unconstitutional, but viewed in context, there was a good deal of ambiguity about the constitutional prohibition on which Marshall rested that conclusion.

Originalists would do well to heed this lesson of *Marbury*. They generally approve of *Marbury* and its embrace of judicial review. But they resist the judicial choice that judicial review inevitably brings over a wide range of real world constitutional questions. There is plenty of room for debate about the proper stance of judges when they resolve constitutional questions in the course of deciding cases. But that debate would be more wholesome if an unrealizable ideal of "objective" originalism were put to the side. The simple fact is that judicial review brings a large quantum of judicial discretion with it. That discretion can be nudged and cabined in various ways, including by lessons of history. But even then, contemporary values will guide the process, making a rather lively Constitution unavoidable.

[14] *Marbury v Madison*, 5 U.S. (1 Cranch) 137 (1803).
[15] Ibid. at 179.

CHAPTER 9

··

AMBIGUITY AND VAGUENESS
IN LEGAL INTERPRETATION

··

RALF POSCHER

FEW topics in the theory of language are as closely related to legal interpretation as the linguistic indeterminacy associated with ambiguity and vagueness. Significant portions of the institutional legal system, especially courts at the appellate level and supreme courts, are for the most part concerned not with disentangling the facts of cases but with the indeterminacies of the law. Such highly developed institutional structures would not be needed if the law contained only clear-cut rules establishing precise legal duties and rights for each case. It is hard cases that lie at the heart of legal interpretation as a professional enterprise, and it is for this reason that penumbral cases are the "daily diet of the law schools" (Hart 1958:615). For law as a professional discipline, ambiguity and vagueness are at the heart of one of law's central topics.

In a colloquial sense, both vagueness and ambiguity are employed generically to indicate indeterminacy. This is the sense in which vagueness is understood in the "void for vagueness" doctrine, according to which a statute is considered void if it is framed in terms so indeterminate that its meaning can only be guessed at (Amsterdam 1960). For this doctrine it is irrelevant whether the indeterminacy of a statute stems from ambiguity or vagueness or generality in the technical sense. It aims to ensure rule of law values like predictability and the prevention of arbitrariness, which are affected by all kinds of indeterminacy. In a more technical sense, though, ambiguity and vagueness are far more specific phenomena.

9.1 VAGUENESS, AMBIGUITY, AND OTHER FORMS OF INDETERMINACY

At first glance, ambiguity is probably the most accessible concept. Ambiguous expressions have multiple meanings, as in the case of the homonym "bank" which can mean both "river bank" and "commercial bank". Ambiguity is rarely an issue in legal interpretation (Solan 2005:79). Usually concepts denoted with ambiguous expressions are so distinct that the context provides the necessary disambiguation. If the law requires a deposit to be made in a bank, it is too far-fetched to assume this requires throwing the money into a river. In law, one more frequently encounters issues involving syntactical ambiguity or amphiboly. For example, a California statute governing the discharge of teachers allowed the dismissal of permanent employees in case of a "conviction of a felony or of any crime *involving moral turpitude.*" It is syntactically ambiguous as to whether the moral turpitude requirement modifies only the last or both preceding expressions[1] (Solan 2005:88f).

In contrast, an expression is vague if it has borderline cases. Borderline cases are cases "in which one just does not know whether to apply the expression or withhold it, and one's not knowing is not due to ignorance of the facts" (Grice 1989:177). We can know everything we want about pudding, but still be uncertain as to whether to consider it a solid.

Vague expressions do not present borderline issues across the board, but only relative to certain cases in which we are not sure whether we should "apply the expression or withhold it." We have no problem classifying rocks, wood, steel, etc. as solid; only cases like pudding give us cause for doubt.

Ambiguity, then, is about multiple meanings; vagueness is about meaning in borderline cases. More technically, ambiguity has been characterized as being about sentences and words—as pre-propositional—and vagueness as being about propositions and concepts as the meaning of words and sentences (Sorensen 2001:413). "Bank" denotes two different concepts, but neither the concept of "river bank" nor the concept of "commercial bank" nor any other concept is ambiguous: most, however, are vague.

Second, only vagueness is reflexive. Vague concepts have borderline cases and borderline cases themselves present higher-order borderline issues, because it can be doubtful if a case still constitutes a borderline case. Ambiguity is neither a borderline issue nor is it reflexive. There are no borderline cases between a river bank and a commercial bank, and ambiguity itself—at least in a technical sense—is not ambiguous.

Third, speakers can resolve ambiguity through context, but the speaker has no power over borderline cases for which, by definition, competent speakers do not know whether they fall into the extension of an expression (Sorensen 2006:§ 2). Since ambiguity and

---

[1] 50 Cal. App. 3d 920, 123 Cal. Rptr. 830 (2nd Dist. 1975).

vagueness are distinct, expressions can have both characteristics. The word "child" is ambiguous between the concepts of "offspring" and "immature offspring"; in the sense of "immature offspring" it presents borderline cases in the dimension of maturity (Sorensen 2006:§2).

Ambiguity and vagueness are distinct from generality. Generality is the graded feature of generic terms, as opposed, for example, to names, to apply to sets of objects or situations. For both ambiguity and vagueness, the distinction from generality can become blurred. Ambiguity can be vague in its relation to generality. There may be borderline cases in which it is difficult to tell whether a general concept comprises certain nuances of meaning or if one word denotes different concepts. Quine's example is "hard" (1960:130): If we talk about "hard cases" and "hard chairs" it is "hard" to decide whether we have a more general concept of "hard" or if the word "hard" is itself ambiguous and denotes two different concepts. There can be a continuum between generality, polysemy, and homonymy (Moore 1981:182).

General terms can be vague, but generality does not imply vagueness (Sorensen 1989, 2001:406; Waldron 1994:522). In law as in life, generality is functional. In life because it makes it possible to speak about large sets of facts; in law because it makes it possible to regulate large sets of situations using one general rule. Generality is highly correlated with under-informativeness (Sorensen 1989:175), but not necessarily with vagueness (Sorensen 1989; Hyde 2008:2). The concept of "tree" is less general than the concept of "living being", but it presents more borderline issues (Waldron 1994:522) despite being more informative. The sentencing rule that allows for imprisonment between 2 and 20 years is precise, but not very specific, and thus not very informative. The convict knows she has to go to jail, but does not know whether she will see her children grow up. H. L. A. Hart is sometimes taken to have confused generality and vagueness in his statement that "uncertainty at the borderline is the price to be paid for the use of general classifying terms" (1994:128). Hart seems to equate uncertainty at borderlines with generality, but there is no necessary relation (Sorensen 2001:407).

German constitutional law even provides different doctrines for questions of vagueness and generalization. Like the Anglo-Saxon tradition it has a void-for-vagueness-doctrine.[2] In addition, however, German law has an essential-issue-doctrine that addresses generality as a specific concern. According to the essential-issue-doctrine in German constitutional law, parliament has to decide essential questions itself.[3] This bars parliament from seeking refuge in highly generalized rules—like allowing the administration to take "appropriate measures"—in essential issues, especially those implicating fundamental rights.

Vagueness is defined not just in terms of borderline cases, but in terms of borderline cases that are "not due to ignorance of the facts" or other surmountable cognitive

---

[2] BVerfGE 6, 32, 42; 56, 1, 12.
[3] BVerfGE 20, 150, 157; 49, 89, 126.

limitations. This additional requirement is sometimes used to distinguish between absolute and relative borderline cases (Sorensen 2004:21–39) with only the former giving rise to vagueness. In comparison to 3, 5, 11 it might be difficult to tell at first glance whether 11.197 is a prime number. The concept of prime number, however, is not vague. 11.197 is only a "relative borderline case" of a prime number—relative to our ad hoc capacities to handle the mathematical complexities of large numbers. Like mathematics, law produces relative borderline cases of this type because of its complexity. Legal rules can be so multilayered and rich in exceptions and counter-exceptions that it can take even a legal specialist some time to find her way through the jungle. Tax codes are a notorious candidate for this type of regulation. But complexity alone does not create vagueness for legal interpretation.

9.2 KINDS OF VAGUENESS

Vagueness may relate to individuation or classification (Alston 1967:219, "vagueness of application"). Vagueness of individuation concerns the precise delimitation of an object. It affects predicates and singular terms (Quine 1960:128). Physical reality is continuous, but we have discrete concepts for different chunks of this continuous reality (Waldron 1994:516). So there will always be borderline issues in individuating physical objects. This is obvious where the continuity of the world is evident to our ordinary sensory perceptions. Where does a cloud or a mountain or—to pick a singular term— Mount Everest begin? But mereological vagueness of individuation is pervasive (Hyde 2008:128). We have only to enhance the discriminatory resolution to run into the same problems with objects that appear discrete to ordinary perception. Determining which molecules at its edge still belong to my desk is at least as hard as deciding the exact delimitation of Mount Everest. Issues of vagueness of individuation can arise in law, too. The distinction in Roman law between *peius* and *aliud* (Schwenzer 2005:414 f.) is a classical example, which reflects the vagueness of individuation. If Theseus' ship is sold, which is the last plank that can be removed before it turns into an *aliud*, with which the sales obligation cannot be fulfilled (cp. Hyde 2008:112–14 on the Theseus example and a set of variations)?

More widespread in law than issues of individuation are issues of classificatory vagueness. It is not merely that the objects of the world are continuous, but they also come in continuous shades, which challenge the discrete terms of our language. There are two kinds of classificatory vagueness (Sorensen 2001:394). One is quantitative—vagueness of degree. Certain qualities of objects come in degrees, leaving us with the problem of drawing a line on a scale. The continuous spectrum of hues between red and orange produces borderline cases for the application of our color concepts.

The second kind of classificatory vagueness is qualitative or combinatory (Alston 1967:219). For some generic concepts we have not made or cannot make up our minds about which properties objects need to possess in order to belong to a certain category of things. Is a glass brick element of a façade a window?[4] Is a boot a "weapon" when kicked at somebody's head?[5] Is the Missouri river a tributary of the Mississippi or vice versa (Quine 1960:128)? Indeterminacies like these are not questions of degree. They stem from our indecision as to certain necessary properties—whether the concept of "window" requires the possibility of opening and closing; whether weapons also include objects not designed as such; whether tributary is judged by volume or length. In these cases, the indeterminacy stems from the number of possible or even established combinations of necessary and sufficient conditions which produce different results for the case at hand.

Most generic terms have combinatory borderline cases; accordingly they are also very common in law. Moreover, the law frequently employs ordinary terms, but gives them a technical meaning that is usually more precise and sometimes even at odds with their ordinary meaning. In H. L. A. Hart's famous example of the "no-vehicles-in-the-park" rule, a fire engine could be regarded as not being a vehicle in the legal sense although it is an obvious example of a vehicle in the ordinary sense. Combinatorial vagueness also results from the widespread disagreement over the precise meaning of legal terms, which leads to diverging legal interpretations of terms like "due process" or "cruel and unusual punishment." Many legal terms have a structure similar to Walter Brice Gallie's (1956) contested concepts.

In the case of combinatory vagueness each of the possible or even established combinatory suggestions could be regarded as a different concept—for example a broader or narrower concept of "window" or "weapon" or a more length- or volume-orientated concept of "tributary." This makes combinatory vagueness similar to ambiguity. In structural terms, combinatory vagueness could be portrayed as a special case of ambiguity between possible or even established, but competing concepts (Pinkal 1995:103–5). In contrast to classical cases of ambiguity, however, in cases of combinatory vagueness the different concepts in play typically share a common core of extensions. The common core of extensions gives combinatory vagueness the core-penumbra structure also typical of vagueness of degree. A pistol is a weapon in both the broader and the narrower sense, but there is no object covered by both of two concepts denoted with a homonymy: There are no objects that are both river and commercial banks. This also holds true for most polysemious terms such as "bank-building" and "bank-corporation." But already the polysemy of "child" as offspring and immature offspring has a core of common extensions. "Visitors accompanied by their children pay a reduced fee" is ambiguous, not vague. What seems to make "child" polysemious, and not vague, is the well-established meaning of the two concepts. But being well-established is a graded feature. This makes the difference between combinatory vagueness and polysemy vague in degree (Pinkal 1995:76–9, 104 f., 248 f.).

The difference between vagueness and ambiguity depends, however, less on the extent to which different concepts are well-established than on the assumptions in play.

---

[4] BGH, NJW 1960, 2092 f.
[5] BGH, NStZ 1999, 616–617.

Ambiguity assumes a precise meaning—although it may be unclear what it is; vagueness presupposes a lack of precision—even in the presence of precise concepts. In a very general context, "democracy" might leave room for doubt as to whether it covers one-party systems, even though well-established socialist and liberal concepts of democracy each deliver a distinct, but different, result. In such a context "democracy" would be vague.

By contrast, in the constitution of the former German Democratic Republic the meaning of democracy was ambiguous in terms of socialist and liberal concepts, with the context settling the issue. The difference in assumptions entails a difference in interpretation. Ambiguity entails a choice between different pre-established alternatives; vagueness allows for creative concept formation even if pre-established concepts are around. If "democracy" is ambiguous between the socialist and liberal concepts, the choice is limited to these two alternatives. If "democracy" is vague, it allows for an—for example deliberative—interpretation alongside previously established accounts. In the past, this has given rise to the suspicion that judges prefer vagueness over ambiguity, because vagueness gives them more discretion in legal interpretation (Azar 2007).

A similar fundamental distinction to that between vagueness of individuation and generic vagueness can be made between semantic and pragmatic vagueness. Generally the pragmatic context helps to disambiguate and precisify utterances. But context can work both ways. Utterances can be vague not only because of the concepts they employ, but also because of the pragmatic context of the utterance. Kettcars are not borderline cases of toy cars, but clear positive cases. If a child is told to bring all her toy cars into the house, it can nevertheless be unclear whether she should also bring her kettcar into the house, given its size. The kettcar becomes a borderline case of "toy car" due to the pragmatic context of the command.

For pragmatic theories of language, the distinction between semantic and pragmatic vagueness might seem less obvious. If all semantics can be reduced to pragmatics, then vagueness is pragmatic to the core. But even in pragmatic theories of language, the difference could be reconstructed on different levels of linguistic practice. In everyday contexts, in which a less elaborate, paradigmatic notion of a concept is pragmatically sufficient, linguistic practices assign a less elaborate semantic content to certain terms. In more specific contexts we draw on the same terms to fulfill more specific pragmatic tasks. The less elaborate everyday notion of a concept may, however, not be up to the specific task or even conflict with it and thus create a specific pragmatic vagueness (Rayo, 2007).

Pragmatic vagueness is central to legal interpretation. Law is not about semantics, but about the pragmatic shaping of social relations in the broadest sense. Law's relation to language is instrumental. The law uses linguistic expressions to establish regulations in order to achieve certain social goals. The instrumental role of language in law explains why the pragmatic purpose of a regulation is such a powerful argument in law. This does not imply that semantics have no import. For whoever has to interpret the law, the semantics of the expressions are the primary means of deciphering the social purpose of a regulation, but the pragmatic social purpose can override semantic conventions— even if certain forms of textualism debate the legitimacy of this ubiquitous feature of legal practice. Hart's no-vehicle-in-the-park rule is not semantically vague as far as fire engines are concerned. Fire engines are not borderline cases of vehicles. In the case of a fire in the park, however, the pragmatic purpose of the statute will overrule its semantics. In the well-worn example of *Riggs v Palmer*,[6] the murderer of the testator met all the requirements for inheriting according to the semantics of the statute. It became a borderline case for pragmatic reasons. It was anything but clear if the regulation governing testaments really intended to let someone profit from his own wrong-doing.

Vagueness is so pervasive in law, because, as a linguistic practice with complex, sometimes conflicting and contested, pragmatic social purposes, it lends itself to all types of semantic and pragmatic vagueness and every imaginable combination thereof. Often the pragmatics of a rule override its semantics. This holds true at least as long as there are no special rules for legal interpretation to limit this effect. In penal law the principle "nulla poena, sine lege" (Hall 1937:165–93) and the rule of lenity (Price 2004: 885–942) leaves wiggle room for pragmatic considerations in borderline cases, but bars the pragmatic overriding of semantically clear positive or negative candidates.

Different kinds of vagueness give rise to different problems. All kinds of vagueness confront us with the issue of how to classify borderline cases. Theoretically, borderline cases challenge basic logical principles like bivalence and the law of the excluded middle. Is a statement about a borderline case true, false, neither, or something else? Tampering with such basic logical principles keeps a whole industry of logical literature busy. For the law, the difficulties caused by borderline cases are equally disturbing since judges confronted with a borderline case must deliver a positive or negative decision: "neither" is not an option in legal interpretation.

Besides this general problem, vagueness of degree holds a more intricate irritation in store: the Sorites paradoxes. These rely on the tolerance principle according to which a minute difference in quantity does not change the quality of an entity. The classical heap paradox is as follows:

> Premise 1: 10,000 grains of sand is a heap.
> Premise 2: A collection of grains of sand minus one grain is still a heap.
> conclusion: 9,999 grains of sand is a heap.

After 9,999 iterations of the syllogism we are left with the false conclusion that 1 grain of sand is a heap (for a Sorites case study in law see von Savigny 1991). We arrive at an obviously wrong conclusion, even though each of the individual syllogisms seems valid and each of the premises true. It goes without saying that not only logicians find this hard to swallow. In law it seems to support a radical skepticism towards legal determinacy. If the indeterminacy of borderline cases is already seen as a threat to the rule of law, Sorites are the abyss. Sorites seem to support the claim that vague legal concepts—pervasive in law—have no boundaries at all. Anything goes. The application of legal rules seems radically indeterminate, the rule of law illusory and solely a question of political *fiat* (cp. Endicott 2000:15 f.).

---

[6] 115 N.Y. 506, 22 N.E. 188 (1889).

9.3 ORIGINS AND ACCOUNTS OF VAGUENESS

There are at least four different vantage points from which to address the problems caused by vagueness: logic, ontology, epistemology, and semantics.

9.3.1 Logic

One obvious way of accommodating the logical problems caused by vagueness is to modify our logic. Maybe it is our standard logic that lies at the heart of the problem; maybe standard logic is not equal to the task and needs enhancement to reflect vagueness (Sorensen 2007). There are two basic logical strategies for enhancing standard logic with respect to vagueness.

One is to extend the number of truth values. The most obvious way of accommodating borderline cases is to introduce a third logical value such as "indeterminate." Fuzzy logic is the finer-grained blend of the same strategy. Fuzzy logic reflects vagueness of degree not only with one additional, but with a continuum of truth values. Depending on its closeness to clear positive and negative cases, a borderline case can be assigned a truth value between 1 and 0. "Glass bricks are windows" could have the truth value 0.723. Multivalued logic seems not to be intimidated by borderline cases—it can simply assign an intermediate truth value—and fuzzy logic could solve the Sorites paradox by refuting the tolerance principle: small changes are not irrelevant, but correspond to small changes in truth value.

Leaving aside all the logical intricacies that stand in the way of a consistent multivalued logic, it should be pointed out that introducing further truth values might not make things easier. If there are borderline cases between positive and negative candidates there will also be borderline cases between positive and indeterminate as well as between indeterminate and negative cases, let alone the masses of borderline cases that are produced in fuzzy logic depending on how fine-grained it is. Multivalued logic merely seems to multiply the boundaries on which borderline cases and thus higher-order vagueness can emerge. For law, then, a multivalued system does not seem very attractive. Though it would be theoretically feasible in legal cases with gradable outcomes, the law does not provide for graded verdicts. Borderline cases of murder cannot be judged 0.6-murder even if the law of the land does not demand the death penalty, but a gradable prison sentence instead.

The second strategy is to admit truth-value gaps. Borderline cases do not have an alternative truth value, but no truth value at all. Aristotle saw a truth-value gap for future contingents. The question as to whether there will be a sea battle tomorrow may have no answer today (On Interpretation, § 9). The idea of truth-value gaps has been adopted for the discussion of vagueness by theories of supervaluation. If the semantics of a vague concept do not provide for an answer in the penumbra of a vague expression, there is nothing to prevent us drawing the line at any given point and thus precisifying the semantic content. Such precisifications are arbitrary, but not excluded by the semantic content of the vague expression. Each arbitrary precisification eliminates all borderline cases. Under each precisification there is a truth value for each former borderline case—but a different one for each different precisification. Even though truth values are unstable in the penumbra, a super-truth value emerges by quantifying over all possible precisifications. Super-true are propositions that are true under each possible precisification of a concept.

Supervaluationism gives up the semantic principle of bivalence, because borderline cases are neither super-true nor super-false, but it does preserve many classical logical principles such as the law of the excluded middle: "This agglomeration of grains is a heap or is not a heap" is super-true even if the agglomeration in question is a borderline case of a heap, because it is true under all precisifications. The logic of supervaluationism remains classic, its semantics are non-classic.

Supervaluationism explains the indeterminacy of borderline cases by embracing it and turning it into a logical feature. The Sorites paradox is solved by rejecting the second premise. The tolerance principle according to which a heap of sand minus one grain is always still a heap is super-false, because under each precisification it will be false at some point. Each precisification draws a sharp line at a given number of grains even though there is no number of grains for which a precisification is super-true. We can stipulate that 75 grains of sand are a heap and 74 miss the crucial grain. But this stipulation would not be super-true, because a stipulation according to which 90 grains are crucial would be equally admissible. Calling 1 Mio. grains a heap of sand would instead be super-true, since 1 Mio. grains is a heap under every possible precisification. Super-truth also seems to capture our intuition that bivalence does not hold true in borderline cases, but that arbitrary precisifications are possible—though not yet agreed on or even contested.

Supervaluationism resembles the standard view of hard cases in law. Hard cases are law's borderline phenomena. According to the standard view—as for example H. L. A. Hart proposed with his metaphor of core and penumbra—there is no right answer to hard cases. They have no predetermined legal truth value. Judges who are obliged to decide hard cases have to make a decision on their own. They have to deliver a precisification for the given hard case and only under this precisification is there a legal answer. To adopt the categories of supervaluationism, the legal answer to a hard case is, however, not super-true. It only delivers one of many possible precisifications for a borderline case (for an application of supervaluationism to the law see Soames 2009; Jónsson 2009).

Besides a whole series of problems with its claim to leave the axioms and laws of standard logic intact—just modifying its semantics—(Varzi 2007:633–75), for supervaluationism as well as for multivalued logic there remains the nagging problem of higher-order vagueness. Is there a super-super-truth to delimit borderline cases of borderline cases? But maybe it misinterprets the logical theories of vagueness anyway, if they are understood as explaining or solving issues of vagueness. Perhaps these are better understood in a more self-referential sense as different technical models for coping with vagueness in logic, however vagueness can be explained in metaphysics, epistemology, or semantics.

9.3.2 Ontic accounts

The most basic approach to explaining vagueness is to regard it as a problem of ontology. Things like clouds, rainbows, waves seem perfect examples of vague objects. For the ontic approach there is no mystery about borderline cases: this is just how the world is. The objects of the world are vague independently of our conceptual schemes. If the objects of the world are ontically vague, we should not be surprised that our language is. It simply reflects a vague reality. If the objects of the world are vague, we need to adjust our binary logic, since indeterminacy is real. So it comes as no surprise that theories of ontic vagueness regularly modify standard logic (Williams 2008). This also allows them to tackle the Sorites paradox in a similar manner to the logical approaches.

One of the major technical problems which ontic vagueness has to confront is "vague identity", to which ontic vagueness seems to commit. For objects like clouds and rainbows the idea of a vague identity might not be counter-intuitive. But should we also commit to Mount Everest having a vague identity because of our problems delimiting it from the neighbouring valleys and mountains? How would vague identity relate to existence claims? If existence requires identity—"No entity without identity" (Quine 1957:20)—ontic vagueness seems like a self-contradicting concept. There is an extended technical debate as to whether we can make sense of vague identities and if any logic could digest them (Hyde 2008:141–7).

Legal interpretation could not easily handle ontic vagueness either. If it is simply the case that the world is vague, what can the law do about it? Contrary to logic, introducing additional legal values alongside lawful and unlawful is not really an option. Legal interpretation is all about deciding cases. There is no room for indeterminate outcomes. The prospect of the world being vague in itself brings the law into conflict with reality. In borderline cases the law would have to precisify objects that are, as objects, ontically vague by definition. Given the pervasiveness of borderline cases, the law would have to misrepresent reality on a regular basis. It comes as no surprise that—so far—ontic accounts of vagueness have not been well-received in law.

9.3.3 Epistemic accounts

This is not so for epistemological accounts of vagueness, which adopt a position contrary to that of ontic accounts. According to epistemic accounts of vagueness, objects and properties only appear vague, because we are—for some even in principle (Sorensen 2004:13 f.)—not able to acquire knowledge of their precise boundaries. It is our limited discriminatory capacities that account for vagueness. We are either unable to discern the discrete features of the world or unable to handle the complexities of our language practices upon which the sharp boundaries of our concepts supervene (Williamson 1994:209). Our epistemic shortcomings also explain the Sorites paradox. They explain why we cling to such inconsistent beliefs as the tolerance principle and the idea that there must be a boundary somewhere along the line. We are right about the boundary; however, we are unable to see it because of our limited epistemic capacities. Even supporters of the epistemic account admit that it is hard to swallow that there is one grain of sand that makes an agglomeration of grains into a heap. But they believe that our irritation corroborates the epistemic account, since this irritation stems from our inability to see the borderlines, whose existence we are forced to admit if we do not want to fall for the Sorites paradox. Moreover, the epistemic solution does not require tampering with standard logic. It can stick to bivalence and all the rest.

The latter feature in particular makes an epistemic account of interest to legal interpretation, which has a certain affinity for bivalence—due to its need to decide every borderline case that is brought before a court. The theories of legal interpretation corresponding to an epistemic account of vagueness are the one-right-answer-theories advanced by Ronald Dworkin (1985a) or by moral realists like Michael Moore (2002), who argues for moral and legal kinds along the lines of the Kripke–Putnam natural kinds argument.

One-right-answer-theorists do not claim that legal rules alone can do all the work. They reach out for legal principles, which open the law to morality and thus provide for sufficient resources. They believe that there are right answers to hard cases even if the complexity of the legal and moral materials might not allow for certainty or consensus. Dworkin's epistemic account is expressed in the metaphor of judge Hercules, who is invested with a super-human intellect (1986:238–58). For Hercules, who masters all the legal and moral materials, there are single right answers to hard cases. Among mere mortals, though, hard cases are contested due to epistemic limitations similar to those which prevent us from finding the last grain in a Sorites series.

One explanatory merit of one-right-answer-theories is that they can explain genuine legal disagreement. Indeed, the law is all about resolving conflicts, a fact which leads us to expect disagreement between the parties involved. Legal decisions in hard cases are, however, also contested between courts and legal scholars with no direct stakes in the matter. They disagree sincerely on the outcome of hard cases. What are they disagreeing about if there is no right answer as a fact of the matter?

9.3.4 Semantic accounts

Closely associated with supervaluationism are semantic accounts of vagueness. Everyone agrees that vagueness is a semantic phenomenon. What makes semantic accounts specific is the belief that the primary origin of vagueness lies in our linguistic practices, too. This does not imply, however, that semantic theories have to regard vagueness merely as a feature of our language. For a semantic account vagueness emerges from a structural discrepancy between language and extra-linguistic reality. On the one hand, the world does not come in prefabricated discrete entities. In spite of Plato, we cannot cut nature at its joints (*Phaedrus* 265d–266a). We confront a world that—most of the time at least—comes in a continuum of shapes and shades. Our linguistic expressions, on the other hand, are discrete. They are faced with the problem of how to accommodate the continuous character of much of reality (Pinkal 1991:251; Waldron 1994:516). Since our linguistic practice cannot simply replicate borderlines prefixed by reality, it would ideally need to develop precise conventions for each linguistic expression. Instead of embarking upon such a tedious task, we work instead with rough and ready linguistic practices that cover paradigm or prototype cases (Endicott 2000:137–58) or some partial definitions that allow us to distinguish clear positive and negative candidates. Our linguistic conventions are thus incomplete, leaving room for borderline cases (for a logical incompleteness account of vagueness see Frege 1964:§ 56; van Fraassen 1970:60 f.; van Heijenoort 1986; Soames 2010: partial definition).

Besides its being tedious, there are various reasons why we do not bother to develop precise conventions. First, drawing sharp borderlines in the continua presented by the world becomes arbitrary at some degree of discriminatory resolution. I have good perceptual reasons to delimit my desk on a macro-level, but the micro-level of molecules or atoms is a different story.

Second, our conventions can be incomplete because of our limited, unstable, and intersubjectively volatile capacities of discrimination. The capacity to discriminate different colors is fairly well-developed and fairly evenly distributed, but when it comes to closely related shades or hues things become less evident and intra- and intersubjectively unstable. Some differences in wavelength we are only able to detect in direct comparison; others we are not able to detect with our natural perception at all. Under these circumstances, establishing a crisp linguistic convention covering every shade and hue is highly unlikely.

A third reason for the lack of precision in our concepts is that there is generally no practical reason for sharpening them to the point. We get along with a rough and ready concept of "heap" fairly well. For purposes that demand greater precision we have developed different techniques. We do not trade sand in heaps, but in cubic- or weight-measurements with all the requisite precision. There is no practical need to determine "heap" down to the grain. If there were, if for example heap were the standard measure for diamonds, we would probably come up with some numbers. The same lack of pragmatic necessity lets us get along with family resemblance concepts (Wittgenstein 1999:§ 66), which are not necessarily vague (Sorensen 2001:407), but which allow for borderline cases if the disjunctive list of properties is only loosely defined.

A fourth reason for the lack of precision in semantic conventions is the lack of consensus. We might be able to agree on some standard features of democracy, like some form of bottom-up political decision making, temporal restraints on the tenure of public offices, etc., but beyond such basic features "democracy" is a contested concept in Gallie's sense. Assigning different terms to the different conceptions is not an option, since contested concepts are symbolically charged. Each contestant claims terms like democracy for his own cause.

A fifth reason has been identified with Waisman's (1945a) notion of open texture. Even if we were to try to sharpen a concept to the point, we could always be confronted with new or surprising phenomena that give rise to borderline cases.

These five reasons are not intended to be an exhaustive list, but taking into account their various combinations, it is not surprising that our linguistic conventions are incomplete most of the time and deliver concepts with fuzzy boundaries and borderline cases. If this picture is roughly correct, demanding an answer in borderline cases does not so much raise questions of truth (Soames 2010:53–9), but of sense. It is like applying a predicate outside its domain of application (van Heijenoort 1986:35–7). Sainsbury's (2001:38) stipulated concept of "minor" illustrates the idea: If we stipulate that "minor" applies to people under 17 and not to people over 18, does it make sense to ask if a 17-year-old girl is a minor in the stipulated sense? 17-year-olds just do not fall within the domain of application of minor in the stipulated sense. It is like asking whether the number 7 is blue (van Heijenoort 1986:36, with a logical reconstruction of the fallacy). "Minor" and "non-minor" in the stipulated sense are only contrary, not contradictory. If we presuppose that they are contradictory, we should not be surprised if we run into logical quandaries (cp. van Fraassen 1970:60 f.). Logic cannot heal nonsensical semantics.

The stipulated case of incompleteness differs from ordinary cases of vagueness, since its borderline cases have sharp borders. "Minor" as stipulated has precise borders bracketing 17-year-olds. But whether the borders of borderline cases are precise or fuzzy does not change the structure of borderline cases (cp. Keefe 2000:191 f.). We can construct a borderline case for window, for example glass bricks, along the lines of an incompleteness account, just as we can analyze the case of a 17-year-old with regard to the stipulated concept of minor. What changes is not the structure of vagueness, but that the additional problem of higher-order vagueness is introduced if the borderline cases of a concept have fuzzy rather than precise boundaries. This additional problem, however, should not invalidate the incompleteness account (Soames 2003 and 2010 for partial definitions). What is called for in borderline cases is not the application of an already existing semantic convention, but its further development, since it hitherto fails to cover the borderline case at hand. It only does so after precisification.

An account along these lines would sit well with widely held views on legal interpretation. Contrary to Dworkin, it is almost universally accepted in legal theory that, at least in hard cases, judges do not merely apply the law, but develop it as they go along. In hard cases—law's borderline cases—judges make law. There are many reasons why legal rules—like semantic conventions—are incomplete. First, the law has to rely on language, which is in itself semantically incomplete. In law, the lack of precision is more likely to become manifest, because of the law's need to decide every conflict with its binary code.

Second, there are independent reasons why establishing legal rules with the help of semantically incomplete conventions can exacerbate incompleteness. Almost all the reasons for the incompleteness of semantic conventions reappear at the level of pragmatic legal regulations. There is the open texture problem of pragmatic rules projected into an unknown future with unknown circumstances and cases. The pragmatic purposes of a statute might be unclear because the legislator did not take borderline cases into consideration or because there was confusion in the complex legislative process or because they were contested and politics only allowed for a compromise, passing the problem on to the courts. In the courts the concepts are necessarily contested, and not only when they have symbolic qualities. Even the definition of commonplace terms—such as window or vehicle—may decide the case at hand. The problem of arbitrariness also reappears on the pragmatic level. Some legal decisions are simply judgment calls (Sorensen 2001:413).

Third, there are cases in which vagueness stems from a conflict between general semantic conventions and the specific pragmatic aims of a legal regulation as illustrated by the "vehicle-in-the-park" example or the case of *Riggs v Palmer*.

Looking at vagueness from the perspective of incomplete linguistic conventions might also help to explain the Sorites paradox by drawing on Wittgenstein's rule-following discussion. The Sorites paradox presupposes that we need a *reason* to reject one of the incremental steps in order to be justified in applying or withholding it in clear positive or negative cases. This presupposition might, however, be misleading. If the application of common language concepts is a matter of linguistic convention then it could be a case of rule-following in the sense famously discussed by Wittgenstein. In this discussion, one of his main points was that rule following is not necessarily a practice which involves giving reasons. " 'How am I able to follow a rule?'—if this is not a question about causes, then it is about the justification for my following the rule in the way I do. If I have exhausted the justifications I have reached bedrock, and my spade is turned. Then I am inclined to say: 'This is simply what I do' " (1999:§ 217). Contrary to the presupposition underlying the Sorites paradox, if challenged by incremental borderline cases there might be no reason for rejecting one of the incremental steps; this is simply what we do when we come to clear positive or negative candidates.

9.4 VAGUENESS AND THE RULE OF LAW: THREAT, VALUE, OR PRICE TO PAY

The rule of law is famously contrasted with the rule of men. The contrast presupposes that under the rule of law conflicts are decided according to legal standards that are only applied, but not made, by the men who are entitled to adjudicate. To such an ambitious concept of the rule of law, vagueness must appear as a threat. In cases of vagueness there seems to be no pre-established legal answer for the case at hand.

Basically, there are three ways in which legal theory tries to accommodate this embarrassment to the rule of law. Some, like the authors of the Critical Legal Studies movement, try to radicalize the embarrassment to expose the rule of law as a liberal ideology. Authors like Dworkin go to the other extreme and cling on to the one-right-answer thesis. The mainstream, however, accepts the embarrassment, tries to marginalize its import and delegates hard cases to other disciplines like politics, economics, or moral philosophy. As for the import of vagueness, theorists point to the vast number of legal transactions and relations that represent clear positive cases of legal regulations. The claim is that, in the overwhelming majority of cases that form the basis of our legal practice, vagueness is not an issue. Compared to the masses of easy cases, hard cases are only an almost infinitesimally small fraction. For cases in which some kind of vagueness is involved, however, they concede that the law is insufficient and that the answer must be found according to some other standard—be it the personal political convictions of the judge, economics, or morality. On the basis of this mainstream account, disciplines like law and economics have emerged in an attempt to develop alternative extra-legal standards for cases in which the legal standards are vague.

While we can concede to the mainstream view that hard cases are numerically marginal in comparison to the entirety of the practices governed by law, the comparison is misleading since most cases that lawyers and judges—at least starting at the appellate level—deal with and care about are ones involving some kind of vagueness. The common view draws a strange picture of our explicit legal practices if we consider most of them as a non-legal issue, as the expression of personal convictions or engaging in politics or economics. Innocent self-deception or malicious deceit on a massive scale on the part of the legal establishment could explain such an account (Leiter 2007).

However, an explanation that does justice to the self-understanding of legal practice would have comparative explanatory merits. Such an alternative interpretation might rest on the idea that, although legal interpretation has to create law in cases of vagueness, the conditions under which law is created in adjudication distance it from politics, economics, and morality in a way that gives it a specifically legal, that is doctrinal, character. Doctrinally developed law—as it developed historically for the first time through the work of the pre-classical Roman jurists—creates a specifically legal sphere of meaning with its own content and structures. Since the creation of law through legal interpretation in hard cases must occur within this specifically legal sphere of meaning, it belongs to a different tradition, with different restraints and path dependencies from politics, economics, or morality. This results in a specifically doctrinal development of the law in the adjudication of hard cases. The doctrinal development of the law preserves the rule of law in the sense that even in hard cases a specifically legal decision is made (Poscher 2009:102–9).

If vagueness does not have to be seen as a threat to the rule of law, might it even have value for the law? Determining the value of vagueness is anything but straightforward. Vagueness is related to other qualities of language like generality and ambiguity, which can feature in the same linguistic expressions. "Child" is ambiguous, vague in the sense of immature offspring and general with regard to boys and girls. This makes the attribution of performances to one of the linguistic features of an expression a complex task. It is indispensable for the law to create regulations that cover large sets of cases. Generality is the feature of language that enables the law to do so. Even though a higher degree of generality is sometimes—but not necessarily—correlated with a higher degree of vagueness, it is not vagueness, but generality that does the work. In a more charitable reading H. L. A. Hart might have been right after all: Vagueness "is *the price to be paid* for the use of general classifying terms"; it is, however, not a value the law is concerned about.

Another value to which vagueness is thought to contribute is the avoidance of the arbitrariness that comes with precision (Endicott 2005:37). With increasing awareness of age discrimination, precise numerical age limits, for example for professional activities, have come under legal scrutiny. Age limits have been replaced with more flexible standards such as "sufficient capacities", that can do greater justice to individual cases, but that are also more vague. Again, however, it is anything but clear that vagueness is the feature that does the work. We choose a more flexible standard because the precise standard classifies things in a way that goes against our intentions. We know that an age limit of 65 for physicians discriminates against doctors who are still competent and whom we clearly do not want to prevent from practicing their profession. The doctors who motivate the choice of a more flexible standard are not borderline cases of professionals with "sufficient capacities", but doctors whom we assume to be clear positive cases of still capable physicians. The motivation might also include relative borderline cases, because the professional capacities in question would have to be examined closely. Absolute borderline cases, which alone constitute vagueness, are, however, not the reason why we choose to adopt more flexible standards. On the contrary, borderline cases are often the reason why we accept the arbitrariness of precision and opt for precise age limits, as in the case of the age limits for drinking, driving, or voting (Sorensen 2001:397). The same would hold for a precise score in a capacity test for the physicians. We do not question the age limit because of its precision, but because it is a bad proxy for the quality that is central to the purpose of the rule. Vagueness can go hand in hand with a more adequate standard, but, again, vagueness is the price we have to pay, not a value we pursue.

Carl Schmitt highlighted another candidate for the value of vagueness with his notion of "dilatory formal compromise" (2008:85). If a legislator is confronted with incommensurable opinions that she has to incorporate into a regulation, she can choose an expression that can be read either way. If the precise amount of a social service is contested, she could legislate that it must be "sufficient" or "reasonable", with each party to the compromise reading its own position into the text. Formal compromises are dilatory, because there comes a time when a decision on the "sufficient" or "reasonable" amount has to be made. In law this usually means that the decision is delegated to judges. In terms of vagueness as incompleteness, in these cases "sufficient" or "reasonable" is a vague standard because of the absence of consensus on the borderline.

Schmitt's dramatic notion of dilatory formal compromise is an example for a more general advantage of vague concepts. Setting precise borderlines always comes with decision costs. In the cases Schmitt had in mind they are insurmountable—at least in the given timeframe for political compromise. But in lesser degrees they also come with everyday concepts in everyday contexts. First, fixing exact borderlines would at least take some time for more social coordination through conventions or more complex kinds of practices—time that can be saved for more useful activities. Who knows if we ever need to determine how many grains make a heap. In the contexts we use the concept we get along well enough with some paradigms or some basic conventions which cover standard cases. In the same vein a legislator might take refuge to a vague concept because he only cares for the paradigm cases and leaves it to the courts to take care of drawing the exact borderlines, to save time for more important legislative acts. Second, even if there comes a time, we might do well to wait for the moment, because we will be able to fix the borderline with much better knowledge of the concrete context and purpose than we could ever anticipate (Soames 2011b:16). Vague concepts allow us to postpone decisions. This not only holds for legislators but also for the courts. It is considered a virtue of a judge not to decide more than needed in a given case. Obiter dicta are a privilege—usually of the highest courts—and to be consumed with utmost moderation.

Again the reduction of decision costs is in part due to the generality of the vague concepts. In the case of the social service a precise range for the amount could already reduce the decision costs. If the parties think that an amount below $5 would be too little and an amount of $50 too much, they could agree on a precise range from $5 to $50. But there are reasons to doubt, that generality does all the work. First, due to higher-order vagueness determining a precise range comes with decision costs, too. Even fixing the range of the number of grains that form a heap will not be easy. Second—and this brings us back to Schmitt—a vague concept can be used to pretend that a decision has been made and not just postponed, it can hide disagreement. It allows the parties to claim that they have come to an agreement by settling on a "reasonable" amount.

The dubious value of hiding disagreement or pretending decision brings us to a last candidate for a value of vagueness of an equally dubious nature: the chilling effect of vagueness in law. Under rule of law standards the chilling effect of vagueness is usually considered a vice, not a virtue. If surveillance regulation is so vague that people cannot predict whether their behavior will be recorded and in which contexts the recordings will be used this might suppress the exercise of constitutionally protected liberties and freedoms. They might refrain from joining assemblies or associations that serve the democratic processes of a community. But in certain contexts some legal scholars also see a virtue in the chilling effect of some vague laws. Vague laws engage the practical reasoning of the people to whom it applies. Vague laws give these persons a reason to think for themselves how a vague standard should be precisified in a given situation. It takes seriously their ability for practical reasoning. A traffic provision that prohibits a speed "greater than is reasonable or proper, having regard for width, traffic use and the general and usual rules of such road or highway"[7] leaves it to the driver to think for himself about the proper speed limit and can guide him to become a more reflective and careful driver than any precise speed limit ever would (Soames 2011a:40f; Waldron 2011:71f). A similar point has been made by behavioral legal scholars who discovered a deterrence effect of uncertainty, which they recommend taking advantage of in criminal or tort law deterrence schemes (Baker et al. 2004).

Leaving the dubious and also more exceptional virtues aside, it seems mostly the reduction of decision costs that constitutes the value of vagueness. This value might also explain, why we find much more vague rather than precise general concepts in language and law. Both may often pay the price of vagueness for the use of more general concepts, but generality does not do all the work, vagueness has some added value of its own.

---

[7]   § 12603 Ohio General Code, for the provision see *State v Schaeffer* 96 Ohio St. 215, 218; 117 N.E. 220 (1917).

CHAPTER 10

LEGAL INTERPRETATION AND THE PHILOSOPHY OF LANGUAGE

BRIAN H. BIX

10.1 INTRODUCTION

LAW is guidance through language, whether the language of statutes, judicial decisions, constitutional provisions, contracts, or wills. It is therefore not surprising that lawyers, judges, and legal commentators have sought whatever assistance they could find from other fields that deal with the meaning and interpretation of words: including literary theory, linguistics, and semiotics. Assistance has also been sought from philosophy of language, and the various philosophical writers on the deeper understanding of truth, meaning, and reference. However, at the end of the day, it is not clear that any of these searches have taught the legal profession useful new knowledge or methods of knowing.

In this chapter, I will offer an overview of some of the attempts to use philosophy of language to alter or resolve questions of legal interpretation.[1] Legal theorists have learned an old truth of philosophy: that philosophical theories rarely give us new answers to our more pressing problems, and often do not even tell us anything we did not (in some sense) already know, but such theories may serve us in other ways, for example by clarifying the problems that lie before us, and by helping us to articulate our ideas in a better and more coherent way.

---

[1] In this chapter, I will be focusing on English-language legal theory in general and American legal theory in particular, though some references will made to other theorists.

10.2 DETERMINACY AND INDETERMINACY

The problems of legal determinacy and indeterminacy raise the issue of whether there are always, usually, sometimes, or never (unique) right answers to legal questions.[2] This is an area where a wide array of philosophical theories and ideas have been brought into legal scholarship, with, at best, mixed results.

The conventional view of most lawyers, and many legal scholars as well, is that there are unique correct answers to the vast majority of cases that come before courts, but that in the hardest cases the law is unclear or unsettled or there is no law, and the judge must make new law. There are legal scholars who have taken positions on both sides of that conventional view: some arguing that law is usually, nearly always, or always indeterminate; while others claim that law is (nearly) always determinate. I will consider those two alternatives in turn, looking at the way scholars in each case have tried to bring in philosophers of language to support their position.

10.2.1 Indeterminacy theorists

Arguments that law is significantly or "radically" indeterminate are associated with the American legal realists of the early decades of the twentieth century,[3] and with the critical legal studies (CLS) movement a few decades later. The CLS version was arguably more systematic and sophisticated than the legal realist version. At least in the more sophisticated versions of the claim, the argument was *not* that courts were chaotic or unpredictable in their decisions, but that whatever order and predictability there were to legal decisions was grounded not on the legal materials, but on the biases (political and otherwise) of judges. The legal sources offered in court opinions as justifications, the argument went, could have been used with equal warrant to justify a contrary outcome (e.g. Kelman 1987: 242–68; Kennedy 1997).

Often theorists in this area, particularly from the CLS tradition, looked to philosophers of language for what support they thought they could find there. Many writers looked to the quasi-philosophical, quasi-literary ideas of deconstruction and postmodernism. Other theorists looked in a more philosophical direction, towards a well-known but controversial reading of Ludwig Wittgenstein's rule-following considerations. (Wittgenstein 1968:§§ 138–242) The reading was a famous skeptical interpretation grounded in or at least loosely based on Wittgenstein's rule-following considerations, and offered by Saul Kripke (1982:2 n.2).

Under Kripke's controversial reading of Wittgenstein's rule-following considerations, meaning is uncertain, made stable only by community agreement. Judgments of

[2] Portions of this section are derived from Bix (1993 and 2010).
[3] There were parallel views among the French and German "Free Law" theorists (from whom the American realists might also have borrowed some ideas). (Herget and Wallace 1987).

"correct" or "incorrect" even in the use of simple color labels (e.g. "red"), or in the continuation of a simple mathematical series ("plus 2": 2, 4, 6, ...), under this view, are based on (and can only be based on) community consensus: the fact that others would use the term or continue the series in the same way. (Kripke 1982: 90–8, 110–12). Legal commentators used this work as grounding for an argument that meaning was always uncertain, and where it appeared certain it was due only to the agreement of elite groups (or the masses after they had been duped by propaganda) (Yablon 1987).

One problem sometimes raised with grounding a legal indeterminacy argument on Kripke's reading of Wittgenstein is that Kripke is wrong, it is claimed, about what Wittgenstein was arguing. However, the objection of fidelity can be brushed aside as irrelevant to present purposes. An argument is valid or invalid, useful or useless, and that status remains regardless of whether it is an exegetically true rendering of some famous philosopher's views. The concern is with the proper understanding of meaning and truth, and their implications for law; intellectual history can be left for others.

However, even putting aside whether Krikpe's view is correct or not (and whether it can be fairly attributed to Wittgenstein or not), there remains the question of the applicability of Kripke's views to what puzzles us within or about law. Wittgenstein had made it clear that his own work was a response to the puzzle of agreement (on basic matters), not the problem of disagreement on hard questions. It was about those areas in which we all "go on" the same way, about those simple questions of arithmetic about which mathematicians "don't come to blows" (Wittgenstein 1968:§ 240).

To move from an explanation of easy cases (in language and mathematical series) to a justification for dissolving or ignoring controversies in hard cases (of legal, moral, and political disputes) would require substantial argumentation, which the theorists of Wittgenstein-inspired determinacy theories seem never willing or able to provide.[4] Whether or not language and meaning must always ultimately be grounded on community consensus does not entail a position one way or the other regarding whether many, most, or all legal disputes currently before the appellate court have a legally right (or, at least, legally "best") answer.

10.2.2 Determinacy theorists

As there have been theorists who have argued that law was more indeterminate than most people believed, so there have also been those (if fewer of them) who have argued that law was far more determinate than most people believed. One such example is Brian Langille (1988), who, ironically, also looked to the later Wittgenstein and his rule-following considerations, to ground his position.[5] He focused on Wittgenstein's view that the

---

[4] I discuss this point at greater length in Bix (1993:36–53) and Bix (2005).

[5] Comparable Wittgensteinian arguments are made by Philip Bobbitt (1991) (as regards constitutional interpretation) and Dennis Patterson (1996) (as regards legal interpretation generally), though neither appears to make the legal determinacy claims one finds in Langille's (1988) work.

"grammar" of language is grounded in human nature and human practices ("forms of life"). Langille then argued that law in general and constitutional law in particular can be similarly said to have a "grammar" grounded in our practices that makes skeptical approaches to law inappropriate. The objection here is much the same as with the contrary use of the rule-following considerations, discussed above (in Section 10.2.1): law is not a good analogy for the simple word references and basic mathematical series ("add 2") on which Wittgenstein focused. He was trying to *explain agreement*, not dissolve disagreement. Questions of legal interpretation are, by contrast, places where "[d]isputes *do*...break out" and where "[p]eople *do*...come to blows" (at least metaphorically) over different and contending positions. (Wittgenstein 1968:§ 240 (emphasis added)) As before, much work needs to be done to show why what is true for simple words and series should be equally true for difficult moral, political, and legal debates, or how the truths in one area illuminate the issues in the other. And it does not appear to be the case that any significant portion of the bridge-work has yet been done.

Michael Moore (1982a, 1982b, 1985, 1987, 1989, 1992a, 1992b), Nicos Stavropoulos (1996), and David Brink (1988, 1989a, 1989b, 2001) have looked to some combination of metaphysical realism and the natural kinds theories of meaning and reference to ground their views of greater legal determinacy. "Metaphysical realism" regarding an area of discourse generally asserts that terms within the discourse correspond to real entities in the world (and not just collective beliefs or social conventions). "Natural kinds" analysis (see Putnam 1975; Kripke 1972; Burge 1979) is a related but distinct view about the connection between meaning and reference. The meaning of "natural kinds" terms are the "real nature" of the item or category of items named by the terms. To determine the meaning and reference of a natural kind term, one looks not to people's conventional beliefs about the object(s) the term names, but rather to our current best (scientific) theory of the object or category of objects. The argument of the theorists like Moore, Brink, and Stavropoulos is that many of the terms used by law makers are, or are like, natural kind terms, that they should thus be interpreted according to the best current understanding of their "real nature," and that this is how law makers would intend them to be interpreted. The meaning of legal texts is determined by the way the world is.

Put in different terms, the argument is that terms in legislation (and constitutional provisions) should be interpreted according to "word meaning" rather than "speaker meaning."[6] As will become clear in this chapter, the need to choose between "word meaning" and "speaker meaning" is a constant theme of discussions of legal interpretation. The objection to the claims of the legal theorists who would use some version of natural kind theory or metaphysical realism is that their views depend on unwarranted effort to ignore or discount the claims of "speaker meaning."

On one hand, lawmaking is about choice, including sometimes the choice, express or implicit, to deviate from the "real extension" (as determined by judges or other observers) of natural kinds or other terms. On the other hand, there are "rule of law" values

---

[6] The same distinction is sometimes offered using different terms: e.g. "utterance meaning" or "expression meaning" or "sentence meaning."

that incline towards the "objective" or publicly accessible meanings of the words enacted, even if the private intentions of the law makers might have been different. There are reasons, important to legal systems and how they operate, both for preferring the speaker's meaning in interpreting legislation and for preferring word meaning. Both claims are present in legal systems, and are recognized to greater or lesser extents by courts in interpreting statutes and constitutional provisions, and neither claim can be extinguished by mere reference to a theory of language, meaning, or reference.

10.2.3 H. L. A. Hart and the "open texture" of language

In some of his earliest works expounding his legal positivist theory, the English legal theorist, H. L. A. Hart, responded to the American legal realists' claims of legal indeterminacy (see 10.2.1, above). He thought that the American realists were overstating a valid point when they argued that judges usually had discretion when deciding cases. (Hart 1958:606–15) Hart argued for what was (and still is) the conventional view, that judges made new law when deciding "hard cases," but not when deciding "easy cases." What was new in Hart's approach is that he borrowed ideas from philosophy of language to support that position.[7]

In particular, Hart argued that language in legal rules has an "open texture" (Hart 1994:127–8). At times, Hart offered this argument as grounded in universal aspects of language. At other times, Hart's argument seems grounded more on the nature of rules, or a focus on legislative intentions. When the law was written, the law makers had certain circumstances in mind, certain harms they meant to prevent or encourage. However, when a fact situation comes before the court that the law makers had not foreseen, Hart argues, the judge must make a new choice (not determined by the law maker's choices, but should be made consistent with the general spirit of those and prior authoritative choices). (Hart 1994:124–36) Additionally, Hart argued that, in any event, an approach recognizing "open texture" and limited judicial discretion against more formalist alternatives would have better policy outcomes (Hart 1994:128–31).

Hart borrowed his term "open texture" from his Oxford colleague, Friedrich Waismann (Hart 1994:249), but it is worth noting how the term changed meaning in the borrowing. Waismann's idea of "open texture"[8] is an application of certain ideas of Wittgenstein that would later appear in Wittgenstein's *Philosophical Investigations*. Section 80 of the *Investigations* reads:

> I say 'There is a chair.' What if I go up to it, meaning to fetch it, and it suddenly disappears from sight?—'So it wasn't a chair, but some kind of illusion.'—But in a few moments we see it again and are able to touch it and so on. —'So the chair was there after all and its disappearance was some kind of illusion.'—But suppose that after a

---

[7] For a detailed critique of Hart's open texture analysis, see Postema (2010).
[8] "*Porisität der Begriffe*" in the original German. (Waismann 1945:121 n.*)

time it disappears again—or seems to disappear. What are we to say now? (Wittgenstein 1968:§ 80)

Wittgenstein adds, in a later section: "It is only in normal cases that the use of a word is clearly prescribed; we know, are in no doubt what to say in this or that case. The more abnormal the case, the more doubtful it becomes what we are to say" (Wittgenstein 1968:§ 142).

In the above quotation from the later Wittgenstein, the question is of the connection between meaning and unusual circumstances. This raises what might be seen as a fairly conventional issue in semantic theory and the philosophy of language: the extent to which conventional meanings assume usual circumstances, and unusual circumstances may unsettle meaning and understanding. However, it is important to note that in Waismann's text (and in the corresponding works from Wittgenstein's middle period (Waismann 1979; Wittgenstein 1975)—works chronologically prior to the *Investigations*)—the idea of "open texture" is an offshoot of a more narrow inquiry relating to verification-ism. Verification theory equated the meaning of a proposition with what would be needed to verify that proposition.[9] Waismann was considering the question of how material object statements could be translated into sense data. When trying to verify the assertion, "There is a cat next door," is it sufficient to see the cat, perhaps touch it, and hear it purr? (Waismann 1945b:121) However:

> What...should I say when that creature later on grew to gigantic size? Or if it showed some queer behavior usually not found with cats?....Again, suppose I say "There is my friend over there". What if on drawing closer in order to shake hands with him, he suddenly disappeared? "Therefore it was not my friend but some delusion or other". But suppose a few some seconds later I saw him again, could grasp his hand, etc. What then?...Have we rules ready for all imaginable possibilities? (Waismann 1945b:121–2)

"Open texture," in this narrow, philosophical sense (later the article will consider a broader and looser sense in which the term has been used in jurisprudential writings), is connected to a particular set of philosophical ideas from the middle decades of the twentieth century. In particular, Wittgenstein and Waismann had both been, at one time, developing an approach towards language and meaning under which material object statements were made more or less probable, but never completely verified or falsified, by our experiences and sense-perceptions. In the case of both writers, the work was discussed in texts that were left unpublished during their lifetimes (and, in Wittgenstein's case, it was clear that he had rejected this approach in moving on to the different approach to language and meaning of the *Investigations*).[10]

---

[9] Verification theory also, controversially, claimed that propositions that could not be verified or falsified (e.g. most propositions of religion and metaphysics) were non-sensical (e.g. Ayer 1936; Waismann 1979).

[10] For Wittgenstein's views, see Waismann (1979:99–101, 158–62, 210–11); Wittgenstein (1975:200–1, 282–97); for Waismann's views, see Waismann (1979:38–59, 1945b). See generally Bix (1993:14–17); Baker (1997).

In Waismann's work (and the work of Wittgenstein on which it is based), "open texture" seems to be not so much vagueness,[11] as conventionally understood, as the mere possibility of vagueness: the uncertainty regarding meaning for logically possible, but realistically highly unlikely, events. The events are so unlikely that it is very improbable that any competent user of the language has even considered how he or she would respond linguistically were the events to occur. For Waismann, "open texture" reflects an essential fact about empirical terms, and our inability to make their meaning entirely precise or conclusively verifiable.

As already mentioned, while Hart borrowed Waismann's term, "open texture," to make a point about the partial indeterminacy of language and (thus, as he saw it) of (legal) rules, his own use of the term indicates a meaning broader and looser than it had for Waismann. Hart uses the example of a hypothetical statute, "No vehicles in the park" (Hart 1958:607–11; Hart 1994:128–9). He argued that the "core" meaning of "vehicle" means that the statute applies unproblematically to a standard car driving through the park. However, when the question comes to someone using roller skates in the park, "roller skates" are on the "penumbra" of "vehicle," and there are thus "reasons both for and against our use of a general term"; asked to decide the application of this statute in such a case, "something in the nature of a choice between open alternatives must be made by" the judge (Hart 1994:126–7).

Terms in a legal rule will have borderline cases of uncertain application, and thus, Hart argued, so will the application of the rule as a whole. On the one hand, common law judicial decisions will clarify some borderline cases through new decisions.[12] Once a judge decides, say, that roller skates *are* vehicles for the purpose of the rule, later courts may be bound to follow that interpretation. On the other hand, however, new practices and technologies will throw up new borderline cases (Hart 1994:126). So there will always be a range of cases in which the application of the legal rule is uncertain (at least until a court's decision settles the question).

For Hart, guidance by legislated rule is not that different from guidance by authoritative example (the latter occurs in common law reasoning, where the court's decision favoring one side or the other under certain sets of facts is binding on (some) later courts, but the deciding court's formulation of the guiding rule and justification is not) (Hart 1994:124–8). In each case, there are paradigmatic cases of clear application, but also borderline applications that will require some choice to be made by the judge (or other decision maker). In these discussions, Hart was affirming the conventional view that judges have discretion in hard cases (under Hart's analysis, because the core meaning of terms used in the rule, or the core meaning of the rule itself has run out).

One can see how in the original context—in the works of Waismann and Wittgenstein—"open texture" refers to a matter of theoretical interest, but of limited

[11] Vagueness is a problem of uncertain borderlines of a category or meaning. "Bald" or "tall" are paradigmatic vague terms. Whether vagueness represents an aspect of epistemology or ontology remains highly controversial among philosophers of language.

[12] Hart also notes that canons of interpretation can reduce, but cannot eliminate, uncertainties in interpretation (in part because those canons of interpretation themselves require interpretation) (Hart 1994:126).

practical application. Open texture is for the extraordinary (cats the size of rooms), not for the merely unusual. What Hart was pointing to was something more mundane, an uncertainty in application that occurs frequently enough for the average lawyer to recognize the judicial difficulty Hart is describing.

At times, Hart seems to change his focus from the clear meaning (in some cases) and (in other cases) unclear application of particular terms to clear and unclear meanings and applications of whole rules. Thus, one can find references both to the "open texture of terms" and to the "open texture of rules" (Hart 1994:123–8). To be sure, uncertainty of terms can lead to uncertainty of the norm as a whole, but this is not necessary or universal. An uncertainty in a particular term might be overcome by reading the term in light of other terms in the rule, in light of the rule's purpose, or in light of other related norms.

Hart also switches from a focus on the terms themselves to references to the uncertain or incomplete intentions of law-makers. On occasion, he ascribes indeterminacy to the fact that some application of a rule was not foreseen, or perhaps was entirely unforeseeable, by the legislators who enacted it (Hart 1994:128–9). However, this assumes that we should be interpreting and applying statutes in line with the law-makers' intentions (only). Whether such a purposive or intentionalist approach to statutory interpretation is required or optimal was, and remains, a controversial topic.

10.3 INTERPRETATION

Legal disputes often concern the proper interpretation of legal texts: determining the meaning and application of constitutional provisions, statutes, contracts, wills, and trusts. The proper methodology for legal interpretation, and the necessary constraints on decision makers, have been points of contention throughout legal history.

With interpreting wills, trusts, contracts, and similar legal documents, most legal systems hold that a court's job is to determine what the drafter(s) intended, and (with some exceptions, sometimes relating to strongly held public policies) to effectuate those intentions. When we move to the interpretation of constitutional provisions and statutes, however, additional levels of complication are added. First and foremost, there is the complication that for most such legal texts, the documents were drafted, approved, or ratified by large groups. Within those groups, individuals are likely to vary significantly in their knowledge of the relevant text, and their intentions regarding it. It is not clear how, if at all, the differing individual intentions can be "summed up" into a collective intention for the legal text.

Second, when one talks about intentions relating to legislation and constitutional provisions, one needs to speak about different levels or types of intentions. For example, those who drafted or ratified the eighth amendment to the United States Constitution (forbidding the infliction of "cruel and unusual punishments") will have had intentions that these words become part of the Constitution. They will have general intentions that "cruel and unusual punishments" will be forbidden. And they will have more specific intentions regarding which punishments would be included in that list (drawing and quartering? being left in stocks? branding with an iron?; many more people today than in the eighteenth century would consider capital punishment to be, per se, "cruel"). They may also have methodological intentions regarding how they think judges should interpret the amendment (according to the general or specific intentions of the drafters? according to the general public understanding of the ratifiers? according to the best understanding of the moral category at the time of adjudication?). Which type or level of intention (if any) should interpreters consult?

Third, there is the complication that these texts are often intended to apply well into the future, to circumstances and issues that were not foreseen, and were likely unforeseeable, at the time of the initial enactment.[13] This relates to the earlier two sets of points (collective intentions, and different types and levels of intentions), pointing us away from the relatively simple model of using intentions to guide understanding and application that one finds in normal conversation and the legal interpretation of wills, trusts, and contracts.

All of the above complications make it hard to determine how (if at all) intentions can or should be used in interpreting statutes and constitutional provisions. Additionally, as discussed earlier (in Section 10.2.2), there are contrary pulls generally in legal interpretation: between the value of authority—giving priority to the choices (and preferences and intentions) of the law-makers—and the rule-of-law values—giving priority to "word meaning," "plain meaning," or the best current theory of an enactment's concepts and categories.

Many prominent legal theorists have discussed the problem of intention in relation to judicial interpretation of legal texts (e.g. Raz 2009:223–370; Dworkin 1985b:146–77), and it seems to be an area where, though help has been sought in philosophy of language (e.g. Searle 1997; Barnes 1988),[14] the indications are that philosophy is no further along in solving the relevant problems. Whatever solutions have been achieved at a philosophical or literary level are not sufficient on their own to respond to all that is troublesome in the legal context.

10.4 US constitutional interpretation: Intentionalism, originalism, textualism, and plain meaning

In the United States, the courts interpret the federal constitution, sometimes using it to invalidate legislation held to be contrary to its provisions. Almost all serious policy disputes—for example abortion, capital punishment, affirmative action (positive

---

[13] Similar issues may arise on occasion for contracts, especially those meant to structure a long-term relationship, and, more rarely, also for wills and trust, especially those which have charitable provisions meant to apply well into the future.

[14] Ronald Dworkin's interpretive theory of law also calls on certain philosophy of language theorists to bolster his approach, in particular, Hans-Georg Gadamer. (Dworkin 1986:55, 62)

discrimination), same-sex marriage, regulation of political campaign funding, and phy-
sician-assisted suicide—have appeared at one time or another before the American
courts with litigants claiming that the United States Constitution requires or forbids
particular policy outcomes.

In this context, it is not surprising that the proper approach to constitutional interpretation remains central to American legal discourse. One prominent approach to constitutional interpretation (associated primarily, though not exclusively, with conservative
political viewpoints) is called "originalism." In its early formulations, this label was associated with the argument that judges should interpret the Constitution in line with what
its drafters intended the text to mean (e.g. Bork 1971; Berger 1977). Supporters of this
approach to constitutional interpretation have sometimes looked for support to "intentionalist" theorists of meaning among both literary theorists (e.g. Hirsch 1973) and philosophers of meaning.

More recent versions of "originalism" have focused instead on the "plain meaning" of
the terms at the time the constitutional provision(s) in question were ratified. Some of
those who have supported this "new originalism" have grounded their approaches on
the philosophical work of H. P. Grice, in particular his theory relating meaning to speaker's intentions and audiences (Solum 2008; Grice 1969, 1989). "New originalism," like
older forms of "originalism," focuses on constraining judicial interpretation by reference
to a stable and unique "meaning" of the constitutional text, though "new originalism"
recognizes that a text's meaning may be only the first step in an interpretive process, by
which that meaning may be modified or subordinated in the process of deciding a case
(Solum 2008).

Debates within and about "originalism" in the United States echo the basic questions
of legal interpretation already mentioned: should one focus on speaker meaning or word
meaning? if one looks at the intentions of the drafters or ratifiers, which level(s) of intention are relevant? and should one give priority to the choices of the law makers or to the
reasonable understanding of those subject to the law?

10.5 POLITICS, LAW, AND PHILOSOPHY

There appear to be contrary temptations. On one side (usually associated with the political Left) is the temptation to assert that law, on its own, resolves little or nothing. This has
been tied with claims of radical legal indeterminacy (discussed in Section 10.2.1), and
the related Critical Legal Studies slogan that "law is [only] politics." This claim is often
connected with a claim that when law does purport to resolve issues, it is only part of a
mystification by the powerful to delude the powerless into thinking that the legal system
in particular, and society in general, are just (Tushnet 1991; see also Kelman 1987;
Kennedy 1997).

On the other side is the temptation to assert that there are unique legal answers to all
(legal) disputes, with no need to fill in gaps with judicial choices and lawmaking. Along

with the theorists of extreme legal determinacy discussed earlier (in Section 10.2.2), there are other theories, most famously that of Ronald Dworkin (1977, 1985b, 1986, 2006), which claim that there are unique right answers to all legal questions that might come before the court.

A different, but related set of questions relates to how judges do or should interpret statutes. Here we have a legal text enacted, usually by majority vote of a multi-member legislature. There is often evidence of some problem to which this legislation was meant to respond, and the manner in which this legislation was meant to respond to that problem, evidence which may include a detailed legislative history. Different legal systems, and different judges within a single legal system (and sometimes even the same judge, over time, when faced with different cases), have offered different responses regarding the relevance and priority of evidence regarding law-makers' intentions, the plain meaning of the words enacted, evidence of purpose, legislative history, and allegations that an otherwise authorized application would be absurd or unjust (e.g. Eskridge et al. 2006).

A better theory of language, meaning, intention, or reference will not save us from having to make what are basically moral and political choices. What general rules of legal (or statutory or constitutional) interpretation we should use cannot be determined by such theories, nor can those theories tell us that we must never (or always) deviate from whatever our general approach is when the result would be contrary to apparent purpose, contrary to morality, or contrary to common sense.

One might say (cf. Solum 2008) that the meaning of a legal text is one thing, its application another, and the above discussion simply indicates that there may be legal, moral, or political reasons for deviating from a law's meaning in resolving certain disputes. However, while a distinction between law and application is sometimes helpful, in the context of the present discussion it may work more to obfuscate the basic point than to illuminate it.

10.6 CONCLUSION

On the whole, the story of legal interpretation and the philosophy of language is a modest one. There have been benefits, where references to philosophical work in meaning, reference, and intentions have given a clearer analytical structure for articulating ideas that were already present in the legal literature, if perhaps in a less well thought-out form. Thus, ideas about intension versus extensions, the interaction of meaning and reference, speakers' meaning versus word meaning, different levels or types of intention, the problems of collective intentions, social and institutional facts, etc., have all increased both the sophistication and the clarity of modern writing about legal interpretation.

Less helpful have been the efforts to find in philosophy of language, and related fields, grounds for believing that legal interpretation is something far different from what is conventionally thought: either far more determinate, far less determinate, or entirely separated from hard political choices. None of those efforts have been persuasive.

PART III

MULTILINGUALISM AND TRANSLATION

CHAPTER 11

....

BILINGUAL INTERPRETATION RULES AS A COMPONENT OF LANGUAGE RIGHTS IN CANADA

....

MICHEL BASTARACHE

11.1 LINGUISTIC RIGHTS OF MINORITIES IN CANADA

....

IN Canada a few groups enjoy explicit constitutional recognition: the inhabitants of Quebec of French expression, as a national minority;[1] certain official language

---

[1] Quebec has a civil law system of private law, based on French law, whereas the private law of the other Canadian jurisdictions is based on the English common law. The existence of the civil law in Quebec is protected by s. 92(13) of the *Constitution Act, 1867* (U.K.), 30 & 31 Vict., c. 3, reprinted in R.S.C. 1985, App. II, No. 5, which assigns each province legislative competence over "property and civil rights in the province." Quebec civil law is further protected by the requirement that three of the judges of the Supreme Court of Canada will come from that province. This requirement was established by s. 6 of the *Supreme Court Act*. It was constitutionalized by s. 41(d) of the *Constitution Act, 1982*, which provides that the composition of the Supreme Court may only be altered by a constitutional amendment with the unanimous consent of the federal Parliament and the legislatures of each province. By convention, three judges are also appointed from Ontario, two from the Western provinces, and one from the Atlantic provinces. But only Quebec's representation is expressly guaranteed in order to protect the integrity of its system of private law. I say that this protection accrues to the francophone inhabitants of Quebec because the civil law is an important symbol of the distinctiveness of the québécois as the only majority francophone population in Canada. In addition to the constitutional protection for Quebec civil law, the francophone population of Quebec enjoys a partial derogation to the minority language education rights granted by the *Canadian Charter of Rights and Freedoms*, Part I of the *Constitution Act, 1982*, being Schedule B to the *Canada Act 1982* (U.K.), 1982, c. 11. Section 23(1)(a) grants minority language education rights to the children of Canadian citizens whose first language learned, and still understood, is the minority official language of the province in which they reside; section 23(1)(b) grants these rights to the children of citizens

minorities;[2] Catholic and Protestant minorities in provinces other than Quebec and Newfoundland and Labrador;[3] provincial and territorial official language minorities with regard to instruction in French or English;[4] aboriginals;[5] and the two official language communities in New Brunswick.[6]

In light of the constitutional history of Canada, the Supreme Court of Canada affirmed in the *Reference re Secession of Quebec* that the protection of minorities forms part of the constitutional order in Canada.[7] This underlying principle is normative and can give rise to substantial obligations for governments. This is an important consideration with regard to the interpretation of the constitution and legislation relative to official languages.[8]

The minority communities in Canada that are officially recognized by the Constitution are thereby entitled to institutions adapted to their cultural needs. Their rights are so important that they are not subject to the override power in the so-called "notwithstanding" clause in the *Canadian Charter of Rights and Freedoms.*[9] These rights also differ from other rights guaranteed in the *Charter* in that they are collective rights. Indeed, except as regards these groups, the *Charter* generally sanctions individual rights, even if their ultimate object is to protect minority groups.[10]

Linguistic rights are part of the more general rights of minorities, but they are of a special nature. In certain cases, language legislation is an instrument for building the nation; this is the case in the province of Quebec. In others, it is a question of ensuring the cultural security and the continuity of a minority; this is the case at the federal level in Canada, and in certain provinces, in particular New Brunswick, the only officially bilingual province. The Canadian approach has multiple facets since it addresses

who received their primary school instruction in Canada in the official language that is the minority language of the province in which they reside. Section 59 of the *Constitution Act, 1982* provides that s. 23(1) (a) will only come into force in respect of Quebec if authorized by the province. Therefore, only the right based on the parent's educational history, not the parent's mother tongue, applies in Quebec.

   [2] *Constitution Act, 1867,* note 1 above, s. 133; *Manitoba Act, 1870,* R.S.C. 1985, App. II, No. 8, s. 23; *Charter,* note 1 above, ss. 16–20.

   [3] *Constitution Act, 1867,* note 1 above, s. 93; and the terms of union with British Columbia, R.S.C. 1985, App. II, No. 10, Prince Edward Island, R.S.C. 1985, App. II, No. 12, and Newfoundland, R.S.C. 1985, App. II, No. 32; and the Acts creating the provinces of Manitoba, R.S.C. 1985, App. II, No. 8, Alberta, R.S.C. 1985, App. II, No. 20, and Saskatchewan R.S.C. 1985, App. II, No. 21.

   [4] *Charter,* note 1 above, s. 23.

   [5] *Constitution Act, 1982,* note 1 above, s. 35.

   [6] *Charter,* note 1 above, s. 16.1.

   [7] *Reference re Secession of Quebec,* [1998] 2 S.C.R. 217 at para. 80.

   [8] *Lalonde v Ontario (Commission de restructuration des services de santé)* (2001), 56 O.R. (3d) 505 (Ont. C.A.).

   [9] Section 33 of the *Charter,* note 1 above, provides that Parliament or the legislature of a province may expressly declare in an Act of Parliament or of the legislature that the Act or a provision thereof shall operate notwithstanding a provision included in s. 2 or ss. 7-15 of the *Charter* for a period of five years following such a declaration.

   [10] Section 15 of the *Charter,* note 1 above, guarantees equality rights to "[e]very individual". This right refers to membership in a group in Canadian case law, since the protection of the group depends on the application of the provision to an individual.

individual needs but often adopts a cultural and community approach. It is important to note that, outside Quebec, the emphasis is not put on non-discrimination, but on the dignity and the equality of the speakers. The protection granted to the minority cannot thus be founded on tolerance; it aims at the full participation of the members of the official language communities in public affairs without having to give up their linguistic and cultural identity.[11]

In Canada, language is regarded as a fundamental element of cultural identity. The linguistic right is in essence the right to resist assimilation; it is distinct from the more general civil and political rights. For example, with regard to the rights of the accused, the members of the official language minority community can obtain a criminal trial in French or in English without regard to their individual linguistic aptitudes, and this right includes the right to be heard by a judge and a jury without the assistance of an interpreter.[12] The notion of fundamental rights must be interpreted in light of the democratic ideals and the understanding of political legitimacy in the country. In Canada, the Supreme Court has ruled that linguistic rights are indeed basic rights, in particular because they are a fundamental element of Canadian democracy and one of the components of the federation. This has great importance because of its implications regarding the applicable rules of interpretation.

When comparing linguistic rights regimes in different countries, one often classifies the various approaches as fundamentally based on either the principle of territoriality (recognition of linguistically homogeneic regions) or personality (recognition of the rights of minority language users in a region). (For a brief overview of these concepts from a Canadian perspective, see Silver 2000:690–2 and Turi 1990:642). This classification is of limited use in describing the Canadian experience because in Canada territorially based linguistic rights do not require unilingualism and personally based linguistic rights are circumscribed by territorial considerations.

In Canada, territoriality is prescribed in two basic constitutional provisions: section 133 of the *Constitution Act, 1867* and section 16 of the *Canadian Charter of Rights and Freedoms*. Section 133 of the *Constitution Act, 1867* provides that either English or French may be used in the debates of the Federal Parliament and the Legislature of Quebec, in all courts of Quebec and in any court of Canada established under the Act. It provides that English and French shall be used in the records and journals of both legislative bodies and that the Acts of both shall be printed and published in both languages. Section 16 of the *Charter* declares that English and French are the official languages of Canada and of New Brunswick and guarantees them "equality of status and equal rights and privileges as to their use in all institutions of" both "the Parliament and government of Canada" and "the legislature and government of New Brunswick".

These linguistic guarantees can be invoked with regard to federal institutions, and with regard to provincial institutions in Quebec and New Brunswick. Similar rights

---

[11] For an overview of State approaches to language rights internationally, see de Varennes 1997.

[12] *R. v Beaulac* [1999] 1 S.C.R. 768 at para. 34.

were recognized in Manitoba under the terms of the constitutional law which created this province, but the province did not recognize their constitutional status until the Supreme Court's decision in the case of *Manitoba (A.G.) v Forest*.[13] These rights belong to "any person" and thus do not provide for protection only to those who have French or English as their mother tongue. The right to obtain services from federal institutions is also partly territorial because it is exerted in particular where there is sufficient demand.[14] In the area of education, particular criteria were adopted with an aim to facilitate freedom of mobility; the right is personal and territorial.[15] It has an obvious collective dimension, however, because it is exerted only in partnership with others and is meant to safeguard the culture of those who are the beneficiaries of the right.

11.2 THE HISTORICAL DEVELOPMENT OF MULTILINGUAL LEGISLATION

Canada was established as a bilingual, bijural, federal "Dominion" with Confederation, in 1867: bilingual because of the linguistic obligations of Parliament and the Quebec Legislature,[16] and bijural because the provinces maintained legislative competence over "property and civil rights in the province," and Quebec remained a civil law province as regards private law.[17]

The linguistic regime which prevails in Canada was radically changed by the adoption of federal and provincial language laws, but those were long in coming. Parliament adopted its first federal *Official Languages Act* in 1969[18] and altered it deeply in 1988.[19] New Brunswick and Quebec adopted the first such provincial laws in 1969.[20] The Quebec legislation sought to promote French, but without making it the province's official language. Quebec's current official language Act, the *Charter of the French Language*, commonly referred to as Bill 101, dates back to 1977.[21] Manitoba had the same constitutional obligations as Quebec when it was created in 1870, because of section 23 of the *Manitoba Act, 1870*, the wording of which was similar to that of section

---

[13] [1979] 2 S.C.R. 1032. See also *Re Manitoba Language Rights* [1985] 1 S.C.R. 721.

[14] *Charter*, note 1 above, s. 20(1)(a); Note, however, that s. 20(1)(b) provides that in some cases is it the nature of the office that will determine that it must communicate with the public and offer services in both languages.

[15] Ibid., s. 23.

[16] *Constitution Act, 1867*, note 1 above, s. 133.

[17] Ibid., s. 92(13) (ss. 91 and 92 of the *Constitution Act, 1867* establish the respective areas of legislative competence of Parliament and the provincial legislatures).

[18] R.S.C. 1970, c. O-2.

[19] R.S.C. 1985, c. 31 (4th Supp.).

[20] *The Official Languages of New Brunswick Act*, S.N.B. 1969, c. 14 and *Act for the Promotion of the French Language in Quebec*, S.Q. 1969, c. 9.

[21] S.Q. 1977, c. 5; R.S.Q., c. C-11.

133 of the *Constitution Act, 1867*, but it ignored its obligations and unconstitutionally repealed the rights of its French-speaking people in 1890.[22] It was not until 1979 that the rights were restored.[23] The Northwest Territories were subject to the same bilingual obligations when created; their obligations were to be assumed by Alberta and Saskatchewan when they were carved out of the Territories in 1905.[24] The Supreme Court judged, however, in *R. Mercure* that these provinces could repeal these rights (which they had never respected) because they were not of a constitutional nature;[25] the repeal was accomplished in 1988.[26] The three current federal territories were forced to adopt linguistic laws by the federal government, but their constitutional obligations are unsettled.

Ontario, which does not have constitutional linguistic obligations, recognized the status of French in the courts in a limited way in 1970 (initially on an exception basis, by the agreement of all parties, see Annis 1985:49–50), in a more important way in 1978,[27] and more importantly again in 1984.[28] In 1990, a much more comprehensive regime was set up.[29] The same year, the *French Language Services Act*[30] came into effect and the *Statutory Powers Procedure Act* was adopted.[31] Those instruments created a partial bilingualism within the public service and administrative courts. Nova Scotia and Prince-Edward Island have also adopted laws on official languages, but they have a very limited range.

11.3 MULTILINGUAL STATUTORY INTERPRETATION

11.3.1 The rules of equal authenticity and shared meaning

The Supreme Court of Canada had to develop rules of statutory interpretation that were consistent with the Constitution. As early as 1891, it affirmed in the case of *Canadian Pacific v Robinson* that the interpretation of statutes would obey the equal authenticity

---

[22] *An Act to Provide that the English Language shall be the Official Language of the Province of Manitoba*, S.M. 1890, c. 14.

[23] *An Act Respecting the Operation of Section 23 of the Manitoba Act in Regard to Statutes*, S.M. 1980, c. 3, enacted in response to *Manitoba (A.G.) v Forest*, [1979] 2 S.C.R. 1032.

[24] *Northwest Territories Act*, R.S.C. 1886, c. 50 (am. 1891, c. 22, s. 18).

[25] [1988] 1 S.C.R. 234.

[26] *The Language Act*, S.S. 1988-89, c. L-6.1 and *Languages Act*, R.S.A. 2000, c. L-6.

[27] With the creation of eight bilingual judicial districts by an amendment to s. 127 of the *Judicature Act*, S.O. 1978, c. 26.

[28] With the adoption of the *Judicature Act*, S.O. 1984, c. 11, s. 135 of which made French an official language in the courts.

[29] In ss. 125 and 126 of the *Courts of Justice Act*, R.S.O. 1990, c. C.43.

[30] R.S.O. 1990, c. F.32.

[31] R.S.O. 1990, c. S.22.

rule and the shared meaning rule.[32] The equal authenticity rule requires that no prefer-ence be given to one or the other language version, and that no version be considered inferior because it may be a translation of the other. The shared meaning rule requires a court to determine, as far as possible, the common meaning of the two distinct language versions. This reflects the idea that although there may be two texts, they are both expres-sions of the same legislative intent. The shared meaning rule has always accompanied the equal authenticity rule.[33] It is commonly accepted that these rules must be applied before any consideration can be given to the general rules of statutory interpretation.

This approach is of course political and ideological. It establishes a moral objective tied to the notion of nation-building. In Canada, as stated earlier, language rights are designed to favour national unity and respect for minorities. The necessity of developing principles of interpretation respectful of the two official languages and the two legal sys-tems is therefore a constitutional imperative. The Court initially inferred the principle of equal authenticity from the fact of simultaneous enactment in both languages, without reference to section 133 of the *Constitution Act, 1867*. It made this inference with regard to Quebec's *Civil Code* in *C.P.R. v Robinson* in 1891 and with regard to federal legislation in *R. v Dubois* in 1935.[34] When the Court specifically affirmed the principle in *Blaikie v Québec (A.G.) (No. 1)* in 1971, it held that it was a constitutional imperative because of section 133's requirement that "[t]he Acts of the Parliament of Canada and of the Legislature of Québec shall be printed and published in both those Languages."[35] The Supreme Court later applied its interpretation of section 133 of the *Constitution Act, 1867* from *Blaikie (No. 1)* to the similarly-worded section 23 of the *Manitoba Act, 1870* and held that the province was equally obligated to enact all legislation in both English and French.[36]

The principle of equal authenticity was more explicitly entrenched in the Constitution with regard to federal and New Brunswick (but not Quebec) legislation in section 18 of the *Charter*. Section 13 of the federal *Official Languages Act* adopted in 1988 is to similar effect as regards federal legislation.[37] The principle is also expressly provided for by ordi-nary legislation in a number of provinces, including Quebec, Manitoba,[38] Ontario,[39] and Saskatchewan.[40] The other provinces have not adopted the rule by legislation. Most of these enact legislation exclusively in English.

---

[32] *Canadian Pacific Railway Co. v Robinson* (1891), 19 S.C.R. 292. (S.C.C.); see also *R. v Dubois* [1935] S.C.R. 378.

[33] The shared meaning rule was affirmed in particular in the case of *R. v Dubois*, ibid., in which the Court had to consider the distinction between a "public work" and a "chantier public." The French expression suggested a space within which works were being undertaken.

[34] Note 43 above.

[35] [1979] 2 S.C.R. 1016 at 1022.

[36] Note 16 above.

[37] Note 30 above.

[38] C.C.S.M. c. I80.

[39] R.S.O. 1990, c. F.32; S.O. 2006, c. 21, Sch. F.

[40] S.S. 1988-89, c. L-6.1, ss. 4 and 10.

How, then, do the equal authenticity and shared meaning rules operate? The present rules are best described in *R. v Daoust*, in which the Supreme Court interpreted the *Criminal Code* provision that creates the offence of laundering proceeds of crime.[41] The two versions of that provision differ in their enumeration of the acts that constitute the offense. The English version lists eight prohibited acts, which are followed by the catchall provision "or otherwise deals with." The French version lists the same prohibited acts but contains no catchall provision. I will first review operation of the two rules, then their application in *Daoust*.

The first step is to determine whether there is a conflict, or, as the Court put it in *Daoust*, a discordance, between the two language versions. If there is no conflict, the common meaning can be tested for compliance with the legislative intent.

The second step is to consider the nature of the conflict where there is one and attempt to determine the shared meaning of the provisions. Three distinct types of conflicts can be discerned in the jurisprudence: There may be an "absolute conflict" regarding meaning, where each version is clear and no shared meaning can be found;[42] there may be a conflict because one version is clear and the other ambiguous;[43] and there may be a conflict because one version is broad and the other narrow.[44] If both versions are clear, the court will decide on a common meaning unless there is an absolute conflict between them. If one version is ambiguous, by which the Supreme Court means reasonably capable of more than one meaning, and the other is not, the clear version is retained.[45] Likewise, if one version is narrow and one broad, ordinarily the narrow version will be retained because it would be the only one capable of incorporating the other to achieve a common meaning.

The third step is to apply the general rules of interpretation in order to verify whether the common meaning, if there is one, is consistent with indicators of legislative intent, and in order to determine the meaning to ascribe to the provision where there is no common meaning (see Sullivan 2008 and Côté 2000). Therefore, the application of the rules of bilingual interpretation is not determinative. A court is not bound to accept a common meaning that is inconsistent with legislative intent.

The *Daoust* Court held at the first step of analysis that there was a discordance between the two versions of the provision. In the second step, it held both provisions were clear.[46] Since one version was narrower than the other, the more restrictive meaning was the only possible meaning shared by both versions.[47] In the third step, the Court found that the legislative history of the provision indicated that

[41] [2004] 1 S.C.R. 217.
[42] As in *R. v Klippert* [1967] S.C.R. 822.
[43] As in *R. v Mac*, [2002] 1 S.C.R. 856.
[44] As in *Deltonic Trading Corp. v Deputy M.N.R., Customs and Excise* [1990] F.C.J. No. 513, 113 N.R. 7 (Fed. C.A.).
[45] *Daoust*, note 53 above at para. 28, citing *Bell ExpressVu Limited Partnership v Rex*, [2002] 2 S.C.R. 559 at para. 29 for the meaning of "ambiguity" in statutory interpretation.
[46] Note 53 above at paras. 33–34.
[47] Ibid. at para. 36.

Parliament's intention was to criminalize all acts in relation to the proceeds of crime where the defendant's intent is to conceal or convert them. The Court nevertheless applied the common meaning that it had found, since the legislative intent revealed by the history was not reasonably supported by the text of the provision.[48] Although the two versions diverged because of an error or omission by Parliament, the Court held that it did not have the authority to amend the clearly drafted French version of the provision.[49]

11.3.2 Selective application by jurists

Despite the fact that the equal authenticity rule always applies to certain legislation in Canada—including all federal legislation, as we have seen—many jurists will use only one version of the legislation. Most counsel and most judges in Canada are unilingual, so the opposite language version will often be consulted only when one party raises it to take advantage of it. This is worrisome because attention to both versions is always relevant and often necessary to arrive at the proper meaning.

The *Mac* case[50] most recently raised the level of awareness of this problem in criminal law (which is an area of federal jurisdiction in Canada).[51] In that case the Ontario Court of Appeal had to determine whether the word "adapted" in the phrase "adapted and intended to be used to commit forgery" in the *Criminal Code* meant "suitable for," or "modified or altered"? The court found that both meanings were equally plausible and therefore determined that the meaning most favorable to the accused had to be retained. The problem was that the Court of Appeal did not consider the French version of the *Criminal Code* provision. The Supreme Court of Canada found that there was no ambiguity when reading the French version of the provision and that, therefore, the meaning found in the French version had to be retained. Whereas the English version of the provision used the same word, "adapted," in two nearby provisions that created similar offenses, the French versions used the word "modifié" where the term meant "modified or altered" and the term "adapté" where it meant "suitable for." This is why the Supreme Court of Canada changed its Rules after the decision in *Mac*. Parties must now present the Court with every provision to be interpreted "in both official languages if they are required by law to be published in both official languages."[52] This requirement is consistent with the application of the equal authenticity rule.

The problems illustrated by the *Mac* case highlight a somewhat ironic result of the principle of equal authenticity: The equality granted to English and French speakers is one of equal obligation to read legislation in a language other than their own. If both

---

[48] Ibid. at paras. 39–44.
[49] Ibid. at para. 45.
[50] Note 55 above.
[51] *Constitution Act, 1867*, Note 1 above, s. 91(27).
[52] *Rules of the Supreme Court of Canada*, DORS/2002-156, art. 25(1)(F)(vii), 42(2)(g) and 44(2)(b).

versions of legislation are equally authoritative, then an individual relying on the law cannot reasonably rely on only one version. Pierre-André Côté notes that producing multiple versions of an Act is designed to give access to more readers in their own language, but this is achieved at the expense of uniformity in the interpretation and application of that same Act (Côté 2005:129). We require a method of bilingual interpretation in order to achieve a uniform interpretation, but we know from the start that it will not be fully accessible to all those who must interpret the law. Obviously, unilingual jurists will do their best to analyze both language versions when a problem is raised, but their ability to identify problems and deal with them will always be limited to some degree. Of course, real problems will only arise where the two versions of a statute say different things.

Still, there is a tension inherent in the Canadian approach: It accords the proper importance to the fact that Canada is a bilingual country, but it functions best when the individual interpreting the law is bilingual, which most Canadians are not. However, it is well understood in Canada that the equal authenticity rule's requirement that both versions be examined is not too problematic because the rule is viewed as sending a clear message that speakers of both official languages are valued enough to have official rules and decisions conveyed to them in their own language. The equal authenticity and shared meaning rules are best seen as the fullest expression possible of the principle of bilingualism in legislation, and the importance of their purpose outweighs the practical difficulties that their application may sometimes present.

11.3.3 Identifying the conflict between language versions

A second difficulty, more specifically tied to the application of the rules, lies in identifying the nature of a conflict; this is to say, determining whether the conflict between the language versions is an absolute conflict or whether it can be resolved by the shared meaning rule. But does every difference between versions constitute a conflict? A few cases will help illustrate the problem.

In *Klippert*, the court was asked to interpret a provision which, in the English text, applied to "any person … who has shown a failure to control his sexual impulses," and in French applied to "une personne … qui a manifesté une impuissance à maîtriser ses impulsions sexuelles."[53] The English version refers to the failure to control one's impulses, while the French version refers to the inability to control one's impulses. This is a case of absolute conflict.

In *Canada (A.G.) v Brown*, the court was asked to decide whether costs could be awarded to non-lawyers acting before the Canadian Human Rights Commission.[54] The English version referred to the payment of costs to "counsel," while the French version

---

[53] Note 42 above.
[54] 2005 FC 1683.

provided for payment of costs to "les avocats." The court found that the English version was ambiguous because "counsel" is not a word that refers exclusively to lawyers. There was no ambiguity in the French version because it referred exclusively to lawyers. This is not a case of absolute conflict; it is a case where one version is clear and the other ambiguous.

In *Côté v Canadian Employment and Immigration Minister*, the court was asked to decide whether unemployment benefits based on "earnings" was the same as benefits based on "rémunération."[55] Here again, the court found that there was an ambiguity resulting from the fact that the word "earnings" can include the payment of interest while this is not the case for the word "rémunération." We therefore have here one version that is broad and one that is narrow.

In identifying language version conflicts, one must not come to a final conclusion by looking at a single word within a provision. It is important to look at the whole provision, but also at the larger legislative context. In looking at related provisions, the meaning of a word that is being scrutinized may become quite clear. This was the case in *Mac*, which was discussed earlier. In order to properly understand how Parliament was using the terms "adapted and intended to be used to" and "adaptés et destinés à servir pour" in that provision, the Court examined the words used in a similar provision, which creates the offense of making or repairing, buying or selling, importing or exporting, or possessing "any instrument, device, apparatus, material or thing that the person knows has been used or knows is adapted or intended for use in forging or falsifying credit cards." Although the English versions of both provisions used the wording "adapted and intended," the French version of the latter provision used the words "modifié ou destiné à cette fin." The ambiguity of the English term "adapted" was easily resolved when the court noted that there was a different meaning in these two provisions.

The rule is in fact quite simple: each version must be read in its own language, but the meaning of a provision as a whole can only be grasped when both versions are read alongside each other.

11.3.4 Erroneous applications of the equal authenticity and shared meaning rules

Although on their face the rules may seem relatively easy to apply, there are many recent examples where they have, in my opinion, been misapplied. One striking example is found in the case of *Cartier v Canada (A.G.)*.[56] In that case, the provision to be interpreted read: "where the board is satisfied that the offender is likely, if released, to commit an offense . . ." in English, and "si elle est convaincue qu'il commettra une infraction . . ."

---

[55] [1986] A.C.F. no 447, 69 N.R. 126 (Fed. C.A.).
[56] 2002 FCA 384 (Fed. C.A.).

in French. The court found that the French version was ambiguous; it also found that the English version was more restrictive. It decided that the French version could be incorporated into the English definition so that the English definition would provide a common meaning. These findings are very confusing. In my opinion, the court must first decide whether one or the other of the language versions is ambiguous in the sense that it is capable of two rational interpretations. Deciding that one version is broad and the other restrictive is a different operation. This determination is made only once a court has established the meaning of each language provision. In this case, there was no ambiguity. There was an absolute conflict: being convinced a person will commit an offense is not the same as being convinced a person is likely to commit an offense. No shared meaning could be found.

Another example is found in the case of *Tupper v R*.[57] In that case the provision to be interpreted established that possession of "any instrument for housebreaking" is a crime. The question was whether the instrument is one that can be used for housebreaking or that is designed for that purpose. In this case, the court was dealing with screwdrivers, flashlights, and a crowbar. The French version of the provision referred to instruments "pouvant servir aux effractions de maisons." The Court examined both versions separately and determined that they have the same meaning. I disagree. I believe the English version is ambiguous, but that the French version is absolutely clear. That version should have been determinative.

11.4 FUTURE CHALLENGES IN CANADIAN BILINGUAL JURISPRUDENCE

11.4.1 Bilingual interpretation of the *Charter*

It will be interesting to see whether the Supreme Court will ever deal with the perplexing question of the bilingual interpretation of section 1 of the *Charter*[58] (see Leckey 2007:571). This section provides, in English, for reasonable limitations to *Charter* rights that are

---

[57] [1967] S.C.R. 589.

[58] The general rules of interpretation are too numerous and complex to be dealt with here. They comprise rules such as the strict construction of penal statutes, the reference to *Charter* values in cases of ambiguity, and reference to the common genus of terms in an enumeration in order to establish the meaning of any individual term. Referring to the general rules of interpretation also means having regard to the legislative history of the provision, the structure of the Act in which the provision is found, attention to the purpose of the legislation and, in some cases, the application of presumptions such as the presumption that the legislature intended to favor the accused, and the presumption that Parliament intended to comply with its obligations under international law. The rules of interpretation

"prescribed by law"; in French, limits established "par une règle de droit." In *Slaight Communications*, the Supreme Court decided that "limits prescribed by law" included limits imposed by a statutory decision maker exercising a discretion arising out of legislation and constrained by legal standards. This interpretation is inconsistent with the French text of the provision. Despite Justice Lamer's reasons to the contrary, and the fact that all members of the Court agreed on this point,[59] the words "ne peuvent être restreints que par une règle de droit" indicate that the law itself must create the limit on the *Charter* right. Although Justice Lamer was satisfied that the limit "provient...d'une règle de droit," this ignored the narrower meaning of the words used in the French text.

11.4.2 Bijural conflicts of law

Canada is, of course, not only a bilingual nation but also a bijural one. As regards statutory interpretation, this is most relevant to the interpretation of federal statutory provisions that refer to or rely on private law concepts that are governed by provincial law.[60]

The existence of two legal systems in Canada presents a unique challenge for the drafter of federal legislation. Federal law, by nature, does not constitute a legal system. Sometimes Parliament provides for a complete set of rules to govern uniformly in one area of the law. But often federal legislation must be supplemented by private law. Canadian private law is not uniform: The common law provinces can adopt different approaches to private law matters and Quebec private law is a civil law system governed by a *Civil Code*.[61] The civil law has traditionally had its principal expression in the French language and the common law in English. However, from a legislative standpoint, Canada is now made up of six English common law provinces, one bilingual civil law province, and three bilingual common law provinces. The difficulty presented to the federal drafter is thus to convey in both official languages when it intends one uniform legal concept to govern as opposed to when it intends the private law of the province to be suppletive to federal legislation. When the latter is intended, it is further necessary to indicate that civil law concepts apply in Quebec and common law concepts apply in the common law provinces. The task is to simultaneously address the needs of different groups of persons: common law anglophones, common law francophones, Quebec

---

are established in the jurisprudence and by the *Interpretation Acts* in the various Canadian jurisdictions. It must be noted that the Supreme Court of Canada has adopted the so-called "modern principle" of statutory interpretation, formulated by Elmer Driedger in *Construction of Statutes* (2nd edn, 1983) as the basic framework for statutory interpretation in Canada. For this approach, see *Bell ExpressVu Limited Partnership v Rex* [2002] 2 S.C.R. 559 and *Rizzo & Rizzo Shoes Ltd. (Re)* [1998] 1 S.C.R. 27. The principal Canadian texts on statutory interpretation are Sullivan (2008) (originally an update of Driedger's text) and Côté (2000).

[59] Justice Lamer dissented in part in the result.

[60] The provinces each have legislative competence over "property and civil rights in the province" under s. 92(13) of the *Constitution Act, 1867*, note 1 above.

[61] *Civil Code of Québec*, S.Q. 1991, c. 64.

civilian francophones, and Quebec civilian anglophones. Each group must be able to read federal statutes and regulations in the official language of its choice and must also be able to find in them terminology and wording that are respectful of the concepts, notions, and institutions proper to the legal tradition of their particular province or territory.

The federal government has strived to find ways to resolve these conflicts of legal language and legal culture. The first method adopted with this in mind was that of co-drafting. This method is defined as follows:

> [A]ctual drafting is followed by a systematic revision of the text by revisers to guar-antee concordance and ensure high linguistic quality. The texts are then scrutinized by jurilinguists, specialists in the language of the law who need not have a law degree. Their task is to ensure that the two texts are equivalent not only in meaning but also from the cultural point of view. The co-drafters openly acknowledge that the work of the jurilinguists helps improve quality and avoid ambiguity. (See Šarčević 2005:281.) (For a detailed review of co-drafting of federal laws, see Labelle 2000.)

Co-drafting takes into account the need to draft legislation with a specific legal commu-nity in mind and the necessity of coherence in the law. Nevertheless, it is very difficult to reconcile drafting practices if one is to be entirely faithful to the civil law and the com-mon law systems. The efforts made to respect both legal cultures has produced texts of great stylistic diversity. Bijuralism has proven difficult to achieve even through this method. A new effort to attain the federal objective is reflected in the adoption of the *Harmonization Acts*[62] (see Allard 2005:217–18).

This principle of derivative bijuralism signifies that federal laws will adopt different notions and concepts referable to provincial legislation incidental to the federal statute, within a single Act, each concept being applicable in a particular province or territory. The context will always determine what concept applies.

This latest technique is that of using "doubles." In both language versions of a provi-sion, terms corresponding to the relevant concepts in the civil and common law are used. This can take the form of the terms and concepts specific to each legal system fol-lowing one after the other. This technique is known as "simple doubles." Doubles can also take the form of "paragraph doubles," which consists in presenting the concepts specific to each legal system in separate paragraphs. A "partial double" is another variant and occurs when one language version refers to both the common law and the civil law concepts, while the other language version contains only one term which is capable of referring to both the civil law and common law concepts. Drafting with doubles is a technique that was purposefully adopted in the federal harmonization program. A few illustrations will facilitate the understanding of the program.

---

[62] *Harmonization Act (No. 1)*, S.C. 2001, c. 4; *Federal Law—Civil Law Harmonization Act (No. 2)*, S.C. 2004, c. 25.

The amended title of the *Federal Real Property and Federal Immovables Act* is itself a double, a simple double.[63] Section 2 of the *Crown Liability and Proceedings Act* provides an example of a paragraph double. It reads:

> "liability", for the purposes of Part 1, means
>
> (A) in the province of Québec, extra contractual civil liability, and
> (B) in any other province, liability and tort;[64]

Section 4 of the *Interest Act* is an example of a partial double:

> Except as to mortgages on real property or hypothecs on immovables, whenever any interest is, by the terms of any written or printed contract, whether under seal or not, made payable at a rate or percentage per day, week, month, or at any rate or percentage for less than a year, no interest exceeding the rate or percentage of 5% per annum shall be chargeable, payable or recoverable on any part of the principal money unless the contract contains an express statement of the yearly rate or percentage of interest to which the other rate or percentage is equivalent.[65]

The French version of the same provision uses only the single expression "hypothèque" because it is capable of referring to both the civil law security interests and the analogous common law interest in real property.

The doubles drafting technique provides the most clarity in terms of parliament's intent to have the private law of the provinces supplement federal law and best achieves this goal while meeting the needs of French-speaking residents of common law provinces and English-speaking residents of Quebec. The danger in using doubles is that the drafter must make certain that the reader of the legislation will be able to recognize and ignore the words that do not apply to his or her jurisdiction, in order to read the provision as it should apply to that jurisdiction.

Another approach which is sometimes used is that of using neutral terminology. This requires the use of terms that are sufficiently general or generic to refer to either legal system. Where this approach is used, the courts are free to interpret and apply the general words to accommodate provincial law. One example of this is found in section 160 of the *Income Tax Act* which provides for the imposition of tax on certain property transferred between spouses.[66] The word "transfer" having no specific legal meaning, the Court was able to apply the provisions of the *Civil Code of lower Canada* to determine when a transfer had taken place between two spouses in the case of *Furfaro-Siconolfi v R.*[67]

There is also a technique which is a sort of hybrid of the double and neutral terms drafting techniques; it is to give a particular definition to a neutral term at the outset of the legislation. This technique avoids repetition of doubles in a statute and the use of

---

[63] S.C. 1991, c. 50.
[64] R.S.C. 1985, c. C-50.
[65] R.S.C. 1985, c. I-15.
[66] R.S.C. 1985, c. 1 (5th Supp.).
[67] [1989] F.C.J. No 1012, [1990] 1 C.T.C. 188. (F.C. T.D.).

potentially ambiguous neutral terms. A related technique is, of course, to create a new concept. Such a concept might draw on both common law and civil law sources, or it can be a truly original creation. One example of this is the notion of "paid" under section 10 (1)9(a) of the insurable earnings and collection of premiums regulations adopted under the *Employment Insurance Act*.[68] This provision deems a person who is not the actual employer of insured employees, but who collects and pays their salaries, to be the employer for the purposes of collecting employment insurance premiums and remitting them to the Minister.

11.5 BILINGUAL PUBLICATION OF JUDGMENTS

I must mention one aspect of bilingual interpretation outside the context of statutory interpretation which presents singular problems—the publication of bilingual judgments. The rules of statutory interpretation do not apply here, but the underlying principles of bilingual interpretation can be referred to usefully. First, the *Official Languages Act* does not provide that the two versions of a court's judgment are equally authentic. In fact, section 13 specifies that both versions of Acts are of equal value while part three, dealing with the administration justice and judgments, does not. It must also be noted that the judgments of the Supreme Court of Canada, while released simultaneously in French and English, are not usually presented as both being original expressions of the judgment of the Court. One version is nearly always presented as a translation of the other. This fact is not determinative but it makes it more difficult to construct a case for equal authenticity of the judgments.

Despite these factors, the importance of ensuring that authoritative legal texts are equally accessible in both French and English, which arises out of the commitment of Canada to the equal value of both these languages, applies to judgments which make law as well as to legislative texts. Both versions of bilingual judgments (which must be published in French and English[69]) should generally be seen as authentic because judgments define and develop the law. Even though an individual discordance between two words in two versions of a judgment ought not to play as large role as it does where two versions of a statute are concerned—since the practical reasoning in a judgment will less often turn on the meaning of one particular word—there is certainly room for an approach to the two versions which searches for shared meaning by reference to the judgment as a whole.

---

[68] S.C. 1996, c. 23.

[69] Meaning judgments of the courts established by Parliament and of the courts of New Brunswick which "determine[ ] a question of law or general public interest or importance": *Official Languages Act*, R.S.C. 1985, c. 31 (4th Supp.), s. 20, *Official Languages Act*, S.N.B. 2002, c. O-0.5, s. 24. All of the judgments of the Supreme Court of Canada should fit this description. Section 25 of the New Brunswick statute deems all of the decisions of the Court of Appeal to fall within the scope of s. 24.

Although I do not have room to discuss them here, I must note two additional aspects of bilingual (and multilingual) interpretation in Canada: First, that the Territory of Nunavut now has three official languages, and second, that Canadian courts are sometimes called upon to interpret international law instruments. In Nunavut, a new approach will have to be developed to deal with three official languages with equal standing. As regards international instruments, international law principles will apply even to domestic legislation if it incorporates international instruments. Addressing these issues is beyond the scope of this chapter.[70]

[70] Parts of this article rely on material from Bastarache et al. (2008) and Bastarache (2004), which explore the subjects of this article in further detail than is possible here.

CHAPTER 12

......

WORD MEANING AND THE PROBLEM OF A GLOBALIZED LEGAL ORDER

......

JAN ENGBERG

12.1 INTRODUCTORY REMARKS

GLOBALIZATION is a central condition in the life of people and companies of today. With it comes the call for some type of globalization of legal orders, especially in the field of business. A number of such attempts have been carried out in different settings and with different degrees of formalization, power, etc. A prominent example is, of course, the highly institutionalized concept of European Union (EU) law with the European Court of Justice (ECJ) playing a systematic role in the interplay between national and communitarian levels of legal organization. But a number of other institutions exist, especially under the auspices of the United Nations (UN), with less institutionalization, but also with the goal of solving problems at an international level and on the basis of a consistent body of their own legal concepts, based again on a consistent system of rulings and/ or rules or treaties.

The degree of institutionalization is not the only criterion for measuring efforts to establish an international legal order. A second relevant criterion is the position of a legal regime to multilingualism. Some systems work with a high degree of multilingualism (e.g. the EU, whose governing documents are formulated in 23 original language versions), whereas other multinational systems (e.g. the Study Group on a European Civil Code) work with only one language, often English. No matter which language approach is taken, whenever we have a globalized legal order, language matters. When cooperation is necessary between people with different mother tongues, some kind of translation or transposition from one language to the other will have to take place. In this chapter, I will concentrate on the way we conceptualize the meaning of words in the context of a globalized, supranational legal order.

In the last part of the chapter, I will elaborate on examples of different types of attempts to form a globalized legal order as mentioned above, and review them in the light of the legal linguistic backdrop against which they exist. I will start, however, by giving an overview of the impact of language, and especially of word meaning, on the problems arising in a globalized legal order. Different approaches to the description of word meaning in (multilingual) law will be presented together with their different takes on the problem.

12.2 BASIC VIEWS OF WORD MEANING

12.2.1 Legal terms as signs

The main challenge to setting up a globalized legal order is overcoming the language problem and solving the subsequent methodological problems. Problems arise in the interaction between language(s) and law in the ascription of meaning to legal words or terms. One problem lies in modeling how the meaning comes about in such an interaction. Another equally central problem lies in conceptualizing the basis of this meaning-creation process. In this section, I will first present a semiotic approach relevant for modeling the first problem. Subsequently, two basic ways to look at the meaning creation process and their different consequences for positions towards globalized legal orders will be presented.

The result of interaction between language(s) and law may be modeled in the form of signs. Following Peirce (e.g. the Peirce Edition Project 1998:478), a sign consists of a triadic relation involving a material entity (here: a word), a meant entity (here: the legal concept) and an interpretant, a meaning ascribed through an interpretive process relating the material entity to the meant entity and thus giving the sign a meaning in actual communication (Poon Wai-Yee 2005:308). This interpretant is created by the receiver on the basis of (not exclusively, but mainly) stored knowledge of conventional relations between the material and the meant entities within the language in which the sign is used. That the relations are conventional means that they are shared with other speakers of the same language. From this it is clear that interpretants (= meanings in communication) emerge from commonalities between the bases on which the receivers relate the two entities and between the access of each receiver to the same meant entity, that is what and how much the receiver knows about the meant entity. When the communicators share the same language, the process is less complicated, as they then share the same knowledge of conventional relations, at least to a relatively high degree. In a globalized and multilingual legal order, the process gets more complicated.

Legal argumentation and legal decision-making (court judgments) as a communicative activity is basically a process of semiosis, viz. a communicative struggle for assessing the exact interpretant to be applied in the communication about a certain case or in doc-trinal discussions about a concept (a meant entity). This struggle, in turn, influences the content of the meant entity (Poon Wai-Yee 2005:311). Raw material for this semiosis comes from statutes, from doctrine (whether accepted or disputed), and from the ongo-ing discussions in the community of legal specialists. What the concept of 'theft', for example, exactly involves is subject to discussion among (groups of) specialists, who are basically attempting to decide what may be subsumed under the meant entity related to the material entity (the word) 'theft', that is what interpretant should be ascribed to the sign. In a national setting, this is normally done with recourse to words and sentences in the monolingual text of a statute. In a globalized legal order, however, such recourse will often be more difficult because of the number of languages involved, which may result from the multilingual nature of the authoritative texts or from the actors in the process belonging to different nationalities and thus not sharing a common linguistic heritage. Whatever the source of the problem, the semiotic process gets more difficult.

12.2.2 Decisive factors for ascribing the interpretant

The second complex of problems is concerned with the basis for ascribing an interpre-tant in the semiotic process. The literature relating to this issue demonstrates a basic distinction between a strong and a weak language theory (Christensen and Sokolowski 2002). This distinction takes as its point of departure the fact that language is a collective and an individual entity at the same time. A language may be seen as a system of signs underlying the communicative activity of members of a (national) speech community. At the same time, a language is represented in individualized formats in the minds of the individuals belonging to this speech community and actually only exists in this form. The language as a collective system is an abstraction only accessible through the obser-vation of the activities of a considerable number of individuals. Depending on the choice of the pole on which the emphasis is put, authors may be said to follow a strong or a weak language theory, respectively:

- Proponents of *a strong language theory* emphasize the collective nature of lan-guage. They see the relation between linguistic elements and their meaning as being stable and basically objective in the sense that it is independent of the actual communicative activity of individuals. Any language as a collective entity governs the way speakers of this language can think and what the words of this language can mean. Thus, if we want to find out what a word in a language means, a sensible solution is to go to some type of centralized source (often a normative dictionary) and look it up. In the context of debates over a globalized legal order, the conse-quence of having a strong language theory is that such an order can hardly be anything but monolingual. A multilingual approach like the one followed by the EU, for example, is virtually impossible from this point of view. For according to the strong language theory, in such an approach a number of equally stable and fixed relations, which are not compatible, will clash as every language tends to characterize the world differently, which, for example, makes automated translation a difficult task. The approach lays much weight on a strict division between language as use (*parole*) and language as a system of rules (*langue*) and sees the latter as the prime factor in the semiosis process and as a collective entity that may not be directly influenced by the individual speakers.

- The *weak language theory* approach, on the other hand, lays more weight on the individual side of a language, on the importance of the *parole*. The communicative experiences and activities of these individuals are of major importance, as each individual experience will possibly have an impact on the 'copy' of the language system present in the mind of the individual. And the individual will use this copy in subsequent communicative interaction and thus has at least the potential to influence the 'copy' of other individuals and thus gradually adjust the collective system, which is seen as inherently unstable and subject to constructions by the individuals. In such an approach, multilingual globalized legal orders are possible in the form of convergence between conventional relations of material entities and meant entities across languages. The primary prerequisite is that there are communicative instances in which communicators may engage with each other and build up experiences, which they will have recourse to in subsequent communicative instances and thus in subsequent semiotic processes.

We thus have a basic dichotomy between, on the one hand, a collective and systematic approach and, on the other hand, an individualistic and constructivist approach. I take the two positions mentioned here to be the two ends of a scale, with the possibility of positioning oneself closer to one end or the other. In the following, I will present work by different authors as examples of positions on this scale.

12.3   APPROACHES TO WORD MEANING AND MULTINATIONAL LAW

12.3.1   Proponents of a strong language theory

One of the most prolific proponents of a strong language theory in the discussions of the globalized legal order of the EU is Pierre Legrand (e.g. Legrand 2008). His basic position, laid out in many publications over the years, is that the emergence of new legal concepts through the convergence of different conceptualizations is not possible because the underlying languages are incompatible.

Another proponent is Petra Braselmann (e.g. Braselmann 1991). Her point of view is that the ways different languages conceptualize meaning, especially at the lexical level, are not in accordance with each other, and that these differences make convergence impossible as a natural process. Instead, different language versions of a text will be inherently inequivalent, and convergence will be possible only if it is imposed by an authoritative institution like the European Court of Justice.

The work of Irene Baron (e.g. Baron 2003) points in the same direction. Her basic assumption is that the way a language structures the world, especially at the basic syntactic level, determines the way we think. She shows a convergence between basic traits of the structure of Danish and French, respectively, and the basic traits of the different types of legal reasoning of these legal cultures. From this evidence she concludes that convergence is going to be very difficult, as there are deeply rooted and almost insurmountable differences in the underlying cultures.

The common denominator of these approaches is that they see languages and their structural aspects at lexical and/or deeper typological levels as so deeply rooted in cultures that they prevent people from understanding each other at deeper levels across linguistic barriers. Language is thus viewed as a barrier, and one which is in principle insurmountable. Proponents of this position see language as a system predominantly detached from the communicative activities among language users (Kjær 2008b:154). They seem to presuppose that language users are not able to change their linguistic behaviors, but are bound to see the world in the way their language requires them to. On the scale mentioned above, I would say that Legrand has to be positioned at one pole of the scale indicating the strongest language theory, as he sees the ties between language, culture, and understanding as so strong that they make convergence utterly impossible. Baron seems to be close to this position, as her arguments work on basic typological traits of languages, whereas Braselmann mainly argues on the basis of differences at the lexical level. But they all seem to agree on a conception of word meaning as quite stable and not subject to substantial change through communicative practices.

12.3.2 Proponents of weak language theory

As stated above, approaches subsumable under this basic position share an emphasis on individuals' communicative activity in semiotic processes. The main challenge for weak language theories is not to explain the development of meaning over time, as already shown in Section 12.2.2, but to explain why this development does not proceed more rapidly than it does in actual fact. The approaches discussed below have been categorized according to the different mechanisms they set up in order to describe the observable stability.

The first type of approach illustrated here relies on the language system, although it takes a weak language position. Viktor Smith's work (e.g. Smith 2003) exemplifies this position. In some respect, he takes a similar approach as those of Braselmann and Baron, discussed above, but reaches a different conclusion. His point of departure, based on the standpoint of Jakobson (1959), is first to distinguish culture from language. Secondly, he proposes that languages force their users to make specific distinctions at syntactic and at lexical levels, but these distinctions do not influence what the language user may conceptualize or express in more general terms (as opposed to a strong language theory position). This approach is mainly based upon taking seriously the distinction between linguistic practice (*parole*) and linguistic system (*langue*), and giving the practice a more important role in actual communication than the system. In his view, the lexicon as the systematic repository of word meanings is generally flexible and subject to changes in practice.

One of his examples is the introduction of the concept of *trust* from English common law into the civil law systems in Germany and France. The trust is foreign to these systems, but has been introduced due to specific legal advantages that made the concept relevant for legal purposes in these jurisdictions, too. So in his view of the language system, communicative practice may influence the system, especially the lexicon, and thus introduce foreign concepts. However, not everything may blend in equally easily. According to his position, concepts mainly relevant for specialized communication in legal settings (like *trust*) are more likely to be accepted into a system than concepts with general relevance in a national culture (like *marriage* including the possibility that the spouses are the same sex). But again, this is not due to linguistic prerequisites, but to deeply rooted cultural views that must be addressed directly, if one wants to change them.

Other propagators of a weak language approach use the characteristics and powers of discourse not only as their motor of development and convergence, but as stabilizers of the process. Examples of this approach to word meaning in a supranational legal order are the works by Anne Lise Kjær and Edda Weigand (e.g. Kjær 2003, 2004; Weigand 2008). The basic approach is that meanings in communication are dependent on the discourses in which they occur, that is they are part of ongoing dialogues. Weigand in particular stresses the basic dialogical character of language and especially of meaning.[1]

The basic idea is that any communicative system is bound to be in a process of constant change, as it is involved in actions where it has to react to impulses from outside the system itself. Legal meaning systems, national as well as supranational, are no exception: The meanings of legal concepts inside the system are subject to legal argumentation outside of it, where the meanings are debated, and the system has to react to these external realities.

This type of discursive action in dialogue is the factor leading to the potential development of system-internal states, like the meanings of legal concepts. The drift towards achieving mutual understanding, especially as described by Gadamer (1960), is the stabilizing factor. Rationality in ascribing meaning in dialogue convergence motivates mutual understanding, which becomes possible if the overlaps between the legal cultures involved are big enough to allow it, as Kjær (2003, 2004) and Weigand (2008) state to be the case in the EU multilingual and supranational legal order. Thus, in this view convergence is not guaranteed, but it is possible, given the right conditions, especially a

---

[1] Central background theories are Luhmann's system theory (e.g. Luhmann 1993), Habermas' theory of communicative action (e.g. Habermas 1981), and Gadamer's theory of understanding in dialogue based on global conceptions of rationality (e.g. Gadamer 1960).

willingness to engage in communicative dialogue and to seek mutual understanding. The main prerequisite is the creation of a discourse community of legal specialists communicating across differences in language. This enables gradual convergence, and thus the development of common word meanings becomes possible (e.g. Weigand 2008:248ff.). Nonetheless, difficulties remain because the different language systems have their roots in different national legal discourse communities. So this approach shares the caveats of the language system approach mentioned by Smith.

López-Rodrígez (2004:1208; 1214ff.) argues in the same direction, focusing upon the necessity of a common legal discourse community in order to achieve a common culture or background upon which to interpret words. In her view, legal research and legal education oriented towards common European questions, the development of a common legal method, and the acceptance of a (limited) number of different languages in which to express the law are the important factors in achieving the necessary dynamics and stability at the same time.

One final way of propagating a weak language theory and to seek instigators and stabilizers of development and convergence is to take as the point of departure relevant characteristics of human cognition. Solan (2009) investigates what he calls the Augustinian interpretation used in the European Court of Justice. He hints at the fact mentioned in my introduction that in a supranational legal order there may not be an actual basic text from which to start legal argumentation, as there is in monolingual national legal orders. Thus, we cannot necessarily go back to one underlying formulation and engage in interpretation (= the ascription of an interpretant) on the basis of a single text. Instead, it is necessary to look at a number of different language versions and try to interpret the meaning underlying these different versions, much the same way as this was done by the Christian church father Augustine when interpreting the Bible (hence the expression "Augustinian interpretation").[2] This works, according to Solan, because human beings have the capacity to form similar concepts from similar experiences. So in his view, what Chomsky has termed our "innate language faculty" enables us to understand each other and creates some stability in word meaning even under the necessary assumption of a weak language theory.

Along the same lines, but without recourse to the Chomskyan assumptions, I have suggested that the so-called "Theory of Mind" ability of humans (Engberg 2009) or the general network structure of the mind (Engberg 2004) explains the relative stability of word meanings in law in general and in supranational or globalized legal orders in particular. The defining factor of this group of approaches is that stabilization of meaning is sought in some characteristic of human cognition.

The state of affairs that Solan terms the Augustinian interpretation (i.e. the fact that in a multilingual legal order meaning is ascribed to legal concepts in a process based not on the formulations of one underlying text, but through a process of mediating between a

---

[2] Burr and Gallas (2004:221–5) describe this state of affairs as a kind of solely intertextual meaning, i.e. meaning that only occurs through the interplay of a number of texts.

number of different texts in different languages) has also been observed by translation scholars. Schäffner, for example, adheres to a weak language theory position. She describes the production process of a (non-official) EU document, which is drafted simultaneously in four languages and then translated into the rest of the EU languages:

> Since each of the four working languages had a role to play in setting up the final version of the [text], actually none of them can legitimately be called a source language. Equally, there was not one particular version of the copies in the working languages that served as a source text for the translations into the other EU language. (Schäffner 1997:194)

Similarly, Kjær (2007) suggests that a specialized theory of translation must be developed in order to account for the characteristics of translation in the framework of the EU as a supranational legal order. She observes that meaning must be ascribed first in a competition between the meanings of words from one language in the national context and meanings in the supranational context (as it is often not possible to coin fully new expressions for concepts at the supranational level), and secondly from the fact that the actual meaning of a statutory text in the EU system is ascribed teleologically on the basis of readings of the different language versions. Describing the process from this weak language theory position presupposes the establishment of a new theory of translation in her view.

By way of conclusion, it is difficult to demonstrate empirically which of the two types of language theory is best in terms of the realities of language and communication. Many propagators of a weak language theory (e.g. Smith and Kjær) state that the propagators of a strong language theory are too skeptical about what is communicated in actual instances of interlingual communication among legal experts, or in instances of converging legal concepts across languages and jurisdictions. It seems demonstrable that over time convergence is possible, and not just through judicial intervention. On the other hand, propagators of a strong language theory are right in pointing to language problems as important in specific instances of communication. So differences lie in both the perspective chosen (synchronic versus diachronic), and in one's ideology concerning supranational legal orders. The question remains: Is law necessarily tied to a national jurisdiction and its national culture, or is it possible to also have law at a supranational level, without direct recourse to any one national culture?

12.4 ATTEMPTS AT GLOBALIZED LEGAL ORDERS

In the light of the deliberations so far, it is clear that when attempting to achieve a globalized legal order it is essential to guarantee a common basis of interpretation across languages and cultures in order to make the semiotic process work in a satisfactory way. In this last section of my chapter, I will present four different approaches that have been chosen as designs for globalized legal orders and show the respective importance of the factors discussed above.

12.4.1 A common code

Within the framework of the EU, a number of different projects have been started to facilitate the development of a common private law system, which would be helpful in further developing commercial transactions inside the Union and across national borders. An example with relevance for this chapter is the so-called "Study Group on a European Civil Code."[3] The main aim of this group is as follows:

> The aim of the Study Group is to produce a set of codified principles for the core areas of European private law (patrimonial law). Although the foundation for our work is detailed comparative law research, the principles which we are fashioning will represent more than a mere restatement of the existing law in the various EU jurisdictions from the standpoint of the predominant trends among the diverse legal regimes. Instead the Study Group seeks to formulate principles which constitute the most suitable private law rules for Europe-wide application.[4]

As the quoted material indicates, the idea behind the initiative is to draft a set of legal rules that may function as a basis for further discussions on the road to an actual and official common European civil code. The first texts for such a code have been published on the Study Group's website. For our purposes, the interesting thing is that the Study Group has chosen a format in which a number of working teams and advisors from different countries are working on drafts of different parts of the code. These drafts are formulated in English and are subject to further discussion at larger meetings. The result is an English text which has been subject to discursive development by people from many different countries and legal systems, speaking a number of different languages, but communicating in English. So the common basis for creating the interpretant for the legal terms is created discursively in a large group of legal specialists and then formulated in one common language, viz. in English. This results in a formulation of the law in one language with the ambition of spanning a supranational system of legal concepts. Although the formulations are in English, they are based on discussed input from a high number of languages and legal systems. This unifying approach may overcome the problems pointed out by propagators of a strong language theory, as the linguistic basis is monolingual.[5] However, this type of development is exactly what they warn against: The hegemony of one legal culture (here: the Anglo-Saxon) over the rest due to the imposition of one language. The weak language position instead relies on communicative interaction to prevent hegemonic developments.

---

[3] <http://www.sgecc.net/pages/en/home/index.htm>, last accessed August 27, 2011.

[4] <http://www.sgecc.net/pages/en/introduction/100.aims.htm>, last accessed August 27, 2011.

[5] Another project with a similar goal, but a different approach is the Common Core Project (<http://jus.unitn.it/dsg/common-core/approach.html>, last accessed August 27, 2011). The idea here is to create a map of similarities and differences between the national rules in the field of contract law, but without setting up a unified code. Thus, the project is just thought of as creating a common basis for semiosis, not suggesting actual mono- or multilingual signs.

12.4.2 Model laws

Another way of achieving a mutual basis for ascribing meaning to words in a globalized legal order is to establish so-called "model laws." An example is the set of statutory regulations suggested by the United Nations Commission on International Trade Law (UNCITRAL) for conducting international commercial arbitration. In 1985, the UN General Assembly adopted a model law for this field (amended in 2006), that is a text that governments can use as a basis for introducing or reforming national statutory regulations in order to assure that the national regulations are in accordance with the evolving international legal order in this field. The model law is formulated in English and is the result of ongoing discussions in the Commission. The amended version of 2006, among other things, reflects developments in contractual practice since the adoption of the original version. The idea behind this approach is to have a basic text written in one language and reflecting the knowledge and insights of global experts of the field and the practice in this field. This text can then be used to create national versions in the official language(s) of a national jurisdiction, which reflect the national systems and national choices, but are interpreted in the light of the basic text. Interpretants for words in different languages are thus constructed by recourse to the same root, but are at the same time embedded in a national context. This state of affairs is normally signaled by stating (e.g. in the *travaux préparatoires*) that the national statute is an instantiation of the model law. Like the common code approach discussed in Section 12.4.1, this approach is possible under the assumptions of a strong language theory, as it respects the idea of the link between language and legal culture. In contrast to the common code approach, it meets the hegemonic problem by giving power to the national legal cultures and their expressions.

12.4.3 A restricted number of official languages

Another type of effort to secure a mutual basis for the semiosis, also applied by the UN, is to work with a limited number of authorized language versions of a single instrument (Cao and Zhao 2008). This is the system adopted in UN Treaties. The UN works with six official languages (Arabic, Chinese, English, French, Russian, and Spanish).[6] In actual fact, there seems to be a tendency to work mainly on the basis of the English and the French versions of the text in the International Court of Justice (Šarčević 1997:218; see also Chapter 14), and English seems to be accepted at least covertly as the main working language of the UN (Phillipson 1999:35). However, according to the Vienna Convention on the Law of Treaties, in treaties authenticated in two or more languages "the text is equally authoritative in each language...". This principle is adhered to officially within

---

[6] <http://www.un.org/en/aboutun/languages.shtml> accessed September 29, 2011.

the UN system (Vienna Convention on the Law of Treaties, Art. 33 (1); Šarčević 1997:199). Thus, at least in principle, UN treaties are multilingual, for which reason they are always issued simultaneously.

Apart from the authenticated language versions, official translations may be produced by the Member States. These will have a weaker status than authenticated versions, as they may function only as guidance in the interpretation of the authenticated versions. The translations can help clarify indeterminacies, but the central, multilingual text is the decisive one. The mutual basis for the semiosis is thus a central text formulated in six languages (probably with the English as *primo inter pares* for all practical purposes). In order to assess the meaning of, for example a word in the official Danish translation of a treaty, the basis is the multilingual text. The multilingual character of the mutual basis in this model makes it incompatible with the assumptions of a strong language theory, whereas it poses no problems in principle for a weak language theory.

12.4.4 Authoritativeness of all languages involved

One last way of setting up a globalized legal order is to establish a supranational and multilingual system, as has been done in the EU. Here, we see a system of (currently) 23 different language versions of the basic documents on which legal interpretants draw. Each version has the status of an original. Consequently, in principle, the mutual basis for the semiotic process is performed on the basis of 23 different language versions and not on the basis of any monolingual official text with a privileged position. In order to solve problems resulting from the different bases of the meaning ascription, the EU has created an institution with a privileged status, that is the European Court of Justice, which adheres to the Augustinian principle of interpretation mentioned above. Again, the radical multilingual approach taken here is incompatible with the assumptions of a strong language theory, whereas it is in full accordance with the assumptions of the power of discourse in the weak language theory.[7]

12.5 CONCLUDING REMARKS

In this chapter, I have attempted to give an overview of positions and approaches to describing the role of word meaning in the context of globalized legal orders, as they have been planned and tested in the last decades. There is general agreement in principle about the attractiveness of such supranational orders, but as I have shown,

---

[7] Luttermann (2009) follows the ideas of a weak language theory, but suggests a distinction between two reference languages, chosen on democratic principles, and a number of mother tongue languages (the rest of the official EU languages) in order to enhance the practical viability of the EU language regime.

differences concerning the role of language as a system in the process of creating an interpretant and concerning the link between language and (national) culture are important for any assessment of the success of such a venture. I consider it an important task for scholars of legal linguistics to monitor and model the semiotic processes in the different attempts at globalized legal orders established over the years. The linguistic approaches described in this chapter can be seen as relevant candidates for such a task.

CHAPTER 13

CHALLENGES TO THE LEGAL TRANSLATOR

SUSAN ŠARČEVIĆ

13.1 LEGAL TRANSLATION: POSSIBLE BUT NOT PERFECT

ON behalf of comparativists Rudolf Schlesinger admits, "Translation difficulties are a prolific source of confusion" (Schlesinger et al. 1998:478). Regarding law as culture, Pierre Legrand goes a step further by denying the translatability of law; however, he deliberately avoids addressing the matter of "legal translation, that is, the actual translation of legal texts" (2005:44, n. 3). J. B. White has called legal translation "the art of facing the impossible, of confronting unbridgeable discontinuities between texts, between languages and between people," yet he stops short of denying the possibility of translation (1994:257). Focusing on the link between law, language, and culture, he reminds us that legal translation is a "necessarily imperfect process" (2005:61).

Despite its imperfections, the need for legal translation has steadily increased over the centuries, as has the variety of text types translated for normative, informative, or judicial purposes. Today, hundreds of thousands of pages of legal translations are churned out daily across the globe, confirming that legal translation plays a significant role in our age of globalization where the mobility of persons, goods, services, and capital across borders has changed the dynamics of law, forcing legal professionals to communicate in a wide variety of multilingual and multicultural settings. As a vital part of this process, legal translation is regarded as an act of communication across legal, language, and cultural barriers enabling the law to function in more than one language at national, international, and supranational levels.

This chapter focuses on challenges to the legal translator caused by the inherent incongruity of legal systems, cultures, and languages. At the same time it attempts to "demystify" the "miracle" of legal translation (cf. Kjær 2008a:69), showing how skilled translators with legal expertise and cultural sensitivity use language effectively to compensate for conceptual incongruity by creating "terminological bridges" (Weigand 2008:248). Following the introductory remarks, the second section presents some of the basics of legal translation with the main emphasis on the special nature of legal texts, their function, and degree of accuracy required to achieve intercultural communication for various purposes. Unable to deal with all aspects of legal translation, the third section is limited to terminological problems in legally binding instruments. Like comparativists, translators need to use methods of comparative law in their search for potential equivalents and to test their adequacy by comparative conceptual analysis. In light of the imperfections of legal translation, the fourth and final section raises considerations about the effectiveness of multilingualism.

13.2 BASICS OF LEGAL TRANSLATION

Legal translation is an interdisciplinary field involving languages, translation studies, and law, especially comparative law, interpretation of law, and legal drafting. Comparative lawyers have long regarded legal translation as a dual operation consisting of both legal and interlingual transfer between different legal systems, in which the main operation is legal in nature (Constantinesco 1974:147). Today, as in general translation, greater attention is devoted to the cultural aspects of legal translation, which is now regarded as a "transcultural venture" (Várady 2006:4) in which the translator's task is to achieve cross-cultural transfer (Pommer 2006; Sandrini 1999, 2009). Adding the cultural element to de Groot's formula for assessing the difficulty of a translation (1992:293), it can be said that the difficulty (and also the degree of translatability) of a given legal text depends primarily on the extent to which the source and target legal systems and their cultural traditions are related and secondarily on the similarity of the source and target languages. According to these criteria, in my opinion, the most formidable translation task with the lowest degree of translatability is the translation of the English common law statutes and case law of Hong Kong into Chinese. Nonetheless, after years of struggling with seemingly insurmountable translation difficulties (see Sin 1998), the Hong Kong Department of Justice[1] has succeeded not only in improving the quality of the Chinese translations but also in establishing an impressive system of legal bilingualism, inspired partly by the Canadian model.

The Canadians deserve credit as the avant-gardes of legal translation in both practice and research (Gémar 1982, 1995). Under mounting pressure to implement equal language rights, the Canadian federal government launched a language reform in the 1970s which later 'revolutionized' translation methods resulting in the introduction of co-drafting, a form of simultaneous text production that goes beyond traditional

---

[1] See *Legislative Drafting in Hong Kong* (2nd edn), 2001, at <www.doj.gov.hk/eng/public/pdf/ldhkv2e. pdf>, last accessed August 27, 2011.

translation (see Šarčević 2005). The growing demand for skilled legal translators world-wide (especially in the European Union) has been accompanied by a sharp increase in the number of scholarly publications by both lawyers and linguists, most of which focus on terminological issues, translation between specific languages and legal systems, or translation of certain text types. As Gémar points out (1995), there is a difference between "translating law" and "translating texts." The translator's task is to translate texts anchored in a specific legal context and intended for a specific purpose. Attempts to provide a systematic approach to the translation of legal texts and the problems con-fronted by legal translators are found in works by Gémar (1995), Šarčević (2000), Alcaraz Varó and Hughes (2002), and Cao (2007b). Publications dealing with transla-tion in the European Union are not mentioned here as this is the subject of the next chapter.

13.2.1 Special nature of legal texts

Legal translation belongs to the branch of translation studies known as specialized translation, which encompasses specialist subjects such as medicine, economics, law, and others (see Gotti and Šarčević 2006). Due to the special nature of law, legal lan-guages, and legal texts, legal translation is generally recognized as the most complex and demanding of all areas of specialized translation (Cao 2007b:85). The subject mat-ter and language of legal texts are complex and often highly technical, thus requiring translators to possess not only language proficiency but also considerable specialist knowledge of both the source and target legal systems. In addition, legal texts differ from other texts for special purposes in their communicative function, a fact often overlooked by linguists. Based on the bipartite system of languages in legal theory, legal texts can be divided into three groups depending on whether their communicative function is primarily prescriptive, primarily descriptive but also prescriptive, or purely descriptive.

Legal texts whose communicative function is primarily prescriptive include legisla-tive texts such as laws and regulations, codes, treaties, and conventions. Such texts are normative instruments containing legally binding rules of conduct which prescribe a specific course of action that an individual ought to conform to or, failing to do so, will be subject to sanction (Kelsen 1979). In legal theory it is generally agreed that normative instruments prescribe how the members of a given society shall act (command), refrain from acting (prohibition), or may act (permission). In addition, legal rules confer pow-ers and/or grant rights (Van Hoecke 2002:94, 101; cf. Cornu (2005) 2000:268). As legally binding agreements giving rise to rights and obligations, contracts also have a primarily prescriptive function.

The second group of legal texts consists of hybrid texts that are primarily descriptive but may also contain prescriptive parts. These include judicial decisions and litigation documents used to carry on judicial and administrative proceedings such as *trials*, pleadings, briefs, appeals, as well as documents used as evidence such as witness statements, expert reports, records, and certificates. Wills also fall into this category. The third group includes purely descriptive texts constituting legal scholarship such as law textbooks, commentaries, and articles written by legal scholars, the authority of which varies in different legal systems.

13.2.2 Role of *skopos* in legal translation

As in general translation, the legal translator should take account not only of the text type and its function but also of the communicative purpose (*skopos*) of the translation, as well as the legal systems involved and other legal factors of the particular communicative situation. As Vermeer emphasizes, there may be a shift of *skopos*, that is the communicative purpose of the target text may differ from that of the source text, as a result of which the same text may be translated in different ways (Reiss and Vermeer 1984:101). The importance of *skopos* in legal translation was recognized long ago by Schlesinger when he remarked in 1950, "A translation may be good enough for one purpose, and not sufficiently accurate for another" (cited in Megale 2008:7). A lawyer with a degree in translation studies, Pommer confirms that the degree of accuracy and reliability required for a given legal translation is determined by its *skopos* (2006:59).

In legal translation the communicative purpose of a translation if often determined by whether it is authoritative (having the force of law) or non-authoritative (without the force of law). Authoritative translations of normative instruments have been authenticated in the manner prescribed by law and have the status of authentic texts. For instance, the Swiss Civil Code was originally drafted in German (*Schweizerisches Zivilgesetzbuch–ZGB*)[2] and translated into French (*Code civil suisse*), and Italian (*Codice civile svizzero*). All three language versions were enacted by the Swiss Federal Assembly and are equally authentic for the purpose of interpretation. The product of equal language rights, the principle of equal authenticity is based on the theory of original texts, according to which all the language versions of a single instrument (called parallel texts) are treated as 'originals' and thus are not referred to as translations. In plurilingual jurisdictions at the national (or regional) level (Canada, Hong Kong, Belgium, Finland, Spain, South Africa, India), in international organizations (UN, UNIDROIT, UNCITRAL, WTO) and in supranational organizations (European Union), the translation of equally authentic texts has developed into a sophisticated process of multilingual text production for normative purposes. Translations of authentic texts of a legally binding instrument require the highest possible degree of accuracy and legal reliability, making them the most restrictive of all legal translations.

On the other hand, the main concern of comparativists is the translation of legal texts for informational purposes (see de Groot 2006:423). For example, to inform foreign

---

[2] SR 210 Schweizerisches Zivilgesetzbuch, at <www.admin.ch/ch/d/sr/210/index.html> last accessed August 27, 2011.

lawyers about Swiss law, the ZGB has been translated into English.[3] The English versions are, of course, non-authentic and as such are intended for information only, thus giving the translators greater freedom, including the opportunity to explain concepts of Swiss law in footnotes and a lengthy commentary. Nonetheless, translations of normative texts for informational purposes should be as accurate and effective as possible. This is particularly important in light of the increasing use of foreign law as evidence in cross-border litigation and international commercial arbitration. For instance, a foreign judge who is required to apply Swiss law and needs information on certain rules of the ZGB is likely to use the new English translation or request the Swiss authorities or an accredited translator to provide a certified translation in English or another language. In the latter situation, it would be clear that the requested translation is to be used for judicial purposes; however, this is frequently not the case. As a precautionary measure, publishers of non-authoritative translations of laws sometimes include a disclaimer freeing them from liability for possible translation errors.

Other texts translated primarily for information may also be used as documentary evidence for establishing facts in court proceedings, hence for judicial purposes. According to Cao, this includes "legal documents such as statements of claims or pleadings, contracts and agreements, and ordinary texts such as business or personal correspondence, records and certificates, witness statements and expert reports" (2007b:11). To this we can add translations of academic works (legal scholarship) and case law, either of which may be used by common law judges when interpreting questions of foreign law (see examples in Domijan-Arneri 2009:353). Since the accuracy and reliability of translated court documents are generally assessed by the degree to which the translation is a mirror image of the original text, sworn translators are required to reproduce the words and form of the original as closely as possible, as a result of which their translations are source-language oriented.

13.2.3 Goal of translators of legally binding instruments

For centuries the primary task of legal translators was to preserve the letter and form of the original by "faithfully" reproducing the words and even syntax as closely as possible, often resulting in a translation that could be "understood" only by reference to the source text. Gradually allowances were made for basic grammar and syntax of the target language; however, all forms of legal translation remained firmly under the grip of literal translation until the twentieth century, when "dissident" translators began to demand equal language rights for lesser-used official languages. When accused of heresy for his

[3] The Swiss Civil Code, first translated by R. P. Shick, annotated by C. Wetherill, corrected and revised by E. Huber (author of German original), A. Siegwart and G. Sherman, Boston: The Boston Book Company, 1915. Later translation by I. Williams, Oxford University Press, 1925; updated and reprinted by ReMaK Verlag Zurich, 1976; new translation by CLS Communication AG, published in M. Amstutz *et al.* (eds), *Handkommentar zum Schweizer Privatrecht*, Schultess: Zurich, 2007.

"liberal" translation of the Swiss ZGB into French in 1907, Professor Rossel insisted that the francophone population of Switzerland had the right to have their code written in "natural" French, thus triggering the debate on the dichotomy between letter and spirit in legal translation (see Šarčević 2000:36–40). Today translators of legally binding instruments are generally allowed to reconstruct the target text in the spirit of the target language, provided the substance remains unaltered. However, the degree of interlingual concordance between the parallel texts of a single instrument varies considerably from jurisdiction to jurisdiction.[4]

Today equal authenticity is a fundamental principle of multilingualism, according to which all authentic texts of a single instrument are deemed to be of equal authority, as a result of which no text shall prevail in the event of a divergence between the parallel texts. While plurilingual jurisdictions at national level (such as Switzerland and Canada) had adopted the principle of equal authenticity at an early date (see Šarčević 2005), it became the general rule in international law by virtue of Article 33(1) of the Convention on the Law of Treaties of 1969.[5] Since multilingual communication in the law can be effective only if the persons affected by a piece of legislation are guaranteed equality before the law in all language versions, all authentic texts of a single instrument are presumed to have the same meaning (Art. 33(3)). Furthermore, this is presumed to be the "true" meaning, that is the meaning intended by the source text producers (States signatories, lawmakers, contracting parties). Lawyers, however, are the first to admit that diversity of meaning is inevitable in the parallel texts of a single instrument, thus reducing the presumption of equal meaning to a fiction (Kuner 1991:958). Going a step further, it is generally agreed that all legal translation is at best approximation (cf. Gémar 1995:154; 2006:77).

Although it is impossible for translators to produce texts with equal meaning, authoritative translations of legally binding instruments are expected to be as accurate as possible and, above all, legally reliable, that is produce the same legal effects in practice. As confirmed by L.-P. Pigeon, late Justice of the Supreme Court of Canada, it is the results that count in legal translation (1982:281). In essence, this is what Beaupré meant when he mentioned legal equivalence in his excellent book *Interpreting Bilingual Legislation*, but he failed to define the term (1986:179). Similarly, Gémar mentions legal equivalence without defining it. In his opinion, translators with no legal training strive for "linguistic equivalence, lawyers for legal equivalence." While he pleads for a "harmonious fusion" of linguistic and legal equivalence, Gémar recognizes that the basic problems of legal translation are legal in nature (2006:76). Accordingly, the translator's main task is to achieve legal equivalence. For our purpose, legal equivalence can be regarded as a synthesis of

---

[4] While stylistic diversity is encouraged in the parallel texts of Canadian federal legislation, Swiss translators of federal legislation are advised to give priority to interlingual concordance and to refrain from altering the length of sentences. Translators of instruments of international law are instructed to strive for a high degree of interlingual concordance, which is often considered the yardstick for measuring the reliability of multilingual instruments.

[5] UN *Treaty Series*, vol. 1155, p. 331.

content, intent, and legal effect, with the main emphasis on legal effect. The importance of achieving legal equivalence is confirmed by Schroth, who stresses that the translator must be able "to understand not only what the words mean and what a sentence means, but also what legal effect it is supposed to have, and know how to achieve that legal effect in the other language" (1986:55–6). This is undoubtedly one of the most serious matters to be considered by translators in their decision-making process.

13.3 INCONGRUITY OF LEGAL SYSTEMS, CULTURES, AND LANGUAGES

Unlike texts of the exact sciences, legal texts do not have a single agreed meaning independent of local context but usually derive their meaning from a particular legal system. This is referred to as the *source* legal system, whereas the *target* legal system is the system (or systems) to which the target text receivers belong. In legal communication a distinction is made between indirect receivers, the persons affected by a piece of legislation, and direct receivers, lawyers who interpret and apply the law, especially judges (Kelsen 1979:34; cf. Van Hoecke 2002:86). Since legal translation is primarily communication between specialists, the success of a legal translation is measured by its interpretation and application by the direct receivers, particularly by the judiciary of the target legal system(s). Perfect communication is said to occur in multilingualism when the parallel texts of a single instrument are interpreted and applied in the same manner by judges of the target legal system(s), thus achieving uniform interpretation and application of all language versions. While perfect communication is the goal, it is rarely, if ever, achieved in practice.

The chances of achieving perfect communication are greatest when the source and target legal systems are identical, that is when the communication process occurs within the same legal system, as in plurilingual states with one legal system, such as Switzerland, Belgium, and Finland. In such cases, the text producers and receivers share the same knowledge base (Swiss, Belgian, or Finnish law) and the terms in all authentic texts derive their meaning from a common conceptual system, thus greatly facilitating the translation process once the terminology has been standardized (cf. Šarčević 2000:15).

Most legal translations involve communication across different languages, cultures, and legal systems. This is the case in plurilingual states and regions with different legal systems or a mixed legal system, such as Canada, India, Sri Lanka, Israel, South Africa, and, more recently, China (Hong Kong and Macau), as well as translations of national legislation, court decisions, court documents, and law textbooks into foreign languages for informational or judicial purposes. As a supranational law, European law is sometimes regarded as an autonomous legal system (de Groot 1999:14); however, in reality it is still very much dependent on the national legal systems of the Member States. As in EU law, instruments of international law often contain technical terms which derive their meaning from a particular national legal system.

Despite the growing emphasis on the convergence of national legal systems, as well as attempts to create uniform international law and to harmonize law at the European level, law remains first and foremost a national phenomenon. Each national law has its own rules of classification, sources of law, methodological approaches, socio-economic principles, its own terminological apparatus, and underlying conceptual system, and thus its own legal language(s). Moreover, every legal system is embedded in a specific culture, which is a kind of gateway through which the translator must pass in order to gain genuine access to the ideas, traditions, thought patterns, institutions, and concepts of a given legal system. Although lawyers often refer to legal translation as a process of *transposition juridique* (Tallon 1995), due to differences in historical and cultural development, the elements of the source legal system cannot simply be 'transposed' into the target legal system. As a result, the greatest challenge to the legal translator is to use language effectively to bridge the incongruity of the different legal systems, cultures, and languages involved in a particular communication act.

13.3.1 Conceptual incongruity

At the heart of the problem is the lack of equivalence between corresponding concepts of different legal systems, making it extremely difficult and sometimes impossible to find an adequate equivalent in the target legal system for a given term in the source text. As in Hjelmsley's analysis (1953) of terminological incongruity in ordinary languages, it can be shown that the boundaries between the meanings of legal concepts are incongruent even in closely related legal systems within the continental civil law family. For example, the concept of *décision* in French law corresponds with two more specific concepts in German law (*Entscheidung* and *Beschluss*) and three in Dutch law (*beschikking, besluit, beslissing*). Although etymological equivalents such as *dettes* and *debts* or *contrat* and *contract* signify the same object, they are not identical at the conceptual level (Sacco 2005:14).

Moreover, within the same language term language, a single term sometimes designates different concepts in different legal systems. For instance, *domicile* has one meaning in English law and quite different meanings in American jurisdictions. Even basic terms such as *Besitz* and *Schaden* have different meanings in German and Austrian law and have been a source of litigation. Conversely, the same concept is sometimes designated by different terms in different jurisdictions having the same official language. For example, a preventive measure consisting of a *retención de bienes* is designated in various Spanish-speaking jurisdictions as *embargo, secuestro, retención, depósito, occupación, anotación preventiva*, and *comiso* (cited in Torres Carballal 1988:449).

In addition, all legal systems contain a number of system-bound terms (also referred to as culture-bound terms, Šarčević 1985:127) designating concepts and institutions peculiar to a particular legal reality and culture. Since no exact counterparts exist in other legal systems, such terms are often said to be untranslatable. In such cases, translators are forced to resort to linguistic equivalents, such as literal equivalents, borrowings, naturalizations, descriptive paraphrases, and other neologisms, in an attempt to partly convey the information content (details in Šarčević 1985:129–32; 2000:250–64; see also de Groot 1999:27–34; 2006:424–428). Generally speaking, the degree of actual transfer varies according to the cognition responses based on the receiver's existing knowledge. For instance, the civil law concept of *Direktklage* (Fr.) / *action directe* (Ger.) / *acción directo* (Sp.) / *azióne dirètto* (It.) does not exist in the common law, but the literal equivalent *direct action* is semantically motivated and thus transparent to common *law* lawyers. On the other hand, the civil law concept of *Geschäftsführung ohne Auftrag* (Ger.) / *gestion d'affaires* (Fr.) / *gestion de negocios* (Sp.) / *gestione di negozio* (It.) is "translated" into English by borrowing the original Latin term *negotiorum gestio*, thus requiring specialist knowledge on the part of the reader. Going the other way, the Anglo-American institution of *equity* is problematic for continental lawyers. In most cases, *equity* is a highly technical term referring to "the principles developed in the Court of Chancery" (Mattila 2006:251). However, it is often translated by the calques *équité* (fr), *equidad* (es), and *equità* (it), which are false friends misinterpreted as denoting the principles of fairness and reasonableness. In its technical sense, *equity* can be translated only by using an explanatory paraphrase. Therefore, Mattila advises continental lawyers to be cautious when signing international contracts with common law technical terms such as *equity*, *equitable remedies*, and *equitable rights* (Mattila 2006:251).

13.3.2   Using methods of comparative law in the search for equivalents

Before resorting to linguistic equivalents, translators should always use methods of comparative law to search for a 'natural' equivalent in the target legal system. In light of the inherent incongruity of the terminology of different legal systems, finding an equivalent in the target legal system that accurately conveys the legal sense of the source term is a formidable and often impossible task. Even with the development of technological aids, such as multilingual term banks, electronic dictionaries, and multilingual knowledge systems, an adequate translation equivalent cannot be found with a mere mouse click. Therefore, de Groot's assertion that all legal translation is an act of comparative law remains true today (1992:287; cf. Pommer 2006:119; Sandrini 2009:152). Like comparativists, translators need to investigate the issue at hand in both the source and target legal systems to identify the concept or institution in the target legal system that has the same or similar function as that of the problematic concept in the source text. This is known as a *functional equivalent*, which I defined in earlier works based on Canadian experience (Šarčević 1989:278; cf. Pigeon 1982). Since then, much has been written on the advantages and disadvantages of functional equivalents in legal translation. Weston goes so far as to say that "the technique of using a functional equivalent may be regarded as the ideal method of translation" (1991:23). However, identifying a functional equivalent is only the first step in a complex decision-making process.

To evaluate the acceptability of a functional equivalent, translators are advised to make an in-depth comparative analysis of the source and target concepts by identifying and comparing their essential and accidental characteristics. The goal of comparative analysis in translation is to establish the similarities and differences of terms at the conceptual level, on the basis of which translators can determine the degree of their equivalence (Šarčević 1989:279–83; 2000:237–47). While some functional equivalents are always acceptable (near equivalence) or never acceptable (non-equivalence), most functional equivalents fall into the category of partial equivalence. Elsewhere I proposed three main criteria for determining the acceptability of partially equivalent functional equivalents: structure/classification, scope of application, and legal effect (Šarčević 1989:284–7). The final decision on the acceptability of a functional equivalent will depend on the particular context, text type, and *skopos* of a given translation. As a rule, if a functional equivalent does not correspond with the source concept in any of the above three aspects, it could lead to different results in practice. In such cases, translators should attempt to compensate for any essential differences by using methods of lexical expansion or contraction. Otherwise, the use of partially equivalent functional equivalents could lead to grave consequences, especially when the incongruent concepts appear in a key provision of a multilingual instrument.

13.3.3 Compensating for conceptual incongruity in practice

A good example of the use, or rather misuse, of partially equivalent functional equivalents is found in Article 25(1) of the Warsaw Convention for the Unification of Certain Rules Relating to International Carriage by Air of 1929,[6] which determined whether the carrier's liability could be limited or excluded. Despite a warning by the English delegate, the term *dol* in the French original was translated by *willful misconduct*, although the scope of application of *willful misconduct* includes acts performed with intention, as well as acts performed carelessly without regard for the consequences. In accordance with the practice at the time, only the French original was authentic, and therefore the French text should have prevailed in all disputes concerning the interpretation of Article 25(1). Nonetheless, in cases involving death and bodily injuries resulting from acts not caused with intention, most American courts declared the carrier to have unlimited liability (in accordance with *willful misconduct*), whereas continental judges ruled in favor of limited liability pursuant to the concept of *dol* (see cases in Mankiewicz 1962:467). Since this provision served as an exclusion clause enabling plaintiffs to evade the thresholds of limited liability provided by the Convention, the conflicting decisions not only frustrated the object of the treaty but also directly encouraged plaintiffs to evade the treaty and shop for a more favorable forum.

---

[6] International Civil Aviation Organization (ICAO) Publication No. 9201.

Later translators and drafters began to use methods of lexical expansion to compensate for conceptual incongruity in an attempt to limit the discretion of national courts when interpreting multilingual instruments. To this end, drafters discarded both *dol* and *willful misconduct* in the Hague Protocol of 1955 amending the Warsaw Convention[7] and incorporated an explanatory definition of *dol* into both texts enumerating the circumstances in which acts or omissions qualify as *dol*. In this sense, the amended French text reads: "*soit avec l'intention de provoquer un dommage, soit témérairement et avec conscience qu'un dommage en résultera probablement*," and the English text: "*done with intent to cause damage or recklessly and with the knowledge that damage would probably result.*" The addition of the qualifier "*recklessly and with the knowledge that damage would probably result*" prevents common law judges from applying the provision in respect of acts that would qualify as *willful misconduct* but not as *dol* (see Mankiewicz 1962:467). Although the drafters succeeded in achieving legal equivalence in the amended texts, it was too late to rectify the damage already done.

The failure of the Warsaw Convention made lawyers aware of the potential dangers of the imperfections of translation which pose a threat to the very goal of multilingualism. The adoption of the principle of equal authenticity made it all the more important for translators and drafters to use innovative methods of lexical expansion or contraction as a means of promoting the uniform interpretation and application of the parallel texts of a single instrument (see examples in Šarčević 1989:287–90; 2000:250). In light of the need to guarantee equality before the law in all language versions, compensating for conceptual incongruity is the greatest challenge to the legal translator and the key to achieving optimal communication in multilingualism at all levels. As Weigand puts it, "Creating *terminological bridges* is the most important issue to be settled in the field of multilingualism" (2008:248).

Today drafters of international instruments (including international contracts) are encouraged to use neutral terms which are easily translatable and widely understood across legal systems and cultures. This, however, is not always possible. Therefore, drafters and translators are required to use descriptive paraphrases or definitions to compensate for conceptual incongruity whenever technical terms of a particular legal system are used in parallel texts. Another option is to use the national term as a borrowing in the various language versions, thus leaving national courts no choice but to apply the foreign concept in question. For this reason, the terms *force majeure* and *hardship* are used as borrowings in the parallel texts of instruments drafted under the auspices of UNIDROIT (Tallon 1995:343, n. 13). To compensate for the incongruity between the concepts of *ordre public* and *public policy*, the drafters of the Hague Convention on the Recognition and Enforcement of Foreign Judgments in Civil and Commercial Matters of 1971[8] retained the terms *ordre public* and *public policy* in Article 5, but broadened the English text to include all elements of due process of law covered by *ordre public*, thus

---

[7] ICAO Doc. (1955) 7632.

[8] Hague Conventions are available at <http://www.hcch.net/index_en.php?act=conventions.listing> accessed October 5, 2011.

achieving conceptual congruency at the expense of interlingual concordance. In later Hague Conventions the term *public policy* is usually followed by *ordre public* in parenthesis in the English text to avoid any misinterpretation (see, e.g., the Convention on the Law Applicable to Trusts and on their Recognition of 1985 (Art. 18) and the Convention on the International Recovery of Child Support and Other Forms of Family Maintenance of 2007 (Art. 22)).

13.4 EXPECTATIONS IN PRACTICE

The incongruity of different legal systems, cultures, and languages causes difficulties in all phases of the translation process, many of which could not be dealt with here. For instance, the first hurdle for translators is to analyze the source text and interpret its legal sense correctly (Gémar 1995:154), which in itself is a disputed endeavor, raising issues of legal hermeneutics (see Legrand 2005:36). Pragmatic considerations also come into play but are often neglected by translators (see Šarčević 2000:133–47). For the purpose of multilingualism, the translator's goal is to strive for legal equivalence with the aim of promoting uniform interpretation and application of the instrument in question. In light of the numerous obstacles facing legal translators, in closing it is legitimate to ask to what extent translators are expected to achieve legal equivalence in order for multilingualism to be effective.

Although the presumption of equal meaning of the parallel texts of a single instrument is a mere fiction, multilingualism is a fact of life in many domains. Like other forms of intercultural communication, legal translation is not perfect. Moreover, according to Cao (a former UN translator), perfect communication is neither expected nor necessary in practice: "No exact equivalence or complete identity of understanding can be expected or is really necessary" (2007b:35). While Cao acknowledges that "practice is satisfied with less," (as Kjær puts it, 2008a:71), she does not pursue the matter, thus raising the question of how imperfect or imprecise legal translation can be without posing a threat to multilingualism. The present chapter attempts to show that there are different standards that translators are expected to meet in practice in order for multilingualism to be effective. While perfect communication is impossible, legal translators are expected to achieve optimal communication as is necessary in the specific communication act. The degree of legal equivalence required for optimal communication depends primarily on the text type and *skopos* of the particular translation. At the top of the hierarchy, the translation of legally binding instruments requires the greatest accuracy and legal reliability.

While Cao claims that all translators need to know law, but not necessarily hold a law degree (2007b:7), lawyers argue either that only lawyers are competent legal translators or that translators need training in both disciplines (Gémar 2006:76). In any case, it is not disputed that both language skills and legal expertise are required in this challenging interdisciplinary profession. Furthermore, the greater the legal expertise, the higher the chances are that the translator will succeed in bridging differences between legal systems, cultures, and languages. Even then, from the lawyer's perspective, the differences remain. As Várady comments, "Translation can bridge differences, but it cannot extinguish them. Differences will appear—and will have to be dealt with" (2006:87). To this end, special rules of multilingual interpretation have been developed in plurilingual jurisdictions, leaving it ultimately to the judiciary to reconcile the imperfections inherent in legal translation (cf. Beaupré 1986). Multilingual communication in the law is a delicate balancing act involving all actors in the communication process—text producers (lawmakers, drafters, translators) and text receivers (judges). As in all intercultural communication, greater interaction between all actors leads to better results. Accordingly, interaction between translators and other text producers and text receivers is instrumental in achieving optimal communication in practice, which is not only expected but also necessary to guarantee the effectiveness of multilingualism in the law.

....

CHAPTER 14

LANGUAGE AND LAW IN THE EUROPEAN UNION: THE MULTILINGUAL JURISPRUDENCE OF THE ECJ

....

KAREN McAULIFFE

THE relationship between language and law has interested scholars for centuries. The use of language is crucial to any modern legal system since, in the most fundamental sense, law *is* language (insofar as, in most legal orders, language is used to make the law—whether in legislation or court decisions; and the use of law relies on language—in communicating, writing, persuading, etc.). On the one hand, it is true that legal theory and the notion of 'the law' involve more than just language—as Endicott states:

> law is not necessarily made by the use of language, and every legal system requires norms that are not made by the use of language. (Endicott 2002)

On the other hand, however, it cannot be denied that any modern social reality, including law, is rooted in language. "The law," certainly in the context of the present volume, is an overwhelmingly linguistic institution: it is coded in language, and the concepts that are used to construct that law are accessible only through language. This particular relationship between law and language becomes all the more evident in legal orders where law is produced in more than one language. The present chapter considers the production of multilingual law in the European Union, and in particular the multilingual jurisprudence produced by the Court of Justice of the European Union (ECJ).

Unlike other international organizations, which appear to function smoothly using only a few official languages,[1] the European Union (EU) currently has 24.[2] There are numerous historical and political reasons for this policy of multilingualism.[3] The most important reason, however, lies in the nature of European Union law: unlike international organizations such as the United Nations or the Council of Europe, whose resolutions are addressed to governments only, the activity of the institutions of the EU is such that it creates a whole new "EU law" in the form of regulations, decisions, and recommendations, which is applicable in each Member State, to each citizen and legal person. Even those texts which are addressed to Member States only can produce rights for individuals which must be guaranteed within their national legal orders and upheld by national courts. As a result it is necessary for such texts to exist in the national languages of the states concerned, that is in a language spoken and understood by each citizen to whom they apply:

> There was a requirement for the political equality of the states, and moreover…for the texts that were to receive direct application in each of the Member States, it was imperative that the governments responsible for their application and the persons to whom they were to be applied could read them in their native language. (Puissochet 1975:58)

In addition to the constitutive treaties and secondary legislation (regulations, directives, decisions, etc.), which are produced and are *equally authentic* in each of the 24 official EU languages,[4] the development of a rule of law within the EU is due in a large part to

[1] For example, the United Nations uses six (Arabic, Chinese, English, French, Russian and Spanish); NATO, with 28 members and the Council of Europe, with a current membership of 47, use only two languages—English and French; EFTA uses only English, a foreign language for all four of its members.

[2] These are, in English alphabetical order: Bulgarian, Croatian, Czech, Danish, Dutch, English, Estonian, Finnish, French, German, Greek, Hungarian, Irish, Italian, Latvian, Lithuanian, Maltese, Polish, Portuguese, Romanian, Slovakian, Slovenian, Spanish, and Swedish. The official order of these languages is to list them according to the way they are spelled each in their own language.

[3] It must be remembered that the institutions of what is now the European Union were created in the aftermath of the Second World War. The founders of the Union were motivated by a desire to avoid such tragedy ever reoccurring. Thus, the very first regulation of the European Council concerned the linguistic regime of the European Economic Community and stipulated in its first article that the official and working languages of the institutions of the Community would be German, French, Italian, and Dutch—four languages covering the six founder members of the Community. With successive enlargements that figure has grown to 23 official languages.

[4] Ideally, EU legislation would be drafted simultaneously in all languages. However, that is neither feasible nor possible in an EU of 28 Member States with 24 official languages and in fact, since the early days of the European Union, legislation has been drafted in one particular language and subsequently translated into all of the other official languages. Most commonly the language of drafting is either English or French (with English having taken over as the more dominant of the two languages in recent years). Drafting of legislation in the EU is strictly governed by an extensive set of rules that have been developed over the years, including: Declaration No 39 on the quality of the drafting of Community legislation, adopted by the Amsterdam Conference in 1997 (OJ 1997 C 340, p. 139); Interinstitutional Agreement of 22 December 1998 on common guidelines for the quality of drafting of Community legislation (OJ 1999 C 73, p. 1); Joint Practical Guide of the European Parliament, the Council and the Commission for persons involved in the drafting of legislation within the Community institutions, Luxembourg: Office for Official Publications of the European Communities, 2003; Interinstitutional Agreement of 31 December 2003 on better lawmaking (OJ 2003 C 321, p. 1); Manual of precedents, drawn up by the Legal/Linguistic experts of the Council (4th edn, July 2002).

the judicial pronouncements of the ECJ. Indeed, much of the 'constitutional law' of the EU is contained, not in the founding treaties, but in the case law of that Court, and it is often claimed that the quasi-federalism of the modern-day European Union has chiefly been brought about not by the express agreement of the states that founded the Community, nor by means of a detailed plan for an integrated legal system, but through the interpretative practice and influence of the ECJ.

As early as 1956, Louis Delvaux, a judge at the then Court of Justice of the European Coal and Steel Community, declared that the jurisdictional powers of that court far exceeded those usually enjoyed by traditional international tribunals and that it possessed in certain respects a "supranational character" (see Delvaux 1956:11–12). Some 35 years later one of his successors, G. Federico Mancini, a member of the ECJ of the European Communities, claimed that the Court "has sought to 'constitutionalise' the Treaty [of Rome], to fashion a constitutional framework for a quasi-federal structure in Europe" (Mancini 1991:178). The Court has done this by developing a series of "constitutional" doctrines, in particular those of direct effect and supremacy.[5] Thus, it is also considered necessary that European citizens (in particular Member State lawyers and judges) should be able to understand the judgments of that Court. The present chapter considers how the multilingual jurisprudence of the ECJ is produced and reflects on some of the changes that have taken place in that Court in recent years.

14.1 LANGUAGE REGIME AT THE ECJ

For every action before the ECJ[6] there is a language of procedure (which can be any one of the 24 official EU languages), which must be used in the written submissions or observations submitted for all oral submissions in the action. The language of procedure of the case must also be used by the Court in any correspondence, report, or decision addressed to the parties in the case. Only the texts in the language of procedure are authentic. In direct actions, the language of procedure is chosen by the applicant.[7] In references for a preliminary ruling under Article 267 of the Treaty on the Functioning of the European Union (TFEU—formerly Art. 234 EC), the language of procedure is the language of the national court that has made the reference. In appeals, the language of the case is that which was used before the General Court (formerly the Court of First Instance of the

---

[5] Cf. Case 26/62 *Van Gend en Loos v Nederlandse Administratie der Belastingen* [1963] ECR 1; Case 6/64 *Costa v ENEL* [1964] ECR 585. Over the years the parameters of those two doctrines have gradually been broadened.

[6] Since the entry into force of the Lisbon Treaty the ECJ of the European Union comprises three courts: the ECJ, the General Court, and the Civil Service Tribunal. The present chapter focuses primarily on the ECJ.

[7] Where a defendant is a Member State or a natural or legal person holding the nationality of a Member State the language of procedure is the official language of that state rather than the language of the application.

European Communities). Member States are entitled to use their own language in their written statements, observations, and oral submissions when they intervene in a direct action or participate in procedures for reference for a preliminary ruling.[8]

Unlike the other EU institutions, the ECJ operates using a single internal working language—French. The Rules of Procedure provide that a judge or advocate general may request the translation of any document into the language of his choice.[9] However, the members have been obliged to forgo that possibility in order not to increase the workload of the translation service.

It is clear that translation must play significant role in the working of the ECJ. However, the production of the multilingual jurisprudence of that court involves far more than translation alone. The case law of the ECJ is shaped by the language in which it is drafted—that is French. Because French is rarely the mother tongue of those drafting that case law, the texts produced are often stilted and awkward. In addition, those drafting such case law are constrained in their use of language and style of writing (owing to pressures of technology and in order to reinforce the rule of law). These factors have led to the development of a "Court French" which necessarily shapes the case law produced and has implications for its development, particularly insofar as it inevitably leads to a type of precedent in that case law (see below). That case law also undergoes many permutations of translation into and out of up to 24 different languages.

14.2 PRODUCTION OF A MULTILINGUAL JURISPRUDENCE: THE DRAFTING STAGE

The jurisprudence of the ECJ consists primarily of collegiate judgments drafted by judges and their référendaires, as well as opinions drafted by advocates general and their référendaires.[10] Each judge and advocate general of the ECJ has a *cabinet*[11]—a small team of personal legal assistants and secretaries working exclusively for him or her. Those

---

[8] Note: there are certain cases where two or more of the official EU languages may be used for all or part of the proceedings; in addition, in certain circumstances, a language other than an official EU language may be used by a witness or expert—a translation into the language of the case will be provided; Cf. Rules of Procedure of the ECJ, Arts 36–42.

[9] Art 39 of the Rules of Procedure of the ECJ.

[10] In the present chapter the term "jurisprudence" is used to refer to the "output" of the ECJ *including* the opinions of AGs. Since those opinions are not binding they are not, in the present chapter at least, considered part of the Court's "case law."

[11] While *cabinet* may be translated into English as *chambers* the French term shall be used here for two reasons: first to avoid confusion with the use of the word *Chamber* for a subdivision of the Court; secondly, unlike the English word *chambers*, '*cabinet*' in the context of the ECJ is used to refer both to the judge's or AG's suite or rooms and to the staff working there.

personal legal assistants are known as *référendaires*, and work very closely with "their" judge or advocate general, carrying out preliminary research on a case, drawing up procedural documents and preparing "first drafts" of judgments, etc. The role of the référendaire at the ECJ has been compared with that of the *Conseiller-référendaire* of the French *Cour de Cassation* (a judge attached to that court to assist its senior members) (see Brown and Kennedy 2000:23) and with the law clerk of the American judicial system. (see Kenny 2000: 93–625). There are currently 65 cabinets at the ECJ (28 judges' cabinets from the ECJ, 28 from the General Court, plus (currently) nine advocates general's cabinets).

The minimum requirement to be a référendaire at the ECJ is to be a qualified lawyer with a good knowledge of EU law and with at least a reasonable knowledge of French. Although they are not required to have a "perfect" command of that language, if a référendaire is not sufficiently competent in the French language it can cause problems for the judge or advocate general in whose cabinet he/she works.

The role of the référendaire is principally to assist the judge or advocate general in drafting documents such as reports for the hearing, judgments, opinions (in the case of advocates general), and, in the case of the presidents of the ECJ and the General Court, orders. However, the role of a judge's référendaire differs to a considerable degree to that of an advocate general's référendaire.

14.2.1 Judges' référendaires

Because of the heavy workload of the Court, it is not always (or even often) possible to allocate cases to cabinets or to individual référendaires on the basis of expertise. For this reason référendaires claim that they have to be "generalists" who are "knowledgeable about every area of EU law". Not only that, they also have to be able to understand and use their knowledge in French—a language that may not be (and indeed in most cases is not) their mother tongue.

The first document to be prepared by a référendaire is the preliminary report (*rapport préalable*). However, the référendaire cannot begin to draft that document until all of the relevant submissions have been lodged at the registry of the Court and, where necessary, translated into French.[12]

The preliminary report, which is written in French, summarizes the facts, law, and relevant arguments. It also contains a section known as the "Observations of the Judge-Rapporteur" (the reporting judge), which comprises the judge rapporteur's opinion on the case and his or her recommendations as to how the Court should rule. Due to the

---

[12] In reality, however, many cabinets begin drafting the preliminary report, and sometimes even the judgment (as reported by a référendaire from one particular cabinet) as soon as all of the parties' submissions have been lodged, i.e. without waiting for translation of those documents.

nature of the document, the report of the judge-rapporteur is often largely "cut-and-paste" from the relevant submissions.[13]

Following the delivery of the advocate general's opinion (see below), the judge rapporteur may begin to draft the judgment.[14] In reality it is the référendaire assigned to the case who drafts, at least the first version, of that judgment. Officially judgments are drafted, discussed, and deliberated on in French. Unofficially, a number of référendaires interviewed during the course of fieldwork research for the present chapter reported drafting "half in [their own mother tongue] and half in French":

> I tend to *translate* what I want to say *into* French instead of *really* working *in* French... (interviewee's emphasis)

> all of my own reasoning and thinking about the case is done in my own language and then put into French when I come to the writing stage...

It appears that, while they certainly draft in French, the *thinking process* behind that drafting, for many référendaires, is done in their own mother tongues. It can also be surmised that consequently the legal reasoning applied by those référendaires is the particular type and method of reasoning applied in their own national jurisdictions.

None of the référendaires or judges interviewed claimed to find it particularly difficult to draft in French. In fact, the only référendaires who expressed any problems or difficulties with that issue were "francophones" who feel that the formulaic style of ECJ judgments and the ensuing "Court French" are almost as alien to the "real" French language as English or German would be!

> The mechanical French that is used at the Court is so far removed from "proper" or "real" French that it is almost like another language entirely...

> The French used at the Court is not "real" French but a type of "Court French"...

Some référendaires noted that having to work in French when it is not their mother tongue "slowed them down", but that, as a result of the rigid formulaic style in which they are required to draft judgments:

> working in "Court French" is actually *easier* than drafting in your own language—provided that you don't actually want to write anything of *your own* (interviewee's emphasis).

As with reports for the hearing, the hands of the référendaire are tied when it comes to drafting judgments. One référendaire went so far as to say:

---

[13] This practice can be "dangerous" however, particularly at the stage of translation of the judgment when the lawyer-linguist responsible for translating that judgment may not be aware of discrepancies between the original submissions and the translations of those submissions (see McAuliffe 2006).

[14] See note 12 above. An opinion is not given in every case before the ECJ (since 2004 if a case raises no new questions of law then an AG's opinion is not necessary (Cf. Article 20 of the Statute of the ECJ [OJ 2013 C 349E, p. 555]).

you are so bound to what has been said before that you can hardly even use a new verb or express the same thing in a slightly different way in case the GTI[15] doesn't pick it up. Judgments are time-consuming but most are easy to draft because it has all already been said by the Court—maybe once in five or six years a case will come along that might have one single paragraph saying something completely new or different.[16]

As well as drafting the various documents for cases for which "their" judge is the judge rapporteur, judges' référendaires also have to work on the cases being heard by the Chamber in which their judge sits but for which he or she is not the judge rapporteur. In general, this involves familiarizing themselves with the case so that they can make written comments on the *project de motif* (the first draft judgment circulated among the Chamber by the judge rapporteur) which will be discussed by the judges during the deliberations.

14.2.2 Advocates general's référendaires

The role of advocates general's référendaires differs greatly from that of their counterparts in judges' cabinets. According to Article 252 TFEU (formerly Art. 222 EC), it is the duty of the advocate general

> acting with complete impartiality and independence, to make, in open court, reasoned submissions on cases which, in accordance with the Statute of the Court of Justice, require his involvement.

He or she does so by delivering what is known as the "opinion"—a document delivered after the case has been heard and normally in open court at a later hearing.[17] In the opinion the advocate general reviews the facts of the case, the relevant law, and critically considers all of the arguments of the parties and submissions of any others. Finally, the advocate general expresses his own opinion as to how the Court should decide the case in question.

Advocates general's référendaires work only on those cases to which their advocate general has been assigned. Just like judges' référendaires, advocates general's référendaires are required to have a wide general knowledge of EU law. Once a case has been assigned

---

[15] The GTI (Generic Text Interface) is a computer program developed by the ECJ to aid and speed-up the translation process at that Court. The GTI is not translation software – it simply searches for words or phrases and cannot identify context. Note: at the time of publication the ECJ is developing its own translation software.

[16] Comments such as this are particularly interesting as they show that référendaires feel constrained by the *language used* by the Court even though, strictly speaking there is no rule of precedent within the EU Court system and in theory the ECJ is not bound by its own previous decisions.

[17] Until 1991 the AG read the entire text of his or her opinion in open court. Since then, however, only the final recommendations of the opinion are read, and that is generally done by whichever AG is sitting in the case to be heard that day.

to an advocate general, the référendaire dealing with that case, just like his or her counterpart in the judge rapporteur's cabinet, will open a file and wait for the submissions to be lodged at the Registry of the Court (and, if necessary, for those documents to be translated into French). Once all of the submissions and other relevant documents have been received, the référendaire may begin to work on the case.[18]

It is at this stage of the proceedings that the role of the advocate general's référendaire differs from that of judges' référendaires: whereas the judge rapporteur and his or her référendaires are first focused on producing a clear and concise report to be circulated among the chamber before the judgment is drafted, the advocate general has the luxury of working on detailed background preparation for his or her opinion in a case from the moment that case is lodged—although the opinion is normally written during the three weeks *following* the hearing[19] (based on interviews with advocate generals and their référendaires, see McAuliffe 2006); and historically that opinion has differed vastly in style, and very often in substance, from the report of the judge-rapporteur and the draft judgment produced by the judge rapporteur's cabinet.

There are three significant differences between the advocate general's opinion and those documents drafted by judges' référendaires. First, while judges and their référendaires are constrained by the collegiate nature of the judgment and the rigid style of both the report of the judge-rapporteur and the judgment, the advocate general's opinion is a different style of document entirely. The comment is often made that the opinion in a case reads very much like an academic document. Whereas the judgment generally sets out only those submissions and recommendations which are necessary to the Court's decision in a particular case (and often does not justify or substantiate them), the opinion is much more free and full—often setting out sources of law, referring in detail to relevant earlier decisions of the Court, commenting on decisions under national law from the courts of EU member states and even citing the opinions of legal academics (*la doctrine*) (see Brown and Kennedy 2000). The référendaires at the Court are acutely aware of that difference:

> Writing an opinion is very different, linguistically speaking, from writing a judgment. An opinion is very free—you can write what you want, how you want, you can include quotes, be humorous—it's more like writing an academic document. With a judgment you are much more restrained.

Secondly, the documents differ from each other in character: while the judgment focuses solely on solving the particular problem at hand, the opinion tends to be a much

---

[18] One référendaire interviewed commented that because of the nature of the document, it is sometimes possible to begin working on the case and even drafting the opinion *before* all of the submissions have been lodged, in particular, in reference for a preliminary ruling (Art. 267 TFEU), which are much more abstract than direct actions and in which the relevant questions can, theoretically, be answered without reference to the parties' submissions (of course, in practice, those submissions are always consulted).

[19] During interviews, AGs' référendaires commented (without exception) that their workload had significantly increased since the 2004 and 2007 enlargements of the EU membership.

more investigative and informative document in which the advocate general can be critical of the previous case law of the Court, etc. The opinion is, in essence, a *dialogue* with the Court:

> the advocate general can, ideally, be the Court's 'sparring partner'—he [or she] can be provocative and critical—and all of this can greatly help the development of the Court's case law.

Finally, until 2004, the opinion was, by convention, written in the advocate general's own mother tongue. Often, référendaires in advocates general's cabinets share the same mother tongue as "their" advocate general, thus, historically, the vast majority of advocates general's référendaires have worked and drafted in their own language. As one such référendaire commented:

> In a judge's cabinet you just have to be able to manipulate French... you get everything fed to you in French and then basically cut and paste it. In the advocates general's chambers you are fed documents in all languages (especially in French) and produce the opinion in [the language of the advocate general]—in some ways it is much easier than drafting judgments, in other ways it is more difficult; but it is always more interesting.

Since 2004, however, a number of advocates general at the ECJ have been drafting their opinions in one of the 'pivot languages' of that Court (English, French, German, Spanish, and Italian; see McAuliffe 2006:chs 6 & 7).[20]

One of the major problems of the pivot translation system introduced at the ECJ following the EU enlargement of May 2004 (See McAuliffe 2006:ch. 3) is that the length of time taken to produce translations necessarily doubles through pivot translation. However, that mainly affects only two types of document: references for a preliminary ruling and advocates general's opinions (i.e. those advocates general who do not draft in one of the pivot languages) (see McAuliffe 2008). Therefore, alongside the introduction of the pivot translation system came an initiative by the director of the translation directorate to encourage advocates general whose mother tongue is a language other than one of the pivot languages to draft their opinions, not in their own language, but in one of the pivot languages of the Court (in particular English and French). The référendaires who, together with "their" advocate generals, draft opinions in one or more of the pivot languages instead of their own mother tongue find their new role very challenging and at times frustrating:

> all discussions with the advocate general are in our own language and therefore you then struggle to find the correct terms in the relevant pivot language when you come to draft the opinion—because you can't say exactly the same thing in another language you have to approximate.

---

[20] In reality, the languages most commonly chosen by AGs in which to draft their opinions are English and French.

At the same time, however, some of those référendaires see a positive side to drafting in a language that is not their mother tongue:

> While it is more difficult for someone to draft in a language that isn't their own, it is also a good idea since working in a foreign language "formalises" the text.

> While it can be difficult to find terms in a foreign language that meet your exact thinking, working in a foreign language can also help you to find answers to legal problems that you wouldn't have found in your own language.

The question that remains, however, is to what extent advocate generals can retain their role as the Court's "sparring partner" while drafting in a language that is not their mother tongue. The discursive, speculative nature of advocates general's opinions is due in no small part to the fact that historically those opinions have been drafted in the language of the relevant advocate general (see Borgsmidt 1988:108). Is there a risk that the advocates general's creativity may be limited by the changes in the language regime necessitated by enlargement at the ECJ?

It is clear that the role of language in the drafting of the ECJ's multilingual jurisprudence is a significant one. However, once the judgments, orders, opinions, etc. have been drafted by judges, advocates general, and their référendaires, that jurisprudence then undergoes further permutations of translation into the language of procedure (where that language isn't French) and the other official EU languages.

14.1 PRODUCTION OF A MULTILINGUAL JURISPRUDENCE—THE TRANSLATING STAGE

The directorate-general for translation of the ECJ deals with translation into French (the working language of the Court) of documents lodged by parties and interveners to a case, and the subsequent translation into all of the EU official languages of judgments and orders of the Court (as well as, where relevant, advocates general's opinions). That directorate is organized into separate "translation divisions" for each of the official EU languages.[21]

With the exception of the French language division, all language divisions do the same work. For each new case the language divisions must:

- translate the application initiating the procedure;
- where the language of a particular division is the language of procedure of the case, that division will also have to translate various essential procedural documents, such as:

---

[21] With the exception of the Irish language, for which there is a 'Cell' rather than a translation division. At the time of going to press there was one person employed in the Irish Cell. Irish has never been used in proceedings before the ECJ.

- Member State observations,
- applications to intervene by third parties,
- advocate general's opinion (where relevant);
- all language divisions (apart from the French language division) must translate:
  - the judgment,
  - the summary,
  - notification of the case in the Official Journal of the EU.

Since French is the internal working language of the Court and thus the language of deliberation and the language in which all internal documents are drafted, it has a special role at the Court. The French language division must translate the application plus *all* of the procedural documents of the case. The French language division translates all opinions not drafted in French, but never translates judgments, since judgments of the ECJ are always drafted in French.[22] Since May 2004 the French translation division has also provided translations from all of the "post 2004" EU languages (see below).

14.3.1 Pivot translation

Until May 2004 the directorate-general for translation provided direct translation from and into all of the official languages of the EU as part of the integral multilingual system of the ECJ. With 11 official languages that meant being able to provide translations in 110 different language combinations. However, following the accession of 13 new Member States between 2004 and 2013 and the addition of Irish to the list of official EU languages, the number of official languages rose to 24, bringing the number of potential language combinations to 552. Provision of translation in 552 different language combinations is quite simply not feasible in an organization such as the ECJ—and so, a solution had to be found. That solution was the introduction of "pivot translation".

The pivot translation system, which has been in use at the Court since May 2004, is actually a mixed translation system—whenever possible direct translation is used instead of translation through a "pivot language". There are five pivot languages: French, English, German, Spanish, and Italian. Because French is the working language of the Court, the French translation division provides translation from all of the "post 2004" official languages while each of the other four pivot language divisions are "partnered" with two or three "post 2004" official languages.[23] While the French language division

---

[22] For an overview of which documents are translated into which language(s) in both direct and indirect actions, (see Tables 14.1 and 14.2).

[23] The German language division provides translation from Bulgarian, Estonian, and Polish; the English language division from Czech and Lithuanian; the Spanish language division from Hungarian and Latvian; and the Italian language division from Romanian, Slovak, and Slovenian. Neither Maltese nor Irish have been assigned to a pivot language division. Since English is the second official language of both Malta and Ireland, it is assumed that the Maltese and Irish lawyer-linguists and those translators attached to the Irish language cell are able to provide English translations of documents in Maltese and Irish where necessary.

must provide translations of all documents originating externally and drafted in any of the "post 2004" languages, the only external documents which go through the pivot translation system are orders for reference for a preliminary ruling, Member State observations and applications to intervene in direct actions. Orders for reference for a preliminary ruling drafted in one of the "post 2004" languages are translated into French and into the relevant pivot language and, from those translations, translated into all of the other official EU languages (note: if there is a lawyer-linguist in a particular language division capable of translating directly from the original language then that is what will happen). Member state observations or applications to intervene drafted in one of the "post 2004" languages are translated into French and, from that translation, into the language of procedure, unless the language of procedure happens to be the relevant pivot language, in which case the document is translated directly into that language. (For an overview of the pivot translation system at the ECJ, see McAuliffe 2008.) The pivot system also applies to the translation of documents drafted in the "pre-2004" languages—again, direct translation is used whenever possible.

While the task of the Court's directorate-general for translation may seem relatively straightforward (translating documents "coming in" into French and those "going out" into all of the EU official languages), as briefly highlighted above, the process behind such a task is more complicated than it may seem.

14.3.2 Lawyer-linguists

While the texts which make up the jurisprudence of the ECJ are drafted by the judges and advocate generals together with their référendaires, that jurisprudence is translated by *lawyer-linguists*. Article 42 of the Rules of Procedure of the ECJ states:

> The Court shall set up a translating service staffed by experts with adequate legal training and a thorough knowledge of several official languages of the European Union

As a result of the rather vague language used in that article, the criteria for becoming a lawyer-linguist at the ECJ are not set in stone. However, lawyer-linguists are typically required to possess a perfect command of their mother tongue and an in-depth knowledge of at least two other official EU languages. They are also usually required to hold a law degree awarded in an EU Member State (usually the state into whose language they translate) and, generally, to have two years professional experience (not necessarily translating experience).

The job description for a lawyer-linguist at the ECJ may appear to be simply to translate the texts of the Court; however, upon closer analysis it becomes apparent that the role of a lawyer-linguist is far more complex and difficult to define than that. In order to be able to translate legal concepts from one language to another, lawyer-linguists need a comprehensive knowledge not only of their own legal systems but also the legal systems of other Member States, as well as a thorough understanding of the law of the EU and the jurisprudence of the ECJ. They are responsible for dealing with legal issues that may arise because of *linguistic* ambiguities in texts. While dealing with the classic problems of transla-tion on a daily basis, the lawyer-linguists at the ECJ also appear to be trying to balance a dual professional identity—that of lawyer *and* linguist. Some lawyer-linguists feel very strongly that they are "lawyers", and feel that their work at the ECJ is actually an exercise in comparative law:

> In order to be able to translate a legal term from one language to another in which that translation will also have force of law the lawyer-linguist must be able to under-stand both the concept in the source language and the meaning of that concept within the relevant legal system as well as the legal system of the country in which the target language is spoken.

Others assert that they are not lawyers, but translators. Interestingly, however, all of those lawyer-linguists interviewed who described themselves as translators immediately qual-ified their statement by pointing out that as translators of judicial texts, with law degrees, they are "much more than simply translators". Without exception, they feel that the job would hold no interest from them "if the law element wasn't there as well as the transla-tion element".

The majority of lawyer-linguists interviewed, however, feel that a lawyer-linguist is something distinct from both a lawyer and a translator:

> a perfect synthesis of a lawyer and a linguist.

The job requires expertise in law *and* expertise in translation, and most find it very satis-fying to be able to "tie-up" their interest in law and their love of languages. Some feel that law *is* a language, that it is an expression of a society and of its history. Those who become lawyer-linguists:

> are lawyers who are more interested in the *theoretical* aspect of law than in the prac-tice of law. Those who practice law actually deal less with concepts of law and more with business and administration—in applying the rules—and rarely deal with any *real* [conceptual] legal problems (interviewee's emphasis).

They feel that the work of a lawyer-linguist involves "working at a deep level of under-standing of legal concepts" and that it is much more than translation:

> in short, it is the manipulation of law as language and language as law.

14.4   SOME DIFFICULTIES IN THE PRODUCTION OF A MULTILINGUAL JURISPRUDENCE

From various interviews and participant observation conducted by the author it is clear that both those *drafting* the multilingual jurisprudence of the ECJ and those *translating* it take their roles very seriously indeed. While very few référendaires interviewed admitted having any difficulty drafting documents in a language that is not their mother tongue, they did comment on a tendency among référendaires to use the same expressions over and again:

> because we are writing in a foreign language there is a tendency to do a lot of "cutting and pasting" and so the style [in which the Court's judgments, orders, etc. are written] reproduces itself.

Thus, it seems that in spite of the majority of référendaires' claims that they find it relatively non-problematic to draft in French, it nonetheless has consequences. This conclusion is supported by comments from lawyer-linguists who complain that because most référendaires generally draft in a language that is not their mother tongue, excessive reliance tends to be placed on stock phrases, frequently causing the meaning of texts to be obscured. One lawyer-linguist interviewed likened the drafting of judgments to constructing a toy house from Lego building bricks with:

> gobbits of words being borrowed from previous cases and inserted into new judgments…[While] the grammatical structure of…French allows this to be done without changing the original wording, it is not always the case that the same can be done in other languages. It is not always possible to anticipate which passages will become "Lego building bricks", and in any case, even where it is possible, it may not be possible to mimic the French sentence structure. Inevitably this leads to inelegant translation and "Eurospeak".

Référendaires also feel constrained as regards the language they believe that they can use when drafting, claiming that they are under pressure to "cite word-for-word when taking material from…past judgments". Many feel that because the ECJ is building up a European case law and rule of law it is necessary to use the same terminology consistently throughout that case law.

Finally, those drafting the judgments of the Court are also restricted by the collegiate nature of those judgments. The judgments of the ECJ are, by their very nature, often compromise documents. However, because the deliberations of the Court are secret and no dissenting opinions are published, it is impossible for anyone other than the judges involved in those deliberations to know where such compromises lie in the text. As many of the référendaires interviewed commented:

> you don't always know which have been the "contentious" parts in the deliberations…or how important a specific wording of a particular phrase may be…therefore it is safer just to stick with phrases that may sound awkward or badly-worded instead of changing them to sound better…

Lawyer-linguists too comment on this particular problem—pointing out that for this reason it is sometimes important to produce a very literal translation, for example, so as not to resolve an ambiguity where the Court has wanted to preserve one:

> often you see a word or phrase that sounds very clumsy and you translate it using something that's not quite literal but sounds neater in [the target language] and then…the phrase comes back to you in another case and you realise you shouldn't

have translated it the way you did in the first place because you've resolved an issue that shouldn't have been resolved at that time...often the wording of a judgment is a compromise formula as a result of disagreement in the deliberations and must therefore be translated very literally.

Such difficulty with translating ambiguity represents the issue at the very core of the lawyer-linguists' role: the reconciliation of the notions of "law" and "translation." It is generally accepted that translation of any kind, including legal translation, involves some measure of approximation (Koller 1989:99–104, 1995:191–222; Šarčević 2000; Steiner 1998). This concept of approximation in translation, however, does not sit easily with traditional notions of law—an authoritative force, necessarily uniform throughout the jurisdiction within which it applies, in particular in the European legal order where the principle of uniformity has formed the basis for the most important doctrines of EU law introduced by the ECJ.[24]

Divergences in the relative ambiguity of texts are particularly significant in the case of judgments of the ECJ, the authentic version of which is in a language other than French (i.e. the majority of judgments!). An authentic version of a judgment that is less ambiguous or more precise than the original language version that has been deliberated over by judges[25] could have widespread legal implications:

> if the translation of a judgment ends up more precise than the French original, and that translation is the authentic language version of the judgment, then presumably lawyers and courts in the relevant member state (and perhaps even in other member states) will follow the authentic language version assuming that that is the correct version.[26]

14.5 CONCLUSION

The relationship between language and law in the context of multilingual EU law and, in particular, the multilingual jurisprudence of the ECJ is one which invites considerable investigation. That multilingual jurisprudence is necessarily shaped by the unique way in which it is produced: drafted in a language that is rarely the mother tongue of the drafter; consisting of a blend of cultural and linguistic patterns; constrained by a rigid formulistic drafting style and put through many permutations of translation. Once the process of production of that multilingual jurisprudence is understood, it becomes

---

[24] See note 5 above.

[25] Although the precaution is usually taken to send the authentic (translated) version of a judgment for review to the member of the Court whose native tongue is that of the language of the case, that member may not necessarily have been in the Chamber of judges that decided the particular case, and therefore could not be aware of the deliberations in that case.

[26] For a recent example of this precise scenario occurring before the UK Competition Appeal Tribunal see McAuliffe (2006, 2009).

Table 14.1 Documents to be translated in direct actions

Translation into:

	Language of procedure	Internal working language (i.e. French)	The other languages
Application / Appeal		✓	
OJ Notification of the action		Internal document drafted in French	✓
Defense / Response (to appeal)		✓	
Reply		✓	
Rejoinder		✓	
Member State observations	✓	✓	
Application to intervene	✓	✓	
Statement in intervention		✓	
Documents lodged during the oral procedure		✓	
Report of the judge-rapporteur	✓	Internal document drafted in French	
Advocate-General's opinion	✓	✓	✓
Judgment	✓	Internal document drafted in French	✓
Summary	✓	Internal document drafted in French	✓
OJ notification of judgment	✓	Internal document drafted in French	✓

Table 14.2 Documents to be translated in references for a preliminary ruling

Translation into:

	Language of procedure	Internal working language (i.e. French)	The other languages
Order for reference		✓	✓
OJ notification of the order for reference		Drafted in French	✓
Observations of the parties to the main proceedings		✓	
Member State observations	✓	✓	
Documents lodged during the oral procedure		✓	
Report of the judge-rapporteur	✓	Internal document drafted in French	
Advocate-General's opinion	✓	✓	✓
Judgment	✓	Internal document drafted in French	✓
Summary	✓	Internal document drafted in French	✓
OJ notification of the judgment	✓	Internal document drafted in French	✓

relevant to consider whether language and translation actually cause problems in relation to the "output" of the ECJ.

The approximation inherent in the production and translation of the case law of the ECJ is illustrative of the limitations of a multilingual legal system. The feature that distinguishes EU law from international law (and the very reason behind the EU's language policy) is the fact that EU law is applicable to individual citizens in individual Member States and therefore must be accessible (and effective) in all of the official languages of the EU. It is often claimed that the teleological method of interpretation developed by the ECJ resolves difficulties relating to the multilingual nature of EU law. The use of such an interpretative method by the Court, together with the inherently approximate and hybrid nature of multilingual EU legal texts, has resulted in the evolution of a "new" EU legal language which does ensure the effectiveness of EU law to a large extent (see McAuliffe 2006). However, the fact remains that different languages offer different accounts of reality. The approximation and imprecision inherent in language and translation do have implications for the case law produced by the ECJ. Thus, an awareness of the problems of language and translation should condition our understanding of the multilingual EU legal order.[27]

[27] This chapter is based on the results of periods of participant observation at the ECJ of the European Communities undertaken between 2002 and 2006; all comments/criticisms are welcome (k.mcauliffe@exeter.ac.uk). Unless otherwise indicated all quotes are taken from interviews with référendaires, judges, advocate generals, and lawyer-linguists at that Court. I would like to thank Dr Robert Harmsen of the University of Luxembourg for his support and valuable comments. I would also like to thank my former colleagues at the ECJ in Luxembourg for their assistance with this research—in particular Mr Alfredo Calot-Escobar and Ms Susan Wright. Any errors are mine alone.

....

CHAPTER 15

FIFTY YEARS OF MULTILINGUAL INTERPRETATION IN THE EUROPEAN UNION

....

CORNELIS J. W. BAAIJ

15.1 INTRODUCTION

....

BOTH the Treaties of the European Union (EU) and the secondary legislation from EU institutions are currently issued in 23 different language versions.[1] Discrepancies between these language versions both jeopardize the equal authenticity of these versions, and make a uniform interpretation and application of EU law in all EU Member States more difficult.

Yet, discrepancies between language versions have come up in the case law of the Court of Justice of the European Union (ECJ). In dealing with these, the ECJ has chosen either a primarily teleological or a literal interpretive method. The ECJ's interpretive canons do not reveal, however, when it will use one or the other method as its principal argument in justifying the interpretation of the legal provision in question. Yet, sometimes the ECJ may justify conflicting outcomes in legal cases by using different interpretive methods. From a viewpoint of legal predictability and thus legal certainty, it is important to gain a better understanding of the circumstances under which the ECJ chooses one method over the other.

---

[1] Article 55 Treaty on European Union (TEU), OJ C 83 of March 30, 2010 (consolidated text) and Article 342 Treaty on the Functioning of the European Union (TFEU), OJ C 83 of March 30, 2010 (consolidated text), jo. Article 1 of Council Regulation No. 1/58 determining the languages to be used by the European Economic Community, OJ B 17, October 6, 1958, p. 385 (consolidated text).

This chapter will use a statistical analysis of 50 years of the ECJ's case law, all relevant judgments between 1960 and 2010, to shed further light on which interpretive method the ECJ is more likely to use in the event of linguistic discrepancies as an argument to justify its interpretation of EU law.

15.2 THE PREDICAMENT OF DISCREPANCIES

Discrepancies between the language versions impede the interpretation of EU law for at least two reasons.

First, from a legal perspective, all language versions of EU legislation (currently 23) are considered to embody the original text. None of the versions should thus be seen as a translation or rendition of one of the other language versions. The Treaty on European Union (TEU) stipulates, as did the treaties that preceded it, that all language versions of the Treaty are "equally authentic."[2] In addition, in its much cited judgments in the *CILFIT* case in 1982, the ECJ for the first time spelled out that language versions of secondary EU legislation are also to be considered equally authentic.[3] In other words, as the ECJ later pointed out in the *EMU Tabac* case in 1998, all language versions must in principle be given "the same weight."[4] As Schilling (2010) points out, when language versions diverge due to discrepancies between them, however, it becomes more difficult to have each version contribute equally to a coherent interpretation of EU law.

Secondly, linguistic discrepancies might hamper the harmonization or unification of national legislation of the EU Member States. As early as in 1969, in its judgments in the *Stauder* case, the ECJ argued that EU law needs to be interpreted and applied in a uniform manner in all Member States and that, therefore, a provision of EU legislation must be interpreted and applied "in the light in particular of the versions in all...languages."[5] The ECJ has repeated its call for a comparison of language versions in the interpretation of EU law in over 30 judgments throughout the years, and recently has been referring to this canon as "settled case-law."[6] However, aiming for a uniform interpretation and application is not as easy as it sounds when different language versions say different things. Diverging language versions may render diverging interpretations in the various Member States that rely on a particular version, and thus potentially cause inconsistent application of EU law. Consequently, in one way or another it is necessary for the ECJ, as Engberg (2004:1157) puts it, to settle on a single meaning for all language versions.

[2] Art. 55 TEU.
[3] Case 283/81 *CILFIT* [1982] ECR 3415, para. 18.
[4] Case 296/95 *EMU Tabac* [1998] ECR-I-1605, para. 36, and repeated in Case C-257/00 *Nani Givane* [2003] ECR I-345, para. 36 and Case C-152/01 *Kyocera Electronics Europe* [2003] ECR I-13821, para. 32.
[5] Case 29/69 *Stauder* [1969] ECR 419, para. 3.
[6] For example in Case C-253/99 *Bacardi* [2001] ECR I-6493, para. 41 and Case C-375/07 *Heuschen & Schrouff* [2008] ECR I-8691, para. 46.

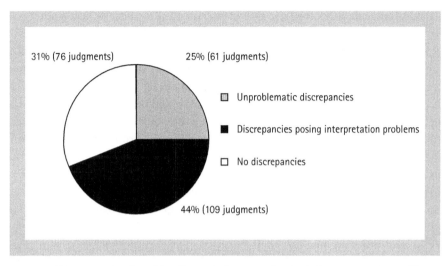

31% (76 judgments)   25% (61 judgments)

▣ Unproblematic discrepancies

■ Discrepancies posing interpretation problems

☐ No discrepancies

44% (109 judgments)

FIGURE 15.1 Discrepancies found in all 246 judgments that include a comparison of language versions

Between 1960 and 2010 the ECJ included a comparison of language versions in the argumentation of 246 of its judgments (Figure 15.1).[7] These, in turn, produced a total of 170 judgments in which the ECJ observed discrepancies between language versions of the provision in question. Of the 246 judgments, in 44 percent (109 judgments) the ECJ detected a linguistic discrepancy that it treated as an interpretive problem that needed to be resolved. In 25 percent (61 judgments) the ECJ discovered discrepancies but did not treat these as problems, but rather as a tool, drawing an argument in support of its preferred interpretation. The use of discrepancies as an interpretive tool is discussed in more detail by Solan (2009:288) and van Calster (1997:370, 375).

In the remainder of this chapter, the focus is on all 170 judgments in which the ECJ claimed to have observed discrepancies between the language versions of the legal provision in question.

15.3 TWO INTERPRETIVE STRATEGIES

15.3.1 The legal reasoning methodology

In analyzing the ECJ's case law, this chapter makes use of the so-called "legal reasoning" methodology as its analytic tool. It considers the arguments that the ECJ uses in its judgments as valid legal grounds for rationally justifying its legal decision. In other words, the

---

[7] These numbers may vary slightly due to the indistinctness of the precise role that a reference to language versions plays in a small number of judgments.

"legal reasoning" methodology focuses on the so-called "context of justification" rather than on the "context of discovery" (Bengoetxea 1993:164–5; Bengoetxea et al. 2001:44–7).

The focus on the "context of justification" avoids relying on variables that are difficult or impossible to measure, such as the *actual* intentions or motivations of individual judges underlying the content of the judgment. Consequently, there is no need to question whether the ECJ's interpretive methods actually led to the eventual decision of its judges, or whether the methods are merely an ex post facto justification.[8] It also makes it unnecessary to evaluate the ECJ's decisions against the background of the *actual* content of the law or the *actual* meaning of the various texts. What matters is merely which factors the ECJ itself takes as valid in coming to its judgment.

In this respect, the interpretive method that the ECJ eventually chooses functions as a "first-order" argument in support of the interpretation of the provision in question; the arguments that the ECJ uses to justify its choice of interpretive method will be referred to as "second-order arguments" (cf. Bengoetxea et al. 2001:57, 65). Discussion below of relevant case law aims to illuminate, in the event of linguistic discrepancies, which interpretive methods the ECJ uses as first-order arguments for its interpretation of the provision in question, and which second-order arguments the ECJ uses to justify its use of these interpretive methods.

15.3.2 The teleological approach to discrepancies

At face value, the ECJ seems to offer a straightforward answer to the question which principal interpretative strategy it chooses in the event of linguistic discrepancies: the teleological approach. This entails, in short, that the interpretation should be guided by the function, purpose, or objective of the provision or legislative instrument (Bredimas 1978:19–21; Bengoetxea 1993:252; Brown and Kennedy 2000:339–43).

Since the aforementioned *Stauder* case in 1969, the ECJ has often taken a teleological approach towards discrepancies between language versions.[9] In the *Régina v Bouchereau* case in 1977, the ECJ first laid out its "second-order" arguments for this approach. It explained that "the different language versions…must be given a uniform interpretation and hence in the case of divergence between the versions the provision in question must be interpreted by reference to the purpose and general scheme of the rules of which it forms a part."[10] Between 1960 and 2010 the ECJ has repeated this canon in 50 of its judgments, and frequently pointed out that its teleological approach to linguistic discrepancies is "settled case law."[11] The second-order arguments that the ECJ thus invokes

---

[8] Such skepticism in the literature on the ECJ is discussed in Bengoetxea (1993:165, 230) and Soriano (2003:298).

[9] Case 29/69 *Stauder* [1969] ECR 419, par. 3.

[10] Case 30-77 *Régina v Bouchereau* [1977] ECR 1999, para. 14.

[11] E.g. C-426/05 *Tele2 v Telekom* [2008], ECR I-685, para. 25. In general the ECJ uses the teleological interpretive method in combination with a "contextual approach", which places the relevant provision or the legislative instrument in the broader context of other EU law (Bredimas 1978:73). The combined teleological-contextual approach will be referred to as "teleological."

to justify the use of teleological interpretation in the event of linguistic discrepancies is the need for the uniform interpretation and application of EU law.

Based on this teleological interpretation canon, one would expect to see a teleological approach applied in all of the 170 judgments in which the ECJ claims to have detected linguistic discrepancies. Derlén (2009:37) points out that in the literature on the interpretive methods of the ECJ, the erroneous assumption persists that the teleological approach is the dominant approach in taking on linguistic discrepancies. This assumption may be due to the common understanding that, as Vogenauer (2005:388) and Pollicino (2004:289) observe, the teleological approach is the ECJ's overall prevailing interpretive method. An examination of the ECJ's case law between 1960 and 2010, however, shows that when it comes to linguistic discrepancies, the teleological approach is in fact not the prevailing approach to the interpretation of EU law.

15.3.3 The literal approach to discrepancies

Amongst others, Schübel-Pfister (2004:233–4) and Derlén (2009:40) observe that the ECJ does not solely take a teleological approach when it identifies discrepancies between language versions. They point out that the ECJ has also dealt with discrepancies by taking a literal approach. Such an approach generally entails comparing the meaning of the various language versions (cf. Brown and Kennedy 2000:327–30).

An examination of all 170 cases between 1960 and 2010 shows that the ECJ's making a principal literal argument in the event of discrepancies is not an exception to the rule. In fact, the ECJ more often took a literal approach than a teleological approach. Between 1960 and 2010 the ECJ took a teleological approach in dealing with discrepancies in 75 judgments, whereas in the other 95 judgments, the ECJ chose a literal approach.[12] Figure 15.2 further reveals that the use of a literal approach is not a tradition of the past or a recent trend; the ECJ has consistently relied on a primarily literal argument in the event of discrepancies throughout the years.

The literal approach can be understood as consisting of at least two categories: the "majority argument" and the "clarity argument."[13] In about two-thirds of the judgments in which the ECJ took a literal approach, it argued that preference should be given to the meaning that it attributed to the majority of language versions. In one-third of the judgments the literal argument entailed giving preference to the language versions that the ECJ considered clearer or less ambiguous than the other versions.

---

[12] In 91 judgments the ECJ uses the literal interpretive method as primary argument; in the remaining four it used the method as a supplementary, secondary argument.

[13] Schübel-Pfister (2004:278–84) and Derlén (2009:41) also discuss the "Gültigkeitsregel" or liberal interpretation; and the "Gemeinsamer-Nenner-Regel" or "most restrictive interpretation" or preferring the "common denominator." Due to its rare occurrence and the controversy as to the status of this approach, this type of literal interpretation will not be discussed further.

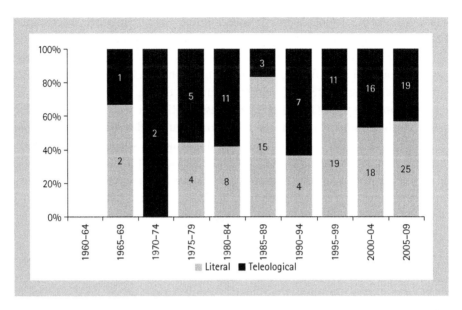

FIGURE 15.2 Interpretive methods in respect of linguistic discrepancies, between 1960 and 2010 (total number and percentage split)

For most of the remainder of this chapter the "clarity argument" will not be further discussed. The reason is that, except for two judgments in which the ECJ interpreted Article 8 of the Council Directive 92/12/EEC,[14] between 1960 and 2010 the ECJ always found the clearer versions to be in the majority.[15] Therefore, unless expressly indicated otherwise, when reference is made to the "literal approach" or "literal interpretive method," it involves the majority argument.

15.3.4 The second-order arguments for the literal approach

The case law of the ECJ suggests that, in the event of discrepancies between language versions, the same second-order arguments that justify the teleological approach, justify the literal approach. In the *Codan* case in 1998, for example, the ECJ justified preferring the meaning it attributed to the majority of language versions by reference to the need for a uniform interpretation and application of EU legislation. There the ECJ found that

---

[14] Council Directive 92/12/EEC of February 25, 1992 on the general arrangements for products subject to excise duty and on the holding, movement, and monitoring of such products, OJ L 76, March 23, 1992, pp. 1–13. Case 296/95 *EMU Tabac* [1998] ECR-I-1605, para. 33 and Case C-5/05 *Staatssecretaris van Financiën v B. F. Joustra* [2006], ECR I-11075, para. 40.

[15] Cf. the comment of Advocate General Stix-Hackle, that the clarity argument does not permit a convincing result when more than one language versions diverges from all the others, in Case C-265/03 *Igor Simutenkov* [2005] ECR I-2579, Opinion of Advocate General Stix-Hackl delivered on January 11, 2005, para. 16.

the Danish and German language versions in question diverged from "most of the other" language versions. Although the ECJ then used as its principal argument a teleological interpretation, it added that "to disregard the clear wording of the great majority of the language versions...would...run counter to the requirement that the Directive be interpreted uniformly."[16]

In its judgment in the *Nowaco* case in 2006, the ECJ used a similar canon to justify literal interpretation as its principal argument. There the ECJ found that a comparison of the various language versions showed that the German version was inconsistent with all others. It then argued that "according to settled case-law, the need for a uniform interpretation of Community law makes it impossible for the text of a provision to be considered in isolation" but that, on the contrary, it was required to be "interpreted in the light of the versions existing in the other official languages." This time, the ECJ drew its interpretation first from this comparison of language versions, before it added supplementary arguments such as the structure and history of the legislative instrument in question.[17]

Although the ECJ has not developed a clearly recognizable and repeatable canon for the majority argument as it did for its teleological approach, it does refers to its legal reasoning in those cases as "settled case law." Advocate General Stix-Hackl confirms that from the ECJ's case law one can indeed derive the interpretive method by which preference is given to the language versions forming the majority.[18] The second-order argument that the ECJ uses to justify its literal approach in the event of linguistic discrepancies is the same as the one it uses for the teleological approach; according to the ECJ it is the need for a uniform interpretation and application of EU law that requires one or several language versions to be interpreted in the light of all the other language versions.

15.3.5 When interpretation strategies lead to conflicting outcomes

The foregoing shows that, when the ECJ detects linguistic discrepancies, it justifies both teleological and literal interpretive methods with the need for the uniform interpretation and application of EU law. Because the same second-order argument is invoked in support of both interpretive strategies, the legal reasoning of the ECJ fails to clearly explicate when it will choose one strategy or the other.

The uncertainty as to which method the ECJ will choose is in itself not necessarily a cause for alarm; the teleological and literal interpretive methods are not mutually exclusive. In fact, often in a single judgment the ECJ uses the literal interpretation as the

---

[16] Case C-236/97 *Codan* [1998] ECR I-8679, paras 23, 29.
[17] Case C-353/04 *Nowaco* [2006] ECR I-7357, paras 41–42.
[18] Case C-265/03 *Igor Simutenkov* [2005] ECR I-2579, Opinion of Advocate General Stix-Hackl delivered on January 11, 2005, para. 18.

principal or primary argument and then a teleological interpretation as the secondary or supplementary argument,[19] and vice versa.[20] There does not seem to be a consistent hierarchy between interpretive methods (Bengoetxea 1993:165).[21] To this extent, the question of when the ECJ would choose one or the other interpretive method does not move beyond the realm of legal dogmatism.

Yet, if the respective interpretive strategies may justify, as first-order argument, conflicting interpretations of the provision in question, determining when the ECJ will choose which method becomes more pressing. Bredimas (1978:70) observes that, in general, even when the ECJ finds a legislative text to be clear, it might invoke a teleological argument to contradict that clear meaning. This might be no different in the event of discrepancies between language versions. As Advocate General Stix-Hackl indicates, notwithstanding the use of the majority argument by the ECJ, in certain circumstances a single language version may need to be favored over the majority of language versions.[22] The case law between 1960 and 2010 includes 17 judgments in which a majority argument would have lead to a different interpretation than the teleological argument that the ECJ eventually chose (see Figure 15.6, second column). These 17 judgments amount to approximately 10 percent of those in which the ECJ identified linguistic discrepancies. In other words, in these judgments the ECJ used a teleological method as its principle first-order argument to support an interpretation that was inconsistent with its reading of the majority of language versions. Consequently, if in these cases the ECJ had invoked the majority argument, it could have rationally justified a contrary interpretation. These 17 judgments emphasize the possibility that, as Paunio and Lindroos-Hovinheimo (2010:410) point out, the ECJ's ability to prefer one interpretive method over the other may undermine the predictability of the outcome of cases, and thus the legal certainty of EU law.

Since the ECJ's explicit second-order arguments do not conclusively explain the circumstances in which either a teleological or a literal interpretation is called for, the next section of this chapter will present a statistical analysis of all 170 judgments between 1960 and 2010 in which the ECJ claimed to have observed linguistic discrepancies. The analysis aims to further illuminate possible implicit second-order arguments. This analysis will remain within the bounds of the "context of justification"; the aim is not to reveal the *actual* motivations of the judges in these judgments, but rather the significance of certain interpretive factors that the judgments themselves reveal.

[19] E.g. Case C-63/06 *UAB Profisa* [2007] ECR I-3239, paras 15–17.
[20] E.g. Case C-298/94 *Annette Henke* [1996] ECR I-4989, paras 13–14.
[21] Cf. the interpretation listed in Case 283/81 *CILFIT* [1982] ECR 3415, paras 18–20.
[22] Case C-265/03 *Igor Simutenkov* [2005] ECR I-2579, Opinion of Advocate General Stix-Hackl delivered on January 11, 2005, para. 18.

15.4 ANALYZING THE ECJ'S
INTERPRETIVE METHODS

15.4.1 The type of legislative instrument

In the literature on the general interpretive methods of the ECJ throughout the years, it has been suggested that the type of legislative instrument may play a role in whether the ECJ is likely to take a literal or a more teleological approach towards the interpretation of EU legislation.

The statistics show that there indeed seems to be a correlation between the nature of the legislative instrument and the ECJ's interpretive methods in the event of discrepancies between language versions. It appears that the more technical the legislative instrument, the more likely it becomes that the ECJ will take a literal approach. Conversely, the ECJ will take a teleological approach when the dispute involves more 'purposeful' legislative instruments.

15.4.1.1 *EU regulations on the Common Custom Tariff*

Bredimas (1978:48) and Bengoetxea (1993:234) found that in general the ECJ is more likely to use literal interpretation when the legislative instrument in question has a highly technical character. They use the EU regulations on the Common Customs Tariff (CCT) as examples.[23] This legislation may be considered highly technical due to the precise definitions of goods, in the (combined) nomenclature and the tariff headings.

As the first column of Figure 15.3 demonstrates, in 12 out of the 13 judgments that involve CCT legislation, the ECJ took a literal approach.[24] Moreover, the second column of Figure 15.3 shows that in judgments that involved *non*-CCT regulations the ECJ did not demonstrate such an obvious preference for the literal approach.

15.4.1.2 *Treaties*

The literature is not consistent when it comes to the ECJ's prevailing interpretive method in respect of the EU Treaties. Bredimas (1978:48) and Bengoetxea (1993:234) argue that the ECJ tends to interpret EU Treaties literally, because these also contain many provisions that have a definitional or technical character. However, Vogenauer (2006:680)

---

[23] Council Regulation (EEC) No 2658/87 of July 23, 1987 on the tariff and statistical nomenclature and on the Common Customs Tariff, OJ L 256, September 7, 1987, pp. 1–675 and, in earlier case law, Regulation (EEC) No 950/68 of the Council of June 28, 1968 on the common customs tariff, OJ L 172, July 22, 1968, pp. 1–402 and Regulation (EEC) No 1798/75 of the Council of July 10, 1975 on the importation free of Common Customs Tariff duties of educational, scientific, and cultural materials, OJ L 184, July 15, 1975, pp. 1–8.

[24] The only judgment between 1960 and 2010 involving the CCT in which the ECJ did not take a literal approach was in Case C-152/01 *Kyocera Electronics* [2003] ECR I-13821, paras 33–36.

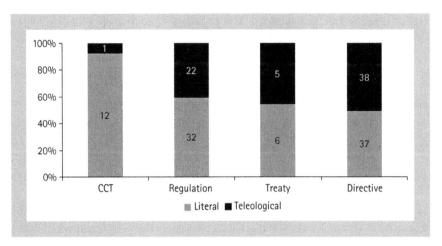

FIGURE 15.3 Interpretive methods in respect of linguistic discrepancies, per legislative instrument, between 1960 and 2010 (total number and percentage split)

reasons that the ECJ is prone to interpret EU Treaties teleologically, because these contain numerous declarations of objectives, particularly in the recitals of the preamble.

Neither hypotheses can be confirmed. The third column of Figure 15.3 demonstrates that when the ECJ is resolving discrepancies between language versions of the EU Treaties, it may either take a literal or a teleological approach.

15.4.1.3 *EU directives*

Hesselink (2001:37–9) and Van Gerven (2004:102) suggest that the ECJ tends to interpret EU directives using a teleological approach. They argue that, unlike EU regulations, EU directives instruct Member States to achieve certain results, rather than to adopt specific legal rules.[25] Consequently, the argument goes, when it comes to interpreting directives, ascertaining the objective or purpose is of greater importance then grasping specific legal concepts.

Returning to Figure 15.3, the fourth column does not indicate that the hypothesis of Hesselink and of Van Gerven applies in the event of discrepancies between language versions of directives. However, this figure includes both judgments in which the ECJ treats discrepancies as an interpretive problem and those in which it treats discrepancies as an interpretive tool (see Section 15.2). As Figure 15.4 shows, when consideration is taken only of the judgments that involved linguistic discrepancies that the ECJ treated as interpretive problems, the ECJ is indeed more likely to take a teleological approach. This seems typical for the interpretation of discrepancies in directives; when it comes to legislative instruments other than directives, the question whether the ECJ considers the discrepancies as an interpretive problem does not significantly affect its choice of interpretive method.

---

[25] See art. 288 TEU, Consolidated versions of the TEU and the TFEU, OJ C 83 of March 30, 2010.

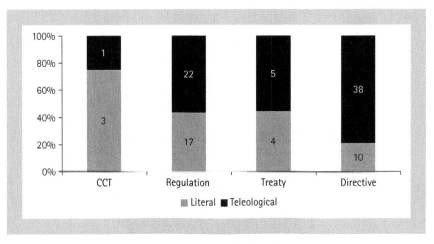

FIGURE 15.4 Interpretive methods in respect of *problematic* discrepancies, per legislative instrument, between 1960 and 2010 (total number and percentage split)

15.4.2 When a minority of versions diverges from the majority

Another factor that seems to be significant in the ECJ's choice of interpretive methods in the event of linguistic discrepancies is the number of language versions that the ECJ determines to be consistent. First, as Figure 15.5 demonstrates, in the vast majority of judgments in which the ECJ found that there is a single or a small number of language versions diverging from the majority of language versions, its eventual interpretation of the legal provision in question is consistent with its reading of the majority of language versions.

Second, there seems to be a relation between the ECJ's reading of the various language versions and the interpretive methods that it subsequently uses as principal first-order argument. The first column of Figure 15.6 shows that the ECJ is more likely to use a literal than a teleological argument to justify an interpretation of a legal provision that is consistent with its reading of the majority of language versions. Conversely, the second column of Figure 15.6 further demonstrates that the ECJ tends to employ a teleological argument to reach an interpretation of a provision that is not consistent with the meaning it attributes to the majority of language versions. The only two exceptions here are the ECJ's judgments in the aforementioned *EMU Tabac* and *Joustra* cases, in which it used a clarity argument to give preference to its reading of the minority of language versions.[26]

Lastly, as (the third column of Figure 15.6 illustrates, the ECJ is also most likely to use the teleological argument when about one half of the versions diverge from the other half, hence, when there exists no clear majority of versions. In almost all judgments in these cases, the ECJ employed a teleological argument to break the "deadlock."

---

[26] Case C-296/95 *EMU Tabac* [1998] ECR I-1605, para. 33 and Case C-5/05 *Joustra* [2006] ECR I-11075, para. 40.

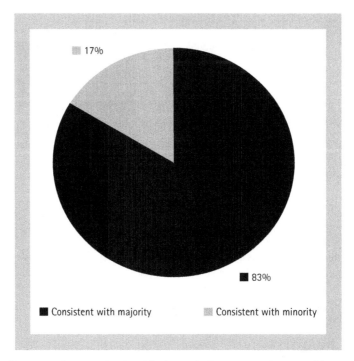

FIGURE 15.5 Interpretation consistent with the majority versus minority of language versions, between 1960 and 2010

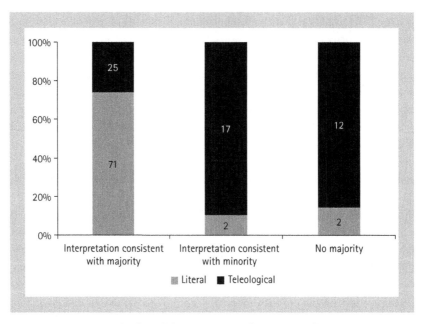

FIGURE 15.6 Interpretive methods and the occurrence of a majority of language versions between 1960 and 2010

15.4.3 The type of discrepancy

15.4.3.1 *Translation errors*

Lastly, when it appears obvious to the ECJ that a translation error was the cause of linguistic discrepancies, the ECJ will more likely take a literal approach. The first column of Figure 15.7 shows that the ECJ used a literal interpretive method in all judgments in which it explicitly or implicitly indicated that the discrepancy in question is the result of a "substantive error"[27] or a "mistranslation"[28] of one or more specific language versions.

In these judgments the discrepancies entailed the use of distinctly different terms in the various language versions. But even when the ECJ does not explicitly believe that a translation error is to blame, it seems that the ECJ is generally more likely to treat these types of discrepancies as textual flaws, which should not be the basis of the interpretation of the legal provision in question. The second column of Figure 15.7 illustrates that in two-thirds of all judgments in which the ECJ found these two types of discrepancies it took a literal approach. For example, in the judgment in the *Ludwig-Maximilians-Universität München* case in 1984, the ECJ found that all language versions of Article 3(1) (b) of Regulation No 1798/75[29] contained the words equivalent to "instruments" and "apparatus" but that only the German language version added the word *Gerate*, "utensils." The ECJ then employed a literal interpretive method to reconcile the discrepancy. It argued that this term could not "confer upon that linguistic version a wider meaning" than implied by the other versions and that therefore "no special significance should be attributed to the word *Gerate* in the German text."[30] Although the ECJ here does not unequivocally state that a translation error was made, it does seem that the ECJ treats this type of discrepancy as an imperfection, which should not play a role in the interpretive process.

15.4.3.2 *Semantic scope*

A different picture emerges with regard to linguistic discrepancies that are less likely to be translation errors or textual imperfections. This seems to hold particularly with discrepancies that involve the semantic scope of terminology. As Šarčević (2000 (1997):238) and Cao (2007a:74–7) point out, it is possible to consider two terms or phrases in different language versions to be equivalent, even though they do not have the same semantic scope or fully overlapping semantic scopes. This suggests that differences in the scope of terminology in the various language versions may not be an error, but merely a natural and unavoidable trait of translation.

The third column of Figure 15.7 confirms that the ECJ is more likely to use a teleological interpretive method in the event the ECJ detects discrepancies involving scope, than

---

[27] Case C-177/95 *Ebony Maritime* [1997] ECR I-1111, para. 50.

[28] Joined cases 424/85 and 425/85 *Frico* [1987] ECR 2755, par. 25.

[29] Regulation (EEC) No 1798/75 of the Council of July 10, 1975 on the importation free of Common Customs Tariff duties of educational, scientific, and cultural materials, OJ L 184, July 15, 1975, pp. 1–8.

[30] Case 45/83 *Ludwig-Maximilians-Universität München* [1984], ECR 267, para. 13.

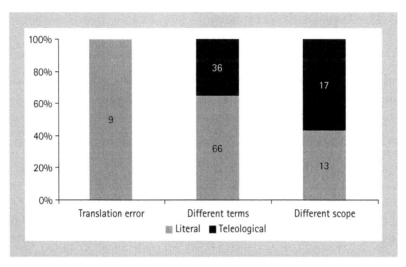

FIGURE 15.7 Interpretive method per linguistic discrepancy between 1960 and 2010 (total number and percentage split)

when it finds discrepancies involving distinct different terms. An example of a discrepancy involving the scope of terminology, appeared in the judgment in the *Abels* case in 1985. There the ECJ stated that a comparison of language versions showed that there were differences as to the scope of the concept of the "transfer of undertakings," and consequently the scope of application of Council Directive 77/187/EEC.[31] The ECJ added that the differences in scope were partly due to differences between the concepts of "contractual transfer" in the various national insolvency laws of the Member States. "In view of those divergences," the ECJ consequently observed that "the scope of the provision at issue cannot be appraised solely on the basis of a textual interpretation" and that "its meaning must therefore be clarified in the light of the scheme of the directive, its place in the system of community law in relation to the rules on insolvency, and its purpose."[32]

15.5 CONCLUSIONS

The 170 judgments between 1960 and 2010 in which the ECJ identified linguistic discrepancies suggest that the ECJ is more likely to use the literal approach when the provision or legislation at hand has a technical nature. It also suggests that when the ECJ observes that a single language version or a small minority of language versions diverges from all others, the ECJ tends to use a literal argument in justifying its interpretation of

---

[31] Article 1(1) of Council Directive 77/187/EEC of February 14, 1977 on the approximation of the laws of the Member States relating to the safeguarding of employees' rights in the event of transfers of undertakings, businesses, or parts of businesses, OJ L 61, March 5, 1977, pp. 26–8.
[32] Case 135/83 *Abels* [1985] ECR 469, paras 11–13.

the legal provision. This holds even more so when the judgment suggests that the dis-crepancy is likely to be caused by a translation error or textual imperfection. Conversely, when the ECJ finds that half the language versions contradict the other half, or that the discrepancies are not so obviously due to error, it is more likely to resort to the teleologi-cal approach.

The statistical analysis used in this chapter might paint a clear picture of the past; it does not provide a look into the future. There is no certainty in predicting what the ECJ will do next. Since the deliberations or personal opinions of the individual judges are not publicly available, a look at the ECJ's past legal reasoning is about all that the legal com-munity has to work with. To the extent that statistical analysis of past cases cannot pre-dict the future with the certainty that one might desire, it may in any event suggest that the legal reasoning of the ECJ is in need of further clarity, at least when it comes to its use of interpretive methods when linguistic discrepancies jeopardize the equal authenticity and the uniform interpretation and application of the language versions of EU legislation.[33]

[33] Many thanks to George A. Bermann and Kent Greenawalt for valuable discussions during the early stages of this study, conducted as a visiting research fellow at the Columbia University School of Law; and to Libuše Vošahlíková for her assistance in setting up the database and spreadsheets for the statistical analysis.

PART IV

LANGUAGE RIGHTS

CHAPTER 16

....

LINGUISTIC HUMAN RIGHTS

....

TOVE SKUTNΛBB-KANGAS

16.1 INTRODUCTION: LANGUAGE RIGHTS AS HUMAN RIGHTS

....

THE history of language rights is probably almost as long as the history of humans as language-using animals, that is tens of thousands of years. As soon as people using different "languages" were in contact with each other, they had to negotiate how to communicate verbally. Many "negotiations" may initially have been physically violent, without much verbal language, oral or signed. The linguistic outcome of negotiations where people wanted to exchange goods and services, rather than, or in addition to conquest, were probably also determined by the amount of physical force and visible material resources that each group could muster. In most encounters it was probably only the stronger party that had any "language rights": they needed to do much less accommodation than the weaker party, if any. The groups with "language rights" may have seen this practice (their "right" to use their own language(s) or the language(s) of their choice) as something self-evident, just as most speakers of dominant languages do now.

Genuine peaceful contact presupposes a mutual will to try to understand the other party's signed or spoken signals and symbols, to accommodate, and to learn at least some of them (often using a pidgin, an auxiliary simplified language), or to learn a common *lingua franca*, foreign to both. For dominant groups, their own rights have often been, and are still, invisible: they take them for granted. Even today, this is one of the problems when discussing and trying to formulate linguistic/language rights (hereafter LRs). Dominant linguistic groups often feel a need to formally codify their LRs only when dominated groups, for example indigenous/tribal peoples, or minorities of various kinds (hereafter ITMs) start demanding language rights for themselves.

Most people connect language rights mainly to ITMs, and most LRs are found among special minority or indigenous rights rather than general human rights (hereafter HRs).

Many states around the world have had legally codified language rights for minorities for centuries (see, e.g., de Varennes 1996, 2008), but summaries of or comparative literature on these rights are still scarce. The literature is often (unconsciously?) Eurocentric: only rights in Europe or Europe's "main" settler countries (e.g. Aotearoa/New Zealand, Australia, Canada, South Africa, the USA) count and are described, even when other parts of the world have had similar debates, codifications, or practices much earlier. Amartya Sen (2005), the economics Nobel laureate, described this bias in relation to peaceful debates and argumentation as ways of resolving conflicts (see also Spivak 2008). Scientific imperialism looms very large here.

Bilateral formally codified language rights started to appear in the West mainly in connection with religious minorities that also happened to be linguistic minorities (Capotorti 1979:2). The first multilateral Western treaty that contained language-related rights was the *Final Act of the Congress of Vienna* in 1815 (see Skutnabb-Kangas and Phillipson 1994 for a short history).

The Peace Treaties that concluded the First "World" War, and major multilateral and international conventions under the League of Nations improved the LRs protection. After the Second World War, the rights formulated by the United Nations were supposed to protect minority persons as individuals, and collective minority rights were seen as unnecessary. Better protection of linguistic minorities only started to develop after Francesco Capotorti, as a UN Special Rapporteur on the Rights of Minorities, published his 1979 report. The protection is still far from satisfactory.

Some LRs started to be described as Linguistic *Human* Rights (hereafter LHRs) relatively late. When I used the concept in a course in Finland in 1969, I had never heard or seen it, but I had an intuitive feeling that some language rights were so important that they should be seen as inalienable human rights. Earlier, language rights and human rights were more unconnected. Both were the domain of lawyers, with few if any linguists involved. Both areas were driven by practical–political concerns, and the research was mainly descriptive, not analytical. Even today, there is a fairly tight separation.

Few lawyers know much about language or education (some exceptions are, e.g,. Fernand de Varennes 1996, 2000; Sandra del Valle 2003; Robert Dunbar 2001; Kristin Henrard 2000; or Patrick Thornberry, esp. Thornberry and Gibbons 1997). Introducing LHRs "did not initially find a great deal of support among legal scholars" (de Varennes 2000:68), mainly because LHRs were seen as *collective* as opposed to *individual* rights. Likewise, many of the sociolinguists, political scientists, or educationalists who are today writing about LHRs know too little about international law (also here there are exceptions, e.g.: May 2001; Phillipson 2009; Tollefson and Tsui 2003).

The first multidisciplinary book about LHRs seems to be from the mid-1990s (Skutnabb-Kangas and Phillipson 1994). De Varennes (1996) and Thornberry's (1991, 2002) pioneering books contain much about LHRs even if they do not use the term. Today this is a fast growing area (as one can also see when googling the term "linguistic human rights"), but further concept clarification and multidisciplinary teamwork is urgently needed. The first concept in need of clarification is of course the main topic of this article: what are LHRs?

16.2 LANGUAGE RIGHTS VERSUS LINGUISTIC HUMAN RIGHTS

Are all language rights linguistic *human* rights? Hardly. A preliminary definition that has been used is: "(Some) language rights + human rights = linguistic human rights." The question then is: which language rights should be included and which should be excluded?

Susanne Mancini and Bruno de Witte define language rights as:

> fundamental rights protecting language-related acts and values. The term "fundamental" denotes the fact that these rights are entrenched in the constitution of a country, or in an international treaty binding on that country. (Mancini and de Witte 2008:247)

I have for some decades defined LHRs as:

> only those language rights are linguistic HUMAN rights which are so basic for a dignified life that everybody has them because of being human; therefore, in principle no state (or individual) is allowed to violate them (e.g. Skutnabb-Kangas 2008a:109).

Mancini and de Witte's (2008) legally oriented definition is more precise than my sociologically oriented one, even if they do not use the term linguistic *human* rights. It is broader than mine. Various constitutions are vague about language rights, stating that their precise formulations are given in separate laws or regulations. If these are also seen as belonging to "constitutions," there would be many "language rights" in these specifications that in my view cannot be considered linguistic *human* rights. One example would be regulations about the size of lettering in each language on product labels, as found in Canada, Latvia, or Slovakia. On the other hand, their definition is also narrower: it does not allow anything that has not yet been codified in any country, meaning new suggestions are, per definition, not (yet?) language rights.

Mancini and de Witte's "fundamental" is defined legally, whereas my "basic" is more a moral judgment. Mine is a very vague definition: even when various central human rights treaties and declarations enumerate fundamental rights, what one sees as basic or fundamental for a dignified life depends on the definer's ethics.[1] On the other hand, it opens possibilities for proposing as LHRs rights which have not yet been codified as such. One example would be an unconditional right to at least elementary education through the medium of one's own language (or mother tongue—see Skutnabb-Kangas and McCarty (2008) for definitions).

---

[1] Katarina Tomaševski, the former UN Special Rapporteur on the Right to Education, has discussed "a dignified life" in several publications. "Dignity" is mentioned in many international human rights instruments (e.g. Article 43 in UNDRIP).

LHRs, just as most other human rights, are to some extent relative. "Full" or "maximal" LHRs (whatever they are) can be seen as one end of a continuum where the other end could be linguicide, linguistic genocide (see the discussion on this in Skutnabb-Kangas and Dunbar, 2010). Many *language/linguistic* rights would come somewhere in the middle of the continuum: those rights that, even if they may be seen as important rights, do not belong in the realm of linguistic *human* rights.

Mancini and de Witte also distinguish between *core rights* and *ancillary rights*:

> The *core linguistic right* is the right to speak one's language, or, more precisely, the language of one's choice. The core right is, or can be, accompanied by a series of *ancillary rights* without which the right to speak a language becomes less valuable for its beneficiaries, such as: the right to be understood by others (for example, by public authorities), the right to a translation or an interpretation from other languages (for example, in the course of a meeting or trial at which those other languages are spoken), the right to compel others to speak one's language, and *the right to learn the language* (Mancini and de Witte 2008:247–8; emphasis added).

One might imagine that their "core rights" could be seen as LHRs, whereas the "ancillary rights" might be "only" language rights. Not so. The "right to learn the language" should obviously be a core LHR; this would follow from Mancini and de Witte's own argumentation. If children are not allowed to learn their parents or ancestors' language at a high level (which presupposes the right to use it as the main medium of education for the first many years), there will be nobody left to "speak one's language" after a few generations. Of the world's over 7,000 mainly spoken languages (7,106; see Lewis, Simons and Fennig 2014), at least some 4,500 are tribal/indigenous (Oviedo and Maffi 2000; Terralingua[2]). Estimates claim that minimally half, maybe up to 90–95 per cent of today's spoken languages will be extinct or at least no longer be learned by children by the year 2100.[3] Learning and knowing one's language/mother tongue is a necessary prerequisite for being able to enjoy the right to speak it. A more strict and principled definition of LHRs is urgently needed. It requires much analytical work, yet to be done.

16.3 LHRs FOR LINGUISTIC MAJORITIES AND MINORITIES

Dominant linguistic majorities are groups that speak the same language and that constitute over half the population. They usually have all rights that can be seen as LHRs; that is, they can use their languages orally and in writing in all situations in their countries.

---

[2] <http://www.terralingua.org>.
[3] The figures come from various writings by Michael Krauss from Alaska; UNESCO uses both 50% and 90–95%.

Still, some of them feel the need to strengthen their LRs—the Slovak Language Law (July 2009) is an example.[4]

Dominated majorities are groups in former colonies where one language group is a demographic majority, or where there is no group that would be demographically over 50 per cent of the population and where all groups are "minorities." They are in a different situation. Often a former colonial language, spoken by a very small elite in the country, is either an or the official language, used for most prestige functions, including parliament, courts, higher education, etc. Local languages are used in homes, on the market, for local politics, etc. This is a typical diglossic situation with a functional differentiation between the High and Low languages.

Dominated majorities are legally in a tricky situation since binding international instruments specifically for demographic but oppressed (or even politically dominant) majorities have not been developed. Although the speakers of the oppressing language are demographically a minority, they do not want to be regarded as such. During the colonial era many of the colonized also internalized the colonizers' views of "local" languages as backward, primitive, not worth anything, and these images still linger strongly. Ngũgĩ wa Thiong'o, a strong advocate of rights for African and other mother tongues,[5] captured the challenges in his 1987 book *Decolonising the mind*.

Linguist-philosopher Sándor Szilágyi (1994) has presented a suggestion for a "Bill on the Rights Concerning Ethnic and Linguistic Identity, and the Fair and Harmonious Coexistence of Ethnic and Linguistic Communities." In principle, it is a non-discrimination bill, but it defines *rights for both majorities and minorities.* Minorities are defined demographically, as consisting of minimally 8 per cent of the population of a local administrative district. His definition of "equality of chances" means that a minority must, for instance, have the same chance as the majority to use its own language in administration, as a teaching language in school and at university, etc., without needing to bear extra costs. Otherwise the minority are forced to finance majority-language-medium services for the majority through their taxes, without getting the same services for themselves—and this is the most common situation today. This would specify majority LRs and make minority LRs equal to them.

Linguistic minorities have some HRs support for various aspects of using their languages in areas such as public administration, courts, the media, etc. (the 1993 and 1994 books edited by Frowein, Hofmann, and Oeter about minority rights in European states give excellent overviews of the situation in Europe). Many of these rights are enshrined in the constitutions or special minority rights bills in a number of countries; some of these are extremely detailed (e.g. Canada, Latvia).

A range of regional instruments grant LRs to minorities—these loom large in the two fairly recent European instruments, the *European Charter* and the *Framework Convention for the Protection of National Minorities*. In the Charter (1998), a state can choose which

---

[4] See, e.g. Schöpflin (2009).
[5] See the Asmara Declaration, <http://www.outreach.psu.edu/programs/allodds/declaration.html> accessed September 1, 2011.

paragraphs or subparagraphs it wishes to apply (a minimum of 35 is required) and the languages it wants to apply them to. The Framework Convention in particular has been criticized by politicians and international lawyers, who are normally very careful in their comments. Law professor Patrick Thornberry's general assessment is:

> In case any of this [provisions in the Convention] should threaten the delicate sensibilities of States, the Explanatory Report makes it clear that they are under no obligation to conclude "agreements".... Despite the presumed good intentions, the provision represents a low point in drafting a minority right; there is just enough substance in the formulation to prevent it becoming completely vacuous (Thornberry 1997:356–7).

16.4 COLLECTIVE LHRs

One of the main legal obstacles to accepting some LRs as LHRs can be placed within the still ongoing debates about the various generations of human rights where only individual rights ("the first generation") have been recognized by some as "proper" human rights. Any linguistic rights "seem to imply some kind of a collective nature" (de Varennes 2000:68), and collective rights in legally binding international treaties have been shunned for political reasons (see Capotorti 1979). Languages are of course only meaningfully used with other people. Legislating about individual inner speech is impossible.

Linguicide, language rights, and LHRs are all phenomena at both *individual* and *collective/group* levels. For instance, the *UN Declaration on the Rights of **Persons** Belonging to National or Ethnic, Religious and Linguistic Minorities* supposedly provides rights to individuals, whereas both the *UN Declaration on the Rights of Indigenous **Peoples*** and the Council of Europe's *Framework Convention for the Protection of National **Minorities*** are about collectives (even if both constantly jump between the individual and collective level). Linguicide also involves both individuals and groups/peoples (see Churchill 1997, final chapter, for discussion). In addition to humans having LHRs, some instruments also treat *languages themselves* (as parts of the intangible human heritage) as right-holders, for example the *European Charter for Regional or Minority **Languages***.

The difficulty in formulating some kind of a collective right while keeping it within the language of individual rights is beautifully (and, for non-lawyers, almost pitifully ridiculously) illustrated by the still most far-reaching *general* article in international law that creates obligations for states about the right to use one's own language, namely Article 27 of the *International Covenant on Civil and Political Rights* (ICCPR).[6] It provides that:

> in those States in which ethnic, religious or linguistic minorities exist, *a child belonging to such a minority* shall not be denied the right, *in community with other members of his*

---

[6] 1966, in force from 1976, <http://www2.ohchr.org/english/law/ccpr.htm> accessed September 1, 2011.

group, to enjoy his own culture, to profess and practise his own religion, or to use his own language. (ICCPR, Art. 27, emphases added)

This provision is echoed literally in Article 30 of the *Convention on the Rights of the Child* (CRC),[7] except "or persons of indigenous origin" and "who is indigenous" have been added in the first and second lines, and "or she," and "or her" have also been added. Female and indigenous children have gained humanity as legal language-using subjects, except in the only two countries which have not ratified the CRC: Somaliland and the USA.

Article 27 was earlier seen in a much narrower way, as only granting some protection from discrimination. However, the UN Human Rights Committee has noted in its General Comment No. 23 of 1994 on Article 27 of the ICCPR[8] that, although phrased in the negative, the Article requires states to take positive measures in support of minorities. Unfortunately, the Human Rights Committee has not spelled out what those measures are. Likewise, the HRC stated that the existence of a minority does not depend on a decision by the state but must be established by objective criteria, an important factor in relation to countries which have denied having (certain) linguistic minorities, such as France, Greece, Turkey, etc. The revised *Human Rights Fact Sheet* on ICCPR from the Committee (2005) sustains these interpretations.

The most important collective LHRs are the rights of indigenous/tribal people and linguistic minority groups to exist as such, without being forced to assimilate, and to be allowed and enabled to transfer their language to the next generation, if they so wish. These rights are included and their contents are spelled out in several HRs instruments. In the *UN Declaration on the Rights of Indigenous Peoples* (UNDRIP),[9] Paragraph 1 of Article 8 provides that indigenous peoples and individuals have the right not to be subjected to forced assimilation or destruction of their culture. And Article 13, para. 1 states:

> Indigenous peoples have the right to revitalize, use, develop and transmit to future generations their histories, languages, oral traditions, philosophies, writing systems and literatures, and to designate and retain their own names for communities, places and persons. (UNDRIP, Art. 13, para. 1)

Article 13, para. 2, continues: "States shall take effective measures to ensure that this right is protected."

The *Framework Convention* provides in Article 5, para. 1 that the Parties to the treaty will promote the conditions necessary for persons belonging to national minorities to maintain and develop their culture, and to preserve essential elements of their identity, including their religion, language, traditions, and cultural heritage, and Article 5, para. 2 requires that Parties refrain from policies or practices aimed at assimilation of persons belonging to national minorities against their will.

---

[7] 1989, <http://www.unhchr.ch/html/menu3/b/k2crc.htm>

[8] 4 April 1996, UN Doc. CCPR/C/21/Rev.1/Add.5. See <http://www2.ohchr.org/english/bodies/hrc/comments.htm> accessed September 1, 2011.

[9] See, e.g. http://www.iwgia.org/sw248.asp, or http://www.tebtebba.org/index.php?option=com_docman&task=cat_view&gid=16&Itemid=27

16.5 Justifications for Linguistic Human Rights

LHRs have been questioned, mainly by political scientists. Researchers debate what kind of language rights can be justified on what bases, that is which *demands* justify what kinds of *supply*. The main issue is whether all or only some (and in that case which ones) of those inequalities that are due to characteristics (in the individual or in society) that are not chosen by the individual should be "compensated for" or "rectified" by the state. Being born to parents who speak a language that is not the dominant language in the society where the person lives, and suffering injustice if this language has low status, could be seen as justifying a demand for "compensation", that is, that the state should offer more supplies, such as mother-tongue-medium education.

Most (neo)liberal political scientists do not recognize, though, that states should support the maintenance of the existence of minority groups beyond present generations. This seems partly to be because they regard speaking a minority language as some kind of a handicap. According to this view, such a "handicap" should not be carried on to the following generations. If parents choose to do it, it is *their* responsibility. The neoliberal view concentrates on individual rights. Therefore, minority groups as groups do not, according to many political scientists, have justifiable demands to continue their existence as minority groups. They are given the choice either to assimilate on an individual basis, or to continue *without* a justified claim to support for collective rights, for instance the right to transfer their languages to the next generation through state education. Thus they deny the validity of what in this chapter are considered as two basic LHRs.

Many lawyers, educationalists, and sociolinguists subscribe to a different analysis. The linguistic protection of national minorities rests according to the former High Commissioner on the Rights of National Minorities of the Organization for Security and Co-operation in Europe (OSCE), Max van der Stoel, on two HRs *pillars*. These have also been called *negative* and *positive rights*, or *non-discrimination rights* and *affirmative rights*. Van der Stoel distinguishes between:

> the *right to non-discrimination* in the enjoyment of human rights; and the *right to the maintenance and development of identity* through the freedom to practice or use those special and unique aspects of their minority life—typically culture, religion, and language. The first protection...ensures that minorities receive all of the other protections without regard to their ethnic, national, or religious status; they thus enjoy a number of linguistic rights that all persons in the state enjoy, such as freedom of expression and the right in criminal proceedings to be informed of the charge against them in a language they understand, if necessary through an interpreter provided free of charge.
>
> The second pillar, encompassing affirmative obligations beyond non-discrimination...includes a number of rights pertinent to minorities simply by virtue of their minority status, such as the right to use their language. This pillar is necessary

because a pure non-discrimination norm could have the effect of forcing people belonging to minorities to adhere to a majority language, effectively denying them their rights to identity. (Van der Stoel 1999:8–9; emphases added)

In a similar vein, Ruth Rubio-Marín (Professor of Constitutional Law in Seville, Spain) distinguishes two kinds of interest in language rights. One is "the expressive interest in language as a marker of identity," the other an "instrumental interest in language as a means of communication" (Rubio-Marín 2003:56). The *expressive* (or non-instrumental) language claims

> aim at ensuring a person's capacity to enjoy a secure linguistic environment in her/ his mother tongue and a linguistic group's fair chance of *cultural self-reproduction.* (Rubio-Marín 2003:56; emphasis added)

It is only these expressive rights (that correspond to van der Stoel's second pillar) that Rubio-Marín calls "language rights in a strict sense" (2003:56); that is, these could be seen as linguistic *human* rights (LHRs). This formulation beautifully integrates individual rights with collective rights, in the sense I suggest below. The *instrumental* language claims (van der Stoel's first pillar) on the other hand

> aim at ensuring that language is not an obstacle to the effective enjoyment of rights with a linguistic dimension, to the meaningful participation in public institutions and democratic process, and to the enjoyment of social and economic opportunities that require linguistic skills. (Rubio-Marín 2003:56)

Negative debates ensue when some instrumentalists falsely claim that those interested in the expressive aspects exclude the more instrumental communication-oriented aspects (for instance, unequal class- or gender-based access to formal language or to international languages). Most ITM groups are interested in both types of rights, expressive and instrumental, and often one is a prerequisite for the other, with both being alternately causal *and* dependent variables. Many of us work with both aspects, and see them as complementary, not mutually exclusive. Individual and collective LHRs presuppose and support each other—"either/or" does not work.

16.6 INDIVIDUAL POSITIVE LHRs

Individual LHRs may relate to a right to

1. identify with languages (identity rights);
2. learn languages (mother tongue, second/official language, foreign languages) through formal education (educational rights);
3. use languages in various situations and for various purposes (functional rights);
4. change/shift languages voluntarily, or not (protection-against-forced-assimilation rights).

All of these rights are in several ways linked and intertwined, and mostly presuppose each other. They cut across the earlier distinctions. Identity rights belong to Van der Stoel's second pillar. Expressive rights and functional rights belong to the first pillar. And instrumental rights, educational rights, and protection-against-forced-assimilation belong to both. I will restrict the rest of the presentation to some of the more important LHRs.

16.6.1 The right to change/shift languages

If an individual (or a group) wants to assimilate into a dominant language group, at the cost of learning, using, and identifying with their own language(s), it should be their right to do so. But very often this kind of assimilation is not voluntary. Many people (are made to) believe that they have to choose: either the mother tongue (and a strong identity, knowledge of their ancestors, and cultural heritage), *or* a dominant language (and better life prospects in relation to jobs, etc). In addition to the promises about a better future often being false anyway, there is no need to choose. It is perfectly possible to learn several languages, including the mother tongue, well, and so to succeed in school and to have a multilingual, multicultural identity. Not having access to mainly mother-tongue-medium education mostly leads to linguistic and other assimilation, even against the wishes of people. The United Nation's 2004 *Human Development Report*[10] linked cultural liberty to language rights and human development and argued that there is

> no more powerful means of "encouraging" individuals to assimilate to a dominant culture than having the economic, social and political returns stacked against their mother tongue. Such assimilation is not freely chosen if the choice is between one's mother tongue and one's future. (UN, *Human Development Report*:33)

Thus not being pressured to assimilate linguistically should be a basic individual (and collective) LHR. Two prerequisites for this are, first, that people have enough solid research-based information about the consequences of their choices. Most ITM people around the world do not have this today. Secondly, alternatives must exist in the educational system.

16.6.2 The right to education through the medium of one's mother tongue

Influential, though non-legally binding principles for mother-tongue-medium (MTM) education have been developed through the office of the OSCE High Commissioner on National Minorities, in *The Hague Recommendations Regarding the Education Rights of*

---

[10] <http://hdr.undp.org/reports/global/2004/> accessed September 1, 2011.

National Minorities of October, 1996.[11] In this document, MTM education is recommended at all levels, including secondary education, and this includes bilingual teachers in the dominant language as a second language (Arts 11–13). In its Explanatory Note, the following comment is made about subtractive education:[12]

> [S]ubmersion-type approaches whereby the curriculum is taught exclusively through the medium of the State language and minority children are entirely integrated into classes with children of the majority are not in line with international standards. (OSCE, *Hague Recommendations Regarding the Education Rights of National Minorities*:para. 5)

The submersion education through the medium of a dominant language that most indigenous/tribal peoples in the world and many minorities undergo today is contrary to recommendations based on solid research, which shows that the more years ITM children study mainly through the medium of their own languages, the better their results are in all subjects and also in the dominant language.[13]

The submersion education approach violates the right to education. It can also sociologically, psychologically, educationally, and economically be seen as genocidal, within the meaning of Articles II(b) and II(e) of the United Nations' 1948 *Convention on the Prevention and Punishment of the Crime of Genocide*.[14] Likewise, forms of this education may legally come within the definitions of a crime against humanity of the Convention (see Skutnabb-Kangas and Dunbar 2010).

16.7 WHY LHRs—THE ROLE OF
INDIGENOUS PEOPLES

The often appalling ignorance among decision makers at various levels about basic language matters is a serious deficiency. As a result, important language status planning decisions are often based on false information, even in situations where the correct

---

[11] <http://www.osce.org/documents/hcnm/1996/10/2700_en.pdf> accessed September 1, 2011.

[12] Subtractive education, through the medium of a dominant language for ITM children, subtracts from their linguistic repertoire: they learn (some of) the new language at the cost of their own language. Instead, teaching should be additive—they should learn the dominant language at a native or near-native level, in addition to developing their mother tongues to a very high level through education. This is perfectly possible through mother-tongue-based multilingual education. For the theoretical background and many examples, see, e.g., Skutnabb-Kangas 1984, 2000; García et al. 2006; Skutnabb-Kangas et al. 2009, Skutnabb-Kangas and Dunbar (2010); Skutnabb-Kangas and Heugh (2011).

[13] See Grin 2008; Mohanty 2000; Nikièma and Ilboudo (2011) show that bilingual education in Burkina Faso gets better results, in a shorter time, and costs less, than French-medium education.

[14] E793, 1948; 78 U.N.T.S. 277, entered into force January 12, 1951; for the full text, see <http://www1.umn.edu/humanrts/instree/x1cppcg.htm> accessed September 1, 2011.

information is easily available and has in fact been offered to the decision makers. More interdisciplinary cooperation between HRs lawyers, sociolinguists, and educationists is urgently needed (see the Introduction in Kontra et al. 1999 and May 1999, 2001). Often Western research additionally suffers from ethnocentricity, and a lack of knowledge of the languages and cultures of others (see, e.g., Hountondji 2002, Smith Tuhiwai 1999).

But a lack of LHRs is not only an information problem. The political will of states to grant LHRs is the main problem. Human rights, especially economic and social rights, should, according to Tomaševski (1996), act as correctives to the free market. She states that

> the purpose of international human rights law is ... to overrule the law of supply and demand and remove price-tags from people and from necessities for their survival. (Tomaševski 1996:104)

These necessities for survival include not only basic food and housing (which would come under economic and social rights), but also basic requirements for the sustenance of a dignified life, including basic civil, political, and cultural rights—and LHRs are a part of cultural rights. Tomaševski and many others write that unless there is a redistribution of resources for implementing HRs, progress will be limited. It is of little or no use to spread knowledge of HRs as a basis for self-directed human development, unless the resources for implementation follow, and that can only happen through a radical redistribution of the world's material resources.

Moreover, state policies leading towards diminishing the numbers of languages are plagued by monolingual reductionism, falsely viewing monolingualism (in a state or dominant language) as something

- *normal and natural*; however, most countries are multilingual;
- *desirable* (more efficient and economical); however, if citizens do not understand the language they are governed in and if huge talent is wasted because children do not profit and are even harmed by formal education, this is inefficient and wasteful;
- *sufficient*: everything important exists in "big" languages, especially English; this is nonsense;
- *inevitable*: only romantics regret the disappearance of languages and linguistic homogenisation; however, linguistic diversity and multilingualism enhance creativity and are necessary in information societies where the main products are diverse ideas and diverse knowledges. (Skutnabb-Kangas 2000)

In addition, states seem to regard the granting of LHRs as divisive. The rationale is that they result in minorities reproducing themselves as minorities. These minorities then supposedly follow the old nation-state mentality and want cultural autonomy, economic autonomy and, in the end, political autonomy: their own state. Thus MTM education for minorities is ultimately seen as leading to the disintegration of "nation-states." These erroneous beliefs are an important causal factor in linguistic genocide and a lack of LHRs in education.

One reason for maintaining all the world's languages, partly through binding LHRs, is as follows: Linguistic diversity and biodiversity are correlationally and causally related. Most of the world's megabiodiversity is in areas under the management or guardianship of Indigenous peoples. Much of the knowledge about how to maintain biodiversity (especially in biodiversity hotspots) is encoded in the small languages of indigenous and local peoples. This knowledge is often more accurate and detailed than the knowledge that scientists have, according to *The International Council of Science*,[15] and it does not transfer to other languages if ITMs shift to a dominant language. Through killing ITM languages or letting them die, we kill the prerequisites for maintaining biodiversity (see Skutnabb-Kangas 2000 for details).

UNDRIP's provision on MTM education does not prevent this: education in the dominant (state) language is "free"[16] for ITMs in the same way as for dominant group children, whereas MTM education is dependent on whether they have the financial resources to "establish" it:

1. Indigenous peoples have the right to establish and control their educational systems and institutions providing education in their own languages, in a manner appropriate to their cultural methods of teaching and learning.
2. Indigenous individuals, particularly children, have the right to all levels and forms of education of the State without discrimination.
3. States shall, in conjunction with indigenous peoples, take effective measures, in order for indigenous individuals, particularly children, including those living outside their communities, to have access, when possible, to an education in their own culture and provided in their own language. (UNDRIP, Article 14)

People who lose their linguistic and cultural identity may lose an essential element in a social process that commonly teaches respect for nature and understanding of the natural environment and its processes. Forcing this cultural and linguistic conversion on Indigenous and other traditional peoples not only violates their human rights, but also undermines the health of the world's ecosystems and the goals of nature conservation.[17]

Cultural diversity is closely linked to biodiversity. Humanity's collective knowledge of biodiversity and its use and management rests in cultural diversity; conversely conserving biodiversity often helps strengthen cultural integrity and values (World Resources Institute, World Conservation Union, and United Nations Environment Programme 1992:21).

Linguistic human rights are a necessary but *not* sufficient tool in the struggle for social justice.

---

[15] <http://www.icsu.org>.
[16] There are school fees in over 100 countries, see Tomaševski 2000.
[17] <http://www.terralingua.org>.

CHAPTER 17

....

LANGUAGE POLICY IN THE UNITED STATES

....

PETER M. TIERSMA

THE United States is often called a nation of immigrants. The earliest migrants were the Native Americans or Indians. Starting in the early 1600s, European immigrants began to arrive on the east coast, mostly from England and other parts of northern Europe. Spaniards explored and colonized the southwest of what is now the United States, and somewhat later Russian traders were active in Alaska and the Pacific coast. Today, of course, English is heavily dominant in almost all of the United States, but it was not always so. Even now, there are substantial linguistic minorities throughout the country.

17.1 NATIVE AMERICAN LANGUAGES

....

When Europeans arrived in what is now the United States, they encountered tremendous linguistic diversity. There were hundreds of languages comprising a number of major language families, including *Algonquian* (such as Cree, Menomini, Micmac, Munsee, and Ojibwa); *Athabaskan* (Navajo and Apache, among others); *Iroquoian* (including Cherokee and Mohawk); *Siouan* (including Lakota and Winnebago); *Uto-Aztecan* (Hopi and some other Pueblo languages, as well as Shoshone and Paiute); and *Yuman* (Mojave, Diegueño) (Mithun 1999:326–605).

The European settlers often had little understanding of the languages they encountered. Some seem to have thought that the Native Americans did not have language at all, or believed that their speech was not comparable to European languages. Columbus, for instance, wrote in his journal that he planned to capture six Indians and bring them back to Spain "that they may learn to speak" (Baron 1990:35). The Spanish, who colonized much of South America, viewed language as a means to establish an empire and aimed to make Spanish the common language and Catholicism the common religion. To a large extent, they succeeded.

The process was similar in the British colonies in North America. Most colonists, unless they were traders or missionaries, saw little reason to learn native languages. Not surprisingly, the indigenous languages spoken in the colonies did not long survive the onslaught of European immigrants (Mithun 1999:1–5).

As the country expanded westward beginning in the early nineteenth century, native Americans were forced to live on reservations. Indians were encouraged to give up their languages and cultures. Treaties made in that period, such as that with the Chippewa, Menominie, and Winnebago, provided for the establishment of schools for Indian children.[1] The schools were intended "to encourage industry, thrift, and morality, and by every possible means to promote their advancement in civilization."[2] Later treaties made attendance of children at these schools compulsory.[3] The reason for these measures was explained by Indian Commissioner Price:

> One of two things must eventually take place, to wit, either civilization or extermination of the Indian.... If the Indians are to be civilized and become a happy and prosperous people, which is certainly the object and intention of our government, they must learn our language and adopt our modes of life. (Prucha 1975:156)

Beginning with the Yankton Sioux in 1858, treaties explicitly required that children at these schools be taught to read in English.[4] The federal policy of "civilizing" the Indian went a step further when, in 1887, it was forbidden to teach the Indian youth "in his own barbarous dialect." The order, which applied to missionary as well as federally funded schools, was propounded because "if any Indian vernacular is allowed to be taught by the missionaries in schools on Indian reservations, it will prejudice the youthful pupil as well as his untutored and uncivilized or semi-civilized parent against the English language" (Prucha 1975:176).

Perhaps the most notorious aspect of this policy was the establishment of boarding schools. Beginning with the first such school in Carlisle, Pennsylvania, in 1879, boarding schools were a mainstay of federal policy for the ensuing 50 or so years (Berry 1968:11). In these schools, where pupils were often hundreds of miles from their parents, the use of the native languages was stigmatized, and students could be and often were punished for using their own language at play (Leibowitz 1969:16).

The 1930s witnessed a change in American Indian policy, championed by John Collier, Commissioner of Indian Affairs from 1933 to 1945. Collier urged that the Indians be allowed to retain their culture, and he reduced the emphasis on assimilation. The use of native languages to promote learning in schools was encouraged (Philp 1977:128–9).

Several decades later Congress passed the *Native American Languages Act*. It recognized that "the status of the cultures and languages of Native Americans is unique and the United States has the responsibility to act together with Native Americans to ensure the survival of these unique cultures and languages."[5]

---

[1] Treaty with the Chippewa, Menominie, and Winnebago, Art. 5. 7 Stat. 303 (1827).
[2] Treaty with the Kickapoo, Art. 9. 10 Stat. 1078 (1854).
[3] See, e.g., Treaty with the Pawnees, Art. 3. 11 Stat. 729 (1857).
[4] Treaty with the Yankton Sioux, Art. 4, cl. 4. 11 Stat. 743 (1858).
[5] 25 U.S.C. § 2901(1).

Unfortunately, the turnabout came too late for many of the tribes. Large numbers of indigenous American languages have become extinct, or are nearly so. Alaska, for instance, is home to approximately 20 native languages, only two of them currently being acquired as a first language by children (Krauss 1992). Revival efforts are under-way, but it will be an uphill battle.

17.2 EUROPEAN LANGUAGES IN EARLY AMERICA

Besides indigenous languages, there were several European languages spoken in the origi-nal thirteen colonies. At the time of the Revolutionary War, many Germans lived in Pennsylvania, Maryland, Virginia, and New York. There was a substantial number of Dutch speakers in New York and Delaware. In the midwestern territories east of the Mississippi, most European inhabitants spoke French (Conklin and Lourie 1983:5; Kloss 1977:11–12).

Yet upon independence none of the original thirteen states found it necessary to declare English its official language. This was true even in Pennsylvania, despite the famous fears of Benjamin Franklin, who worried that the many Germans in the state were not assimilating linguistically. "Few of their children in the Country learn English; they import many books from Germany; and of the six printing houses in the Province, two are entirely German." In a few years, Franklin mused, it might become necessary to use interpreters in the state Assembly, "to tell one half of our Legislators what the other half say" (Franklin 1753:484–5).

Franklin's worries seem not to have been broadly shared. During the late eighteenth and early nineteenth century, the state published statutes and other official documents in German. Pennsylvania, along with some other states, even allowed the establishment of German-language public schools during this period (Kloss 1977:143–50). Despite leg-ends to the contrary, which persist to this day, German never came close to becoming the national language of the United States or of any individual state (Heath 1981:9).

The founders of the United States likewise seem to have felt no need to make English the official language of the federal government. As in some of the states, the federal govern-ment sometimes employed languages other than English for official purposes. The Continental Congress had many of its proclamations translated and printed in German. It also authorized a German translation of the Articles of Confederation (Kloss 1977:26–7).

Of course, authorizing an occasional publication in German does not mean that Pennsylvania or the federal government was endorsing official bilingualism. The found-ing fathers—who were almost all native speakers of English—probably considered it self-evident that English would be the language of government. At the same time, most of them were apparently not threatened by the presence of other languages in their midst.

In retrospect, the relatively tolerant approach to European languages during this period was quite successful. Language was never a particularly contentious issue in early America.

And the role of English as the de facto national language was never seriously challenged. Even though millions of German speakers dwelt on American soil at various times, the German language in America is now virtually extinct, spoken only by a few recent immigrants and a small number of historic religious communities (Kloss 1966:248–9).

17.3 INCREASING IMMIGRATION AND WORLD WAR I

The relatively tolerant attitude towards immigrant languages weakened during the period from around 1880 to the end of World War I. This was a time of great immigration to the United States, much of it from southern and eastern Europe. Anti-immigrant sentiment grew (William Ross 1994).

World War I added fuel to the fire. On the federal level, the government enacted the Trading with the Enemy Act after the United States entered the war in 1917. The law made it illegal to print or circulate a news item, editorial, or other printed matter in any foreign language if the topic was the government of the United States or any nation engaged in the war. An exception was created if the publication, including a true and complete translation in English, was filed with the local postmaster.[6]

Many school districts banned the teaching of German. Some people went so far as to try to abolish the German word *sauerkraut*, replacing it with *liberty cabbage*. Oregon prohibited any foreign language publications, unless accompanied by a literal English translation. And the governor of Iowa issued a proclamation in 1918 against the use of any foreign language in the schools, in public, or on the telephone! Over 18,000 people were charged under this and similar laws by 1921 (Baron 1990; Crawford 1992:55–60).

Even in wartime, the constitutionality of such laws seems highly questionable. In fact, it was right around this time that a major case on language rights, *Meyer v Nebraska*,[7] reached the United States Supreme Court. In 1919 Nebraska had passed a law forbidding the teaching of any subject to schoolchildren in a language other than English. Furthermore, children could be taught to speak, read, or write other languages only after they had passed the eighth grade. A teacher at a parochial school was convicted of violating the act by teaching a ten-year-old boy to read Bible stories in German. The Nebraska courts affirmed the conviction.

The state defended the law on the ground that it was necessary to promote civic development and American ideals. In the words of Nebraska's Supreme Court:

> The salutary purpose of the statute is clear. The Legislature had seen the baneful effects of permitting foreigners, who had taken residence in this country, to rear and educate their children in the language of their native land. The result of that condition was found to be inimical to our own safety. To allow the children of foreigners, who had

---

[6] 40 Stat. 411, §19 (1917).
[7] 262 U.S. 390 (1923). For background on the case, see Ross (1994:74–95).

emigrated here, to be taught from early childhood the language of the country of their parents was to rear them with that language as their mother tongue. It was to educate them so that they must always think in that language, and, as a consequence, naturally inculcate in them the ideas and sentiments foreign to the best interests of this country.... The obvious purpose of this statute was that the English language should be and become the mother tongue of all children reared in this state.[8]

The United States Supreme Court viewed the matter differently. It held that a state can do much to regulate the lives of its citizens, but it must respect certain fundamental rights of the individual. Using the constitutional jurisprudence of the time, the Court emphasized the teacher's right to carry out his occupation, as well as the right of parents to educate their children as they see fit. "The protection of the Constitution extends to all, to those who speak other languages as well as to those born with English on the tongue."[9]

The Court was sympathetic to Nebraska's desire to "foster a homogeneous people with American ideals."[10] But that goal did not justify the means used to achieve it. "Perhaps it would be highly advantageous if all had ready understanding of our ordinary speech, but this cannot be coerced by methods which conflict with the Constitution—a desirable end cannot be promoted by prohibited means."[11]

Another language case, *Yu Cong Eng v Trinidad*, arose a few years later in the Philippines, which at the time was under American rule. The Philippine legislature passed a law known as the Chinese Bookkeeping Act. The law required that all account books be kept only in English, Spanish, or any "local dialect." Presumably, *local dialect* referred to indigenous languages such as Tagalog or Cebuano. As the name implies, the statute was aimed at Chinese merchants, who typically kept their books in Chinese. The stated reason for the law was to allow authorities—who could not read Chinese—to determine that these merchants paid their fair share of taxes.

The Supreme Court observed that the Philippines was in a "polyglot situation" that presented many difficulties for government. There were 43 native dialects or languages. A number of people spoke Spanish, and younger people increasingly knew English. In addition, Chinese merchants had operated in the islands for centuries and accounted for a large part of the trade in the Philippines. Very few of them spoke English, Spanish, or a native language. Most communicated with the local population by means of signs or a patois. Consequently, the act would impose a substantial hardship on them, and the need to hire translators or bookkeepers might drive some of them out of business.

The Court concluded that the law was unconstitutional. As in *Meyer*, the Court's concern was not so much the right to speak or write Chinese per se, but the right of Chinese businessmen to engage in a lawful occupation. Nonetheless, the case reinforced the principle that discrimination based upon language should not be tolerated.[12]

---

[8] 187 N.W. 100, 102 (Neb. 1922).
[9] 262 U.S. 390, 401 (1923).
[10] Ibid. at 402.
[11] Ibid. at 401.
[12] 271 U.S. 500 (1926).

During the 1920s and 1930s, immigration declined considerably and language issues receded from the national consciousness. By now, the children of earlier immigrants were mostly speaking English. Moreover, with the collapse of the stock market, the Great Depression, and World War II, the nation had more serious concerns.

17.4 THE OFFICIAL ENGLISH MOVEMENT

During the 1980s and 1990s there was another large wave of immigration to the United States. Millions of immigrants from Asia and Central America entered the country (Alba and Nee 2003). This has—perhaps predictably—led to renewed controversy regarding language rights and the role of English as the country's national language.

Before this time, the only significant attempt to make English an official language was an Illinois statute that gave this status to the "American" language. A court later held that the English and American languages were equivalent, and several decades later the state amended the law to change "American" to "English" (Baron 1990:128–30).

Then, in 1981, Senator S. I. Hayakawa from California proposed the English Language Amendment to the US Constitution. Besides holding some hearings, however, Congress took no action (Baron 1990:18). Because the Constitution is very hard to amend, other members of Congress have from time to time introduced ordinary legislation to the same effect. To date, none of these bills has passed.[13]

The momentum of the movement then shifted to the states, where it has been quite a bit more successful. To date, about half of the states have made English their official language. The individual statutes or state constitutional provisions vary quite a bit, however. Many of them do little beyond declaring that English is the state's official language.[14]

17.4.1 Arizona's law and resulting litigation

Some states have enacted language laws that are more than symbolic. Probably the most restrictive is Article XXVIII of the Arizona constitution ("Article 28"), adopted by the state's voters in 1987. Not only did Article 28 declare English to be the official language of Arizona, but it expressly provided that it is "the language of the ballot, the public schools and all government functions and actions." It applied to "all political subdivisions, departments, agencies, organizations, and instrumentalities of this State, including local governments and municipalities." In fact, its scope included "all government officials and employees during the performance of government business."

---

[13] The most recent attempt was the English Language Unity Act of 2009. <http://www.govtrack.us/congress/billtext.xpd?bill=h111-997> accessed October 18, 2010.

[14] *Alaskans for a Common Language, Inc. v Kritz*, 170 P.3d 183, 189 (Alaska 2007).

Only days after voters passed Article 28, Maria-Kelley Yniguez challenged it in federal court. Yniguez worked for the Arizona Department of Administration, where she handled malpractice claims against the state. Fluent in both English and Spanish, she had previously communicated in both languages. Yniguez asserted that by forbidding her to speak Spanish to clients, Article 28 violated the United States Constitution. The court of appeals agreed and struck down the provision.[15]

The *Yniguez* case then went to the United States Supreme Court. Ultimately, however, the Court dismissed the case on procedural grounds and vacated the opinion of the court of appeals.[16] The status of Article 28 therefore remained unresolved.

At about this same time, there was a lawsuit wending its way through the Arizona state courts, entitled *Ruiz v Hull*. In it, some elected officials and state employees asked the Arizona state courts to declare Article 28 unconstitutional. The case eventually reached the Arizona Supreme Court, which held that Article 28 violated the free speech clause of the state and federal constitutions.[17] In particular, it interfered with the ability of state legislators to discuss matters of public concern with their constituents, as well as the right of citizens to petition the government. The court also held that Article 28 was a violation of the Equal Protection Clause of the Fourteenth Amendment. Because it related to a fundamental right—the freedom of speech—the court subjected the measure to what is called *strict scrutiny*, which requires the government to have a compelling state interest to justify limiting the right in question. Here, the state's interest in enforcing Article 28 would be to promote English as the state's common language. The court pointed out, however, that even if that interest is compelling, Arizona can easily promote English without banning the use of other languages.

Ruiz has become the most important modern case on language rights in the United States. It clearly establishes that a restrictive law like that of Arizona, which broadly prohibits government and its employees from using languages besides English, is unconstitutional. On the other hand, the many laws that simply declare English to be the official language of a state are almost certainly valid. What would change the situation, incidentally, is if the English Language Amendment were to be adopted at the federal level. Because such an amendment would be part of the Constitution itself, it might well override some or all constitutional protections of languages other than English. As noted above, efforts to adopt such an amendment have so far failed.

17.4.2 The *Kritz* case in Alaska

A somewhat less draconian statute was passed as an initiative measure by the voters of Alaska in 1998. The Official English Initiative (OEI) requires the state to use English in all government functions and actions. Also, official records must be in English. The OEI

---

[15] *Yniguez v Arizonans for Official English*, 69 F.3d 920 (9th Cir. 1995).
[16] *Arizonans for Official English v Arizona*, 520 U.S. 43 (1997).
[17] *Ruiz v Hull*, 957 P.2d 984 (Ariz. 1998).

applies to the legislature, all state agencies, local governments, school districts, public corporations, and the university. There are exceptions for dealing with, among other things, international trade, emergencies, and criminal inquiries. Other languages may also be used to comply with federal law.[18]

Local officials who conducted government business using native languages like Yup'ik and Inupiaq, as well as Spanish, challenged the OEI in Alaska state courts on constitutional grounds. In 2007 the Alaska Supreme Court issued its opinion. It rejected the arguments of proponents that the OEI would only apply to "official" or "formal" acts of the government. At least one part of the OEI requires all government officers and employees to use English in all government functions and actions, not only at the state, but also at the local level. Moreover, it limits the ability of Alaska citizens to petition the government or to receive information from it. The OEI also restricts the right of legislators and public employees to speak to the public in their chosen language. These rights are protected by the US and Alaska constitutions.[19]

As in *Ruiz*, the court inquired whether the state had a compelling interest that could justify these restrictions. Although it agreed that encouraging the acquisition of English and promoting unity are compelling, it held that those goals could be advanced in ways that would not violate the free-speech rights of citizens. The court thus concluded that the restrictions on activities such as petitioning the government in one's own language, or the right of legislators to address the public in their chosen language, could not be justified. Other provisions of OEI (such as the requirement that official state acts and records must be in English) could stand.[20]

An important observation is that neither *Ruiz* nor *Kritz* holds that the US Constitution *requires* the states to provide information or services in languages other than English. They merely hold that the government may not bar employees and legislators from doing so. In the following sections we discuss when the government has—or should have—an affirmative duty to provide bilingual services.

17.5 Governmental services to non-English speakers

When should a government provide bilingual services to those who do not speak, or have limited knowledge of, the predominant or official language? Until the last century, most states offered relatively few services to their citizens, so the issue may not have seemed urgent. With the widespread availability today of public education, social

---

[18] *Kritz*, 170 P.3d at 187.
[19] Ibid. at 197–206.
[20] Ibid. at 204–215. The court declined to decide whether other sections of the law were constitutional. Ibid. at 214–215.

welfare programs, and similar services, the question has become more pressing. An important issue that we will not cover is when people with limited English have a right to an interpreter, which is discussed in Chapter 30.

17.5.1 Medical care and social services

In the United States, courts have generally been reluctant to require the government to provide social services in languages other than English. Perhaps the best-known example is the California case of *Guerrero v Carlson*.[21] The plaintiffs were receiving welfare benefits (Aid to Families with Dependent Children) when they received a mailed notice that their benefits were about to terminate. It also explained that they had a limited time to appeal. Although social workers knew that the plaintiffs spoke Spanish, they nonetheless sent the notice in English. The plaintiffs claimed they failed to understand the notice and thus lost their chance to appeal.

The state supreme court noted that in spite of the early Spanish culture in California, "the United States is an English speaking country."[22] More to the point, the court commented that when people receive an official notice that they do not understand, they should ask bilingual relatives or a legal aid office for a translation. Finally, the court turned to the "slippery slope" problem: where would the process stop if it held that these documents should have been translated into Spanish? Would it mean that all state forms would have to be published in Spanish? Moreover, speakers of many different languages reside in California. The Court specifically mentioned Chinese, Japanese, Russian, Greek, Filipino, and Samoan. Would every government notice have to be published in these—and also in dozens or hundreds of other languages currently spoken in the state?

For all of the above reasons, the Court decided that the state was not required to provide these welfare forms in any language besides English. Most other state courts to consider the matter have come to the same conclusion (Piatt 1990:97–103).

People with no English proficiency (NEP) or limited English proficiency (LEP) have generally fared better under federal law, in particular under Title VI of the Civil Rights Act of 1964, which provides that citizens of the United States may not be excluded from the benefits of a program receiving federal financial assistance because of their race, color, or national origin.[23] Language, though not expressly listed in the statute, is closely related to national origin. As a means of implementing Title VI, the federal Department of Justice has issued guidelines that apply to any entities that receive federal funding, requiring that they offer "language assistance" to their LEP and NEP clients. These guidelines apply to a broad range of medical and social welfare programs throughout

---

[21]   512 P.2d 833 (1973).
[22]   Ibid. at 835.
[23]   42 U.S.C. § 2000d.

the United States.[24] The guidelines do not have the force of law,[25] and can be withdrawn by a subsequent administration, but they have nonetheless been influential as a statement of federal policy.

17.5.2 Ballots and voting

Voting is another area where non-English (or limited English) speakers tend to be at a disadvantage. In the past, requiring that voters be able to read and write English was sometimes aimed at preventing certain racial or ethnic groups from participating. For example, English literacy requirements in New York effectively denied the vote to many Puerto Ricans.

In 1965 Congress passed the Voting Rights Act. Part of the act was directed at English literacy laws. Section 4(e) provided that anyone who completed the sixth grade in an American flag school could not be prevented from voting by an English literacy test, even if the school was conducted in a language other than English.[26] This was largely meant to benefit Puerto Ricans living in the United States (Leibowitz 1969).

Later the act was extended to cover other linguistic minorities. As the act pointed out, language minorities have been effectively excluded from participation in the electoral process. Among other factors, the denial of the right to vote to such citizens is ordinarily related to the unequal educational opportunities afforded them, resulting in high illiteracy and low voting participation.[27]

The bilingual provisions of the act cover language minorities consisting of American Indians, Asian Americans, Alaskan Natives, and Spanish-heritage citizens. They come into play when over 5 percent of voting-age citizens in a jurisdiction are members of a single language minority and have limited proficiency in English. The provisions also apply when over 10,000 people in a particular jurisdiction meet the standard, even if they constitute less than 5 percent of the total population. Also covered are Indian reservations where more than 5 percent of the residents speak native American languages. In all cases, the literacy rate of members of the language minority group must be lower than the national literacy rate. If these conditions are met, the jurisdiction must provide voting materials, including ballots and instructions, in that group's language.[28]

17.5.3 Education

Although there has been some controversy regarding the use of bilingual ballots, the debates about language rights have been even more heated with regard to bilingual

---

[24] Guidance to Federal Financial Assistance Recipients Regarding Title VI Prohibition Against National Origin Discrimination Affecting Limited English Proficient Persons, 67 Fed.Reg. 41455-01 (June 18, 2002).

[25] See *Alexander v Sandoval*, 532 U.S. 275 (2001).

[26] 42 U.S.C. § 1973b(e).

[27] 42 U.S.C. § 1973aa–1a. See also Piatt (1990:132–5).

[28] Ibid.

education. For quite some time, American educators did relatively little to address the linguistic needs of schoolchildren who spoke little or no English. Most immigrant children (including the author of this chapter) found themselves in English-speaking classes, where they were expected to "sink or swim."

This situation began to change in the 1970s. A group of Chinese children sued the San Francisco school district in *Lau v Nichols*.[29] There were at the time around 3,000 LEP and NEP children of Chinese ancestry in the district. A majority of them did not receive any particular help in learning English. The students argued in the United States Supreme Court that the district's failure to address their linguistic needs violated the US Constitution and the Civil Rights Act of 1964.

The Court began its analysis by noting that treating all children alike did not necessarily produce educational equality. "There is no equality of treatment merely by providing students with the same facilities, textbooks, teachers, and curriculum; for students who do not understand English are effectively foreclosed from any meaningful education." Despite the references to equality, however, the Court did not impose a specific remedy. Rather, it held that the Civil Rights Act required the school district to take affirmative steps to rectify the "language deficiency" of non-English speaking children.[30]

What sorts of affirmative steps must a school district take? Clearly, "sink or swim" is ruled out. Beyond that, the Supreme Court left the field open to any educationally sound approach. Courts have since clarified that *Lau* does not require that all children receive bilingual education (Rodriguez 2006:759).

Consequently, in the years since *Lau* various methods have been undertaken to teach English to LEP and NEP children. These include:

- *Immersion*: LEP and NEP children are placed into an English-speaking classroom. The basic idea is that the more a child is exposed to English, the faster the child will learn it. Of course, immersing oneself in a language is much more effective when it is accompanied by teaching. Such an approach (sometimes called *structured immersion*) involves placing LEP or NEP children in English-speaking classrooms, but with bilingual aides or teachers who explain or translate some or all of the content. Unlike the old "sink or swim" approach, an instructor is in the water with the children, showing them how to swim.
- *English as a Second Language* (ESL): Another approach is to place LEP or NEP children in ordinary classes, alongside English speakers, and to provide them with ESL instruction outside of the classroom (often after school, or children may be taken out of their classes for a while during school hours). It may be the easiest option for the school, because all it has to do is hire one or two ESL instructors; the rest of the curriculum is unaffected. On the other hand, the LEP and NEP children may start to fall behind in their coursework because they may not understand their teachers very well and will have to devote some of their learning hours to ESL instruction.

[29] 414 U.S. 563 (1974).
[30] Ibid. at 566, 568.

- *Bilingual education*: The basic idea behind bilingual education is that children should initially be taught in their own languages, so that they do not fall behind in learning substantive materials. At the same time, they receive instruction in the English language. In most cases, the goal is to "mainstream" students into an English-speaking class after a few years (Clair 1994).

Thus, in the United States bilingual education has almost always been *transitional*. Its purpose is to convert LEP or NEP children into speakers of English. Critics sometimes call this *subtractive bilingualism*, because it often leads to children losing their ability to speak their native languages.

An alternative is *two-way bilingualism*, sometimes also called *additive bilingualism*. Speakers of English and those who speak another language are placed in one class with a bilingual teacher. The language of the class alternates, and each group of students helps the other group learn its native language. Ideally, all the children will become fully bilingual in both. Unfortunately, although it sounds like an attractive option in theory, it is difficult to implement in practice, often due to a lack of qualified teachers or other resources (Crawford 1995:209–22).

During the 1980s, bilingual education programs of various kinds were widely implemented throughout the United States. But they quickly became controversial. The same groups that supported making English the official language of the states tended to support elimination of bilingual programs, in favor of the ESL and structured immersion approaches. The battle was especially fierce in California.

California was once renowned for its educational system. During recent decades, however, scores on standardized tests by elementary and middle school students dropped dramatically. Many Californians were convinced that the cause was bilingual education. Thus, in 1998 California voters approved an initiative that, subject to certain exceptions, prohibits school districts from educating children bilingually.[31] Other states, including Massachusetts, have also abolished bilingual education in public schools (Lisa Ross 2007). Whether additional states will follow these examples remains to be seen. One factor that is almost never taken into account in the United States, however, is how well these programs maintain the child's native language. It is highly ironic that in a country where relatively few people learn to speak foreign languages well, children who speak such languages natively are subtly encouraged to abandon them.

17.6 A HUMAN RIGHT TO LANGUAGE?

The development of linguistic rights in the United States—and many other countries—has been tortuous. Fortunately, there seems to be an emerging consensus among the

---

[31] An *initiative* in this context is a proposed law placed on the ballot by citizens, who can usually adopt it by majority vote.

world's nations that minority languages must be respected and allowed to maintain themselves (see Chapter 16). To date, however, a human right to language is scarcely recognized in the United States.

The right to preserve one's language is especially critical for indigenous minorities. If Chinese or Korean or Spanish dies out in the United States, those languages and their related cultures will continue to flourish in their native lands. But if indigenous languages like Hopi or Navajo or Sioux disappear, they will be lost forever, along with much of the cultures that they embody. Indigenous languages are facing extinction in unprecedented numbers, especially with the ubiquitous availability of electronic devices that disseminate mass culture—mostly in English—to the most remote parts of the country. It has been estimated that, as of 1992, there were 187 native languages still spoken in the United Stated and Canada. Of those, only 40 or so were being naturally passed on to children (Krauss 1992).

Fortunately, there are ongoing efforts to maintain and even revitalize endangered languages (Hinton et al. 2002). Recognizing linguistic rights is an important aspect of that effort. If we do not act quickly, the world will soon be a far less interesting place culturally and linguistically.

CHAPTER 18

....

LEGAL RIGHTS OF LINGUISTIC MINORITIES IN THE EUROPEAN UNION

....

DURK GORTER
JASONE CENOZ

18.1 INTRODUCTION

IN 1957 the Treaty of Rome established the European Economic Community (EEC). It established the equal treatment of the (dominant) languages of all Member States as "official and working languages of the Community" (Nic Shuibhne 2002:4). The first six Member States had four languages among them (Dutch, French, German, and Italian). Since then, the European Union (EU) has increased to become an organization of 28 Member States with 24 official languages. However, the linguistic diversity among the states does not take into account the vast diversity of languages spoken across Europe because it does not consider linguistic minorities. Although it is not easy to come to a precise count, Pan (2009:29) lists 191 minorities inside then EU-27 (see also Benedikter 2006:6-7; Extra and Gorter 2008). All Member States have at least one minority, except Malta, but then Maltese is the smallest of the official languages of the EU. Rumania has 18 minorities and Hungary and Poland have a substantial number (with 13 minorities each). Outside the EU there are another 162 minorities in 20 other European states, including 45 in the European part of Russia and 23 in Ukraine. Those 20 states also include mini-states like Andorra, Lichtenstein, Monaco, San Marino, and the Vatican City that have no minorities. A complex system of language rights with a lot of variations applies to this mosaic of linguistic minorities in the 28 EU Member States.

The policy developments and legal measures at the level of international organizations (in particular the United Nations), and the European institutions (EU, but also the Organization for Security and Co-operation in Europe (OSCE) and the Council of Europe) have become more important in recent years in developing legal standards regarding language rights. However, the level of the state is still by far the most important. Although there are no clear boundaries between the competence of the Member States and the EU in the field of language, it is the states that largely determine which level of rights is given to linguistic minorities. Some states, for example Finland and Spain, have provisions in their constitution that anchor basic legal rights of the minority languages on their territory. For other groups there are special laws or legal arrangements to protect and promote the language, for example Welsh in the United Kingdom or German in South Tyrol, Italy. Other minorities may enjoy a modest degree of legal rights, for example Frisian in the Netherlands, or there may be some mainly symbolic recognition, for example Friulian in Italy. There are also states such as France or Greece that nowadays admit the existence of minority groups on their territory, but are reluctant to provide any rights at all. Many linguistic minorities in Europe are vulnerable or severely endangered (Moseley 2009) and in need of protection.

Although there are still many weaknesses, there is a trend in Europe toward the improvement of minority rights. Inside the EU, the UK and Spain have taken the lead in devolving central power to minority-dominated regions. The examples of Welsh and Gaelic as well as Catalan and Basque illustrate best practices for language rights at a regional level. They can be compared to other well-protected minority languages, such as Swedish in Finland and German in Italy.

This chapter focuses on the level of the EU as a whole and on general trends regarding legal rights of linguistic minorities. The Treaty of Lisbon, adopted in 2009, is a new foundation for the EU. It introduces for the first time the word "minorities" in EU-primary law (Toggenburg 2008:12). Although its impact remains to be seen, it has the potential to improve the protection of European minority languages.

18.2 Definitions

Minority language groups are predominantly defined in relation to a state. Each language group has its own unique history and linguistic, social, political, and economic development, also in terms of language rights. Historically the issue of minorities is closely related to the development of the modern system of "nation-states" since the middle of the seventeenth century. Majorities and minorities came into existence because of policies aimed at national homogeneity and cohesion, based on an ideology of "one state, one nation, one language" (Judge 2000; Beswick 2007:29).

A distinction should be made between "language minorities" and "minority languages." The former refers to the social group or community and the latter to a specific category of languages, for which sometimes also terms such as "lesser used," "heritage," "stateless," or "ethnic" language are used. Thus, minority languages should be distinguished from majority languages, also referred to as "dominant," "national," or "state" languages (Gorter 2006).

In itself the concept of *minority* is quite problematic. The term is an issue of controversy among academics, policymakers, and minority activists. There are many definitions of minorities and they often overlap to some extent. The difficulty in arriving at an acceptable definition lies in the diversity of situations in which minority languages exist. What constitutes a minority depends on who defines a minority and who are the beneficiaries of minority rights.

In international law a lot of work has been done about minority protection. The special rapporteur of the United Nations, Francesco Capotorti, defines a minority, including a language minority, as:

> a group numerically smaller than the rest of the population of the State to which it belongs and possessing cultural, physical or historical characteristics, a religion or a language different from those of the rest of the population and shows, if only implicitly, a sense of solidarity, directed towards preserving their culture, traditions, religion or language. (Capotorti 1991:96)

Although later studies tried to improve on this definition, it reflects the general understanding of minority in international law (Pentassuglia 2002:72) and covers most minority situations (Thompson 2001:130). This definition combines 'objective' and 'subjective' approaches. The approach is objective to the extent that membership in a minority group is seen as a demographic fact independent of the will of the members. It is also subjective to the extent that the free choice and will of the group members are decisive. Up to the present day the term *minority* is not defined in most instruments of international law, because a definition may serve certain ideological or political goals.

In contrast, a definition for "regional or minority languages" in the European Charter for Regional or Minority Languages has gained wide acceptance in recent years. The text refers to minority languages as:

> languages that are traditionally used within a given territory of a State by nationals of that State who form a group numerically smaller than the rest of the State's population; and different from the official language(s) of that State; it does not include either dialects of the official language(s) of the State or the languages of migrants. (Council of Europe 1992)

The definition shows the decisive role of the nation-state in determining which language varieties obtain minority rights (and protection) and which do not. The answer to the layman's question on the status of a variety as "language or dialect?" depends on political recognition by a state. At the same time, a basic idea in international law is that what constitutes a minority should not depend on a state but on objective criteria.

In a more sociological sense the term *minority* is also used to refer to groups with less status and less power (May 2001). This usage may be preferred over the commonsense understanding of minority as "less than half" or "a smaller number." Language minorities differ very much in size—there can only be a handful of speakers or there can be millions. The number of individuals that speak a language seems a simple fact, but it is not always the case (cf. Fishman 1991:45–6). When drafting a list of minority languages and the numbers of speakers, one inevitably runs into a lack of consensus about the question of which varieties belong on the list as separate languages and which are subvarieties of another language (Wei 2000:6–11; Lewis 2009). Who is counted as a speaker is likewise not straightforward because there are different criteria to count someone as a "speaker" of a language. The most common criterion is mother tongue (i.e. the language acquired as a child), but language competence (the language that someone is able to speak), and the main language used (the most important daily means of communication) are also often used as criteria (Kloss and Haarmann 1984:34). The size of a language minority can be quite different depending on whether the mother tongue speakers are counted or whether instead it is all persons able to speak a language.

Another important distinction can be made between so-called "unique minority languages," which are not the dominant language in any state, and "cross-border minority languages," which are the official dominant language of one state and a minority language in one or more other states. Basque and Frisian are examples of the former, and Swedish in Finland and German in Italy illustrate the latter.

Yet another distinction can be made between regional minority languages and the languages spoken by immigrants (Extra and Gorter 2008). The first refers (chiefly) to minorities that arose during state-formation or because of the migration of population groups in the distant past. Immigrant minority languages are the consequence of more recent migration. In Western Europe this process dates mainly from the 1960s. Due to an influx of migrants, expatriates, refugees, and asylum-seekers, in many European states today, in particular in the larger urban areas, easily over 100 languages are spoken as home languages. The difference between regional and immigrant minority languages can be gradual, as is shown by the example of Finnish language speakers in Sweden. Immigrant minority languages are hardly if ever protected by legal measures.

18.3 EMERGING EUROPEAN NORMS

Some major international human rights instruments, such as the European Convention on Human Rights (1950) of the Council of Europe (COE) and the International Covenant on Civil and Political Rights (1966) of the United Nations include a number of provisions which are important for minorities, although they are not specifically directed at minorities (Henrard and Dunbar 2008:3). The COE has played a crucial role in developing language rights for European language minorities, as has the OSCE.

The OSCE is a security organization with members not only in Europe, but also in Central Asia, the USA, and Canada. It has 57 participating States. In 1992 the OSCE established the position of High Commissioner on National Minorities (HCNM). His mandate was created largely in reaction to ethnic conflict in Europe, in particular the situation in the former Yugoslavia. The OSCE states are bound by United Nations obligations on human rights, including minority rights, and most OSCE States are also bound by the standards of the Council of Europe. For the HCNM the linguistic rights of national minorities are a recurrent issue. In 1996 the HCNM consulted a group of experts to ascertain their recommendations on the linguistic rights of persons belonging to national minorities. It led to the development of the "Hague Recommendations Regarding the Education Rights of National Minorities" (1996), followed two years later by the "Oslo Recommendations Regarding the Linguistic Rights of National Minorities" (1998). Whereas the former document focuses on the use of language in education (the right to proper knowledge of the mother tongue), the latter deals more broadly with rights in regards to issues such as names, community life, media, economic life, administrative authorities, public services, and judicial authorities. The two sets of recommendations together form a standard that is being used by the High Commissioner. Over the years the OSCE has expanded this series of recommendations. Now it also includes "The Lund Recommendations on Effective Participation by National Minorities in Public Life" (1999), the "Warsaw Guidelines on Minority Participation in the Electoral Process" (2001), the "Guidelines on the Use of Minority Languages in the Broadcast Media" (2003), and most recently "The Bolzano/Bozen Recommendations on National Minorities in Inter-State Relations" (2008). Generally those recommendations are based on provisions in international law. They do not have legal force in themselves, but they are important in shaping the debate and in giving the outlines of what is regarded as normal.

The COE today comprises 47 Member States, including all 28 EU states. The work of the COE was probably even more important for linguistic rights than the OSCE, because between 1984 and 1992 the COE developed the European Charter for Regional or Minority Languages (ETS 148) and later, between 1993 and 1994, the Framework Convention for the Protection of National Minorities (ETS 157). Both treaties came into force in 1998.

The European Charter for Regional or Minority Languages is an important instrument for the development of language rights and language policy. The Charter was drafted over a long period of time, starting in 1981[1] with recommendations from the Parliamentary Assembly of the COE as well as the European Parliament. They recommended drawing up a charter of regional or minority languages and cultures (Ó Riagáin 2002; see also Woerhling 2006:23–4). Its drafting was a long and tedious process, but due to the important political changes in Central and Eastern Europe in the early 1990s the process was speeded up and the Charter was accepted by the COE in 1992 by the then 27 members. By 2015 the Charter had been ratified by 25 states and another 8 had signed but not ratified it. This implies that 14 other states are not party to this treaty; among them, for different reasons, are Belgium and Ireland, countries that have a long tradition of dealing with language rights.

English and French are the official language versions of the treaty, but the interest among minority language groups is high as can be seen from the fact that the official text has been translated into 45 different languages, official state languages as well as several unique minority languages. According to Woerhling (2005:27–8) the Charter has

---

[1] Resolution 928 (1981), adopted in October 1981. Incidentally, only nine days later, also in Strasbourg, the European Parliament adopted the now historical Arfé Resolution, launching for the first time a European Communities' policy on Europe's lesser used languages.

several characteristics that make it an original approach to promoting respect for regional or minority cultures.

The Charter has a preamble and five parts:

Part I. *General Provisions*. This part deals primarily with definitions, undertakings, and practical arrangements.

Part II. *Objectives and Principles*. All ratifying states are obliged to accept these general objectives and principles.

Part III. *Measures to Promote the Use of Regional or Minority Languages in Public Life*. Part III is the substance of the Charter. There are seven articles in this part and each article has paragraphs and sub-paragraphs: Article 8—Education; Article 9—Judicial authorities; Article 10—Administrative authorities and public services; Article 11—Media; Article 12—Cultural activities and facilities; Article 13—Economic and social life; Article 14—Transfrontier exchanges.

Part IV. *Application of the Charter*. This concerns the monitoring, periodical reports, and the task of the Committee of Experts.

Part V. *Final Provisions*. Contains the procedure for signing, ratifying, and the coming into effect of the Charter.

A ratifying state must apply a minimum of 35 paragraphs or sub-paragraphs from the provisions of Part III to each minority language, including at least three paragraphs or sub-paragraphs from Articles 8 and 12 and a minimum of one from Articles 9, 10, 11, and 13. Ratification of the Charter is a serious undertaking and not merely an expression of good intentions.

The states party to the European Charter have to deliver a periodical report every three years. The Committee of Experts examines these reports and prepares recommendations for the Committee of Ministers, the highest body of the COE. The Committee of Experts thus plays a central role in the monitoring process. Although the Committee can clarify ambiguities in the Charter, it cannot give a definitive legal interpretation. Dunbar (2008:61) suggests that the role of the Committee of Experts should not be that of a quasi-judicial body, but a "policy advisor on good language planning."

The European Charter functions as an international instrument for the comparison of legal measures and facilities of Member States (Craith 2003), and is aimed at the protection and the promotion of the historical regional or minority languages of Europe. The Charter offers the adhering states the opportunity of choice between different alternatives. The degree of protection is not prescribed; thus, a state can choose loose or tight policies. The result is a wide variety of provisions across EU Member States (Grin 2003).

The second important treaty that provides support for minority language groups is the Framework Convention for the Protection of National Minorities (Council of Europe 1995). The Framework Convention was drafted in a much shorter period of time and is even more strongly related to the political transitions in Central and Eastern Europe in the 1990s. It was adopted in 1995 and entered into force in 1998. As of 2015 there were 39 states that had ratified the Framework Convention and another four signed it but did not follow by ratification; another four states are not party to this treaty: France, Monaco, Andorra, and Turkey.

The Framework Convention is not completely satisfactory because it was drafted with a lot of compromises between different views of the Member States. A criticism is that the provisions add little to existing international law. Furthermore, they are vaguely worded with many phrases such as "as far as possible." Troebst (1999: 3) compares it to "a wide-meshed net which contains a great number of large holes. Each government which intends to slip through will no doubt succeed." Although Troebst is also convinced that this "leaves room for interpretation in a more positive direction," the treaty needs to be implemented in "good faith" with the political will to support minority rights.

The Framework Convention contains a preamble and five sections with 32 articles:

- Section I, articles 1–3, sets out several general principles. Article 1 states that the protection of national minorities is part of the international system for human rights protection.
- Section II, articles 4–19, is the main operative part of the text and contains the program-type provisions, particularly in the fields of education, media, and public administration.
- Section III, articles 20–23, concentrates on issues regarding the interpretation of the principles in Section II.
- Section IV, articles 24–26, and Section V, articles 25–32, set out the principles for the monitoring and entering into force of the Framework Convention.

Similar to the European Charter, an Advisory Committee of independent experts monitors the implementation of the Framework Convention and reports to the Committee of Ministers. The monitoring process consists of four stages: (1) a periodical report by the state (every five years); (2) an opinion by the Advisory Committee on the state report; (3) comments on the Advisory Committee opinion by the state; and (4) a resolution of the Committee of Ministers.

The aim of the Framework Convention is to ensure respect for the rights of national minorities and it is "the first (and still only) international treaty specifically and exclusively directed at minorities" (Henrard and Dunbar 2008:5). The implementation of the rights from the Framework Convention, however, may still leave much to be desired (Gal 2000).

The Framework Convention is a different instrument from the European Charter. Its aim is to protect minorities (thus groups) and the Charter is concerned with languages as cultural assets. The Framework Convention is about establishing rights, whereas the European Charter requires states to develop a policy to promote minority languages. The Framework Convention is also much less detailed on the use of language in different social fields than the European Charter (Woerhling 2005:32–4). However, because of the interpretations of the periodical reports by the Advisory Committee, De Varennes (2008:29) opines that the Framework Convention "may become a much stronger instrument than the European Charter."

18.4 EU LANGUAGE POLICY AND
LINGUISTIC RIGHTS

The European Charter and the Framework Convention are instruments developed by the COE and thus they are not part of the *acquis communautaire* (current law) of the EU. Nonetheless, they have been influential in the development of EU policies towards linguistic minorities. In the last decades important developments have taken place inside the EU that pave the way for more attention being given to linguistic minorities, their legal protection, and their promotion by active policies.

The earliest political involvement with minority languages of the EU (then still European Communities) dates back to October 1981, when the first directly elected European Parliament adopted the so-called Arfé Resolution. The resolution called on the Member States and on regional and local authorities to promote regional and minority languages, particularly in the domains of education, mass communication, public life, and social affairs.[2] The political and cultural support for minority languages expressed in the Arfé Resolution enabled the European Commission to open a small EU budget line and to develop a program of activities for minority languages. It led, among other things, to the establishment of the European Bureau for Lesser Used Languages (EBLUL) based in Dublin, Ireland. The EBLUL was a non-governmental organization (NGO) which aimed at seeking political and financial support for lesser used languages in European institutions and has been particularly active in the European Parliament and the COE. In January 2010 the EBLUL closed as funding was no longer available. The EBLUL collaborated with the Mercator network of three specialized centers (Mercator-Education in Friesland, Mercator-Media in Wales, and Mercator-Legislation in Catalunya). These are centers for information, documentation, and research about minority languages in the EU. Recently the Mercator network has been extended with centers in Sweden and Hungary.

Another important development took place in 1983 with the establishment of the Intergroup for Minority Languages and Cultures, an informal working group comprising Members of the European Parliament from different political parties. The next initiative on behalf of lesser used languages in the European Parliament was the Kuijpers resolution, adopted in 1987. This resolution was more wide-ranging and it went into greater detail on specific actions than the Arfé Resolution. It recommended various measures in the areas of education, language use before local authorities, mass media, cultural infrastructure, and transborder cooperation.

It is difficult to say how important these resolutions of the European Parliament in the 1980s were, because they were not related to the priorities of the Commission or the European Council. Stolfo (2009:40–2) concludes that the European Parliament has

---

[2] However, a similar initiative, the Goppel-report on legal rights, did not get past the stage of the Legal Affairs Committee.

played an important role since the 1980s. Toggenburg (2008:3), however, criticizes the resolutions as being "idealistic," "unrealistic," "non-legally binding," and "a means for fostering [the] institutional profile [of the European Parliament]".

During the 1990s two important lines of development took place, the first internal to the EU and the second triggered by external processes.

Among the internal developments, the Killilea report of 1994 stands out. The text shows the influence of the Maastricht Treaty (1993), which created the European Union. Member States are called upon to recognize their linguistic minorities and create the basic conditions for their preservation and development. The Killilea report differs from the earlier Arfé and Kuijpers reports because it focuses completely on the European Charter for Regional or Minority Languages, which it wholeheartedly supports. It was adopted by an overwhelming vote in the Parliament, which seemed to reflect a positive shift in public opinion in favor of linguistic diversity.

It is also worth noting that there are several references to minority languages in other resolutions adopted by the European Parliament, relating to matters such as cable television networks, regional policy, and radio and television production.

However, inside the EU there was a rather negative development that resulted from a general decision by the European Court of Justice in June 1998. The Court held that the Commission did not have the right to fund any program unless it was based on a legal act agreed to by the Commission, the Parliament, and the Council. Because it did not qualify under this standard, the budget line for Regional and Minority Languages and Cultures was blocked. To reinstate a budget line would call for a new legal base. However, it also would require unanimity, which was something impossible to achieve because some states would veto any program supporting minority languages. Even during the European Year of Languages (2001), a thematic year organized and supported by the EU and the COE together, no solution was found and nothing happened. The European Commission contracted the SMiLE report, which investigated how the EU can best support minority languages. The report provides an overview of language policy, activities, and instruments (Grin and Moring 2002). However, the end result was that minority languages did not remain as a separate policy, but were "mainstreamed" as part of the Action Plan 2004–2006 to promote language learning and linguistic diversity.

The most important external process in the 1990s was the political transition of Central and Eastern Europe and as a consequence of the enlargement of the EU. The so-called "Copenhagen criteria" (1993) define whether a country is eligible to join the EU. These conditions included "the respect for and protection of minorities." In this way the European Council (by deciding on accession) and the European Commission (by monitoring the candidate states) became directly involved with minority issues. The policy shifted from a focus on language and culture to wider issues of political participation and citizenship. In the end, Estonia and Latvia were able to join the EU without fully complying with the spirit of the Copenhagen criteria (Adrey 2005). According to Toggenburg (2008:7) the Copenhagen criterion of respect for and protection of minorities "remains hopelessly vague." The addition of 10 new Member States became a fact in

2004 and in 2007 Bulgaria and Rumania also became EU Member States. Thus, the many linguistic minorities in those 12 new Member States also became part of the EU. Croatia became the 28th member-state in 2013.

With this enlargement in 2007, Irish was made an official and working language of the EU, which means it has the same status as the other national languages of the Member States. A further recognition and extension of the use of minority languages at the European level was accomplished with the approval of the use of additional languages. This concerns minority languages that have an official status in a particular Member State and it requires special agreement with that Member State, which has to be ready to take upon itself the costs and the responsibility (Arzoz 2008:7). So far Basque, Catalan, and Galician in Spain and Welsh and Scottish Gaelic in the United Kingdom have profited from this legal measure.

Meanwhile the European Parliament accepted a resolution based on the so-called Ebner Report (2003). This document calls for the establishment of a European Agency for linguistic diversity and language learning, including regional and minority languages, as well as a multiannual program. To date neither proposal has been realized. In its next legislative period (2004–2009) the European Parliament reaffirmed its support for linguistic minorities by adopting the Moraes Report (2005). This report contains the most encompassing and far-reaching resolution thus far. The text calls on the European Commission and the EU Member States to treat linguistic minorities in accordance with the principles laid down in the European Charter, the Framework Convention, and the Hague and Lund recommendations. It shows the continuing importance of the two COE treaties and the OSCE recommendations for the further development of EU policy (see also Henrard and Dunbar 2008:9). Today the Commission sees minority protection as a part of the *acquis communautaire*.

Since the beginning of 2007 the EU has had a special Commissioner who deals with all issues related to multilingualism, including linguistic minorities. The importance of multilingualism for Europe and of minority languages as an integral part of linguistic diversity has been emphasized by him in several reports. The Commissioner has published his general strategy under the title "Multilingualism: an asset for Europe and a shared commitment." Multilingual speakers of minority languages are seen as acting "as the glue between different cultures" (European Commission 2008:6). In the European Commission of 2010 this special post was reintegrated with the mandate of the Commissioner for Education, Culture, Multilingualism, and Youth. Among the priorities for the next five years, the Commissioner mentions the support for "Europe's 60 regional or minority languages." The 2014 Commission abolished the post.

18.5 CONCLUSIONS—OUTLOOK FOR THE FUTURE

In the EU linguistic minorities are more valued today than they were only a few decades ago. Linguistic diversity and multilingualism are now on the political agenda. After the acceptance of the Charter of Fundamental Rights in 2000, the EU committed itself in

Article 22 to respect for cultural, religious, and linguistic diversity (Arzoz 2008:5). With the adoption of the Treaty of Lisbon (2009) it becomes legally binding. In Europe in the twenty-first century a basic assumption is that the preservation, protection, and promotion of linguistic and cultural diversity are important. It is an idea that is backed up by the population in general. In a survey in the then 25 EU Member States, a positive answer was given by 63 percent of the respondents to the statement "Regional and minority languages should receive greater support" (Eurobarometer 2005).

Over the years a widely supported set of standards in the area of linguistic minorities has been developed. The role of the COE and the OSCE has been very important. "Europe" has also contributed in a constructive way to the development of national state policies. The development of legal standards is, however, heavily constrained by political considerations.

Despite all the progress made, as Benedikter (2008:3) remarks "Europe is not yet a 'heaven' for minorities". In terms of language rights what can be observed is quite complex and in need of further elaboration and clarification. In the end the implementation of language rights is of greatest importance (Thornberry and Martin Estébanez 2004). The essential question is, do such rights contribute to the revival and the improved maintenance of a minority language, or do they encourage a transition to the dominant language? If the recognition of the minority language is only symbolic, that may work as a stimulus for assimilation to mainstream society, instead of being a safeguard for the language concerned.

Overall, the policies of the EU are of major importance, but the EU has lacked leadership on this issue due to constitutional limitations. With the entry into force of the Treaty of Lisbon this might change. The treaty refers to "the rights of persons belonging to minorities" as a basic European value. Moreover the Charter of Fundamental Rights uses the term "national minority," which via the Treaty of Lisbon becomes a term of EU law. The Treaty of Lisbon is thus an important step forward for the protection of the rights of linguistic minorities in the EU, because in legal terms it becomes a value on which the EU "is founded" and which is "common to the member states" (Toggenburg 2008:14). How far this protection will go is still an open question.

CHAPTER 19

......

INVESTIGATING THE LANGUAGE SITUATION IN AFRICA

......

TUNDE OLUSOLA OPEIBI

19.1 INTRODUCTION

FROM one decade to another, and through many generations, there appears to be a general consensus among language scholars all over the world that among symbols and badges of national identity, language remains the most profound, most unique, and the most treasured. Rousseau, the French linguist and philosopher, in his treatise, *Essay on the Origin of Languages*, argued that language distinguishes nations from one another (quoted in King 1997). And in multilingual societies, "language is a central and defining feature of identity" particularly for those in minority language groups (Patten 2001:697).

Whether colonized or independent, each country treats language as a resource for actualizing the essence of its existence. After nationhood[1] is attained, language continues to permeate every aspect of the national life as it helps members of the community to contract and transact inter- and intra-relationships; share identity and engage in other human activities for the survival and progress of that society. Apart from its communicative function, language is also closely linked with the people's culture, religion, or religious activities, administrative and legal systems, as well as socio-political and geographical configurations, among other things that uniquely define that society.

The situation in most parts of Africa supports scholars' argument that for any group of people to share a sense of common identity, a certain minimum level of communication between them must be guaranteed (Barbour 1998:195). And the incontrovertible

---

[1] Nationhood is used here in its loose sense to refer to a community of people with its unique language.

evidence shows that language has remained one of the most visible and enduring senses of that shared identity.

In Africa, there is a quantum of evidence that shows that language has become a very strong factor for ethno-national identity with the ethnic loyalty overriding national interest. Beardsmore (1980) observes that, next to religion, language loyalty overrides all other questions that impinge on Nigerian life, uniting conflicting ideologies and drawing together social classes with contradictory interests.

A new trend in the linguistic situation emerged when the West[2] came in contact with Africa through slave trade, colonialism, missionary activities, and other factors. The status of the languages, language rights, allocation of roles among the foreign and indigenous languages, and the impact of language policies on nation-building became serious issues in many African nations.

As the winds of independence blew across most colonized territories in Africa in the late 1950s and 1960s, language issues began to engage the attention of scholars and policymakers in these new nations. Ndhlovu (2008:139) identifies the presence of multiple language varieties and ethnic groups as one of the key issues in the difficulties that African countries face in the construction of stable national identities. Often major languages are pitched against minority languages. And because language involves the cultures and ethnic identities of its users and can act as a social bond as well as a social barrier, each language group strives to protect this inalienable cultural heritage (Opeibi 2000:190). Often, the language policies that have evolved in most African countries have not gone unchallenged, especially when they favor one language above another.

Previous scholarly contributions on the complex linguistic situation in Africa have discussed strategies adopted in language planning and types of language policies in many of the nations in Africa. Drawing on these contributions, as well as incorporating recent developments, this chapter uses a sociolinguistic perspective to discuss aspects of language policies in Africa and how these policies are a reflection of the language situation in Africa.

19.2 THE LINGUISTIC LANDSCAPE OF AFRICA

Africa is a culturally diverse and linguistically heterogeneous continent. It presents a classic example of linguistic diversity with almost 2,000 indigenous languages, which are grouped into the following language families: (1) *Afro-Asiatic* (approximately 200 languages covering nearly all of Northern Africa, including the horn of Africa and the central Sahara at the top of the Nile); (2) *Nilo-Saharan* (consisting of about 140 languages with some 11 million speakers scattered in central and eastern Africa); (3) *Niger-Saharan* (covering about two-thirds of Africa with about 1,000 languages and some 200 million

[2] Refers to European countries and other developed nations whose languages have been adopted in Africa.

speakers, and including the Bantu languages of central, southern, and eastern Africa); and (4) *Khoisan* (about 30 languages in the western part of Southern Africa) (see Bamgbose 1991; Adegbija 1994).

A graphic picture of the multilingual situation in Africa is painted in a working document by UNESCO, cited in Wolff (1998):

> According to the definition of languages and dialects there are between 1,250 and 2,100 languages in Africa.... It is a trivial statement to say that monolingual countries are more the exception rather than the rule if we are to adhere to strict criteria. Even in an apparently monolingual setting, the geographical distance (dialects), the social distance (sociolects), the historical and other codes and registers will make the situation more complex.
>
> Homogeneity is a fiction in the linguistic field more than in any other. Taking an arbitrary threshold of 90 per cent as the defining landmark of a monolingual country, only a handful of countries meet this criterion in Africa. The ones generally cited are Botswana (language: Setswana), Burundi (Kirundi), Lesotho (Sotho), Madagascar (Malagasy), Mauritius (Creole), Rwanda (Kinyarwanda), Seycelles (Creole), Somalia (Somali), Swaziland (Seswati).
>
> The degree of multilingualism varies greatly. About 105 million people speak around 410 languages in Nigeria, 30 million people in [former] Zaire use 206 languages and Ethiopia has 97 languages for a population of about 45 million. Diversity is not the characteristic of giants alone. In Cameroon, 185 languages are used by 8 million people, giving an average of 50,000 persons per language; 3 million inhabitants of Benin are spread over 58 languages while 2 million Congolese [Congo Brazzaville] have at their disposal 31 languages. On the other hand, Mauritania has four languages, Niger ten.
>
> ...These figures need to be scrutinised further, and they yield interesting and useful information. With a population of about 28 million, Tanzania has 120 languages, among them Kiswahili which as a lingua franca is used by the vast majority of the population. Mali has 12 languages and 90 per cent of the population use four of them and 60 to 65 per cent use only one language, Bamanan, as first (L1) or second (L2) language. Twenty years ago this percentage was around 40 per cent; the increase is due more to growing numbers of users of Bamanan as L2 rather than the demographic increase of the ethnic Bamanan. Burkina Faso has about 60 languages for a population of 9 million, half of which is Morephone (speaker of More language).
>
> The numbers also conceal facts which need to be brought to light for a better understanding of the context and the challenge of multilingualism as a problem. In Nigeria 397 languages out of 410 are 'minority' languages, but the total number of their speakers accounts for 60 per cent of the population. Among them are several languages with more than 1 million speakers, with a few of them having a number of speakers close to 10 million. Similar phenomena are observed elsewhere and compel a departure from 'numerical muscle' as a decision criterion in language planning...
>
> Even in world terms, a mother tongue of another language with some 200,000 or so speakers is by no means a small language, given the fact that the overall population of the country of its usage may be much greater. Where, as in much of Africa,

speakers of a certain language are not dispersed but tend to be restricted to well-defined geographical areas, even languages of some 50,000 speakers become significant for the purpose of development and use in national life. By the time one gets down to this level of language with 50,000 speakers, one has taken into account well over 90 per cent of the population of almost any Africa country. (UNESCO Working Document, Intergovernmental Conference on Language Policies in Africa, Harare, March 17–21, 1997:3)

A cursory look at the demographics of Africa vis-à-vis the language situation shows that of the 890 million people in Africa (as of 2005), about 20 percent speak an Arabic dialect (used in major parts of north Africa), about 10 percent speak Swahili, the *lingua franca* of southeastern Africa, and about 5 percent speak Hausa, a west African *lingua franca*. Other important west African languages are Yoruba (3 percent), Igbo (3 percent), and Fula (2 percent). In northeastern Africa, about 4 percent speak Oromo and 2 percent speak Somali, while Zulu and Afrikaans are two major languages in the South African region.[3]

As mentioned previously, there are African countries that are virtually monolingual, these include Burundi, Somalia, Madagascar, Botswana, Cape Verde, Seychelles, Rwanda, Mauritius, Lesotho, and Swaziland. Nonetheless, multilingual countries dominate the continent. Such countries may be broadly divided into three groups:

1. Multilingual countries with one dominant language, e.g. Tanzania (Swahili), Senegal (Wolof), Central African Republic (Sango), Niger (Hausa), Zimbabwe (Shona), Malawi (Chichewa).
2. Multilingual countries with more than one dominant language, e.g. Nigeria, Democratic Republic of Congo, Zambia, Kenya, Ethiopia, Guinea.
3. Multilingual countries that have no dominant language: Sierra Leone, Liberia, Cote d'Ivoire, Benin, Cameroon (Bamgbose 2000:99).

Perhaps one virtue of the bilingual/multilingual nature of many African communities is that "bilingualism, as a strategy, encourages a blending of cultures in the quest for identity, since it enhances the standing of both the languages concerned and the cultures they convey in the various stages of personality formation" (Ndoye undated). The choice of language policy by each nation has, however, influenced the pace of nation-building and national development.

19.3 LANGUAGE AS POWER IN AFRICA

In virtually every part of the world, the challenges of language recognition, language rights, and attitudes arise in jurisdictions where language diversity exists. Recently in Nashville, Tennessee, USA, a proposal to legislate English as the city's only official

---

[3] <http://cn.wikipedia.org/wiki/African_language> accessed September 8, 2011.

language suffered a setback because those who voted against it argued that it would diminish the provision of emergency services in languages other than English.[4] This is based on the belief that a citizen is able to exercise his/her rights only if he/she receives communications from government officials or service providers in a language he/she understands (Patten 2001:696). Language rights become more contentious when dealing with multilingual nations with a great diversity of languages and cultures.

Long before factors such as conquest, slave trade, missionary activities, colonialism, and migration came to alter the linguistic configuration of Africa, the local languages of the natives were the subject of convenient choices depending on the region and location of the speakers. Each nation has continued to adapt her individual peculiar socio-cultural and socio-political experience to manage linguistic issues arising from the factors mentioned above. At best, many countries have opted for a multilingual society to support the traditional socio-cultural landscape and contain the potential spill-over crisis that may arise from an unfavorable language policy by those in power.

The linguistic situation became more complex when the colonial powers that shifted the national borders of the nations in Africa paid little or no attention to the existing linguistic, religious, and cultural affinities and political organizations of the ethnolinguistic groups. The convergence of several diverse languages in these new nations inevitably created the challenges of language management, language rights, language attitudes, allocation of roles, and the development of language policies that would adapt to the circumstances that are prevalent in individual nations.

Whether in the English and French-speaking west Africa, or the Portuguese-speaking nations in central and part of southern Africa, or Arabic and French-speaking North Africa, language issues have continued to generate debates that have led to the emergence of different language policies.

The subsisting multilingual situation has also given rise to classifications such as *official languages* (in most cases the imported languages), *national languages* (e.g. Swahili in Tanzania), *network* or *broadcast languages* (e.g. Tiv, Nupe in Nigeria), and *indigenous languages*. In Africa, the official languages are often the languages of government, the mass media, and medium of instruction in schools. National languages are indigenous languages that also share the functions of official languages. Broadcast or network languages, on the other hand, are languages used for limited communicative purposes within a region, while indigenous languages are used for personal and intra group communication within the locality where they are spoken and across regional boundaries where language affinity exists or where speakers of those indigenous languages are found.

The implication of choosing the imported languages as the official languages is that most children in Africa come into contact with the official languages for the first time in primary school. By implication then, only a marginal population with access to formal

---

[4] <http://www.gather.com/viewArticle.action?articleId=281474977582637>.

education will acquire some level of competence in the language used to conduct the affairs of their nations. As is the case in Mozambique with the Portuguese language, so it is in Nigeria with English and in Benin Republic with French. "The imported official and dominant language is effectively controlled by only a minority, which, by virtue of this control, also has access to political and economic power" (Bamgbose 2000:44). The language power thus creates inequality at virtually every stratum of the society, bifurcating the society into those that have language power and those that do not.

The emergence of different language policies has often taken into consideration the critical role of the imported languages against the background of the numerous indigenous languages in Africa. The controversies that language selection procedures often generate have supported the position of those who favor the retention of the imported languages as the languages to be used for official communications. However, it is believed that such language policy (e.g. in Nigeria) will continue to perpetuate the dominance of the imported language over all the indigenous languages.

Gilbert Ansre (1976) was very blunt in criticizing the choice of the language of the colonial master. He argued:

> Any country which takes seriously the need to develop its human resources maximally cannot afford to under-use such resources. Much less can it afford to do so on linguistic grounds. If the language or languages selected to be used for resource exploitation and wealth acquisition are those mastered only by a small minority of the population, the unemployment and the emergence of an exploiting and wealthy minority can be the only results expected.... A nation-state in which the constitution is an obscure document written in a language understood well by a small minority and used for communication by even less cannot be said to be politically developed. (Ansre 1976:6)

Although the challenges of socio-economic development in Africa may not be solely blamed on the language situation, it is a fact that language, to a large extent, impacts on socio-economic and educational policies that in turn underpin progress towards national development. The complex language situation in Africa notwithstanding, each nation has been exploring ways to successfully manage the peculiar situations in its communities.

19.4 Language planning, language policy, and nation-building in Africa

It has been argued that apart from the existence of several natural language groups, the present language situation in Africa was further shaped by the importation and implantation of languages that came through slave trade, colonization, and forced migration. Language planning is thus a natural and inevitable consequence. Language planning has been defined as a government-authorized long-term sustained and conscious effort to alter a language function in society for the purpose of solving communication problems (Weinstein 1982). If communication problems exist anywhere, they exist in most multilingual African countries. To ease communication challenges in those nations, successive governments have been formulating deliberate policies that will assign roles to the various languages in their societies.

Thus the issues of authority, choice, and allocation of roles for each language within the multilingual community, the duration of the policy, as well as well-articulated and clearly-communicated language policies all impact on language planning in Africa. The continent has had a fair share of all the challenges associated with these phenomena. As pointed out by Bamgbose (2000:99), multilingualism, the colonial legacy, the role of education as an agent of social change, low levels of literacy, concerns for communication, and nation-building constitute some of the factors influencing language planning in Africa.

Usually choices and decisions made with respect to language issues are viewed with serious concern because they affect the identities, rights, opportunities, welfare, and the prosperity of the citizens. Whenever a language is placed in public domains and receives the official stamp of government, it becomes a powerful instrument for social mobility and socio-economic advancements for those who speak it. It is natural, therefore, for people in multilingual jurisdictions all over the world to become worried about a language policy that selects one language above the other as the official medium of communication in public institutions, the economy, and civil society.

Furthermore, as a result of the entrenched ethnic relationship between language and culture in many of the communities that make up the African nations, cultural loyalty and language loyalty appear to be very strong. The interests of the regional cultures and ethnic languages may override those of the national and central culture and the language of national solidarity (Adekunle 1990:243). Speakers of minority languages may then prefer the choice of the imported language(s) as the official language in order to reduce the overbearing influence of any of the indigenous languages over theirs. Nigeria is a case in point, where English is still preferred over the three major (national) languages (Hausa, Igbo, and Yoruba).

Multilingual settings as found in Africa have been shown to present a situation where language may serve as instruments of *inclusion* or *exclusion*, depending on the type of language policy adopted by the government. In most cases, authorities of nations with a diversity of languages and ethnic groups embark on language planning and language policy as a result of the need for national integration. In countries like Nigeria, with different ethno-linguistic communities that have diverse cultures and religions, the only way to unify the various communities would be to choose as the official language one that is not indigenous and/or assign official functions to the various languages spoken by the people. For instance, in order to mitigate the scars of apartheid and forge national cohesion, South Africa adopted a policy that replaced the two former official languages (English and Afrikaans) with eleven languages that function as official languages to be used at all levels. The previous policy, which marginalized all indigenous languages, thus gave way to an inclusive community to integrate various interests and ideals and to reach mutual agreements (see Bellamy 1999, cited in Ngcobo 2007).

It is worth noting that as a result of the multiplicity of languages in Africa, the official language of each country usually carries the main functional load while the indigenous languages perform limited intra-group communicative roles. English in Nigeria, French in Benin Republic, and Portuguese in Mozambique are typical examples of such official languages that also play the role of language of wider communication (LWC). Sometimes some selected national languages, such as Swahili in Tanzania, Sesotho in Lesotho, Yoruba in southwest Nigeria, Hausa in the north and Igbo in the east of Nigeria, as well as Afrikaans in South Africa, are languages of socialization in their respective nations, especially in major cities.

Unfortunately, political instability in Africa and other factors have undermined the goal of a sustainable long-term language policy. Bamgbose (2000:103) observes that "language planning in Africa is characterized by a number of features that include non-conformity with rational processes of decision-making, pre-occupation with policy, lack of continuity, bureaucratic monopoly of planning, elite domination of policy-making, and restriction of the focus of language planning mainly to education." Some countries such as Guinea, which promoted mother tongue education in early primary education, abandoned the policy when Sekou Toure died in 1984. Burkina Faso also practiced mother tongue education from 1979 to 1984 and then switched to French when there was a change of regime (Sanou 1990:76–7, cited in Bamgbose 2000:111). And Ghana changed its language education policy five times within the period of 24 years as a result of changes in government. Because language planning has been limited to government alone and its implementation to its agencies, most of such policies have suffered serious setbacks or have been totally abandoned because of a lack of political will and/or continuity in government. The absence of a viable and stable institutional framework, as well as a well-focused sustainable policy, and lack of governmental determination to systematically implement language policy are issues hampering language development on the continent.

Tollefson's assertion that "language policy is one mechanism available to the state for maintaining its power and that of groups which control state policy" (1991, cited in Bamgbose 2000:115) provides another interesting dimension. The elite class in Africa has been accused of formulating and implementing deliberate language policies to limit the social mobility of the masses who may not possess the language power, and then to disempower them politically, socially, and economically. They create language bars or barriers by preferring a minority official language to a more widely spoken indigenous language. Scotton (1990:27, cited in Bamgbose 2000:115) describes the phenomenon as "elite closure," and examples may be found in Senegal where French is preferred above Wolof, Ghana with English instead of Akan, and Niger with French preferred to Hausa. Tanzania, on the other hand, presents a situation where the dominance of the elite group is reduced because a lack of proficiency in the exoglossic language does not limit the social and economic progress of the citizens. In Tanzania, English shares its official status with Swahili, an endoglossic language which also serves as the national language.

In an attempt to address the challenges of linguistic diversity in Africa, the 1997 Intergovernmental Conference of African Language Policies made the following observations and recommendations:

1. a democratic Africa...seeks to enhance the active participation of all citizens in all institutions—social, economic, political, etc.;
2. [in] a democratic Africa...development is not construed in narrow economic terms, but within a broader context of justice for all, fairness and equity; respect for linguistic rights as human rights, including those of minorities;
3. [it] acknowledges its ethno-linguistic pluralism and accepts this as a normal way of life and as a rich resource for development and progress, an Africa that promotes peaceful coexistence of people in a pluralistic society; where pluralism does not entail replacement of one language or identity by another, but instead promotes complementarity of functions as well as cooperation and a sense of common fate;
4. an Africa where democratisation in a pluralistic context seeks to produce through sound and explicit language policies Africans who are able to cooperate effectively at local levels as well as at regional and international levels;
5. an Africa that provides the environment for the promotion and preservation of an African identity as well as the cultivation of a proud and confident African personality;
6. an Africa where scientific and technological discourse is conducted in the national languages as part of our cognitive preparation for facing the challenges of the next millennium. (Intergovernmental Conference of African Language Policies 1997:1f.)

The above recommendations have, in recent times, encouraged some positive moves towards fashioning acceptable and workable language planning programs and policies in most African nations.

Ndoye (undated) has summarized the three main trends in language policies that have emerged in Africa:

1. Some countries have adopted a Western language as the only official language in government institutions, the public sector, as well as the language of instruction in the school systems.
2. There are countries that have put in place a form of bilingual system with a gradual blending of the indigenous languages with the Western language. Some of them have introduced African languages in non-formal or adult literacy education, and also for the first years of primary education. Such countries, including Nigeria, are taking government-backed policy measures to promote the use of local languages and are opening up new, broader contexts for the use of national languages without really challenging the official status of the Western language. In fact, the National Policy on Education (1981) and the 1979 and 1999 Constitutions give overt recognition to the importance of three major languages (Hausa, Igbo,

and Yoruba) in Nigeria over and above the others, while English remains the official language.

3. The third group of African countries have embarked on a rather radical language policy initiative that has seen the restriction of the use of the Western language to the benefit of African languages. Such countries as Mali and Burkina Faso, and recently, South Africa, have been using local languages as the medium of learning in both formal and non-formal education, thus promoting bilingualism and multilingualism. In South Africa, before the abolition of apartheid rule in 1994, the regime permitted only the use of English and Afrikaans as the media of instruction, while other numerous local languages were neglected. As a deliberate policy, no single national language was allowed to evolve and each African ethnic group was encouraged to live in their so-called homelands, where they were to promote their own ethnic languages within the confines of their various individual communities. The learning of other ethnic groups' languages was discouraged. However, the new South African Constitution adopted in 1996 recognises eleven official languages, nine of which are the previously marginalised African languages (Kamwendo 2006:57).

In addition, the influence of globalization and the phenomenal expansion of English as world language, as well as other political considerations, have made nations like Rwanda reconsider the choice of their official language. Recently, the Rwandan government formulated a new language policy that will replace French with the English language as a medium of instruction in schools, arguing that English will make Rwanda become an international financial hub in Africa and also enhance its educational, technological, and economic development.

Similarly, a new language policy that will make the learning of French compulsory by Nigerian school children has been proposed for immediate implementation.

These developments show that the issues of language situation and language policy are in an evolving and on-going process of adapting to the various circumstances, needs, and challenges that shape the national life and the development of each country as a member of the international community.

19.5 LANGUAGE OF THE LAW IN AFRICA: A BRIEF OVERVIEW

Legal activities anywhere in the world need the instruments of language to fufil their purposes. In most African nations, the language of legal communication has, in most cases, been the official language of administration instituted before gaining nationhood. Depending on the official language adopted, the language of legal documents and communication in superior courts of the land has always been the imported language.

While it may be true that the multilingual nature of some of these countries has left them with no other choice, the fact remains that English, French, Spanish, Portuguese, and even Arabic, which are non-indigenous to any state in Africa, have often carried the functional load of administrative and official activities. Usually, the prevailing language of the government environment determines the language employed by legal professionals. For instance, on gaining independence from British colonial rule in 1960, Nigeria adopted English as the language of law. This is not surprising because long before independence English had already assumed the status of official language of administration in this British territory. English "is the language in which legal business is done and documented." English has also carved for itself an indispensable role in Nigerian courtrooms. For instance, "it is the language of proceedings in Nigerian law courts at the federal and state courts" (Awonusi 2004:48).

The only exception, perhaps, will be the Alkali or Sharia courts in northern Nigeria, where Hausa or Arabic (a non-indigenous language) is the medium, as well as in the Customary Courts in the south where local languages of the area are used primarily because of the low level of education of the litigants that patronize the courts (Opeibi, forthcoming).

The same situation may be applicable in other parts of the continent, with the official languages functioning as the language of legal communication at the superior courts and national or indigenous languages at the courts (e.g. Customary Courts) that have jurisdiction to handle other, less serious civil litigation, such as divorce. Where this is not obtainable, interpreters are provided for parties that are not proficient in the language of the courts. Legal documents, including the constitution, executive orders, contracts, deeds, affidavits, and documented court rulings are usually drafted in the official language of each nation.

19.6 CONCLUSION

In the foregoing chapter, we have discussed aspects of the linguistic situation in Africa, highlighting the multilingual nature of the continent. It has been posited that the linguistic density in many African nations and its interplay with foreign languages has challenged governments in various countries to alter the status of the language(s) and/or allocate functions to the various languages in those nations. We have shown that the multilingal linguistic situation in Africa, on the one hand, and the specific situation of each country, on the other, dictates the language policies adopted in different countries. Reasons that include administrative and political convenience, utilitarian status of the language(s), number of speakers, codification, availability of institutional frameworks, and relevance to national or international roles, among other factors, have converged to impact decisions on language policies.

While some nations have chosen the imported language as the language for official businesses, others like South Africa are promoting the use of multiple languages, many of them indigenous, as their official languages.

We align with the view espoused by some experts that Africa stands to benefit from its diverse language structures because language is often tied to the pace at which a nation develops its socio-economic, political, and technological potentials. This view is supported in Humphrey Tonkin (2003:6):

> The diversity of language is an asset: it helps build cohesion in small communities and sustains unique cultures, thereby bestowing distinctive identities on individuals and reducing alienation and homogenization. The rich variety of linguistic idioms carries with it an equally rich variety of cultural forms and ways of thought, and maintains for humankind a diversity of devices for coping with the uncertain challenges of human existence. And who knows what cultural and intellectual tools we will need in tomorrow's world? In this sense, linguistic diversity resembles biodiversity.

Fortunately, the African Union, the umbrella body for all countries in Africa, has already taken a positive step by adopting all languages in Africa as its official languages. We believe that this initiative will further promote the use of the local languages in their various communities for the purposes of nation-building and to elevate the sense of nationhood of the people.

The Asmara Declaration on African Languages and Literatures (2000) also reflects the true perspectives of African languages and captures the aspirations of scholars concerning the linguistic situation in Africa.

- African languages must take on the duty, the responsibility and the challenge of speaking for the continent.
- The vitality and equality of African languages must be recognized as a basis for the future empowerment of the African peoples.
- The diversity of African languages reflects the rich cultural heritage of Africa and must be used as an instrument of African unity.
- The effective and rapid development of science and technology must be used for the development of African languages.
- African languages are essential for the decolonization of African minds and for the African Renaissance.

Confronted with the grim effect of global economic challenges and the ever-advancing development of science and technology in other parts of the world, the continued survival and preservation of African civilizations and development may, to some extent, rest on adopting the right language policy. Such a policy should, primarily, promote the development and use of the indigenous languages alongside the imported languages.

Although the hegemonic status of the imported languages, the effects of globalization, and the growing influence of English as a global language have continued to put

African languages on the defensive, the linguistic diversity in Africa can still become the catalyst that will promote cultural, socio-economic, political, and technological development, as well as sustainable growth and good governance in Africa.

While South Africa's model is not perfect, it remains a commendable initiative worthy of emulation by other African countries.

PART V

LANGUAGE AND CRIMINAL LAW

CHAPTER 20

....

THE MEANING OF SILENCE IN THE RIGHT TO REMAIN SILENT

....

JANET AINSWORTH

20.1 INTRODUCTION: A VENERATED RIGHT HONORED MORE IN THE BREACH THAN IN THE OBSERVANCE?

....

THE right to remain silent is one of the cardinal principles of American criminal jurisprudence, rooted in a long history of Anglo-American legal policy and practice. The origins of our right to remain silent can be traced back to seventeenth-century England and the backlash against the Star Chamber, which had required accused persons brought before it to answer whatever questions were put to them on pain of flogging (Rybnicek 2009:409–10). The American colonies, too, considered the right to be free from compulsory questioning as a fundamental natural right (Alschuler 1996:2649–51). The centrality of this right can be seen in its universal adoption in the founding charters of the former colonies upon independence. All of the twelve states writing constitutions prior to the adoption of the federal Bill of Rights included the protection of a right against self incrimination, though several failed to provide for freedom of speech (Rybnicek 2009: 410).

Expressions of esteem for the right to remain silent have continued to the present day. Noted constitutional scholar and former Harvard Law School Dean Erwin Griswold described the legal privilege against self incrimination as "one of the great landmarks in man's struggle to make himself civilized" (Herrmann and Speer 2007:1). In the jurisprudential literature, the right to remain silent has been justified as essential to the preservation of human dignity (Greenawalt 1992; Easton 1998) and to the fulfillment of human expressive freedom (Seidman 2007). Not only is the right to remain silent celebrated by legal scholars, but it is also probably the single most widely recognized principle of criminal law amongst members of the general public. In fact, given the global reach of the American entertainment industry and its cops-and-robbers movies and television dramas, the *Miranda* warning, beginning with the phrase, "You have the right to remain silent," may be the most well-known criminal law tenet in the world. In semiotic terms, police recitation of the *Miranda* warning has come to stand for the meaning of the concept of arrest itself (Winn 1992:421). Even conservative Supreme Court Chief Justice William Rehnquist conceded that the *Miranda* formulation of the right to remain silent has become so ingrained in the public imagination that it is now part of the fabric of American culture.[1]

Surprisingly, then, current American legal doctrine as actually applied embodies an attitude toward the right to remain silent that is at best ambivalent and at worst aggressively hostile towards the exercise of this right. Treasured in the abstract, the right against self-incrimination is too often given short shrift in its concrete application when individuals attempt to avail themselves of it. For example, the rules governing the exercise of *Miranda* rights require such precise niceties of expression as to make it extremely difficult for non-legally trained people to successfully invoke the right to remain silent during police interrogation (Ainsworth 1993, 2008). The Supreme Court has held that, ironically, simply remaining silent in the face of police questioning does not count as a legally effectively exercise of the right to remain silent.[2]

Why should there be this judicial hostility to such a historically rooted, normatively celebrated constitutional right? One powerful explanation is that the right to remain silent is a right which is ordinarily exercised only in the course of a criminal investigation, and American courts have been increasingly unsympathetic to the exercise of constitutional rights in criminal cases since the heyday of the Warren Court in the 1960s. Doubtless this is true. However, the tenor of recent judicial decisions also reflects the law's conceptualization of the meaning of silence in communication—a simplistic conceptualization at odds with the far more complex and nuanced sense of the meaning of silence found in the works of linguists and anthropologists studying the role of silence in communicative interaction.

20.2 A LINGUISTIC VIEW OF THE MEANING OF SILENCE

At first consideration, it might seem that language researchers would have little interest in examining silence—that is, the absence of verbal expression—just as those studying the meaning of printed texts likely pay little or no attention to the blank white spaces on the page as opposed to that spent on the black symbols making up the textual message.

[1] *Dickerson v U.S.* 530 U.S. 428, 443 (2000).
[2] *Berghuis v Thompkins*, 176 L.Ed.2d 1098 (2010).

Silence in verbal interaction, however, is not just the "white space" setting off the verbal elements of spoken language. In fact, speech and silence each mutually frame the other, and it is this reciprocal framing that gives both silence and utterances their fullest meaning (Eckert and McConnell-Ginet 2003:119). As language scholars have come to appreciate, silence serves a myriad of communicative functions—semantic, pragmatic, and socio-pragmatic (Saville-Troike 1985:7–11; Jaworski 1993:66–97; Lakoff 1995:26). Not surprisingly, perhaps, in light of the complexity of its use in interaction, the appropriate deployment and understanding of silence occurs quite late in a child's acquisition of communicative competence (Sobkowiak 1997:51). Consideration of silence is so crucial to interactional analyses grounded in the discipline of Conversational Analysis that its transcription conventions measure pauses to tenths of a second, with micro-silences too short to measure indicated in transcription by the use of dots (Psathas 1995:11–13).

Silence has been called the "least semantically determinate" linguistic element (Sobkowiak 1997:54). Although all linguistic practices are context-dependent, silence is particularly so, with an interpretation of silence truly impossible without the discursive and interactional context to give it meaning (Saville-Troike 1985:11; Gal 1991:176, 2001:422–3). As Penelope Eckert and Sally McConnell-Ginet (2003:19) have noted, "Silence is never neutral. We talk about awkward silences, ominous silences, stunned, strained, awed, reverent and respectful silences." Which of those glosses is to be mapped onto any particular silence cannot be determined absent a consideration of context. Silence only becomes a communicative act when it occurs within a communicative context—that is, within a structured interaction with others governed by distinct social norms of behavior (Tiersma 1995a:21–2). Thus, silence can only be accorded meaning in the light of those communicative norms.

The ascription of meaning to silence varies culturally, since conventions on the appropriate degree and deployment of silence within interaction are not universal but instead culturally contingent (Sifianou 1997:69–72). In some cultures, interpersonal interaction is largely structured through talk, with silence often serving subsidiary functions as boundary markers, junctions, and turn-taking signals. In other cultures, however, interaction is more frequently structured through nonverbal means, with silence a primary source of interactional mediation (Philips 1985:209–12). Cultural norms differ both in the pragmatic use of silence (see, e.g., Chon (1995) on Asian American active use of silence in interaction) and in the interpretations accorded to silence when it occurs. Naturally, cross-cultural differences in this regard create a serious potential for misunderstanding and misinterpretation of intended meaning (Tannen 1985; Houck and Gass 1997:298–301).

Even in interactions between persons sharing a single cultural set of interactional norms, the semantic and pragmatic aspects of meaning ascribed to silence (Jaworski 1993:66–97) are so sensitive to the multiplicity of dimensions of context that miscommunication between interactors is all too common (Jaworski 1993:3–7). Miscommunication is particularly pernicious in contexts marked by power asymmetries between the parties to the interaction, in which one party may be constrained in his responses and limited in his range of interactional options (Walker 1985:55–75; Lakoff 1995:26). Another source of miscommunciation is the fact that, unlike utterances, which are generally intentionally produced by their speakers, silence is in some instances intentional, with an incumbent meaning intended by the silent party, but in other cases inadvertent, with meaning given to the silence only through ascription rather than intent (Kurzon 1995; Tiersma 1995a: 6–23). In cases of unselfconscious and unintended silence, inferences accorded to that silence by external hearers are frequently unreliable as accurate reflections of the internal state of mind of the silent person.

Of course, even when silence is quite deliberate on the part of the non-speaker, its ascribed meaning by external observers may be quite different from its internal intended meaning. For example, the person who remains silent during a group pledge of allegiance to the flag at school may intend to express her religious qualms about expressing allegiance to God or to an earthly government, or she may mean to express her objection to a particular government leader or policy, but her silence may be interpreted by observers as a lack of patriotism on her part or as an expression of immature anti-authoritarianism against school administrators. Context certainly helps narrow the plausible interpretations of this silence, but context can never be finely grained enough to completely determine meaning, whether internally intended meaning or externally ascribed meaning.

Linguistic researchers have developed taxonomies of more than twenty different interpretations of the meaning of silence in response to an utterance (Johannesen 1974:29–30; Chafe 1985; Eprhatt 2008). Perhaps as a consequence, some scholars consider silence irreducibly ambiguous in most instances (Sifianou 1997:63–5). Given the semantic indeterminacy, the contextual sensitivity, and the cultural variability in ascribing meaning to silence, linguistic researchers are understandably reluctant to ascribe definitive meaning to specific instances of silence without a highly particularized examination of the context in which the silence at issue occurred. Still less would a linguist posit global ascription of meaning to responsive acts of silence in general. Legal doctrine, however, is much less diffident about doing so, due in part to the law's impoverished sense of the range of meanings that silence can have.

20.3   ADOPTIVE ADMISSIONS—WHEN SILENCE CAN BE TREATED AS A CONFESSION

The law's often inadequate sense of the range of socio-pragmatic meaning of silence in interaction becomes apparent in cases in which the meaning of a person's silence is directly at issue. One such situation occurs when the legal rules of evidence construe a person's silence that follows an accusation by another. Under the evidentiary rules,[3] when someone is confronted with an accusatory statement under circumstances in

---

[3] Federal Rule of Evidence 801 (d) (2) (B).

which it is assumed that the appropriate response would be to object, and instead the hearer remains silent, that silence is admitted as a tacit adoptive admission of the truth of the accusation. In other words, silence in the face of accusation is interpreted as an affirmative agreement by the accused person that the accusation is true.

Before this kind of evidence can be admitted at trial, it must be shown that the person heard and understood the accusatory language and had an opportunity to respond. In addition, the accusation must be one that, in the context of its utterance, would have called for a denial under the circumstances if it were untrue (McCormick et al. 1999: 168–9). If these threshold requirements are met, the rules of evidence permit the fact of silence in the face of an accusation to be weighed as identical in evidentiary force to a confession to the charge. The assumption behind the rule is that, when confronted with an accusation of wrong-doing, the only reasonable response is to issue an explicit, unequivocal, and unambiguous denial.

Although this interpretation of silence is firmly rooted in common law evidentiary law, a few courts over the years have expressed skepticism about its soundness and urged that judges exercise restraint in presuming that silence be treated as though it were an admission of guilt.[4] Linguistic research suggests that courts would be right to be skeptical about interpreting the meaning of silence following accusatory language. What counts as an accusation is often unclear, and what kind of response is warranted even less clear. Even a purely surface semantic analysis of accusatory language cannot be performed in the absence of social context, including who is making the accusation and to whom it is being made—often the subject of supposedly accusatory language might well interpret the utterance in question as something that he need not respond to (McCawley 1979:136–8).

Linguistic analyses of communicative interactions tend to undermine the law's assumption that the natural response of a person accused of wrong-doing is an immediate and unhesitating denial, suggesting instead that silence is at least as plausible a reaction as denial to such an event. In fact, silence may itself be a denial. Linguists studying communicative interactions observe that they are marked by turn-taking within the interaction, and that turn-taking is governed through a system of social conventions of floor-holding, floor-ceding, topic raising, and the like. (Sacks et al. 1974; Brown and Yule 1983:226–31). Pairs of turns are referred to as adjacency pairs, with the second turn seen as the response to the first. Thus, after one person has concluded his turn and has ceded the conversational floor to the other, either speech or silence by the party who now has the "floor" would be considered a response turn. Whether that turn involved an utterance or not, it would constitute the second element of the adjacency pair in question.

Anita Pomerantz' (1984) work on adjacency pairs compared what she called "preferred" responses with "dispreferred" responses. Preferred seconds in an adjacency pair are responses like agreement or approval, whereas dispreferred seconds are responses like disagreement or objection. What Pomerantz found in looking at contrasting adjacency pairs is that preferred seconds—agreements with the first speaker—tend to be

---

[4] See, e.g., *People v Bigge*, 285 N.W. 5 (Mich. S. Ct. 1939); *Commonwealth v Dravecz*, 227 A.2d 904 (Pa. S. Ct. 1967); *State v Clark*, 175 P.3d 1006 (Ore.2008).

more fluid and rapid than dispreferred seconds—disagreements with the first speaker. The latter are marked by long pauses, hesitations, false starts, discourse markers, and the like. In other words, a response in an adjacency pair which disagrees with the first utterance is likely to be non-fluent, hesitant, or even non-existent—that is, expressed through silence. Dennis Kurzon's (1994b) examination of question and answer adjacency pairs in police interrogation found similar patterns. In short, silence is well within the range of expected second elements in an adjacency pair that begins with an accusation if the second person disagrees with the accusation, since as a dispreferred response it will tend to be non-fluent or even totally absent.

Nevertheless, the overwhelming judicial practice has been to permit the introduction of adoptive admission evidence liberally—even unreflectively—as proof of wrong-doing by the silent party. Courts often utilize this doctrine even in cases in which the required foundational facts for admissibility are doubtful. For example, despite the requirement that the statement cannot be admitted unless the party in question was able to hear the accusation, in some cases adoptive admissions have been used in situations in which it is unlikely that the defendant actually heard the statement in question because he may not have been in the room when it was uttered[5] or he was in the back seat of a car when the statement in question was made by people in the front seat.[6] In another case, the testifying witness conceded at trial that he could not remember whether the defendant responded to the supposedly accusatory statement or not, but despite the lack of proof that the defendant actually was silent in the face of the accusation, an adoptive admission was construed against the defendant nonetheless.[7]

The inherent unfairness of this doctrine is compounded by the fact that it is frequently applied in contexts in which the supposed link between the fact of silence and a presumed admission of guilt is extraordinarily thin. For example, in many cases, the purported accusation is not directly made to the person accused, but merely made within his earshot in a conversation in which he is not necessarily a participant. Apparently, the law of evidence expects people to pay attention to the substance of any conversations that happen to be within range of hearing, to be vigilant in detecting any suggestions of wrong-doing, and to interrupt with a firm denial.

It is not enough to be wary of direct, obvious accusations. Indirect or ambiguous language that could possibly be interpreted as an accusation is sometimes also construed as the kind of utterance that must be expressly challenged, particularly if the speaker uses pronouns of ambiguous referential scope such as "we"[8] or "they"[9] in describing actions. Innocent sounding comments that conceivably could have an incriminating interpretation must be objected to as well, at the risk of their being used as adoptive admissions. For example, in a conversation between two corporate officers, the words of

---

[5] *Alvarado v State*, 912 S.W.2d 199 (Tex. Ct. Crim. App. 1995).
[6] *U.S. v Carter*, 760 F.2d 1568 (11th Cir. 1985).
[7] *Commonwealth v Braley*, 867 N.E.2d 743 (Mass. S. Jud. Ct. 2007).
[8] *People v Sneed*, 653 N.E.2d 1349 (Ill.App. 1995).
[9] *People v Riel*, 998 P.2d 969 (Cal. S. Ct. 2000).

one that "I'll see if we can get anything for this work," was interpreted as possibly a suggestion that illegal bid rigging be undertaken. Despite the lack of any explicit language regarding illegal activity, the defendant's failure to anticipate and object to that possible interpretation at the time of the utterance was considered an admission that he was indeed aware of the illegal nature of the bid.[10]

Remaining silent in the face of even a non-accusatory statement can potentially result in a later judicial finding that the silence is an adoptive admission when, at some point in the future, that innocuous statement turns out to have an incriminatory implication. For example, being referred to as "John" by a stranger was found to be an admission that the defendant went by that name because he did not register an objection to the moniker.[11] In another case, the defendant was present and failed to challenge an allegation in a conversation to which she was not a party that she habitually carried a gun. Her silence was held to be an admission that she was, in fact, in possession of a gun at the time of the crime in question, notwithstanding that the supposed "admission" occurred long before the crime took place.[12]

Likewise, the person who chooses to ignore name-calling is risking adoption of the insulting characterization. In the case of a defendant who was called a "butcher," his failure to argue with the name caller was held to be an admission.[13] In another case, a corporate officer asked by a reporter at a press conference if the corporation had been "cooking the books" responded by saying, "Next question, please," instead of denying the colloquial allegation of wrong-doing. Later at trial, the court found that his failure to explicitly deny the allegation at the press conference constituted an admission on his part because he should have directly addressed the reporter's charge without attempting to avoid it.[14] Nor is it sufficient merely to react angrily to an accusation, as when a defendant told an accuser to "shut the f—up."[15] A more direct and explicit denial, in the view of the law, would have been the appropriate way to rebut an accusation.

Even a direct and explicit denial of an accusation may be legally insufficient if the defendant fails to repeat it often enough. In one such case the defendant was asked if he had committed the crime, and he responded with a denial. In response, the questioner told him that a third party believes that he did commit the crime. The defendant reacted by turning his head and staring out the window. The court could well have interpreted his response as shock or dismay that someone could believe that he was guilty, but it instead chose to construe it as an adoptive admission because he failed to repeat the denial that he had made just seconds earlier.[16]

Telephone conversations present a particularly problematic situation because the participants' inability to see each other's facial expressions and body language can create a false impression of acquiescence to an accusation. In one such case, a defendant's

[10] *U.S. v Basic Construction Co.*, 711 F.2d 570 (4th Cir. 1983).
[11] *State v Wallingford*, 43 S.W. 3d 852 (Mo. App. 2001).
[12] *State v Browning*, 485 S.E.2d 1 (W.Va. S. Ct. 1997).
[13] *State v Gorrell*, 687 A.2d 1016 (N.J. App. 1996).
[14] *U.S. v Henke*, 222 F.3d 633 (9th Cir. 2000).
[15] *State v Gilmore*, 22 S.W.3d 712 (Mo. App. 1999).
[16] *State v Gomez*, 848 A.2d. 221 (R.I. S. Ct. 2004).

silence during a recorded jailhouse telephone call after a friend read him a newspaper account of the details of the crime was admitted as an adoptive admission of those details on the theory that he should have interrupted his friend to deny inaccuracies in newspaper account.[17] In another case involving a recorded jailhouse telephone call, a friend of the defendant told him that the police had asked him "twelve times" whether he had seen the defendant shoot the victims, to which the defendant replied, "Oh man, twelve times." From this response the court inferred that, by not expressly denying that he was the shooter, the defendant had adopted the substance of the police belief that he was the shooter as true, despite the fact that the friend gave the defendant no reason to think that he, the friend, shared that police belief. Apparently, in the court's view, the reasonable response by the defendant would have been to deny guilt, not to express shock in the persistence of a false police theory of his involvement or to express empathy for the persistent police questioning that his friend had undergone.[18]

Given the ambiguity of pronoun references, sometimes being present while someone plans a crime or brags about past crimes can result in adoptive admissions that one is or was involved in those crimes in the absence of overt disassociation. For example, one defendant nodded his head while someone at a party boasted about the crimes he, the braggart, had committed. Although the braggart did not link the defendant to those crimes in his narrative of them, by silently nodding his head the defendant was held to have admitted that he too had participated in them.[19] In another case, a racketeering kingpin, present in the defendant's home, ordered an underling to commit arson. By remaining silent in the face of the kingpin's order, the defendant was tacitly admitting his culpability in the arson plot, said the court, since "an innocent man would not let others sit in his house and plan arson."[20] The court ignored the very real possibility that the defendant might simply have been afraid to object. His silence is at least as plausibly construed as his unwillingness to confront a powerful kingpin as it is his willing participation in the crime. In another such case, a defendant who testified that he was in no position to object to inaccurate inculpatory statements made about him by a Mexican Mafia boss because of his fear of the boss was nevertheless saddled with those statements as adoptive admissions.[21]

Power imbalances may inhibit the possibility of a denial of accusatory statements in contexts beyond those involving violent and dangerous criminals. For example, when a judge made statements describing the details of a crime in the course of accepting a plea agreement, the defendant was later held to have made adoptive admissions of those characterizations by not objecting to them at the hearing. The appellate court apparently expected the defendant to jeopardize the guilty plea agreement and thereby risk a harsher sentence by interrupting the judge and objecting to the way in which the judge represented the circumstances of the crime.[22]

---

[17] *U.S. v Higgs*, 353 F.3d 281 (4th Cir. 2003).
[18] *People v Davis*, 115 P.3d 417 (Calif. S. Ct. 2005).
[19] *U.S. v Price*, 516 F.3d 597 (7th Cir. 2008).
[20] *U.S. v Manzella*, 782 F.2d 533, 545 (5th Cir. 1986).
[21] *Paredes v State*, 129 S.W.3d 530 (Tex. Ct. Crim. App. 2004).
[22] *U.S. v Miller*, 478 F.3d 48 (1st Cir. 2007).

As cases like this show, evidence law insists that people not only confront accusations made directly to them but also be on the alert for any statements that they might overhear that might impugn them, directly or inferentially, with regard to bad acts that have occurred or that might occur in the future. Failing to defend one's reputation with an explicit denial in any of those situations will be treated as the legal equivalent of a confession. Because it is treated as a confession, it will be sufficient to sustain a conviction even where there is little or no other evidence of guilt of the crime in question.[23]

Further, because it is the defendant's silence, not the accuser's statements, that are taken to be the "statement" admitted in court, there is no hearsay problem with admission of the evidence even if the accuser never appears in court.[24] In short, inflammatory, highly prejudicial, and quite possibly completely false allegations can be put before the jury without the defendant ever having the right to confront and cross-examine his accuser in court.

20.4 ADOPTIVE ADMISSIONS DURING POLICE QUESTIONING

The adoptive admission rule can become a particularly dangerous trap for those suspected by the police of involvement in a crime. Because the familiar *Miranda* warnings communicate the message that citizens have the right to remain silent in the course of a police investigation, it would be reasonable for the lay person to assume that this silence, if chosen, could not later be used against him to imply his guilt. And indeed, in some situations, that assumption is a valid one. The Supreme Court recognized that, having told a suspect that he has the right to remain silent and warned him that anything he does say can be used in evidence against him in the *Miranda* warning, it would be unfair to then use silence resulting from the reading of that warning as substantive evidence of guilt through the adoptive admissions rule.[25]

Since the adoptive admissions rule requires that the context of the interchange be one in which it would be natural for the accused to affirmatively deny the accusation, it might appear that the adoptive admissions rule could have no application at all in a *Miranda*-governed interrogation system, with its guarantees of the right to remain silent. Yet, surprisingly, in a number of American jurisdictions, this is not necessarily the case. In many cases, failure to respond to police accusations runs the risk of inadvertently adopting them by silence.

---

[23] See, e.g., *Commonwealth v Braley*, 867 N.E.2d 743 (Mass. S. Jud. Ct. 2007); *State v Tolliver*, 765 N.E.2d 894 (Ohio App. 2001).

[24] *U.S. v Kehoe*, 310 F.3d 579 (8th Cir. 2002).

[25] *Wainwright v Greenfield*, 474 U.S. 284 (1986).

The *Miranda* warnings, as the Supreme Court itself recently acknowledged, have become an iconic part of American popular culture, familiar to almost all Americans.[26] Keeping that in mind, consider the common situation in which someone is being confronted by the police with allegations of wrong-doing, but where the *Miranda* rights have not been recited—perhaps because the police have not yet formally arrested the suspect or perhaps because the police have arrested the suspect but intend to postpone the reading of the *Miranda* warnings for a time. In such a case, the target of police suspicion might well be aware that he has the right not to respond to police accusations, either from earlier police interactions in which he had been read his *Miranda* rights or from his general cultural understanding of the right to remain silent. Under those circumstances, his silence in the face of police accusations could be motivated by the knowledge that anything said could be used against him.

However reasonable that choice might seem to the suspect, it is fraught with peril. For example, the Supreme Court has permitted the prosecution to use evidence of pre-arrest, unwarned silence by a suspect to impeach his credibility if he later takes the stand at trial.[27] In other words, if the accused testifies in his own defense, the prosecutor will be permitted to introduce evidence that the defendant chose not to answer police questions and further to argue to the jury that the defendant's silence at that time should lead them to conclude that his testimony now in court should not be believed, since if it were true, he should have told his story to the police earlier rather than choosing to remain silent. Even silence once a person is formally arrested can legally be used for impeachment as long as the record does not show that *Miranda* warnings had been given at the time of the silence in question.[28] Given this doctrine, the person who takes his right to remain silent seriously and who decides to exercise it early on in his dealings with the police will be hard pressed later to take the stand in his own defense. Despite the fact that most people already believe that they have the right to remain silent in the face of police accusations, they are not justified in relying on the right to remain silent, according to current Supreme Court doctrine, unless they can prove that the *Miranda* warnings had actually been read by the time of the police confrontation.

Although the Supreme Court has made it clear that pre-warning silence may be admissible to suggest that the defendant's courtroom testimony should not be believed, the high court has left open the question of whether such silence could be used not just to impeach a defendant's credibility but in addition as substantive evidence of guilt. Because adoptive admissions are treated identically to explicit confessions, the question here is whether failing to answer police allegations is tantamount to a confession as long as the allegations were made prior to reading of the *Miranda* warnings. The federal circuits have split on this question. The Fourth, Fifth, Eighth, and Eleventh Circuits have held that pre-warning silence can indeed be used by prosecutors as substantive proof of guilt; the Seventh, Ninth, and DC Circuits have held that it is constitutionally

---

[26] *Dickerson v U.S.*, 530 U.S. 428, 443 (2000).
[27] *Jenkins v Anderson*, 447 U.S. 231 (1980).
[28] *Fletcher v Weir*, 455 U.S. 603 (1982).

impermissible. A similar split exists regarding silence in the face of police accusations prior to arrest (Macchiaroli 2009:16).

Thus, despite the knowledge of virtually everyone that they have the right to remain silent when confronted by the police, exercising that right in some jurisdictions can lead to the highly unexpected and fundamentally unfair possibility that such silence will be construed as a confession. The problem is compounded by the fact that current case law permitting the prosecution use of pre-warning silence gives police a positive incentive to ignore the mandate of *Miranda* and to delay giving the warning as long as possible, hoping that the suspect may naively exercise what he believes to be his right to remain silent in the face of police insinuations of guilt (Hennes 2007:1015; Willis 2008:742). Ultimately, the use of the adoptive admission doctrine in the context of a police investigation means that, prior to arrest, suspects should actually be warned, "Anything you say can be used against you. And if you don't say anything, that will be used against you, too." Small wonder that police interrogation has come to be seen as a game of "heads we win, tails you lose."

Some legal commentators have urged the Supreme Court to back away from its doctrinal framework that permits guilt to be proven from evidence that the defendant simply did not verbally contest police accusations during the investigatory phase of the criminal process (Strauss 2001; Skrapka 2006). Some judges have likewise recognized that silence in the face of accusation is often ambiguous and that it may be unfair to infer that this silence is an acknowledgment of guilt. For example, Justice Thurgood Marshall expressed skepticism about the inevitability of the linkage between a suspect's silence and the inference that such silence constitutes acquiescence to the truth of police allegations. He argued that there are a host of reasons other than consciousness of guilt that might lead someone to choose to be silent under those circumstances, including being confused, being intimidated, misunderstanding the import of the allegations, being unwilling to implicate other persons, and so forth. Marshall stressed that the meaning of suspect silence needs to be assessed contextually, in the light of the atmosphere inherent in custodial police interrogation—an atmosphere that Marshall characterized as confusing, highly emotionally charged, and hostile.[29] Marshall's analysis of this situation reads like an opinion by a judge familiar with the linguistic analysis of the communicative meaning of silence. In the thirty-five years since that opinion, however, few courts have matched his intuitive grasp of linguistic principles. American legal doctrine continues in the grip of a cramped view of the pragmatics of silence in which silence has an easily determined meaning and in which that meaning tends to favor incrimination.

Sadly, the situation is no better in the birthplace of the right against self-incrimination, the United Kingdom. The caution given to arrestees was amended in 1994 to read, "You do not have to say anything *but it may harm your defence if you do not mention when questioned something which you later rely on in court.* Anything you *do* say may be given in evidence"[30] (1994 amendments in italics) (Cotterill 2005:7–8). As in the United

---

[29] *U.S. v Hale*, 421 U.S. 171, 177 (1975).
[30] Criminal Justice and Order Act of 1994, amending the Police and Evidence Act of 1984.

States, adoptive admissions are liberally admitted as concessions of criminal liability in Britain (Cotterill 2005:15–21). The concept of adoptive admissions—that an accused person has an affirmative duty to speak to rebut an accusation—is far better suited to legal regimes in which the burden of proof is on the accused than in criminal justice systems such as those in Britain and the United States, where the defendant has no burden to establish his innocence (cf. Ephratt 2008:1928–30). It is ironic, then, that admission through silence has come to play a major evidentiary role in undermining the right to remain silent in two legal systems that both assert the centrality of that right in maintaining the presumption of innocence.

CHAPTER 21

POTENTIAL IMPACT OF JUVENILE SUSPECTS' LINGUISTIC ABILITIES ON *MIRANDA* UNDERSTANDING AND APPRECIATION

NAOMI E. S. GOLDSTEIN
SHARON MESSENHEIMER KELLEY
CHRISTINA L. RIGGS ROMAINE
HEATHER ZELLE

IN *Miranda v Arizona*,[1] the US Supreme Court established procedural safeguards for custodial interrogations that also serve as a rule of admissibility if the prosecution wants to use a suspect's statements as evidence at trial. Specifically, the suspect must be informed of the right to silence, of the government's intent to use the suspect's statements against him or her, of the right to counsel, and of the right to appointed counsel for indigent suspects. Many jurisdictions have also added a fifth warning to their *Miranda* rights, explicitly informing suspects of the continued privilege of their rights.

The *Miranda* Court also held that suspects may waive these rights, but in order for a waiver to be considered valid, it must have been made knowingly, intelligently, and voluntarily. The knowing and intelligent requirements refer to a suspect's overall comprehension of his rights, which the Court has defined as "full awareness of both the nature of the right being abandoned and the consequences of the decision to abandon it."[2] Some researchers have equated the legal constructs of "knowing" and "intelligent" with the

---

[1] *Miranda v Arizona*, 384 U.S. 436 (1966).
[2] *Moran v Burbine*, 475 U.S. 412, 421 (1986).

psychological constructs of "understanding" and "appreciation," respectively (Grisso 2002). Whereas understanding requires a basic comprehension of what the rights mean, appreciation requires a deeper level of comprehension that is reflected in a suspect's ability to apply the rights to his own situation and to grasp the potential consequences of waiving the rights.

The voluntariness requirement, primarily, refers to the absence of police coercion in securing a *Miranda* waiver (*Colorado v Connelly*[3] 1986). Suspects' language abilities do not directly affect voluntariness (although police, theoretically, can use coercive techniques to take advantage of suspects' poor linguistic skills). Therefore, this chapter will focus on the language of *Miranda* and its impact on juvenile suspects' capacities to meet the "knowing and intelligent" requirements of a valid waiver.

When evaluating the validity of a *Miranda* waiver, courts consider the *totality of circumstances* surrounding the warnings, waiver, and interrogation.[4] There are two broad categories of factors: (1) suspect characteristics (e.g. age, intelligence, prior experience with police, education); and (2) interrogation characteristics (e.g. length of the interrogation, police interrogation strategies)[5] (Grisso 1998). Factors such as the defendant's age and education at the time of the waiver, the methods police used to administer the *Miranda* warnings, and the complexity of the *Miranda* warnings administered can all be considered by courts when determining the validity of a *Miranda* waiver and the admissibility of the statement that followed. Thus, this chapter focuses on juveniles' *Miranda* comprehension and linguistic abilities, variability in the administration and language of *Miranda* warnings, and the potential impact of these suspect- and interrogation-related factors on juvenile suspects' capacities to provide knowing and intelligent waivers of rights.

21.1 SUSPECT-RELATED TOTALITY OF CIRCUMSTANCES FACTORS: AGE AND EDUCATION

21.1.1 Age and juveniles' *Miranda* comprehension

Approximately 90 percent of juvenile suspects waive their rights (Ferguson and Douglas 1970; Viljoen, Klaver, and Roesch 2005), and research across many decades has consistently revealed that juveniles' *Miranda* comprehension is generally poor (Abramovtich, Peterson-Badali, and Rohan 1995; Ferguson and Douglas 1970; Goldstein, Condie, Kalbeitzer, Osman, and Geier 2003; Grisso 1981; Oberlander and Goldstein 2001). Using data collected in the 1970s, Grisso (1981) found significant levels of impairment among boys who had recently been taken into police custody. Specifically, youth under age 15,

---

[3] *Colorado v Connelly*, 479 U.S. 157 (1986).
[4] *Fare v Michael C.*, 442 U.S. 707 (1979).
[5] *Coyote v United States*, 380 F.2d 305 (10th Cir. 1967).

and youth aged 15 to 16 with IQs scores below 80, rarely demonstrated adequate under-standing of the *Miranda* warnings. Furthermore, one-third to one-half of youths with average IQ scores also failed to demonstrate adequate understanding. A twenty-first-century study revealed similar levels of performance among pre- and post-adjudication boys in juvenile justice facilities, suggesting that youths' *Miranda* comprehension did not improve during the intervening three decades (Riggs Romaine, Goldstein, Zelle, Heilbrun, and Wolbransky 2008). These widespread deficits raise questions about youth-ful suspects' capacities to provide knowing and intelligent waivers of rights (e.g. Grisso 1981; Goldstein et al. 2003; Viljoen, Klaver, and Roesch 2005).

21.1.2 Education and juvenile justice youths' linguistic abilities

When courts consider education as a totality of circumstances factor, they may review information about a defendant's reading level and listening abilities. Generally, research has shown that language continues to develop through adolescence and into early adult-hood (Nippold 1993). Semantic abilities, those concerned with meaning and most relevant to *Miranda* comprehension, advance during this time. The accurate comprehension and use of sophisticated vocabulary continues to progress through the college years (Astington and Olson 1987; Nippold 1993). Comprehension of figurative expressions also improves throughout adolescence (Nippold 1993). As a result of this incomplete linguistic develop-ment, adolescents may have difficulty understanding words or expressions with abstract or multiple meanings (Nippold 1993). In the context of *Miranda* comprehension, children and adolescents may be able to understand the word "right" as meaning "correct," but they may lack sufficient linguistic development to recognize that "right" is also an entitlement.

More specifically, research has shown that juvenile offenders have more linguistic def-icits than their non-offending peers and that these deficits permeate all facets of lan-guage (Davis, Sanger, and Morris-Friehe 1991). The reading abilities of juvenile offenders are often several years behind their peers. One study (Texas Youth Commission 2006) found that the average reading levels of delinquent youth (median age of 16 years) ranged from 5.8 to 6.0. The general vocabulary and grammar skills of juvenile offenders are significantly lower than non-offending adolescents, as well (Davis et al. 1991).

Juvenile offenders also demonstrate problems with language processing, interpreta-tion of ambiguous stimuli, and verbal memory. In one study (Humber and Snow 2001), juvenile offenders performed significantly worse than non-offending adolescents on two tests: one requiring them to indicate, as quickly as possible, whether statements were true or false; and the other requiring them to decide whether presented words were real or not. The offending group also showed significant deficits when asked to interpret ambig-uous statements and figurative expressions. Similarly, juvenile offenders performed sig-nificantly worse than a community sample on a test requiring them to recall three short stories after a small time delay (Olvera, Semred-Clikeman, Pliszka, and O'Donnell 2005).

Research on the listening comprehension of children generally suggests that pre-existing topical knowledge predicts understanding (Hare and Devine 1993). Notably, juveniles' general legal knowledge, and, more specifically, their knowledge and under-standing of the *Miranda* warnings, is poor (e.g. Goldstein et al. 2003; Grisso 1981, 1997); consequently, juveniles lack a useful foundation for comprehending orally delivered warnings. General listening comprehension research has also shown that individuals tend to understand and recall comparative and causative passages better than descrip-tive passages (Meyer and Freedle 1984). Because the *Miranda* warnings fall into the latter category, juveniles are placed at yet another disadvantage for understanding their rights.

Juvenile offenders frequently have language and learning disabilities (Dunivant 1982), and adolescents with such disabilities tend to experience difficulties with listening comprehension skills. For example, following a social studies lecture, adolescents with language-learning disabilities performed significantly worse than did adolescents with-out disabilities when responding to literal and inferential questions (Ward-Lonergan, Liles, and Anderson 1998). In addition, juvenile offenders did not perform as well as non-offending youth on listening comprehension tasks that required them to make inferences from orally-delivered information (Humber and Snow 2001) or that required them to follow complex oral instructions (Olvera et al. 2005).

In addition to the receptive language abilities described above, juvenile offenders also demonstrate problems with their expressive abilities (Davis et al. 1991). Juvenile offend-ers in one study made significantly more errors than non-offending adolescents on a narrative discourse task that required them to coherently describe a series of events depicted in cartoon frames (Humber and Snow 2001). Juvenile offenders in another study performed significantly worse than a community sample when asked to formulate sentences (Olvera et al. 2005).

Overall, the linguistic difficulties of juveniles impair both their receptive and expres-sive language abilities. Therefore, juveniles are likely to have problems (1) understanding the information provided to them in *Miranda* warnings and (2) communicating their understanding of their rights (or lack thereof) to police, parents, or attorneys. Given the combination of juvenile offenders' poor linguistic abilities with the high linguistic demands of juvenile warnings, juvenile suspects are at risk for failing to provide knowing and intelligent rights waivers.

21.2 INTERROGATION-RELATED TOTALITY OF CIRCUMSTANCES FACTORS: ADMINISTRATION AND LANGUAGE OF THE WARNINGS

Although the Supreme Court dictated the content of the *Miranda* warnings, it held that no specific wording is required.[6] The warnings merely need to be stated in "clear and unequivocal language" and impart a comprehensible statement of the individual's

---

[6] *California v Prysock*, 451 U.S. 1301 (1981); *Duckworth v Egan*, 492 U.S. 195 (1989).

rights.[7] As a result, a wide variety of *Miranda* warnings and administration methods has emerged across jurisdictions. Recently, Rogers and colleagues found 560 unique, English versions of the warnings across the United States that varied dramatically in length, readability, sentence complexity, and vocabulary (Rogers, Harrison, Shuman, Sewell, and Hazelwood 2007b; Rogers, Hazelwood, Sewell, Harrison, and Shuman 2008b). When examining the variability of *Miranda* warnings, differences can be described in four broad areas: administration methods, structure of the warnings, and population-specific versions.

21.2.1 Administration of the warnings

A recent survey of police practices revealed that most *Miranda* warnings are delivered orally (67 percent), but that warnings are also frequently administered in exclusively written form (Kassin et al. 2007). Oral warnings, generally, appear to be understood less frequently than their written counterparts (Rogers 2008), potentially due to problems with memory and recall (Rogers, Harrison, Shuman, Sewell, and Hazelwood 2007b). However, for defendants with limited reading abilities, such as juvenile offenders (Davis et al. 1991; Texas Youth Commission 2006) and other offender populations (Klinge and Dorsey 1993), oral delivery may be preferable (Rogers 2008). Of course, if suspects also have listening comprehension deficits, as is common among juvenile justice youth (Humber and Snow 2001; Olvera et al. 2005), oral delivery may not facilitate comprehension.

Beyond the oral versus written formats of administration, little is known about the details of how police deliver *Miranda* warnings (Oberlander and Goldstein 2001). Nonetheless, details about the delivery (e.g. speed of administration, whether police ask suspects to waive each right individually or the entire set of rights at once, whether police ask suspects to paraphrase the warnings before waiving them) could, theoretically, affect suspects' understanding and appreciation of rights.

21.2.2 Language of the warnings: structural variability

21.2.2.1 *Warning length*

Rogers et al. (2007b) found that the average warning and waiver was 146 words, with a notably large range of 49 to 547 words. On average, each statement within a warning was longer than the statement that preceded it (Rogers et al. 2007b). Long passages can pose problems for recall and comprehension (Miller 1956), particularly when the suspect either is not given the opportunity to read along or does not have the requisite reading ability. Rogers et al. (2007b) estimated that, generally, adults cannot adequately comprehend *Miranda* warnings that exceed about 73 words. Juveniles, who have particular difficulty

----

[7] *Miranda*, 384 U.S. at 467–8.

comprehending *Miranda* warnings, would probably struggle even with 73-word warnings (e.g. Goldstein et al. 2003). Yet, as the following sections detail, other characteristics of the warnings impact comprehensibility, and warnings that are longer in length may be more easily understood if they incorporate simpler language, lower reading levels, and contextual information.

Consistent with this suggestion, Rogers and colleagues (2008a) found that longer warnings do not necessarily have higher reading levels. In their analysis of juvenile versions of the warnings, they found that, on average, juvenile warnings exceeded adult warnings by more than 60 words. However, they also found a slight inverse relationship between warning length and a warning's reading level. If the goal is to provide critical information while keeping reading levels low and sentence length short, perhaps the simplest and most informative warnings would consist of several short, simple sentences with commonly used vocabulary.

21.2.2.2 *Reading level*

Reading level can be established with the Flesch–Kincaid formula, which estimates the grade level required for reading comprehension of a text by analyzing average sentence length and average number of syllables per word for that text (Flesch 1950). For material to be classified at a particular Flesch–Kincaid grade-level, readers of that grade level must be able to comprehend 75 percent of the material (DuBay 2004). Although the Flesch–Kincaid formula may not fully account for the presence of unfamiliar words or legalistic terms (Rogers et al. 2007b), it is a commonly used tool for evaluating the reading level of *Miranda* warnings (e.g. Kahn, Zapf, and Cooper 2006; Rogers et al. 2007b).

A variety of factors about the individual and the text can impact readability, such as motivation of the reader, legibility of the material, complexity of words and sentences, and an individual's reading ability (Johnson 1998). These final two factors, and the interaction between them, are particularly significant in the context of *Miranda* warnings.

The reading level of warnings varies tremendously, both across jurisdictions and across the different statements of the warnings. In one study, the grade level of the warnings, in their entirety, varied from 5.7 to 12.0 (Kahn, Zapf, and Cooper 2006); in two larger studies, they varied from grade level 3 to 18 (Rogers et al. 2007b; Rogers et al. 2008b). On average, the first two warnings (right to silence and intent to use a suspect's statements against the suspect) required less than a sixth-grade reading level. The overwhelming majority of jurisdictions (91 percent for the first warning, 81 percent for the second warning) used versions of these warnings that have reading levels of less than sixth-grade (Rogers et al. 2007b). In contrast, the last three warnings (right to counsel, right to an appointed counsel for indigent suspects, and continued privilege of the rights) in most jurisdictions required an eighth-grade reading level or higher (Helms 2007; Rogers et al. 2007b; Rogers et al. 2008b).

21.2.2.3 *Sentence complexity*

Sentence complexity of the *Miranda* warnings and waivers can directly impact oral and written comprehension, as well. Grammatik is a tool that measures sentence complexity on a scale from 0 to 100 by taking into account compound sentences, clauses, and prepositional phrases. The average *Miranda* warning, in one study, had a sentence complexity of 48.96 (Rogers et al. 2008b), with the complexity of the individual rights ranging from 12 to 100 (Rogers et al. 2008b). Although subject-relevant examples are unavailable, some perspective on the meaning of these values can be gained from two examples that are available in the literature: (1) instructions for the IRS 1040-EZ form obtained a score of 42 (Rogers et al. 2008b), and (2) the content of a college-level introductory financial accounting textbook obtained a score of 61 (Davidson 2005).

21.2.2.4 *Vocabulary*

The vocabulary used in *Miranda* warnings also varies widely, from words requiring a fourth-grade education for understanding to words requiring a college education (Rogers et al. 2007b; Rogers et al. 2008b). Although most words used in the warnings can be understood by individuals with a fourth-grade education, Rogers and colleagues (2008a) identified 60 words that require at least a tenth-grade education for comprehension, including 14 words that have specialized legal meanings. Some of the more difficult *Miranda* vocabulary words included "coercion," "leniency," "retain," and "waiver" (Rogers et al. 2008b).

In addition, words that are infrequently used may be difficult to understand, regardless of their grade levels (Stalh and Nagy 2006). Of the 60 words identified by Rogers and colleagues (2008b) that require at least a tenth-grade education, 23 of them also occur "very infrequently" (i.e. less than 1 per 1 million words) (Rogers et al. 2008b).

The variability in *Miranda* warning length, readability, sentence complexity, and vocabulary underscores the need to consider a particular warning and waiver as part of the *totality of the circumstances* when evaluating the validity of a *Miranda* waiver and admissibility of an inculpatory statement.

21.2.3 Language of the warnings: population-specific versions

The findings and discussion above refer to standard versions of the *Miranda* warnings. Some jurisdictions also have juvenile versions of the warnings, created to address juveniles' comprehension difficulties. During the course of two nationwide surveys, Rogers and colleagues collected 122 different juvenile *Miranda* warnings (Rogers et al. 2007b; Rogers, Hazelwood, Sewell, Shuman, and Blackwood 2008a). Studies that examined juvenile warnings found that these "simplified" versions were not necessarily easier to comprehend (e.g. Ferguson and Douglas 1970; Messenheimer, Riggs Romaine, Wolbransky, Zelle, Serico, Wrazien, and Goldstein 2009). One study found that juvenile warnings had a mean length of approximately 214 words, exceeding standard warnings by an average of 60 words (Rogers et al. 2008a). The first warning (right to silence) required, on average, less than a fifth-grade reading level, but the remaining four warnings required an average of a sixth-grade education for 75 percent comprehension and nearly a ninth-grade education for full comprehension (Rogers et al. 2008b). Finally, vocabulary content of the juvenile versions was similar to that of adult warnings, with 49 words requiring at least a tenth-grade education (Rogers et al. 2008b). Overall, juvenile *Miranda* warnings appear to be either *as* difficult to understand or *more* difficult to understand than adult versions.

Ferguson and Douglas (1970) administered two different versions of the warning to a group of adolescents, one standard version used by the San Diego Police Department and a "simpler" version created by the authors. There were no significant differences in comprehension between the adolescents who received the standard warning and those who received the simpler version. A more recent study (Messenheimer et al. 2009) compared juveniles' comprehension using three different versions of the *Miranda* warnings: Grisso's (1998) *Instruments for Assessing Understanding and Appreciation of Miranda Rights* and two versions of the revised instruments, the *Miranda Rights Comprehension Instruments* (MRCI Goldstein, Zelle, and Grisso, in preparation). When juveniles' scores were compared on the two MRCI versions, which are similar in wording but vary in length, understanding of the shorter and longer versions did not differ. However, when comparing juveniles' scores on the original and revised versions of the instruments, which differ substantially in reading level, total scores differed significantly. Notably, youth better understood the first two warnings (right to silence and intent to use a suspect's statement against the suspect) of Grisso's instruments, warnings which *exceed* the reading level of those warnings on the revised instruments by two grades.

21.3 POTENTIAL IMPACT OF LINGUISTIC ABILITIES AND *MIRANDA* WARNING LANGUAGE AND ADMINISTRATION PROCEDURES ON JUVENILE SUSPECTS' CAPACITIES TO PROVIDE KNOWING AND INTELLIGENT RIGHTS WAIVERS

In *Miranda v Arizona* the Court held that "[i]n order to ... permit a full opportunity to exercise the privilege against self-incrimination, the accused must be adequately and effectively apprised of his rights."[8] And, as the 10th Circuit noted in *Coyote v United States*,

> Miranda is not a ritual of words to be recited by rote ... [it requires] meaningful advice to the unlettered and unlearned in language which he can comprehend and on which he can knowingly act. ... The crucial test is whether the words in the context used, considering the age, background and intelligence of the individual being interrogated, impart a clear, understandable warning of all of his rights.[9]

[8] 384 U.S. 467.
[9] 380 F.2d 308.

Clearly, if a *Miranda* warning is administered in written form, and the reading level of the warning exceeds the reading abilities of the suspect, the suspect is unlikely to understand and appreciate his rights. The suspect, therefore, should be unable to provide a valid rights waiver that meets the knowing and intelligent requirements. Similarly, if a *Miranda* warning is administered orally, and the level of the warning exceeds the suspect's listening comprehension skills, the suspect would be insufficiently aware of his rights. The length of a warning, its sentence complexity, and/or the difficulty of the vocabulary in the warning can all exceed the linguistic abilities of the suspect, thereby making the warning relatively meaningless to the suspect.

Given the potential incongruity between juvenile suspects' linguistic skills and the complexity of *Miranda* warnings, would lowering the required reading level of *Miranda* warnings solve the problem? Currently, simplified, juvenile-specific versions of the warning are being created to address this issue. Although a reading level within a suspect's linguistic capacities should be a prerequisite for comprehension, we caution that it may not be sufficient to produce the understanding and appreciation needed for a juvenile suspect to validly waive rights. Even if a juvenile suspect can decipher the language of a very simplified warning, the suspect may be unable to comprehend the basic meaning of the rights or the significance of waiving them due to developmental immaturity or mental illness.

21.3.1 Developmental immaturity

Consistently poor *Miranda* comprehension by youths across studies and over time, as well as findings that simpler versions of the warning have not aided understanding, have led some researchers to postulate that *Miranda* comprehension may be developmentally related (Goldstein et al. 2003; Rogers et al. 2008b; Viljoen, Zapf, and Roesch 2007). Adolescents differ from adults in their cognitive abilities (e.g. Levin et al. 1991; Davies and Rose 1999), psycho-social maturity (e.g. Cauffman and Steinberg 2000), and neuro-anatomy (e.g. Baird and Fugelsang 2004; Kambam and Thompson 2009). Although a comprehensive review of developmental factors is beyond the scope of this chapter, some relevant factors are listed here to demonstrate the likely role development plays in *Miranda* comprehension.

21.3.1.1 *Cognitive developmental limitations on* Miranda *comprehension*

In terms of cognitive abilities, verbal fluency (e.g. Levin et al. 1991), memory and learning (e.g. Levin et al. 1991; Ryan 1990), sustained attention (e.g. McKay, Halperin, Schwartz, and Sharma 1994), abstract thinking (Baird and Fugelsang 2004), and executive abilities (e.g. Davies and Rose 1999) largely develop during adolescence and into adulthood. These skills are required for youth to pay attention during the administration of *Miranda* warnings, to process and retain the warnings, to decipher the meaning of the warnings, to evaluate the significance and consequences of waiving rights, and to make a final decision about whether or not to waive the *Miranda* rights.

In addition, the ways in which youth think about the concept of a right seems to differ from that of adults. Youth generally define rights concretely, rather than in abstract terms (Ruck, Keating, Abramovitch, and Koegl 1998). A fundamental component to understanding and appreciating the *Miranda* warnings is the conceptualization of a right as an entitlement—something that cannot be revoked (Grisso 1997). Yet, fewer than one-quarter of juvenile offenders in one study adequately defined the word "right," with almost half of youth defining it as something one "can" do (Goldstein et al. 2008), and failing to recognize, even with probing, the privileged nature of a right.

21.3.1.2 *Psychosocial maturity limitations on* Miranda *comprehension*

Research has identified psychosocial characteristics that develop throughout adolescence that also affect legal judgments (Grisso et al. 2003; Scott, Reppucci, and Woolard 1995; Steinberg and Cauffman 1996; Colwell et al. 2005). These characteristics include: Responsibility (the ability to make independent decisions, as well as exhibit internal control, independence, and self-esteem); Perspective (the ability to consider long- and short-term consequences, as well as to consider the perspective of others); and Temperance (the ability to delay action and limit impulsive actions).

In theory, youth low on Responsibility would have difficulty making an informed decision about whether to waive their rights. Given their low self-esteem, lack of independence, and lack of internal control, their valuation of the *Miranda* rights and their waiver decisions may be easily influenced by police pressure or parents' encouragement to cooperate with police. In fact, in one study, Responsibility significantly predicted juvenile offenders' understanding and appreciation of the *Miranda* warnings (Colwell et al. 2005).

Similarly, youth low on Perspective are likely to have difficulty appreciating their rights because they tend to focus more on short-term consequences than on long-term ones (Steinberg and Scott 2003), and they tend to emphasize the benefits of options, rather than the costs (Steinberg 2008). Therefore, a youthful suspect may have difficulty appreciating the long-term consequences of waiving rights over the short-term consequences of withstanding police pressure during an unpleasant interrogation. Limited Perspective may also result in errors about the role of the defense attorney, such as a failure to view the lawyer as an advocate or the belief that a lawyer reports information directly to the police or judge (Grisso 1997).

Temperance also may impact the ways in which youth understand and appreciate the *Miranda* warnings. Before waiving rights and answering police questions, impulsive youth may not attend to, attempt to comprehend, or evaluate the rights-related information presented to them in the warnings—regardless of the linguistic simplicity of the *Miranda* warnings administered.

21.3.1.3 *Neuroanatomical limitations on* Miranda *comprehension*

Brain maturation occurs throughout adolescence and into the early 20s, with the frontal lobe, the region responsible for executive functioning, developing last (Giedd et al. 1999; Sowell, Thompson, Holmes, Jernigan, and Toga 1999; Gogtay et al. 2004). In addition, tracts between the frontal and parietal regions of the brain develop during adolescence and are thought to be responsible for observed improvements in working memory (Baird and Fugelsang 2004). Working memory deficits could interfere with retention of the *Miranda* warning, comprehension of the basic information in the warning, and manipulation of more complex information presented in the warning about the *Miranda* rights.

The increased sensitivity of the dopaminergic system during adolescence may enhance the reinforcing nature of certain activities or situations (Steinberg 2008). This may explain the increased susceptibility to peer influence observed during adolescence (Steinberg and Monohan 2007), which could impact a juvenile suspect's consideration of his *Miranda* rights. Adolescents also rely more on the amygdala and other socio-emotional areas of the brain than on the pre-frontal cortex in their decision making (Kambam and Thompson 2009). Warnings too complex for youthful suspects to comprehend might generate frustration, heighten emotional arousal, and decrease the rational processing of rights and decision making about the waiver.

In addition, variability in development is common among same-aged youth (Baird and Fugelsang 2004), and individuals can develop complex skills before they develop simpler ones (Oberlander, Goldstein, and Ho, 2001). Nonetheless, research indicates that youths are developmentally different from adults in ways that limit *Miranda* comprehension. These differences may explain why simply shortening *Miranda* warnings is not sufficient to produce adequate understanding and appreciation of rights.

21.3.2 Mental illness

As with developmental immaturity, symptoms of mental illness may interfere with a suspect's abilities to understand and appreciate rights, regardless of whether the wording of the warning is within the suspect's linguistic capacities. Although most research on the relationship between mental illness and *Miranda* comprehension has involved adults (e.g. Cooper and Zapf 2007; Rogers, Harrison, Hazelwood, and Sewell 2007a), many of those findings may apply to mentally ill juveniles, as well.

It is difficult to obtain stable prevalence rates of mental illness in juvenile offenders for a number of reasons (e.g. variation in the timing of studies; variation in gender, ethnicity, and age of subjects). However, research has typically indicated that rates of mental illness in delinquent youth are substantially higher than in the general population (Goldstein, Olubadewo, Redding, and Lexcen 2005; Cocozza and Skowyra 2000). Conduct disorder is the most prevalent disorder among delinquent youth, with rates ranging from 87 to 91 percent among chronic juvenile offenders (Goldstein et al. 2005). Depression (estimates range from 21.6 percent (Teplin et al. 2002) to 67 percent (Myers, Burket, Lyles, Stone, and Kemph 1990)), substance abuse (approximately 50 percent of delinquent youth in one study abused substances; Teplin et al. 2002), and attention-deficit hyperactivity disorder (in one study, 16.6 percent of boys and 21.4 percent of girls met ADHD criteria; Teplin et al. 2002) are also common.

The presence of mental health symptoms appears to interfere with understanding and appreciation in adults. For example, approximately 25 percent of defendants with severe mental disorders were unable to produce coherent, non-psychotic reasons for exercising the right to silence, and 16 percent were unable to produce such a reason for exercising the right to counsel (Rogers et al. 2007a). Similarly, in a study with adult inpatients, patients with a psychotic diagnosis scored lower than patients without such a diagnosis on measures of *Miranda* understanding and appreciation (Cooper and Zapf 2007). Whereas some linguistic abilities, such as the ability to paraphrase and define words, appear to be less affected by mental illness (Gold and Harvey 1993; Heinrichs and Zakzanis 1998; Lezak 1983), other relevant abilities, such as attention and working memory, appear to deteriorate as a result of mental illness (Viljoen, Roesch, and Zapf 2002).

Mental disorders other than psychosis are also associated with cognitive deficits (Mineka, Rafaeli, and Yovel 2003) that could impair *Miranda* comprehension. For example, researchers have suggested that depressed individuals may be less assertive in exercising rights and more acquiescent to interrogators' challenges (Follette, Davis, and Leo 2007). Follette and colleagues (2007) also theorized that clinical anxiety may lead individuals to escape the stressful interrogation context by making inculpatory statements. In addition, research has demonstrated that anxiety interferes with cognitive processing (e.g. Covington and Omelich 1987) and that stress can increase suggestibility (Gudjonsson and Singh 1984; Richardson, Gudjonsson, and Kelly 1995). Substance use has the potential to inhibit *Miranda* comprehension, too, as it can interfere with executive functioning (e.g. Elias, Elias, D'Agostino, Silbershatz, and Wolf 1999; Fromme, Katz, and D'Amico 1997), theoretically resulting in interference with *Miranda* comprehension.

Similar to the concerns raised in the earlier section on developmental issues, ADHD-related deficits in attentional abilities, impulse control, and self-monitoring (Redding 2006) may impact *Miranda* capacities. It would appear that such deficits would limit a suspect's ability to focus on the warnings during delivery, interpret the warnings, and consider waiver consequences. Juvenile suspects with ADHD may also have difficulty inhibiting verbal responses and considering the consequences of their statements. One study demonstrated that youth with deficits in attention, hyperactivity, and psychomotor agitation were more likely to waive the right to counsel (Viljoen, Klaver, and Roesch 2005). Attention was also examined in a study of *Miranda* comprehension with adolescent defendants and was found to be significantly related to deficits in *Miranda* understanding and appreciation (Viljoen and Roesch 2005).

Overall, individuals with mental illness, like juveniles, appear to struggle with warnings as a result of difficulties with conceptual understanding and abstract thought. In one study, adult psychiatric inpatients demonstrated similar levels of understanding on two versions of the *Miranda* warnings, one simpler and one more complex (Cooper and Zapf 2007). Notably, the inpatient sample had considerable problems comprehending both versions. These results suggest that comprehension problems reflect poor underlying conceptual understanding rather than effects of warning language. Again, although the research in this area was conducted with adults with mental illness, these findings also may apply to mentally ill youth.

In sum, even if a youthful suspect has the reading and/or listening comprehension skills required to decipher the linguistic meaning of a particular *Miranda* warning, the youth may still not adequately comprehend that warning. As a result of characteristics associated with developmental immaturity or symptoms associated with mental illness, youthful suspects may have difficulty understanding the concept of a right, applying rights to their own interrogation situations, recognizing the consequences of waiving rights, and restraining their impulsivity to waive rights and talk to police.

21.4 POLICY IMPLICATIONS

Clearly, the *Miranda* warnings are susceptible to misunderstanding and misinterpretation. The warnings and the suspects who receive them are often unevenly matched in terms of reading level, sentence complexity, and vocabulary. In light of these problems, some researchers have suggested the need for research-based, standardized warnings to be used across jurisdictions. Suggested recommendations include: warnings with Flesch–Kincaid reading levels at or below a sixth-grade reading level, Grammatik sentence complexity no greater than 40, avoidance of words requiring a tenth-grade education or higher, and avoidance of words that occur "very infrequently" (Rogers et al. 2008b).

The creation of warnings that follow these recommendations may improve comprehension for a substantial number of adult suspects. Nonetheless, police, judges, and policymakers should be cautious about assuming that such changes would result in improved comprehension for the majority of juvenile suspects. Although many juvenile offenders read near the sixth-grade level (Foley 2001), their linguistic deficits make comprehension of the warnings unlikely even when they are written at an appropriate level (e.g. Davis et al. 1991). Furthermore, adolescent characteristics associated with developmental immaturity seem to impact *Miranda* comprehension in ways that create unique challenges for youths attempting to comprehend their rights. These characteristics may interact with language factors, suggesting that a sufficiently low reading and complexity level of the warnings may be necessary but not sufficient for comprehension.

Overall, effective *Miranda* warnings must strike a balance between providing enough information to promote understanding and appreciation, and doing so in a way that is comprehensible to most suspects. Although we caution against simplifying the warnings by shortening them, we also caution against creating warnings that are so long that they exceed the attentional, working memory, or reasoning abilities of the individuals likely to receive them.

Research-informed change to the language of the warnings is an essential area for reform. Whether this reform is performed jurisdiction by jurisdiction, or on a nationwide level, we must ensure that individuals, including juveniles, are given adequate opportunities to understand and appreciate their Constitutional rights.

....

CHAPTER 22

THE CAUTION IN ENGLAND AND WALES

....

FRANCES ROCK

> Another fundamental right I then contended for, was, that no man's
> conscience ought to be racked by oaths imposed, to answer to questions
> concerning himself in matters criminal, or pretended to be so.
>
> John Lilburn (1637)[1]

22.1 INTRODUCTION

....

You are in a small room which is lit rather too brightly by harsh fluorescent lighting panels. A strange smell hovers. It reminds you of something unpleasant but you are not sure quite what. The room is furnished with a metal toilet and a wide, thigh-high bench covered by a thin mattress encased in very thick, very cold, blue plastic. There is a piece of paper beside you covered in tight-set type which you cannot bring yourself to concentrate on. You have a nagging, queasy feeling, however, that you should have read that paper and you should have read it carefully. You are particularly concerned that the words at the top of the page, the same words which you heard when you were arrested and brought to this police cell, might be some of the most important you'll ever encounter as they might affect the rest of your life. However you just cannot face reading them.

Those words are the police caution and the scenario described is that of the anxious suspect in a police cell. The caution is recited by police officers in England and Wales to members of the public "whom there are grounds to suspect of an offence" (Home Office

---

[1] Cited in Haller and Davies (1944:454).

2008:S10.1, p33) as well as those "attending a police station voluntarily to assist with an investigation" (Home Office 2008:S3.2.1, p13). The caution is presented when individuals are arrested and immediately before they are interviewed. A similar wording is recited if they are charged. On entering custody, suspects will also be offered access to a written version of the wording, as described in the scenario, above, along with information on other rights, most importantly the right to legal advice.

The caution runs as follows:

> You do not have to say anything. But it may harm your defence if you do not mention when questioned something which you later rely on in Court. Anything you do say may be given in evidence. (Home Office 2008:S10.5, p34)

Detainees' decisions about how to respond to the caution can be life-changing. As Solan and Tiersma note in relation to *Miranda* rights, their delivery is "the critical first step in a long legal process that may involve interrogation, trial, sentencing and prison" (2005:73). In the case of the caution, the specific set of implications and upshots from speech and silence in a police interview are extremely consequential but also subtle and complex. According to Government figures, 1,482,000 people were arrested in England and Wales in the most recent year of measurement (Ministry of Justice 2008:4). This equates to, on average, 4,060 arrests per day. Due to this extensive use of the caution and its prominence in the UK legal system, it is worthy of the attention of the forensic linguist. Three main aspects of cautioning have been studied in relation to language.

First, linguists have studied the official wording of the caution itself with both a social agenda and a more individual one. At the social level, the official wording, if misunderstood, can cause huge yet potentially invisible problems for the justice system and ultimately for society; most obviously, creating miscarriages of justice or unnoticed injustice. At the individual level, people in police custody use the wording every day to inform decisions. For them, understanding it correctly, whatever that may entail, is crucial. These aspects of the influence of the official wording have prompted research on how "easy" or "difficult" that wording might be to understand (its comprehensibility) and whether people appear to understand it (its comprehension).

The caution's context of use has emerged as a second important focus. This is because, as well as reciting the official wording, police officers in England and Wales are advised by their Codes of Practice that they may also be required to explain it in their own words (Home Office 2008:Note 10D, p37). This means that those 4,060 people who hear the official wording of the caution every day might also hear an explanation from the officer who arrested or will interview them. These explanations are largely unregulated and, in giving them, officers can elaborate on both semantic and pragmatic aspects of the caution. Thus, in England and Wales, the official wording is only part of the story of the caution's comprehension, comprehensibility, and use. If we are to study cautioning we must include the caution's explanation by police officers.

Finally, cautioning interests linguists because it leads speech and silence to function in rather particular ways—ways which differ from their functioning in other areas of daily life. Indeed, the caution requires speech and silence to be interpreted in ways so marked that they are explicitly specified in the Police Codes of Practice, in concert with acts of Parliament including the Criminal Justice and Public Order Act 1994 and the Youth Justice and Criminal Evidence Act 1999. The Codes of Practice describe "significant statements" as those "capable of being used in evidence against the suspect," and "significant silences" as featuring "failure or refusal to answer a question or answer satisfactorily when under caution, which might . . . give rise to an inference" (Home Office 2008:Note 11.4A, p38). Through the caution, judges, juries, and magistrates are enjoined to view silence not *necessarily* as the legitimate choice of someone unsure of their situation or too nervous to explain themselves, for example, but *potentially* as the deliberate, perhaps duplicitous, choice of the dishonest.

These three aspects of cautioning—its official wording, its explanation in context, and its upshots during the extended legal process—structure this chapter's examination of current knowledge on the caution. They will be followed by consideration of the particular issues surrounding non-native speakers when encountering cautions and warnings. First, a little history is needed because the caution's meaning has changed over time, a fact which may surprise those being cautioned and accordingly challenge those who caution.

The caution in use before the current wording read:

> You do not have to say anything unless you wish to do so, but what you say may be given in evidence. (Home Office 1991:57)

How and why was it extended? The right to silence originates in the activism of John Lilburn, cited at the beginning of this chapter, which ultimately created a number of principles of immunity and in turn a privilege against self-incrimination (Munday 2009:543). The right to silence, as it relates to investigative interviews, took shape as professional policing developed, following the founding of the Metropolitan Police in 1892. The right became sturdy under the influence of the 1912 Judges' Rules, which clarified the relationship between police powers and civil rights (revised in the 1930s and 1960s) (McBarnet 1981:109), and the Police and Criminal Evidence Act 1984, which introduced such practical measures as the audio-recording of police interviews (Easton 1998:3–4).

However, as Easton observes, even from the early days of policing, "courts seemed to take the view that if all suspects exercised their right to silence valuable information would be lost which would undermine the fight against crime" (1998:4). This perspective too developed over time, fueled by prolonged terrorist activity. Eventually concerns about the risks of a consequence-free right to silence became too potent. Through the enactment of the Criminal Justice and Public Order Act 1994 the caution gained its middle sentence, which introduces the potential for courts to draw negative inferences from significant silences.

It is worth noting a few key differences between the caution and the US *Miranda* warnings in view of the volume of research on language and *Miranda* (e.g. Shuy 1997; Brière 1978). First, *Miranda* articulates more rights than the caution, such as that to free, independent legal advice. These are also part of the Anglo-Welsh system, though not stated in the text referred to as "the caution." Focusing then on the overlap between the caution and *Miranda*, clearly both offer a right to silence, but only *Miranda*'s is unrestricted. More subtly, *Miranda* and the caution operate differently in that US detainees, by invoking their right to silence, can halt the interrogation.[2] Conversely, the Anglo-Welsh "suspect... may choose not to answer questions but police do not require the suspect's consent or agreement to interview them." Even suspects who refuse to enter an interview room or walk out mid-interview "shall be advised their consent or agreement to interview is not required" (Home Office 2008:12.5, p43). In turn, being silent "is not a permanent, irrevocable decision" (Cotterill 2005:11).

Turning to formulation, the caution "does not use the word 'silence' at all, referring instead to 'failure to mention.' This contrasts with Miranda, which includes arguably the more direct phrasing: 'You have the right to remain silent' " (Cotterill 2005:9). That said, the caution's wording also encodes silence as *not* having to *say anything* and some would argue that this is more comprehensible than the hidden negative, *silence* (Gibbons 2003:171). Unlike *Miranda*, which varies across jurisdictions (e.g. Rogers, Hazelwood, Sewell, Harrison, and Shuman 2008b), the caution wording is standard throughout England and Wales (although see Rock 2007:37–8 regarding its presentation in writing).

Despite all of these differences, research on *Miranda* is extremely relevant to the study of cautions and cautioning because it shares a focus on the formulation, use, and influence of a standard wording. In particular, Shuy's (1997), "ten unanswered questions" about the *Miranda* warnings catalyzed rights communication research in England and Wales by foregrounding such central issues as the very meaning of "to understand" (1997:182–5), a theme taken up by Rock (2007:209), and of "remain silent" (Shuy 1997:187–91), developed by Cotterill (2005:10).

22.2 THE STANDARD WORDING OF THE POLICE CAUTION

Two distinct strands of research on the caution's official wording are usefully distinguished. The first strand focuses on the wording itself, asking whether that wording is inherently easy or difficult to understand, to the extent that those questions are open to investigation. The second strand focuses on whether people understand the official wording. These two strands, respectively concerning *comprehensibility* of the text and *comprehension* by readers and hearers, are examined in the two sub-sections below. Section 22.3 moves on to consider how contextual factors come to bear on the official wording during its *administration* in real police interviews, and Section 22.4 examines its influence throughout police interviews and in the wider legal system.

---

[2] 384 U.S. 436 (1966).

22.2.1 Comprehensibility of the caution

There has been what can only be described as a wealth of research on the official word-ings of cautions and equivalent warnings both in the UK and worldwide. This research has examined, typically critically, official formulations' lexis; syntax; semantics; discourse features; pragmatic features; or all of these (e.g. Gibbons 1990, 2001; Kurzon 1996; Shuy 1997; Godsey 2006; Pavlenko 2008:6; Rogers et al. 2008b). In other words, research has examined both the wording of cautions and their meanings.

Perhaps the most influential work on these aspects of the Anglo-Welsh caution is by Kurzon (1992, 1995, 1996). He identifies and discusses characteristics of the current cau-tion which readers might misunderstand, particularly those with low IQs. For example, he highlights the modal auxiliary verb *may* in *it may harm your defence*. Understanding this *may* is important because the degree of likelihood it entails indicates how worried detainees should be about silence being understood negatively in court. Yet, as Kurzon notes, incomprehensibility is built into this word. *May* has an epistemic meaning indi-cating possibility (the court might or might not choose to draw inferences from your silence) and a deontic meaning indicating permission (the court is permitted to draw inferences from your silence) (1996:8–9). Ultimately, he asks whether this really chal-lenges comprehension, as courts are *permitted* to draw inferences and then might or might not *choose* to do so (1996:14). Nonetheless, he claims, later on the same page, that "the caution should be as explicit as possible" and, in this spirit, the potential for such ambiguities to distract is real. Kurzon, however, is more concerned about such features as the heavy clause at the end of the caution's middle sentence and the way that *it* at the beginning of that sentence refers to the conditional clause at its end (*if you do not men-tion when questioned...*). These are, Kurzon claims, unusual structures which require extensive processing and memory work. Kurzon's ideas, like Shuy's, influenced scholars such as Cotterill (2000:15–20) and Rock (2007:166–79), who both re-examined words and phrases which he discussed, testing his assertions using empirical evidence, as we will see when we turn to talk in real and simulated police interviews in Section 22.3.

Taking a different approach, psychologists have used readability tests, particularly the Flesch Index, to measure the comprehensibility of the caution (e.g. Clare, Gudjonsson, and Harari 1998). However, use of readability scores to assess a wording that is so short, administered in such particular circumstances, and delivered orally has attracted criti-cism (Owen 1996). The value in assigning linear and immutable measures to texts irre-spective of their diverse uses and users is limited in view of the situationally constituted nature of texts themselves. Additionally the very fact that texts like the caution should be intended to be *used* not only *read* within this diversity illuminates the value of a socio-linguistic perspective (see Rock 2007:17–39 for discussion).

22.2.2 Comprehension of the caution

Psychologists have been rather ahead of linguists in assessing actual or likely compre-hension of the caution and similar wordings (e.g. Cooke and Philip 1998). In particular,

Gudjonsson and colleagues have dedicated considerable attention to assessing comprehension of actual and proposed caution wordings in experimental settings. The populations they have investigated represent a cross-section of abilities and backgrounds. They include students, embodying "at least average intellectual ability" (Gudjonsson and Clare 1994:110); individuals with mild learning disabilities or mental health difficulties who might struggle to understand, particularly unassisted, in custody (1994:110); police officers, reasonably expected to understand the caution as a result of their work (Clare et al. 1998) and suspects in police custody, the caution's target audience (Fenner, Clare, and Gudjonsson 2002). Their findings have overwhelmingly identified shortcomings with the official wording and indeed with other versions of the caution, suggesting that both the content and form present problems. For example, amongst suspects "when the caution was presented in its entirety, as it would be in real life, no one provided a correct explanation of all three sentences," despite 52 percent of respondents claiming to understand the wording (Fenner et al. 2002:89).

The method employed by psychologists to assess comprehension has relied on subjects (1) deciding whether they understand the caution by responding to a yes/no question, and (2) demonstrating understanding by explaining the caution in their own words either as a whole or sentence-by-sentence. This two-part method, as Fenner, Clare, and Gudjonsson themselves note, replicates police procedure (2002:325). It has two major shortcomings. First, when used by police and by experimenters, it assumes that self-assessment of comprehension will be *honest*. The method cannot acknowledge that one might claim comprehension for reasons other than understanding, for example, to avoid appearing stupid or weak. Similarly, it is entirely possible for speakers to agree that they understand cautions just to seem agreeable and, perhaps, escape interview speedily (Cooke 1996; Eades 1997:20).

Furthermore, the method assumes both that self-assessment of comprehension will be *accurate* and that if one thinks one understands something, one will be able to demonstrate that understanding in any situation. The method does not acknowledge that one might understand but find oneself unable to explain due to performance anxiety, distraction or discomfort with the very activity of explaining something to a stranger, for example.

Research on both the comprehensibility and comprehension of the caution's standard wording has necessarily worked from the assumption that the wording is always recited uniformly by police officers. However, officers are not, in fact, required to stick to the official wording slavishly (Home Office 2008:S10.7, p35). Audio-recordings of police interviews reveal that the wording is certainly not always reproduced faithfully, with typical changes including contractions, alteration of modal verbs, and substitutions of relative pronouns. The Codes state that changes are acceptable "provided the sense... is preserved" (Home Office 2008:S10.7, p35). Unfortunately this is not easily established. Berk-Seligson cites a US case, *People v González*, where a detective explained rights to a suspect in Spanish. The defendant later claimed he had "not been given his *Miranda* warnings," yet the appeal court found that the explanation "conveyed the substance" of *Miranda* (Berk-Seligson 2000:223). In any case, examining an official wording is helpful only to the extent that the text is administered verbatim. Therefore studies which go beyond the official formulation are crucial.

22.3 ADMINISTRATION OF THE CAUTION

The first substantial study examining the caution's delivery in monolingual police interviews was Cotterill (2000). This paper was driven by the requirement that "if it appears a person does not understand the caution, the person giving it should explain it in their own words" (Home Office 2008:Note 10 D, p37). Cotterill was thus motivated by a pragmatic desire to examine how cautioning materializes in interview situations rather than only to examine what *might* happen as embodied in the official wording.

Without naturally occurring interview-room data, Cotterill obtained simulated explanations by asking police officers about particular lexical items from the caution. She selected items which present "comprehension difficulties" stemming from their combination of "real world meaning" outside custody and specifically legal meanings in context. She stressed that officers' caution explanations should "translate" between detainees' existing knowledge and legal reality (2000:15). Difficulties in this kind of "translation" present problems in naturally occurring interviews, as Pavlenko illustrates. She cites a detainee whose everyday understanding of "detained" led her to misunderstand the seriousness of the legal process she was engaged in. "Because she thought she understood the term, she did not question its meaning" (Pavlenko 2008:13). Thus, interference from the suspect's "real world" understanding had dire yet concealed consequences.

Cotterill's simulated interviews, despite a potentially problematic use of self-reporting about linguistic practices, raise important themes. For example, she explains that . . . *harm your defence* . . . provides an inanimate referent for both the object of *harm* (*your defence*) and its cause ((inconstant) silence). Cotterill proposes that officers' explanations "should" maintain the sense that harm is "abstract." Instead, they emphasize potential harm to the detainee (e.g. *it could be damaging to you*), highlighting personal relevance (2000:15–16). She also demonstrates the difficulty for officers of explaining *mention when questioned* when they themselves appear unsure of how substantial or vague talk on a topic needs to be in order to constitute a *mention* and whether a *mention* must be in response to specific questions or spontaneous. Finally, in reviewing explanations of *something which you later rely on in court*, she notes that officers varied in the degree to which they implied that *rely* denoted information crucial to a case (2000:19). One officer suggested that relied-on information would be very generally *anything that you want the court to know*; another, that it would be very specific information *important to your defence*. It seems that explaining the caution is not only about legal terms but also about referring to things which simply cannot be known at the time of interview because they depend on later events, such as whether a *mention* or its absence will ever be at issue and whether particular information will form part of a future defense.

Rock (2007) is the first book-length study of the language of rights in custody. The book uses naturally occurring data from real police interviews and my presentation of some of its themes below uses similar audio-recorded data which is novel to this chapter. Rock offers a different take on the strengths and weaknesses of officers' explanations. Rather than problematizing non-literal "translations" which, for example, personalize, she conversely considers the potential value in explanations which might make the caution's implications more tangible to detainees. To develop this theme, consider an officer who explains the caution's words *when questioned* using the string *now when I'm asking you questions*. This officer's explanation indicates the immediate relevance of the caution (questioning takes place *now*) and the local character of questioning (questioning is between speaker and hearer: *I'm asking you*).

Such specificity can have further advantages. The caution's final sentence advises about talk which may be *given in evidence* but does not specify how this happens. Kurzon, whilst concerned about this lack of explicitness, notes that if such details were specified in the caution, the wording would become too long for officers to remember and for detainees to understand and use. He concludes that this may evidence a "linguistic version of the law of diminishing returns" which necessitates balancing the needs for the text to be sufficiently detailed with the need for it to be short enough to work (Kurzon 1996:14–15). The alternative to such a compromise, of course, is to provide several texts. For example, one could be short enough for police officers to memorize and detainees to hear quickly and another could be longer in words and duration. Alternatively, officers could receive guidance on parts of the caution which should be fleshed out in their explanations. Even without such guidance, officers frequently take it upon themselves to make the processes implied within the caution explicit when they explain the wording. In explaining *anything you do say may be given in evidence*, officers frequently explicate the process of presenting evidence, saying, for example:

> anything that's said (.) here (.) is on tape and it can be played to a court if need be

or:

> it's being tape recorded every sound in the room there and should you appear in court at a future date (.) that tape (.) can be used as evidence

or:

> everything's being tape recorded (.) so (.) tapes can be used and that's evidence yeh?

or, rather more mysteriously:

> the content of these tapes we might have to use to do some writing about OK?

This set of explanations, all administered in authentic police interviews, illustrate the variety which detainees might encounter. The first might be said to be clearer than the original wording itself whilst the last potentially introduces more puzzles than it solves. This diversity suggests both the potential for officers to benefit from sharing good practice and the need for focused, practice-led training in how to explain the caution to suspects.

Rock also notes instances when officers explain incompletely, leaving parts of the caution out. In her data almost a fifth of explanations were incomplete (2007:183), most often omitting the propositional content of the caution's final sentence (2007:200), potentially leaving detainees unclear on whether and how interviews were being recorded. More worrying are explanations which are potentially persuasive being delivered in ways which might suggest that the caution prefers or even requires a certain response from detainees. For example, explanations which cast interviews as an *opportunity* or *chance* to speak might lead detainees to infer that speaking might be desirable because one normally aspires to take opportunities and chances which generally offer something good (2007:172), an ethos which is supported by collocations (2007:173–4). Explanations which proclaim the *opportunity* or *chance* to speak in interview contrast sharply with those which instead present the interview as a time when *you may be silent if you wish . . . or only say so many little things to us it's entirely up to you*. This emphasis on interviews as a time when silence is a genuine, available strategy was frequently inventive; some officers even explain how to accomplish silence with detainees told, for example, *you can just stare at the ceiling if you want*. Explanations which are explicitly pressurizing, and legally incorrect, are more than a worry:

> if you do say something (.) you're expected to say:: everything that you know about
> it and tell the truth about it

The utterance above bears little relation to the caution and there is an argument, voiced by both Cotterill (2000:21) and Russell (2000:45), that such crass mangling of sense should be eradicated by introducing a standard explanation of the caution. However, Rock counters that officers' opportunity to explain using a dialogic form is beneficial to them and to detainees (2007:205–21). Consider the following example:

> D   it means (.) you get a caution (.) and you just get it on the criminal record
> P   nah that's a different type of caution
> P2   ((you're thinking of))

Here, the detainee has heard the caution recited yet still believes that he is being cautioned in a different sense—the caution he has in mind is a form of reprimand which can function as an alternative to a more serious charge once the interview is complete. If the detainee believes he is being cautioned or *let off*, a common collocate of this kind of caution, he will not be able to respond appropriately in interview. The use of genuine dialogue here enables the two interviewing officers to address this misapprehension, which might have remained had he simply recited a further standard wording.

Dialogue also offers opportunities to explore understanding:

> P   just explain to me what you think the caution means
> D   um it means that I have the right to remain silent unless you know (.) I wish to
>   speak um (.)

P yeh =

D   = it will be used in evidence //against me//

P   //yeh   yeh// you don't have to say anything now when I'm asking you questions if you fail to mention something now and bring it up in court

D it wouldn't be listened to as

P yeh well (.) they would listen but they'd say why didn't you mention it in court it might carry less weight

D yeh

Here, the officer and detainee work together to establish an account of the caution's meaning through a process which would not have been possible without dialogue.

There has, nonetheless, been much discussion about the wisdom of allowing officers to explain the caution in their own words. Cotterill (2000:21) and Russell (2000:45) both argue for a "standard explanation" to be issued to officers and read aloud by them after they have recited the caution's official wording. Whilst it is true that errors need to be addressed, examples like those above suggest there is value in allowing officers to explain in a way which attends to the detainee in front of them, as far as possible. Furthermore, free explanations can be tailored to the circumstances of the particular arrest and interview situation. For example, explaining the use of evidence by a judge is irrelevant if the content of the interview will only be considered by a magistrate's court. In the example below, flagging context indicates the caution's familiarity:

> before I start the interview (.) I've got to <u>say</u> (.) what I said to you at the house

Allowing officers to explain the caution in their own words provides for dialogic exchanges around the caution's meaning, which may facilitate very particular comprehension-related activities that complement those made available via recitation of the official wording. It is also the case that providing a standard script is not infallible, as the following recitation of the caution shows (major deviations and repetitions marked in bold):

> I must also tell you hhh you do not have to say anything but it may harm your defence (.) if you do not **mention when qu-** (.) mention when questioned something which you later **rely in court** (.) **God I always get that wrong don't I?** (.) I must tell you ((**sniggers**)) hhh you do not have to say **a thing** but it may harm your defence...

Needless to say, if people in authority are to explain anything to people over whom they have power, they should be given guidance on how and what to explain and be monitored and mentored as they do so (Cameron 2000). This seems a better solution to cautioning problems than simply overlaying multiple standard scripts.

Shuy points out that if the component parts of a warning or caution are re-sequenced, meaning will change (1997:177–8). The idea was examined in relation to naturally occurring data by Russell, who noted that six out of the thirteen officers in her data re-ordered the caution's sentences when delivering explanations. Rock explored the functions of reordering and the way that it materialized in over 140 examples of cautioning (2007:180–99). She observed that even an orientation to the caution as consisting of three sentences leads officers to use metalanguage which flags and evaluates those three sections with a potential knock-on effect on comprehension and persuasiveness of the caution (2007:185–91). In the excerpt below, for example, the officer marks the *first part* (the caution's first sentence) as being *quite simple*:

first part's quite simple you don't have to answer any of my questions (.) OK?

Quite simple might function as a move to downplay the importance of this section or to suggest that the detainee is somehow defective if he does not understand. Yet the utterance as a whole also potentially signals the relationship of the caution's parts, indicating that the wording can be considered as small units rather than one daunting monolith and indeed marking some kind of semantic boundary.

For Pavlenko (2008), themes raised in the studies described above have become the basis of expert testimony. She illustrates how an interviewer systematically distorted the image he presented of questioning and the *Miranda* warning in explaining and re-presenting rights during an interview. The interviewer did this in three ways:

- personalizing in order to present important matters as only of concern to him, not to the suspect (for example in introducing rights, the officer said *I'm going to read something to you here and then I've got to read something else to you* (2008:17);
- hedging and mitigation to downplay the importance of rights (for example explaining important legal information as *laws and all that stuff* (2008:17); and
- explicitly misrepresenting processes and activities in order to suggest that the interview was informal and inconsequential (the officer introduces the interview with the suspect, in which he was to accuse her of murder, as a time when *I'll have my coffee and you can have some more water*) (2008:20).

Even though US police officers are not encouraged to explain the *Miranda* warning, explanation can be inherent in interviewing, providing another argument for training in this activity.

22.4 THE CAUTION'S INFLUENCE ON SPEECH, SILENCE, AND THEIR INTERPRETATION

The caution's ramifications for interviews and trials are huge. Turning first to interviews, as I noted at the end of this chapter's introduction, these can proceed without the interviewee's consent. This creates severe interactional pressure. As legal commentators have put it: we do not "all suffer from a compulsion to confess but . . . we are subject to powerful norms not to remain silent" (Hepworth and Turner 1982:32) as "exposure to questioning can undermine the will" for silence (Easton 1998:251). In more linguistic terms, such forces as adjacency pairs (Sacks, Schegloff, and Jefferson 1974) and silence as an interactional device (papers in Tannen and Saville-Troike 1985; Jaworski 1993) are potent during police interviews. Not only do they make it difficult to resist relevant talk, but they also potentially trap detainees. Having not responded to particular accusations during interview, "it may prove difficult for the suspect to later address any further assertions that the interviewer makes on the basis of inferences from the suspect's 'absent denial'" (Heydon 2007:151). Beyond proving "difficult" later in the same interview, due to interactional constraints which all but prevent suspects from asking questions (Heydon 2007:151), there is no routine opportunity for suspects to "address" events in their interview later in detention or at any point between detention and trial.

Silence in an interview potentially influences the important later overhearing audiences—juries, judges, and magistrates. This fact may weigh heavily on detainees. As one legal scholar puts it, "because silence may be construed as so abnormal in everyday interaction...this common sense view may spill over into the legal context, so that silence in police interrogation...may be viewed with suspicion" (Easton 1998:251). Again, linguistics can articulate the processes at work here. Through the Conversation Analytic notion of preference, following accusations, denials are preferred. If a denial does not materialize after an accusation, its absence can be taken to indicate acceptance of the accusation (Atkinson and Drew 1979). As a consequence, "a person who exercises their right to silence will be seen as 'failing to deny', and so to be accepting the allegations against them" (Heydon 2007:147).

Cotterill explains, after Mirfield (1997:239–40), that juries potentially read silence as implying one of three things: First, that the defendant is guilty as s/he would have offered any defense available otherwise; second that the defendant's silence corroborates prosecution evidence; and finally that silence in an interview followed by raising a defense at court results from an "ambush" attempt rather than anything more innocent, such as fear, a desire to protect others, or a lack of comprehension (2005:12–14). Cooke highlights the benefits of explaining to interviewees why they might wish not to answer police questions and stating that there are "reasonable grounds for an otherwise cooperative person to refuse to answer" (1996:273). This might usefully be highlighted for juries too. Certainly, "in cases involving a 'silent' suspect, it is crucial that jurors grasp the legal consequences of that silence and are able to rationally interpret its significance in the case" (Cotterill 2005:15).

The caution changes silence's meaning by destroying "the oppositional and binary distinction of 'speaking' versus 'silence'...because it is possible to speak at length and yet, somewhat paradoxically, still be deemed to have 'remained silent'" by speaking irrelevantly (Cotterill 2005:9–10). Cotterill combines Mirfield's (1997:239) distinction between silence and relevant silence with Shuy's (1997:189) notion that it may be difficult for interactants to be certain about what constitutes "crime relevant talk" and therefore to know whether silence has been maintained. She concludes that there is no neat distinction between talking and silence in interviews under caution, and indeed that this distinction is best seen as gradable rather than binary (Jaworski 1993). Ultimately, "whether appropriate facts have been mentioned in sufficient detail and at the right time" is "highly subjective" (Cotterill 2005:10–11).

The implication is that during an interview, detainees will have to make instant decisions about whether they have "mentioned" facts adequately to form the basis of a possible future defense. If the accused has a mental impairment this requires a high degree of subtlety. Consider the case where, although the defendant had an IQ of just 51, the judge did not instruct the jury regarding inferences from his silence (Munday 2009:549).

The caution further influences later legal processes by determining how records of interview talk will be used. *Anything you do say may be given in evidence* warns that "de- and re-contextualisation will take place" (Hutton 2009:181). This implies a "legally constructed identity" between a suspect's original utterance and all subsequent written and spoken versions produced or discussed—that all versions are "deemed to be 'the same' " (Hutton 2009:182). This notion of identity is nonsensical (Polanyi 1981) but likely to bolster the prosecution's position.

Courts are increasingly paying attention to whether the caution has been understood (e.g. Eades 1997:20) and whether it was administered when it should have been or even at all.[3] As Solan and Tiersma (2005:73–93) report, US courts sometimes order the suppression of evidence gathered in interview because defendants were felt to have inadequately understood their rights or their exercise. Because attention is increasingly drawn to this problem, courts in England and Wales might eventually encounter appeals on this point (see e.g. Brown-Blake and Chambers 2007).

22.5 CAUTIONING NON-NATIVE SPEAKERS

Police cautions present particular challenges to non-native speakers (e.g. Russell 2000; Nakane 2007; Pavlenko 2008). Importantly, the requirement to issue a caution is not internationally universal, so some detainees have no "cultural equivalent" (Russell 2000:43). In England and Wales, the Home Office has made some progress towards providing for speakers of languages other than English, at least in relation to the official wording. A Welsh version of the caution is now incorporated into the Police Codes of Practice for use "where...appropriate" (Home Office 2008:S10.5, p34). The printed information given to all detainees is currently published in 42 written languages in addition to English and Welsh (Home Office 2011) and in versions for blind and partially sighted people (De Pablo 2001). Providing these texts does not mean that they will be read or used.

The situation for many detainees depends heavily on interpreters. Of course, translations of standard wordings are not infallible. In the *People v Márquez* (1992) particular

---

[3]   See *R v Shukla* [2006] EWCA Crim 797.

words were challenged in a Spanish translation of the *Miranda* warning (Berk-Seligson 2000:222). Crooker explicitly warns interpreters against using versions of *Miranda* which have been translated by someone else "in case of errors in the translation" (1996:18). To ward against such problems, translations or even audio recorded translations could be agreed upon by collectives of "certified court interpreters, forensic linguists, and legal experts" (Pavlenko 2008:27).

Interpreters' involvement in cautioning can also complicate delivery of an explanation. Various measures have been proposed to assist interpreters in this situation. These include training in legal terminology, caution implications, turn-taking during cautioning, and the influence of comprehension checks (Nakane 2007:108) and assistance in switching between monologic and dialogic interpretation which occurs in unusual ways in cautioning (Russell 2000:28–32). Even more support is needed for the interpreter when interpreting for deaf participants because of the shift between modalities (Hoopes 2003; Brennan and Brown 2004).

22.6 CONCLUSION

Caution wordings and cautioning explanations provide rich and fascinating data for linguists. Yet because of the legal situation in which both operate, they also offer an important applied focus. Reconsidering the official wording and explanation practices with linguistic advice in mind is an obvious first step. In addition, there is a growing feeling that information on the law, including rights in custody, should be more prominent within schools' curricula (Rock 2007:325) and adult education programmes for those learning English as a second language (Pavlenko 2008:2; 27–8). The instructive potential of dramatic representations of cautions, which are frequent in police and courtroom dramas in the media, should also be harnessed (Rock 2007:149–51; Pavlenko 2008:3).

CHAPTER 23

··

THE LANGUAGE OF CONSENT IN POLICE ENCOUNTERS

··

JANICE NADLER

J. D. TROUT

A police officer who is certain to get his way has no need to shout.

Souter J, dissenting, *Drayton*, 536 U.S. 194 (2002).

23.1 INTRODUCTION

IN this chapter, we focus on public encounters between citizens and police officers in the United States. More specifically, we examine encounters in which police question and search citizens without probable cause or even reasonable suspicion of criminal activity. These encounters are legally permitted because courts deem them "consensual." Legal consent depends on whether a reasonable person, when confronted by the police, would feel free to end the conversation and leave, which itself turns in part on the nature of the conversation and its context. It is these conversations, embedded in their social and physical contexts, which we explore in this chapter.

We argue that when police officers seek permission to conduct a search, citizens often feel enormous pressure to say yes. But in most criminal cases, judges do not acknowledge these pressures, generally choosing instead to spotlight the politeness and restraint of the officers' language and demeanor. By ignoring the pragmatic features of the police–citizen encounter, judges are engaging in a systematic denial of the reality of the social meaning underlying these encounters, and are thereby constructing a collective legal myth designed to support current police practices in the "war on drugs." Because consent searches are very common, and because the vast majority of people subjected to consent searches are innocent,[1] the practice of conducting frequent consent searches comes with social and political costs. It is possible that these costs are worthwhile, at least in some cases, depending on the threat at hand. But the US Supreme Court has declined to engage in any serious analysis of this question. We begin with the practical importance of consent searches as a crime investigation tool.

23.2 THE ROLE OF CONSENT SEARCHES IN CRIMINAL INVESTIGATION

Law enforcement practices in the United States today frequently include on-the-fly searches to detect evidence of crime. These searches are not a result of an ongoing investigation, but rather the result of police acting on their instincts and training regarding a person's appearance or behavior or even presence in a particular place. For example, in locations where intercity (e.g. Greyhound) buses make stopovers, local police sometimes make a practice of boarding every bus as it arrives and requesting consent from passengers to search their bags and/or their persons. In airports, law enforcement officers use "drug courier profiles," consisting of a list of behaviors and characteristics, to decide which passengers to approach, question, and perhaps request consent to search for drugs.

Consent searches often follow on the heels of a routine traffic stop. Police pull over drivers for burned out tail-lights, unsignaled lane changes, and speeding. Police incentives to attend to such administrative violations often rest not on the risk posed by the violations themselves, but rather on the opportunity such stops provide for investigating "suspicious" citizens. Which citizens appear suspicious is, of course, in the eye of the beholder. Unfortunately, recently uncovered evidence demonstrates that the race and ethnicity of the driver sometimes influence police judgments about which cars to stop (Ayres 2008; Garcia and Long 2008).

The incentives to engage in this type of "drug interdiction" are now quite powerful, with the advent of federal programs that pay large sums of money to local police departments to fund the war on drugs (Bascuas 2007). As part of this federal program, some small towns located near an interstate highway have generated millions of dollars in revenue from seized cars and cash after local police succeeded in stopping drivers transporting illegal drugs (Bascuas 2007). As a result, violations of minor traffic violations are routinely parlayed into consent searches. Thus, the real purpose of many traffic stops is

---

[1] Because of the absence of systematic record keeping, it is difficult to calculate the proportion of consent searches in which the target is innocent of any crime. There are, however, scattered statistics for individual localities. For example, the sheriff in one Florida county arrested only 55 of the 507 motorists subjected to consent searches over a three-year period (Brazil and Berry 1992). An analysis of over 1,900 consent searches of motorists concluded that illegal drugs are discovered in about one of every eight searches (Lichtenberg 2001).

drug interdiction, and minor traffic violations will suffice to justify such stops,[2] even though minor violations are committed by virtually every driver on virtually every trip.

In the absence of probable cause that a crime is being committed, officers rely on the driver's consent to find out what is in the car. In some localities, consent searches have become routine, and are accomplished not only through traffic stops, but also by boarding intercity buses and searching bags. As a tool for ferreting out possession offenses, consent searches are extremely effective. First, consent searches permit police to search when they otherwise would be prohibited from doing so. By some estimates, over 90 percent of all searches are consent searches (Simmons 2005). Second, once police decide to request consent to search, they are remarkably successful in obtaining consent—one study found that over 95 percent of people asked to consent to a search did so.[3] Third, consent searches are low cost—no investigation, wiretaps, or warrants are needed. And consent searches are effective in much the same way junk mail or spam email is effective. If police stop and search enough people, it is just a matter of time until they find evidence of crime. In the next section, we discuss the circumstances under which it is legally permissible for the police to conduct a consent search.

23.3 LEGAL STANDARDS FOR CONSENT SEARCHES: THE "FREE TO TERMINATE" TEST

Government searches and seizures are governed by the Fourth Amendment to the United States Constitution, which guarantees the "right of the people to be secure in their persons, houses, papers and effects, against unreasonable searches and seizures." A search is likely to be considered reasonable if there is probable cause to believe that a crime is being or has been committed. But in practice, police often search without probable cause if the citizen has consented to the search.

To be valid, consent must be given voluntarily. If the citizen merely accedes to the authority of the officer, then consent is not valid and the search is unreasonable. Anything obtained during an unlawful search is excluded from evidence. Additionally, if the police unlawfully seize someone, and then obtain consent to search, anything obtained following the unlawful seizure is excluded. As a practical matter, excluding contraband from evidence results in the dismissal of a charge of possessing that contraband.

The two key issues, then, are: (1) whether a consent search lacks sufficient voluntariness, and (2) whether a person who consented to search had been unlawfully seized. The first issue focuses on the extent to which a citizen's consent to search was voluntary or

---

[2] That the real reason for the stop in the first place was the officer's mere hunch that he might find something illegal does not invalidate the enterprise—so long as the police can hang their hat on a provable violation of traffic regulations. *Whren v United States*, 517 U.S. 806 (1996).

[3] *State v Carty*, 170 N.J. 632 (2002).

was the product of duress. The analysis requires the judge to decide, under the totality of the circumstances, whether a reasonable person would have felt free to refuse consent. To decide this question, courts examine, among other things, the manner in which the police requested consent. If consent is requested in a manner that indicates "to a reasonable person that he or she was free to refuse,"[4] the courts consider this to be strong evidence the search was consensual. Courts point to factors such as the police speaking in a polite manner, and asking for permission to search, as indications that the person voluntarily consented. We will return to these factors later.

The second issue, regarding unlawful seizure, is analyzed in a similar manner. The judge's task is to decide whether a reasonable person in that situation would believe that she is free to leave, or to terminate the encounter. Note that both of these tests require the courts to interpret the social meaning of behavior—to ascertain what is implicit in a social interaction. For example, a police officer who orders a car to pull over acts with an implicit claim of right, and so a driver or even a passenger in the car would not feel free to leave once the car has been pulled over.[5] We understand this implicitly only because we have internalized certain norms of social behavior; a visitor from another culture might not understand this. Similarly, when a police officer says, "May I please see your license and registration?" we understand this utterance to be not a request, but a command. This understanding is gleaned from our social and cultural understanding of what a police officer means and intends when he utters those words in that context. In the next section, we examine more closely the ways in which contextual implicatures are understood in ordinary conversation between people, and specifically in encounters between police and citizens.

23.4 LANGUAGE

Language is usually the first point of contact between police and citizen. These encounters are dense with meaning, and fraught with the potential for deception. In the hands of a seasoned communicator, clever use of language can gain anyone an advantage over their peers. And when that person has a badge, uniform, gun, and the power to change the course of your days, language becomes his or her soft restraint. To appreciate the controlling power of language, we will cover general pragmatics first; then we will turn to its application to police encounters.

23.4.1 Pragmatics basics

Language is far more than a tool for communicating descriptive facts. Language pleases and cajoles, it scolds and questions. And when it is embedded in a cultural setting, it can

---

[4] *Drayton*, 536 U.S. at 197.
[5] *Brendlin v California*, 551 U.S. 249 (2007).

intimidate, control, or liberate. But this won't be obvious if we only look at the superficial structure of language. Fifty years of work in the philosophy of language has delivered an elaborate roadmap of the origins of meaning in communication, from posture and gesture to types of meaning, like conventional and speaker meaning. Leaving aside phonetics and phonology, linguistics is usually carved up into three main areas: syntax (the rules of linguistic well-formedness), semantics (the theory of meaning), and pragmatics (the contribution of context to meaning).

In philosophy, the chief preoccupation has been with what philosophers call "truth functional semantics," or the conditions that have to be met in order for descriptive claims (normally, declarative, factual sentences) to be deemed true or false. Accordingly, the meaning of a sentence is given by the conditions that would make it true. The sentence "The earth has magnetic poles" is true if and only if the earth has magnetic poles. For these kinds of statements, it doesn't matter who says them, or how they are said. Their meaning is entirely a function of what states of affairs would make them true.

By contrast, pragmatics takes into account the potential impact of social norms and subtle cues that are typically expressed in language, and is informed not only by linguistics and philosophy, but also psychology and anthropology.

Many linguistic expressions, such as commands, promises, or questions, have meaning but not truth conditions. "Would you leave her alone?" is a question (and interestingly, can also be a command of sorts), and has no truth conditions. In the case of some linguistic expressions, like questions, the same person can imply different meanings by uttering the same sentences with stress on different words. There is nothing at all surprising or exotic about this fact. We see it in exchanges in every walk of life. In order to see that the very same expression can provoke very different reactions, consider that classic question: "Why did Sutton rob the bank?" Now place the accent on the capitalized word, and note the answer, ratified by convention and common sense:

> WHY did Sutton rob the bank? (He needed the money.)
> Why did SUTTON rob the bank? (He was the one who needed the money.)
> Why did Sutton ROB the bank? (He asked for the money nicely, but they wouldn't give it to him.)
> Why did Sutton rob the BANK? (That's where the money was.)

If the appropriate answer is different for each of the questions, the implicatures of emphasis go well beyond descriptive meaning. In addition, one has to be steeped in a culture to know the permissible interpretations of this question as a function of stress.

The philosopher of language Paul Grice identified and characterized the phenomenon of implicature. His theory explained and predicted what he called the "conversational implicatures" that arise in ordinary conversations. Grice (1975) postulated a general "Cooperative Principle," which posits that conversational partners cooperate with each other and will contribute what is required by the accepted purpose of the conversation. People expect that communication will, in general, conform to this principle, so violations can be powerfully manipulative. Any individual prepared to deviate from this norm can exploit the listener's unwitting expectation of cooperation.

Grice also postulated four "maxims" specifying how to be cooperative in communication. These maxims (quantity, quality, relevance, and manner) all document the way that subtle mechanisms of language—often together with the broader context—can imply meanings that go beyond the sober, descriptive use of language (Grice 1975). Using a vintage example: Imagine a friend telling you "A man came to my office" only for you later to find that the man was her fiancé, whom you know. You assume that your friend is being cooperative and adhering to the maxim of quantity, which specifies that a speaker should provide enough information for the purposes of a conversational exchange. If your friend had been cooperative, she would have specified that her fiancé came by the office. Therefore, the use of the indefinite article with a noun, "a man" creates an implicature that the person who came to the office is not known to you (or possibly that he is but would not be of interest to you).

Notice what the friend has done here. She has controlled the meaning of the expression by saying something that is strictly true, but she has also manipulated you by correctly predicting your reaction to her violation of selected rules of cooperative communication. In these cases, there is little honor in merely telling the truth, because it is not the whole truth, anything less than the whole truth will mislead, and the speaker designed the statement with the intent to mislead. The violation of these conversational maxims would seem a powerful tool for manipulation.

23.4.2 Pragmatics of police encounters

These pragmatic features of language play an important role in citizen–police encounters, including vehicle stops, bus sweeps, airport stops, and street stops. In these encounters, the police officer's main purpose is to get information about what the person is doing, and get permission to do something else, like search their person, house, car, bags, etc.

With the idea of pragmatic implicature now in hand, we can examine the way in which police language can be used to deprive citizens of their sense of control. If the police officer says or does something to diminish the citizen's sense of control, the citizen will not feel that consent could be refused. First, consider the contrast between declarative statements and other kinds of utterances. Much communication is achieved through simple declarative sentences, like "It is raining" or "Electrons have a spin of plus or minus one half." The meaning of declarative statements, like "The cat is on the mat" is given by its truth conditions. But questions don't have truth conditions. As we mentioned earlier, a substantial portion of communication does not invoke declarative sentences. Indeed, what would it mean to say that a question is true? Instead, questions ("May I look in your bag?"), commands ("Hand over your valuables"), promises ("I promise to repay the debt"), recommendations ("Always pay your taxes"), etc., have what linguists and philosophers call "felicity conditions" (Austin 1962; Alston 2000).[6] But once you concede

---

[6] This is Austin's (1962) original terminology.

that the meaning of such utterances is not a simple function of their truth conditions, you must examine all of the relevant contextual factors that contribute to their meaning in order to fix their interpretation. In addition, because contextual factors can affect meaning in limitless, even if systematic, ways, there is no sense to be made—either scientific or folk—of claims about the "literal meaning" of some linguistic sequence. Its meaning can change with the identity of the speaker, tone and accent, location of the utterance (church, courthouse), and a host of other indexes.

23.4.3 Pragmatics and police authority

During traffic stops, bus sweeps, and the like, the conversation between the police officer and the citizen tends to be dominated by the kinds of utterances whose meaning varies widely with context (Solan and Tiersma 2005). Yet, courts often analyze police encounters as if the conversation that took place has a fixed meaning, which can be readily gleaned without reference to the context.

One way to debunk the contention that there is some obvious, literal, or uncontested interpretation of a police officer's request is by the following example. Consider a backpack owner's reaction to the same linguistic utterance, constituted by sound alone, when delivered by a shabbily dressed passerby. Suppose such a person stops and says, "Would you mind if I look in your backpack?" Most people would feel freer to refuse the shabbily dressed passerby than the person who has identified himself as a police officer. But if the same acoustic sequence engenders two different responses depending upon the speaker, which is the "literal interpretation"? Another way to debunk the contention is to imagine how the backpack owner might respond to other sorts of communication from a police officer. Suppose a police officer says "Drop the backpack and raise your hands in the air." The owner obeys. Now suppose the shabbily dressed passerby issues the same command. The owner laughs it off.

It may be rational to comply with a police officer's command (like "put your hands in the air"), but that doesn't make it voluntary. We assume that the command is backed by force. Similarly, when the police use request language, we hear this as a command and similarly assume this is backed by force. Because people perceive discourse originating from an authority to be coercive regardless of assertive linguistic cues, authority figures need not use highly face-threatening language—part of that burden is carried by the badge and gun.

People in positions of authority can control the message conveyed by linguistic expressions in a number of ways. The cues of threat go well beyond speaker intentions. Posture, mode of dress, physical proximity, location, identity, and the authority of the speaker all contribute to meaning. The same question may carry different force, or imply different meanings, when uttered by different people. Suppose you are sitting on a bus, with an empty seat next to you. Suppose further that someone approaches you and says: "Would you like to move over?" Consider your reaction when the question is asked by each of the following people:

1. a child;
2. an adult passenger;
3. the bus driver;
4. a police officer.

We could explore the different implications in each case, but for the moment it is enough to observe the difference in your reactions, and that we are quite used to sentences having different meanings when asserted by people in different stations in life.

The meaning of social exchanges also depends on whether the speakers were invited or unsolicited by chief parties to the exchange. When a citizen summons the police, police presence is a welcome relief. But when officers approach uninvited, it is seldom a happy event for the citizen. Without a clear idea of where this encounter is going and how it will turn out, a citizen would feel irresponsible to treat this exchange like any other. People know that they should be courteous to the police, that police carry guns and handcuffs, that they make mistakes that can cause you harm, and that additional police are just a radio call away. They know that the police can handcuff you and take you to the station for processing, and that it can take hours or days to sort out a misunderstanding. So, if a police officer asks to check my backpack or luggage—even if they inform me that I have the right to refuse—I would naturally worry that a refusal would be viewed as grounds for suspicion.

23.4.4 Judicial misunderstandings of pragmatic implicature in police encounters

Courts routinely conclude that searches that ensue during police–citizen encounters are voluntary (Nadler 2003). To justify this conclusion, judges highlight the language of the exchange and minimize important contextual features, like the fact that the speaker is armed. For example, the US Supreme Court has stated that when an armed police officer approaches and asks to search, "[t]he presence of a holstered firearm . . . is unlikely to contribute to the coerciveness of the encounter absent active brandishing of the weapon."[7]

Judges often note that, in requesting consent, the officers made a request rather than a demand. They also note that the officers used a polite tone of voice. Judges routinely conclude that these aspects of language give rise to the inference that the citizen was free to decline to talk to the officers or to decline the request to search. As the Supreme Court put it, a police–civilian encounter is consensual so long as the police do not convey a message that compliance with their request is required.[8] Indeed, the Supreme Court has lionized the kind of exchange that takes place between police and citizens in consent searches:

---

[7] *Drayton*, 536 U.S. at 204.
[8] *Florida v Bostick*, 501 U.S. 429, 435 (1991).

In a society based on law, the concept of agreement and consent should be given a weight and dignity of its own. Police officers act in full accord with the law when they ask citizens for consent. It reinforces the rule of law for the citizen to advise the police of his or her wishes and for the police to act in reliance on that understanding. When this exchange takes place, it dispels inferences of coercion.[9]

But is the Court correct that consent searches are typically characterized by the notion of a voluntary agreement between the citizen and the officer (akin, perhaps, to two corporate executives negotiating a licensing agreement)? Do citizens really "advise police of [their] wishes" when they agree to searches that are devoid of probable cause? In short, is it plausible to conclude, as the Court does, that the language of the exchange itself dispels inferences of coercion? Contrary to the Court's conclusion, our discussion in the previous section suggests that this kind of police–citizen exchange heightens, rather than dispels, inferences about coercion.

Fortunately, not all judges advance the implausible position that consent searches arise from a dignified understanding between citizens and police. In an early landmark case, the police stopped a car in the middle of the night. The police asked permission to search the car, and when they were through, the officer asked, "Does the trunk open?" The defendant opened the trunk, and police found stolen checks. The federal court of appeals judge was concerned that the defendant might not have realized that he had the option of refusing the officer's implied request to open the trunk. The judge acknowledged that, "[u]nder many circumstances a reasonable person might read an officer's 'May I' as the courteous expression of a demand backed by force of law."[10]

In bus sweep cases, too, some courts have acknowledged that passengers approached by officers requesting permission to search might not feel free to leave or to terminate the encounter. In one case, the Florida Supreme Court found that sheriff's officers who boarded the bus wearing raid jackets, blocking the aisles, and questioning passengers about their destinations had unlawfully seized the passengers, rendering invalid the passengers' subsequent consent to search.[11] And in other Florida bus sweep cases, considered by federal appellate courts, judges found that reasonable passengers would not have felt free to refuse the consent to search, because they had no indication that consent could be refused.[12]

Remarkably, in each of the cases just described where the judge has recognized the coerciveness of the police request to search, the US Supreme Court has reversed the lower court's decision and held that there was no unlawful seizure and that consent was freely given. The Supreme Court has made it very clear that considerations about pragmatic implicature are to be ignored in consent search cases, no matter how compelling those considerations might be. Instead, it has signaled to lower courts that an utterance

[9] *Drayton*, 536 U.S. at 207.
[10] *Bustamonte v Schneckloth*, 448 F.2d 699 (1971).
[11] *Bostick v State*, 554 So. 2d 1153 (1990).
[12] *United States v Drayton*, 231 F.3d 787 (11th Cir. 2000); *United States v Washington*, 151 F.3d 1354 (11th Cir. 1998).

phrased in the form of a question, and spoken in a polite tone, is to be considered a request that can be freely refused, regardless of whether the context of the conversation strongly suggests otherwise.[13]

Consider the following example. In the last bus sweep case mentioned above, *U.S. v Drayton*, three police officers boarded a Greyhound bus during a scheduled stopover in Tallahassee, Florida. The driver had collected all of the passenger's tickets and taken them into the terminal to complete paperwork. One police officer knelt backwards in the driver's seat; one police officer stood at the back of the bus; and one officer began questioning passengers. As he asked questions, the officer stood over the seated passenger and leaned toward them, placing his face 12–18 inches from theirs. He held up his badge and explained that he was conducting drug interdiction, and said that he would like their cooperation. He then asked permission to search their bags.

During oral argument in the case, Justice Scalia made clear his opinion that the police officer's utterance was merely a request, and that the words uttered would "counteract" contextual cues suggesting compulsion, such as the placement of one of the officers in the driver's seat of the bus. Specifically, Justice Scalia asked, "Why... is it that the most immediate expression of the police officers does not counteract whatever other indications of compulsion might exist under the circumstances?... There's a policeman in the front of the bus. Who cares? He... has made it very clear that he's asking for your permission."[14] To answer Justice Scalia's facetious question, the bus passengers are the ones who care, because they could not help notice the following: the driver and tickets were absent, one police officer was now in the driver's seat, the police had effectively commandeered the bus, and the bus was apparently going nowhere until the police got what they wanted. But Justice Scalia and the rest of the majority in *Drayton* appear to see things differently. Pragmatic implicature falls to the wayside, and instead an officer's asking of permission "counteract[s]... other indications of compulsion." According to this view, the authority of armed police officers simply fades away when they express their desire to search in the form of a question.

Ever since *Drayton*, lower courts have had no choice but to follow the lead of the US Supreme Court. In doing so, those courts routinely and mechanically point to the police officer's polite tone of voice as a key basis for finding that the defendant voluntarily consented to being searched.[15] *Drayton* portrayed the questioning police officer as

---

[13] Note that the US Supreme Court's consent search decisions have not been unanimous, and some judges of the Court do recognize the coercive effects of powerful contextual factors. For example, Justice Souter, in his dissent in *U.S. v Drayton*, argued that the fact that the police asked politely and said "Do you mind" is irrelevant, concluding that "a police officer who is certain to get his way has no need to shout," Drayton, 536 U.S. at 212.

[14] Official Transcript of Oral Argument, *U.S. v Drayton* 2002 U.S. Trans LEXIS 37 at 46.

[15] *United States v Awoussi*, 2009 U.S. Dist. LEXIS 45680 (consent to search apartment was voluntary in part because officers were polite); *State v Rathjen*, 16 Neb. App. 799 (2008) (consent to search locked toolbox in pickup truck was voluntary in part because officer was "cordial and polite" when he requested consent); *United States v Johnson*, 2005 U.S. Dist. LEXIS 712 (2005) (consent to search car was voluntary in part because officers were polite); *People v Palomares*, 2008 Cal. App. Unpub. LEXIS 1452 ("[t]he tone of the encounter was conversational, not accusatory").

courteous and courtly: "He spoke to passengers one by one and in a polite, quiet voice. Nothing he said would suggest to a reasonable person that he or she was barred from leaving the bus or otherwise terminating the encounter.... There was ... no threat, and no command, not even an authoritative tone of voice."[16]

Indeed, lower courts now seem hesitant to ever find that the defendant's grant of consent to search was coerced, unearthing voluntariness even when the officer issues a direct command. In one recent case, the police pulled over a car and arrested the driver for driving without a license. The officer then asked the passenger if he had any drugs, and asked, "Well, do you mind if I check?" The passenger did not answer and did not gesture. The officer ordered the passenger out of the car. The passenger complied, placing his hands in the air. The police officer then searched the passenger and found drugs. Unbelievably, the court held that the passenger had consented voluntarily to the search by raising his hands in the air.[17] Apparently, when the officer uttered the magic words, "Well, do you mind if I check?" this rendered the remainder of the encounter voluntary.

Although lower courts applying the Fourth Amendment have little choice but to routinely find consent searches voluntary under the tightly constrained precedent that the US Supreme Court has constructed, each state has its own constitution with its own version of the Fourth Amendment. A few states interpret their own constitutions to be more restrictive than the US Constitution on matters relating to government searches and seizures.

New Jersey courts, for example, have interpreted their state constitution to require a higher level of scrutiny for consent searches.[18] Under this standard, the prosecution must prove that the person consenting knew that she had a choice in the matter. Further, a police officer making a traffic stop is prohibited from requesting consent to search unless he or she has a "reasonable and articulable suspicion" to believe that a crime is occurring.[19] The New Jersey Supreme Court acknowledged that "many persons, perhaps most, would view the request of a police officer to make a search as having the force of law."[20] Several other states follow a similar rule for traffic stops.[21] The Supreme Court of Hawaii has gone further and applies a similar "reasonable suspicion" rule for requesting consent during any police encounter, not just traffic stops.[22] The highest courts of these states have each acknowledged that when a police officer says, "Do you mind if I search?" the pragmatic implicature is often that cooperation is not just requested but required.

---

[16] *United States v Drayton*, 536 U.S. at 204.
[17] *People v Tupper*, 2009 Cal. App. Unpub. LEXIS 4908.
[18] *State v Carty*, 170 N.J. 632, 639 (2002).
[19] *State v Carty*, 170 N.J. at 647.
[20] *State v Carty*, 170 N.J. at 644.
[21] These states include Indiana (*State v Washington*, 875 N.E.2d 278 (Ind. App. 2007)); Minnesota (*State v Fort*, 660 N.W.2d 415 (Minn. 2003)); and North Carolina (*State v McClendon*, 350 N.C. 630, 517 S.E.2d 128 (N.C. 1999)).
[22] *State v Quino*, 840 P.2d 358 (1992).

23.5 EMPIRICAL EVIDENCE REGARDING THE LANGUAGE OF CONSENT IN POLICE ENCOUNTERS

Given the nature of police authority and the context of the citizen–police encounter, it is highly likely that police requests to search are often interpreted as commands to permit the search to take place. But the extent to which citizens feel compelled to accede to a police request is an empirical question (Nadler 2003). Not much empirical evidence is available to help answer that question. But there is some, which we will review next.

First, consider an illustration used by courts as the paradigmatic example of when no seizure takes place: a police office approaches a citizen on a sidewalk and asks a question. Recall that if a police officer unlawfully seizes someone, then any subsequent search is deemed invalid. The US Supreme Court has characterized this kind of sidewalk encounter as a "perfect example of police conduct that supports no colorable claim of seizure."[23] That is to say, the Court assumes the citizen in that situation clearly feels free to terminate the encounter or to leave.

But do people in fact feel free to terminate that type of sidewalk encounter? Kessler (2009) conducted a survey to find out, and it turns out the answer is mostly, no. Respondents read a scenario in which they are walking on the sidewalk when a police officer approaches and says, "I have a few questions to ask you." Respondents indicated how free they would feel to walk away or decline to talk with the officer. About half of the respondents indicated that they would not feel free to leave in this situation.[24] Remarkably, only about 20 percent of respondents indicated that they felt free to leave or decline.[25] Thus, most people do not in fact feel free to terminate the very type of police encounter that the Supreme Court considers the clearest example of a completely consensual conversation. It is clear that the Court's conception of the level of coercion present in ordinary citizen–police encounters is greatly at odds with the conception of ordinary people when they think hypothetically about interacting with police.

Moving from the hypothetical to the actual, consider next Lichtenberg's (1999) survey of Ohio motorists who had been stopped recently by police for traffic violations and asked for their consent to search. Of the 54 drivers interviewed, 49 reported that they had agreed to the request to search. Of these 49, all but two said they consented because they were afraid of what would happen if they said no. Their fears included having their trip unduly delayed, being searched anyway, incurring property damage to their car if they refused, being arrested, being beaten, or being killed. Some of these concerns were

---

[23] *Drayton*, 536 U.S. at 209 (Souter, J, dissenting).

[24] The response scale ranged from 1 to 5, where 1 was labeled "Not free to leave or say no," 3 was labeled "Somewhat free to leave or say no," and 5 was labeled "Completely free to leave or say no." For each scenario (sidewalk and bus), about 50% of respondents chose 1 or 2. Kessler (2009) repeated this with a scenario in which the respondent is on a bus when the officer approaches, and the results were the same.

[25] That is, only about 20% of respondents selected 4 or 5.

apparently well founded: of the five motorists who declined to consent to the search, two reported being searched despite their explicit refusal to consent. Another motorist who refused to consent was not searched but was threatened with future retaliation, which left him so shaken that he avoids driving on the road near his home where he was stopped.

The fact that such a large percentage of this sample reported feeling afraid to decline the officer's request to search suggests a possible solution: require the police who request consent to search to advise citizens of their right to refuse (Solan and Tiersma 2005).[26] Although on its face this requirement might seem promising, it is not a panacea. There is no reason to believe that giving a warning would dispel the coercion inherent in police encounters. In fact, there is empirical evidence suggesting that such warnings have no effect on people's willingness to refuse consent. Lichtenberg (2001) examined all Ohio highway stops between 1995 and 1997. For part of the period studied, police were not required to advise motorists of their right to refuse consent, and for part of the period, police were required to do so.[27] Remarkably, the same percentage of motorists consented with the warnings as without the warnings. Apparently, people are unaffected by the warnings because they do not believe them—they feel that they will be searched regardless of whether or not they consent, as illustrated by the interviews just discussed.

23.6 CONCLUSION: HOLLOW POLITENESS AND ITS CONSEQUENCES FOR INNOCENT CITIZENS

No one knows precisely how many innocent people are subjected to consent searches each year, but there is little doubt that the number is staggering. One officer conducting bus sweeps testified that he had searched 3,000 bags in the previous nine months.[28] In some localities, police officers ask every motorist they stop for consent to search.[29] One officer in Ohio made, in one year, 786 requests for consent to search motorists pulled over for routine traffic violations.[30]

But consent searches are not costless. People are shaken by them and don't forget them quickly. The vast majority of people subjected to consent searches are innocent. This is a fact that is easily forgotten because consent searches often come to our attention via

---

[26] The US Supreme Court has already considered and rejected the notion that police are required to advise citizens that they have the right to say no to requests for consent. *U.S. v Drayton*, 536 U.S. 194 (2002).

[27] During that time period, the Ohio Supreme Court ruled that police who stop motorists for traffic violations must advise them that they are free to leave prior to asking for consent to search the vehicle. *Ohio v Robinette*, 653 NE2d 695 (Ohio 1995). Subsequently, the US Supreme Court reversed and held that no such warning was necessary. *Ohio v Robinette*, 519 U.S. 33 (1996).

[28] *State v Kerwick*, 512 So. 2d 347 (1987).

[29] See *Harris v State*, 994 SW2d 927, 932 n 1 (Tex Crim App 1999).

[30] *State v Retherford*, 93 Ohio App 3d 586, 591–92 (1994).

published exclusionary rule cases, in which the defendant was factually guilty. How do consent searches affect the lives of innocent people—that is, people who possess no illegal drugs or guns, are not engaged in illegal activity, yet find themselves submitting to a search?

The Supreme Court paints a wholesome picture of a citizen and a police officer engaging in polite conversation, in which the officer and the citizen amicably agree that the officer is free to search her person or possessions, after which the citizen bids the officer good day and goes on her way. But in the real world, people subjected to searches do not live happily ever after. The Lichtenberg (1999) survey reveals that a large majority (76 percent) of citizens whose consent was requested from the Ohio Highway Patrol felt negatively about the experience. Here are some examples:

> I don't know if you ever had your house broken into or ripped off… [it's] an empty feeling, like you're nothing (Lichtenberg 1999:285, subject #11091).

> It was embarrassing. It pissed me off…they just treat you like a criminal and you ain't done nothing….I think about it every time I see a cop (Lichtenberg 1999:283, subject #14735).

> I feel really violated. I felt like my rights had been infringed upon. I feel really bitter about the whole thing (Lichtenberg 1999:285, subject #15494).

> I don't trust [the police] anymore. I've lost all trust in them (Lichtenberg 1999:288, subject #12731).

When police question citizens or rummage through their possessions and find nothing, they leave in their wake a flood of shaken people. Those feelings of contingency or personal insecurity frustrate well-being. At best, subjecting citizens to suspicionless searches amounts to a loss of liberty. At worst, it threatens the legitimacy of the police and the legal system more broadly (Nadler 2003, 2005). People who feel that the legal system is worthy of respect are more likely to comply with legal rules regulating their everyday experiences (Tyler 1990; Nadler 2005).

We have demonstrated in this chapter that the power of language and context to intimidate is well established. By choosing to ignore the intimidating power of language in a commanding context, the courts have adopted an interpretation of police exchanges with citizens that favors expedience over justice, and the interests of an unsustainable war on drugs—politically motivated and historically datable—over the rights of citizens, inalienable and eternal.

CHAPTER 24

....

THE LANGUAGE OF CRIME

....

PETER M. TIERSMA
LAWRENCE M. SOLAN

24.1 CRIMINAL SPEECH ACTS

MOST crimes require that the defendant commit a certain type of wrongful act (often referred to as the *actus reus*) while having a particular mental state (the *mens rea*). Many wrongful acts involve physical violence, such as assault and battery, rape, or homicide. It is not unusual, however, for wrongful acts to be committed by speech or writing. They are the focus of this chapter. We will survey a number of crimes that are perpetrated primarily by means of language. Most of our data will come from American jurisdictions, although similar principles apply in most of the world's legal systems.

As we will see, language crimes are all about illegal speech acts. As the name suggests, speech acts involve using language to perform certain types of actions. Speech act theory was initially developed by the English philosopher J. L. Austin (1962) and elaborated by John Searle (1969), among many others. They pointed out that utterances can function as acts that do things besides communicate information. Among the acts performed by speech are promising, questioning, threatening, lying, soliciting, and agreeing. Some of these are illegal in specific circumstances. Speech act theory is relevant not just to the criminal law, but also to certain areas of the civil law, such as contracts (see Chapter 7).

Some speech acts are characterized by the intent of the actor (referred to as the act's *illocutionary force*), others by the effect that the act has on the hearer (referred to as the act's *perlocutionary effect*). All language crimes concern themselves with the actor's intent. One has to have intended to solicit a crime in order to be guilty of solicitation. But others also concern themselves with the perlocutionary effect of the act. A statement that does not leave the recipient feeling intimidated is not a threat, whatever the intent.

Two other aspects of speech acts are worth noting for the purposes of this chapter. First, some speech acts are *performatives.* Just saying it is to do it. If a mother says to a child, "I don't have time today, but I promise to fix your bicycle tomorrow," the mother has promised—that is, she has performed the speech act of promising—merely by saying those words. In contrast, the verb *fix* cannot be used as a performative. It can describe actions, but cannot perform them. Unless she has magical powers, Mom cannot repair the bicycle by saying, "I hereby fix the bicycle." Some illegal speech acts discussed in this chapter are performative (e.g. agreeing to commit an illegal act, or asking someone else to commit one). Others, like lying under oath, are not. You cannot lie by saying "I hereby lie."

Often people engage in performative speech acts by using explicit speech act verbs like *ask*, *order*, or *promise*. Yet it is entirely possible, and in fact very common, to engage in performative speech acts without announcing so explicitly. If the mother were to say to the child, "I will fix your bicycle tomorrow—you can count on it," she has made a promise without using that word. This leads to the second aspect of speech act theory that recurs in our discussion of crimes of speech: Speech acts, including illegal ones, can be accomplished indirectly. I can threaten you by saying something that I know will leave you feeling threatened, whether or not I use the word *threaten*, as when I make an intimidating statement that I will do something harmful to you. The same holds true for other crimes discussed in this chapter.

24.2 SOLICITATION

The crime of *solicitation* involves asking or inducing someone else to commit a crime. That crime does not, in fact, have to be performed. Usually the government need only prove that the solicitor *intended* the crime to be committed. What is essential, at least under the federal law of the United States, is that the solicitor "solicits, commands, induces, or otherwise endeavors to persuade" someone else to commit a crime.[1] Thus, the essence of solicitation is language.

The crime of solicitation is often performed via the speech act of requesting. Someone can explicitly solicit the crime of murder by saying to a hit man, "I request that you kill my boss." Of course, we typically make requests without using the word itself, as in "please kill my boss" or "I want you to kill my boss" or even by means of a question like, "Would you please kill my boss?" Note also that some forms of solicitation refer only to the illocutionary force of the act ("solicits," "endeavors to persuade"), while others ("induces") require that the solicited party actually be convinced to participate.

A final preliminary issue is whether the solicitor must be sincere. Linguists and philosophers of language generally agree that subjective sincerity is not required to perform a speech act successfully (Searle 1969). If a child promises her parents to stop swearing, she has made a promise, even if she secretly does not intend to keep it. Yet when it comes

---

[1] 18 U.S.C. § 373 (2011).

to the crime of solicitation, the statute specifically requires that the state prove that the defendant intended to solicit the crime.

24.2.2 Examples of solicitation

We now apply these principles to some actual cases. Often enough, the issue in a solicitation case revolves around what type of speech act the defendant made. Sometimes there is very little doubt. Consider the case of Sheik Omar Abdel Rahman, a blind cleric from Egypt who had been living for some time in the United States. He was at one point accused of soliciting the murder of Hosni Mubarek, the then president of Egypt. He was convicted and sentenced to life imprisonment for this and related offenses.[2]

Abdel Rahman's conviction was affirmed on appeal. The evidence (recorded conversations) made it quite clear that the sheik was requesting or urging his followers to assassinate President Mubarek. For instance, he told someone that he "should make up with God...by turning his rifle's barrel to President Mubarak's chest, and kill[ing] him." Referring to the pending visit of Mubarek to the United States, Abdel Rahman counseled one of his followers: "Depend on God. Carry out this operation. It does not require a fatwa.... You are ready in training, but do it. Go ahead."[3] These statements are clearly requests, and their goal is obviously to induce the addressees to engage in murder.

Of course, people do not always solicit crimes so directly. The distinction between actually requesting that someone engage in a criminal act and, on the other hand, simply contemplating it aloud or just talking about it can be elusive. Consider the case of a Colorado man named Hood who decided to rid himself of his wife. Hood met with a friend, Michael Maher, and began to discuss his unhappiness with his marital state, concluding with the statement that his wife was "better off dead." Hood went on to describe several schemes he had considered to kill his wife, such as staging a robbery, during which his wife would be killed, but added that he needed a third person to "pull the trigger." When Maher told Hood he should seek psychological help, Hood retorted: "No, she needs to die." Maher testified that Hood seemed completely serious.

But did Hood really solicit or request Maher kill his wife? He seems to have sincerely wanted her killed, but that is not enough. Maher testified on cross-examination that Hood never directly asked him to kill his wife. Nonetheless, Maher assumed that when Hood suggested he needed someone to "pull the trigger," he was referring to Maher. Hood was speaking to Maher, who was the only other person in the room. The jury agreed, and the Colorado court of appeals affirmed.[4]

To see how indirect a solicitation can be, consider the case against white supremacist Matthew Hale.[5] Hale was the "Pontifex Maximus" of the World Church of the Creator

---

[2] *United States v Rahman*, 189 F.3d 88 (2d Cir. 1999).
[3] 189 F.3d at 117.
[4] *People v Hood*, 878 P.2d 89, 94-95 (Colo. Ct. App. 1994).
[5] *United States v Hale*, 448 F.3d 971 (7th Cir. 2006).

("World Church"). Another religious organization, the Church of the Creator, sued World Church for trademark infringement because the names were so similar. The Church of the Creator won, which provoked Hale to become so angry at the judge who ruled against World Church that he agreed to a subordinate's suggestion that she be killed. The subordinate, it turned out, was a government informant named Evola, who had been put in place after a follower of Hale had gone on a shooting rampage, which left two people dead and brought the World Church to the attention of the FBI.

Informant Evola, whose conversations with Hale were recorded, had been trying over time to get Hale to agree to a killing but Hale refused to take the bait. When it came to the judge, however, Hale kept less distance between himself and the plan. Hale had asked Evola for the judge's address, and then had this conversation with him:

HALE: That information, yes, for educational purposes and for whatever reason you wish it to be.
EVOLA: Are we gonna ... I'm workin' on it. I, I got a way of getting it. Ah, when we get it, we gonna exterminate the rat?
HALE: Well, whatever you wanna do ...
EVOLA: Jew rat?
HALE: ... basically, it's, you know? Ah, my position's always been that I, you know, I'm gonna fight within the law and but ah, that information's been pro-, provided. If you wish to, ah, do anything yourself, you can, you know?
EVOLA: Okay.
HALE: So that makes it clear.
EVOLA: Consider it done.
HALE: Good.[6]

Hale hoped that his indirect approval of a plan hatched by a subordinate would not be sufficient to get him into trouble. But he was wrong. He was convicted, and the appellate court affirmed the conviction. Apparently, when an individual has sufficient authority to ensure that an illegal act not occur, his approval of it becomes legally tantamount to his requesting (or ordering) the act, which constitutes a solicitation, albeit an indirect one. Thus, recognition of the power relationships among the players converts acquiescence into solicitation, and rightly so, we believe.

Not only must the solicitor request someone to commit a crime, but the request must be sincere. A man named Rubin once held a press conference, waved $500 in the air, and offered it to anyone who killed or injured a member of the American Nazi Party. After being arrested, he argued that his words were a type of political hyperbole, and that he therefore was not sincerely soliciting murder. The court of appeals held that even though the utterance was made at a press conference, it could potentially constitute solicitation to murder. Its decision rested in large part on Rubin's own statement that "we're deadly serious. This is not said in jest, we are deadly serious."[7]

[6] Ibid., at 978–79.
[7] *People v Rubin*, 158 Cal. Rptr. 488 (Cal. Ct. App. 1979), *cert. denied*, 449 U.S. 821 (1980).

Solicitation typically involves one person trying to induce someone else to commit a crime, typically via a request or similar speech act. What if people agree to commit a crime? That brings us to conspiracies.

24.3 CONSPIRACY

Conspiracy involves two or more people agreeing to commit a crime. Evidence of an explicit agreement is relatively rare and is not normally required. Tacit agreement is sufficient. This means that the agreement can be proven by circumstantial evidence.

Perhaps because the evidence is often indirect, many jurisdictions require that the agreement be followed by an *overt act*—a physical act intended to further the conspiracy. This requirement helps ensure that the conspirators were serious, as well as providing concrete evidence that the conspiracy did indeed exist.

Oftentimes there may be linguistic cues from which a jury can infer that there was an agreement, or lack of one. For instance, use of the plural pronoun *we* once helped establish the presence of a conspiracy to rig bids at auctions and to avoid paying federal income taxes. The participants allegedly sold property to each other, paying in cash to conceal the transactions from tax authorities. A critical statement by one of the conspirators, captured on tape by an informant, was that "we don't want any check writing between us. If we get caught by IRS, we'll be dead."[8] This suggests not only that the participants were acting in concert, but that they were aware that the scheme was illegal.

Covert tape recording by government informants can provide compelling evidence of conspiracies and other language crimes. But, as illustrated by linguist Roger Shuy (1993), use of such recordings can be problematic. The quality of the recordings can make it hard to understand exactly what was said. Even when someone is heard agreeing to certain propositions on tape, it may be difficult to determine whether he agreed to engage in a conspiracy or simply agreed with a more innocuous proposition. Often the wired informants explicitly discuss various criminal activities, casting a pall of illegality on all the participants in the conversation.

A related problem is that people engaged in criminal activity often use street slang and coded language, aware that law enforcement officials may be eavesdropping. In a Texas case, the court cited evidence that the defendant used terms like *longs*, *shorts*, and *apples*, which referred to a gram, a half-gram, and an ounce of cocaine, respectively, as evidence that he was involved in a conspiracy to sell drugs.[9] Judges sometimes permit expert testimony by narcotics investigators to define such street talk for the jury.[10] In one case, the court held that a narcotics investigator was not competent as an expert to interpret the word "speakers" as a technical word in the manufacture of PCP, but

---

[8] *United States v Romer*, 148 F.3d 359, 364 (4th Cir. 1998).

[9] *Childress v State*, 807 S.W.2d 424, 433 (Ct. App. Tex. 1991).

[10] See *Burton v United States*, 237 F.3d 490, 499–500 (5th Cir. 2000)(testimony that "a five price" means "$500 per pound").

permitted testimony relating to "grignard," "yardstick," and "yards," apparently all terms of art in the trade.[11] Of course, street slang and even coded language can be used for purposes that are not criminal. There is a danger that use of these terms will lead to guilt by linguistic association. If, in the ears of the jury, you talk like a drug dealer, you must be one.

24.4 BRIBERY

The crime of bribery involves giving someone an item of value with the intent to induce that person to act in a particular way in her official or professional capacity. Accepting an item of value can also constitute bribery. In addition, the item of value must be "corruptly" offered or received for the purpose of influencing official action (Lowenstein 1985; Solan 2010). Finally, the recipient of the bribe must belong to a specified class of people, typically government officials or witnesses in court cases.[12]

Bribery is often accomplished by physically giving or receiving an item of value. But it can also occur through words alone. The briber might *offer* to give something of value, rather than giving it directly. Moreover, it is illegal for government officials to *request* a bribe or to *agree* to accept one. There are thus at least three different speech acts that can be involved in bribing: offering, requesting, and agreeing.

Because bribery is a criminal act, the language of bribing may be quite indirect. In *People v King*, a juror approached one of the parties to a lawsuit and said that the case was "down the drain" but that "for peanuts" it could be "turned your way." The court held that this was a request for a bribe.[13] Likewise, for an official to suggest that a bidder on a government project should "take care of him" or make a "gesture" towards him has been held to constitute a request for a bribe.[14]

24.5 THREATENING

Threats are not always criminal acts. For instance, one spouse can to threaten to divorce the other without fear of prosecution. Only certain categories of threats are criminal. Thus, to ask a person on the street for money is usually nothing more than begging. But if it is accompanied by a threat that causes the victim to hand over property against his will, the action may constitute robbery. Threats are also involved in the crimes of extortion and blackmail, where the victim consents to give money or property to someone, but only because of a threat to do something bad to the victim if he does not consent

[11] *United States v Reed*, 575 F.3d 900, 923 (9th Cir. 2009).
[12] See, e.g., Cal. Pen. Code §§ 67–68; 92–95 (2011).
[13] 32 Cal. Rptr. 479, 481 (Cal. Ct. App. 1963).
[14] *People v Vollman*, 167 P.2d 545 (Cal. Ct. App. 1946).

(Shavell 1993). Blackmail is especially interesting, because the threat may be that the blackmailer, if not paid by the victim, will reveal something that it is perfectly legal to reveal in any event (see Robinson, Cahill, and Bartels 2010). Likewise, using threats to cause another person to engage in sexual intercourse is generally considered rape.

24.5.1 The speech act of threatening

Threats are similar to warnings and predictions. All of these speech acts deal with events or states of affairs that are likely to happen in the future. Threats must therefore be carefully distinguished from these other speech acts (Fraser 1998). The important distinction is that a person who makes a threat expresses an intention to bring about or cause the event or state of affairs. Thus, one requirement for a threat is that the speaker must state or imply that he will cause something to happen in the future.

Consider the case of a young man who sent a letter to the White House when Ronald Reagan was president. It contained the words: "Ronnie, Listen Chump! Resign or You'll Get Your Brains Blown Out." Below was a drawing of a gun with a bullet emerging from it. He was convicted of threatening the life of the president and sentenced to four years in prison. Was he just announcing that the population was so angry at Reagan that someone would assassinate him sooner or later? If so, his words were either a warning or a simple prediction. The jury, however, concluded that he was not just speculating about the future, but was suggesting that he would help bring the result about, a decision affirmed on appeal. On the other hand, as the dissenting judicial opinion pointed out, the young man used the passive voice ("you'll get killed"), which suggests that he did not plan to be personally responsible for the killing.[15]

A second requirement is that the speaker must believe that the future event or state of affairs will be bad for the addressee. In this regard threats are like *warnings*, which also refer to a bad future state of affairs. The difference is that warnings are typically aimed at protecting someone from a potential harm caused by natural forces or by someone else (Tiersma 2002). If you tell a sailor who plans to go out in a boat that it will be a nice day for sailing, it is neither a threat nor a warning, but merely a prediction. If, on the other hand, you tell the sailor that a hurricane is approaching, it is a warning because it is a statement regarding a future state of affairs that is bad for the addressee and aims to alert the person to the danger.

Crucially, just because a speaker "warns" someone, the speech act is not necessarily a warning. It might be a threat, depending on whether the requirements for making a threat have been met. If I "warn" someone against a harm that I intend to cause myself, it is usually a threat. Suppose that Larry and Peter share a secretary. Peter tells her that Larry is exasperated with her shopping on the Internet while pretending to work and will fire her if it happens again. That is most likely a warning. But if Peter "warns" the secretary that he (Peter) will fire her, he has in reality made a threat, albeit a perfectly legal one.

---

[15] *United States v Hoffman*, 806 F.2d 703 (7th Cir. 1986).

In like fashion, the word "promise" can act as a threat under some circumstances. A promise expresses an intention to engage in an act or create a future state of affairs. Unlike a threat, however, the act or state of affairs is beneficial to the addressee. If I promise to let you go for a swim tomorrow, it is usually a genuine promise, because most people enjoy a swim. But if I am a pirate who has kidnapped you, and we are on his boat in the middle of the ocean, his so-called "promise" is really a threat because in this case it involves something harmful.

The third requirement is that the speaker must intend his utterance or statement to intimidate the addressee. Suppose that an African-American family moves into a previously all-white neighborhood. A local skinhead gang places a noose on the street in front of the house, or burns a cross there during a midnight rally. In light of American history, these are highly symbolic acts that would almost certainly be intended to intimidate the residents of the house. In contrast, burning a cross as part of a political rally at a remote location would be less likely to intimidate anyone in particular, and is likely to be permissible under American law as a legal, albeit hateful, expression of opinion, protected by the Free Speech Clause of the US Constitution.[16] Or consider *Watts v United States*. During an anti-war rally, a young man stated to a group of people that if he was forced to carry a rifle in Vietnam, "the first man I want to get in my sights is [President Johnson]." The Supreme Court held that, given the circumstances, he had not made a "true threat" on the life of the president.[17] If he had said these words while parading with a loaded rifle in front of the White House, the outcome would almost certainly have been different.

A final requirement, common to many speech acts, is that a threat must appear to be sincere. (See Chapter 7, discussing sincerity conditions as they relate to the law of contracts). It is important, however, to emphasize that to make a threat, the speaker does not *actually* have to be sincere, but need only *appear* sincere. To be more exact, the speaker must intend the addressee to believe that the speaker intends to carry out the threatened act. Below is a New Jersey statute making it a crime to threaten to kill another person. The statutory language makes just this point:

> A person is guilty of a crime of the third degree if he threatens to kill another with the purpose to put him in imminent fear of death under circumstances reasonably causing the victim to believe the immediacy of the threat and the likelihood that it will be carried out.[18]

People often jokingly make statements that might literally be considered threats, but that are not meant to be taken as such. In one case a firefighter claimed that his superior threatened him by saying, "I should just shoot you." In light of the circumstances and the firefighter's own testimony that he did not take the comment seriously, the court held that the statement was merely intended as a joke.[19]

---

[16] See *Brandenburg v Ohio*, 395 U.S. 444 (1969).
[17] *Watts v United States*, 394 U.S. 705, 706 (1969).
[18] N.J.S.A. § 2C: 12–3(b)(2011).
[19] *Cignetti v Healy*, 89 F. Supp. 2d 106, 125 (D. Mass. 2000).

In contrast, if a robber approaches you in a dark alley, shows you a gun, and tells you that he will kill you unless you give him your wallet, it does not matter that the robber might have absolutely no intention of carrying out his threat. He has made a threat nonetheless, because his intention was to appear sincere and thereby intimidate you into handing over your money.

24.5.2 Indirect threats

Like other speech acts, threats can be made indirectly or nonverbally, as long as the requirements discussed above are met. An example of a nonverbal threat is a case in which a defendant made hand gestures in the shape of a gun to a prosecution witness entering the courtroom.[20] Observe that the defendant expressed—in gestural form—an intention to commit an act that would be bad for the addressee, and that act was meant to intimidate the addressee. There is no doubt that in the proper circumstances, gestures that mimic acts of violence against a person can be very threatening.

Even when expressed verbally, threats are frequently indirect. Suppose that someone involved in a crime tells witnesses that if they say anything to the police, "something [is] going to happen to them."[21] Things continually happen to people, both good and bad. Here, however, the circumstances are critical. Assuming the statement was meant to intimidate the witnesses, the court's decision that this was a threat seems justified.

Threats can also be made indirectly by means of questions. A woman in Nebraska was being harassed by a man and reported his activities to the police. A month later the man called the woman, told her that he had been forced to pay a fine, and continued by asking: "What should I do to retaliate?"[23] Superficially, this was merely a question. But note that the man's asking what he should do to retaliate presupposes that he intends to do so. Communicating this intention to the victim can reasonably be considered a threat (see also Yamanaka 1995).

24.6 PERJURY

Perjury normally involves lying under oath. Under US federal law, a person commits perjury if he "willfully and contrary to such oath states or subscribes any material matter which he does not believe to be true."[22] This is often called the *false statement* requirement.

Perjury also requires that the false statement be material. If it relates to a minor matter—something that would not be expected to influence a trial or other official

---

[20] *Mickens v United States*, 926 F.2d 1323 (2d Cir. 1991).
[21] *State v Myers*, 603 N.W.2d 300, 388 (Neb. 1999).
[22] 18 U.S.C. § 1621(1).
[23] *State v. Methe*, 422 N. W. 2d 803, 806 (Neb. 198).

proceeding—it does not constitute perjury. Marginally relevant misstatements are not likely to disrupt the truth-finding function of the courts (Solan and Tiersma 2005).

To decide whether a statement is false, we need to determine its meaning. As we will see, in perjury cases judges take a relatively literal approach to interpretation.

24.6.1 The *Bronston* case and literal truth

The most important American case on the false statement requirement is *Bronston v United States*, decided by the US Supreme Court. The issue in *Bronston* was "whether a witness may be convicted of perjury for an answer, under oath, that is literally true but not responsive to the question asked and arguably misleading by negative implication."[24]

Samuel Bronston was the president of a movie production company. His company petitioned for bankruptcy. At a hearing, lawyers for creditors were allowed to question Bronston under oath regarding the nature and location of his assets:

Q. Do you have any bank accounts in Swiss banks, Mr Bronston?
A. No, sir.
Q. Have you ever?
A. The company had an account there for about six months, in Zurich.[25]

In fact, Bronston had once had a large personal bank account in Switzerland, where over a five-year period he had deposited more than $180,000.

Bronston was convicted of perjury. The prosecution apparently convinced the jury that although Bronston's reply to the second question was literally true (his company did once have an account there), it falsely implied that he had never had a personal Swiss bank account.

The Supreme Court admitted that people might indeed infer from Bronston's answer that he had never had a personal account in Switzerland. But Bronston never said so directly. The Court emphasized that the perjury statute refers to what the witness "states," not to what he "implies." It is the job of the examining lawyer to clarify a vague or ambiguous answer. If a witness gives a literally true but unresponsive answer, the solution is for the lawyer to follow up with more precise questions, not to initiate a federal perjury prosecution.[26] Bronston's perjury conviction was reversed.

Unfortunately, it is not always easy to determine whether an answer to a question is literally true. In actual conversation people convey much information by means of implication, as explained by philosopher H. Paul Grice's *Cooperative Principle*. The Cooperative Principle consists of several maxims, one of which is the *maxim of relation*. It requires that one's contribution to a conversation be relevant to what went on before (Grice 1989). Assume Peter asks Larry how much money Larry has with him and Larry

[24] 409 U.S. 352, 353 (1973).
[25] Ibid., at 354.
[26] Ibid., at 358.

answers, "I have a dollar," although he is carrying $23 with him. Whether we regard this statement as true or false depends on the context in which the question was asked. If Peter needs a dollar to put into a soda machine, then Larry's response seems true and helpful: Peter wanted to know whether Larry had enough money (in a useful denomination) to enable Peter to buy a soda. If, however, Peter is wondering whether he will be getting back the $20 that he lent Larry last week, then we would regard Larry's answer as false, because the question is understood as asking for the sum total of the money in Larry's possession at the time. In both instances, we read relevance into the answer, and judge its honesty accordingly.

Now let us return to Mr Bronston, who was asked about any bank accounts in Switzerland; the Supreme Court assumed—as would most people—that this meant personal accounts. Bronston responded by mentioning that his company once had a business account there. Because the questioner assumed that Bronston's answer was relevant, he thought that Bronston was testifying that he had no personal bank accounts in Switzerland, but that—in an effort to be helpful—Bronston volunteered the unrequested information that his company once had an account. This is how we would normally interpret such a response. If Roger asks Janna if she has any brothers, and she replies that she has a sister, most people would take her answer to mean, or at least suggest, that she does not have a brother (Solan and Tiersma 2005:ch. 11; Tiersma 1990).

As mentioned, the Supreme Court assumed in *Bronston* that the lawyer's question referred to personal bank accounts. But suppose that it referred instead to any bank accounts, personal or business, that he might have had in Switzerland. In that case Bronston's answer was relevant but incomplete, which can also be problematic because it can lead to another false inference.

Suppose that Roger asks Janna, "How many siblings do you have?" and she replies, "I have a sister." If she also has a brother, has she told the truth? People tend to be quite divided on these sorts of judgments. Again, Grice's Cooperative Principle helps explain why. The *maxim of quantity* requires that a person give enough information for the purposes of the conversation or exchange. It is true that Janna has a sister. Yet because the audience will assume that Janna is obeying the maxim of quantity and giving sufficient information, it will infer that Janna intends to communicate that she has only one sibling, a sister. In contrast, if Roger had simply asked Janna *whether* she had any siblings, most people would deem the response somewhat less misleading, or even true.

Thus, the nature of the question can be critical in determining the meaning, and hence the truthfulness, of the response. For that reason, the *Bronston* court's holding that it is the responsibility of examining lawyers to clarify their questions and to follow up on incomplete or ambiguous answers is understandable, even if it exposes a rather simplistic notion of the concept of literal truth.

The *Bronston* case created what is now often called the *literal truth defense*. It is often used by defendants accused of perjury. They commonly argue that while their testimony may have been somewhat misleading, it was literally true. In fact, this strategy was used with some success by President Clinton during his impeachment hearings (Solan and Tiersma 2005:ch. 11).

24.6.2 Perjury and intended meaning

Many perjury cases involve questions of meaning. Linguists and philosophers have identified various types or categories of meaning, but in a perjury case what should matter most is how the defendant intended an utterance to be understood. If he intended his testimony to be understood in a way consistent with the facts that he believed to be true, his testimony should not subject him to criminal liability. On the other hand, deviation between his testimony and his understanding of the truth, if it was material and intentional, should lead to a guilty verdict.

Thus, defendants commonly argue that allegedly false testimony was either not material or that a discrepancy was unintentional (and therefore a mistake). In the alternative, they may argue that their testimony as they intended it to be understood was not, in fact, inconsistent with the facts (and thus, did not contain a false statement). Typically the prosecutor will allege that the defendant meant one thing, while the defendant will argue that he meant something else.

Initially, it might seem that just about any defendant could avoid a perjury conviction by arguing that he intended to communicate some claimed meaning that was not false. No one knows what was in his or her mind while testifying. Yet, with few exceptions, people commit perjury by means of language, which presupposes a speech community that shares a substantial body of knowledge (or conventions) regarding the meanings of words and how they can be combined to create sentences and larger units of discourse.

Consequently, what a person means by an utterance (sometimes called the *speaker's meaning*) depends on how that person intends the recipient to understand it. A rational speaker realizes that the recipient will assign a meaning to his utterance using the knowledge they share regarding their language.

The Clinton impeachment proceedings provide a nice illustration of these principles. At one point, President Clinton was placed under oath and forced to answer questions before a grand jury. Monica Lewinsky, with whom Clinton was alleged to have had an affair, had earlier filed an affidavit stating that she did not have a "sexual relationship" with the president. In a previous proceeding, Clinton had testified that Lewinsky's statement in the affidavit was true. During the grand jury testimony, the special prosecutor suggested Clinton had lied in affirming Lewinsky's statement. Clinton responded:

> I believe at the time that [Lewinsky] filled out this affidavit, if she believed that the definition of sexual relationship was two people having intercourse, then this is accurate. And I believe that is the definition that most ordinary Americans would give it.

He later continued:

> I believe, I believe that the common understanding of the term, if you say two people are having a sexual relationship, most people believe that includes intercourse. So, if that's what Ms. Lewinsky thought, then this is a truthful affidavit. I don't know what was in her mind. But if that's what she thought, the affidavit is true. (Solan and Tiersma 2005:233)

As Clinton correctly pointed out, the critical issue is what Lewinsky meant by the phrase "sexual relationship." How she actually intended her audience to understand the phrase is very hard to determine. Yet, Clinton argues, we know the usage of the average person, and we can assume that her audience would have shared that usage (that a "sexual relationship" involves intercourse). Lewinsky thus must have intended her audience to understand "sexual relationship" to refer to intercourse and not less intimate sexual activity. Clinton's analysis is correct, although his assumption about ordinary usage of the phrase is subject to debate.

To say that the meaning of words and phrases is shaped by ordinary usage and understanding is helpful, but it only goes so far in resolving questions. One of the most vexing problems for everyday discourse as well as perjury law is ambiguity: many words can be used in more than one sense, and thus have multiple meanings. Suppose that a witness's testimony is truthful under one construal but false under another; can she be convicted of perjury?

Some American jurisdictions have held that if a question contains an ambiguity, the answer can never support a perjury conviction. In *United States v Wall,* a woman was asked, "Have you ever been on trips with Mr. X?" She denied it. The prosecution could only prove that she had been in Florida with Mr. X, not that she traveled with him from Oklahoma to Florida. The court held that the meaning of being "on trips" with someone was ambiguous—it could refer to traveling somewhere with someone, or to being away from home with someone. Thus, the woman could not be convicted of perjury.[27]

Other jurisdictions follow a different approach: if there is evidence of what the defendant meant by his answer, the judge or jury should be allowed to resolve the ambiguity. An illustration involved an officer in the Kentucky National Guard. He was asked whether he attended a "Preakness party" in 1991; such parties had sometimes been the scene of illegal political fundraising. He admitted to being at the party, but denied that there had been any political fundraising. In fact, he had attended a Preakness party in 1990, during which illegal fundraising took place. The 1991 event was a small dinner party. Because other questions and answers revealed that the defendant understood the questions as referring to the 1990 party, his conviction was upheld[28] (see Solan and Tiersma 2005:218–19).

A final category of cases deals with ambiguities that cannot readily be resolved, even with reference to context. During the 1950s, the US Congress held hearings to expose people thought to have Communist sympathies. A witness denied being a "follower of the Communist line." When he was prosecuted for perjury, the court rejected the accusation because the phrase did not have a meaning "about which men of ordinary intellect could agree." When testimony, or the question upon which it is based, is vague or fundamentally ambiguous, it cannot form the basis of a perjury conviction.

[27] 371 F.2d 398 (6th Cir. 1967); see also Tiersma 1990:414.
[28] *United States v DeZarn,* 157 F.3d 1042 (6th Cir. 1998).

24.6.3 Perjury: the bottom line

Witnesses must tell the truth in court, or the entire justice system would collapse. A witness who intentionally makes a false statement on a material issue should be subject to prosecution. Unfortunately, it is not always easy to determine what witnesses mean in response to queries by lawyers.

In the common law tradition, it is the lawyers who ask the questions, and when witnesses do not cooperate, judges can force them to respond. Given the tremendous power that lawyers have over the questioning process, they share with witnesses a responsibility to find the truth. Too often lawyers and prosecutors manipulate the examination of witnesses to suit their own trial strategies, rather than the loftier goal of determining what actually happened.

Witnesses should tell the truth. And lawyers who examine those witnesses should promote that goal by asking clear questions that avoid ambiguities. When uncertainties arise, as they inevitably will, it is the duty of the examining lawyer to try to clarify the testimony. Perjury prosecutions should occur only when what a witness intended to communicate is clearly inconsistent with the facts that she believed to be true.

24.7 CONCLUSION

We have discussed five language crimes in this chapter. They have a great deal in common. Other than perjury, they are all susceptible to commission both directly and indirectly; they all require some kind of intent; and most importantly, they are all committed—at least for the most part—through speech acts. They also differ, not just with respect to the elements of each crime, but also with respect to the extent to which the speech acts must affect the recipient, and whether the speaker must actually be sincere, or merely appear sincere (a difference between solicitation and threatening, for example). The vocabulary of speech act theory goes a long way toward providing an analytical framework for understanding and evaluating these crimes of language, as we have seen.

CHAPTER 25

INTERROGATION THROUGH PRAGMATIC IMPLICATION: STICKING TO THE LETTER OF THE LAW WHILE VIOLATING ITS INTENT

DEBORAH DAVIS
RICHARD A. LEO

THROUGHOUT American history, police-induced false confessions have been among the leading causes of wrongful conviction (Leo 2004, 2008). In recognition of the potential for physical and verbal coercion to induce false as well as true confessions, and in the wake of some highly publicized examples of police-induced false confessions, the law in the United States has evolved over time to protect suspects from police coercion and to discourage the use of physical violence or explicit threats or promises of leniency contingent upon confession.

In a series of cases beginning in 1897, the US Supreme Court offered protections against coercion in interrogation.[1] These included prohibitions against physical coercion and against the use of *explicit* threatened consequences of a failure to talk to the police or to confess, or promises of leniency tied to talking or confession. Some seventy years later, in *Miranda v Arizona* (1966) the Court ruled that custodial suspects must be informed of their right to refuse questioning by the police, their right to the advice of counsel (free of charge for those who can't afford to pay counsel), and of the fact that any statements they offer can and will be used against them in legal proceedings.[2]

---

[1] In 1897, the US Supreme Court constitutionalized the common law rule against the use of threats and promises, holding that any confession induced by a "direct threat or promise, however slight," violated the Fifth Amendment. *Bram v United States*, 168 U.S. 532 (1897).

[2] *Miranda v Arizona*, 384 U.S. 336 (1966).

In response, however, police have adapted and developed pre-interrogation and inter-rogation procedures designed to circumvent these protections while still inducing sus-pects to talk to police and to offer incriminating statements, including full confessions (see Leo and White, 1999, for a review of tactics for inducing suspects to talk, notwith-standing the requirement of *Miranda* warnings; see Davis and O'Donohue 2004; Kassin et al. 2010; Leo 2008 for a review of tactics promoting confession).

Largely, these tactics adhere to the prohibition against explicit threats or promises, but nevertheless are specifically designed to convey the forbidden messages indirectly, through the process of pragmatic implication. They very deliberately use indirect impli-cation both to negate *Miranda* warnings and to convey the forbidden explicit promises or threats contingent on the suspect's choice of confession or continued denial. These indirect strategies of implication violate the intent of the law while adhering to its literal content. They very clearly convey the message, despite *Miranda* warnings, that the sus-pect actually has no choice other than to talk to police, and/or that *failure* to talk to police will be held against the suspect, instantly, and in later legal decisions and proceedings—and therefore are quite effective in convincing him to talk to his interrogators. These messages are supplemented during the interrogation with implied incentives for giving self-incriminating statements, including full confessions.

At all stages, specific words, labels, and linguistic implications function to define the nature and purpose of the interaction, to set the agenda for what will be discussed, to define the roles of the interrogator and suspect, to suggest possible and probable choices and outcomes, and, more generally, to mislead and actively deceive the suspect as to the nature of his choices and their long- and short-term consequences. Interrogation train-ing manuals and seminars offer very specific guidance concerning the exact wording and phrasing that will best promote crucial misperceptions in the suspect, while not stating these messages in legally impermissible explicit form (e.g. Inbau, Reid, Jayne, and Buckley 2001; www.Reid.com).

The ability of the interrogator to convey these messages *implicitly*, through *pragmatic implication*, without violating the letter of the law, is based in the principles of speech act theory (e.g. Austin 1962; Grice 1975; Searle 1969). The theory specifies that much of what is conveyed in conversation is accomplished through inference rather than explicit wording. That is, the speaker assumes the hearer will arrive at his intended meaning in part through a series of inferences, and in turn the hearer does make such inferences, albeit in a predictable fashion, given the speaker's literal wording and the context in which it takes place (see Holtgraves 2002; Turnbull 2003 for reviews).

Grice, for example, suggested that interlocutors abide by the "cooperative princi-ple" in conversation, to "Make your conversational contribution such as is required, at the stage at which it occurs, by the accepted purpose or direction of the talk-exchange in which you are engaged (1975:5). To achieve this, Grice proposed that participants abide by four maxims: "quality" (Say what's true. Don't say what's false.); "quantity" (Say enough and no more.); "relation" (Be relevant.); and "manner" (Be clear, concise, to the point.). To determine what is meant, Grice proposed that par-ticipants make "conversational implicatures," in which they fill in, amplify, or revise the *literal* meaning of statements to arrive at the *intended* or *implied* meaning. These implicatures are intended to preserve the assumption that the cooperative principle is indeed being followed by the speaker. Even when the speaker appears to flout the cooperative principle by being irrelevant or obviously not truthful, the hearer may first attempt to preserve the assumption of cooperation through attributing meaning such as humor or irony before concluding that the statement is uncooperative or incomprehensible.

Perhaps the most important of Grice's maxims for the police interrogator is that of "relevance." That is, a hearer expecting the speaker to follow the cooperative principle will expect the speaker to be relevant to the situation and topic at hand. In a police interrogation, the suspect is likely to assume that statements made by the interrogator are relevant to the situation as the suspect understands it. In the sections to follow, we review common police interrogation tactics, with particular emphasis on those conveying implicit messages beyond their literal content. As we shortly illustrate, most such implied messages are (1) conveyed through specific wording that defines the purpose of the interrogation and the agenda for carrying it out, and misrepresents the interrogator as an ally rather than an adversary, and/or (2) are conveyed indirectly by the interrogator and understood by the suspect through conversational implicatures based on the presumption of relevance.

25.1 THE "INVITATION" TO ENGAGE

Influence professionals of all stripes realize that they will be better able to influence a target whose resistance has not been raised (Davis and O'Donohue 2004). Recognizing this principle, police interrogators often seek to begin the interrogation of a suspect with the ruse that they wish to solicit the suspect's "help" with the investigation. The suspect is asked if he is willing to come to the police station to discuss the case and "help" get "this thing" or "this situation" "straightened out" or "cleared up."

Notice the many implications incorporated into such a request. First, the use of a request, rather than command, implies the interview is voluntary—even though, in fact, few will feel free to refuse. This illusion is then furthered during the interrogation. When the suspect arrives, the interrogator may immediately ask if he understands that he is there voluntarily and that he is free to go at any time, and will typically remind him of these points throughout the interrogation, until or unless it becomes necessary to place the suspect under arrest. This illusion of voluntariness serves both to undermine the suspect's natural resistance to being interrogated as a suspect, and to avoid raising resistance further (or even triggering an outright refusal to continue to talk) by reading *Miranda* rights—a requirement that would apply only if the suspect were under arrest.

Moreover, by casting the nature of the interaction as "helping," police may, at least until the accusatory stage of the interrogation begins, further promote the illusion that the suspect is not under suspicion, thereby diverting the suspect's natural resistance to an interrogator perceived as an adversary working to incriminate him. ("Surely, they aren't asking me to *help* incriminate myself!"). The request for "help" can also place additional pressure on the suspect to talk to police. After all, refusing to "help" seems much less justifiable than refusing to submit to questioning by the "enemy"—and might even be viewed as likely to cast suspicion on oneself!

To further reduce suspects' resistance to talking, interrogators are trained to avoid reminders of the criminal nature of the events in question, as well as of any legal consequences. There are many recommendations for how to keep the suspects' focus away from these issues (see Inbau et al. 2001), but the use of such phrases as "this thing" or "this situation" (rather than this "rape" or this "murder," etc.) to refer to the event, and to getting this "cleared up" or "straightened out" to refer to the purpose of the interaction are prominent among them. While the phrase "this thing" can serve to keep the link between a named crime and the consequences less salient, references to getting it "cleared up" or "straightened out" are designed to promote the illusion that there may be minor consequences or perhaps none at all.

25.2 *MIRANDA* AND "ANTI-*MIRANDA*": "ACTUALLY, YOU *MUST* TALK TO US, AND EVERYTHING YOU SAY CAN AND WILL BE COUNTED IN YOUR FAVOR"

The purpose of *Miranda* is to protect the accused from the inherently compelling pressures of police-dominated custodial questioning. According to the Supreme Court's logic in *Miranda*, these inherently compelling pressures are dispelled if (1) police inform suspects of their Fifth Amendment rights to remain silent and to appointed counsel, and (2) the suspect waives these rights knowingly and voluntarily. Absent properly issued warnings or a properly obtained waiver, a custodial suspect's incriminating statements cannot be admitted into evidence at trial. These procedures (both the warnings and the exclusionary rule) are intended to protect the suspect's rational and voluntary decision-making ability within the interrogation environment and, by implication, the reliability of the suspect's statement. According to the Supreme Court's logic, then, *Miranda* should offer some protection against the admission of involuntary and/or unreliable confessions.

Although one writer has argued that *Miranda* has exerted negative effects on the ability of police to investigate and solve crimes (Cassell 1996; but see Schulhofer 1996; Donahue 1998; Feeney, 2000), police have, in fact, developed a number of strategies either to avoid the necessity of administering *Miranda* warnings or to render them ineffective (e.g. Leo and White 1999). The pretext of voluntarily helping described above is a prominent strategy when police are able to interview the suspect without the necessity of first detaining and arresting him. Many interrogations begun in this way proceed unchecked until *after* the suspect has provided incriminating statements or a full confession. At that point, the suspect may be *Mirandized* and placed under arrest.

If the suspect is placed under arrest before the interrogation begins, police must administer *Miranda* warnings before proceeding. At this point, they may make a number of statements that either imply that the suspect actually does not have the right to refuse to talk, despite the statements in the warnings, or directly state or imply negative effects should the suspect choose to invoke his rights to silence or to an attorney. For example, the detective may say something like "We need to talk to you to get 'this thing' 'straightened out,' but before we can do that we need to get this form out of the way," "We want to talk to you about 'this thing,' but we've got this formality we've got to take care of first," or "*Before we can talk*, I need to get your signature on some forms…"

By including the diverting language of "this thing" and getting it "straightened out" these statements imply that the situation is less serious with less serious potential consequences than it in fact is. And, they further imply that the suspect doesn't really have the choices implied in the reading of his rights by such phrases as "We need to…" or "Before we can…" Essentially, they say "We're going to talk about this, but first we have to take care of this technicality" (implying that the suspect's rights aren't real or aren't wise for him to exert in this situation).

If the suspect does refuse to talk or asks for an attorney, detectives may say something like "Well, we can get you an attorney, but we have to wonder why you think you need one," or "You can ask for an attorney, but you're just going to be drawing attention to yourself," implying that the suspect will be under greater suspicion than he already is (clearly not the case!). Such explicit and implicit messages can be so strong as to make the suspect doubt that he actually can invoke his rights and/or to make him afraid of the consequences should he do so.

Although such statements often occur before the interrogation begins, it is important to note that *Miranda* warnings can be administered at any point during the interrogation, at any time the detective considers them necessary to serve legal purposes (such as ensuring that the interrogation is not suppressed as involuntary), or to detain the suspect (if he wants to leave at some point during the interrogation, but cannot be released). The suspect may also raise the issue of his rights to decline to talk or to an attorney as the interrogation proceeds, thereby triggering attempts by the detectives to discourage the suspect from invoking his rights.

It is also important to note that if *Miranda* rights are administered or discussed during the interrogation proper, the suspect's decision can be strongly influenced by standard interrogation tactics preceding the warnings that are intended to encourage confession. As we have noted in other contexts, the entire interrogation serves as an extended "Anti-*Miranda* warning" to the effect that failure to talk to police will work against the suspect's best interests, whereas talking to police, and particularly a full confession, can and will work to his benefit (Davis and O'Donohue

2004; Davis and Leo 2006; Leo and Davis, in press). Given that all aspects of police interrogation practices are designed to convey this anti-*Miranda* message, and that the interrogation can last hours or even days, the messages conveying incentives for talking far outweigh those conveyed in *Miranda* warnings that often last less than one minute (almost always less than five), that are often referred to as an insignificant formality, and that are administered in a rushed, unclear, and/or perfunctory manner.

25.2.1 Setting the stage to facilitate confession

Though the suspect may begin by coming to the police station voluntarily to "help" "clear things up," the detective will, at some point, transition from the relatively nonthreatening, pre-interrogation "interview" to the accusatory "interrogation" (e.g. Inbau et al. 2001). During this earliest stage of the interrogation, the interrogator attempts to undermine resistance to himself and to effectively smooth the way to persuade the suspect to confess by communicating five crucial messages to the suspect: "(1) 'I know you're guilty; your guilt has been established beyond any doubt;' (2) 'Nevertheless, there may be a resolution that doesn't involve serious consequences;' (3) 'I have the authority to affect what happens to you;' (4) 'I like you and want to try to help you;' and (5) 'I can't help you unless you explain what happened, now, before we finish here'" (Davis in press). In other words, these messages serve to define the nature and purpose of the interaction, the roles of the participants, and the agenda for carrying it out.

That is, these messages collectively (1) define the interrogation as a negotiation in which the interrogator will have significant influence on whether and what charges are filed, (2) minimize resistance to the interrogator by casting him as a benevolent ally who wants to help the suspect, (3) define the potential outcomes of the situation, such that they take the potential of establishing innocence off the table, yet suggest that there may be a way to minimize the consequences of guilt, and finally, (4) offer the essentials of how to achieve the best outcomes: that is, to offer a full confession, including the details of how and why the crime was committed, during the interrogation, before the case is turned over to the District Attorney. Thus, the way is paved for latter stages of the interrogation to convince the suspect that confession is, indeed, the pathway to the most desirable legal outcomes. Although some elements of these claims are conveyed directly, many are conveyed through implication.

25.2.1.1 *The "Set-up Question"*

The popular Reid Nine-Step method of interrogation (Inbau et al. 2001) suggests that just before beginning the accusatory interrogation, the detective should ask the suspect a question such as the following: "Tell me Harry, what do you believe should happen to the person who did this? Are there any conditions under which he should get a second chance, maybe get counseling or help? Or should he just go to jail?" Inbau et al. suggest that answers to such questions are diagnostic of guilt. Presumably an innocent person will simply recommend jail, whereas a guilty person will suggest leniency. But such a question is not simply a diagnostic tool. To a suspect likely to assume the detective is obeying the Gricean principle of "relevance," it is likely to provide the first misleading hint that the alleged crime may not result in criminal charges at all, and that the detective may have some authority to affect his outcomes. That is, the suspect is likely to infer that there must be a reason the detective is asking such a question (i.e. it must be relevant to the situation), with the most reasonable inference being that there is potential for leniency. Recognizing this, interrogation training materials suggest use of the set-up question as a means of "influencing the perceived flexibility of consequences" (Jayne and Buckley 1999:161).

Indeed, this "set-up question" appears to have exactly these effects. Davis, Leo, and Follette (2008) asked participants to read a transcript of the interrogation of an innocent suspect accused of child molestation, and then to answer questions regarding the motives, authority, and intentions of the detectives. If the transcript included such a set-up question, participants believed (incorrectly) that the detective had significantly more options regarding the seriousness of any charges filed and whether to charge the suspect at all than if it did not include the question.

25.2.1.2 *The Borg Maneuver: taking innocence off the table*

If the detective concludes the suspect is guilty of the crime, he will proceed to Step 1 of the accusatory interrogation—"Positive Confrontation"—in which he confidently states that "our" (implying consensus) investigation has definitively established the suspect's guilt. He may explicitly refer to both true and false "evidence" against the suspect, including confronting him with an allegedly failed polygraph, claiming to have eyewitnesses, fingerprints, DNA, claims of alleged co-perpetrators, or other incriminating evidence. Moreover, he may *imply* the existence of such evidence with questions such as the following: "Is there any reason why we *would find* your finger-prints on the murder weapon?" "*Think very carefully before you answer this question.* Could anyone have seen you near the scene of the fight that night?" "We've been talk-ing to lots of people, and we know what happened. We just need to hear it from you." Such "evidence" may be brought up throughout the interrogation, at any time the sus-pect attempts to deny culpability. Such tactics are intended to establish in the suspect a sense of hopelessness that he might convince anyone of his innocence, thereby sweep-ing away the (arguably) most powerful source of resistance to the interrogator and to confession. Once having instilled this sense of hopelessness, the interrogator turns to the task of convincing the suspect that confession will result in the best legal outcomes.

25.2.1.3 *The "pretext" for the interrogation*

Quite rightly, given the apparently overwhelming evidence of guilt claimed by the inter-rogator in the "Positive Confrontation" phase of the interrogation, the suspect might wonder why further interrogation is necessary. Hence, interrogation manuals recom-mend that the interrogator provide the suspect with a "pretext" for continuing. As we will see, however, the recommended pretext statements convey much more than simply a reason to continue. Essentially, they convey the message that the interrogation is not really about "investigating" what happened, or even the suspect's role in what happened, but rather it is about "deciding what to do about it." In other words, the nature of the situation is redefined as a negotiation that will determine what will happen to the suspect *as a result of his guilt*, rather than an investigation as to *whether* he is guilty. The Inbau et al. (2001) manual recommends such statements as the following:

- "The reason I wanted to sit down and talk with you about this is to find out what the circumstances were surrounding this thing. The reason why someone did something is often much more important than what he did."
- "Now Sam, there is absolutely no doubt that you did this. What I need to establish with you right now is what kind of person you are" (2001:225).
- "...There's no question that you went into the home on Wilson Avenue last weekend. My concern is that we have over 20 unsolved burglaries within a two-mile radius of that home...if you're not involved in all of those others, if it was a lot less than 20, we need to know that because it means that there is someone else out there responsible for those. The last thing I want to have happen is for you to be blamed for something you didn't do. That's why I'm talking to you now" (2001:226).

Through such statements, the interrogator sets the agenda for what will be discussed, and frames the underlying issues to be addressed by the discussion. He casts this agenda as relevant to what will happen to the suspect as a result of his actions ("We're going to talk about why you did this, and in doing so we're going to learn about what kind of person you are—things that are important to know!"). Reinforcing the messages of the "Sympathetic Detective" (see below) and "Set-up Question" tactics, he implies there are choices about how he may handle the suspect ("The reason why someone did something is often much more important than what he did" or "What I need to establish with you right now is what kind of person you are."), and that there may be a way to minimize the seriousness of the consequences. Following Grice's (1975) Cooperative Principle, a reasonable hearer would assume such statements to be *relevant* and therefore assume that one would not want to know these things in this legal context if they didn't matter for legal outcomes.

The detective further attempts to cast himself as a benevolent ally by "arguing against self-interest," suggesting he is there only for the suspect's benefit ("The last thing I want to have happen is for you to be blamed for something you didn't do. That's why I'm talking to you now"), thereby again invoking the reciprocity principle of influence (Cialdini 2008) to obligate the suspect to talk in return. The pretext is integral to the process of establishing the "authority" of the detective to influence the suspect's outcomes. Why would the detective be the one to try to investigate why the suspect committed the offense, determine what kind of person he is, and ensure that the suspect wasn't blamed for something he didn't do unless he had at least some authority to make decisions concerning what happens to the suspect as a result?

Having once established the purpose of the interrogation as the suspect's opportunity to explain what happened, the interrogator turns to the task of persuading the suspect that providing this "explanation" will actually be in his best legal interests. This task begins with a tactic we have dubbed the *"sympathetic detective with a time-limited offer"* (Davis et al. 2006; 2007b; Davis 2008).

25.2.1.4 *The "sympathetic detective with a time-limited offer"*

The natural inclination of a suspect faced with an interrogator who has accused him of a crime, particularly a serious crime such as rape or murder, would likely be to mistrust the interrogator and resist the interrogator's attempts to influence him. Thus, an important step in setting the stage for the interrogator to effectively influence the suspect is to sweep away this potential source of resistance by casting himself as a benevolent ally rather than as an enemy. With this in mind, the interrogator may say something like "Listen Jack, I think you're basically a good guy—not a career offender—a good guy who got himself in a bad situation. I'd like to help you out with this thing. But I can't do it if you don't tell me the truth. Once we leave here no one's going to be interested in what you have to say. The wheels are gonna turn and they're just gonna go with what they have. I can't help you after we leave here..." The detective flatters the suspect, states his desire to help the suspect, and makes this offer of help time-limited and contingent on confession. Though no explicit promise of leniency is offered in exchange for confession, these statements clearly imply that the detective *knows* what will help the suspect, and that he *can* and *will* "help" the suspect if he "tells the truth" (i.e. tells a story consistent with what the detective believes to be true—entailing, obviously, the suspect's guilt). Help, in the situation at hand, can only refer to help in achieving better legal outcomes.

Our research (Davis et al. 2006; Davis 2008) has clearly demonstrated that these messages are more than clear to the hearer. Research participants who read a transcript of an interrogation including the sympathetic detective tactic were more likely than those reading one without the tactic to believe that the detective (1) had more options concerning whether and with what to charge the suspect (even though charging decisions are not up to the detective), (2) liked the suspect, (3) wanted to help him, and (4) would actually help him more if the suspect confessed, but not if he refused to confess. Further, if the sympathetic detective tactic was included in the transcript, participants were more likely to conclude that the suspect would actually receive more lenient outcomes if he confessed than if the tactic was not included.

The detective also typically states or implies that once the interrogation is completed the case will be handled by others with less sympathetic motivations, and therefore failure to confess and explain during the interrogation will do far reaching damage to the suspect's case. For example, "Once we leave here there's nothing that you're going to have to say that the DA's going to be interested in hearing. They'll just go with the information they got." Though explicit, such messages clearly convey the idea that the charges and outcomes will be more serious if the suspect fails to "explain" (confess) during the interrogation and others who are less sympathetic take over.

25.3 MAKING THE SALE: LOWERING THE PERCEIVED COSTS OF CONFESSION

The tactics thus far, if effective, will have convinced the suspect that establishing innocence is unlikely, that the purpose of the interaction is to decide what to do about his established guilt, that the interrogator is a benevolent authority with the desire and ability to "help" the suspect, and that the only way to achieve this help is to offer a full confession of guilt. The suspect's remaining resistance is likely to derive from the inherent implausibility that a full confession could result in anything but the most serious legal charges and sentencing outcomes. The interrogator's remaining task, then, is to convince the suspect that a confession is, indeed, in his best interests, as clearly acknowledged in interrogation manuals (e.g. Jayne and Buckley 1999:207).

The interrogator has cast the interrogation as a negotiation in which the suspect provides information or explanations that can result in leniency—even potentially release without charges, as the set-up question implies, and has convinced the suspect that he has the authority to exert significant control over the suspect's fate, thereby rendering the suspect particularly motivated to please the detective and get his "help," and very attentive to any cue that will tell him what he needs to say or do. The suspect is convinced that what kind of person he is and what exactly happened and why he did it can matter. But he doesn't yet know exactly how it matters or what would be the best story to tell. His clues can only come from the one person in the room who has these answers.

The detective, of course, favors confession. Knowing that the suspect will be trying to assess the relative costs and benefits of confession versus denial, the interrogator must endeavor to enhance the perceived "benefits" of confession (and costs of denial) and minimize the apparent "costs" of confession (and benefits of denial). Since explicit promises of legal benefits or threats of legal costs can be grounds for exclusion of the confession from evidence at trial, these arguments must be done through implication, and can be supplemented by reference to non-legal costs and benefits—such as "doing the right thing," being a "stand-up guy," and "making family proud," or other appeals to moral or social values. These alleged costs and benefits are conveyed through implication, using strategies consisting of one or both of two related prongs: "minimization," in which the interrogator suggests scenarios for how and why the crime was committed that appear to be less legally serious; and/or "maximization," in which he engages in scare tactics designed to suggest that failure to confess will result in harsher outcomes.

This process begins with the second step of the Reid Nine-Step method of interrogation (Inbau et al. 2001), known as "theme-development." Interrogation manuals suggest a number of "themes" specific to individual crimes (e.g. Jayne and Buckley 1999; Senese 2005). Essentially these themes suggest scenarios for how and why the crime was committed that imply that the alleged actions are not as legally serious as they appear to be— perhaps not even criminal at all. In some cases, the interrogator may directly suggest the scenario, such as the self-defense theme used in a case of alleged first degree murder:

> Even if you did shoot somebody, sometimes that happens for a reason. I mean sometimes there's such a thing as self-defense, you know....Maybe those guys started it, and I believe they did because those guys are knuckleheads. Yeah, maybe they didn't deserve to die. But sometimes, you know, sometimes these guys bring it on themselves. If that's how it happened, I can understand that. It's no big deal. We can work with that.[3]

In this case, the detective has directly suggested that the killing occurred in self-defense, that this is understandable and no big deal—implying that the alleged killing is less legally serious, or not criminal at all. The commonly used phrase "We can work with that..." further implies that the detective can do something to help the suspect *if* the suggested version of the crime is true.

But the self-defense theme and its implied consequences may also be suggested more indirectly, in the form of relevant stories and illustrations, such as the following:

> I'll give you another little example what I had happen one time when I was investigating a homicide. Um, I had people telling me that this guy pulled a gun and he shot and killed another guy. That's a pretty simple thing, right? I mean, just, "Boom, boom." Pulls a strap, shoots a guy dead. So what do you think about that? What do you think about that guy, the guy who shot the other guy? Stone, cold killer, right? You—that's somebody you probably wouldn't want on the street. You wouldn't want to meet up with that fool, just going to pull a gun and kill somebody right in front of you for no reason. But then pretty soon we found out that the gun that the victim had had fallen in the...storm drain. The victim had a gun as well. And the victim was pulling this gun when the other guy shot and killed him. That's a little bit different scenario, isn't it? That guy got a voluntary manslaughter. People understood because they have the whole story about what happened out there. And the DA understood when he evaluated the case. And he filed the appropriate charges. That's what we're trying to tell you. We're trying to understand what happened out there so that we can tell the DA what really happened.[4]

In either form, the detective has suggested a less serious and potentially non-criminal version of the target events, and has further implied that the DA would respond to an "explanation" in these terms by filing the "appropriate" (i.e. less serious) charges, if any. Further, he is implying that confession is necessary to achieve this leniency—that the DA must "understand what happened" in order to take the appropriate lenient action.

The detective will pursue his theme, leading up to the "alternative question," in which he contrasts the more and less serious versions of the crime and asks the suspect which of them is true (Step 7 of the Reid Technique). For example, in following up the above story about the self-defense versus unprovoked version of homicide, the detective might say: "If this was something you had to do to protect yourself, I can understand that. That's no big deal. We can work with that. But if this is a case where you just decided to

---

[3] Data taken from *People v Montecinos* by co-author Davis, who was an expert witness in the case (2005 WL 3036458 (Cal. Ct. App. 2005)).

[4] Ibid.

kill this guy just cause he looked at you wrong, that's different. I don't want to talk to you anymore. So which was it, did you do this to protect yourself, or did you do it just because you felt like it. This is important to know. Which was it?" This "alternative question" technique reinforces the notions that the two versions of the event differ in seriousness and consequences and that the less serious version may not be criminal at all, and is often effective in eliciting a first admission of involvement.

These "minimizing" themes can be supplemented by "maximization," in which the detective implies that the suspect will be subject to more serious outcomes if he refuses to confess. For example, the detective may refer to a number of potential costs of refusal to confess. He may imply that judges and juries will react with little sympathy to a person who refuses to admit responsibility, for example.

> Would you feel better about a guy who just flat out lies to us and tells us he had nothing to do with this when the evidence clearly proves that he did? Or would you feel better about the guy who stands up like a man and takes responsibility for what he did. A guy who says "Yeah, I did this thing. It was a mistake, and I'm sorry." Which one do you think the judge and jury are going to feel better about.[5]

Or, he may imply that refusal to confess can lead to more serious penalties through statements such as the following:

> Listen Jack, you're at a crossroads here. One way is life and the other can mean death. The choices you make today are gonna put you on one of these paths. You need to work for your future here Jack. You need to explain this thing...

The detective has made no direct threat that failure to confess can result in the death penalty, but nevertheless has clearly conveyed the message. It is this difference between direct and indirect communication that can explain how the detective can truthfully testify in later proceedings that he made no explicit threats or promises to the suspect, but yet the suspect can also truthfully testify that he did.

25.4 CONCLUSIONS

As we have shown, interrogation tactics rely heavily on the use of pragmatic implication to convey threatened costs of refusal to confess and promised legal benefits of confession. Yet, while the law forbids the use of such threats and promises, the courts have generally refused to recognize that they are conveyed just as effectively through indirect implication as through direct explicit statements (see Russano et al. 2005 for a test of this assumption; see Leo 2008; Kassin et al. 2010 for reviews).

While the courts have failed to recognize the implied messages of tactics such as minimization or theme development, they have been even less sympathetic to claims that

---

[5] State of *Nevada v Eddie Torbio-Ruiz*, Case No. CR03-2287.

tactics such as the sympathetic detective, the set-up question, or the use of flattery and offers for help can convey promises of leniency (see Davis, in press). We can only believe that this reluctance is rooted in a motivation to preserve the admissibility of confession evidence that would perforce be routinely excluded should the judges recognize the clarity of threats and promises conveyed through implication.

Clearly, all of us, judges included, would recognize the threat conveyed by a statement made by a mafia man to a store owner:

> Just last month Mr Smith, who's just like you—he owns that deli over on 6th street— thought he didn't need to pay his protection money. But you know what happened to him. Somebody done went and burned his store down. I don't know as I'd wanta take that risk myself. But it's up to you.

That same judge, however, would likely rule that the following statement, made by an interrogator to a suspect, did not constitute a threat:

> Just last month, we had a guy in here just like you. We had the evidence showing he was implicated in a murder. He thought he didn't need to explain himself. But you know what happened to him? The DA had to go with the story other people were telling, and the guy was charged with first degree murder, and he's askin for the death penalty. I don't know if I'd want to take that risk myself. But it's up to you.

As long as this situation endures, both guilty and innocent suspects will be led to confess against their self-interest by the deceptive use of implied threats and promises of leniency contingent on the decision to confess.

PART VI

COURTROOM

DISCOURSE

CHAPTER 26

......

DISCOURSE IN THE US COURTROOM

......

GAIL STYGALL

26.1 INTRODUCTION

......

SOMETIMES ordinary people just do not understand the meaning of the language that they hear in courtrooms. This is problematic because courts are places of great power: a person's liberty can be restricted or life taken or a person's property lost. The words in a courtroom have real world outcomes following the utterance or writing of language in the courtroom. Upon hearing or reading language in a legal context, laypeople often attribute difficulties in understanding to the law itself. Attorneys may attribute the lack of understanding to their use of "legal jargon," but this is a legal version of folk linguistics. Unfortunately, it is more than legal jargon. A trial is a specialized genre of language activity, governed by a large number of discourse rules that are completely unfamiliar to ordinary people. Discourse studies of American courtrooms demonstrate that the language used in courtrooms is patterned, structured, and in many ways predictable, both at the aggregate level of a trial and in specific procedures that are a part of the trial. Legal discourse is, in large part, based on written texts, texts which are invisible to laypeople in contact with the legal community, but in a trial, this discourse becomes prominent. For the attorneys, the structure of the prototypical legal event—the trial—is second nature.

Yet trials' language and procedures are opaque to ordinary people. Because the language itself can be difficult, the operation of power can be masked. Until there was a substantial baseline of research on ordinary conversation emerging in the 1960s and 1970s,[1] it was difficult to say how legal language worked in the courtroom interaction, or how power was a factor in that operation. Once a baseline was established permitting

......

[1] See, for example, the work of Sacks et al. (1974).

comparison, it became possible to describe courtroom discourse and to identify what aspects of the discourse were sensitive to lay confusion and to the operation of power. Ordinary conversational turn-taking, for example, disappears in a courtroom. The attorneys control the topics of conversation. Topic choice for conversational partners also disappears in a courtroom. Attorneys also control the pacing of the questioning and how long the topic they selected stays on the conversational floor. Judges control what the attorneys can say and what the jury will hear. Witnesses cannot ask questions of their own to the attorneys or the judge. And witnesses cannot refuse to answer. These are not the ordinary discourse rules of everyday life.

In the US system, there are many opportunities for interaction in the courtroom between legal participants and laypeople. After an arrest, for example, an accused person is arraigned and interacts with attorneys and the judge. After filing a civil action, the participants, legal and lay, may come together in the court-like setting of a deposition. In criminal and many civil cases, the participants are entitled to a trial by jury. Prospective jurors undergo the selection process, *voir dire*, which consists of questioning by the attorneys or by the judge. A judge reads preliminary instructions to the jury. Attorneys make opening statements in which they outline their cases. Evidence is presented through witnesses who testify by being asked questions by an attorney. Each attorney may object to the other's questions and stop the testimony until the judge rules on the acceptability of the objection. A judge may rule on whether these questions are acceptable under a set of legal discourse rules, which are not accessible to lay jurors, such as the concept of "laying a foundation" or the nearly complete ban on hearsay. The trial ends with attorneys' making closing arguments, followed by the judge reading a more extensive set of instructions to the jury. If the outcome of the trial is appealed by either side, a transcript of the proceedings will be produced by the court reporter.

This chapter explores the research focused on US courtrooms and how discourse operates in that particular setting. The research on discourse in courtrooms has moved from a relatively straightforward analysis into a more nuanced and complicated understanding of the operation of power. This chapter examines the development of these ideas through trial chronology: pleas and pleading; jury selection or *voir dire*; opening statement; questioning and narrative in the evidence portion; and closing arguments. The need for laypeople to understand the language in trials is a part of the legitimacy of law in the United States. If trial language moves further away from ordinary language, the need for explanations to laypeople increases. Jury instructions will not be discussed here (see Chapter 31 for a detailed account). This chapter takes as a given discourse inequalities among members of different social and economic classes, gender, race, and ethnicity.[2]

---

[2] See Conley and O'Barr (1998) for a sustained discussion of the ways in which power threads through legal discourse.

26.2 Pleas and pleadings

The initial pleas and pleadings in a case take place before the full trial begins. Yet in both pleas and pleadings, there is a narrative to be told. For this chapter, the primary narrative structure refers to the Labov and Waletsky framework of abstract-orientation, complicating action, evaluation, and coda (Labov and Waletsky, 1989). The *abstract* announces what the story is about, a kind of topic marker. *Orientation* sets the context for the event. The *complicating action* is the series of actions or what happened. *Evaluation* is the assessment of why the story is important, and *coda* shifts the talk back to conversants. This formal narrative structure is the background against which the varied narrative structures of trial are described in this chapter. Researchers disagree about the extent to which narrative concepts may control a trial, some preferring a conceptual framework. Others suggest variations on this Labovian structure to better fit the legal setting.

26.2.1 Pleas

A *plea* is a defendant's formal response (usually "guilty" or "not guilty') to a criminal charge. Several issues relating to pleas have received attention from the community of language scholars. One is an examination of plea bargaining in California municipal courts, in which the prosecutor and defense lawyers try to negotiate a plea before trial. The researcher identified a set of three narrative types, which included a story entry, stories, and an defense segment, often an excuse (Maynard 1990). The story entry functions as a kind of synopsis or abstract of the case at hand. The story itself includes both a kind of orientation to the setting of the story, an action report, giving the temporal and sequential organization, and a reaction report, typically giving the unresolved issues with the police or prosecutor. Defense segments consist of two types, denials and excuses. The narratives in this study were presented much more frequently by the defense attorneys. Collectively, prosecutors and defense attorneys used narrative structures that included all the basic narrative parts described in the introduction to Section 26.2 above. Successful attorneys could use the narratives at the same time that they were able to negotiate the regular legal discourse of the formalization of a plea bargain. So while narrative is not a formal part of plea bargaining, the attorneys presented narratives that followed a prototypical structure associated with plea bargains.

Although pleas may have been negotiated outside of a courtroom, they still must be ratified inside the courtroom before a judge. An Arizona study (Philips 1998) focuses on the moment in court in which a criminal defendant must answer questions from the judge about the defendant's understanding of the consequences of a plea bargain, the conditions under which the plea agreement was reached, whether the facts actually support the plea and the sentencing possibilities as a result of the plea agreement. The procedures associated with the plea bargain follow Rule 17 of the *Arizona Rules of Criminal Procedure*. The judge and attorneys are well aware of Rule 17. Judges are also required to establish the factual basis of the crime as part of accepting the plea. Defense attorneys are supposed to explain the factual basis to their clients. Interestingly, there is little evidence in this study that the factual basis of the crime plays a role in the plea bargains. The criminal defendants have little or no understanding of the relationship between the textual form of Rule 17 and the oral genre of the plea bargain in court. The discourse then produces markedly different understandings of the process, one for attorneys heavily anchored in written genres, the other for laypeople experiencing an unfamiliar oral event in the courtroom.

26.2.2 Pleadings

The initiation of a civil lawsuit begins with the plaintiff's filing of a pleading, called a *complaint*. Complaints tell a story, another narrative, but unlike traditional narratives, the pleadings may contain incomplete stories or stories which contain allegations not yet proven (Tiersma 1999:148). A complaint must follow legal rules for filing a lawsuit and these rules will shape the narrative. The complaint must have a legal cause of action and whatever narrative is told must conform to the outline of the cause of action. Other aspects of the narrative may be irrelevant and eliminated. Jurisdiction must also be established, telling the story in the correct venue. The defendant usually responds to the complaint by means of another pleading, usually an *answer* that admits or denies the allegations of the complaint. Other responses are also available.

The pleadings described above are typically produced by an attorney after his or her client has discussed the problem with the attorney. Small claims courts are different in that in most cases, the pleadings are written and filed by individuals who are not attorneys. Unlike the description of the civil lawsuit above, the complaint in a small claims court action may be just a few lines handwritten on a form by an actual plaintiff. In a small claims court, filing a case is usually less expensive, the procedures to file a case appear simple, and the litigants do not need to have attorney represent them. It is also the litigants who argue their own cases orally when the case is heard. The downside is that these complaints sometimes lack a legal cause of action and may be rejected.

The small claims court has been a very productive site for examining the intersection of legal discourse with the discourse of laypeople. In a major study of small claims courts, John Conley and William M. O'Barr (1990) find that laypeople approach their cases in one of two basic ways: either they seek relationship remedies, posing their claims in social terms, or they seek rule-based remedies, posing their claims as rule violations, asking for legal remedies and remuneration. Although there is also some variation in how small claims court judges react to these approaches, the rule-seeking plaintiffs tend to fare better in these courts. Conley and O'Barr also note that the rule-based approach was more likely to come from white males, while the relationship orientation was more apparent with women and various ethnic and racial groups. One notable aspect of the plaintiffs' approach to the litigation was that they wanted to be able to tell their story, even when the story was not legally relevant.

Similarly, in victims' accounts of domestic violence and domestic sexual violence, the original narrative told by the victim does not typically highlight aspects of the incident that are required for prosecution. When the orally reported event is transformed into a written affidavit, changes occur in victims' accounts that make them conform to legal discourse rules, such as the focus on an individual event rather than a series of events. Tense changes are necessary in the accounts, the organization of the narrative may be changed, and sexual terms must be included, despite the reluctance of victims (Trinch 2003). The original narrative—compelling, emotional, and disordered—must be transformed into legally acceptable discourse in order to be prosecutable.

26.3 *VOIR DIRE*

In order to seat a jury, jurors must be examined through the process of jury questioning, or *voir dire*, determining if they can be fair and reasonable jurors who will follow the judge's instructions. Although an extensive consulting industry has arisen around *voir dire*, little attention has been paid in the literature to the discourse of the process. In this process, jurors experience their only interactive discourse in the courtroom (with the exception of a possible poll of the jurors after a verdict).

Voir dire is conducted in one of three ways: the judge conducts all the questioning (with the possibility of attorney questions submitted to the judge), the judge begins the process and the attorneys ask follow-up questions, or the attorneys ask the jurors all the questions. In federal district courts, the judge is likely to ask all of the questions. In any version of the questioning period, the conversational power is asymmetrically distributed. The judge or the attorneys control the questions; prospective jurors can only answer them. There is also an imbalance in the amount of information that the judge and attorneys have in contrast to the information that the jurors have. Most jurisdictions use jury questionnaires, filled out by prospective jurors in advance. Some of these jury questionnaires may be general; others may be quite long and case-specific. In the O. J. Simpson criminal trial, an unusually public and widely viewed trial, prospective jurors filled out a questionnaire that contained "294 questions and was over 80 pages long" (Cotterill 2003:13). The prosecution hoped that the some of the questions would identify prospective jurors who admired Simpson as a football player or media star. The defense hoped to identify prospective jurors who retained subtle racial biases.

Many times the *voir dire* will begin with questions that are likely to be answered in unison, as a group. Typically, these are initial questions asked by the judge, such as "have you ever served on a jury before?" and the jurors collectively answering "no." Judges are especially interested in having a jury that will pass appellate scrutiny. This means that the judge is concerned about potential juror knowledge that might bias the outcome of the case. In a criminal case, this might be a juror who has a family member who is a police officer. In a civil case, it might mean a juror who works in the insurance industry or who has had a similar experience to the one that is being litigated. One concern that may emerge from a discourse perspective is the social force of answering questions in unison several times before there is a question which an individual juror must answer differently. This situation will require that the prospective juror speak up, against the stream of the unified discourse. Because this can be hard to do, it may result in a juror being seated who has not fully responded to all the questions (Stygall 1994).

If the attorneys are allowed to ask or to submit questions, the questions are likely to relate to issues of their respective cases. A plaintiff's attorney may attempt to introduce legal concepts into the jury questioning; a defendant's attorney may attempt to make strategic responses to the plaintiff's expected case. *Voir dire* is typically not on the record, not recorded by the court's official reporter, except in unusual or well publicized cases. Though official, the questioning period is thus more open to typical conversational strategies, such as overlap, interruption, self-repair, repetition, and other moves. The degree to which these normal conversational strategies are present may make the difference as to which jurors are seated on the jury. One study suggested that the fewer overlaps in questioning, the less likely the prospective juror was to be seated (Wood 1996).

Prospective jurors may be challenged for cause by the judge or the attorneys. A challenge for cause might be the demonstration of a prospective juror's belief in law enforcement officers always being correct. Another challenge for cause might be a juror's belief that the death penalty is always wrong. The attorneys can also make a limited number of peremptory challenges. Attorneys, especially those working closely with jury consultants, will try to remove potential jurors who are likely, by their own demographic characteristics, to favor or disfavor their client. After all of the challenges have been made, the jurors are then sworn in and remain silent observers for the rest of the trial.

26.4 OPENING STATEMENT

The opening statement, when each side presents the case it intends to make, can raise the perennial psychological question of recency versus primacy. One school of psychological work argues that the jury makes sense of the case early in the trial, as soon as the opening statement, and having made that decision, "hears" the evidence that supports the early sense of the case. This is primacy. Others argue that jurors, as the legal system would prefer, hear all of the evidence, making tentative decisions at the end of the trial, possibly in final argument. This latter version is recency. Although jury instructions require that jurors hold their decision in abeyance until all the evidence is heard and the jury has been given final instructions, cognitive studies suggest that "jurors do not make decisions in the manner intended by the courts regardless of how they are instructed" (Devine et al. 2001:699).

Opening statements outline the evidence that each side will present and explain how this evidence will support the case. Insofar as they are able, attorneys will attempt to bind the evidence together into a narrative. Discourse analysts have generally followed one of two proposals on the structure of opening statement. One group describes the discourse of the opening statement as a structured narrative. The goal for either attorney is to put the client's "story" into words for the jury. There are some differences in how that may occur, but both the plaintiff and the prosecution must tie the story to pieces of evidence and the legal requirements in jury instructions. The ordering of witnesses in the trial may not conform to the chronology of the narrative and it is in opening statement that these discontinuities may be addressed early in the process (Stygall 1994).

The other proposal for the structure of opening statements is that of themes, as contained in "lexical representations of the acts and actors" (Cotterill 2003:65). Cotterill argues that narratives must be constructed from lexical choices. Lexical choices have implications, through their association with semantic prosody. Semantic prosody is the collection of the senses of the collocated words and phrases. Cotterill's tracking of collocations in the O. J. Simpson trial demonstrates how the prosecution's lexical choices portray Simpson as someone who is negatively *encountered* and participates in a *cycle of* X, while the defense portrays the interaction between the Simpsons as *incidents* and *discussions* (Cotterill 2003:65–90). Similarly, Matoesian (2005) examines a semantic network of terms associated with payment to a witness by a media source—terms such as *dollars, payment, maximize your profits*—in order to diminish the value of that witness's testimony. The themes and lexical choices in opening statements may carry through into the questioning strategies of each side's planned witness examinations.

26.5 TESTIMONY

The evidence stage of a trial has its own set of discourse rules. Although lawyers may know these as rules of evidence, they are at the same time rules about how language may be used in this portion of the trial. There are rules about who starts the questioning. There are rules about the turn-taking, both in relation to the stages of questioning—direct examination, cross-examination, redirect, and recross-examination—and in relation to the ways witnesses are allowed to answer.

The evidence stage can be quite confusing to jurors because they will not hear a conventional narrative. What narrative there is comes in bits and pieces in question and answer form. Witnesses testify out of the order with respect to the chronology of events leading to the trial.

Attorneys are less concerned with narrative coherence than they are with using witnesses and pieces of evidence to construct a legally viable case. Instructions to the jury will include which legal elements are necessary to prove the case. But there isn't an opportunity in the evidence stage for an attorney to stop and say "Ladies and gentlemen of the jury, what he just said is one of the required elements of proof for this case." Telling a good story may work against constructing a viable legal case. These necessary elements are drawn from the legal text world which are not salient to jurors. There is a substantial difference between what attorneys need to do to establish their case and what jurors think is more important or more credible.

26.5.1 Judges

The discourse role for judges in the evidence phase of trials is quite limited, usually confined to admonishing the jury at breaks and at the end of the day, ruling on objections, and conducting sidebar conferences with the opposing attorneys. In one of their most ritualized roles, judges tell the jury not to discuss the case with their fellow jurors or with anyone else and tell them not to read or listen to any media accounts of the trial. Because this admonition comes at every break and at the end of every day of a trial, it becomes a speech event on its own, a spoken ritual to bracket the jury's leaving the courtroom.

Another role for judges is to rule on objections. Attorneys make objections both to the other lawyers' questions and to witness's answers. There are many objections that are actually discourse rules at the same time that they are legal rules. The objection discourse sequence is what a conversational analyst might call an *adjacency sequence*, an ordered and reoccurring stretch of talk which, in this case, begins with a question to a witness by an attorney, followed by the other attorney objecting, and the sequence is closed by the judge ruling on the objection. It is both the required sequence for the legal discourse and a recognizable adjacency sequence. This kind of sequence is not common in ordinary conversation.

After an objection, witnesses may become less cooperative, in large part because they were not expecting to have their answer interrupted by an objection. Moreover, ordinary witnesses may be quite confused about why they have been stopped. In ordinary conversations, it is not unusual to provide further evidence for a story by saying something like "and my sister said when she saw it...". In a courtroom, unless the sister was going to testify, the answer would be objectionable as hearsay. Hearsay is a common evidential in ordinary speech and its prohibition in the courtroom may be unsettling for the witness, who may be stopped several times by objection before he or she understands what cannot be said. In many cases, a witness continues answering when an attorney has interrupted with an objection before the judge rules on the objection. If the judge affirms the objection, and the witness has already answered, the judge may tell the jury to ignore the answer and tell the court reporter to "strike" the answer from the official record, although it is unlikely that jurors will actually ignore what the witness said.

Another speech role of trial judges is to call or to oversee bench conferences or sidebars and to rule on the issue raised. The O. J. Simpson criminal trial provided an unusual opportunity to observe a wide variety of sidebars. The topic of most sidebars is a question of the admission of evidence. Sidebars should be limited in number, calm in style, and always out of the hearing of the jury (Gaines 2002:214). The beginning of the sidebar is announced by the judge for the court reporter's record. The judge can be the one requesting the bench conference, but it is more likely that counsel on one side or the other will make the request. The judge controls the topic and the focus and these utterances are typically directives or imperatives (Cotterill 2003:101).

26.5.2 Testimony

Narrative coherence is difficult to attain within trials, given the necessity of each side presenting its story through various witnesses and question and answer sequences. This is clearly unlike most discourses that adults experience in their ordinary lives. The question/answer pair is called an adjacency pair; that is, participants in conversations have a structural expectation that a question will be followed by an answer. This is typically in the next turn in the conversation, but it is possible that the answer will not be heard until several turns have passed. Adjacency pairs are normative, as are the expectations that they generate. Thus, numerous violations of that expectation will have an impact on the jurors' assessment of witnesses.

While narrative is present in some parts of testimony, it is not likely to be sustained narrative. Harris argues that narrative is more likely to appear in a trial in a reduced form, consisting of just an orientation, the core narrative, and the point (Harris 2001:60). These narrative fragments are necessary when the story of the trial is heard from multiple witnesses, perspectives, and competing points of view.

26.5.2.1 *Direct examination*

Testimony starts with the "moving" party: in a civil trial, it will be the plaintiff; in a criminal trial, it will be the prosecution. The plaintiff or the prosecution will present witnesses who will first undergo direct examination. There are two types of witnesses in many trials: ordinary witnesses and expert witnesses. The discourse rules for the testimony of each are slightly different. Ordinary witnesses are limited by and large to the evidentials of induction, seeing, smelling, tasting, hearing, and touching. Evidentials are a way of our signaling how we know and how sure we are of what we know. Witnesses may also use hedges, another evidential category that modifies certainty in a response, as in "it was sort of loud," with "sort of" qualifying "loud." Expert witnesses have a wider range of evidentials available to them on the topic of their expertise. Experts are allowed greater leeway to signal the degree of reliability, belief, deductions, and expectations, in contrast to the limits in the testimony of ordinary witnesses.

At the beginning of direct examination, a witness may be answering a somewhat open-ended question, allowing the witness to tell a short narrative that is constrained by how the attorney asks the question. These kinds of questions are often technically posed as yes/no, which typically require a "yes" or "no" answer, but in this context they are made in such a manner that they invite a more extended response, as in "Would you tell the jury what you saw when you opened the envelope?" The scope of the answer is limited to "what" the witness "saw when" the witness "opened the envelope." The "what" is narrowed to an evidential of sight, something to which an ordinary witness can testify.

In conventional thinking about trials, attorneys limit what witnesses can say through the type of question that is asked. Linguists have spent some time examining the forms of questions asked in trials. WH-questions (introduced by question words such as "who" or "what") are dominant in direct examination and witnesses give longer answers to them. In contrast, answers to SUBJ-AUX inversion questions ("was she driving?"), questions marked only by intonation ("she was driving?"), and tag questions ("she was driving, wasn't she?") tend to be considerably shorter (Stygall 1994:149). Tiersma observes that questions become increasingly narrow in direct examination, starting from questions that invite short narratives to much more constrained questions (Tiersma 1999:160–1). This process of narrowing puts the attorney in control of the narrative, sometimes to the frustration of the witness. Direct examination must be a phase of building that supports the party's case. Each witness called by the plaintiff or prosecutor gives a piece of the account, gradually building the party's case.

A number of attorney strategies and practices have been observed in direct examination. Strategic expansions of information in direct examination are often marked with lexicalized clauses. A lexicalization takes place when the phrase or clause is used so commonly that it becomes a unit. An example of this is the clause "when you say…" and the open slot may be filled with any number of details. The details could be about observed changes, location, pronouns, and time (Cotterill 2003). There is also the use of "repair" strategies, such as "Excuse me, I'm not sure that I understood…" aiming perhaps for the repetition of and emphasis on an important point. The use of the non-question—"would you share with us…?"—often invites a longer, more detailed, and possibly helpful response (Cotterill 2003: ch. 5). Other lexicalized phrases and clauses include *I'll hand you what has been marked as ____ Exhibit ____ and ask you to identify it*, or *Is that a fair and accurate representation of ____* and others like these that are required to introduce exhibits into the trial record. Jurors are not told that there are specialized ways of introducing trial exhibits and sometimes conclude that the attorney repeating these phrases is not competent (Stygall 1994).

Direct examination is a good deal more complicated than it first appears. Not only do the attorneys need to manage a story that is told through questions and answers and multiple witnesses, but they must also conduct formal legal activities such as entering exhibits into the trial record. Even if attorneys control the topics and form of the question, it is not necessarily the case that witnesses are simply pawns of attorney strategies. Witnesses may answer in unexpected ways, sometimes stubbornly avoid a preferred answer, and become quite forgetful.

26.5.2.2 *Cross-examination*

Cross-examination is usually what non-lawyers think of when they imagine a trial and courtroom. People imagine an attorney asking sharp questions, cutting off answers, trying to lead witnesses into saying something not intended, and giving long speeches about the evidence in the form of a question. It's great drama. As Cotterill notes, cross-examination takes clear precedence over direct examination in recent films (2003: 128–9).

The questioning type often associated with cross-examination is the leading question. Traditionally, there are no leading questions allowed in direct examination, with a handful of exceptions. Leading questions do not have one form and instead may appear as one of the following: a negative yes/no question ("she wasn't driving?"); a tag question ("she was driving, wasn't she?"); a question formed by making a statement with a rising intonation at the end ("she was home?"). Sometimes a witness is asked a question and, after answering, the attorney reads the witness's sworn testimony on the same topic from a deposition or a previous hearing. Thus, a leading question may be formed by asking the witness to explain any discrepancies between the two, even if they are quite minor (Tiersma 1999:166), and asking after that reading, for example, "you were wrong, weren't you?".

Attorneys may also ask multiple questions at the same time in cross-examination. Although these types of questions may be objectionable, attorneys don't always register an objection. An example of a question asked of a medical doctor might be "Did you see Mr Smith on October 1 and make an evaluation of whether these injuries had been treated in line with standards of practice for this injury?" Here the doctor has been asked both about a specific date when she saw Mr Smith and a much more complicated question about whether she had evaluated the injuries in a particular way. These multiple questions are often difficult to answer and the witness may need to answer at some length, providing opportunities for the attorney to pick up on inconsistencies. Witnesses may become quite cautious after leading or multiple questions and begin to self-monitor their answers, hedging or otherwise equivocating, possibly lowering their credibility with the jury.

An additional strategy used by attorneys in cross-examination is the turn-initial *so* question. In this question form, the attorney inserts the *so* at the beginning of the question, as in "So you don't have any specific information about the time the incident occurred?" Thus, with the *so* question, the attorney is able to emphasize the lack of information from the witness.

26.5.2.3 *Expert testimony*

Experts witnesses also use *so* in their testimony, typically making reference to a professional judgment by summarizing with *so*. As mentioned above, expert witnesses face slightly different evidentiary rules than the ordinary witness. They are in court to testify about their expertise and thus are allowed to draw conclusions from their professional judgment. Experts who are psychiatrists or psychologists are likely to have more opportunities to speak about someone's state of mind than the ordinary witness. Expert witnesses also have the opportunity to provide amplification in their testimony, especially during direct examination. They are in the process, when testifying, of "translating" a professional language into one that is accessible to the jury. Expert witnesses also politely disagree on both direct and cross, with the use of the discourse marker *well*, which can be used to signal doubt or disagreement. These polite disagreements typically occur when the attorney asking the question has misstated or misunderstood part of the testimony of the witness and the witness works to answer and to correct the question by starting with *well* (Stygall 2001).

Expert witnesses are also interrupted less often and their responses are much longer than ordinary witness responses, in both direct examination and cross-examination, by a factor of almost ten to one (Cotterill 2003:159). Expert witnesses are also given more leeway to interrupt the attorney questioning them. Experts have their credentials established in direct examination to a far greater extent than any lay witness. In order to use the testimony of experts effectively, attorneys must on the one hand learn at least some of the language and knowledge of the expert, while on the other hand ensuring that jurors will understand. An expert may be less effective when it appears to the jury that the attorney and the expert are having a conversation in the professional language of the expert without adequate explanation or definition for the jury.

26.6 CLOSING ARGUMENT

The closing argument is an opportunity for the attorneys to engage in persuasion. It is also the time when recency becomes important. These arguments are the last speech heard by the jury before deliberation. It can be such a powerful moment that some defense attorneys contend that the prosecutor should not get the last word (Mitchell 2000). It is the time when attorneys may use full narrative sequences and make the narrative more immediate by using the historical present tense. In the alternative analysis of trials as themes or metaphors, the closing argument is the time when a theme or metaphor can be thoroughly developed and expanded.

Some additional linguistic strategies used by attorneys in final argument include reformulating ideas relevant to the case through the use of synonyms and antonyms, using active or passive voice depending upon the desired position for the actors in the case, the use of specific pronouns to be inclusive or exclusive, and a number of rapport building approaches (Tiersma 1999). Closing argument may include references to the jury's final instructions, with each attorney presenting those instructions most important to each side and suggesting that, if jurors apply those instructions to the narrative the lawyer has built, the verdict should be in his or her side's favor.

26.7 CONCLUSION

It is said that the vast majority of the world's jury trials take place in the United States. Those jury trials are a fundamental part of a system of law and the popular understanding of law. We could certainly do more to prepare both jurors and citizens for the discourse differences that a trial presents to ordinary citizens. We could also certainly do more to make it clear to the legal community that "their" discourse is very different from ordinary language and that some effort to address those differences should be made.

CHAPTER 27

....

COURTROOM DISCOURSE IN JAPAN'S NEW JUDICIAL ORDER

....

MAMI HIRAIKE OKAWARA

27.1 INTRODUCTION

THE implementation of the *saiban-in* (lay judge) system in 2009 has opened the way, not only to lay participation but also to some participation by linguists in Japanese courts. In this chapter I will show how differences between lay and professional views are mingled in the deliberations. I will first explain the *saiban-in* (lay judge) system. Next, I will briefly introduce some studies of court proceedings in Japan. Then, I will discuss how the intent to murder is determined in Japanese courts. Finally, I will focus on a discourse connective and analyze the discussion on the degrees of murder during the deliberation stage in a mock trial. As we will see, lay people do not understand an important legal concept—*mihitsu no koi*—which means "willful negligence." Furthermore, in determining a defendant's state of mind, lay people tend to look for motives, while the legal system asks them to examine circumstantial evidence instead. The result is a complicated negotiation between the professional and lay judges in which the professional judges play more of a role of educator than of an equal colleague.

27.2 THE *SAIBAN-IN* (LAY JUDGE) SYSTEM

The *saiban-in* system is not the first lay judge system in Japan. Japan previously had a jury system, which was introduced in 1928 and suspended in 1943. The current lay judge system was proposed as a pillar of judicial system reform in 2001. The *saiban-in* system is expected to make court procedures more efficient and comprehensible through public participation.

The *saiban-in* system is a middle-of-the-road system between a common law jury system and the Roman law lay judge system. Like the common law juries, Japanese lay judges serve a term of only one case. However, unlike the jury system of common law countries, Japanese lay judges deliberate together with professional judges. If they reach a guilty verdict, they then decide on what kind of penalties, fines, or prison terms they need to impose. Not all cases are heard using the lay judge system. Only criminal cases involving serious offenses are subject to the new system, and in those cases it is mandatory. *Saiban-in*s serve in trials in the first level district courts. Not only defendants but also prosecutors can appeal the decisions of lay judge trials to higher courts.

*Saiban-in*s are chosen randomly by computer from the electoral roll. However, not all voters are qualified to serve as *saiban-in*; those who have not finished compulsory education and those who have been imprisoned are disqualified from serving, along with various people employed in the legal system or in government. Finally, people over 70 years old or students have the right to be excused from the duty.

The deliberation body consists of three professional judges and six lay judges. Trials are open to the public, but deliberations are held behind closed doors. Lay and court judges are not allowed to discuss their deliberations in public.

To prepare for the new system, district courts, together with district public prosecutors' offices and local bar associations, have held about ten mock trials in each prefecture throughout Japan using the same mock case scenarios. The total number of mock trials held nationwide has surpassed 500.

In each of these mock trials three court judges in their own district court played the role of professional judges. Attorneys of the district public prosecutors office took on the role of prosecutors. Lawyers of the prefectural bar association performed the role of defense attorneys. Court staff members acted as defendants and witnesses. The *saiban-in*s were recruited from ordinary citizens through connections within the legal profession in the area. In these mock trials the argumentation was very heated.

Although real trials are open to the public, the mock trials are held *in camera* to avoid criticism about poor performance from those strongly opposed to the implementation of the lay judge system. Academic access to the courtroom discourse of mock trials is limited to a few researchers.

27.3 STUDIES OF COURTROOMS IN JAPAN

Studies of Japanese courtrooms have traditionally been conducted by legal experts, but in recent years other professionals have become involved. As the legal profession has been preparing for the introduction of the *saiban-in* system since 2005, there has been a growing interest in making courtroom language plainer for lay judges, and in analyzing the discourse of deliberations in mock trials to assist judges, prosecutors, and lawyers.

Thus, for the first time in Japan, linguists have begun to make contributions to studies of courtrooms.

27.3.1 Courtroom language

There have been several efforts to promote the use of plain courtroom language. Public prosecutors published a guidebook (Maeda 2006). A project on Plain Courtroom Language in the Preparation for the Mixed Court system was launched in *Nihon Bengoshi Rengoukai* (the Japan Federation of Bar Associations) resulting in the publication of two guidebooks (Nihon Bengoshi Rengoukai 2008a,b). It is noteworthy that the project includes not only legal experts but also non-jurists such as a socio-psychologist, linguists, and journalists. An introductory book on legal language from the perspective of lay persons has also been published (Okawara 2009b). In addition, some work has been done on persuasive language in the courtroom (Okawara 2008b, 2009a,b).

27.3.2 Courtroom discourse

While the controversy surrounding these mock trials has limited academic access to a few researchers, some studies have been conducted to develop guidelines for judges, to examine interpreting concerns, and to do quantitative and qualitative studies of deliberations and courtroom documents.

Hotta and Fujita conducted a quantitative study of the deliberations of mock trials held nationwide (Hotta 2009). They carried out contrastive quantitative analyses of utterances by trial and lay judges in 13 mock trials. They found that chief judges produced the highest number of utterances, in contrast with those of associate judges and lay judges. Using a communication network model, Hotta and Fujita emphasized the importance of verbal exchange among lay judges, rather than the classroom-style exchange of communication from a chief judge to a lay judge.

Hotta and Fujita also found that professional judges argue using evidence more frequently (52 percent) than lay judges (25.1 percent). In contrast, the use of one's imagination based on evidence was the preferred form of argumentation by the lay judges (53.2 percent), with a lower percentage for professional judges (32.8 percent). For both groups the use of one's own experience was the least frequent form of argumentation.

Hotta, Hashiguchi, and Fujita (2008) found that professional judges frequently used legalese, while lay judges used expressions with onomatopoeic words (e.g. "and he shot her, bang!") and ambiguous statements. Hotta and Shudo (2009) discuss the influence of trial judges' use of speech acts on lay judges.

Okawara (2007) conducted a contrastive discourse analysis of an indictment used at the Judicial Research and Training Institute, and of an indictment appearing in a novel. The study focused on comprehensibility. Using a television script from a *saiban-in* trial, Okawara (2006a,b,c) discussed the characteristic features of the deliberations. In the

Okawara study all data were edited. In contrast, in this chapter I will analyze non-edited data from a mock murder trial. Before presenting the analysis, I will explain the issue of "murderous intent," which is a critical concept in the deliberations.

27.4 INTENT TO MURDER

27.4.1 Homicide

In Japan there are several types of homicide, stipulated in the Penal Code of Japan of 2008 (EHS Law Bulletin Series) as follows:[1]

- *Intent.* Article 38: An act without intention of committing a crime shall not be punished. Provided that, this shall not apply when otherwise specified by law.
- *Homicide.* Article 199: A person who kills another shall be punished with death or penal servitude for life or not less than five years.
- *Manslaughter caused by negligence.* Article 210: A person who causes the death of another by negligence shall be punished with a fine of not more than five hundred thousand yen.

Homicide is therefore classified into two main categories: "intent" (*koi*) and "negligence" (*kashitsu*). "Intent" (*koi*)[2] is further divided into two types: "definite intent to murder" (*kakutei-teki koi*) and "murder through willful negligence" (*mihitsu no koi*). "Negligence" (*kashitsu*) is then subdivided into two types: "recklessness" (*ninshiki aru kashitu*) and "inadvertent negligence" (*ninshiki naki kashitsu*). Legal experts use these four notions when they judge a homicide case.

The notions of "definite intent to murder" and "inadvertent negligence" are easily understood. However, lay persons seem to find it difficult to make the distinction between "murder through willful negligence" and "recklessness," though this distinction is the boundary between "murder" and "manslaughter." The distinction between "definite intent to murder" and "murder through willful negligence" is also difficult to determine. This is because lay persons may lack the notion of "murder through willful negligence," which depends on whether or not a defendant knew the consequences that would probably result from his actions. Ramseyer and Nakazato (1998:153) succinctly explain that to be liable for murder, one need not intend to kill the victim; instead, one need only intend to kill *someone*. If so, he can be convicted of murder.

---

[1] "Death or bodily injury, etc. caused by negligence in conduct of business" is also stipulated in Article 211 in the Penal Code. As the Article 211 is not relevant to the discussion of this paper, Article 211 is not included in this section.

[2] "Intent" *(koi)* includes "intent to injure" as well as "intent to kill." However, in the context of homicide, "intent" is conventionally used as "intent to murder."

It is not sufficient to rely on accessing a defendant's mind through his confession or statement in court (Ono 1992:1). Legal experts, therefore, have worked out a conventional way of judging "intent to murder" from the external facts of a homicide rather than the internal feelings of a defendant. More concretely, they use circumstantial evidence: the region of an injury, the degree of an injury, the type of weapon, how a weapon was used (e.g. randomly stabbing or making a lunge), an action after a criminal act, and motive. The first four types of evidence relating to injury or weapon are considered to be the most important. Ono (1992:2) emphasized the importance of circumstantial evidence, in particular with respect to "murder through willful negligence" (*mihitsu no koi*).

27.4.2 "Murder through willful negligence" (*mihitsu no koi*)

The term *mihitsu no koi* is a legal phrase coined in the Meiji era (1862–1912), when new western legal concepts were introduced. *Mihitsu* means "not necessarily," but is not used in Japan except in this legal sense (Okawara 2009a:28). "*Koi*" (intent), however, is used in ordinary Japanese, though the legal usage of "*koi*" includes a more precise definition. Attaching an unknown term "*mihitsu*" to "*koi*" has created a new term, "*mihitsu no koi*", totally unintelligible to ordinary citizens.

At a lecture on the *saiban-in* system offered at Masoho Culture College for citizens on 27 February 2005, I asked 30 participants to write down legal terms which I dictated (Okawara 2008a:27–30). "*Mihitsu no koi*" was one of the legal transcription test words. None of the participants gave a correct transcription; rather, there were several curious answers such as "*misshitsu no koi*" (romance in a locked room) or "*misshitsu no kooi*" (conduct in a locked room). As the participants had never heard the term "*mihitsu*," they thought my pronunciation was wrong and wrote down a different word with a similar sound "*misshitsu*" (locked room). Needless to say, the legal concept of "*mihitsu no koi*" is quite alien to lay persons.

27.4.3 Differences in reasoning: legal experts and lay persons on "intent to murder"

A questionnaire survey from October 2006 to February 2007 was conducted to determine if there are differences in the understanding of "intent to murder" between lay persons and experts (Okawara 2008a). The legal expert respondents were 73 attorneys of the Gunma Bar Association. The lay persons consisted of 159 respondents between the ages of 16 and 78 (75 males and 84 females) in Central Nagano Prefecture.

The question was whether a respondent could understand "intent to murder" based on a murder mock trial case in a television program (NHK Special "Can you pass on a judgment?"), broadcast on February 13, 2005.

In both groups 45 percent rendered a judgment of "no intent to murder" (33 attorneys and 71 lay persons). However, 80 lay persons (50 percent) gave the judgment of "intent to

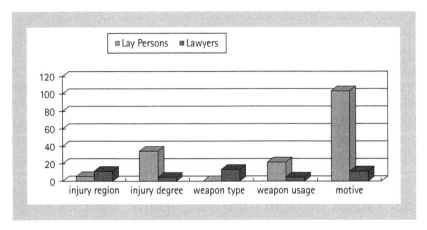

FIGURE 27.1 Reasons for finding intent to murder

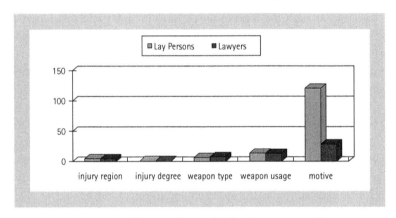

FIGURE 27.2 Reasons for not finding intent to murder

murder," whereas only 21 lawyers (29 percent) gave that judgment. The other 19 lawyers (26 percent) stated they could not answer due to limited information about the case.

The questionnaire also asked respondents to write the reason for their judgment. I classified their answers into five categories: the region of an injury; the degrees of injury; type of weapon; how a weapon was used; and motive. As multiple answers were accepted, the numbers given are of responses, not the number of respondents. Figure 27.1 shows the reasons for judging "'intent to murder," while Figure 27.2 shows the reasons for not judging "intent to murder."

In the answers of the lay persons, "motive" (103) was the highest, then came "the degree of injury" (34) and "usage of a weapon (how a weapon was used)" (21). For "motive," lay persons gave these reasons: "the defendant was carrying a knife before his visit to the victim" (72); "the defendant visited the victim late at night" (11); and "the defendant visited the victim while intoxicated." Among the lawyers, the reasons for determining "intent" varied more widely: "type of weapon" (13), "region of an injury" (11), "motive" (11), "the degree of injury" (4), "usage of a weapon (how a weapon was used)" (4). "Motive" is the predominant reason for determining "intent" by lay persons; however, attorneys also tend to use other circumstantial evidence.

In the case of judging "no intent," the survey results are similar to those for finding "intent" to murder. Lay persons judged almost solely on "motives" (120), while lawyers used "motives" (28) as well as "weapon." In conclusion, for lay persons "motive" is the most important source for reasoning, while "motive" is only one of the reasons for lawyers.

With these two different perceptions in mind, in the next section I will discuss the verbal exchanges between lay and professional judges when deliberating on a charge of "murder through willful negligence."

27.5 COMING TO AGREEMENT IN A MOCK SAIBAN-IN TRIAL

27.5.1 The Mistress Case

The Mistress Case is one of the mock trial cases held in all district courts in Japan. The defendant (Junko Yamamoto) met the victim (Goro Ikeda) at a bar where Junko was working as a barmaid. Later, she became his lover and was financially supported by Goro. Goro was a violent man with a criminal record. On the day of the crime, the two had a quarrel over their relationship. Goro was beating her violently. Junko then stabbed him in the right side of his back with a kitchen knife (the 1st stab), upon which he pulled the knife out of his back and continued to beat her. Junko grabbed the knife from Goro and in the same motion she stabbed Goro in the abdomen (the 2nd stab). Goro died.

27.5.2 Mock trial

I observed a Mistress Case held at a district court for three consecutive days in late October 2007.[3] The case highlighted two issues: intent to murder and self-defense. The prosecution demanded 16 years' imprisonment for the accused. The court imposed a six-year sentence. The court acknowledged excessive self-defense, "murder through willful negligence" for the 1st stab, and "definite intent to murder" for the 2nd stab.

---

[3] Due to limited space in this chapter, the transcription provided here is only the English translation.

27.5.3 Deliberations

In this analysis of the deliberations, I will focus on two questions:

(1) What kind of "words" did professional judges try to draw out of lay judges?

(2) How did lay judges try to respond to professional judges?

An important aspect of the analysis is the discourse connective *tada* ("except that…", "the only thing is that…").

27.5.3.1 *Discourse connective* tada

Japanese *tada* ("except that…", "the only thing is that…") is a discourse connective which adds an exceptional or supplementary clause to the previous clause (Morita 1980:265), as shown in the following:

27.1   (a) Aji   wa   ii   ga,
            taste   topic marker   good   but

       (b) tada   shoushou   ne   ga   haru.
            the only thing   a bit   price   subject marker   cost
            "The taste is good. The only thing is, it's a bit expensive."

The use of *tada* marks a proposition in which the speaker believes that proposition (27.1a) requires a supplementary explanation or an explanatory note. After *tada*, the speaker gives a proposition (27.1b) as a form of supplementary comment.

Kawagoe (2003) notes that *tada* is used as a communicative strategy to be considerate of the hearer, referring to Brown and Levinson's (1978a) discussion of politeness strategies to save the hearer's "face." The use of *tada* indicates the speaker is not imposing on the hearer, allowing the hearer to save face. Kawagoe (2003:86) suggests that *tada* is used when the hearer partially opposes the speaker's statement in a polite and mitigated way. While use of "*tada*" indicates the speaker agrees with the other's utterance partially, it also points out a problem or a difference.

In the deliberations in the mock trials, professional judges frequently used *tada* when they were trying to convince lay judges of *mihitsu no koi*. As mentioned earlier, the notion of "murder through willful negligence" is barely comprehensible to the minds of ordinary people because lay persons lack the concept of "knowing the consequences that would probably result from the actions one took." Therefore, lay judges did not mention the notion of "murder through willful negligence" when professional judges expected to hear it. In such cases, a judge would first paraphrase a lay judge's opinion ("no intent to murder") as proposition (27.1a), then the judge's opinion ("murder through willful negligence") would be expressed after *tada* as proposition (27.1b).

The important point is that the lay judge's proposition (27.1a) ("no intent to murder") is contrary to the trial judge's proposition (27.1b) ("murder through willful negligence").

Unlike the use of *tada* in ordinary Japanese, as discussed above, trial judges are not opposing proposition (27.1a) *partially*; they are presenting a completely different proposition (27.1b). Thus, professional judges use *tada* as a means of opposing a lay judge's opinion.

27.5.3.2 *Deliberations on the first stab*

The following discourse is a 30 minute segment of the deliberations in the morning of the third day. The issue is to decide whether the defendant's first stab constituted *mihitus no koi* ("murder through willful negligence"). The six *saiban-in*s are Mrs A (a housewife in her 60s), Mr B (a professor in his 50s), Mr C (a government employee in his 40s), Mrs D (a housewife in her 50s), Mr E (an administrative scrivener in his 60s), and Mr F (a college student in his 20s). Trial judges consist of a Chief Judge (a male in his 50s), a senior associate judge (a male in his 40s), and a junior associate judge (a male in his 30s).

(27.3)   Chief Judge: ... When the defendant made the first stab, as I explained many times, can you say that she was aware of the fact that because of her action the victim would die or might die? I would like to focus on the defendant's mind. What about this, Mrs A?

(27.4)   Mrs A: I don't know what to say.

(27.5)   Chief Judge: As I mentioned a little while ago, we cannot read people's hearts. It is impossible to grasp correctly what the other person is thinking. So, as I said a little while ago, we infer from the external circumstances.

(27.6)   Mrs A: The external circumstances mean the violence the defendant received or the injury she got?

(27.7)   Chief Judge: In other words, it is something like this, the defendant is aware that the victim would be killed or might be killed by her stab, something like that.

(27.8)   Mrs A: I don't think she was thinking at that level, "will die" or "may die."

(27.9)   Chief Judge: You are thinking she did not recognize "will die" or "may die," aren't you?

(27.10) Mrs A: yes.

The Chief Judge tried to determine Mrs A's opinion on the definite intent or willful negligence based on circumstantial evidence in (27.3). Mrs A could not answer in (27.4) because she was still unfamiliar with the distinction of the intent. Then, the Chief Judge suggested external evidence would give some clues in (27.5). In (27.6), Mrs A was confused about the external evidence and mistook the injury of the victim for that of the defendant. The Chief Judge returned her to the issue of the defendant's intent in (27.7), but Mrs A flatly rejected the notion of intent to murder in (27.8). In (27.9) the Chief Judge repeated Mrs A's response; the use of a tag question implies his doubt about her response, but she did not change her answer in (27.10). The Chief Judge gave up, and then moved to another lay judge, Mr B.

(27.11) Chief Judge: Mr B, what do you think of this?

(27.12) Mr B: The defendant has been beaten for a while. So, there must be some kind of lesson or punishment, in addition to counterattack. I'm thinking she wanted to show she was taking some revenge on him.

(27.13) Chief Judge: Well, you are thinking she had the will to protect herself, and moreover she had the intent to counterattack. The only thing is that (*tada*) the content of her intent to counterattack. Had she gone as far as thinking of murdering him?

(27.14) Mr B: I don't think she was thinking to that extent.

(27.15) Chief Judge: The only thing is that (*tada*), otherwise, how do you answer if you were asked whether she must have recognized he would die or might die?

(27.16) Mr B: Well, I also might do, just threatening someone, just showing a knife, that's all. I don't have any intention to kill…

(27.17) Chief Judge: No intention to kill means the strong intent to kill?

(27.18) Mr B: Not at all.

(27.19) Chief Judge: Well, not that level. Well, how about her recognition of "will die" or "might die"?

(27.20) Mr B: I don't think she had that sort of recognition. That must be a lesson, pressing down the other party's violence. The term "pressing down" might not be the right word, but counterattacking and teaching a lesson, something like that.

Mr B repeated his opinion that the defendant was teaching the victim a lesson in (27.12), (27.16), and (27.20); on the other hand, the Chief Judge also repeated two types of intent to kill, using the term "tada" in (27.13) and (27.15). Both were talking along parallel lines. The Chief Judge then asked the opinion of the senior associate judge, who indicated he believed the first stabbing was done with "'willful negligence." The Chief Judge then asked another lay judge the same question in confirmation.

(27.27) Chief Judge: Mr C, what do you think of this?

(27.28) Mr C: I think at her first stab she [the defendant] had not realized anything about the possibility that he [the victim] might die. Rather, her feelings were mostly occupied with her desire to stop the violence from the victim, I think.

(27.29) Chief Judge: Well, that was an immediate attack. So, you are thinking that was a counterattack. As I said just a little, for example, about a situation of stabbing someone in a frenzy of the moment, it is true that in such a moment one cannot grasp what he is thinking.

(27.30) (Chief Judge, cont.) The only thing is that (*tada*), even in such a case, if we follow the way courts think, from the act which appeared externally, for example, random stabbing.

(27.31) (Chief Judge) Yeah, in a frenzy of the moment, feeling a rush of blood to the head, yelling noisily, in such a case the feelings such as "will kill" or "may die" would disappear somewhere in the midst of a frenzy

(27.32) (Chief Judge) The only thing is that (*tada*), even in such a case, in a case of random stabbing, when we try to view the inside of the heart of the accused, we have so far conjectured "may die" from external evidence.

(27.33) (Chief Judge) So, I *personally* don't think an immediate act does not include "may die".

(27.34) (Chief Judge) The only thing is that (*tada*), in a chain of events, because of the immediate act the defendant was simply thinking of an immediate counteract, or, as Mr B mentioned, she might be thinking of threatening him. I don't think it isn't impossible to think that way, though.

(27.35) (Chief Judge) The only thing is that (*tada*), as Senior Judge mentioned, the position of the stab, how she stabbed him, that was not a straight way, she did this, she did that, those kinds of things…

Mr C could not recognize any specific kinds of "intent" in (27.28) in spite of repeated explanations from the judges. In (27.29) the Chief Judge repeated and paraphrased the lay person's views of "no intent." However, in (27.30) the Chief Judge started to talk about the court's conventional way of recognizing "intent" by the use of *tada*. But, he changed his approach in (27.31), probably because he was trying to be careful not to persuade lay judges to his way of thinking. In (27.32) by the use of *tada* he returned and reiterated the court's way, using "we," which does not include lay persons. In (27.33) he mentioned his personal view in line with the court view, in a mitigated way by using double negatives. In (27.34) by the use of *tada* he repeated the lay view citing a previous comment of Mr B, again using double negatives. But, in (27.35), he once more started with *tada*, and he presented the traditional court view, citing the comment of the Senior Judge. The Chief Judge was careful not to give plain and straightforward conclusions, but with repetition he was hoping that the lay judge would understand the court's way of inferring a defendant's state of mind from the circumstances. As he realized that was not an easy task, he changed his approach and continued with a less controversial question.

(27.36) Chief Judge: Let me see, the defendant said she had not recognized where she was stabbing…that it was his back. What do you think of her utterance?

(27.37) Mrs D: I cannot believe her.

(27.38) Chief Judge: It is only natural that you cannot believe her.

(27.39) Mrs D: Since part of his shirt was ripped in the back, she probably thought that was good timing.

(27.40) Senior Judge: I remember her saying that.

(27.41) Chief Judge: Whether she really thought that or not is disputable, though. It is only natural you don't believe her utterance. We would like to see her heart to determine the credibility of her utterance. What do you think of this, Mr E?

The Chief Judge was successful in starting with an undisputable question and has confirmed common ground with one lay judge. He then returned to the intent issue, calling on another judge, Mr E.

(27.42) Mr E: Well, she perceived neither "will kill" nor "may die" at this point.

(27.43) Chief Judge: You are saying she did not have that kind of perception. How about Mrs D?

Contrary to the expectation of the Chief Judge, Mr E did not recognize any "intent," either. He returned to Mrs D, hoping to extract "intent" from her answer.

(27.44) Mrs D: I don't think she had the intent to kill. She was just in despair. Both were quarreling over a divorce. She was almost in despair. She might not be thinking that he would die. She might be thinking that if his violence would continue, she would end the relationship. If you take up a kitchen knife in the quarrel, you won't get away with it. So, as the defendant said, she just wanted to end his violence. So, her intent is to stop the violence.

(27.45) Chief Judge: Mr B said she had the intent of a counterattack and the intent to threaten him. And Mrs D said she had the intent to end the relationship because by taking up a knife, they cannot continue the relationship any more.

(27.46) (Chief Judge) This means, it may be too harsh, but she had *the intent of that kind*.

(27.47) (Chief Judge) The only thing is that (*tada*), it does not mean the intent of death, that's how you are thinking.

(27.48) Mrs D: The only thing is that (*tada*), *she was aware that he would be badly wounded*.

(27.49) Chief Judge: She had *the intent of that level*, all right. Mr F, what do you think of this?

In (27.45) the Chief Judge repeated the opinions of Mr B and Mrs D. After that, the judge introduced the intent of "injury," rather than the intent of "death." As Mrs D thought the intent of "injury" was related to the defendant's desire to stop the violence or to end the relationship, she recognized the defendant's intent to injure. Mrs D's comment (27.48) is certainly a turning point on the intent issue in the deliberations. It is interesting to note that Mrs D also used *tada* when she met the Chief Judge halfway. The Chief Judge then tried to obtain an opinion on "the intent" from another lay judge.

(27.50) Mr F: Regarding the opinion on the intent to end the relationship, I don't agree with it. That was a simple, as Mr B mentioned, an immediate action. But it is something caused by a reflex action.

(27.51) Chief Judge: A reflex action means a counterattack?

(27.52) Mr. F: That's right. Something caused by a reflex action, counterattack, self-defense. But, by looking at her action of stabbing him with a kitchen knife, I have a feeling that she must have some kind of "intent."

The intent to cause injury was again confirmed in (27.52). After a few exchanges between Mr F and the Chief Judge, omitted due to space limitations, the Chief Judge talked about "intent" again in (27.53).

(27.53) Chief Judge: The only thing is that (*tada*), I asked Mrs D's opinion about this, but you are thinking she did not have the intent of death, are you?…not the level of his death?

(27.54) Mr F: If she had had that intent, she would have stabbed him in a different place. It was just like random stabbing.

(27.55) Chief Judge: The only thing is that (*tada*), you are talking about a more definite intent to kill. Not that level of the intent, something like a feeling that he may die if she does such…how about this intent?

(27.56) Mr F: Well, I do not think she had the presence of mind, after all.

(27.57) Chief Judge: From the circumstance, you think that way?

(27.58) Mr F: Yes.

(27.59) Chief Judge: Junior Judge, Junior Judge…

The Chief Judge tried to extract a perception "willful negligence" based on the intent to injure, but it ended unsuccessfully. He asked the Junior Judge for help. After a seven minute long explanation by the trial judges, the lay judges began to understand the notion of "willful negligence."

(27.60) Mr B: Well, that's a gap between professional judges and ordinary citizens. Your way of asking is whether the defendant had a will to kill or not.

(27.61) Chief Judge: Not a will to kill, but the intent to kill. Because I feel that a will to kill means a definite intent to kill, it is the intent to kill.

(27.62) Mr B: Well, you are asking whether she had the intent to kill, but the intent to kill includes what Senior Judge stated, but we are simply looking at only how she was feeling.

Mr B is getting the point of "willful negligence" in (27.60). The Chief Judge gave a more precise definition of the intent. In (27.62) Mr B clarified the different approaches of the lay and professional judges. After some supplementary explanation from the Chief Judge, Mrs D also recognized the defendant's intent to kill. Her reasoning was that a gambler-mistress of an ex-convict is so different from herself that Mrs D could assume that that kind of woman could have had an intent which ordinary people would not have. After that, Mr B expressed his opinion in (27.63).

(27.63) Mr B: If I can round off the discussion, my personal view is my perception of her heart and in such a narrow sense she did not have the intent to murder. But in a more broad sense including legal interpretation, I think I can perceive the intent to murder.

This is how "willful negligence" regarding the first stab finally came to be shared with professional and lay judges.

Now let me return to the two questions posed at the beginning of this section. The answer to the first question is that professional judges wanted to extract the words, "the intent that the victim might die" from the lay judges. Because the lay judges lacked the notion of "willful negligence," they could not differentiate between "definite intent" and "willful negligence." As they could not perceive the definite intent in the first stab, they could not see any other kinds of "intent." Therefore, they replied "no intent." The Chief Judge reiterated the lay responses of "no intent" and then carefully provided the conventional notion of "intent that he might die," using *tada*. As mentioned before, *tada* is used when one adds supplementary information or partially opposes what the other has said. Although the Chief Judge was completely opposing what the lay judges said, he presented his opinion as if he were only partially opposing the lay judges' perception. His use of the communicative strategy was so successful that the lay judges began to differentiate between their notion of "intent" and the legal notion of "intent." They ultimately agreed to use the legal notion in the deliberations.

27.6 CONCLUSION

Because heinous criminal cases are deliberated under the *saiban-in* system, lay judges are often involved in hearing murder cases. When a defendant admits to "intent to murder" (definite intent), the deliberation is on the assessment of culpability. However, when the defendant claims "no intent" (negligence) to a murder charge, lay and professional judges need to decide whether the defendant had the required intent at the time of enacting the crime or not. The courts' conventional way of judging intent is based on external circumstances; in contrast, it appears that lay persons may focus more on the defendant's motives to understand the story of the crime. Thus, as lay persons lack the notion of "willful negligence," opinions of the panel of judges very well might be divided.

As Japanese courts begin to incorporate lay judges, professional judges will have to learn how to educate lay judges regarding important legal distinctions, without placing too much pressure on them to simply agree with the professionals. Lay judges will also have to learn how to express their opinions and participate in a meaningful way.[4]

[4] I would like to mention with gratitude that this research was supported by Takasaki City University Grant Program. I also would like to thank Margaret van Naerssen for her comments and suggestions.

CHAPTER 28

COURTROOM DISCOURSE IN CHINA

MEIZHEN LIAO

28.1 INTRODUCTION

IN this chapter, I will approach Chinese courtroom discourse in terms of its three components: the contextual, the interactional, and the propositional, so as to present a relatively comprehensive picture. In the contextual component, I will give a brief introduction to the Chinese legal culture and system as a background against which readers, especially those of the West who do not share this background, can come to understand courtroom discourse in China. In regard to the interactional component, I will focus on courtroom questioning and interaction patterns. As for the propositional component, I will analyze a courtroom judgment. The transcription of one typical criminal trial was used as the data for the analysis of the interactional component. The trial involved a charge of destruction of private property. The defendant, a farmer in one of the districts of Beijing, was accused of blowing up the new car of his business partner out of revenge for the partner's not sharing the contracted dues to the production brigade. The trial took place in a lower court in Beijing. The data for the analysis of the propositional component is a judgment from a lower court in Shanghai. Before we come to the discussion proper, a caveat is in order. Courtroom discourse in this chapter means criminal courtroom discourse, rather than courtroom discourse in general, as it is impossible to give an adequate treatment of the latter within the space available.

28.2 CHINESE LEGAL CULTURE AND SYSTEM

28.2.1 *Fa* (法) versus *li* (礼)

Fa and *Li* are two core concepts in traditional Chinese legal culture. They represent a conceptual dichotomy which is traditional in China. They also represent the debate between the doctrines of the Legalists and Confucianism. The standard word for law in classical Chinese was "*fa*" (灋). The Chinese character for "*fa*" denotes a meaning of "fair," "straight," and "just," derived from its water radical (the left componential part of the character) (*Shuo Wen Jie Zi*[1]). The ancient Chinese people discovered that water is always straight or flat wherever you put it and accordingly they thought that law should be as just and straight as water (Wang Guiyuan 2008:49). According to Yan Fu (严复) (1981), a famous Chinese scholar in the Qing Dynasty, the Chinese "*fa*" and Western *law* are not the same thing: The word "law" in Western languages has four different interpretations in Chinese: "*li*" (理: "order"), "*li*" (礼: "rites," "rules of propriety"), "*fa*" (法: "human made laws"), and "*zhi*" (制: "control"). Only *fa* corresponds to English *law*.

A term which predated "*fa*" was "*xing*" (刑), which originally referred to decapitation. '*Xing*' later evolved to be a general term for laws that related to criminal punishment (Guo Chengwei 2001:46), which, according to the early history *Shangshu* ("尚书"), was embodied in the 'five penalties'—tattooing, disfigurement, castration, mutilation, and death. Once written law came into existence, the meaning of "*xing*" was extended to include not only punishments but also any state prohibitions whose violation would result in punishment.

Different from "*fa*" or "*xing*", "*li*" consisted of rules of propriety (Xia Zhengnong 1989) or a set of generally accepted social values or norms of behavior. Early in the latter part of the primitive society of China, when Yao, Shun, and Yu, the three legendary sage kings, ruled, both punishment and inculcation of rules of propriety were employed in the government of the people. What is more, unlike many other major civilizations where written law was held in honor and often attributed to divine origin, the law in China was viewed in purely secular terms and its initial appearance was greeted by many with hostility as indicative of a serious moral decline, a violation of human morality, and even a disturbance of the total cosmic order. Ordinary people's awareness and acceptance of ethical norms was shaped far more by the pervasive influence of custom and usage and by inculcation of moral precepts than by any formally enacted system of law.

28.2.2 The Confucian school and the Legalist school

The Chinese legal tradition also developed from Confucianism and Legalism, two rival schools of thought during the Spring and Autumn Warring States periods (770–476 BC). Confucianism held that human behavior was subject to formation and reformation through the educational process. It advocated rule by moral persuasion in accordance with the concept of "*li*" (禮: "propriety"). For Confucians, "*li*" was rooted in innate human feelings, those which people in general would instinctively feel to be right. *The Book of Rites*[2] ("礼记") describes "*li*" as "forbidding trespasses before they are commit-

---

[1] *Shuo Wen Jie Zi* is a dictionary of ancient Chinese characters.
[2] *The Book of Rites* (礼记), a Confucian classic recording rules of propriety before the Qin and Han Dynasties.

ted, whereas '*fa*' punishes criminal acts after their commission." Thus, "*fa*" could supplement "*li*" by providing people with appropriate models via a mixture of rewards and penalties.

While the Confucian school relied on "*li*" to maintain the social order, Legalists invoked "*fa*" (law) for the same end and employed punishment as the enforcing agent. "*Fa*", as used by the Legalists, referred to several ways in which state power could be organized and exercised: through laws and punishments, administrative and military systems, policy planning, statecraft, or methods of personnel management. Legalists rejected traditional ethical values and chose to emphasize government by law. They conceived of a totalitarian political order in which the state would be ordered by a set of laws administered with complete regularity and impartiality. The state of Qin utilized Legalist policies, famously implemented by Shang Yang, to unify China under the Qin dynasty.[3]

28.2.3 The modern Chinese legal system

China's legal system blends a variety of legal traditions: Roman law, particularly the version transmitted through Germany to Japan; traditional law, notably the legal system developed in China over the millennia; the communist legal tradition, especially the Soviet-influenced system of socialist law; and more recently (notably in contract law) common law.

Two important features of the Chinese legal system are its socialist characteristics and its particular emphasis on the educational function of the law. For example, the *Criminal Procedure Law of the People's Republic of China* (Article 1) prescribes that "Pursuant to the Constitution and for the purposes of guaranteeing the correct operation of the Criminal Law, punishing crime, protecting the public, safeguarding the security of the State and the public safety of society, and *ensuring the socialist order*, this law is enacted."[4] Article 2 says that

> The tasks of the *Criminal Procedure Law of the People's Republic of China* shall be: to ensure accurate and prompt ascertainment of the facts of crimes, to correctly apply laws, to punish criminal offenders, to guarantee any innocent person from criminal prosecution, *to educate citizens to voluntarily observe the law and actively struggle against criminal acts*, so as to uphold the socialist legal system, to protect the citizens' rights of person, rights over their property, democratic rights and other rights, and to guarantee the smooth progress of *the socialist modernization*.[5]

The Supreme Court of China has a tradition of emphasizing the three functions of a trial: (1) exposing crime and punishing those who commit crimes; (2) educating both

---

[3] <http://en.wikipedia.org/wiki/Laozi> accessed September 23, 2011.
[4] *The Criminal Procedure Law of the People's Republic of China*, revised on March 17, 1996 and put in force January 1, 1977 (italics mine).
[5] Ibid.

the defendant and the general public; (3) publicizing of the law.[6] Leaders of the Chinese Communist Party and the Chinese government such as Mao Zedong, Deng Xiaoping, Jiang Zeming, and Hu Jintao have emphasized the use of two hands in running the country, that is, the rule of law and rule by moral virtues.

28.2.4 Judicial proceedings

Let us introduce some of the key points about judicial proceedings. First, under Article 13 of the *Criminal Procedure Law*, China has adopted the system of people's assessors instead of the jury system. People's assessors, either selected or appointed, sit together with the judge, may ask questions, and participate in deliberation. There is usually one people's assessor per trial.

The whole judicial process consists of five stages or parts. Stage 1 is ascertainment of the presence of parties concerned and informing them of their rights. At the time when a court session opens, the presiding judge will ascertain whether the parties have appeared before the court, announce the subject matter of the case, list the names of the members of the collegial panel (the judge and people's assessor), the court clerk, the public prosecutors, the defender, the agent ad litem, the expert witnesses, and the interpreter, inform the parties of their right to apply for the withdrawal of any of these participants, and notify the defendant of his right to present a defense.

Stage 2 is examination. After the public prosecutor reads out the bill of prosecution in the court, the defendant and victim may make their respective statements on the crimes charged in the bill of prosecution, and the public prosecutor may interrogate and question the defendant. Judicial personnel also may interrogate and question the defendant.

Stage 3 is evidence presentation and identification. The public prosecutor and the defense lawyer present their material evidence to the court and have the parties identify it. The judicial personnel solicit the opinions of the public prosecutor, the parties, and the defenders as well as agents ad litem.

Stage 4 is argument and self-defense. The public prosecutor, the parties, and the defenders and agents ad litem may, with the permission of the presiding judge, express their opinions on the evidence and the circumstance of the case, and may debate with each other. After the presiding judge declares the conclusion of the court debate, the defendant has the right to make a final statement.

Stage 5 is judgment and sentencing. After the defendant has made his final statement, the presiding judge will announce an adjournment, and the collegial panel will conduct deliberations and render one of the following judgments on the basis of the evidence and relevant provisions of law: (1) if the facts of a case are clear, the evidence is reliable and sufficient, and the defendant is found guilty in accordance with law, he shall be pronounced guilty accordingly; (2) if the defendant is found innocent in

---

[6] The Research Section of the Supreme Court of China, 1997. Focusing on Courtroom Trial. Law Press.

accordance with law, he shall be pronounced innocent accordingly; (3) if the evidence is insufficient and thus the defendant cannot be found guilty, he shall be pronounced innocent accordingly on account of the fact that the evidence is insufficient and the accusation unfounded.[7]

28.3 COURTROOM QUESTIONING

Whether in the common law or continental law system, a courtroom trial is a process of questions and answers and it is the same in the Chinese legal system (Liao 2003). Discourse space in terms of the distribution of questions is a very important and a reliable indicator of a judicial system and its discourse (Adelsward et al. 1987).

Before we quantify the distribution of questions in our data, it is necessary to explain three aspects of Chinese courtroom questioning. First, in the Chinese language, there are six types of questions:

- wh-questions (WH), which can be further divided into broad and narrow ones;
- yes/no (Y/N) questions;
- declarative (DEC) questions;
- alternative (ALT) questions;
- tag (TAG) questions;
- affirmative/negative (A/N) questions,[8] which are unique to the Chinese language.

Second, in order to better understand the judge's role in court, we distinguish between procedural questions (P.Q.) and substantive ones (S.Q.), the latter of which are aimed at investigation of the substantial facts of the case or at substantial justice while the former are for the administration of the court procedures or procedural justice. Finally, questions in the first stage are excluded as they are pure procedural ones.

Table 28.1 illustrates the types of questions asked by the judge, the people's assessor, the prosecutor, and the defense lawyer.

First, let us look at the distribution of questions. From Table 28.1 we can see that the distribution of questions is seriously imbalanced. There are 447 questions, for which the judge accounts for 17.6 percent, the prosecutor 75 percent, and the defense lawyer about 5 percent. The distribution of questions reflects the distribution of discourse space occupied by the participants or the degree to which they are engaged during the trial. More questions mean more discourse space, more interaction, and more involvement. That a prosecutor asks the most, and the defense lawyer the least, indicates that the prosecutor enjoys the most discourse space and the defense lawyer the least. Discourse space indicates the status of a participant in a trial. Thus, the imbalance in the distribution of questions is an important indicator of an imbalance between the status of a prosecutor

---

[7] Refer to Article 162 of *The Criminal Procedure Law of the People's Republic of China*.
[8] Such as "*shi bu shi*", "是不是" (literally translated as English "yes not yes").

Table 28.1 types of questions put by the judge, the people's assessor, the prosecutor, and the defense lawyer

Questioner	Types of Q \ Trial Stages	Investigation		Evidence presentation		Debate and statement		Sentencing		Total
		S.Q.	P.Q.	S.Q.	P.Q.	S.Q.	P.Q.	S.Q.	P.Q.	
Judge	WH	2	0	0	2	0	0	0	0	4
	Y/N	0	1	0	31	0	1	0	0	33
	A/N	0	1	0	31	0	2	0	0	34
	DEC	2	0	0	1	0	0	0	0	3
	TAG	0	0	0	0	0	0	0	0	0
	ALT	5	0	0	0	0	0	0	0	5
	Sub-T	9	2	0	65	0	3	0	0	79
	TOTAL	11		65		3		0		79
People's assessor	WH	2		0		0		0		0
	Y/N	0		0		0		0		0
	A/N	1		2		0		0		4
	DEC	2		0		0		0		2
	TAG	2		0		0		0		2
	ALT	0		0		0		0		9
	TOTAL	7		2		0		0		9
Prosecutor	WH	182		0		0		0		182
	Y/N	42		0		0		0		42
	A/N	36		0		0		0		36
	DEC	59		0		0		0		59
	TAG	15		0		0		0		15
	ALT	2		0		0		0		2
	Sub-T	336		0		0		0		336
	TOTAL	336		0		0		0		336
Defense lawyer	WH	9		0		0		0		9
	Y/N	6		0		0		0		6
	A/N	3		0		0		0		3
	DEC	5		0		0		0		5
	TAG	0		0		0		0		0
	ALT	0		0		0		0		0
	Sub-T	23		0		0		0		23
	TOTAL	23		0		0		0		23

WH: wh-question; Y/N: yes/no question; DEC: declarative question; ALT: alternative question; TAG: tag question; A/N: affirmative/negative question; P.Q.: procedural question; S.Q.: substantive question.

and a defense lawyer in Chinese courtroom discourse. We see that the people's assessor, who is part of the collegial panel, did ask some questions but his questions account for only 2 percent. This means that on the one hand the people's assessor is no mere puppet, but on the other hand his involvement is minimal.

Second, let us examine the distribution of the questions in terms of their types. Different types of questions mean different strategies, as questions vary in their level of control (Dunstan 1980) and their function. Of the 79 questions asked by the judge, almost 89 percent are procedural ones. This means that, although he has a dual duty of being a substantive investigator and a procedural administrator, most of the time the judge is performing his procedural duty and his function as a procedural administrator far outweighs his function as a substantial investigator. This results from the legal reforms of the past few decades, which draw more on the common law system, where the trial process is more transparent and adversarial with the judge being a neutral arbitrator. That is, their traditional focus of Chinese judges has shifted from substantial investigation to procedural administration. We also see that most of the judge's questions are yes/no and affirmative/negative ones. Most of the judge's questions are procedural ones, suggesting that his questions are non-information-soliciting.

Of the 336 questions by the prosecutor, more than half are wh-questions. The distribution is significantly different from that in criminal trials I observed in the United States, where examination of the defendant by the prosecutor when the defendant takes the witness stand is characterized by yes/no questions or declarative questions, which are regarded as more effective than wh-questions in controlling the person being questioned (Harris 1984; Dunstan 1980).

The difference in the choice of form of questions results from differences in the two countries' different judicial systems. In China, leading questions are not allowed in either direct or cross-examinations. As we know, leading questions are usually yes/no, declarative, or tag questions (Loftus 1975). As a result of this prohibition, Chinese prosecutors must employ wh-questions, especially broad wh-questions such as "why" and "how" (Liao 2003). In the American judicial system, leading questions, though not allowed in direct examination, are extremely common during cross-examination. This enables lawyers to exercise control through the form of their questions. Thus, the Chinese prosecutors' questions are not as strategic as those of their American counterparts (Liao 2009a). And of the 23 questions by the defense, nearly 40 percent are wh-questions. That is, most of the time, the defense lawyer let the defendant have his say, as is the same in the trials in the USA.

We can also see that all the questions were addressed to the defendant and there was no witness. Thus, the distribution of questions presents a picture of the Chinese judicial system: a defendant occupies the center of the court and is the focus or the target of discourse, and there is little or no interaction between a judge, a prosecutor or a defense lawyer, and a witness. In China, the defendant in a criminal trial is never regarded as a witness (Liao 2009a). Traditionally, witnesses are reluctant to appear in court to testify and their testimony is usually written down and later read in court by the prosecutor or the defense lawyer.

28.4 COURTROOM INTERACTION PATTERNS

A trial is also a process of interaction among the trial participants. Consequently, the patterns of interaction among different participants will reveal quite a lot about the nature of the courtroom discourse as well as the judicial system. In this part I will focus on courtroom interaction patterns.

It has been found that interaction patterns vary with different social activities. Hence, an examination of interaction patterns will help to reveal the nature of a social activity. Merritt (1976:315–57) found that the following embedded structure characterizes service encounters:

> A: Do you have Marlboros?
>> B: Hard or soft pack?
>> A: Soft, please.
> B: OK (turns to retrieve)

There is usually an embedded pair within the pair. For example, in service encounters you need to make sure exactly what the customer wants, because there are different brands or varieties of the same thing.

Sinclair and Coulthard (1975) found that the following "three-step" pattern characterizes classroom discourse:

TEACHER:	What's the name of this cutter?	(The first step: Initiation)
PUPIL:	Hacksaw.	(The second step: Response)
TEACHER:	The hacksaw.	(The third step: Follow-up)

And they found that the third step, the follow-up, cannot be omitted as it has a very important educational function. That is, if the teacher does not give feedback to the pupil's answer, the pupil will be puzzled.

In everyday conversation, the following pattern is very popular (Stenstrom 1984):

> A: Will you be in tonight?
> B: Yes/Why do you ask?
> A: Can I come and see you?
> B: Yes.

Here the first pair is preparatory and the second pair is primary. As we need to save face in daily interaction (especially in Western culture), the question initiating the first pair has a very important face-saving function.

We found that the above three patterns do not characterize Chinese criminal courtroom discourse though they do appear in our data (Liao 2003). Rather, it is the two other patterns that characterize our data. The first is Q (question)—R (response)—F1 (feedback 1)—F2 (feedback 2), which is exemplified by the following:

PROSECUTOR: Did you go to him later?	Step 1: Question
DEFENDANT: No.	Step 2: Response
PROSECUTOR: No?	Step 3: Feedback 1
DEFENDANT: Yeah.	Step 4: Feedback 2

Where the first step is a question, the second step is the response, the third step is ambiguous, in that sometimes it sounds like a question and sometimes it seems to be just an echo of the response, and the last step is the follow-up to the echo or question.

The second pattern is Q (question)—R (response)—Qr (question repeated)—Rr (response repeated) as exemplified by the following:

PROSECUTOR: What did you take with you when you went to blow up his car?
DEFENDANT: I didn't know.
PROSECUTOR: What did you take when you went there?
DEFENDANT: I didn't know then. My brother just asked me to go with him.

Here, the first step is a question, the second is a negative answer, and the third and fourth step repeat the first pair.

What is more significant is that as the interaction relationship changes, the interaction pattern will change accordingly. A simple Q (question)—A (Answer) pattern dominates the interaction between the judge and the other participants. As already mentioned above, most of the time the judge focuses on his procedural duty and there is no substantive confrontation between the judge and the others; his interaction with others tends to be matter-of-fact, smooth, and clean.

A three-step Q—A—F pattern prevails in the interaction between the defending counsel and the defendant. But the third step here does not have any educational function. Instead, the third step here is simply a solidarity marker, which is absent from the interaction between the prosecutor or judge and the defendant.

The four-step pattern Q—R—Qr—Rr dominates the interaction between the prosecutor and the defendant as the relationship between them is adversarial and non-cooperation is the rule, especially when the defendant has not pleaded guilty. And the more the pattern repeats itself, the fiercer the confrontation is. But, it is Q—A—F1—F2 that distinguishes courtroom discourse from everyday conversation or other institutional discourses.

The four-step pattern appears not just in the interaction between the prosecutor and the defendant, but also sometimes between the defense lawyer and the defendant. However, it occurs more often in the former. And what is more significant, there is a very important distinction in what can appear to be the same structure, that is the third step in the interaction between the prosecutor and the defendant is more often a question (usually with a rising tone), showing the doubt of the prosecutor as to the truth or credibility of the defendant's answer, while in the interaction between the defense lawyer and the defendant the third step is more likely to be a confirmative echo (*with a falling tone*).

It can therefore be seen that analysis of the interaction pattern of a discourse can provide profound insights into the nature of a discourse.

28.5 Courtroom judgment (sentencing)

Now let us turn to examine the propositional component based on a criminal court judgment made in a court in Shanghai. The English translation of the original Chinese version is represented here to facilitate our analysis.

Hongkou District Court, Shanghai
2004, No. 60
The public prosecutorate: the People's Prosecutorial Office
of Hongkou District, Shanghai

PART 1

Section 1 Information about the defendant and trial[9]

(1) The defendant is Li Zhaoqing, male, born on Oct. 24, 1975; his nationality, Han; his birth place, Shanghai; his education, university graduate. (2) He was an employee of XXX Clothing Company limited, Shanghai and lives at Room 203, No. 8, Lane 565. (3) Suspected of robbery, he was held in criminal detention on Dec. 16, 2003, and was arrested on Dec. 26. (4) He is presently held in a detention house in Hongkou District. (5) In its bill of prosecution No.73 (2004) the People's Prosecutorial Office of Hongkou District, Shanghai charged the defendant Li Zhaoqing with robbery and instituted the case to this court on Feb. 25, 2004. (6) In line with the law, the court formed a collegial panel of judges, and held a public hearing. (7) The People's Prosecutorial Office of Hongkou District, Shanghai sent a prosecutor, Fu Weiqin, to the court to support the prosecution, and the defendant Wu Yong attended the hearing.

Section 2: Findings and verdict

(1) The trial has been concluded. (2) During the trial, it was found that at around 9 pm, on December 12, 2003 the defendant Li Zhaoqing, having made considerable premeditation, invited Wu Yanrong, a woman he acquainted himself with through the internet, to room No. 1520 of Haihong Hotel of Shanghai, which he had reserved by using a forged identity card with the name of Shen Jun. (3) Hereafter, he made Wu Yanrong drink a glass of juice with sleeping pills. (4) As soon as she fell into lethargy, Li Zhaoqing robbed Wu Yanrong of a mobile phone (Model Motorola T189) worth 541 yuan (renminbi), 50 yuan (renminbi) in cash, a leather bag, a Buddhist jade article, and absconded with the booty. (5) About eight o'clock, the next morning, Wu woke up aware of having

---

[9] The words in bold type and the numbers in the text of the judgment were added by the present author to facilitate the analysis.

been robbed and reported it to the public security station. (6) After examination, it was found that Wu's urine contained diazepam. (7) The policemen tracked down and found all the stolen money and goods, and returned them to the victim. (8) The defendant Li Zhaoqing raised no objections to the above charges during the trial, and we have a record of the victim's statement and identification, the testimony of the witnesses Miao Yun and Shen Jun, the registration sheet at the hotel, the forged identity card, the report of the urine test by the public security bureau, the record of the search of the defendant's home by the Shanghai Public Security Bureau, Hongkou Branch, a list of the goods seized and returned to the victim, the expert's report of the value of the goods produced by the Shanghai Price Authentication Center as sufficient and true evidence. (9) The court holds that the defendant Li Zhaoqing, in order to possess Wu Yangrong's goods illegally, robbed her of her goods by anaesthetizing her, which constitutes a crime of pillage. (10) The charge of the defendant by the People's Prosecutorial Office of Hongkou District, Shanghai, with the crime of pillage is tenable. (11) Having been held in custody, Li Zhaoqing pleaded guilty and his attitude was positive, and his family volunteered to pay the penalty for him. (12) Therefore, the punishment could be commutable.

Section 3: Sentencing and appeal

(1) In order to maintain the social order and protect legal private property from encroachment, the court issues the following sentence in accordance with Article 263 and Article 23 of the Criminal Law of People's Republic of China. (2) First, the defendant Li Zhaoqing committed the crime of pillage and is sentenced to a 4-year term of imprisonment and a penalty of 5,000 yuan (The imprisonment term starts from the day of the execution of the sentence. The time of detention before the execution of the sentence will be taken as part of the imprisonment term and therefore subtracted from it. Consequently the actual imprisonment term commences on December 16, 2003 and concludes on December 15, 2007). (3) Secondly, the seized forged identity card will be confiscated and destroyed. (4) If the defendant objects to this sentence, he may, within ten days dating from the second day after reception of the paper of the sentence, appeal via this court or directly to the Shanghai Second Intermediate People's Court. (5) If the defendant chooses to appeal in a written form, one original copy and 2 duplicates of the appellate petition should be submitted.

> Judge: Zhou Jun
> Acting judge: Bian Biao
> People's assessor: Xu Yaping
> Secretary: Cai Yi
> Secretary: Tang Chenjie
> March 9, 2004

PART 2

Postscript by the judge

(1) Li Zhaoqing, you were born in an intellectual's home. (2) You worked very hard for many years and went through countless difficulties in your schooling until you successfully graduated from the university. (3) You are 28 years old and this is the

golden time of your life. (4) You should have been working harder and using what you have learned to serve society and your parents, but because of a moment's greedy desire, you went the wrong way and committed a crime. (5) Think of your parents, who have endured countless sufferings and borne numerous hardships in raising you and supporting you in your education. (6) Actually, parents expect no repayment from their children for what they have done. (7) They simply want their children to develop and grow happily and healthily and be people of integrity. Because of a moment's foolish action, you failed to live up to their expectations. (8) The lesson is too expensive. (9) However, as the saying goes, it is not too late to mend the fold after the sheep is lost. (10) It is hoped that you draw a lesson from this bitter experience, try to reform yourself, learn and abide by the law and try to come back to our society and be a useful man.

Now let us discuss the judgment's structure, style, diction, and content. In terms of the structure and content, we can see that there are two major parts. Part 1 is primary, dealing with the legal aspect of the case. It is a sentencing speech act consisting of the following sub-acts:

(1) information about the defendant and the trial (7 sentences);
(2) findings and verdict (12 sentences); and
(3) sentence and appeal (5 sentences).

It is, in effect, verdict, sentence, and judgment all in one.

Part 2 is secondary, dealing with the moral aspect (10 sentences). It is a moralizing speech act consisting of three sub-acts:

(1) pointing out what is good as well as what is bad about the defendant;
(2) pointing out the sacrifices made by the parents and their expectations; and
(3) giving the defendant encouragement and expressing the judge's hope.

In terms of the style, the first part is written and formal. There are no personal pronouns like "you," etc. Rather, full names or full names plus legal addresses such as "Defendant Zhang Wenxiang" are used. Archaic words such as "hereafter," "conclude," "commence" are used. The sentences are fairly long. A cold and matter-of-fact tone is assumed. It is typical of bureaucratic language. It appeals to reason and law. As opposed to the first part, the second part is spoken language and is very informal. It is personal, conversational, and interactional, as shown in the use of the pronoun "you." The sentences are fairly short and ordinary words are used. It has a warmer tone. It appeals to emotions, ethics, and morality as well as folk wisdom.

We should point it out here that this way of rendering the judgment or sentencing is by no means the most popular one adopted in China. That is, the second part, the judge's postscript, is optional and even those judges who do adopt this practice do not always include it. There is much controversy over the practice because most law professors or jurists, especially those who received their law degrees in the West, think that the second part simply has nothing to do with the case. Yet these different styles of judgment reflect the dichotomy in the Chinese legal tradition between the rule of law and rule by moral virtues, or "*fa*" and "*li*".

28.6 CONCLUDING REMARKS

Susan Ehrlich (2001:4) is right in writing: "Central to an investigation of language as it is embodied within institutional settings is both an understanding of the relationship between linguistic practices and speakers' social identities and an exploration of the institutional and cultural backdrop against which speakers adopt such practices." So, in order for the reader to understand Chinese courtroom discourse, I briefly introduced the Chinese legal culture and system. The dichotomy of "*fa*" and "*li*" in the Chinese legal tradition explains very well why there are two different parts in the judgment, one devoted to sentencing and one devoted to moralizing. The Chinese legal system is responsible for the peculiar distribution of questions, question types, and interaction patterns in Chinese courtroom discourse, which is so distinct from those of the court-room discourse in the United States.[10]

As reform in the Chinese legal system and practices moves on, linguistic practices in the courtroom will change accordingly. Continuing analysis of the distribution of questions and interaction patterns and the particular configuration of judgments in terms of style, structure, and content will contribute to a better understanding of Chinese legal culture, reflecting the changes and reforms of the legal system and culture that have taken place in the past and are likely to continue in the future.

[10] The remark is based on my observation of three criminal courtroom trials in New York when I was a Fulbright scholar at Brooklyn Law School 2006–7.

CHAPTER 29

....

THE LANGUAGE OF CRIMINAL TRIALS IN AN INQUISITORIAL SYSTEM: THE CASE OF THE NETHERLANDS

....

MARTHA L. KOMTER
MARIJKE MALSCH

29.1 INTRODUCTION

....

THE way cases are handled in court is related to characteristics of the legal system in which they take place. Some legal systems are highly professional, while others rely predominantly on lay decision making. In some systems the centre of gravity lies with the judge, and in others the parties play the most dominant role in the trial of cases (Damaška 1997; van Koppen and Penrod 2003; Malsch 2009). In highly professionalized systems there is a greater reliance on paper documents than in systems involving lay adjudication. In the latter systems more attention is paid to a presentation of all the evidence at trial in a way that makes it comprehensible for the lay adjudicators and, thus, less use is made of documentary evidence (Malsch 2009). These differences have an influence on the type of language that is used during the trial.

This chapter discusses the role of language in inquisitorial systems, also known as civil law systems. It will concentrate on the highly professionalized inquisitorial Dutch criminal justice system, where the dependence on documentary evidence is noticeable the moment one enters a Dutch courthouse. Ushers can be seen pushing trolleys stacked with files and papers, on their way to the courtroom or to the archives. The prominent role of the case file is also evident inside the courtrooms, not only as a central source of information around which the events are organized, but also as material presence, as a physical object that is leafed through, pointed at, read from, etc., by the legal professionals: judges, public prosecutors, and defense lawyers (cf. Komter 1998).

Compared with the relatively passive role of judges in adversarial criminal justice sys-tems, judges play an active role in Dutch courtrooms. They not only organize courtroom proceedings, they are also actively involved in questioning suspects and witnesses (if any). Thus, an inspection of the language used in Dutch courtrooms inevitably requires directing attention to the judges. The activities of judges and the central role of the case file in Dutch courtrooms will be the core of our discussion in this chapter.

We start with a short discussion of the main differences between adversarial and inquisitorial criminal justice systems. Next, we describe some typical features of Dutch criminal trials, and position these in relation to adversarial and to other inquisitorial criminal justice systems. We then proceed with our main business: a description of the language of Dutch criminal trials focused on the central position of the case file for the activities of the judges.

29.2 ADVERSARIAL AND INQUISITORIAL CRIMINAL JUSTICE SYSTEMS

In adversarial systems, legal proceedings are essentially contests between equivalent parties. This model emphasizes an oral presentation of evidence, and lay participation often plays a substantial role in such criminal justice systems (van Koppen and Penrod 2003; Malsch 2009). As a consequence of the lay adjudication, considerable emphasis is placed on rules of evidence that are aimed at assuring reliable proof to jurors. In adver-sarial systems the parties present their own evidence to the trier of fact. The principle of "immediacy," which requires that all evidence is presented in court in its most original form, is strongly adhered to in these systems. The adversarial system is found mainly in England and Wales and countries that have adopted the English common law: largely the Commonwealth countries and the United States.

In inquisitorial systems the police, prosecution, and the judge generally gather and present the evidence, both of an incriminating and an exculpatory nature. It is ultimately the judge who decides whether to admit evidence (Malsch and Freckelton 2005). In con-trast to the adversarial model, judges in an inquisitorial system are non-passive: they take an active role in the collection and the review of evidence during the hearing of cases. Once a case is brought before it, the court takes on the responsibility for finding "the truth" (Damaška 1997; van Koppen and Penrod 2003). Although some inquisitorial systems, such as those of Spain, Italy, France, and Belgium, sometimes have lay adjudica-tion in the form of a jury, most cases in these systems are tried by professional decision makers (Malsch 2009).

In inquisitorial systems there is a preference for documentary evidence (Malsch and Nijboer 1999). Related to this is the fact that these systems adhere to a substan-tially smaller degree than adversarial systems to the principles of immediacy and oral-ity. Inquisitorial systems tend to sustain the principle of "free proof," where any type of evidence may reach the judge; the judge is trusted to give any weight considered appropriate to this evidence (van Koppen and Penrod 2003). Inquisitorial systems are found predominantly on the continent of Europe and in South or Latin American countries.

An important consequence of the differences between the two types of systems is that the trial in open court in adversarial systems plays a far more dominant role, while in inquisitorial systems there is a greater emphasis on the pre-trial stages. Adversarial systems stress the importance of questioning witnesses and investigating other types of evidence in open court, whereas inquisitorial systems often satisfy themselves with the written reports of the interrogations and investigations by officials that were produced before the hearing of the case in court (Malsch and Freckelton 2009).

29.3 TYPICAL FEATURES OF DUTCH CRIMINAL TRIALS

Although the Dutch criminal justice system can be described as inquisitorial, it also has adversarial elements (cf. Jörg et al. 1995). Inquisitorial features are most prominent in pre-trial stages: Suspects are still not fully allowed to have a defense lawyer present at police interrogations, and items from the case file can remain undisclosed to the defense until the hearing of the case in open court. Adversarial elements come to the fore in the trial stage. Although the prosecutor and the defense lawyer don't cross-examine suspects or witnesses in the same manner as in some adversarial systems, they do present their vision of the case in their closing statements, with the aim of influencing the outcome of the case. The defense may also, at trial, adduce new evidence or ask the court to do so.

The Dutch criminal justice system also has certain characteristics that distinguish it from other inquisitorial systems, such as a heavy reliance on paper documents, an explicit focus on finding the truth, a certain emphasis on reaching consensus,[1] and the absence of a jury. The Dutch criminal justice system relies on documentary evidence. Most of the investigation in a case is done by the officials of the system: the police, the prosecution, and the (investigative) judge;[2] the defense plays a relatively restricted role here. These officials give an account of the actions they have performed or of the decisions they have made before the actual trial (Malsch and Freckelton 2009).

During the "preliminary investigations" evidence is collected that is necessary to sufficiently inform the judges and the parties during the trial. During the trial, judges

---

[1] Although lately there appears to be more of a fighting spirit in the relations between defense lawyers and prosecutors than before.

[2] In inquisitorial criminal law systems an investigative Judge may be requested by either the prosecution or the defense to conduct certain investigations prior to the hearing of the case.

conduct the "main investigation" by reviewing this evidence, and by comparing it to the direct evidence produced on the spot by the testimony of suspects and witnesses. If, in the course of the trial, judges feel that the case file is incomplete, they may adjourn the trial and give orders to the investigative judge and experts to conduct additional investigations. The time spent on the pre-trial investigations is one reason why the Dutch hearing of cases in open court lasts a relatively short period of time. Witnesses are seldom summoned to appear in court, as their written statements can be used in lieu of their appearance.[3] Trials rarely take more than one day to be concluded; routine cases usually take no more than an hour. Another reason for a quicker dispatch of criminal cases is the fact that most of the suspects confess to at least some of the charges. This is related to the fact that the Dutch criminal justice system does not make use of the kind of plea bargaining that is common in some adversarial systems.

It has been observed that the Dutch criminal justice system is more compromise oriented than adversarial systems (Malsch and Nijboer 1999; de Groot-van Leeuwen 2006). Dutch court sessions in criminal cases are generally not characterized by fierce debates between the two sides; they can be more effectively portrayed as discussions of the case file by the participants, in which the independent judge plays a dominant role (Malsch and Freckelton 2009). As interrogations are conducted in a less aggressive manner than in adversarial systems, finding common ground and seeking solutions to a conflict are features of Dutch court sessions.

In contrast to adversarial systems, where the parties play the dominant role in presenting their version of the truth, the Dutch and other inquisitorial systems seem to assume that only one "truth" exists and that it is the task of the court to "find" it (Malsch and Freckelton 2009). The general assumption that only one truth exists can be expected to promote an early acceptance of a state of affairs. Participants at trial in the Dutch system tend to readily accept a scenario of how the crime took place, if this has been made plausible by the prosecution.[4] In contrast, parties in an adversarial system generally attempt to undermine the arguments of the other side throughout the trial.

As mentioned above, Dutch judges play an active role at trial in interrogating the suspect and witnesses, as well as investigating other items of evidence.[5] The case file is used to examine the suspect, to confront him or her with contradictions with prior statements and statements of certain witnesses, and to focus more exclusively on those aspects of the case that seem relevant in the eyes of the judge who conducts the interrogations. Although this "documentary method of interrogation" is by no means restricted to inquisitorial systems (cf. Lynch and Bogen 1996), it is one of the notable features of Dutch trials.

---

[3] Recently, however, Dutch courts' dependence on documentary evidence and the relative absence of direct spoken testimony in the courtrooms has come under some pressure from European case law, which favors a move towards greater "immediacy."

[4] However, this has slightly changed under the influence of decisions by the European Court of Human Rights (ECHR).

[5] Serious cases are tried by a panel of three judges, of which one acts as presiding judge; simple cases are handled by a single judge.

Case files (dossiers) consist of—among other things—the following documents:

- the indictment containing the charges;
- suspect and witness statements made to the police and to the investigating judge;
- the suspect's criminal records;
- reports on the suspect's personal life and mentality by probation officers, psychologists, or other expert witnesses; and
- other pieces of evidence such as situation sketches, photographs, etc.

The law requires that the verdict must be based on evidence that has been brought up at the trial. As a consequence, judges have read these dossiers beforehand in view of the decisions they ultimately have to make about the suspects' guilt and punishment. During the trial, as part of the examination of the suspect, judges read or summarize those passages from the case file that they think they may need for their verdict. Consequently, when the judges enter the courtroom, they will have already formed some idea of the suspects' guilt and of the probative value of the evidence.[6]

The suspects' and witnesses' statements in the case file are typically written as first person monologues. Because the questions that elicited these statements are left out, the interaction between suspects or witnesses and the police (or investigative judge) has become invisible. Yet, these documents are treated in court as representations of what the suspect or witness has said to the police or to the investigative judge (Komter 2006). Thus, suspects' and witnesses' statement are transformations of what was originally said, and they are therefore products of the institutional and bureaucratic activities of police officers and investigative judges.

29.4 THE LANGUAGE OF DUTCH CRIMINAL TRIALS

Globally, Dutch trials are organized around the following events in the following order:

- the opening of the trial by the presiding judge;
- the presentation of the indictment by the public prosecutor;
- the hearing of the suspect (consisting of two topics: "the facts" and "the person") by the judge;
- the summing up of the public prosecutor;
- the summing up by the defense lawyer;
- the last word by the suspect; and
- the closing of the trial by the presiding judge.

---

[6] One of the drawbacks of such a focus may be the risk of "confirmation bias": the judge who conducts the questioning only seeks confirmation of certain beliefs that have materialized as a consequence of reading the case file prior to the actual trial.

Every phase in the trial is marked by references to the dossier; for the management of the different topics there are different documents in the case file. For example, "the facts" are discussed mainly by reference to statements of suspects and witnesses; "the person" is discussed by reference to expert reports and to the suspect's criminal record.

In the following sections we shall discuss how judges typically conduct the business of the trial. The materials were collected for earlier research (Komter 1998, 2002).[7] From this corpus we have chosen one trial to illustrate the typical features of the language in Dutch criminal trials. This trial is typical in that the suspect is heard by the judge on the basis of the written documents. The witnesses are not summoned to appear in court;[8] their statements as written down in the case file are summarized or quoted by the judge in the course of his hearing the suspect.

The case concerns a suspect who is accused of having threatened to kill two social workers in charge of distributing methadone to drug addicts from a so-called "methadone bus." The suspect was angry because he did not get his methadone, as he arrived after closing time. When the two social workers left the social center after work, the suspect almost ran them over with his car. According to the two social workers the suspect drove toward them at high speed, so that they could barely save themselves by running away and jumping between parked cars. Other witnesses corroborated this version. According to the suspect he drove carefully and behaved normally on the road. Eventually the suspect was found guilty and received a prison sentence of ten months.

29.4.1 STRUCTURING THE TRIAL

Part of the job of the presiding judge is to act as "chairman" of the court proceedings. The presiding judge starts and concludes the trial, allocates the speaking turns, and structures the different phases of the trial. For these structuring activities judges rely on the dossier as an object of reference. An inspection of the materials reveals that judges typically refer to the case file to open the hearing and to mark the transitions between the different phases or the different topics in the trial. In our case, after the public prosecutor's presentation of the indictment, the suspect's questioning starts as follows:

(29.1)

(1) J: Then uh we'll get to the uh first count,
(2)   that is something that happens on uh April the 10th 1990,
(3)   and uh so you are suspected mister uh Berlage
(4)   of threatening a certain Fongers,
(5)   and a certain Zeeman.

---

[7] These materials consist of 31 audio-taped trials of violent crime in three district courts in the Netherlands.

[8] Apart from a social worker who is invited to talk about the suspect's chances of rehabilitation.

(6)   Did you- so did you uh tell the truth to the police?

(7) S: Yes, I did not see that Mr Fongers at all.[9]

(14, p. 3)

At the start of the hearing the judge recapitulates the charges as laid out in the case file (lines 1–5). He continues with another, implicit, reference to the case file: the suspect's statement to the police (line 6). At the beginning of hearings, judges often verify whether suspects stick by their earlier statements, in order to determine how to proceed with the questioning (cf. Komter 2002). In this case the suspect stands behind his statement to the police, as written down and included in the case file. He justifies this by adding that he did not see the alleged victim, Mr Fongers. Thus, the references to the information in the dossier at the beginning of the trial anticipate and structure the business on the judge's agenda: finding "the truth" about what happened on April 10, 1990, and ascertaining the suspect's plea.

Later in the trial the judge recapitulates the testimony of the social worker, Mr Fongers, which contradicts the suspect's story. After the judge has recounted the alleged victim's version of the events he asks the suspect:

(29.2)

(1) J: Do you think he's lying or uh

(2) S: Well, that uh I don't say that.

(3) J: No.

(4) S: (overlaps) But I haven't seen him so I-
       I assume that it isn't like that.

(6) J: The testimony of Henk Schipper,

(7)   ... page 17,

(8)   (17 seconds of rustling of paper)

(9)   well so he was in that bus,

(10)   and that is then the previous history I'll just skip it,

(11)   the problem inside I'll just skip it, and uhm

(12)   "Jan Willem [Fongers] crossed the street, ... "

(13)   (continues reading from the case file)

(14, p. 11)

---

[9] The translations of these fragments have been made to capture the conversational style of the original Dutch text. The names have been changed for reasons of privacy.

Transcription conventions:

J	judge
S	suspect
under<u>lined</u>	stress
(14, p. 5)	e.g. trial no. 14, page 5 of transcript
. full stop	falling intonation
, comma	slightly rising intonation
? question mark	rising intonation

The suspect's conclusion of his side of the story (lines 4–5) is followed immediately by the judge's reference to the statement of Henk Schipper, another witness. This illuminates again how the dossier serves the judge to structure court proceedings. He uses the dossier to move on with the court session without entering into a discussion with the suspect.

All the professionals in the courtroom (judges, prosecutor, and defense lawyer) have a copy of the dossier in front of them. After the judge's reference to the page number in the dossier (line 7), he waits for 17 seconds in order to allow the others to find the required page, and to give them the opportunity to "co-read" the dossier with him. After this he mentions the location of the events (the bus, line 9), and then indicates how he is going to proceed. His repeated "I'll just skip it" (lines 10 and 11) shows how the judge is reading the case file: he is selecting the most relevant items from the dossier by passing over others. He appears to be thinking aloud on what is important information in the dossier and what is not, on what items to highlight and what to leave out. When he has found the passage he was looking for he starts reading aloud (line 12). The passage he reads subsequently describes how the witness saw that the social worker, Jan Willem Fongers, could only just save himself from being hit by the suspect's car by running away. In retrospect this contradicts the suspect's version, in which he had claimed that he did not see the social worker at all (see example 29.1, line 7).

These fragments illustrate how the case file serves the judge as a basic foothold to structure the talk and to manage topic shifts. Moreover, references to the case file serve to make his actions transparent and accountable, in the sense that the participants in the courtroom are offered the opportunity to verify and follow the judge's line of thinking. And finally, references to the case file enable judges to avoid discussions or arguments with the suspect (see also the sections below).

29.4.2 Finding the truth

As mentioned before, a central task of judges in court is to find "the truth." This task is complicated by the fact that the evidence is often conflicting, which means that the judges must reject some pieces of evidence and endorse others. A result of the combination of the inquisitorial and adversarial elements of Dutch trials is that suspects have an ambiguous position in the courtroom. As interested party they are expected to defend themselves against an accusation; as objects of inquiry they are required to assist the judges in their truth finding. Consequently, the suspect is both the best and the worst source of information. The best because he presumably has first-hand knowledge of the events he is accused of; the worst because he has a stake in the outcome of the trial. Judges also have a double commitment. They must be objective and neutral, yet they must be investigative and find out the truth from a potentially unreliable source. In the following sections we shall examine how the judge invites the suspect to explain his side of the story, how he confronts the suspect with counter versions of the events, and how he attempts to establish common ground.

29.4.2.1 *Inviting the suspect's version*

After the presentation of the charges by the public prosecutor, the judge must make the transition from the essentially adversarial propositions of the public prosecutor to the inquisitorial mode of interrogation of the suspect. Let us examine the beginning of the suspect's hearing again (see example 29.1):

(29.3)

    (1) J: Then uh we'll get to the uh first count,
    (2)   that is something that happens on uh April the 10th 1990,
    (3)   and uh so you are suspected mister uh Berlage
    (4)   of threatening a certain Fongers,
    (5)   and a certain Zeeman.
    (6)   Did you- so did you uh tell the truth to the police?
    (7) S: Yes, I did not see that Mr Fongers at all.
    (8)   And I mean it is a busy street Biltstraat is,
    (9)   so I carefully looked around me whether I could cross,
  (10) J: Hm.
  (11) S: and I didn't see anyone on the road.
  (12)   So I thought that was rather strange.
  (13) J: And that Mrs. Zeeman?

(14, p. 3)

The judge tells the suspect what he is charged with, after which he asks him whether he told the truth to the police (line 6). The problem is, of course, that the suspect's confirmation that he told the truth to the police does not necessarily make the judge believe him. It is undoubtedly in the court's interest that suspects tell the truth, and in the suspects' interest that judges believe them, but neither the judge not the suspect can explicitly induce the other to do so.

Our suspect tries to convince the judge of why he could not have committed the crime he is accused of by adding to the account. His point is that he did not see Mr Fongers, one of the two alleged victims, so he could not have attempted to run him over with his car. He elaborates on this by suggesting that he would not have crossed a busy road without looking carefully around him. This implies that if Mr Fongers had walked in the street he must have seen him. In this way he presents the contrasting versions to the court as a puzzle, which he does not attempt to solve but which he acknowledges as "rather strange" (line 12). The judge continues:

(29.4)

  (13) J: And that Mrs. Zeeman?
  (14) S: She was standing between posts,[10]

---

[10] Later on it appears that these "posts" were parking meters.

(15)   and I didn't drive into those,
(16)   I drove toward it, until I was beside her,
(17)   and then I only <u>looked</u> at her,
(18)   and then I drove <u>on</u>,
(19)   yes so uh an attempt- attempt of this or that
(20)   I just find that a little yes exaggerated let's say.

(14, p. 3)

In answer to the judge's question regarding the other alleged victim, the suspect again describes his actions as those of a normal driver. First of all, the fact that she was standing between posts made it practically impossible for him to try and run her over. Second, he claims only to have looked at her, after which he drove on. Again, the suspect describes his actions as nothing out of the ordinary, and offers the description of the scene as evidence that he could not have committed the crime he is accused of.

The fact that the suspect's explanations are preceded by the judge's mentioning of the charges (lines 2–5) makes his statements sound like defenses (cf. Atkinson and Drew 1979). The suspect underlines this with his final evaluation ("… an attempt of this or that I just find that a little yes exaggerated," lines 19–20). This refers to the fact that, when the suspect was first arrested by the police, he was told that he was accused of attempted manslaughter. Thus, in response to the charges, the suspect describes his actions as those of an attentive and well-behaved citizen, who concludes that the accusation is "a little exaggerated."

The two questions asked by the judge thus far (lines 6 and 13) could be described as factual questions. Yet, their sequential placement, after the presentation of the charges, makes them also interpretable in relation to the accusation for which the suspect is on trial. Similarly, the suspect not only responds to the factual contents of the judge's questions, but also to their blame-implicative nature by offering a description of the scene (cf. Drew 1992). Thus, negotiations of blame and assertions of innocence are done implicitly, on the basis of inferences that can be drawn from "the facts." The suspect talks from the perspective of a "theorist" who logically derives what might have transpired from the elements of the situation (Brannigan and Lynch 1987). He tries to convince the judge of the veracity of his version by appealing to logical inferences and common sense notions.

29.4.2.2 *Presenting counter versions*

Thus far, in the course of the suspect's examination, the judge has remained relatively quiet. He produces a minimal response "hm" (example 29.3, line 10), and asks a question (examples 29.3 and 29.4, line 13). When the suspect's description has recognizably reached a conclusion (line 20), the judge continues:

(29.5)

(19) S: yes so uh an attempt- attempt of this or that
(20)   I just find that a little yes exaggerated let's say.
(21) J: Well I'll briefly put to you what it says in the documents about that,

(22)   that uh Mrs. Zeeman, she is an uh employee of uh
(23)   Biltstraat 211 right, [the center for drug addicts]

(14, p. 3)

The judge chooses not to respond to the suspect's evaluation of his case, but proceeds by referring to "the documents" (line 21). As mentioned before, the judge counters the suspect's claims by referring to alternative versions of the events as recorded in the case file (see example 29.2, line 6). The phrase "I'll ... put to you ... " is often used by judges, as if to say that they are merely passing on the information that is in the dossier. However, if we consider the substance of what the judge presents from the statement of Mrs Zeeman, it will be seen that it is in stark contrast with the suspect's version:

(29.6)

(1)   J: ...and there she walks on the sidewalk,
(2)   and then she is by the gas station
(3)   and then she hears the noise of screeching tyres.
(4)   "I heard someone call out something,
(5)   that's the voice of Jan Willem, of eh 211,
(6)   I looked around,
(7)   saw on the Biltstraat from the direction Berekuil
(8)   a blue car heading in my direction
(9)   I saw that this car started driving on the sidewalk,
(10)   and was driving straight at me.
(11)   I saw that behind the wheel was Igor Berlage."

(14, pp. 4–5)

The judge initially summarizes the information in the case file, but at a certain moment (from line 4 onwards) he continues by quoting directly from the alleged victim's statement. Note that the personal pronoun "she" is changed into "I" (line 4), reflecting the first person narrative style of Dutch testimony, as recorded by the police or the investigating judge (Komter 2002).[11] The understanding is that both of these pronouns refer to the witness, and that the personal pronoun "I" signifies that the judge is relaying the witness' text as a direct quotation written down by the police.[12]

The judge's serious consideration of this contrasting version reveals an active assumption of the "investigative stance": a thoroughgoing skepticism meant to display a hardheaded commitment to establishing the "facts of the matter" (Zimmerman 1969). The reference to the case file enables the judge to give voice to alternative versions of the events without going on record as endorsing those versions (Clayman 1992). It also

---

[11] Goffman describes these activities as shifts of "footing," that is, as changes in the alignment of an individual to a particular utterance (1981:128).

[12] As research has shown (Komter 2002) there is a considerable difference between what suspects or witnesses state in interaction with the police and the first person monologues that are written down and form part of the case file.

allows him to proceed with the questioning without responding to the suspect's evaluations and conclusions. Thus, the case file serves the judge not just as a source of information, but also as a means to question the suspect's version of the events, to avoid entering into a discussion with him, and to maintain his appearance of objectivity.

29.4.2.3 *Offering compromise*

The discussion above shows how the judge uses the case file to offer alternative versions without directly contradicting the suspect, or without openly calling into doubt the veracity of his version of the story. Apart from quoting or summarizing the case file, the judge also enters into episodes of directly questioning the suspect. After having read some lengthy passages from the case file, the judge delves into the suspect's motives for driving towards the social workers:

(29.7)

    (1) J: yes, <u>why</u> then did you drive in that direction?
    (2) S: Well simply to show that woman that I was <u>angry</u>.
    (3) J: But why
    (4) S: I mean I could also have driven on the road,
    (5)   and simply drive on,
    (6)   but then she wouldn't have paid any attention so
    (7) J: Yes if I understand correctly,
    (8)   then yes then you wanted to frighten her,
    (9) S: Well, frighten her,
    (10)   I simply wanted to show her that I was <u>angry</u>.

(14, p. 6–7)

The suspect's initial answer to the question (line 2) apparently does not satisfy the judge, because he responds by asking for the suspect's motivation again ("But why," line 3). After the suspect's elaboration, the judge offers his own characterization of the suspect's story thus far (lines 7–8). Although the formulation of the judge ("then you wanted to frighten her") may be easier to agree with than the official accusation of "threat to kill," the words could still be interpreted as threatening. The suspect shows, in his response, that he is aware of the availability of these kinds of inferences and he repeats his prior position of portraying the activities as a normal course of events: "I simply wanted to show her that I was angry" (line 10, see also line 2). This description offers a more innocuous interpretation to the potentially damaging implications of the judge's question. The judge offers a version that downgrades the description in the charges, but that nevertheless allows for more harmful interpretations; the suspect does not overtly dispute the judge's version, yet he dissociates himself from its more harmful implications (Drew 1992).

    The mitigated formulation of the charges demonstrates the judge's efforts to get the suspect to agree to a version of the events that is less damaging for the suspect, yet not wholly incompatible with the accusation as formulated in the indictment. The suspect's version is not necessarily incompatible with the judge's suggestion, yet it manages to withhold confirmation of the blame implied in it.

29.5 CONCLUSION

The conduct of the trial discussed here is typical of the Dutch way of dealing with criminal cases in open court, in that it exemplifies how features characteristic of the Dutch criminal law system affect the language of trials. We are aware that we have left the activities of the public prosecutors and the defense lawyers out of consideration. We chose to focus on the activities of judges and suspects as we intended to highlight the inquisitorial elements of Dutch trials.

We have argued that the case file is important, not only as a source of information, but also as an instrument for organizing the trial and for structuring the activities that take place within it. Because judges prepare the trial beforehand by selecting from the case file those points that they find important, the trial is highly structured and leaves little room for improvisation. The dependence of the judges on case files renders their activities transparent for the other participants in the courtroom, and it illuminates their professionalism and objectivity. However, their practice of reading or summarizing the case file does not make for a very lively performance.

The judge's main substantive business in the courtroom is "truth finding." That is, the judge is supposed to ask the suspect about "the facts" and the suspect is supposed to inform the judge. Such a focus ignores the obvious interests of suspects to avoid or minimize punishment. As a result, while the activities of judges and suspects may at one level be described as eliciting and providing information, at a deeper level their actions can be seen as accusing and defending. Judges avoid openly accusing suspects, yet their factual questions can in context be interpreted as accusations. Similarly, suspects tell stories that describe a "normal" course of events, yet these stories can be seen as directed at denying or minimizing blame.

References to the case file help judges to interrogate the suspects because the authoritative voice of the dossier, and its presumed factual nature, allows them to question the credibility of the suspects' statements while maintaining their stance of neutrality, and it allows them to avoid entering into discussions with the suspect. Thus, the case file is a versatile resource for Dutch judges in organizing activity in the courtroom.

CHAPTER 30

LINGUISTIC ISSUES IN COURTROOM INTERPRETATION

SUSAN BERK-SELIGSON

30.1 INTRODUCTION

COURT interpreting, in its broadest sense, involves the conversion of source language material into its closest target language equivalent in a legal context. The notion of legal context, or domain, in turn, is broadly construed by court interpreting specialists. In fact, the term "court interpreting" itself is used interchangeably with labels such as "judiciary interpreting" and "legal interpreting," and while many experts in the interpreting field consider the distinctions among these concepts to be fuzzy (Pöchhacker 1997; Roberts 1997), some (Colin and Morris 1996:xii) use only one term, "court interpreter," referring to persons who conduct interpreting both in the courtroom setting as well as in other types of legal contexts. Others, such as Benmaman (1997), however, consider "court interpreting" to be synonymous with "judiciary interpreting" and distinguish between these, on the one hand, and "legal interpreting" on the other. For Benmaman,

> Legal interpreting refers to all situations in the legal domain in which interpreter services are performed. These situations include: interviews in law enforcement offices at the local, state and federal levels; attorney–client interviews, which may occur in the attorney's office, in a public service agency, or at a jail; depositions; administrative hearings in state and federal agencies dealing with such issues as social security, worker's compensation, unemployment and disability, and immigration and naturalization; interviews with probation and other court-related agencies; and all court appearances in the various stages of civil and criminal litigation. Court interpreting refers normally to simultaneous and consecutive interpretation, and sight and written translation provided for court officials and minimal-English speaking litigants during evidentiary and non-evidentiary proceedings. This term

includes interpreting during interviews in case-related matters outside the court-room. (Benmaman 1997:181)

González, Vasquez, and Mikkelson (1991), too, consider the more general concept to be "legal interpreting," and distinguish between two subtypes: "quasi-judicial" and "judicial interpreting," the latter being synonymous with "court interpreting." For González et al. (1991:25), quasi-judicial interpreting refers to "the interpretation of interviews and hear-ings that typically occur in out-of-court settings (extra-judicial) but may have a bearing on in-court proceedings." "Judicial interpreting," in contrast, refers to interpreting that occurs in a courtroom (González et al. 1991:25). In this chapter, I will use the term "court interpreting" in its broader sense, synonymous with "legal interpreting," following Colin and Morris (1996).

The term "simultaneous interpretation," referred to by Benmaman, designates a mode in which the interpreter speaks at the same time as the speaker for whom she is interpreting, albeit lagging behind somewhat. Thus, while in simultaneous mode, the interpreter is listening to the source language and simultaneously speaking in the tar-get language. "Consecutive interpretation," in contrast, involves waiting for the source-language speaker to complete his or her turn, before beginning the interpretation. Simultaneous interpreting is generally performed in a hushed voice, so that only the party for whose benefit the interpreter is acting will hear the interpretations (this is usually the defendant or plaintiff), whereas consecutive interpreting is done aloud, for everyone present to hear. The consecutive mode is routinely used for persons testifying at a trial or specifically addressing the judge at a hearing. While these two interpreting modes tend to be separated functionally along these lines, in practice, some interpret-ers use a modified form of consecutive interpreting for persons who are testifying, something that is mid-way between consecutive and simultaneous in nature. This is because consecutive interpreting is considered by skilled interpreters to be more diffi-cult than simultaneous, in that it requires a great deal more reliance upon memory, and since it is done out loud, for everyone to hear, any interpreting errors can potentially be noticed by bilingual people who are present. Any inaccuracy emerging during simulta-neous interpreting will go unnoticed by the person receiving interpreting services, par-ticularly if s/he has highly limited proficiency in the language of the judicial institution.[1]

Since court interpreters are assigned to both quasi-judicial and judicial speech events, each will be given equal attention in this chapter. Specifically, I will explore two com-monly used quasi-judicial venues for interpreting, the police interrogation and the asylum application interview, as well as the informal judicial context of the small claims

---

[1] Although interpreters are generally required for criminal defendants who do not speak English, the decision to assign an interpreter is otherwise within the purview of the presiding judge. Some judges are very generous in providing interpreting services to parties, although this generosity sometimes stems from an effort to minimize the possibility of future appeals on the grounds that interpreting services had not been provided and that the party therefore had not understood what was being said about him or her.

court. Finally, I review research from the formal setting of the trial court. The reason that I begin with quasi-judicial and informal interpreting contexts is that in the USA a greater number of people experience the judicial process in these less formal settings, since approximately 75 percent of persons arraigned for criminal matters opt for a plea bargain rather than subjecting themselves to a trial. Nevertheless, they do appear in trial court for brief proceedings such as initial appearances or arraignments, changes of plea, and sentencing.

30.2 INTERPRETING IN QUASI-JUDICIAL, INFORMAL, AND SPECIALIZED JUDICIAL SETTINGS

This section will deal with interpreting in three contexts: police interrogations, immigration and asylum cases, and small claims courts. Within the context of immigration I will include the more formal role of interpreters in an immigration court, as well as the less formal interpreting contexts of asylum application interviews and the immigration detention process.

30.2.1 Interpreting in police interrogations

Perhaps one of the most important quasi-judicial contexts in which interpreting occurs is in police interrogations. Many European countries provide for the services of professional interpreters in such speech events (Kredens 2009; Russell 2000, 2002; Wadensjö 1998). In the USA, however, the rapid expansion of immigrant communities beyond the traditional urban coastal venues has resulted in a growing trend for police to rely on the interpreting services of police officers, some of whom are relatively proficient in a language other than English—primarily Spanish—but others of whom have learned the second language either in high school or through brief crash courses, and who therefore have very limited proficiency in the second language. Berk-Seligson (2009) presents evidence of the communicative failure that all too frequently occurs when such police officers serve as interpreters for detectives conducting custodial interrogations. An example of such miscommunication can be seen in Extract 30.1, below. The case deals with a 25-year old Mexican man suspected of sexually molesting a six-year old child, specifically, engaging her in oral sex. His claim is that he had just gotten out of the shower and had walked into his bedroom when a child who routinely visited his house to play with his children rushed over to him as he was drying himself off, put her arms around his waist, and told him that she wanted to suck his penis.

Extract 30.1[2]

RYAN: You are gonna try to tell me that a six years old girl came onto <u>you</u>? She came
on to <u>you</u> and wanted to do that? <u>She</u> wanted to suck your pee pee?

LÓPEZ: No, what you say?

RYAN: That's what he's tellin' us.

BAXTER: *La bambino, es posible para ella, que tú chupe su pine. La bambino se dice
"quiero chupe su pine".*
   "The little girl, is it possible for her, that you would suck your peenay? The
little girl says to herself 'I want suck your peenay'."

LÓPEZ: Yeah, *la bambino* telling me. *La bambino dice, "quiero chupar tu pine." Porque
era así con la toalla (unintelligible) "me quiero chupar tu pine" cuando (unintelligible) la bambino ya así* here *conmigo.*
   "Yeah, the little girl telling me. The little girl says, 'I want to suck your peenay.'
Because look, like this with the towel (unintelligible) 'I want to suck up your peenay' when (unintelligible) the little girl now like this here with me."

BAXTER: *La bambina él dice, "quiero chupe su pine" en inglés o en español?*
   "The little girl he says, 'I want suck your peenay'" in English or in Spanish?"

LÓPEZ: *No, en, en español, no en, en inglés.*
   "No, in, in Spanish, no in, in English."

BAXTER: He stated,

LÓPEZ: *Me dice,* "You suck your pipi, you suck your pipi," is telling me.
   "She says to me, 'You suck your pipi, you suck your pipi', is telling me."

BAXTER: He states that the little girl say, "I wanna suck your pee pee."

LÓPEZ: Yeah, is telling me.

Communication between the interrogating detective, Ryan, and the suspect, López, is
fraught with misunderstanding. One of the major sources of difficulty is that Baxter, the
police officer acting as interpreter (and "mediator" according to Officer Ryan), does not
carry out the role that he is expected to play, namely, rendering in the target language
everything that is said in the source language, and when he does finally perform his
interpreting duties, he does so very poorly, so poorly that the limited English speaking
suspect has difficulty understanding him. Seeing how badly the officer communicates in
Spanish, López resorts to communicating directly with the interrogating detective on
his own, albeit with great difficulty and unable to make himself completely comprehensible to his interlocutor. Thus, what is evident in this extract is that there is a great deal of
negotiation for meaning going on, mainly in the form of communicative accommodation on the part of the suspect.

At the root of the need for such negotiation and accommodation is the police interpreter's limited proficiency in Spanish and the suspect's equally limited proficiency in
English. In fact, each interlocutor's second language utterances exhibit characteristics of

---

[2] Throughout this chapter, all names of people or places related to the legal cases analyzed have been
changed, to protect their privacy.

pidginization. Evidence of Baxter's low proficiency in Spanish are (1) his failure to use gender concord between article and noun in noun phrases (e.g., *la bambino* rather than *la bambina*), and the lexical choice of *bambina* for 'child' is itself highly unusual for most dialects of Latin American Spanish, as it is an Italian-origin word; (2) incorrect selection of pronouns (*que tú chupe su pine* "you to suck your peenay" instead of *que ella chupe su pine* "that she suck your peenay"; *La bambina se dice*, "The little girl says to herself," rather than *le dice* "says to you"; and (3) syntactic errors (use of the conjugated verb rather than its infinitival form in verb phrases consisting of two consecutive verbs (*quiero chupe su pine*, "I want to suck your peenay," rather than *quiero chupar su pene*).

López's efforts to communicate in English are equally problematic. He has difficulty in forming verb phrases, especially periphrastic constructions,[3] in which he usually omits the auxiliary verb ("No, what you say?" for "No, what are you saying?"; "Yeah, *la bambino* telling me," rather than "*la bambina* was telling me"). Most striking about the suspect's efforts to communicate in English with Detectives Ryan and Baxter is his accommodation to the faulty renditions of Baxter's interpretations. For example, once Baxter uses the phrases *la bambino* and *pine* (for *pene* 'penis'), López uses these non-standard forms in his own speech, and continues to do so throughout the interrogation. In addition, López freqently resorts to code-switching, the use of two languages within a given stretch of discourse, either intra-sententially or inter-sententially. Thus, he prefaces the English quotation of the child's purported statement expressing her desire to suck his penis with the Spanish pre-quotation, *Me dice* ("She says to me"), he then switches to English for the quote, and completes his turn in English by saying, "is telling me" ("she was telling [saying to] me").[4]

While inadequate command of the second language is one of the major causes of communicative failure on the part of police officers who have not grown up as bilinguals, another important cause of communication difficulties is the failure of police interpreters to interpret all source language substance for the limited English speaker. This can be seen in Extract 30.1, where Detective Ryan's first question goes uninterpreted, which induces López to ask Ryan what he has meant. When Baxter finally makes an effort to render Ryan's question in Spanish, it is nowhere close to being a faithful equivalent of what Ryan has said. Similarly, when Baxter interprets López's lengthiest turn for Ryan's benefit, he reduces it to a summary: "He states that the little girl say, 'I wanna suck your pee pee.'" Crucially, Baxter omits López's explanation that he was drying himself off with a towel after coming out of the shower, when the child ran over to him and put her arms around his hips.

Perhaps more dangerous for the person undergoing custodial interrogation is the fact that police officers who take on the role of interpreters often see themselves essentially as police detectives rather than as interpreters, and for this reason frequently change footing

---

[3] Periphrastic constructions are ones that are constructed by using an auxiliary word rather than an inflected form; for example, *of father* is the periphrastic possessive case of *father*, but *father's* is the inflected possessive case, and *did say* is the periphrastic past tense of *say*, but *said* is the inflected past tense (Houghton Mifflin e-reference dictionary).

[4] López usually uses the verb "tell" when he means "say," as he reports the speech of others. He does this because in Spanish there is one verb, *decir*, meaning both "tell" and "say."

between the two roles.[5] The interpreter, who may easily be perceived by the suspect as being there to help him or her (Morris 1999), steps out of interpreter role and begins to act as an interrogator (Berk-Seligson 2009). Extract 30.2, below, provides an example of such a shift in footing. The case involves an 18-year old Mexican man arrested for the murder and attempted rape of a young woman whom he was trying to pick up outside a metro station.

Extract 30.2

CALHOUN: I'm sorry for you Luis. A very bad thing that happened to you here. (Pause) You didn't want to hurt her, did you?

ALVAREZ: *No entiendo lo que dice.*
"I don't understand what he is saying."

LARSON: *¿Usted no quiso hacerle tanto daño?*
"You didn't want to hurt her so much?"

ALVAREZ: *No quiero hablar más. No quiero hablar más de nada.*
"I don't want to talk more. I don't want to talk more about anything."

LARSON: *¿No sabía que estaba muerta?*
"You didn't know that she was dead?"

ALVAREZ: *No. No quiero hablar más. No quiero saber nada más.*
"No. I don't want to talk more. I don't want to know anything more."

LARSON: *¿No quiere saber nada más?*
"You don't want to know anything more?"

ALVAREZ: *No, no quiero (u). No sé.*
"No, I don't want (u). I don't know."

Calhoun is the interrogating detective and Larson the police officer assigned the role of interpreter. As can be seen from the extract above, once Larson has rendered Calhoun's question into Spanish, he switches over into interrogator role. Such behavior is considered to be completely out-of-bounds for court interpreters. According to interpreting norms, the only time when court interpreters are permitted to ask a question is when they need to clarify a point that bears on their ability to interpret accurately (e.g. to clarify the meaning of some word or phrase that they do not understand). Larson, however, is moving the interrogation forward. In the process, he is prodding the suspect to answer questions that he does not want to answer. In fact, the suspect has been resisting answering questions all along, and several times has tried to claim his *Miranda* right to silence. In this particular case, an appellate court later ruled that the police in question had been coercive in their questioning, and for this reason overturned the ruling of the trial court, which had found the defendant guilty of both crimes. Ultimately, his sentence for the murder was reduced, although the sentence for attempted rape was affirmed.

---

[5] The concept of "footing" comes from Goffman (1979:173). According to Goffman, footing refers to "the multiple senses in which the self of the speaker can appear, that is, the multiple self-implicated projections discoverable in what is said and done." And so, "A change in footing implies a change in the alignment we take up to ourselves and others present as expressed in the way we manage the production or reception of an utterance" (Goffman 1979:5).

Even under the best of circumstances, when interpreters assigned to police interroga-tions are professionals, and therefore are assumed to be impartial, problems arise in a three-party interaction such as an interpreted police interrogation. Russell's (2000) study of police administering the "caution," the British equivalent of the *Miranda* rights, to French speakers detained in the UK, found that interpreters have a great deal of diffi-culty rendering into the target language what the police are saying because the police do not use a standard form of the caution—in essence, they tend to paraphrase it. This means that every police officer is issuing the caution somewhat differently, and that in uttering its various components, the police change the sequence in which those elements are intended to be communicated. In addition, in paraphrasing the caution police offic-ers often simplify it and repeat elements of it, which in turn provokes checking responses from the detainee (Russell 2000:35). All of this produces a loss of logical progression in the source language, English, and consequently results in difficulties for the interpreter, and impaired comprehension on the part of persons being read their rights.

30.2.2 Interpreting in immigration and asylum cases

Immigration and asylum hearings are usually held in tribunals separate from ordinary trial courts. Research carried out in the USA, Canada, Austria, and Italy demonstrates that people assigned to interpret for immigration and asylum applicants play a multi-plicity of roles. Most significantly, in contrast to certified interpreters who interpret in trial courts, and who therefore are aware that impartiality and fidelity to source language speech are expected of them in the performance of their work, many immigration inter-preters tend not to perceive their role as necessarily encompassing these features.

Zambrano-Paff (2008:130–1), in her study of US immigration courts, found that inter-preters mitigate the intimidating atmosphere of hearings by adding polite forms when addressing immigration applicants; they similarly add polite forms of address when direct-ing their utterances to judges (e.g. "sir," "judge," "your honor"). Zambrano-Paff considers the polite interpreting style of interpreters with respect to Hispanic applicants, in particu-lar, to be related to a conversational contract adhered to by many Hispanic cultures, which requires such politeness in interaction. In addition, immigration interpreters often become parties to cross-examinations in their own right, thereby becoming members of the "fact-finding committee," to put it in Zambrano-Paff's terms (2008:135). In the process, they turn source language utterances (specifically, English ones) into target language renditions that are more deferential than the source. In a related study based on the same database, Zambrano-Paff (2008) found that interpreters, when converting judges' and lawyers' ques-tions, make third-person reference to women more polite in Spanish. Extract 30.3, below, presents an example of this phenomenon (Zambrano-Paff 2008:372):

Extract 30.3

J: In addition, the government charges that you sought to get permanent residence in the United States through fraudulent marriage to a woman named María Gertrudis.

I: *También el gobierno lo acusa de que usted trató de conseguir la residencia casándose con un matrimonio falso con <u>una señorita</u>, María Gertrudis.*

The extract shows that while the judge (J) refers to the woman in question as "a woman," the interpreter renders the phrase as "*una señorita*" ("a young lady"), which is far more polite. Other polite variants for "woman" that were used by interpreters are *señora* and *doña*, Zambrano-Paff finds. Her explanation for the use of phrases such as "a woman" and "that woman" by judges and attorneys is that they are intended to distance the American woman from the non-US national who has married her, and to make their marriage one of convenience, namely, aimed at securing residency status for the non-US spouse. Beyond that, Zambrano-Paff concludes, such English phrases serve to portray the woman as a victim of a deliberately deceitful and unlawful strategy of the defendant. Residence through marriage is one common device used by non-nationals to live and work legally in the USA, and immigration judges are highly suspicious of marriages between nationals and non-nationals. They generally presuppose nefarious motives behind such relationships.

Immigration cases make use of interpreting in speech events far less formal than the courtroom proper. We have seen that in the US immigration/asylum context—at least with respect to Hispanic immigrants—interpreters have been shown to be sensitive to the applicant's positive face needs—in Brown and Levinson's (1978b) sense.[6] Interpreters working in asylum interviews in Italy and Austria, however, have been found to be attentive not only to the applicant's face, but to their own face and to that of the authorities as well. They do so by using a variety of politeness strategies.

In an empirical study of interpreted asylum hearings recorded at the Federal Asylum Office in Graz, Austria, Pöllabauer (2004:175) found that interpreters working with police officers at asylum interviews are not regarded by them or by the asylum seekers as "'invisible', neutral mediators," but rather as "highly visible—and in most cases—equal participants in the hearings." In the process, "They shorten and paraphrase statements, provide explanations, try to save their own—and if possible, also the other participants'—face and intervene if they deem it necessary." In particular, interpreters perceive that their face is threatened when one of the parties to the interaction questions either their ability to interpret or their impartiality (Pöllabauer 2007:42). In fact, while these interpreters sometimes appear to exhibit a kind of "pseudo-loyalty" to the asylum seekers during the moments when they are not interpreting, "this supposed loyalty turns out to be disingenuous or at least transient" (Pöllabauer 2006:158).

In an analysis of a "mediated encounter" between a French-speaking man from Cameroon seeking political asylum in Italy, an Italian service provider working in the Foreign Advice Bureau of the Department of Social Care located in a major Italian city, and a Moroccan man who is designated as "mediator" (as opposed to "interpreter"), Merlini (2009:84) found that such encounters are zones of "cultural mediation," and that

---

[6] For Brown and Levinson, "positive face" is the universal desire to be valued, respected, and accepted by others in society. It the desire that the self-image that the individual has created for him/herself be acceptable to others.

cultural mediation itself represents a "zone of instability," one of uncertainty. Her conclusions merit a detailed review, because of their broad theoretical implications.

The asylum application interview analyzed by Merlini (2009) demonstrates that a cultural mediator will exhibit different degrees of involvement with an asylum seeker. In the case that Merlini studied, the mediator's behavior was primarily that of a co-provider of the service, but in addition, he acted as a fully ratified participant when he acted as interpreter, and as such demonstrated his interactional power by managing both conversational topic and floor (Merlini 2009:85). Furthermore, he was placed into the role of "linguistic support" for the asylum seeker. In effect, the mediator was seen to be constantly shifting his position vis-à-vis the asylum applicant, depending upon whether the interaction was dyadic or triadic (i.e. depending upon whether the service provider was present or absent at the moment). For all of these reasons, Merlini concludes that interaction observed in the asylum application interview was

> an extraordinarily heterogeneous space, where alternative and at times conflicting discourses constituted and re-constituted the interlocutors' identities. From the opening sequences, interactional dynamics established a joint positioning of the mediator as a knowledgeable and competent advisor, on a par with the Bureau's employee. Within this position, the mediator was able to help the asylum seeker transform his personal narrative into an institutionally acceptable one.... To turn the asylum seeker's narrative chaos into a linear account, the mediator pointed out potential inconsistencies and eventually synthesized the original narration in a first-person dramatization of the applicant's speech before the Refugee Commission. Besides the logical and chronological restructuring of events, improving on the narrative required a foregrounding of the political motives over the economic ones. This was most effectively achieved through a simulated interrogation, in which the mediator was seen to appropriate the discursive practice of the legal institutions. (Merlini 2009:85)

By shifting functions and thus speaking in a manner acceptable to the dominant ideology, the mediator in effect was speaking "strategically" in an effort to "help a member of the minority culture overcome the strictures of the legal process" (Merlini 2009:85).

Merlini's findings are remarkably similarly to those of Barsky (1994, 2000), whose analyses are based on Canadian political refugee hearings. Barsky found that interpreters assigned to such hearings appropriately act as "intercultural mediators." For him, interpreters in political refugee cases should be "facilitators," in the sense that they should be able to "interpret language and intention, the verbal and the non-verbal, and then assist in the difficult process of contextualizing testimony and rendering it appropriate to the circumstance" (Barsky 2000:78). In short, he espouses the position that competent interpreters at political refugee hearings should take on a role that goes far beyond merely converting source language utterances into target language equivalents (Barsky 2000:62). He gives the example of a Canadian-born English/Russian interpreter who brings narratives—even dull narratives—to life, by adding relevant details to the short, terse statements of Russian-speaking claimants, and in the process making their stories compelling and more believable (Barsky 2000:73).

The role of interpreters as advocates in immigration matters has been brought into stark relief by a 2008 event that shocked many in the USA, so much so that one of the 26 interpreters who were called on to serve in this case spoke out publicly against what he, and many others, considered to be a grave injustice. It was the detention and incarceration by approximately 900 agents of the US Immigration and Customs Enforcement (ICE) of 390 undocumented persons who were working illegally in the largest slaughterhouse and meat-processing plant in the USA, located in a small town in Iowa. The specific charges against them were the crimes of "knowingly using a false Social Security number" and "aggravated identity theft." Erik Camayd-Freixas, a federally certified interpreter and professor of interpreting/translating at a Miami, Florida university, published a 13-page article in the newsletter of the National Association of Judiciary Interpreters and Translators (NAJIT), the highlights of which were reprinted in one of the most prestigious of US newspapers, *The New York Times*, and much of which was reiterated in his testimony before the House of Representatives Subcommittee on Immigration, Citizenship, Refugees, Border Security and International Law of the US Congress (July 24, 2008). Camayd-Freixas's outrage at the way that these men and women were treated for merely living and working without documentation in the USA is clear from his description (Camayd-Freixas 2008:1–2) that it was

> the saddest procession I have ever witnessed.... Driven single-file in groups of 10, shackled at the wrists, waist and ankles, chains dragging as they shuffled through, the slaughterhouse workers were brought in for arraignment, sat and listened through headsets to the interpreted initial appearance, before marching out again to be bused to different county jails, only to make room for the next row of 10. They appeared to be uniformly no more than 5 ft. tall, mostly illiterate Guatemalan peasants with Mayan last names,... some in tears; others with faces of worry, fear, and embarrassment. (Camayd-Freixas 2008:1–2)

The painstakingly detailed account of what these undocumented persons went through is extraordinary because it was written by an interpreter who participated in the judicial process. Professional court interpreters are expected to maintain a stance of neutrality in the course of their work. The ethical codes of conduct of interpreting associations routinely point out this expectation (Berk-Seligson 2002; González et al. 1991; Hewitt 1995; NAJIT Code of Ethics and Professional Responsibilities). For an interpreter who has impeccable credentials, namely certification at the highest level in the USA and experience as a professor of interpreting at the college level, to express a personal opinion via the mass media of the way in which justice was carried out in a particular case represents an act of courage, all the more justifiable because the press and television reporters were prohibited from coming close to the place of the mass arrest and therefore had no way of capturing images of it. The passionate desire of this highly regarded interpreter to describe the event in which he participated highlights the point that despite the theoretical ideal that interpreters are sworn to uphold, maintaining one's impartiality is sometimes impossible, and ultimately even unethical. There are times when interpreters must speak out against what they perceive to be a miscarriage of justice.

30.2.3 Interpreting in the informal courtroom

While cases involving immigration and asylum issues will employ interpreters both in formal courtrooms as well as in bureaucratic settings such as the Austrian and Italian ones described by Pöllabauer and Merlini, respectively, there are cases that are tried in a type of court less formal than either the state or federal trial court, yet one that has something in common with the immigration court. Conley and O'Barr (1990:24) have called them "informal courts," and "depending on the state, this court may be called a small claims court, a magistrate's court, a justice of the peace court, or a *pro se* court." According to Conley and O'Barr, formal courts can be distinguished from informal courts in that the former "observe procedural and evidentiary formalities, and in which lawyers customarily represent the litigant," whereas informal courts do not (Conley and O'Barr 1990:24). Court-supervised and community-based mediation or arbitration would be included within the purview of the informal justice system, according to Conley and O'Barr. In contrast to formal courts, informal courts often do not allow the presence of lawyers (Conley and O'Barr 1990:25).

An important study of interpreting in small claims court by Angermeyer (2006) brings to light a number of unexpected and highly interesting findings. Observing proceedings in New York City Small Claims Court, Angermeyer discovered that this court in many ways is different from small claims courts in much of the USA. The most important difference, according to Angermeyer, is the frequent use of arbitrators rather than judges, and the fact that lawyers are allowed to represent litigants. Indeed, in some types of cases lawyers are required to do so (Angermeyer 2006:67). Angermeyer observed 208 disputes, 187 of which involved a participant who used a language other than English (for whom Angermeyer coins the acronym LOTE). The languages were Spanish, Russian, Polish, and Haitian Creole, and the cases involved such issues as landlord/tenant disputes, unpaid wages, property damages, and damage from car accidents.

When interpreters were present at disputes involving LOTE speakers, a number of problems arose. First, interpreters often omitted crucial parts of the testimony, and pragmatically misrepresented others (Angermeyer 2006:230). Second, some arbitrators expressed impatience with the interpreting process and would interrupt litigants who used the services of an interpreter (Angermeyer 2006:261). This was especially the case when the LOTE-speaking litigant was accompanied by a lawyer. In such cases, the lawyer would often take over the testimony from the claimant, and the discourse would become one between arbitrator and lawyer, without the participation of the claimant (Angermeyer 2006:251). In effect, the claimant's speaking rights were revoked as a result of this restructuring of the dispute process.

One reason that arbitrators become impatient with interpreted testimony, Angermeyer found, is that when interpreters use the consecutive mode, which requires that interpreters wait until the speakers have completed their turn before beginning their interpretation, the questioning process takes far longer than it does when it is conducted entirely in English. As a result of this general impatience with interpreters, "Most English-speaking litigants and attorneys, but also many arbitrators, don't pause for translation while they hold the floor, and thus they force the interpreter into simultaneous interpreting by interrupting English-speaking litigants" (Angermeyer 2006:266). Angermeyer was told by the interpreters he observed that the simultaneous mode is far more arduous than the consecutive mode; however, my own conversations with federally certified interpreters, who represent the most highly qualified interpreters in the US context, drew exactly the opposite conclusion. Irrespective of whether consecutive interpreting is cognitively more taxing than is simultaneous, the outcome for the LOTE-speaking litigants in a New York City small claims court was that consecutive interpreting forced them to pause during their testimony, which resulted in their narratives appearing less coherent and more fragmented. As O'Barr (1982) and Harris (2001) have noted, fragmented testimony can cause jurors and judges to evaluate witnesses more negatively than does a narrative style testimony. Angermeyer's important finding is that

> The distribution of interpreting modes thus creates an imbalance between English-speaking litigants and non-English-speaking litigants, as the former are more likely to be able to give uninterrupted, narrative-style testimony than are the latter. This imbalance is amplified by a further difference between simultaneous and consecutive interpreting, namely in the degree to which each enables interpreters to produce close renditions of the original talk.... When interpreters translate simultaneously, they are often unable to produce close renditions of all that has been said, and as a consequence, relevant information may be left untranslated for the non-English-speaking litigant. This is far less likely to occur with consecutive interpreting. (Angermeyer 2006:271)

In sum, Angermeyer concludes, litigants in small claims courts who communicate through an interpreter are at a distinct disadvantage compared to English-speakers.

30.3 INTERPRETING IN TRIAL COURT

For court interpreters, the trial court represents the highest level of expectation of accuracy.[7] Accuracy, in turn, is conceptualized as pragmalinguistic and cultural equivalence. The concern for equivalence is driven by the fact that in the trial court, the speech of defendants, witnesses, lawyers, and judges is preserved for the record. Transcripts by a court reporter are invariably in English. The court reporter transcribes either the original utterances in English, or the English interpretation of utterances in other languages. Foreign language testimony is thus not part of the court record, although it may be retrievable when doubts about interpreter accuracy arise in courts where proceedings are audio-recorded (something that is usually done because court reporters are not employed there).

A number of empirical studies have addressed the question of pragmatic equivalence in court interpreting (e.g. Berk-Seligson 1990, 2002; Hale 2004; Hale and Gibbons 1999;

---

[7] The following discussion draws heavily on Berk-Seligson (2005).

Rigney 1999; Russell 2000). Berk-Seligson's (1990, 2002) ethnographic study of Spanish/ English interpreting in American federal, state, and municipal courts revealed that interpreters alter the style of witness testimony, turning unmarked speech into what O'Barr (1982) and O'Barr and Atkins (1980) have called "powerless speech style." Specifically, interpreters were found to add hedges, insert into the target language linguistic substance perceived to be underlying or "understood" in the source utterance, use uncontracted forms, rephrase what they themselves had just uttered in their interpretation, and add polite forms of address, particles, and hesitation forms. The use of uncontracted forms, combined with the insertion of linguistic material normally deleted in surface syntax, creates a hyperformal speech style, that is, a stilted style not usually used in spoken American English. This style had been found by O'Barr to produce negative social/ psychological evaluations of witnesses. When used by interpreters, however, hyperformal style enhances the image of a witness in the eyes of mock jurors (Berk-Seligson 1990, 2002).

Hale's (2004:156) study of interpreting in the Australian courtroom supports the essential findings of Berk-Seligson, namely, that interpreters regularly alter the speech styles of witnesses. However, she found that although interpreters generally omit features characteristic of powerless style, they also sometimes add features of powerless speech to their English renditions of Spanish testimony when no such features were present in the Spanish.

Furthermore, court interpreters not only alter witness testimony, but they also affect lawyers' questioning strategies, often having a negative impact on the degree of control that lawyers have over witnesses' answers (Berk-Seligson 1990, 1999, 2002; Hale 2004; Rigney 1999). Both by interrupting lawyers and by turning their leading questions into ones that are either not leading at all or are far weaker in their degree of coerciveness, court interpreters have been shown to reduce the power that lawyers normally hold over the witnesses they are questioning. In addition, interpreters have been found to adversely affect the ability of lawyers to control the flow of information coming from witnesses when they omit from their interpretations discourse markers such as "well," "now," and "you see," all of which are used by lawyers to preface their questions.

30.5 Conclusions

This review has attempted to demonstrate that the role of court interpreters is complex and multi-faceted. By viewing their efforts in four distinct settings, we have seen that the contexts themselves introduce variation into the performance of interpreters. Thus, in relatively informal settings such as the asylum interview, interpreters have been seen to shift between demonstrating to asylum seekers that they care about a positive outcome of the application process, and demonstrating to the police officers who are conducting the interviews that they—the interpreters—are concerned about the institution for which the police work. At the same time, asylum application interpreters care about preserving their own positive face. In contrast, police officers acting as interpreters at custodial interrogations apparently have only the institution at heart, and have great difficulty remaining in an interpreter footing. Only in the most formal judicial setting, the trial court, do interpreters feel highly constrained by the role that they are expected to play, yet even there, feelings of solidarity with non-English speaking witnesses can affect their interpretations (Berk-Seligson 2002). Thus, if impartiality is one of the prerequisites of professional court interpreting, it should be viewed more as an elusive ideal than as a realistically attainable goal.

CHAPTER 31

....

INSTRUCTING THE JURY

....

NANCY S. MARDER

31.1 INTRODUCTION

....

IN the American legal system, a defendant in a serious criminal case and parties in certain types of civil cases are entitled to a trial by jury. In both criminal and civil jury trials, jurors are drawn from a "fair-cross-section" of the community.[1] Although they are usually untrained in the law, they provide the "common-sense judgment" of the community.[2] A defendant in a criminal case or a party in a civil case might prefer a jury trial to a bench trial (in which the verdict is reached by the judge), even though both jury and judge are required to be impartial, because the jury is drawn from a broad swath of the citizenry, the jurors serve in only one case, and the jurors bring to their deliberations a variety of perspectives, backgrounds, and life experiences. As Justice Byron White, writing in one US Supreme Court opinion explained, if a criminal defendant prefers "the common-sense judgment of a jury to the more tutored but perhaps less sympathetic reaction of the single judge, he was to have it."[3] The jury trial is a protection afforded to the parties in the American legal system and is guaranteed by the Sixth[4] and Seventh Amendments[5] to the US Constitution. The jury, particularly in a criminal case, is seen as an "inestimable safeguard against the corrupt or overzealous prosecutor and against the compliant, biased, or eccentric judge."[6]

Even in a jury trial, however, the judge performs many key functions. For example, a judge in a federal court typically conducts the *voir dire*,[7] or questioning, of prospective jurors

---

[1] 28 U.S.C. § 1861.

[2] *Duncan v Louisiana*, 391 U.S. 145, 156 (1968).

[3] Ibid.

[4] See U.S. Const. amend. VI (providing the right to a jury trial in criminal cases).

[5] See U.S. Const. amend. VII (providing the right to a jury trial for certain civil claims brought in federal court).

[6] *Duncan*, 391 U.S. at 156.

[7] See Fed. R. Civ. P. 47(a); Fed. R. Crim. P. 24(a).

in order to determine who is impartial and can serve on the jury and who is partial and must be excused for cause. The judge also supervises the attorneys' exercise of peremptory challenges, by which each side can remove a certain number of prospective jurors without having to give a reason.[8] Throughout the trial, the judge maintains order in the courtroom, rules on objections, protects the jury from prejudicial remarks by either side, guards against attorneys' badgering of witnesses, and serves as a gatekeeper, deciding which exhibits and testimony will be admitted into evidence. The judge is seen as a neutral, authority figure in the courtroom. Jurors often look to the judge to provide guidance as to their proper role (Marder 2005:118–20). In some courtrooms, the judge provides such guidance by offering jury instructions early in the trial. These preliminary instructions can provide jurors with some background about the case, the trial, and their role in it (Dann and Logan 1996:281).

At the end of a jury trial, whether in a civil or criminal case, the judge instructs the jury on the relevant law. The jury is supposed to use the jury instructions in the course of its deliberations. It is supposed to find the facts and apply the law to reach its verdict. But what if the jury does not understand the instructions, either because of the language or the presentation of the instructions? Much of the empirical and anecdotal evidence suggests that juries have difficulty understanding the instructions.[9] The consequences of jury misunderstanding can be dire, particularly in capital cases. Thus, jury instructions need to be written in language that jurors can understand and presented in ways that reach jurors so that they can use the instructions correctly during their deliberations.

This chapter will examine why jury instructions are so difficult to grasp and what steps can be taken to make them more accessible to jurors. Part of the problem is that jury instructions are typically drafted by a committee of professionals whose goal is to produce a pattern instruction that accurately encapsulates the law. Such an instruction is written for members of the legal community, but not necessarily for laypersons. Another part of the problem is the way that judges deliver instructions. Typically, judges simply read the instructions aloud, no matter how lengthy they are. It is difficult for jurors to grasp legal language and concepts from instructions delivered in this manner. This chapter will explore a range of steps—big and small—that judges and committees can take so that the language and presentation of jury instructions are no longer barriers to juror comprehension.

31.2 LANGUAGE OF THE INSTRUCTIONS

Many state and federal courts now use pattern (or standardized) jury instructions.[10] The main advantage to pattern instructions is that they tend to be reliable and accurate statements of the law. Instead of each judge writing instructions from scratch for each jury

---

[8] There are several instances in which an attorney has to give reasons for the exercise of a peremptory challenge and the reasons cannot be based on race, gender, or ethnicity of a prospective juror. For the prima facie test that an attorney seeking to challenge a peremptory challenge must meet, see *Batson v Kentucky*, 476 U.S. 79, 96–98 (1986).

[9] See Section 31.4.

[10] See, e.g., Hannaford-Agor and Lassiter (2008).

trial, judges can turn to books containing pattern jury instructions and thus save time and reduce the risk of reversal. Pattern instructions are usually written by a committee and they have the approval or recommendation of the state judges. In some states, such as Ohio, the committee that drafts the instructions consists solely of judges; in other states, such as Illinois, the committee consists of judges and lawyers. In either case, the committees are made up of professionals who have been trained in the law.

Typically, the committee drafts boilerplate language that can be used in different types of cases. To use a pattern instruction, the lawyers and judge in a case might make minor adjustments to the pattern instruction so that the general language fits more closely the particulars of the case. For example, wherever the pattern instruction offers several options, the judge will select the ones that are relevant to the case. Although judges fill in blank spaces and tailor the instruction to reflect the particulars of the case, in general they use the language of the pattern instruction.

The language of the pattern instruction often relies on legal phrases and concepts that are familiar to lawyers and judges but not to jurors. For example, "preponderance of the evidence," "a violation of the standard of care," and "proximately caused" are phrases that a lawyer or judge learned in law school, but that a juror is unlikely to have encountered before. Legal concepts and phrases are used throughout the instructions, and even when the instructions explain them, the explanation is not one that a layperson will necessarily understand. For example, Illinois' jury instructions define "contributory negligence" as "negligence on the part of the plaintiff that proximately contributed to cause the [alleged] [injury]."[11] Although jurors are likely to need a definition of contributory negligence, they are unlikely to understand the one offered unless "negligence," "proximately contributed," and "alleged" are also explained.

There are several reasons why a committee is likely to use legal terms in an instruction and to adhere closely to the language of a statute even if the meaning is difficult for a layperson to discern. Perhaps, most importantly, the committee wants to get the law right. One way to do this is not to deviate from the language of the case law or statute. A second reason is that these instructions are drafted for several audiences. One audience consists of the legal community, including trial and appellate judges and lawyers. Another audience consists of the jurors, who serve in only one trial. The committee drafts instructions that are supposed to address the needs of both audiences; however, that is a difficult task. It is easier for a committee of professionals to write for fellow professionals than it is to write for laypersons. Lawyers and judges, immersed in the culture and language of the law, often forget how arcane it sounds to those who have not studied it. Moreover, if the committee makes a mistake and writes an instruction that states the law incorrectly, as declared by an appellate court, that will lead to a reversal and possibly a new trial. The costs of an error are great. A prudent committee will err on the side of caution and adhere to the language of the case or statute. If the committee drafts an instruction whose meaning eludes the jury, the jurors are unlikely to complain. The losing party can potentially

---

[11] Ill. Sup. Ct. Comm. on Pattern Jury Instructions in Civil Cases, Illinois Pattern Jury Instructions—Civil § 11.01, at 52 (2006 edn) [hereinafter IPI].

raise the issue, if it could find out about juror confusion, but that is difficult to do (Tiersma 2006b:7). Moreover, a reviewing court might well decide that the instruction is a correct statement of the law even if this particular jury had trouble understanding it. The instruction might remain part of the pattern instructions, whether jurors understand it or not.

31.3 PRESENTATION OF THE INSTRUCTIONS

Typically, the judge instructs the jury on the law either immediately before the attorneys' closing arguments or immediately afterward. Although the judge waits until the close of the case to deliver the final instructions, the judge might instruct jurors on preliminary matters throughout the trial. One reason for preliminary instructions is that jurors benefit from learning about certain concepts as they arise during the trial. Empirical studies have found that instructions given at the beginning and end of the trial help jurors to focus on the relevant evidence and to remember it (Elwork et al. 1977), to follow the law, and to feel more satisfied with their experience (Heuer and Penrod 1989). Final instructions are supposed to leave jurors with the law fresh in their minds as they begin their deliberations.

Traditionally, the judge instructs the jury by reading aloud from written instructions. The instructions are presented like a lecture, and like some lectures, the instructions can be difficult and lengthy. In many courtrooms, the jurors are simply expected to absorb the information. They are supposed to understand the instructions even though many of the words and concepts are foreign to them. They are also supposed to remember what they have heard—sometimes without any of the aids available to students, such as taking notes or asking questions.

Once the jury has begun its deliberations, the foreperson can submit a note to the judge if the jury has a question about the instructions. In most courtrooms, the judge will respond by interrupting the jury's deliberations, reassembling everyone in the courtroom, and rereading the relevant portion of the instructions, rather than actually answering the jury's question.[12] The judge is reluctant to deviate from the written script for fear that any explanation might be in error. The judge might reread the relevant portion of the instructions or ignore the jury's question altogether, but either response is frustrating to the jurors. As one juror in a first-degree murder trial explained: "It was really frustrating because we were not getting any help on how do you go about this, how do you approach the situation. You're supposed to decide the outcome of a man's life—blind—and that's not acceptable" (Emery 2002:1A). Jurors often feel that they have been given a tremendous responsibility, but then when they seek the court's assistance they are rebuffed. At this point, rather than turning to the judge for further clarification of the instructions, they attempt to cobble together their own explanation (Sundby 2005:50).

---

[12] See, e.g., Connor (2004:7).

Traditionally, jurors were not given a copy of the written instructions to take into the jury room and to consult during their deliberations. Originally, this may have been because jurors were illiterate, though that is no longer the case. Today, one of the eligibility requirements, at least in federal court, is that a juror has the ability to read and write in English.[13] Another explanation that has been given is that if jurors were provided with a written copy of the instructions, then they might give too much weight to one portion of the instructions, rather than considering the instructions in their entirety. Without a written copy of the instructions, though, it is difficult for jurors to remember the instructions, particularly if there are a lot of them.

31.4 PROBLEMS WITH THE INSTRUCTIONS

The key problem with jury instructions is that jurors have a hard time understanding them. The instructions use legal phrases and concepts that are foreign to the layperson. The explanations of the legal phrases and concepts, when they are provided, are also given in legal language. The instructions should be written with jurors in mind. Instead, jury instruction committees, faced with competing pressures, draft instructions for the legal community rather than for the jurors.[14]

At least 30 years of empirical studies support the conclusion that juror comprehension of instructions is modest (Marder 2006:454–8). This is not surprising given the prevalence of pattern instructions and their use of abstruse legal language. Although deliberation improves juror understanding of the instructions, there is still room for jury instruction committees to take further steps (Forston 1975). In several studies in which researchers rewrote the instructions in plain language, mock juror and mock jury comprehension improved (Elwork et al. 1977:176). Thus, committees, if committed to increasing juror and jury understanding of the instructions, could rewrite the instructions so that laypersons could understand them. As an illustration, one traditional instruction in California was as follows: "Failure of recollection is common. Innocent misrecollection is not uncommon."[15] A new committee, striving for plain language, created a new instruction, which is straightforward and easy for jurors to understand. California judges can now instruct jurors as follows: "People often forget things or make mistakes in what they remember."[16]

Judges' anecdotal experiences, gleaned from years in the courtroom, are consistent with the empirical studies that show that jurors have a hard time understanding the

---

[13] See 28 U.S.C. § 1865(b)(2).

[14] See, e.g., *Foreword to the Fourth Edition (1995)* of IPI (note 11 above), at ix ("At times, the committee has been forced to choose between simplicity and accuracy, and it has been necessary to come down on the side of accuracy.").

[15] Civil Comm. on Cal. Jury Instructions, California Jury Instructions—Civil (BAJI) §221 (2005).

[16] Judicial Council of Cal. Civil Jury Instructions, California Jury Instructions §107 (2003).

instructions. Judges admit that as they read the jury instructions aloud, they can almost predict when the jurors' eyes will begin to glaze over (Wascher 2005:52). They know that jurors have a difficult time focusing on and following the instructions, and yet they read the instructions aloud as they have always done.

Even judges reveal their boredom when they read the instructions. The judge in the movie *12 Angry Men* is an illustration, albeit a fictional one, of this phenomenon.[17] We, the viewers, listen to him as he reads some of the instructions aloud to the jurors before they deliberate. He delivers the instructions in a bored, monotone voice. He conveys to the jurors and viewers that he is not interested in the case. The case involves a 19-year old boy who has been charged with the murder of his father. If the boy is convicted by the jury, he will be executed by the state; the death penalty is mandatory. The judge's rote delivery suggests to the jurors that the case before them can be easily dispatched. The jurors vote almost immediately. Eleven jurors vote to convict, but one juror, played by Henry Fonda, votes to acquit. His decision to vote not-guilty requires the other jurors to engage in earnest deliberation, in spite of the example set by the judge.

Even if in most cases juries reach verdicts with which judges would agree (Kalven and Zeisel 1966:56), juries do so in spite of the instructions. However, jury instructions should be an aid, not a hindrance, to jurors' performance of their role.

In capital cases, in particular, jurors feel that they are asked to perform a daunting task—deciding whether someone should live or die—and that they should at least be given instructions they understand. Jurors who vote for the death penalty feel an enormous responsibility. If they discover afterward that they did not understand the instructions properly, they can experience a lifetime of regret.

Empirical studies of capital case instructions reveal a number of mistakes by mock jurors, and yet it is hard to convince appellate courts that these instructions need to be rewritten. For example, there is confusion about "aggravating" and "mitigating" circumstances,[18] two concepts that are critical in deciding whether to impose the death penalty. Jurors may not understand what the words mean (Tiersma 1995b), or how much agreement there has to be among jurors to find either set of circumstances (Haney and Lynch 1994:420). There is also a tendency among mock jurors to import the ordinary, commonplace meaning of words into the death penalty context (Eisenberg and Wells 1993:8). They fail to understand that for some words, such as "aggravating," they need to use a specific meaning provided by statute, rather than the ordinary meaning of "annoying."

One problem is that appellate courts have regarded empirical studies, particularly mock jury studies, with skepticism. Although there are several ways in which mock jury studies fail to capture the actual jury experience,[19] sometimes they are the best available method. In addition, some of the findings of mock jury studies have been supported by interviews with actual jurors (Sundby 2005). Although interviews have their own

---

[17] *12 Angry Men* (Orion-Nova Productions 1957).

[18] See, e.g., Burgins (1995: 30, 31).

[19] For example, mock jurors know their decision will have no real-world consequences. Also, studies that do not include deliberations omit a key component of the jury experience.

limitations, such as the self-interest or faulty recollections of the interviewees, the use of multiple methods helps to counteract the limitations inherent in any one method. Even when jury-eligible citizens were used in another empirical study examining capital case instructions, an appellate court doubted the efficacy of the study because there was no control group and the results were based on tests of individuals' understanding of the instructions rather than a group's understanding, and jurors work in groups.[20]

Although there are limitations with any particular study, in light of the myriad empirical studies finding that mock jurors have trouble understanding the instructions, and the interviews with actual jurors who expressed their frustration with not understanding the instructions, what steps should judges and committees take to make jury instructions more understandable to jurors?

31.5 NEXT STEPS

State and federal courts have taken different approaches to improving jury instructions. Some states, like Arizona, have rewritten their jury instructions using plain language and have used language appropriate for a sixth-grade reading level (Woo 1994:B5). Arizona's efforts to rewrite its instructions were part of a large-scale effort to reform the state's jury system. Arizona's efforts required the leadership of its chief justice, who formed a committee to recommend jury reforms and gave it a broad mandate for change (Dann and Logan 1996). Other states have taken more modest steps. For example, Delaware sends its jury instructions to a professional linguist for review and revision (Munsterman et al. 2006:147–8). There are a range of steps that state and federal courts can take to make the language of their instructions more understandable to jurors and to enhance the way in which instructions are presented.

31.5.1 Small steps

There are a number of small steps that state and federal courts can take to improve juror comprehension of jury instructions. One is that judges can give jurors an individual written copy of the final instructions that they can follow as the judge reads the instructions aloud.[21] Some people absorb new material more readily by reading it, others by listening to it, and still others by reading and listening to it.[22] Providing jurors with individual written copies of the final instructions takes into account these different learning styles. In addition, judges should permit jurors to take notes as the instructions

---

[20] See *Free v Peters*, 12 F.3d 700, 705-06 (7th Cir. 1993) (criticizing the methodological weaknesses of a study testing the instructions in an Illinois capital case).

[21] See Connor (note 12 above), at 7.

[22] See, e.g., Hansen (2003:26).

are read aloud so that they can mark on their written copy any questions they have. Jurors should take their individual, annotated copies of the instructions into the jury room so that they can answer each other's questions, or the jury can send a note to the judge with the jury's questions.

Another small step that judges can take is to include the headings for each instruction in the written copies that are given to jurors. When lawyers and judges look through a book of pattern instructions, they have headings to guide them. The headings serve as a roadmap for the instructions.[23] They look at the heading and know that the instruction will be about "negligence," "products liability," or another specific topic. However, when jurors are given a written copy of the instructions, the headings have usually been omitted. Jurors see only pages of text. There are no indications of which block of text corresponds to which instruction, where one instruction ends and another begins, or why one instruction precedes or follows another. The headings serve as guide-posts for lawyers and judges, and if they were made available to jurors, they could serve a similar function for them.

Judges can also follow the practice that a number of states have adopted and give some of the instructions as they become relevant during the trial. For example, if a law enforcement officer is about to testify, the judge should instruct the jury that even though a law enforcement officer will be a witness, his or her testimony is not to be given any more or less weight because of that position.[24] It is useful for the jury to hear that instruction right before the law enforcement officer testifies rather than to hear it for the first time at the very end of the trial when so many other instructions are given.

Another small step that judges can take is to make an audiotape or videotape[25] of the reading of the instructions and to permit jurors to replay it during their deliberations. When a question arises about an instruction, the jurors can turn to their written copies or to the audiotape or videotape without interrupting their deliberations. An audiotape or videotape provides more information than a hard copy of the instructions and may help the jury to understand the instructions without having to send a note to the judge. Tone of voice and inflection can make an audiotape helpful, and a videotape provides even more detail. Body language and tone can convey much information and jurors should have this information available to them without having to reconvene in the courtroom.

Finally, judges need to be open to new ways of delivering jury instructions. The judge's reading of the instructions, no matter how tedious some jurors find it, is useful because it ensures that all jurors will have heard the instructions from beginning to end. However, there are different ways to supplement the reading to make it more engaging to jurors. One judge accompanies his reading with PowerPoint slides that highlight what he is

---

[23] See, e.g., Kimble (2007:50, 51) ("Good headings and subheadings are vital navigational aids for the reader.").

[24] See, e.g., 1 Leonard B. Sand et al., Modern Federal Jury Instructions: Criminal § 7–61 (2005) (Law Enforcement Witness).

[25] A DVD is another option, but I refer to audiotapes and videotapes because some courts are slow to adopt new technology.

saying (Marder 2006:504). One lawyer has suggested using illustrations as an aid to conveying difficult concepts in the instructions (Dattu 1998). Younger judges trying to reach younger jurors may think of new ways to make the reading more interesting without compromising the seriousness of the reading. Trial judges should experiment and appellate courts should support these experiments (Cate and Minow 1993:1111).

31.5.2 Big steps

Perhaps the biggest step that a court can take to make its jury instructions understandable to jurors is to rewrite all of the instructions using plain language. Some states, such as Arizona and California, have taken this approach. For example, in California, a committee of lawyers, judges, academics, and laypersons rewrote the civil jury instructions, while another committee rewrote the criminal jury instructions. Both committees had to start from scratch because there was a copyright on the existing jury instructions.[26] The civil jury instruction committee took six years to complete its work (Ward 2004:38), and the criminal jury instruction committee took eight years (Tebo 2006: 36).

The California jury instruction committees were unusual in several respects. First, they included linguists, who were able to focus on drafting instructions that communicated effectively with laypersons. Second, they initially included laypersons who could potentially provide feedback as to whether the new instructions were understandable to them or not. Third, the committees engaged in a process that gave the public an opportunity to comment on proposed instructions before they were published and made available for use in the courts.

There have been several first-hand accounts that capture just how labor-intensive this process was (Tiersma 2001). Writing instructions from scratch required extraordinary effort by the committee members and chairs, as well as extraordinary leadership by the state supreme court's chief justice. Only those states that have a supreme court willing to lead the effort and committee members willing to perform this yeoman's task should consider such an undertaking. Even with all of the effort, and with an end result that most agree is far more understandable than the earlier instructions, there were still complaints. Some lawyers criticized the new instructions, which were written for a tenth-grade reading level, as being a "dumbed down" version of the earlier instructions.[27]

31.5.3 A middle course

For those judges and jury instruction committees that want to take significant action but are unable to engage in the massive undertaking of rewriting their entire book of jury instructions, there are at least two steps that offer a middle course. One addresses the

---

[26] See, e.g., Post (2004:1, 19).
[27] Ibid. (quoting plaintiffs' attorney William Weiss, a San Francisco solo practitioner).

language of jury instructions and the other step addresses the way in which instructions are presented.

As to the language of jury instructions, committees could agree to test any new jury instruction using laypersons to see whether they understand the instruction or whether the instruction needs to be revised (Marder 2006:489). The jury instruction committee would take any new or newly revised instruction that it had completed to its satisfaction, and instead of publishing it immediately, the committee would send it to a social scientist or other academic who would test the instruction using jury-eligible citizens to see whether they understood it. Testing would reveal whether any words or phrases caused confusion. The academic could replace those words or phrases and test the rewritten instruction to make sure laypersons understood it. After the testing and rewriting, the committee could review the instruction to make sure that it still conveyed the law accurately.

This process would still leave responsibility for the instructions in the hands of the committee, but the committee would have the benefit of laypersons' responses to the instruction before it was published. Admittedly, the testing would add another step and more time to the process of writing an instruction. But jury instruction committees are usually willing to take as much time as they need to work on an instruction, so this might not be a significant drawback. The testing of only a new or newly revised instruction, rather than of all existing instructions, would mean that change would happen slowly. There would not be a major overhaul of the instructions. On the plus side, however, states choosing this option would not need their jury instruction committees or chief justices to take extraordinary measures. The committees could function as they always had, but simply add this new step to their process.

As to the presentation of jury instructions, judges should allow jurors to ask questions about the instructions immediately after the judge has read the final instructions aloud (Marder 2005:501–2). Rather than the instructions being offered as a lecture, they would become an opportunity for a dialogue. If a juror had a question, the judge could simply answer it. Currently, a juror with a question has to go into the jury room and hope that other jurors will know the answer. If other jurors do not know the answer, the jury might send a note to the judge. The judge might ignore the question or might respond by simply rereading the relevant portion of the instructions. In either case, the question remains unanswered. Alternatively, the jurors might try to answer their own question and arrive at a correct or incorrect answer.

This added step of allowing jurors to ask questions would undoubtedly be greeted with skepticism by some judges who would worry that any answer they gave would open the door to reversal on appeal. However, the questions could be submitted in writing, giving the judge more control over his or her response and time to consult the lawyers. Lawyers are also likely to resist this practice because after they have argued over the precise wording of an instruction they are unlikely to want the judge to deliver off-the-cuff explanations to jurors. But from the jurors' perspective, the opportunity to have their questions answered would be very useful. One empirical study found that when a judge answered jurors' questions about instructions, their understanding of the instructions reached "fairly high levels" (Reifman et al. 1992:551). Just as a student should not have to go through a course without understanding a key term or concept, so too a juror should not have to go through deliberations without understanding the governing law.

In some states, jurors are permitted to ask questions of witnesses, and the practice has usually been well-received (Mott 2003:1105). For example, some states allow jurors to submit written questions anonymously to the judge to be asked of witnesses before they step down from the witness stand. The judge, in consultation with the lawyers, first decides whether the question is appropriate. If it is, the judge asks it; if it is not, the judge explains to the jurors that it cannot be asked (Lucci 2005:17). Lawyers had worried about interrupting the flow of the proceedings and judges had worried about lengthening the trial, but in courtrooms that have tried this practice neither of these problems has come to pass. The judge does not invite questions until the witness has finished testifying and is ready to step down. Researchers have found that jurors do not ask many questions and the questions they do ask have not lengthened the trial process (Mott 2003:1120). In fact, the questions might shorten the trial because deliberations proceed more quickly. Lawyers and judges who were resistant to the idea initially were usually won over when they actually had experience with the practice. This is also likely to be the case when jurors are permitted to ask judges questions about the instructions.

31.6 CONCLUSION

The key challenge with jury instructions is how to make them more understandable to jurors. The language is abstruse and the presentation can be mind-numbing. Although jurors have performed admirably in spite of the instructions, they have expressed frustration with them. They have been summoned to perform the difficult task of judging, and yet when they look to the court for guidance, they do not find it in the instructions.

Judges and jury instruction committees have a range of options when it comes to improving the instructions. They can take small steps, like making sure that every juror has an individual written copy of the instructions to follow as the judge reads them aloud. They can take big steps, like rewriting all of their instructions in plain language and focusing on the needs of the layperson rather than the professional. Or, they can take a middle course and arrange for every new or newly revised instruction to be tested by a social scientist to ensure that laypersons can understand it. At the same time, judges can allow jurors to ask questions about the instructions so that jury instructions are no longer a lecture by the judge, but rather a dialogue between judge and jury.

PART VII

INTELLECTUAL
PROPERTY

CHAPTER 32

USING LINGUISTICS IN TRADEMARK CASES

ROGER W. SHUY

32.1 LINGUISTICS AND LAW

WHEN linguists apply their knowledge and skills to another field, it is prudent for them to begin with the problems, assumptions, perspectives, and specialized language of that other field. In the relationship of linguistics and law, this means that linguists need to begin with the lawyers where *they* are and to not expect lawyers to begin where linguists are.

Lawyers' training, concepts, and content cause them to think about and deal with categories such as trademarks, product liability, contracts, wills, copyrights, defamation, bribery, murder, and other types of cases that they learned in law school. It is safe to say that they are not dealing with or even thinking about the linguistic categories of syntax, phonology, semantics, speech acts, discourse analysis, or dialects in the same way linguists think about and use them. Linguists have to begin with (and first learn about) the way lawyers think, their language, their assumptions, and even their professional vision (Goodwin 1996:606–33).

One of the current useful applications of linguistics to law is in trademark disputes, where the legal issues offer a good fit for linguistic tools. So far, at least, linguistic contributions to trademark disputes seem to have surfaced primarily in North America and Australia, although there has been some activity in Japan as well (Hotta and Fujita 2007; Okawara 2006d).

The ongoing efforts of The International Trademark Association show hopeful signs that lawyers are making steady progress toward standardizing trademark law and procedures throughout the world, making this a fruitful area for international applications of linguistics. But first we should know how lawyers view their trademark cases.

32.2 PERSPECTIVES ON TRADEMARKS

A trademark is a distinctive sign associating and distinguishing a product or service that indicates its commercial origin (Blackett 1998:1). Trademark law tries to protect the owner of the mark from "referential confusion" (Tiersma 1999:121). Unless the mark is lost through lack of use, the owners have a property right that is perpetual. Trademarks "play a central role in defining corporate personality through image-manipulation or 'branding'" (Hutton 2009:121).

In most jurisdictions, trademark law deals with the proprietary use of product names, services, logos, and slogans, using categories to describe them such as *generic, descriptive, suggestive, fanciful, arbitrary* (McCarthy 1984:436–502). More recently, focus on these categories has been accompanied by the trademark concept of *dilution*. Cases that utilize these trademark categories offer the potential for linguistic interest and are capable of being analyzed and measured linguistically.

The focus of most trademark disputes is whether consumers will become confused about the origin and ownership of a product or service. To resolve this question, lawyers focus attention on the relative strength of the marks. Strong marks are protected from use by others because they do not confuse consumers about the quality, nature, and manufacturer of the product or service, while weak marks are not protected. But many marks fall between the polarities of strong versus weak and invite litigation. In many such cases, lawyers argue about whether a mark is either descriptive or generic, therefore weak, or suggestive, therefore strong (McCarthy 1984:434). In contrast, linguists and other social scientists view trademarks as a prescriptive form of language planning with the admirable purpose of bringing order to otherwise chaotic business practices (Shuy 2002:3). The basic assumptions of linguists are sometimes very different from those of lawyers, especially about who owns language, about who has or does not have the power to use it, and about who has the authority to control natural language variation, change, and diversity (Hutton 2009:126–7). From the perspective of the legal system, a basic purpose of trademark law is to protect the consumer (Westerhaus 2003:295), and to ensure that the products they buy are authentic. In contrast, the linguist's common concern is about the consumer's right to use the language freely, whether trademarked or not (Shuy 2002:55, 199).

Because both fields have compelling reasons for believing as they do, linguists who decide to work with lawyers in trademark infringement cases need to be aware not only of these differing disciplinary assumptions and perspectives, but also of the need to focus attention on only the linguistic relevance to the case, not on their conflicting ideologies (Shuy 2002:192). Otherwise, their efforts to assist lawyers can be counterproductive.

32.2.1 Trademark categories

Although it might seem that trademark categories are well-defined pigeon-holes, it is prudent to understand that trademark categories exist on a continuum that has less-than-sharp boundaries.

32.2.1.1 *Generic marks*

Generic is a category name borrowed from the fields of logic and biology, in which the noun, *genus*, is a term used to depict a major class or kind of things that includes several subclasses called *species*. The corresponding adjective forms are *generic* and *specific*. For example, the applicable laws regard trademarks as a species within the genus of intellectual property. A mark like *Bicycle* for the name of a wheeled vehicle called a bicycle is an example of a generic name because it depicts a *genus*, a major class of self-propelled vehicles. But when a manufacturer uses *Bicycle* as a trademark for a brand of playing cards, the word is no longer used generically, opening the door to being labeled suggestive.

32.2.1.2 *Descriptive marks*

Descriptive marks describe the qualities, ingredients, and characteristics of a product or service, such as *Raisin Bran* cereal, which contains raisins and bran in the form of small flakes. It's hard to imagine anything more descriptive. Since its name is descriptive, the producer cannot prevent other cereal makers from using the same name. Laudatory names are also considered descriptive, such as *Gold Medal* flour and *Blue Ribbon* beer, since they describe the character or quality of their products. A rule of thumb is that descriptive marks convey information directly with no denotative or connotative association required that might suggest any other possible meaning.

Trademark lawyers consider descriptive marks weak unless these marks have achieved fame among consumers. Many descriptive trademarks that are protected have achieved *secondary meaning*, which means that the owners of the product or service have used the name exclusively and successfully for a long time or have promoted their products or services so vigorously that the public does not register their literal meaning in their minds and therefore associate the mark with only that product or service.

32.2.1.3 *Suggestive marks*

Suggestive marks are protected more than descriptive marks but less so than fanciful or arbitrary ones. They suggest or connote something other than the denotation of the words used as their marks. In the history of trademark categories, the suggestive designation came later than descriptive, fanciful, and arbitrary.

According to trademark law and practice, suggestive marks require consumers to make an instantaneous "mental leap" in order to associate the product or service with the name. For example the name of *Tide* laundry soap is said to be suggestive. The common noun, "tide," does not denote a soap product, but when it's used as the name for one, it calls up the image of a large, active body of water, such as the ocean that washes onto the shore. It's not clear how an oceanic flow causes customers to imagine a positive image of a soap product, but somehow they do. Perhaps the suggestion of water washing onto the shore is the clue, but whatever mental process is involved, marks like *Tide* cause consumers to make a "mental leap," a process requiring them to make use of their imaginations.

Despite the efforts of international trademark law conventions to determine what makes a mark distinctive, the law is still a long way from being clear (Ladas 1995:974).

But context plays an important role in distinguishing between things that are descriptive and suggestive. For example, *Brilliant* is considered descriptive as a name for diamonds but suggestive when used in the context of a furniture polish. The name of a bus service called *Greyhound* recalls the attributes of the type of dog that runs very fast. Associating a bus service with fast dogs may be an incongruous interconnection of the thought processes but its incongruity makes an effective claim of suggestiveness. The more incongruous the connection, the more the mental process has to work to find it, thus creating a strong reason to call it suggestive.

In disputes about whether a mark is suggestive, lawyers often use three tests: the imagination test, the competitors' use test, and the dictionary test. Linguists can offer help in all three of these tests.

(a) The imagination test

The "mental leap" that consumers have to make in order to associate a product or service with its name is measured by the imagination test (McCarthy 1984:491–2). The more that imagination is required by the consumer to get some connection between the product's name (or service) and the product, the more likely that mark can be judged suggestive. While descriptive names directly convey the ingredients, qualities, or characteristics of the named product (*Raisin Bran Flakes, Tasty Bread, Yellow Pages*), suggestive marks indirectly suggest these things in some kind of rapid, multi-stage processes of the mind, as with *Greyhound* bus line and *Tide* laundry soap. The question often comes down to how immediate this imaginative mental process is from the moment when consumers first see the mark to imagining its particular characteristic or service.

(b) The competitors' use test

The competitors' use test grows out of the imagination test (McCarthy 1984:493). The more imagination is required to associate the mark with the product, the less likely are competitors to use that mark when they describe their own products. Mentioning it would seem to strengthen their competition but it implies that this mark actually might be descriptive. For example, if *Ricoh* photocopiers described their product as "the best way to xerox," this could be evidence that *Xerox* is descriptive, with only a weak claim to protect to its mark. But *Ricoh* is unlikely to even say this because doing so could advertise its competitor, *Xerox*. Despite this possibility, some manufacturers occasionally use their competitors' marks in their own advertisements and promotions to borrow their prestige or to portray the competitor's mark as merely descriptive.

(c) The dictionary test

Since dictionaries are often revered as authoritative, they are frequently cited in trademark trials in the dictionary test (McCarthy 1984:493–5). Trademark lawyers frequently rely on dictionaries to determine the meaning and pronunciation of words used in marks or slogans. Although dictionaries may do a fine job providing general information, they cannot capture all of the ways a word is used or said, all of its possible meanings, or all the contexts in which a word can appear. Some dictionaries are better than others at this, some are outdated, and some are too abridged to be authoritative. Linguists who are knowledgeable about the quality and usefulness of dictionaries can serve as quality control experts in trademark cases and also provide ways to find useful lexicographical information not provided by many dictionaries.

32.2.1.4 *Fanciful and arbitrary trademarks*

These marks are distant from any imaginative connection with their products. Fanciful marks are coined words, such as *Exxon* (the oil company), while arbitrary marks are existing words that convey meanings very different from their usual senses, such as *Shell* (gasoline and oil), and *Camel* (cigarettes). Although it requires a leap of imagination to associate a suggestive mark with its qualities, the process of associating products with arbitrary names such as *Exxon*, *Xerox*, or *Kodak* requires more than imagination. Owners who select fanciful or arbitrary marks risk placing their name so far away from its association with their product or service that consumers may not see any connection at all. When *Xerox* and *Kodak* first created their names, consumers had no easy way to associate *Xerox* with photocopying machines or *Kodak* with camera products. But these manufacturers found that after consumers began to associate those names with their products, there were business advantages created by fanciful and arbitrary names. Fanciful and arbitrary marks can become far stronger than the names of competitor's marks, thereby protecting them against any efforts to infringe them.

32.2.1.5 *Trademark dilution*

Although concerns about preserving the uniqueness of marks were voiced as early as 1927 (Schechter 1927), trademark dilution laws are relatively recent (The Federal Trademark Dilution Act of 1995; The Trademark Dilution Revision Act of 2006). These acts require mark owners to prove that the quality and reputation of their marks have been diluted, tainted, blurred, or eroded by another mark, thereby causing consumers to be confused about the quality and ownership of the original mark (Butters 2008a:101–13). Blurring is said to involve the activation of two different referents for the mark if and until the consumer sorts out the proper referent, a process that can diminish the sales power of the original mark. Tarnishment is the persistent negative association caused by blurring (Beebe 2006:1147–51). That is, the blurred mark remains active in the consumer's mind and tarnishes it. Obviously, the junior mark would need to be similar enough to the original mark for the latter to be able to claim that its name had suffered dilution through blurring or tarnishment (Swann 2003:585–625).

It is difficult for the owner of an allegedly diluted mark to prove that such dilution has occurred, which may be the reason dilution is not often charged in trademark cases. In 2003 *Victoria's Secret*, a manufacturer of ladies' sexy garments, charged a pornography shop, named *Victor's Little Secrets*, with dilution. This case went all the way to the US

Supreme Court,[1] but many questions remain unresolved, leading Beebe to observe that dilution "is probably the most muddled concept in all trademark doctrine" (Beebe 2006:1144). Some unresolved issues are cognitive and linguistic in nature, including ways to measure what is meant by "similar," how degrees of alleged dilution can be measured, and what role language context plays in making such distinctions (Shuy 2003a: 13.1–13.19). To my knowledge, linguists have not yet been involved in trademark dilution cases, although they have begun presenting linguistic analyses of the nature of such cases (Hotta 2007a; Butters 2008a).

32.3 THE MAJOR QUESTIONS IN
TRADEMARK DISPUTES

In most trademark disputes there are three standard questions. Do the marks sound alike? Mean the same thing? Look alike? To prove the answers, scientific measurements are always helpful. Often these proof measurements are accomplished by linguist's phonetic, grammatical, semantic, and graphemic analyses. Sounds and meaning are the clear territory of linguistics but the similarity of the way trademarks look is often a question for semioticians, especially when the "look alike" question is addressed by non-linguistic issues such as trade dress, the colors used, and packaging. But the study of letters and symbols (graphemics) also falls within the scope of linguistics and can provide helpful answers to questions about whether marks look alike.

32.3.1 Using phonetics

A well-trained phonetician can make distinct contributions to the question of whether marks sound alike. Many people have no idea, for example, that letters such as "s" can represent more than one spoken sound. To them, the "s" at the end of Bran Flakes, /s/, is the same as the "s" at the end of Boston Baked Beans, /z/.

One tool used by linguists is called distinctive feature analysis. It appears that the first time this analysis was applied to a trademark case was in a 1988 dispute between the manufacturers of the competing cupcake products called *Little Dolly* and *Little Debbie*. Analyzing the phonetic components of the consonants and vowels of the two names, linguist Jerry Sadock testified that these two marks contained many different distinctive features based on consonantality, vocality, relative fronting or backing, articulation at a high or low point in the mouth, coronal or grave quality, voice or voicelessness, and stridence. Sadock demonstrated clearly how such analysis provides useful quantitative comparisons of what otherwise would look like only four words, two of which are the same.[2]

---

[1] *Moseley v V Secret Catalogue, Inc.*, 537 U.S. 418 (2003).
[2] *McKee Baking Co. v Interstate Brands Corp.*, 738 F. Supp. 1272 (E.D.Mo. 1990).

I followed Sadock's example in 1991, when ConAgra, the producer of *Healthy Choice* microwave lunches, challenged the trademark of its competitor, Hormel, producer of a similar microwave lunch called *Health Selections* (Shuy 2002:69–80). There are some obvious phonetic similarities in the first words of the two names but totally different phonetics in the second words of each. Distinctive feature analysis of the two names showed 228 phonetic features, 89 percent of which were different. Although to the average listener, the two names would appear to be rather similar, distinctive feature analysis measures the degree of similarity or difference in a more detailed and scientific manner, where an 89 percent difference argued strongly for Hormel's position.

Similarly, in 2006 linguist Ronald Butters used distinctive feature analysis in the case of two pharmaceutical companies, *Aventis v Advancis*, in a creative way (Butters 2008b:233–7). Consumers can say the names either as isolated words or in normal conversational sentences. Butters first transcribed the marks in a conventional phonetic transcription and compared the slowly isolated pronunciations with their pronunciations in a continuous conversational mode. He found 63 percent similarity in the isolated mode and 73 percent similarity in the conversational mode. He then used distinctive feature analysis and found that 84 percent of the phonetic features in the two marks were the same in the isolated mode and 89 percent were the same in the conversational mode. Distinctive feature analysis can be a very powerful instrument for measuring the similarity or difference in trademark sounds.

32.3.2 Using grammar

The grammatical differences between ConAgra's microwavable lunch cup, *Healthy Choice*, a pluralized noun phrase, and Hormel's similar product, *Health Selections*, with an adjective modifier preceding a singular noun, can be apparent to laypersons in a surface way at least. They can see two differences: the "y" at the end of *Health* and the "s" at the end of *Selections*. But was this difference of two consonants enough for consumers to consider the products as separate and different? Linguistic analysis showed that these two consonants represented much more than letters. They also convey grammatical differences. *Healthy Choice* is a noun–adjective noun phrase while *Health Selections* is a compound noun phrase. We stress the first word of compound noun phrases, and the second word of noun–adjective noun phrases. Many people might see the similarities of the two words without understanding that they contain very different grammatical constructions.

32.3.3 Using semantics

The dispute between ConAgra and Hormel also provides an example of the way linguists employ semantics. Hormel disputed ConAgra's claim that "choice" and "selections" have identical meanings. If its claim was accurate, ConAgra could have said that consumers would be confused, believing that ConAgra was the manufacturer of Hormel's microwave lunch cup, or *vice versa*.

I pointed out that there is a semantic difference between the noun, "choice," which conveys making a decision between two things, and "selection," which signals a decision to be made between an array of things (more than just two). To make this clear, I called attention to the exclusively different prepositions that normally occur before "choose" and "select." One chooses *between* good and evil, *between* two boyfriends, and many other groups of two. In the movie, *Sophie's Choice*, the mother had to choose *between* her two children, not *among* her two children.

In contrast, we select from *among* an array of more than two things. The lyrics of one formerly popular song include the lyrics, "I find a broken heart among my souvenirs." Unless this song was about only two items in a collection of memorabilia, it would be ludicrous to sing, "I find a broken heart between my souvenirs." Even brilliant lawyers do not usually consider the way "between" and "among," which were not even present in the trademarks, can play a role in determining the differences between *Healthy Choice* and *Health Selections*.

32.3.4 Using graphemics

Graphemics, an area of language that borders on and complements document design, is a tool that some say is different from linguistics. But graphemics is an integral part of linguistics. In trademark disputes, linguists use graphemics to address the issue of whether marks look alike. Characteristics such as spelling, font size, typeface, and overall design are used to compare and quantify disputes about the similarity or difference.

Because linguistics has more detailed units of measurement than are familiar to most lawyers, there are distinct advantages to using a forensic linguist in such cases. The case of *Warren v Prestone* provides an example of how graphemic analysis was used effectively (Shuy 2002:56–68). Both companies produce antifreeze/coolant products for motor vehicles. Warren called its antifreeze *LongLife*. Somewhat later, Prestone named its product *LongLife 460*.

Writing systems are, in every sense, language systems. It is linguistically significant, therefore, when two trademarks use the same graphemes similarly or identically, such as capitalizing where lower case is common, the size and font of the letters, and the spacing in the words. These graphemic features also can signal similar kinds of features that intonation, loudness, and pauses convey in spoken language.

In this dispute, two common English words, "long" and "life," were combined into a single word without the usual spacing between them. In both names the second word was capitalized in mid-word position. This much alone constituted graphemic evidence that 73 percent of the two names were identical. It is true that Prestone added "460" to its *LongLife* mark, but as researchers show, the beginning portions of words are very crucial in word identification and memory storage (Cutler 1982:573). This suggests that

Prestone's added "460" played only a minor role in consumers' ability to distinguish between the two marks.

Butters provided a similar graphemic measurement in the case of *Aventis v Advancis* in 2006, showing not only that the two names were 67 percent the same, but also that there was a high degree of similarity in the placement of the letters in the two marks (Butters 2008b:234–7).

32.4 ANALYZING GENERIC, DESCRIPTIVE, AND SUGGESTIVE MARKS

Having outlined the categories commonly used by trademark law and some examples of how linguistic analysis can help resolve disputes, I now offer case examples in more detail.

32.4.1 Generic versus descriptive marks

Let us continue with the case of *Warren v Prestone*, which pitted against each other two manufacturers of antifreeze/coolant products for vehicles. Relying on a 20-year old compact dictionary, Prestone's lawyers attempted to show that the name, *LongLife*, was generic. They cited the definitions of "long" and "life" separately, primarily because they could not locate dictionary entries for either the compound noun, "longlife," or for the adjective–noun combination, "long life." Nor could they find these in any other dictionaries. The single words "long" and "life" are undoubtedly generic, but that was not the real issue here. Warren had created a new compound noun phrase with no space between the two words and with capitalization in both morphemes, exactly what Prestone did.

Not only did Prestone's lawyer select only those senses of "long" and "life" in their compact dictionary, but they also selected only those senses of those words that best suited their case. They cited only one of the 12 senses of "long." Their first problem was that when lawyers use the dictionary test for meaning (noted earlier), it is not prudent to use only the one sense that they prefer. This constitutes selection bias. They have to tell the whole lexical story if they're going to tell the story at all.

Things got even more difficult for Prestone when their lawyers used that same selectivity in their compact dictionary's senses of "life." By contrast, in all of the *Oxford English Dictionary*'s 18 senses of "life," only one part of one of the senses was in any way related to an inanimate object. All the rest refer to living things, like people or animals. It's obvious that antifreeze is an inanimate object and the *OED*'s single subsection with an inanimate sense was metaphoric: "he was the life of the party."

Clearly "life" primarily refers to living things. All else is metaphoric. Since Prestone's lawyers cited only the single, highly selective and metaphoric sense of "life," their argument collapsed, because the law's major definition of suggestive marks is that they require a leap of imagination. And what better motivator for such a leap can there be than a metaphor?

Webster's Third International Dictionary included two subparts of the 18 senses that were in any way associated with animate existence, confirming my thesis that Warren had used "life" metaphorically. This case was a good example of how the opposing lawyers tried to capitalize on the dictionary test, but failed miserably in the attempt.

After Prestone's lawyers failed to establish that Warren's *LongLife* was a generic mark, they then tried to show that the mark was generic because "long life" was used to describe a class or type of things—the class of all antifreeze/coolant products containing newer additives that extend the engine's life. Trying to prove this, Prestone cited some of Warren's advertisements that referred to its new and improved *LongLife* as a product that would give "a long life" to the engines of vehicles that used it. If "long life" were the actual name for this class or type of antifreeze, Prestone could claim that Warren's *LongLife* was a generic mark.

My broad Lexis/Nexis search yielded all the expressions and names used by the industry to describe this class or type of antifreeze in its advertisements, bulletins, correspondence, and brochures. It produced 32 references to "extended life antifreeze" as the type and class of this product. Two other competitors actually used "extended life antifreeze" as part of their brand names. "Extended life" also was used in some of Prestone's own advertisements and even in its own catalogue, all of which clearly used "extended life" to refer to this type or class of antifreeze product. Prestone's claim that "long life" was the generic name of a type or class of antifreeze was defeated.

Another case in which a mark was linguistically tested as generic was the 1987 case of *McDonald's Restaurants v Quality Inns International* (Lentine and Shuy 1990:349–66; Shuy 2002:95–109). For reasons that seem illogical and counterproductive (to me at least), Quality Inns wanted to name a new hotel chain "McSleep Inns," and asked for linguistic help.

The dispute was whether McDonald's had the sole right to use the patronymic prefix, "Mc-" in names of retail businesses of all kinds. Most trademarks are words or phrases, but in this case McDonald's lawyers claimed that only McDonald's could use the bound morpheme prefix, "Mc-" when it is used before a generic word or personal name.

A linguist first collects data about how this "Mc-" prefix was currently being used. In this case, the data were collected via a Lexis/Nexis computerized search, along with results from a national clipping service, creating a large corpus of words containing the "Mc-" prefix. All were published at around the time of the trial. In all of the 150 articles, none of which were about McDonald's or hamburgers, the writers used "Mc-" before a generic or descriptive word many times, including these examples: McArt, McBook, McCinema, McFashion, McFood, McHistory, McTelevision, McHospital, McLaw, McJobs, McMedicine, McOil Change, McPaper, and many others.

This list excluded all media articles specifically about McDonald's and all instances in which "Mc-" was used in front of proper names or as acronyms. Nor did it include articles about Macintosh brand computers, simply because McDonald's and Apple Computers had previously worked out an arrangement for peaceful co-existence.

The next step was to determine the semantics of "Mc-" in the long list of media uses. The writers actually did this themselves. They made it very clear that by using "Mc-" before art, surgery, lawyers, newspapers, jobs, etc., they meant basic, convenient, inexpensive, and standardized. If anything identifies the product and characteristics of McDonald's method of making, selling, and advertising its food, it is these four characteristics. Fast food is basic (not gourmet). The stores are everywhere (convenient). Their food is said to fit any budget (inexpensive). And if you ever bought one McDonald's hamburger, you know that the next one you eat will be just like it (standardized).

In terms of the defining qualities of generic words, this little bound morpheme, "Mc-," was extremely active, productive, flexible, and recent, covering everything from automotive tune-ups to major surgery. Surprisingly, McDonald's own marketing expert supported this redefinition of "Mc-" when he testified that the company's advertising icon, Ronald McDonald, had gone around the country teaching children to add "Mc-" before many words, such as McFries, McShakes, and McBest. McDonald's Vice-President testified that the purpose of this campaign was to create a "McLanguage" that would dominantly associate the prefix with McDonald's. It was obvious that McDonald's had encouraged the wide extension of "Mc-," but apparently the company had not anticipated that the new meaning of "Mc-" would embrace the company's characteristics of standard, basic, convenient, and inexpensive. No one can challenge the success of McDonald's huge promotion and advertising program. It also extended far beyond the children that Ronald McDonald taught, and encouraged the media to do the same— only with unintended consequences.

It was clear to Quality Inns that McDonald's played a major role in "Mc-" becoming generic. It had entered into the lexicon of English with a new recognized meaning of its own—basic, convenient, inexpensive, and standardized. The exclusivity of "Mc-" referring to McDonald's alone was fading fast because of McDonald's own promotion and advertising.

Before the trial, McDonald's hired an advertising firm to survey the public's perception of the "Mc-" prefix. Among this survey's major findings were that the terms, "reliable," "prepackaged," "consistent," "fast," "processed," "simplified," "uniform," "cheap," and "easy" were characteristic of the way the public viewed McDonald's. These results confirmed my own analysis of the lexical shift reflected in the media's four main meanings of "Mc-."

Despite my linguistic testimony at trial, the judge did not agree that "Mc-" had become generic. He invoked another concept in trademark cases: secondary meaning. In his decision, the judge considered the fame of McDonald's, due in part to the millions of dollars it spent on promotion and advertising. He also opined that if Quality Inns were to adopt the name, McSleep Inn, this would be likely to confuse the public into thinking the hotels were owned or operated by McDonald's.

So Quality Inns lost the case and had to choose another name instead. The company quickly dropped the "Mc-" and decided on Sleep Inns, which would have been a better choice in the first place. Ironically, this hotel-chain is now thought to provide rooms that are basic, convenient, inexpensive, and standardized.

32.4.2 Descriptive versus suggestive marks

In *ConAgra v Hormel* one issue was whether ConAgra's product, *Healthy Choice*, was descriptive or suggestive. Hormel's lawyers claimed it is descriptive because it informs the buyer about the quality of the product and wouldn't help consumers distinguish between different products. ConAgra countered that its mark was suggestive. If the Court ruled that the name was descriptive, ConAgra would then claim that the two names are so similar that consumers would be confused or deceived about their source and sponsorship.

The judge ruled that *Healthy Choice* was a laudatory mark ("puffing"), which is one characteristic of being descriptive, meaning it was not strong. The judge ruled: "In this case I conclude that the 'mental leap' between the words and the product's attributes is almost instantaneous." The judge also found that *Healthy Choice* and *Health Selections* sounded significantly different (supporting my testimony) but that they meant essentially the same things (supporting the opposing linguist's testimony). However, his ruling on the similarity of meaning did not support ConAgra's claim that Hormel had infringed ConAgra's trademark. He ruled that there was little chance of consumer confusion.

In most trademark cases the dispute is over whether the product names and services are generic or descriptive, illustrated by the cases described above. It's easier to see the effects of the mental leap that defines a mark as suggestive than to convincingly identify the process of imagination that allegedly takes place. This points out that considerably more research is needed about the workings of the mind.

This suggests that linguists need to learn more about the sequential steps consumers must process when they infer. For example, perhaps in the *LongLife* dispute consumers might have gone through something like the following mental processes after they encountered the word "LongLife":

(1) they imagine human life, such as a baby;
(2) they imagine the baby living to adulthood, a long time;
(3) they imagine how this antifreeze is like the old person;
(4) they imagine antifreeze living a long time; and
(5) they may also imagine antifreeze giving a long life to their engine.

We have no idea whether or not consumers go through these or other imaginative leaps in this or any other sequence. If we want to describe the difference between a small or large "imaginative leap," we need more cognitive and linguistic research to provide some answers, making it possible, for example, to compare a mark that causes a five-step mental leap of imagination with one that causes only a two-step leap. Until something like this can be shown, trademark cases will have to slog along as best they can. Fortunately for linguists, trademark litigation still needs their help.

32.5 Objections

Linguists' efforts to work on trademark cases, however, have met with criticism. Some critics would discard linguistic analysis entirely in trademark cases: "The pronouncements of linguists about language are not likely to be of much use to the practice of trademark law" (Davis 1996:261). Three specific objections are commonly made about using linguistics in trademark disputes. While considering these objections, it is useful to recognize that a trademark is the message in the communication context of a sender, a message, and a receiver.

One objection is that linguists cannot aid in determining whether consumers will be confused: "The judgments of linguists as to what are identical or similar linguistic forms (e.g. in arguments about confusion of trademarks) are of no relevance unless they can claim to mimic the perception of ordinary consumers" (Hutton 2009:129–30). Most trademark cases use survey experts to address consumer perceptions. Although there is no way that linguists can prove consumer confusion, it is equally questionable that anyone else can do so with certainty, including survey experts commonly used in trademark cases, and it is unclear why surveys are generally acceptable while linguistics deserves criticism.

Surveys normally focus on a sample of representative receivers of the message who self-report their possible confusion with the product's name, manufacturer, and uses. In contrast, linguists focus on the illocutionary force of the message itself as well as on its possible perlocutionary effect on its receivers (Austin 1962:99–108). It is noteworthy that linguists have made similar points about language evidence in other types of cases, including defamation (Tiersma 1987:54–71).

Properly conducted consumer surveys can provide useful clues about *possible* confusion by a representative sample of receivers of the message. This is exactly what linguistic analysis provides about the language of the message. It seems prudent for trademark lawyers to use both types of analysis. The decision about whether or not consumers are actually confused must be made only by the triers of the facts, not by either type of experts, whose only job is to provide whatever clues there are in the language of the actual message and through their surveys of representative consumer/receivers. Gilson and Lalond make this point specifically: "it is the understanding of the public and not that of the linguist or other language expert which is controlling" (Gilson and Lalond 1999:26).

A second objection to linguistic experts is that they analyze language out of context, "effectively removing this time and perception element" (Hutton 2009:129–30). It is difficult to understand what Hutton means here, since the language of the trademark (its message) is timeless and its form creates the receiver's perception. Hutton further claims that the linguist's use of synonymy is "an artifact of linguistic theory" (Hutton 2009:129). This odd observation seems to say that the existing synonymy of a trademark (context) is not important as readers try to understand its message.

A third objection, also made by Hutton, is that the ideology of linguists differs from the ideology of law. Linguists clearly recognize this difference (Philips 1998:116–23; Shuy 2002:2–3), although they are certainly not alone in believing that language is owned by the people who use it. Even trademark lawyer Westerhaus comments on the danger of trademark law's control of language use: "But if law is indeed king over language, it is important to remember that sometimes the subjects revolt" (Westerhaus 2003:295). My point, however, is that ideological differences about the ownership of language are irrelevant to the use of linguistics in analyzing trademarks. Linguists' ideology may differ from that of lawyers, but the three major questions of trademark cases (sound alike, mean alike, look alike) are clearly unaffected by this. The linguist's only concern is to help lawyers sort out and measure the linguistic characteristics of the marks, not to change their belief systems.

Linguists can work effectively with lawyers in their trademark cases, but they need to take the lawyers' perspectives and steer clear of conflicting ideologies. All applied linguists need to do this. Linguists need to know and select appropriately from among the standard tools in which they are well trained and competent.

CHAPTER 33

··

LANGUAGE AND COPYRIGHT

··

RONALD R. BUTTERS

33.1 LEGAL ASPECTS OF COPYRIGHT

A copyright is one of four legally enforceable limitations on the general public's freedom of expression with respect to a wide variety of creative productions, legally termed "intellectual property", including works of visual art, music, and language. A copyright differs from a "patent", which is intended to limit the freedom to manufacture specific inventions to the creator of those inventions (or the inventor's assignees); and it differs from "trademarks" and "service marks", which are legal means of restricting the public's use of specific words, phrases, and designs insofar as they are used as designators of products and services (see Chapters 32 and 34; see also Butters 2008b, 2010b). "Trade secrets" are also a kind of intellectual property which the owner has taken measures to keep "secret for the purpose of getting a jump on competitors" (Elias and Stim 2004:3, 6); it may, for example, be potentially copyrightable material that is granted special protection before it has actually been published. Other types of legal limitation on language use (e.g. laws forbidding pornography, threats against the life of public officials, defamation, the communication of state secrets) apply to all citizens equally. In contrast, the laws that govern intellectual property create specified, exclusive rights that permit only specific individuals to use particular creations if those individuals can claim to have had a significant creative role in their origination; all other citizens are denied the specified uses, or in some instances have the right to use the material but must pay to do so. Granting a monopoly for a limited time to authors, inventors, and other owners of intellectual property is justified as a means of promoting the invention of new devices or the production of literary and artistic works.

As the result of several important international agreements (i.e. the Berne Convention of 1886, the 1952 UNESCO Universal Copyright Convention, the 1995 World Trade Organization's TRIPS agreement, and the 2002 WIPO Copyright Treaty), copyright limitations are transnational in scope. In the United States, the Constitution (Article I,

Section 8, Clause 8) gives the federal government the power to grant copyrights (and patents) under a fundamental principle of law:

> To promote the Progress of Science and useful Arts, by securing for limited Times to Authors and Inventors the exclusive Right to their respective Writings and Discoveries.

Through the centuries, the American Congress has specified the number of years that "limited Times" specifically means; in the United States today, the life of a copyright normally extends from the date of its publication and for 70 years after the "Author" dies. In the case of works with no clear "Author," such as, for example, most movies, the copyright extends for 95 years after the work is first used in public. Other countries limit the length of copyright protection differently, but (by international treaty) for most countries it is in no case less than 50 years or more than 100 years after the author's death.[1]

33.1.1 Copyright and other types of intellectual property

The distinction between copyright and other types of intellectual property is not always crystal clear. National laws make a distinction between copyright violations, which involve "original works of authorship," often works of art, and the "counterfeiting" of "goods," which is generally treated as a trademark violation, not a matter of copyright (Zaichkowsky 2006). For example, the sale of clothing and accessories that duplicate styles of famous brands—no matter how expensive, and even if the famous-brand makers consider them one-of-a-kind "works of art" in the colloquial sense—cannot usually be sanctioned by the original designers as violation of their trademarks, but only as copyright violations.[2] Even so, the border between "works of art" and "goods" is somewhat fuzzy: the architectural designs of buildings are generally copyright-protectable (see Elias and Stim 2004:84).

At the other end of the intellectual property continuum, the distinction between what is eligible for a copyright and what is eligible for a patent may also sometimes seem unclear. For example, computer software may be largely (or perhaps even wholly) translatable into linguistic form—expressed on paper or fixed in concrete form in a computer disk, and thus copyrightable (Elias and Stim 2004:74); yet its essential function is that of

---

[1] For summaries of the copyright laws of various countries, see the website of The World Intellectual Property Organization at <http://www.wipo.int/copyright/en/> accessed October 5, 2011.

[2] Prosecution of counterfeiters is of course clear-cut if the counterfeiters actually attach a registered trademark label to the product (e.g. putting "ROLEX" or "ROLEXX" on the face of a watch); however, even if a product uses its own, quite different label and product name but very closely imitates the product of another, it may be said to violate what is called the imitated product's "trade dress", which in itself can violate trademark rights (Elias and Stim 2004:479–80). Another common term that is often applied to counterfeiting is "piracy" (see note 8 below). Criminal prosecution of counterfeiters and pirates is also possible.

a process used to operate a computer in carrying out certain tasks, which would seem to make it patentable (Elias and Stim 2004:227).

Relatedly, although it is not a copyright violation, the publication of the private linguistic or semiotic material of others may lay one open to invasion-of-privacy, "right to publicity," and/or "misappropriation of identity" sanctions.[3] Thus the unauthorized use of even a person's mere likeness may be actionable—even if the likeness is a drawing or a photographic image of a look-alike. In one famous case, attorneys for Jacqueline Kennedy Onassis successfully prevented the continued public display of a magazine advertisement that contained the photograph of a woman who merely looked like Mrs Onassis, arguing that the use of the image suggested that Mrs Onassis herself endorsed the contents of the ad.[4] Indeed, the ad has been reconfigured with Mrs Onassis's image cut out of the replacement ad—even in the archived websites of publications in which it first appeared.[5]

33.1.2 The scope of copyright protection

As noted, the US Constitution gave Congress the right to grant copyrights. Congress subsequently gave copyright protection to "original works of authorship fixed in any tangible medium of expression, now known or later developed."[6] Thus, only original material is protected. "Authors" is broadly conceived of today as including writers, painters, sculptors, choreographers, the makers of film-, video-, and sound-recordings, and those who generate other scholarly, scientific, religious, journalistic, and artistic expression (including visual arts such as painting and sculpture). "Works of authorship" is likewise broadly conceived (including not only publications and recordings, but also the right to perform a play or show a video). Because of copyright protection, the right to use certain language (e.g. a short story, novel, poem, play, script, song lyrics, video-game dialogue, or magazine article)—and even to translate it into other languages—becomes something that one can own, buy, sell, and acquire through inheritance.

Copyright ownership extends not only to authors of published works, but also to the authors of unpublished materials—for example, private letters, manuscripts, personal

---

[3] See Gaines (1991). See also <http://www.law.ed.ac.uk/ahrc/personality/uscases.asp> accessed September 25, 2011 for some history of case law in these domains.

[4] "When a photograph of a celebrity 'look-alike,' who is an instantly recognizable public figure and who has not consented to the use of her likeness for promotional purposes, is published for commercial use in an advertisement, the celebrity has sufficient grounds for a misappropriation claim" *Onassis v Christian Dior*, 472 N.Y.S.2d 254 (N.Y. Sup. Ct. 1984). These rights do not stem directly from copyright laws, but they come about in the United States as the result of various state laws and common-law precedents.

[5] Display Ad 194—No Title / *New York Times (1957–Current file)*; October 9, 1983; ProQuest Historical Newspapers The New York Times (1851–2006), p. SM52. Also removed from the ad were images of other celebrities (the actress Ruth Gordon, the film critic Gene Shalit, and the television personality Shari Belafonte), who actually posed for the ad themselves, presumably for pay.

[6] 17 U.S.C. § 102(a).

business records, home videos, and tape recordings—whether or not they have been registered with the appropriate governmental copyright office. If you write your sweetheart a steamy letter and then later the two of you have a falling out, his publication of that letter without your permission violates your copyright, even though he and not you are in material possession of, and actually own, the physical letter itself.

Certain types of works belong to the public and cannot be copyrighted or have lost their copyright protection. Works that have outlasted copyright protection are said to be in the "public domain"; in the United States, works may also enter the public domain if the work is a federal government document of any kind, or if the "author" specifically renounces copyright ownership (Elias and Stim 2004:170).

33.1.3 Infringement

Issues of language and copyright law arise when the owner of copyrighted linguistic material (e.g. a book, story, or indeed any published or even unpublished work containing language as an important part of its communicative function) alleges that someone else's later work infringes on the owner's copyright. Infringement requires that (1) the defendant actually copied the plaintiff's work; and (2) a "substantial similarity" exists between the defendant's work and the protectable elements of the plaintiff's work.[7] Violations may result in either civil or criminal sanctions.

In civil matters, sometimes the copyright owner will simply request that the putative violator cease further use. If that does not work, or if the copyright owner has suffered financial loss as a result of the infringement, the situation may well result in a civil lawsuit. If a violation occurred, the infringer may be required to compensate the owner for losses suffered as a result. Even if the owner did not suffer an economic loss, the law in some circumstances permits "statutory damages," which can be quite significant.

In the criminal area the violation may amount to nothing more than "piracy," a lay term that is often applied to the full-scale reproduction of a work and the sale of such reproductions for profit without the copyright owner's permission, as, for example, in the case of music CDs and video DVDs.[8] Copyright violations that are piracy may be punishable under national and international law as crimes for which the pirate may be fined or imprisoned as well as required by courts to make financial restitution for actual and punitive damages to the copyright owner's rightful owners.

---

[7] *Street Wise Maps, Inc. v Vandam, Inc.*, 159 F.3d 739, 747 (2d Cir.1998).

[8] See, e.g., the *New Oxford American Dictionary* (2001), s.v. **piracy**: "[1] the practice of attacking and robbing ships at sea. [2] a similar practice in other contexts, esp. hijacking: *air piracy.* [3] the unauthorized use or reproduction of another's work: *software piracy.*" The term is also frequently applied to the private copying (without paying royalties to the copyright owners) of CDs and DVDs for private use, whether by unauthorized duplication of a borrowed, legally obtained hard copy or by unauthorized downloading from the internet. See Elias and Stim (2004:168); Peters (2005). The term "piracy" is also sometimes loosely applied to trademark violations that involve counterfeiting of goods (see note 2 above).

The likelihood of prevailing in a civil copyright infringement suit depends upon a number of factors, including whether actual copying occurred. Because there is usually no direct evidence of copying, it can be proved or disproved indirectly. If I publish a short story that bears a resemblance to an extensive unpublished diary entry that you have kept in a trunk in your attic and never shown anyone, it is unlikely that you will have a viable infringement case against me.

The requirement that the works be "substantially similar" requires making a difficult decision that can sometimes be considered arbitrary or vague. Copying one and a half sentences from a 140 page book was once held to be de minimis, whereas taking 300 words out of 200,000 has been deemed infringement. Of course, taking one or two sentences from a large work would likely be an infringement only if the copied material was very distinctive and important. Otherwise the copying would be protected as fair use (Nimmer 2010:§ 13.03[A]).

The notion of "fair use" is an important limitation upon what constitutes a copyright violation.[9] Under fair use, a person may, even without seeking permission of the owner, make a limited (but legally unspecified) number of copies of a limited (but unspecified) number of pages of a copyrighted work, especially if the nature of the use is "educational" and not in itself primarily "commercial."[10] One may also quote a limited (but unspecified) number of words from another's copyrighted text in a publication of one's own, if in doing so one is using the copied material as support or illustration, not as the text itself. The U.S. Copyright Office specifically mentions as examples of activities that courts have regarded as fair use:

- quotation of excerpts in a review or criticism for purposes of illustration or comment;
- quotation of short passages in a scholarly or technical work, for illustration or clarification of the author's observations;
- use in a parody of some of the content of the work parodied;
- summary of an address or article, with brief quotations, in a news report;
- reproduction by a teacher or student of a small part of a work to illustrate a lesson;
- reproduction by a library of a portion of a work to replace part of a damaged copy;
- reproduction of a work in legislative or judicial proceedings or reports;
- incidental and fortuitous reproduction, in a newsreel or broadcast, of a work located in the scene of an event being reported.[11]

Unanswered questions concerning fair use have been raised as the result of recent technological advances in scanning and internet archiving of works on sites such as Google Books and NewspaperArchive.com. Out of fear of violating copyrights of the original

[9] See "US Copyright Office—Fair Use" <http://www.copyright.gov/fls/fl102.html>; and "US Copyright Office—Copyright Law of the United States, <http://www.copyright.gov/title17/> accessed September 23, 2011. See also Newman (2007).

[10] According to "US Copyright Office—Fair Use" (ibid.), the basic criterion concerning amount of quoted material is "the amount and substantiality of the portion used in relation to the copyrighted work as a whole."

[11] <http://www.copyright.gov/fls/fl102.html> accessed September 23, 2011.

authors and their publishers, Google and others have been reluctant to allow internet searchers access to many works that seem to have little actual monetary value unless those books are clearly in the public domain. Similarly, websites such as YouTube and Facebook are constantly faced with removing what is or seems to be copyright-protected material that users have uploaded to the sites, even when a legitimate fair use defense might be available.

33.2 THE ROLE OF LINGUISTS WITH RESPECT TO COPYRIGHT INFRINGEMENT

Fifty years ago, a discussion of language and copyright would have been far less complex than it is today. Three historical developments have created new complexities that are of significance in considering the relationship between linguistics and copyright.

First, copyright law has been impacted by various technological innovations that combine spoken language with visual images in movies, television commercials, and on the internet. Moreover, important new media have come into existence for the dissemination of the printed word, including chat-room and list-serv discussions, social websites such as Facebook and MySpace, instant messaging, internet blogging, twittering, and cell-phone texting. The domain names of internet websites have come to have such immense financial value that website owners seek to protect them as intellectual property.[12] The linguist may be forgiven some amount of confusion about what is or is not subject to copyright ownership in the new media, because the law is still coming to terms with these issues.

Second, while in earlier generations "language" would have been construed in the strict linguistic sense of "the sentences of human languages used as the medium of expression in writing and recorded speech," today, the notion of "language" has expanded, owing to developments within linguistic science in such areas of inquiry as sociolinguistics and dialectology, pragmatics, discourse analysis, and semiotics. While the linguistic aspects of copyright law may still center upon sound structure, word structure, syntax, and dictionary meaning, there has been an increasing understanding of features of language and communication that involve the interaction of sentential language and pragmatic context. Moreover, while copyright law does not allow anyone to copyright ideas or mere facts per se, the ideas that underlie (for example) a particular novel, short story, play, magazine article, or movie script can be a de facto part of the linguistic structure of

---

[12] Neither trademark law nor copyright law protects domain names. According to the US Copyright Office, "The Internet Corporation for Assigned Names and Numbers (ICANN), a nonprofit organization that has assumed the responsibility for domain name system management, administers the assignation of domain names through accredited registers" <http://www.copyright.gov/help/faq/faq-protect.html> accessed September 23, 2011.

the work itself,[13] and could be open to analysis using methodology from the subfields of linguistics that extend beyond the narrow consideration of sentences and their component parts.

Finally, developments in forensic linguistics have created methodologies in author identification techniques that have been applied (often controversially) to a number of different criminal and civil questions in courts of law, for example, the authenticity of wills, suicide notes, text messages used as alibis, confessions, anonymous defamatory letters, and witness statements. Many of these methodologies are essentially quantitative in nature, and all have been the subject of a good deal of debate among forensic linguists (notably Chaski 2001; Coulthard 1994; Howald 2008; McMenamin 2004; Tiersma and Solan 2002; see especially Chaski, "Authorship Identification in the Forensic Setting"; and Coulthard, "Corpus Linguistics in Authorship Identification," Chapters 35 and 36 in this volume). Such methodology has also been turned to questions of plagiarism (see Chapter 37).

Copyright violations are sometimes, though by no means always, instances of "plagiarism," and vice versa.[14] Plagiarism is the unacknowledged use of the work of another (or, in the case of what is often called "self-plagiarism," the use of one's own previous publication without acknowledging the fact of previous publication),[15] and the term implies an intent to deceive the reader concerning the original authorship of the work in question. Thus it might be plagiarism, but would not be a copyright violation, if the copied material is in the public domain, as for example if the real author denies copyright ownership, if the copyright has expired, or in the case of a student who writes a paper for another. On the other hand, even the fully acknowledged use of copyrighted material, which would generally not constitute plagiarism, can be a copyright violation. For example, if a professor photocopies an entire textbook and distributes it to her class, even if she notes the name of the author and even if she distributes the book at no cost to her students, she will still have violated the copyright of the textbook's author and publisher and is legally (if not criminally) culpable.

Tiersma (2004) suggests that the considerable thought that forensic linguists have given to how to use the methodologies for authorship identification in matters of plagiarism should be turned to the strictly legal issue of copyright infringement:

[13] According to the US Copyright Office (ibid.), "Copyright ... protects original works of authorship including literary, dramatic, musical, and artistic works, such as poetry, novels, movies, songs, computer software, and architecture. Copyright does not protect facts, ideas, systems, or methods of operation, although it may protect the way these things are expressed."

[14] See Turrell (2008:271–2), who also notes that some countries (Spain, for example) create, in addition to copyright protection (which "is strictly limited to the piece of work"), a category of author's rights, "based on the author's personal and non-transferable right established in the relationship between the author and his/her creation." In such countries, an author may thus be able recover damages from someone who "plagiarizes" the author's work, even if the plagiarism does not constitute actual copyright infringement.

[15] See, e.g., Ahmad (2005). Linguistic purists sometimes term this "dual submission" or "redundant publication," reserving the word *plagiarism* strictly for the unacknowledged use of the work of another as if it were one's own. See, e.g., Bird (2002), Samuelson (1994).

There is nothing wrong with studying plagiarism…—it is a serious topic in academia. But plagiarism is not a crime, nor is it a civil wrong (tort) in most countries. It is purely a matter for discipline within the academy, or subject to moral censure. What matters for the law is copyright. I am actually rather surprised that so many [forensic linguists]…study plagiarism when, from the law's perspective, copyright is the only relevant issue (with some possible exceptions). I'd like to strongly encourage those…looking at plagiarism to start investigating copyright law as well, because there are some very interesting linguistic issues to be researched, and no one to my knowledge has ever looked at them. There may also be some interesting consulting opportunities, because the similarity of one text to another is a critical issue in copyright law, and a corpus-type analysis might have much to offer. (Tiersma 2004)

Linguists have rarely taken up Tiersma's challenge[16] (perhaps because few attorneys have actually called upon linguists to assist them in copyright cases); one important exception is Roger Shuy, who discusses several factors involving plagiaristic violations of copyright upon which lawsuits most often center, noting which are, in his view, most likely to be of forensic linguistic consequence. Shuy (2008:131–2) identifies three important issues that linguistic plagiarism and copyright violation have in common (what I am terming here the "senior" work is the one in which the owner claims copyright violation; the "derivative" or "junior" work is the putatively infringing work).

Issue 1. *The amount of putatively plagiarized material that makes up the allegedly violating work.* This corresponds to the criteria of "amount and substantiality" set forth by the United States Copyright Office, as discussed above. In adjudicating a copyright infringement claim, then, a court would ask, "Is the percentage of overlapping material a large or small percentage of the senior work?" "Is the percentage of overlapping material a large or small percentage of the junior work?" and "How substantial is the overlapping material in terms of quality and importance?"[17] The larger and more important the overlapping material, the more likely it is that it constitutes copyright infringement. This analysis also can help to determine whether the defense of "fair use" applies in a case.

Issue 2. *The degree of similarity of the passages in the junior and senior works.* The court would ask, "To what extent is the supposedly plagiarized portion of the 'derivative' work a word-for-word copying of the senior work?" Again, the greater the similarity, the more likely that it constitutes copyright infringement (if only because it is all the more likely not to have happened by chance).

---

[16] Introductory texts in forensic linguistics and related fields generally do not even index the word *copyright*, e.g., Tiersma (1999), Kaplan (2002), Gibbons (2003), Olsson (2004), Solan and Tiersma (2005), Coulthard and Johnson (2007), and Kniffka (2007).

[17] See Rich (1996): "The quantity, as well as the quality and importance, of the copied material must be considered. One criterion that courts frequently evaluate is to make certain that the user of the copyrighted material has taken no more than was necessary to achieve the purpose for which the user copied the materials."

Issue 3. *The independent originality of the works both from each other and from generally accepted knowledge or format.* The court would want to consider the extent to which clearly non-derivative portions of the junior work are of central importance to the junior work; and whether the "derivative" work appropriates the core of the original contribution of the senior work and not merely some incidental part. Similarly, if the supposedly plagiarized portion merely presents established facts or makes use of language or structure that is commonplace, then the work is not likely to be considered a copyright violation.

As Shuy notes (2008:132), "These are indeed difficult issues for the courts to consider," in large part because they depend greatly on judgments with respect to what are essentially quantitative criteria for which no specific metric is established. Shuy believes that "the major areas in which linguistic analysis can be helpful in copyright infringement disputes are in what constitutes 'substantial similarity' and how 'expression of idea' is defined."

Shuy (2003b) discusses in greater detail the linguistic criteria that may determine "substantial similarity." His criteria are phrased in terms of "plagiarism," but they would seem to apply equally well to copyright issues. He comments also, "Without some sort of guidelines answering these (and possibly other) questions, it will be difficult for forensic linguistic experts to stand up to energetic cross-examination in court":

Words

(1) How many/what percentage/what ratio of identical words must occur in the second document in order for us to say that the original is plagiarized?
(2) If synonyms replace some of the words, by what linguistic justification can we call this plagiarism?
(3) Since all documents are capable of containing same or similar words, how do we take into consideration the occurrence of alleged plagiarized words and expressions in terms of their possible everyday use?
(4) If we allege that certain allegedly plagiarized words are so uncommon that the document must be a plagiarism, how do we define common and uncommon words?
(5) How similar/identical is enough?

Sentences

(1) How many/what percentage/what ratio of identical sentences must occur in the second document in order for us to say that the original is plagiarized?
(2) What weight do we put on the fact that some topics are difficult to express without using the same words, even sentences?
(3) What do we do with sentences that change the original by reversing such things as the order of main and dependent clauses? Is it plagiarism to take a compound sentence and reformulate it into two simple sentences?
(4) How similar/identical is enough?

Discourse

(1) How many/what percentage/what ratio of identical discourse units, such as top-ics, topic sequence, illustrations/examples must occur in the second document in order for us to say that the original was plagiarized?

(2) Do certain topics or genres by their very nature suggest a common discourse structure?

(3) How similar/identical is enough?

In the remainder of this chapter, I will describe three cases in which linguists have attempted to apply linguistic principles to copyright issues as expert consultants in liti-gated cases. The first is a summary of the only instance I have found in which a linguist, Roger Shuy, has published a case summary concerning copyright. The second is a dis-cussion, drawing on my own consulting experience, of a case in which the plaintiff alleged a number of different civil wrongs related to and partially stemming from what were, linguistically, multiple putative copyright violations involving "self-plagiarism." Other linguists may well have consulted and even given testimony in copyright-related cases,[18] but none of them have, to my knowledge, published their results or discussed their methodology. The third case is a decision by a federal judge on the admissibility of linguistic evidence in copyright cases.

Case I: *St. Martin's Press and Robert Sikorsky v Vicker's Petroleum Corporation*

Roger Shuy reports on this case in a brief (nine-page) chapter in a book (2008) that treats a number of applications of linguistics to civil law cases. He consulted with attor-neys for the plaintiffs, who in 1978 published (and registered the copyright for) a 111-page paperback book, *How to Get More Miles per Gallon*; the plaintiffs sued Vickers Petroleum Corporation for copyright violation owing to Vickers' publication of a "one-page foldo-ver pamphlet called 'Savin' Gas is Easy' as a part of a new promotional and advertising campaign" (2008:133). Because Sikorsky's "book was obviously much longer than the pamphlet, the issue concerned the proportionality of the alleged borrowings, along with issues relating to the degree of expressiveness that might favor the pamphlet over the previously published book" (2008:134).

---

[18] For example, the website of the Centre for Forensic Linguistics at Aston University in Birmingham, England, posts the following on its website (<http://www.forensiclinguistics.net/flair. html> accessed September 23, 2011): "In plagiarism cases, copyright infringement and intellectual property theft we have provided evidence of the relationship between texts including whether or not one has been based upon another. Such cases have involved accusations of literary and academic plagiarism including work on books, journal articles, PhD theses and student essays. It has also included work on links between patent applications and internal research documents in the banking and financial sector."

Using "whatever linguistic tools might be available for the task" (2008:133),[19] Shuy demonstrates that, because a linguist is especially equipped with the vocabulary for discussing language, a seasoned, well-organized linguist can at least present an analysis of allegedly copyright-infringing material in a clear and informed fashion. For example, when the junior publication uses the word "harm" in a sentence which, in the senior publication uses the word "damage," Shuy the linguist knows that this can be scientifically labeled "lexical substitution/deletion"; and when the junior publication contains a sentence that is identical to one in the senior publication except for the "substitution" of a singular for a plural noun, Shuy the linguist knows that this can be labeled "grammatical variation" (2008:135). Likewise, Shuy the linguist is surely better equipped than a layman or lawyer to identify, interpret, and compare "topic sequencing"; and Shuy also uses linguistic knowledge that would not have been available to a non-linguist when he compares speech-act sequences of the junior and senior documents (2008:135). Given that the proper role of the expert witness is to aid the judge and jury in interpreting facts in ways that non-experts cannot do on their own,[20] Shuy's chapter demonstrates that the linguistic expert seems to have something of real and legitimate jurisprudential value to offer to the courts in a copyright infringement case such as the one that Shuy discusses.

At the same time, it should also be noted that the greater part of the reported results of Shuy's actual methodology does not seem much, if at all, beyond the reach of a lawyer to put together. In what presumably is a summary of his projected courtroom testimony, the chapter lists—junior and senior extracts side-by-side—longer passages with lexical substitutions of synonyms or deletions (2008:136–7); shorter passages with lexical substitutions of synonyms or deletions (2009:136–8); and passages with grammatical changes (2008:138–9). Shuy also presents a brief analysis of topic-sentence sequences that show that, out of some 54 possibilities, "twenty of the pamphlet's tips present and develop the book's topic sequence exactly" (2008:139–40. He notes that this is apparently a contribution that only a linguist would think of making: "The extent to which topic sequencing can be used as an indicator of copyright infringement has not, to my knowledge, been presented or tested in court" (2008:140). What may not be so clear is the significance of a ratio of 20 to 54 (perhaps Shuy intended to leave this to the judge or jury to decide).

Even more interesting and linguistically specialized is Shuy's suggestion (2008:140) that the issue of "speech-act borrowing" could be a fruitful contribution that linguists

---

[19] "If scientific, technical, or other specialized knowledge will assist the trier of fact to understand the evidence or to determine a fact in issue, a witness qualified as an expert by knowledge, skill, experience, training, or education, may testify thereto in the form of an opinion" (Rule 702 of the Federal Rules of Evidence; see, e.g., <http://www.law.cornell.edu/rules/fre/rules.htm> accessed September 23, 2011).

[20] Shuy makes only passing reference in the case summary to the Three Issues framework set forth in the immediately preceding pages of the same book, and he makes no reference to his 2003 discussion of linguistics and plagiarism. Shuy also makes no reference to the forensic linguistic scholarship on authorship or plagiarism, and it is not at all clear that the data in the case was particularly amenable to such methodologies.

could make to copyright infringement cases. Yet the single paragraph in which Shuy discusses "speech-act borrowing" contains little more than a brief tally of raw numbers, without specifics, except for the concluding sentence:

> The pamphlet consistently changes the most common speech act in the book, offering advice, to giving a directive and, in the case of one tip, a warning. (Shuy 2008:140)

Of course, this is in fact a *difference* between the junior and senior publications. Oddly, this would seem to support the contention that the junior publication might not be a copyright violation—which was surely not Shuy's intent (note the somewhat question-begging implication of Shuy's assertion that the pamphlet "changes" the language of the book). Because Shuy gives so little discussion of the "speech-act borrowing" he found in preparing for testimony in *Vickers*, the suggestion of the potential use remains intriguing, but impossible to evaluate.

Shuy concludes by noting that "the dispute was settled through negotiation before a trial took place, [so] it is not possible to tell how effective this analysis might have been in the courtroom"—or even whether a trial judge would have allowed a linguist to testify in a copyright case. At the very least, Shuy's suggested comparisons present a roadmap for research for linguists interested in determining the extent to which these measures can be used as technical descriptions of substantial similarity.

Case II: *Eli Research, Inc. v United Communication Group*

This, too, is a case that was settled between the parties before a trial could take place, so the value to the court of the linguistic analysis (a brief report and a lengthy deposition) was never tested. According to the extant, publicly available legal documents, the case appears to have begun in about 2003 and involved a series of intertwined allegations, as the court described it in a 2004 decision involving preliminary motions:

> [The] action filed by plaintiffs, two corporations that published medical coding newsletters, against defendants, former editors and their new employer, alleg[ed] claims under the Lanham Act, 15 U.S.C. § 1125 et seq., and various tort claims.... [¶] After the former editors left plaintiffs' employ and began publishing newsletters for their new employer, plaintiffs filed suit, alleging that the editors used plaintiffs' trade secrets in doing so.[21]

The exact legal issues in the case were not of direct concern to the task that the plaintiffs' attorney set for the linguist, which was essentially the examination of certain articles that the "new employer" published on topics that were highly similar to topics that were written by the same contract workers who moved with the "former editors" to the "new employer." Trade secrets included subscription lists, style manuals, and contact

---

[21] *Eli Research, Inc. v United Communications Group*, LLC, 312 F. Supp.2d 748 (M.D.N.C., 2004).

information for medical experts who would be willing to be interviewed for articles. The linguistic issues, however, involved the question of "self-plagiarism": Did the contract workers essentially engage in "dual publication" of their work (and receive payment twice), first in the old journals, then in the new, competing ones? Thus even if the legal foundations for Eli's claims of damages did not in the end depend largely on copyright infringement,[22] it was nonetheless in the interests of the plaintiffs' claims to establish that the defendants' writings were a part of a pattern of the transfer of the know-how of the senior publishing company to the junior one. It was thus important to determine to what degree the junior company fared with respect to the three salient issues that Shuy notes in his 2008 book: *Did a substantial amount of putatively plagiarized material make up the allegedly violating work? Was there a substantial degree of similarity of the passages in the junior and senior works? Did the junior and senior documents display independent originality of works both from each other and from generally accepted knowledge or format?* That is, the linguist's task was to proceed by confronting the issues that normally underlie claims of plagiarism and copyright infringement.

However, the authors of the putatively corresponding junior and senior articles were already known and acknowledged. Furthermore, in none of the materials that I reviewed in the case did I find the kind of pragmatic linguistic evidence that would normally exist to enable a writer to argue that he or she has not actually copied from a senior work. A student, for example, might argue that highly similar passages in two different essays that he or she had written were merely the product of unconscious memory and the unique aspects of an individual writing style; such a student, however, might be able to support this argument by presenting two substantially different outlines, sets of reading notes, and early drafts, proving that they were independently created works. No such evidence was forthcoming in the materials presented to me, and no such detailed arguments were made in the depositions of the defendants. Indeed, evidence found in the depositions points in the opposite direction. For example, some of the junior articles that I judged to be highly similar to the senior articles purported to have interviewed the same persons of authority and received substantially the same quotes, yet these interviewees reported under oath that they had not been interviewed a second time, and one of them was dead at the time the junior article was written.

As for the linguistic analysis of the data, the key question was indeed that of substantial similarity: *Was there a substantial degree of similarity of the passages in the junior and senior works?* My report stated broadly that, in my opinion, multiple instances of material in the junior publications had been copied and paraphrased from the senior publications. Such material frequently duplicated word for word, or with small variations in syntax and diction, material that had been previously published by the same contract authors in the senior publications. The substance of a major portion of my day-long deposition was simply the side-by-side comparison of a number of the documents of

---

[22] One of United's defenses appears to have been that the contract authors retained copyright republication rights to their own work because they did not specifically assign such rights to their earlier employer at the time of the senior publications.

alleged self-plagiarism, and it was clear that, had the case gone to trial, my role would have been similar to the ones that the attorneys in Shuy's case seems to have envisioned for him: to organize the material within the framework of linguistic science and to characterize linguistically the similarity of the putative infringing passages.

Case III: *Mowry v Viacom International, Inc.*

There is only one known US copyright case in which a judge ruled in detail on the value and admissibility of linguistic evidence: *Mowry v Viacom International, Inc.*[23] Mowry had written an unpublished but copyrighted screenplay. He claimed that a motion picture made by the defendants infringed his copyright. To prove his case, he had to show not just that the works were substantially similar, but also that the defendants actually copied material from his screenplay. Mowry could produce no evidence that the defendants ever had access to it.

Mowry's only hope was to prove that the works were so "strikingly similar" as to raise an inference of access and copying. He offered the testimony of a linguist, who used a cladistic (or phylogenetic tree) method for detecting the ancestral properties of derived authorship. The judge noted that this method had apparently never been used in a copyright case and that it also had never been tested or subjected to peer review. He ruled that the analysis was more confusing than helpful and proceeded to read the junior and senior works himself, concluding that they were not strikingly similar.

Mowry v Viacom is just one case, and it was not officially published, but it suggests that courts feel that they or ordinary jurors are competent to make their own judgments regarding similarity. In another case, *Stromback v New Line Cinema*,[24] a federal appellate court, without detailed analysis of any proffered expert testimony, also suggested that evaluating the degree of similarity between two documents was well within the competence of judges.

Nonetheless, linguists can still play a useful role in organizing the data, pointing out similarities and differences, as well as providing statistics on how much of each work is identical, or nearly so, to the other. Even if such expertise is not admissible in court, it can be helpful to lawyers in preparing the case for trial. The ultimate questions—whether there was copying and whether the works are substantially similar—must be answered by a judge or jury.

33.3 CONCLUSION

Tiersma's (2004) suggestion that forensic linguists would find copyright issues worthy of further attention has yet to bear much fruit, though it is clear that linguistic issues are central to copyright law and copyright litigation, and that there is considerable overlap

---

[23] 2005 WL 1793773 (S.D.N.Y. 2005).
[24] 384 F.3d 283, 295–96 (6th Cir. 2004).

between copyright and two fields that forensic linguists have spent considerable time investigating: author identification and plagiarism. The consideration of the trademark issue of likelihood of confusion, long a staple of linguistic expert-witness consultation, is a further indication that linguists are equipped to think in terms of the issues of similarity and difference that are central to copyright litigation.

Given also that linguistic issues are so central to copyright, it would seem logical that those who teach courses on language and law would offer instruction on copyright issues, and that future introductory forensic linguistic textbooks would add material that would facilitate such instruction. Moreover, to the extent that additional research would add a level of additional certainty to linguistic analysis, the time is ripe for such inquiry to commence.

CHAPTER 34

....

THE PSYCHOLINGUISTIC BASIS OF DISTINCTIVENESS IN TRADEMARK LAW

....

SYÛGO HOTTA
MASAHIRO FUJITA

34.1 INTRODUCTION

A Supreme Court justice once remarked that "[t]he protection of trademarks is the law's recognition of the psychological function of symbols."[1] For a trademark to be legally protected, it must be sufficiently distinctive from others in the market. Whether a given mark is distinctive or not is essentially a matter of our cognition of words. Therefore, it is indispensable to scrutinize trademarks in terms of how we "understand" and "perceive" the language in trademarks.

This chapter aims to develop a linguistic analysis that helps examine distinctiveness in a trademark. The proposed analysis adopts well-known linguistic concepts and principles such as markedness and Grice's Conversational Maxims (Grice 1975) in scrutinizing the linguistic aspects of a mark. We will first illustrate how the proposed linguistic analysis works to identify the source of distinctiveness in a trademark. Then, we will test the proposed analysis with a reaction time experiment in which participants are visually exposed to stimulus words that differ in their phonological, morphological, and semantic structures. Our analysis will contribute not only to linguistics but also to trademark practice in that it will provide more consistent and empirically-grounded standards for the analysis of linguistic aspects of trademarks.

---

[1] *Mishawaka Rubber and Woolen Mfg. Co. v S.S. Kresge Co.*, 316 U.S. 203 (1942).

34.2 LINGUISTIC ANALYSIS OF TRADEMARKS

The principal functions of a trademark are to indicate the source of the products or wares associated with that mark and to guarantee their quality. These functions are attainable only if consumers associate the mark with a single source, even though the source may be anonymous. To meet this requirement, a mark must be unique and distinctive. A trademark's registrability and eligibility for legal protection essentially lie in the distinctiveness that it carries. Language communicates a large amount of the information that renders the trademark distinctive. This study is an attempt to identify the source of distinctiveness in trademarks from a linguistic point of view and to apply some basic notions and theories in pragmatics and other areas of linguistics.

As a legal matter, the degree of distinctiveness in trademarks is divided into five categories. From least protected to most protected, they are: generic, descriptive, suggestive, arbitrary, and fanciful.[2] Examples within each of these categories are provided in Table 34.1.

Generic marks are common names or refer to an entire group or category of goods or services. Descriptive marks are those that, while not simply terms for products or services, describe their features, qualities, ingredients, or uses. Suggestive marks refer to marks that imply the features, quality, ingredients, or uses of a product or service. Unlike generic or descriptive marks, suggestive marks indirectly express the features or characteristics of a product or service. Arbitrary marks are marks whose terms are in common usage but have no direct semantic relation to the products or services. Fanciful marks are terms that are made up or are some "combination of letters or other symbols used to describe a product or service" (Buccieri 2004:§14).

Generic and descriptive marks are generally unregistrable. However, the borders between categories are often unclear, and accordingly, courts frequently fail to identify an appropriate category for a mark.

Table 34.1 The distinctive spectrum

Categories	Generic	Descriptive	Suggestive	Arbitrary	Fanciful
Definition	class of goods	only descrtibes characteristics or ingredients of goods	suggests a characteristic or ingredient of goods	an arbitrary word as applied to goods	a made-up word
Example	CAR	TASTY BREAD	STRONGHOLD	APPLE	KODAK
Goods	car	bread	nails	computers	photographic supplies

Shuy (2002:65).

[2] *Abercrombie & Fitch Co. v Hunting World Inc.* 537 F.2d 4 (2d Cir. 1976).

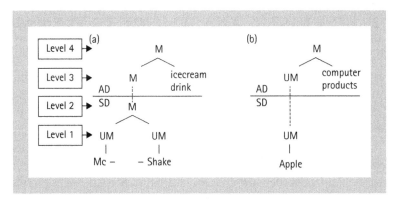

FIGURE 34.1 Representations of associative and structural dimensions

(AD = associative dimension; SD = structural dimension; M = marked;
UM = unmarked) (Hotta 2007b)

Hotta (2007b) has proposed an analysis that links pragmatic and structural aspects of trademarks, then extracts and illustrates the properties of those trademarks more accurately. Consider the representations of the marks shown in Figure 34.1.

In general, a distinctive part of a mark is defined as one that attracts consumers' attention more than any others (Kakuta and Tatsumi 2000:187). The part that "draws attention" is, in other words, a cognitively salient part of the mark. The saliency can be captured in terms of *markedness* in the sense of McCawley (1985:23). Markedness is defined, following McCawley, as follows: something is marked if it is abnormal, deviant, idiosyncratic, or specific in a given context, while something is unmarked if it is general, standard, or neutral in the context. The distinctive part of the trademark is salient because it has a marked property. The marked property of a trademark can come from any of the mark's features, for example phonological, morphological, syntactic, pragmatic, or orthographic.

The marked property of a mark is attributable to a violation of Grice's Conversational Maxims (the Maxim of Quality, the Maxim of Quantity, the Maxim of Relevance, and the Maxim of Manner) (Grice 1975). These maxims follow from Grice's Cooperative Principle: "Make your contribution such as is required, at the stage at which it occurs, by the accepted purpose or direction of the talk exchange," which basically says that people work cooperatively in conversation to convey and to acquire new, relevant information. Ordinarily, people anticipate, for example, that what they are being told is relevant to the subject under discussion. They therefore draw normal inferences and resolve ambiguities in favor of a relevant construal of utterances as they hear them. By the same token, speakers know that hearers will draw those inferences and resolve ambiguities in that manner, and therefore structure what they say accordingly. The Cooperative Principle and corresponding maxims were originally proposed as a conversational principle, but are now applied in many other types of linguistic settings.

Returning to our understanding of trademarks, *McShake* in Figure 34.1a above is distinctive because the prefix *Mc-*, which canonically combines with a personal name, has formed a word with a drink name, *Shake*. The combination violates the Maxim of Relevance, since there is no direct relationship between the two morphemes.[3] The distinctive part of the mark in this example is the whole word, that is the combination of the morphemes.

We assume two dimensions in the analytical scheme in Figure 34.1: a structural dimension and an associative dimension.[4] The markedness observed in a mark's phonology, morphology, syntax, orthography, etc., is all structural, whereas that observed in the association between a product and the name is associative. Although we have discussed only the structural markedness brought about by violation of Grice's maxims so far, those maxims apply to the associative markedness as well. For example, *Apple* for computer products in Figure 34.1b is structurally unmarked, because the word *apple* is part of the ordinary English vocabulary. On the other hand, the association between the word and the product—computers—is marked, because *Apple* is not a generic name for computers. Accordingly, the association between them violates the Maxim of Relevance, since there is no direct relationship between the mark and the product. The trademark is thus distinctive, as it is a marked form in the associative dimension.

In contrast, the example in Figure 34.1a (*McShake*), which illustrates structural markedness, works differently. The trademark, which is marked in the structural dimension, is also marked in the associative dimension. That is because it is not a normal thing to say, and thus becomes marked as a result of its violating Gricean principles. Accordingly, the resulting association between the mark and the product is marked. Hence, the mark is distinctive.

The relationship between the distinctive spectrum and markedness in each dimension is summarized as in Table 34.2.

Besides correspondence with a distinctive spectrum, we would like to assume that generally as a trademark becomes more marked, use of that same trademark for different

Table 34.2 The distinctive spectrum and structural/associative markedness

Categories	Generic	Descriptive	Suggestive	Arbitrary	Fanciful
Definition	class of goods	only describes characteristics or ingredients of goods	suggests a characteristic or ingredient of goods	an arbitrary word as applied to goods	a made-up word
Example	CAR	TASTY BREAD	STRONGHOLD	APPLE	KODAK
Goods	car	bread	nails	computers	photographic supplies
Structural markedness	Unmarked	Unmarked	Unmarked	Unmarked	Marked
Associative markedness	Unmarked	Unmarked	Marked	Marked	Marked

[3] It may be also true that the combination of the two morphemes violates the Maxim of Quality.

[4] What is dealt with in the structural dimension may seem oversimplified. However, the audience of this analysis is not only linguists but also non-linguists such as lawyers. Therefore, it is preferable to simplify the model as much as possible. See Shuy (2002).

products and services becomes less coincidental. Thus, identical fanciful trademarks are less likely to occur than identical suggestive trademarks.

34.3 AN EXPERIMENTAL STUDY

From a psycholinguistic point of view, recognition of a marked part of a trademark imposes more "load" on our cognition. Such cognitive load manifests itself upon human memory and perception. While Sweller's (1988) proposal concerning the role of cognitive load applied to learning processes, the concept is applicable to a variety of situations in which learning new information is involved, including, we suggest, the association of trademarks with products. Such a cognitive viewpoint makes sense because the confusion that results in associating a product with the wrong trademark is essentially a matter of cognition.

In trademark disputes, it is important to identify the "distinctive part" of a trademark. The distinctive or salient part of a trademark is defined as that part of a trademark that draws consumers' attention most (Kakuta and Tatsumi 2000) and is likely to qualify for legal protection. The part that "draws attention" is, in other words, the part that imposes some load on cognition. Thus, recognizing a marked entity and "drawing attention" share a very important feature: they both increase cognitive load. Put differently, the distinctive part of a trademark is the marked part, since it produces cognitive load. Under present trademark law practice in Japan, for example, the definition of "the part that draws consumers' attention" is not based on any scientific ground and even lacks definitive standards. However, if the distinctive part of a trademark is redefined in terms of markedness, as proposed in the previous section, we can identify it in a more systematic, predictable way with scientific grounding. In this section, we will show with an experimental study that the cognitive load caused by the distinction between marked and unmarked elements of a trademark is psychologically real.

We assume, for the purposes of this study, that such linguistic deviancies as marked characteristics found in trademarks would require extra computation or processing, and accordingly result in a longer reaction time (cf. Sweller 1988). For example, using a reaction time (RT) task, Rubenstein et al. (1970), found that the processing of nonsense words takes longer than that of lexical words. In their experiment, nonsense words were divided into two kinds: phonologically legal ones and phonologically illegal ones. They showed that the processing of phonologically legal nonsense words, such as *FLINK*, result in longer reaction times than do phonologically illegal ones, such as *FLNIKI*, while the processing of lexical words produced the shortest RT. This result suggests the following: (1) a phonologically legal nonsense word sets off a search in the lexicon and quantization,[5] but the lexical search continues until it finds out that there is no entry of the word in the lexicon; (2) a phonologically illegal nonsense word incurs and continues the

---

[5] Quantization is the process that divides the stimulus into segments and assigns these segments to phonemes.

quantization process without search in the lexicon until it is discovered that there is no applicable rule for it; (3) a lexical word sets off quantization and lexical search, and these processes are immediately terminated once the matches are found. We assume that the words that involve a violation of the maxim(s) should incur longer RT, because they undergo three processes: quantization, lexical search, and computation of the violation of the maxim(s). Accordingly, it is expected that these four types of words will differ in RT as follows: words with a violation of the maxim(s) > phonologically legal nonsense words > phonologically illegal nonsense words > lexical words.

34.3.1 Method

Stimuli were presented using a PC-based apparatus: Cedrus SuperLab Pro and Response Pad RB-530. The participant (*S* hereinafter) was seated in front of a 10.4″ LCD display of a Windows laptop PC, and was told to respond with the above-mentioned Response Pad. Fifteen participants (9 males and 6 females) whose ages range from 19 to 31 (mean age, 23.67; SD 4.29) participated in the experiment. They all speak Japanese as their native language. Each participant was asked to look at four-character *hiragana* words as they individually appeared on the display. Each visual stimulus was presented to *S* after a beep, which signaled the beginning of each task. *S* then heard the audio stimulus through the built-in speakers of the laptop computer. For each expression, the following were presented in order on the display: (1) "+" as the point of regard (1000ms); (2) blank (black) screen (500ms); (3) a single stimulus word (which was kept displayed until the participant responded correctly). *S* was given a chance to practice before the real experiment began. *S* was asked to respond to all tasks presented on the display: Press the left button on the Response Pad if the given stimulus is a word, and the right button if it is not a word. The RT was measured, recorded, and stored automatically in an electronic file on the computer. The unit of measurement was 1/1000 second. Results were interpreted by comparing the average response times of each group of the words within each *S*.

Four kinds of linguistic patterns all consisting of four morae[6] were presented to *S* on the display: (A) 7 phonologically illegal nonsense words (e.g. *ngozuku*); (B) 7 phonologically legal nonsense words (e.g. *sumo-zumo* voicing occurs on the first consonant of the third mora); (C) 7 words consisting of two morphemes in which each morpheme is lexical but the collocation or combination of the morphemes renders the resulting word nonsense (e.g. *make-mizu*, "defeat-water"); (D) 21 lexical words (more precisely, compounds in most cases) in Japanese (e.g. *kane-mochi* [money-have] "rich person").

Groups A–D correspond to some of the categories in the distinctive spectrum: (A) represents fanciful trademarks that are phonologically marked; (B), fanciful trademarks that are phonologically unmarked but semantically marked because they are nonexistent in the language (e.g. *Nikon* for photographic equipment); (C), trademarks that are

---

[6] A mora is a phonological unit used in some language, equivalent to a syllable in English and other languages.

phonologically unmarked but semantically and structurally marked fanciful marks (e.g. *McShake* for icecream drink and *Toys"Я"Us* for toys); (D), completely unmarked and equivalent to generic or descriptive marks.

The linguistic patterns in the third and fourth category, that is (C) and (D), were selected according to their familiarity: The familiarity of each morpheme was checked for both (C) and (D), but that of the whole word was checked only for the first category. The familiarity of morphemes was determined in reference to the list created by Amano and Kondo (1999). The familiarity of each word was 4.5 or higher on Amano et al.'s seven-point scale. The list of stimuli actually used in our experiment is available in the Appendix to this chapter.

34.3.2 Results

The mean RTs of the words categorized by phonological legality and meaningfulness of stimulus words are shown in Figure 34.2. They were significantly different over all the groups. [$F(3, 243) = 19.40, p < .001$] The multiple comparison test was also conducted to examine the results further. Again, significant differences were observed among all of the groups except for the pair of (A) and (B). As expected, the processing of words involving a violation of the maxim(s) took the longest time.

34.3.3 Discussion

Our prediction was borne out by these results: the computation of a violation of the maxim(s) requires extra processing beyond quantization and lexical search, and is reflected in the reaction time. It is not very clear at this stage, and accordingly we will not explore

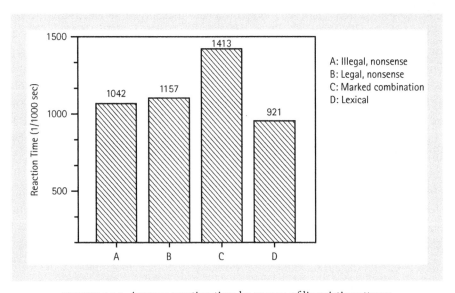

FIGURE 34.2 Average reaction time by groups of linguistic patterns

further, exactly what kind of processing the computation of the violation of the maxim(s) involves. Nevertheless, it is reasonable to conclude from the results that the processing of the marked combination of meaningful morphemes, which involves the violation of the Gricean Maxims, involves a process in addition to the quantization and lexical search. Our finding that words with marked parts have a special property that slows language processing *per se* contributes to the scholarship in language processing. In addition, this study contributes to establishing an empirical foundation for the linguistic analyses of trademarks utilizing markedness (Hotta 2007b). As discussed above, the distinctiveness of a trademark is founded upon irregularities, or marked properties, of the linguistic expression involved in the sound, form, or meaning of the trademark. At the very least, phonetic, phonological, and semantic irregularities of the linguistic expression are reflected in increased RT.

It would be an error, however, to conclude that our experiment can determine the markedness or distinctiveness of all trademarks. For example, while our analysis applies to newly created marks that have not acquired consumer familiarity,[7] it does not apply to trademarks that are distinctive with regard to their association with products (e.g. *APPLE* for computer products) and trademarks that have been lexicalized (*XEROX* for copiers). Scrutiny of those marks which our analysis does not examine will be left open for future research.

34.4 CONCLUSION

People believe that they know a language, merely because they speak it. They routinely and confidently analyze language from their own viewpoint, experience, and knowledge. However, linguistic knowledge is tacit knowledge. It is intangible and difficult to grasp without a means to "visualize" it. Linguistics provides our tacit knowledge with a mechanism that enables us to access, understand, and present it. When research grounded in the disciplines of linguistics and cognitive science enables this tacit knowledge to manifest itself before a court, that knowledge becomes scientific evidence. In the discussion above, we have presented an analysis of trademarks in terms of markedness and Grice's Conversational Maxims, and have shown how this analysis helps to uncover the features of (common and) foreign language trademarks. In addition, we have offered an experimental analysis that adds additional support to our claim that the proposed analysis is on the right track from a psycholinguistic point of view.

Although the proposed analysis has focused mainly on the linguistic aspects of trademarks, other aspects of trademarks undoubtedly play a significant role in courts' decision-making processes regarding trademark actions. The proposed approach is still in its infancy and is far from comprehensive. Further elaboration of the analysis is envisaged in our future research.

---

[7] Typically, marks that are inherently distinctive from others can be registered.

Appendix: List of Stimuli

A. Phonologically illegal nonsense words: ngo-zogu (illegal consonant pattern), wozo-zenu (illegal consonant pattern), sobi-tose (violation of rendaku), zumo-ggo (violation of geminization), kka-woyo (violation of geminization, etc.), kad-daro (violation of geminization), dae-aa (illegal geminate vowel).

B. Phonologically legal nonsense words: sare-zari (rendaku "a consonant-voicing rule"), tak-keni (geminization), wako-garo (rendaku), iko-hazu (no special rule), nebi-dasa (rendaku), sumo-zumo (rendaku), sas-sha (geminization).

C. Words consisting of semantically unrelated lexical morphemes: [Stimulus (Morpheme 1, Familiarity; Morpheme 2, Familiarity)] mono-iro (mono 6.250; iro 6.500), hiku-oni (hiku 6.094; oni 6.094), haya-tori (haya 5.031; tori ["bird"] 6.344), nama-musi (nama 6.094; musi 6.312), oka-hebi (oka 6.000; hebi 6.312), make-mizu (make 6.312; mizu 6.531), huda-ziki (huda 5.531; siki 4.812).

D. Lexical words: [Stimulus, Familiarity (Morpheme 1, Familiarity; Morpheme 2, Familiarity)] sawayaka 5.375 (sawa 5.500; yaka N/A), yamadori 4.438 (yama 6.500; tori 6.344), yakiguri N/A (yaki 5.781; kuri 6.031), kane-moti 6.344 (kane 6.375; moti 5.812), hiki-dashi 5.844 (hiki 5.500; dashi 5.938), hude-bako 5.250 (hude 5.969, hako 6.156), oo-oba 4.750 (oo N/A; oba 5.438), oki-mono 5.656 (oki N/A; mono 6.250), siro-gane 4.562 (siro 6.438; kane 6.375), naga-buro N/A (naga N/A; huro 6.156), asa-meshi 5.656 (asa 6.719; meshi 5.969), ai-uchi 4.750 (ai N/A; uchi N/A), sato-oya 5.094 (sato 5.719; oya 6.531), huyu-huku 5.688 (huyu 6.438; huku 6.250), uki-kusa 4.654 (uki 5.531; kusa 6.406), naga-ame 5.331 (naga N/A; ame 6.531), rok-kaku 5.031 (roku 5.594; kaku 5.812), yoko-yure N/A (yoko 6.344; yure 5.344), ama-gasa (hiragana) 5.406, (ama N/A; kasa 6.281), hana-taba 6.031 (hana 6.594; taba 5.312), naka-niwa 5.375 (naka 5.750; niwa 6.3129). (Familiarity of some lexical words or morphemes was not available, but no significant difference from other words in RT was found.)

PART VIII

IDENTIFICATION OF AUTHORSHIP AND DECEPTION

CHAPTER 35

AUTHOR IDENTIFICATION IN
THE FORENSIC SETTING

CAROLE E. CHASKI

> A "No" uttered from the deepest conviction is better than a "Yes" merely
> uttered to please, or worse, to avoid trouble.
>
> Mahatma Gandhi

Author identification can play a role in the investigation of many different types of
crimes, civil transactions, and security issues. Some documents have an obvious legal
significance: anonymous threatening letters, ransom notes, anonymous missives to
the Securities and Exchange Commission. But in a more subtle way, other
documents—diaries, business and personal emails, business memoranda, personal
letters, employee manuals, blog posts, website copy—can also directly relate to
determining a person's involvement in a situation with criminal, civil, or security
implications.

Authorship identification methods have developed out of many different disciplines,
with each one bringing its own set of literary, historical, linguistic, or computational
tools to the workbench (Chaski 1998; 2008). A multitude of potentially useful methods
are available. Within the computational-linguistic paradigm, research in author identification has boomed since 2000. Stamatatos (2009), Koppel et al. (2009), and Juola
(2008, 2009) provide reviews of this activity.

Forensic authorship identification poses specific challenges to any method. First,
there is usually far less data than non-forensic contexts require. The huge novels-and-
newspapers datasets used for comparison in solving non-forensic problems allow non-
forensic methods to test ideas that could never be implemented with forensic datasets.
Second, the data are far less clean or grammatical than non-forensic methods require.
Again, novels and newspapers provide clean, grammatical data. Most standard tools for
natural language processing or content analysis expect data to be spelled correctly and
grammatically composed. Forensic methods should expect just the opposite. Third,

the method must meet legal requirements that most non-forensic methods need never consider. Error rates are generally foreign to literary discussions but essential to forensic methods in the post-*Daubert* judicial system. Thus forensic authorship identification methods can and should draw upon the research and insights of non-forensic studies, but in the end methods employed in forensic authorship identification must be shaped, evaluated, and vetted within the forensic science community and approved by the courts.

Over the last 15 years, author identification has become increasingly recognized by research funding agencies, investigative agencies, the forensic science community, and the courts, as a forensic science that deals with pattern evidence. Pattern evidence relies on the identification of patterns on suspect or questioned material that can be matched with patterns on comparable known material. It includes both biometric and non-biometric data, such as fingerprints, palmprints, handwriting, voice, gait, shoe prints, tire treads, toolmarks, and ballistics.

Any analysis of pattern evidence requires methods that can answer the following questions:

(1) What kinds of patterns are significant and reliable?
(2) Are these patterns detectable or countable in specific ways that can be taught, learned, and processed by humans and/or machines?
(3) What amounts of data are required to get significant and reliable patterns?
(4) Are there other conditions, besides quantity, which affect the recovery of significant and reliable patterns from data?

This chapter presents a review of currently available and emerging methods for identifying authorship in the forensic setting. In Section 35.1, features which help to compare and contrast current methods are presented. Section 35.1 also covers validation testing methodology. Section 35.2 presents some current methods based on the categorization scheme in Section 35.1. Section 35.2 also provides some ideas about why some methods fail to obtain high accuracy. Section 35.3 provides some future directions for forensic author identification. It is an exciting time for forensic author identification because the field poses so many research questions, and validation testing provides a clear paradigm in which to answer them.

35.1 COMPARING AND CONTRASTING CURRENT METHODS

Forensic authorship identification methods, despite their differences, require that similar steps be taken: choosing an appropriate linguistic level, coding, engaging in statistical analysis and decision making, and conducting validation testing.

35.1.1 Linguistic level: which linguistic units are used?

Linguists often focus their analysis on specific linguistic levels, such as the phonemic, morphemic, lexical, syntactic, semantic, discursive, and pragmatic. Forensic author identification methods, which deal with written data, have focused on analytical units at the character, word, sentence, and text levels. At the character level, analytical units include single characters, punctuation marks, or character-level n-grams (units of adjacent characters). At the word level, analytical units can be function words, content words, word-level n-grams (units of adjacent words), lexical semantics, lexical overlap, vocabulary richness, average word length, and variants thereof. Sentence-level analytical units include part of speech (POS) tags, tag-level n-grams, constituent structures, anaphoric dependencies, marked and unmarked constituent structures, sentence type, average sentence length, and variants thereof. At the text level, analytical units can be text length, paragraph length, and discourse strategies.

For some linguistic levels, it is extremely easy to detect patterns by machine. For instance, character and word level features can almost always be extracted and analyzed automatically, even for messy forensic data. For these reasons, methods based on character and word features will be highly valued if and when they are shown to work reliably.

Other linguistic levels are fairly difficult for machine pattern detection with forensic data. Sentence level features can be extracted automatically, but most parsers cannot deal with messy forensic data very well. An intern at the Institute for Linguistic Evidence was testing the Stanford parser, one of the state-of-the-art parsers available, and discovered, much to his chagrin, that the parser could not properly parse the sentence: "I'll meet him at the libary tonight." The parser tagged "libary" as an adjective, "tonight" as a noun, and the prepositional phrase as "at the libary tonight." Most parsers are built to generate grammatical tags and constituent structures based on morphological and positional information. The morpheme "-ary" is very common for adjectives, and clearly the parser was tripped by the misspelling of "libary."

Some discourse features can be even more difficult to extract automatically, while other discourse features are so clearly lexicalized that they can be extracted accurately. Consider, for instance, how lexicalized politeness is in contrast to irony or sarcasm.

Since features on all linguistic levels might contribute to a very robust method of author identification, both machine and human coding may be necessary for high accuracy, and more importantly, for the minimization of mechanical errors. On the other hand, totally automated systems might attain slightly less accuracy than mixed machine–human methods, but fulfill a screening or ranking operation, as will be suggested below.

35.1.2 Coding: how is the linguistic analysis recorded?

Coding refers to the spectrum of methods for keeping track of linguistic features in a text. Coding includes: a list of examples, binary codes for the presence or absence of features, frequency counts (or even better, frequency counts normalized to text length so that texts of different lengths can be directly compared), and a mixture of the frequency counts and binary codes.

Example listing and presence/absence codes are purely qualitative (and also known as binary variables). Frequency counts are purely quantitative (also known as interval or count variables, depending on whether they have been normalized or not). A method might exploit both quantitative and qualitative coding, and some statistical procedures, for example logistic regression, allow for both interval and binary types of variables.

Sometimes analysts conflate example listing and frequency counting in their analysis. Recently I was asked to review an authorship identification report. There were four potential authors whose known documents were compared to the questioned document, an anonymous whistleblower letter. The client for whom the report was issued claimed that of the four potential authors, A, B, C, and D, the questioned document was authored by A or B. The first selected stylemarker was the presence of an apostrophe in plurals, for example "vendetta's, fee's, doc's, FAQ's." The report listed an example of this in the questioned document, and then listed examples of this in the known documents from authors A, B, C, and D. For author D, the report states that the pluralizing apostrophe is attested but not frequently. The examples were not counted in any of the known authors. The report states that authors A, B, and C "frequently use apostrophe and s for plurals on nouns." With this feature as one of the supporting arguments, the report concludes that authors A and/or B authored the questioned document. How did authors C and D—who each also exhibit this feature—not get caught in the same net that caught A and B? If frequency really mattered, then counts should have been recorded and compared to some baseline of pluralizing apostrophes in current American English. Since the mere presence of a pluralizing apostrophe cannot differentiate the four authors, but frequency might really serve as the differentiator among the authors, then the counts should have been taken and subjected to some kind of statistical analysis. If binary coding (presence/absence) is applied, the four authors cannot be differentiated and two cannot be singled out as authors. This vignette illustrates how important coding schemes can be, and how they are connected to decision making and statistical analysis.

35.1.3 Statistical analysis and decision making: how is the identification/elimination made?

Whether a method does or does not use any statistical analysis, all methods require some kind of decision making. The decision making might be as simple as majority rules (there are more matches to the questioned document in X than in Y, so X is counted as the author of the questioned document). For example, the examiner could make the decision about authorship based on his/her listing of matching points (i.e. similar examples) between a set of known documents, or segments of one long known document, and a questioned document.

Alternatively, the decision making could be the output of a statistical procedure, or the statistical output along with other qualitative observations which align with or contradict the statistical procedure. Statistical procedures are applied to the coding of linguistic analytical units in a set of texts and determine the decision making for identification or elimination (inclusion or exclusion).

Using statistical procedures for decision making is one way to minimize the possibility of confirmation bias—the propensity to reach conclusions that confirm the researcher's initial hypothesis. Although confirmation bias can, first, influence the selection of features, and, second, influence the coding of features, it can finally influence decision making. The example of the pluralizing apostrophe, described earlier, shows confirmation bias at each of these analytical stages.

Statistical procedures can be fairly simple or complex. For example, the decision making could be based on a threshold: X exceeds the threshold, Y does not, so X wins, or based on a rank: X has a lower/higher score than Y, so X wins.

More complicated statistical classifiers actually make the decision regarding authorship by assigning the questioned document to one of the known author classes. Advantages to using statistical classifier output as the basis for decision making are objectivity; simultaneous use of multiple variables; and simplicity. The statistical output is based on the coding from the data at hand; an analyst cannot easily predict what the statistical output will be just by eyeballing the coding, especially if the features being coded are abstract. Since almost all methods use multiple variables (on one or more levels of linguistic analysis), the classification is multivariate: this kind of hyperdimensional feature space is usually very difficult for us to visualize but easy for multivariate statistics to handle. Finally, reliance on the statistical output for decision making is simple, as long as some standard protocols have been developed. For instance, if the accuracy of a statistical classifier is only 70 percent, then a standard protocol could preclude going to the next step of classifying any questioned documents, based on a model which has such low accuracy on known documents.

One disadvantage of statistical classifiers is that they do not always perform well on some datasets. Some statistical classifiers, logistic regression in particular, perform very poorly or halt if there is a clear 100 percent separation between classes (documents or authors). On the other hand, some statistical classifiers such as discriminant function analysis work perfectly when there is complete separation between the classes (documents or authors) but cannot work with binary data. Calculating frequency base rates is also tricky because the multiplication rule (which is what allows DNA analysis to get such astronomically small probabilities) can only be applied if the items are truly independent of each other. For many linguistic features, this kind of strict independence cannot be justified. For instance, multiplying the frequency of verbs and the frequency of particles does not meet the independence criterion because some of the verbs require the particles, or the particles are dependent on the verbs. So it is important to select the right kind of statistical procedure for the kind of available data and coding.

Whether a statistical procedure is included in a method or not, any method should use cross-validation to check its conclusions, as discussed later. Cross-validation is one component of validation testing.

35.1.4 Results of validation testing: how well does the method work on ground truth data?

Forensic author identification methods can also be compared with respect to the results of validation testing. Validation testing may be for the courts one of the most important aspects of the method, since it speaks to the legal requirements for admissible scientific evidence.

Validation testing is an empirical technique that determines how well a procedure works, under specific and manipulable conditions, on a dataset containing samples with known provenance and characteristics. Chaski (2009) identifies four steps for validation testing:

(35.1.4.1)   Get a database of known samples.
(35.1.4.2)   Apply a repeatable analytical method to all texts in the database.
(35.1.4.3)   Apply a cross-validation scheme.
(35.1.4.4)   Compute the error rate based on hits and misses, analyzing the errors, in relation to the amount of data and other characteristics of the data.

35.1.4.1 *Datasets: get a database of known samples*

A dataset of known author documents—ground truth data for the authorship identification question—is essential. The point of using ground truth data is that we are trying to find out how often a method is correct at assigning authorship; if we do not know the correct authorship of known documents, we will never be able to tell if the method is accurate or not. Any mixture of known and unknown documents will make the calculation of error rates meaningless.

Ground truth data is all too often overlooked or undervalued. One intriguing study of the "writeprint" claimed a high degree of accuracy at identifying the authorship of emails, with over 97 percent accuracy for English, and over 92 percent accuracy for Chinese (Li et al. 2006). This impressive result, however, is undermined by the fact that the dataset was not ground truth data, as revealed by the researchers' comment about a substudy of three authors in their English dataset: "Clearly, Mike's distinct writeprint from the other two indicates his unique identity. The high degree of similarity between the writeprints of Joe and Roy suggests these two IDs might be the same person" (Li et al. 2006:82). Joe and Roy's 'writeprints' are almost identical. Yet it is also possible that Joe and Roy are distinct people, and the method cannot clearly recognize the difference between Joe's and Roy's documents. We will never know which explanation is correct because a dataset of ground truth data was not used. If a ground truth dataset had been used, if known authors were attached to one or more screennames before validation testing was begun, the accuracy of the method could have been legitimately tested.

The dataset of known author documents also needs to be tuned to the particular task at hand. For instance, Brennan and Greenstadt (2009) wanted to test whether non-professional writers could disguise their writing, either through obfuscation or imitation, to such a degree that stylistic analysis would fail to assign the disguised documents to the correct author. They designed a ground truth database specifically for this purpose, and found that non-professional writers could indeed fool a few methods they tested, which focused on punctuation, letter usage, vocabulary richness, readability, sentence length, and synonyms. Most of these features have already been shown to be very poor performers (Chaski 2001) or argued to be potentially poor discriminators because they rely on features with high linguistic salience and imitability (Chaski 1997). Nonetheless, the dataset is an important contribution because it can be studied to determine and to document the most frequent ways in which non-professional writers disguise their styles or imitate others' styles.

Chaski (1997, 2001) designed a ground truth dataset to be used specifically for author identification in forensic setting. The writing tasks spanned a wide range of text types, including love letters, apologies, business letters, narratives, fact-based essays, opinion-based essays, angry letters, complaints, and threat letters, for each author. The range of text types reflects the fact that in many authorship cases, the type of document which is questioned and the types of comparable known documents are not the same. A suspect suicide note might necessarily be compared to love letters and school essays. An anonymous threat letter might necessarily be compared to business letters and personal emails. This dataset has been released for use by researchers in Switzerland, France, Canada, Spain, and the United States. Through case work, Chaski has also has collected a dataset of ~1,500 spontaneously produced, topically unconstrained, known-author documents, which has been used for validation testing, as reported below.

Koppel and his colleagues harvested a dataset of blog posts from ~19,000 bloggers, which is available for research (Schler et al. (2006)). The bloggers are identified by a numerical identifier, gender, age, industry, and zodiacal sign. As with any data collected from the web, there is an assumption that the screenname belongs to one person at the keyboard, but the sheer size of this dataset makes it a valuable contribution to authorship research in the forensic setting.

Funded by the National Science Foundation, Juola and Argamon (2008–11) extracted and cleaned a set of emails from the famous Enron email database. The Enron email database is approximately 2 gigabyte of emails authored by known adults in a business environment, the authorship of which has, to the best of my knowledge, never been disputed; it is available for download from several sites including www.cs.cmu.edu/~enron/ and http://enrondata.org/. Email datasets are initially difficult to work with because emails often include emails from the author to whom the enveloping email is addressed; hence, cleaning the emails makes the data easier to work with when testing authorship methods.

35.1.4.2 *Analytical method: apply a repeatable method to all texts in database*

Once a dataset has been designed, collected, and organized for analysis, an analytical method can be applied to each document in the dataset. No matter what method is being

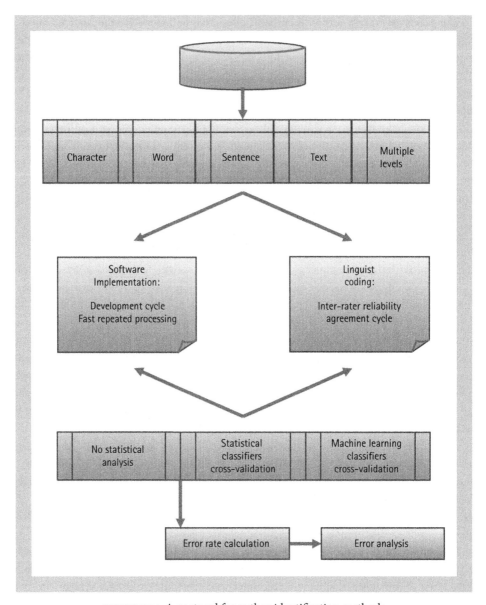

FIGURE 35.1 A protocol for author identification methods

tested, in validation testing the method is applied to each document in the dataset. There are basically two ways to apply a method to a document: computer software or human analysis.

Forensic authorship identification requires a repeatable method that can be consistently applied by different analysts. The units measured in both qualitative and quantitative analysis must be explicit enough to be operationally defined. Software-implemented (quantitative) methods can produce rapid validation testing results once the methods have been programmed. Qualitative methods can also produce validation testing results, but they require a team of trained linguists, inter-rater reliability, and a longer time commitment than software-implemented methods.

If the analytical units are explicit, then it may be possible to implement the method in computer software. Software implementation of a method provides instant repeatability because the software implements the same method every time it runs. Software implementation of a method also provides speed and efficiency, since most linguistic analysis performed by humans is time consuming and can be exhausting mentally. Once an authorship identification method has been implemented in software, each document in any dataset can be processed automatically and subsequently subjected to statistical analysis.

But sometimes qualitative methods are necessary, and software implementation may not be available, for example identifying a particular discourse strategy such as sarcasm or irony. When the analytical method cannot be implemented using software, then it should be subjected to inter-rater reliability testing. Several analysts are given the same task and the same dataset. Their analyses are compared to determine how often the analysts agree with each other. This agreement level indicates the inter-rater reliability. There are several statistical procedures for measuring the agreement level (Cronbach's alpha, Cohen's kappa), but the important point is that qualitative methods can and should be subjected to validation testing, with the first step being inter-rater reliability. If the analysts are in high agreement with each other, then they can proceed to apply the qualitative method to each document in the dataset. If the analysts have very low agreement, then they need to hammer out their differences, re-test themselves with new data, and determine their inter-rater reliability, iteratively, until they have reached a high enough level of agreement to apply the method to the entire dataset. If they do not test for inter-rater reliability first, then the entire dataset is being used just for inter-rater reliability, rather than validation testing.

35.1.4.3 *Apply a cross-validation scheme*

Once the linguistic units have been accounted for in a text, whether through computer software or human coding, the next step in validation testing is discovering how well the method works by checking the method's answers against the correct answer known from the ground truth data.

The general idea behind cross-validation is simple. First, run a statistical procedure over a dataset, building a statistical model which differentiates two (or more) authors. The accuracy of this model may not generalize to any other dataset, so cross-validation is a way to find out how robust the model really is. If one removes some data from the dataset, and builds a statistical model with the remaining data, will the removed data be classified accurately when reinserted into the dataset?

Even if no statistical modeling is used, cross-validation can and should be applied. For instance, one could apply discourse analysis, qualitatively, to two sets of known documents to determine which set a questioned document belongs to. The two authors of the known documents first need to be differentiated from each other, at the discourse level. If author A and author B show two different clusters of discourse strategies, how stable are their different clusters across each author's own documents? If I remove author A's document 1, do I find the same cluster of discourse strategies across the remaining known documents? This kind of procedure would, first, show the analyst how consistent the known documents are, and second, go a long way toward minimizing confirmation bias in feature selection. If only one of the known documents contains the selected discourse features, then the discourse features are not consistent and stable among the author's known documents, and this kind of instability weakens any conclusion about authorship. If none of the known documents contains the same cluster of selected discourse features, then the discourse features are clearly not consistent and stable among the author's known documents, and this kind of instability weakens any conclusion about authorship, or makes the selected features unemployable as identifying features.

Cross-validation applied in the traditional statistical way allows us to minimize over-fitting for statistical procedures but, applied in this novel way I am suggesting for forensic linguistics, also allows us to identify and minimize over-generalization for non-statistical procedures.

35.1.4.4 *Error rate calculation and error analysis*

Error rates are calculated from the mis-classifications. When Authors A and B are being compared, any A documents which jump over into the B bin, and any B documents which jump over into the A bin are misses: the method missed the true author classification.

At some point, any method will fail to distinguish different authors or the method will assign documents to the wrong author. Any method which never fails—no matter what the data quantity, no matter what other characteristics of the data are varied—is most likely over-fitted to the dataset and needs to be tested on different datasets.

In the forensic setting, failure can easily be caused by not having enough data to run the method robustly. The worst part of this is that there is usually no way to get any more data. In this scenario, the method cannot be applied with confidence. The forensic data problem certainly motivates researchers to develop methods which can work on very small amounts of data. The forensic minimal-quantity requirement also means that most methods for authorship identification based on literary data or newswriting data often cannot be applied to forensic data because they require far more data than most forensic cases supply.

At other times in the forensic setting, failure can occur because some quality shared by the known documents from different authors makes them difficult to differentiate. All of the different authors may each use a specific, highly-constrained jargon (drug dealing, numbers running, prostitution, corporate culture) which results in very

formulaic language. When everyone is writing three sentence emails that begin "Dear
____," "Your order has been scheduled... see below," and "please feel free to contact me
directly," the difficulty of detecting differences between authors obviously increases. The
different authors might be professional writers with high metalinguistic awareness or
one author might demonstrate a distinctive substyle.

Much more work is needed in error analysis to determine how any particular method
is failing. Brennan and Greenstadt's (2009) work offers a good place to begin error analysis for the methods they tested, and shows, for example, that lexical choice is a highly
salient linguistic feature which most people will manipulate when they are disguising or
imitating authorship.

35.2 CURRENT FORENSIC AUTHOR IDENTIFICATION METHODS

There are two methods which are currently used in investigations and trials: forensic
stylistics and software-generated analysis. There are also other methods in development,
which have real potential for being tested on forensically-feasible datasets and in the
near future employed forensically. These will be discussed in Section 35.3.

35.2.1 Forensic stylistics

The forensic stylistics method is best represented by McMenamin (1993, 2002), although
it has many other practitioners who borrow extensively from McMenamin's work.
McMenamin (2002) offers the best statement of the method and the fullest list of potential stylemarkers.

Using forensic stylistics, the examiner selects linguistic features from multiple linguistic levels as well as formatting and spelling. Examples of these features are listed from the
texts, and the lists from the known and questioned documents are compared. The
authorship decision is based on the matching of examples from the known and questioned documents.

There are no published validation testing results from any practitioner of forensic
stylistics. Chaski (2001) tested some linguistic features which are common in forensic
stylistic analyses but did not combine them with other linguistic features; when the
singular results are combined, the forensic stylistics features would have achieved only
54 percent accuracy. St Vincent and Hamilton (nd post-2001) did combine forensic stylistics features from Chaski (2001) and found that the method performed very poorly,
the highest accuracy being 51.46 percent. Koppel and Schler (2003) also tested forensic
stylistics features and achieved poor identification results, with the highest accuracy of
72 percent using part of speech tags in addition to the usual forensic stylistics features.

Chaski (2007b) used 42 punctuation and abbreviation features on 9,000 bloggers from the Koppel blog dataset and achieved only 60 percent differentiation among the bloggers, showing that merely recognizing punctuation and abbreviation features is not enough to differentiate authors from each other at a high enough rate to serve the justice system.

35.2.2 Software-implemented methods

35.2.2.1 *ALIAS SynAID*

The ALIAS SynAID method (Chaski 2001, 2005, 2007c) is a software-implemented method which extracts and normalizes frequency measurements at the character, word, and sentence levels from known and questioned documents. At the character level, punctuation is classified for its syntactic edge (clause, phrase, or morphemic). At the word level, average word length is calculated. At the sentence level, within each sentence, marked and unmarked syntactic structures for each syntactic head (noun, verb, adjective, etc.) are categorized based on POS tag n-gram sequences and regular expression programming which allow for non-adjacent tags to be considered in patterns. The marked and unmarked category examples are then counted within each sentence, and summed for document level quantification. Once each document is quantified, the numerical output is processed through linear discriminant function analysis using leave one out cross-validation. The authorship decision is based on the classification results, as long as the statistical model attains an accuracy which is in the very high 80s or better.

Independent of any litigation, ALIAS SynAID has achieved 95 percent accuracy in pair-wise tests among ten authors from the Chaski dataset, and 94 percent accuracy in pair-wise tests among ten authors from the Chaski dataset and known case dataset. In 23 litigation-related cases, ALIAS SynAID has created statistical models ranging from 93 to 100 percent cross-validated accuracy at differentiating the known authors' documents, so that classification of the questioned document(s) was possible.

ALIAS SynAID has also been tested, independent of litigation, with ten authors chosen at random from samples produced by 175 known authors) each represented by 20 five-sentence chunks. The accuracy rate is much lower with these very short texts (from 30 to 75 words), as shown in Table 35.1, from Chaski (2007c). Author 16, tested against the nine other authors, has documents correctly assigned to her ~95 percent when linear discriminant function analysis (LDA) and support vector machines with different kernels (SVM 1 and SVM 2) are used, but only ~92 percent with logistic regression (LR) and decision tree forest (DTF). Author 91's five-sentence chunks are much more difficult to assign to him correctly, as shown by the fact that the best classifier overall, LDA, achieves only 74 percent cross-validated accuracy.

The computational method, as implemented in ALIAS SynAID, has been scrutinized by *Daubert* and *Frye* hearings (Washington DC, 2001 (Federal); Atlanta, GA, 2008

Table 35.1 Results of SynAID with very short samples

Author	LR	LDA	SVM 1	SVM 2	DTF
16	91.67	95.28	95.28	95.83	92.50
23	85.28	88.33	85.28	80.56	82.78
80	80.00	85.56	80.56	77.78	81.39
90	72.22	76.67	81.94	80.28	76.11
91	81.39	74.17	81.94	78.89	75.28
96	79.17	83.61	78.61	76.11	76.11
97	85.56	85.83	83.61	79.44	82.22
98	79.72	84.17	79.44	76.11	82.50
99	70.00	82.50	78.06	74.17	80.83
168	83.33	88.89	76.39	79.72	86.39
Overall	80.83	84.50	82.11	79.89	81.61

(State); Annapolis, MD (1998)). Presented by one expert, computational linguistics evidence has attained full admissibility, meaning that the expert was allowed to state a conclusion about the authorship of the document in question.[1]

Given the current interest and research activities, other computational linguists, or law enforcement officers trained in the use of specific software, will be presenting evidence based on validated, litigation-independent techniques in the near future.

35.2.2.2 *POS (part of speech) trigrams*

Hirst and Feiguina (2007) tagged ten authors from the Chaski dataset (the same authors used in Chaski (2005)) and used a Support Vector Machine with 10-fold cross-validation to classify documents based on POS trigrams. This method achieved 88 percent accuracy. Hirst and Feiguina (2007) do not manually check the assigned POS tags and they use a parser designed for standard English. It is highly likely that at least some of the POS tags have been incorrectly assigned. It is thus possible that they might achieve higher accuracy with the trigrams if trigrams were checked for containing the correct tags.

Baayen (2008:154–9) reports the results of his statistical analysis of POS trigrams from Spassova's (2006) dataset of three Spanish writers. There are 15 texts, each of approximately 3,000 words, so this dataset is on the high side for forensic casework. Applying

---

[1] *Green v Dalton/US Navy*, 164 F. 3rd 671, District of Columbia District Court, Washington DC; (for related material see <http://caselaw.findlaw.com/us-dc-circuit/1436391.html> accessed September 23, 2011); *Arsenault v Dixon*, Fulton County Superior Court, Atlanta, GA (certified transcript of ruling available from author); *Zarolia v Osborne/Buffalo Environmental*, Anne Arundel County Superior Court, Annapolis, MD. Since most opinions in forensic author identification are unpublished, please contact the author for further information about these cases and others.

discriminant function analysis, Baayen shows how the initial result is perfect, with each text assigned to its true author with high probability. But then Baayen applies leave-one-out cross-validation, and shows that the cross-validated accuracy is 9/15 correct assignments, or ~70 percent. This rather low result is most likely due to the fact that the data were not run in pair-wise tests, but run as a multi-class problem. The best results are always obtained through pair-wise comparisons (Chaski 2005; Grieve 2007).

35.3 FUTURE DIRECTIONS FOR FORENSIC AUTHOR IDENTIFICATION

New methods are continually being developed, especially in the computational paradigm. In this section, I will mention a few and point out some areas of consensus that have developed in the past decade with respect to authorship identification research.

The ALIAS UniAIDE method (Chaski 2007a, 2010) is a software-implemented method which extracts the frequencies of single characters (including punctuation and whitespace) in a questioned document and each known document. The questioned–known frequencies are subjected to a variation of the chi-square statistic that enables the method to overcome length bias. Independently, Chaski (2007a) and Stamatatos (2008) realized that the unigram methods as described in Peng et al. (2003) and Keselj et al. (2003) would rank the longest documents as most similar to the questioned document. In the forensic setting, the chief suspect would typically have more documents collected, and thus end up with the longest merged document, and then end up as most similar to the questioned document based on sheer size, unless the length bias is corrected. Stamatatos's (2008) fix involves text sampling; Chaski's fix is a simple variation on how the chi-square is calculated, allowing raw counts which are normally not allowed in the use of chi-square for calculating a probability.

Character-based methods are especially intriguing because, in a Unicode-compliant system, they can be applied to any language which has a Unicode-compliant script. This means that a reliable character-based method could be run on languages for which no linguistic expertise was available to sort and rank documents before being sent to linguistic experts.

Koppel et al. (2011) have recently published a character-based method based on trigrams that include no spaces. The choice of three non-space characters is prudent and clever, linguistically, since this window will capture almost all function words and roots, in both Indo-European and Semitic languages. The method currently can achieve high accuracy if a threshold for false positives is implemented; false positives can run as high as 30 percent, but once these are filtered out, the method achieves a high accuracy. Whether this can be implemented in a forensic setting remains to be seen, but the work is important because it opens the door for ways of discovering when a document cannot be matched to any in the known set.

Argamon et al (2007) are developing a method based on function words and lexical categories within Halliday's (1994) Systemic Functional Grammar. On a dataset of nineteenth-century novels, the method extracts and counts the lexical categories and applies Weka's SMO learning algorithm with 10-fold cross-validation. On the literary dataset, the method is able to distinguish different authors at near 90 percent accuracy.

Some points of consensus and experimental replication have already been attained. For instance, we know that author pair-wise comparison achieves more accurate results than multi-author comparisons. We know that methods which combine multiple linguistic levels are more accurate than methods which focus only on one level. We know that character-based and word-based methods can show topic bias that must be controlled for in the known document data collection. We know that syntax-based methods, whether POS tags or more sophisticated structures, work across topics and registers better than word-based methods do. We know that there are data requirements for different methods in terms of known characters, words, or sentences.

The immediate future for forensic author identification is intensely exciting as research teams collaborate by data sharing, validation testing, and learning what we can and cannot do with the data at hand. As linguists in service to the legal communities, it is equally as important for us to say "no" as it is for us to say "yes."

....

CHAPTER 36

CORPUS LINGUISTICS
IN AUTHORSHIP
IDENTIFICATION

....

KRZYSZTOF KREDENS
MALCOLM COULTHARD

36.1 INTRODUCTION

'THIS semantic prosody stuff is really amazing' is how a police officer in the UK responded to a recent presentation on the investigative and evidential potential of forensic linguistics. His was not an uncommon reaction. When we train individuals working in law enforcement, their polite interest invariably gives way to considerable animation when, using examples from corpora, we demonstrate how normally "invisible" patterns of language use become clearly manifest once one has access to sufficient data. Importantly, in the context of forensic linguistics, corpus linguistics offers much more than explanatory possibilities.

Corpus linguistics is basically "an empirical approach to studying language, which uses observations of attested data in order to make generalisations about lexis, grammar, and semantics" (Stubbs 2006:107). In a popular introduction to the field, McEnery and Wilson (1996:21) write that in the context of modern linguistics the term "corpus" most frequently has connotations of sampling and representativeness, finite size, machine-readable form, and a standard reference, while according to Biber et al. (1999:4), a corpus is "[a] collection of spoken and written texts, organized by register and coded for other discourse considerations." However, "corpus" is increasingly being used to refer to any digitally stored collection of texts that has been put together with some exploratory purpose in mind; for this reason Sinclair's (1991:171) less restrictive definition—"a collection of naturally occurring language text, chosen to characterize a state or variety of a language"—is perhaps the safest for us to use here, not least because of the possibilities afforded by the internet when it comes to data collection and analysis (see Section 36.5 below).

Terminological considerations aside, what is of most importance in the present context is the fact that corpus linguistics provides methods for processing naturally occurring language data with a view to describing the nature of particular instances of language use and the behavior of particular (groups of) language users. Language corpora can thus be used for a variety of forensic linguistic tasks. In this chapter we set out to explore and exemplify ways in which corpora and corpus methodology can aid the forensic linguist to, for instance:

- analyze texts comparatively in order to comment on the authorship of questioned documents;
- interpret the meaning of disputed utterances; and
- investigate and describe language use in legal and forensic settings.

36.2 AUTHORSHIP ATTRIBUTION

The interest of linguists in questions of authorship is comparatively recent, but there has been a continuing recorded interest in assigning authorship since the days of Ancient Greece—Davis (1996, as reported in Coulthard and Johnson 2007:163–4) recounts humorously an early unsuccessful attempt in Greece in the fourth century BC. For an excellent historical survey of authorship attribution see Love (2002:14–31).

During the next two millennia considerable effort was expended on attempts to resolve disputes about the authorship of crucial religious texts, like the Gospels and some of the Pauline letters (Morton and McLeman 1964, 1980); of significant literary texts, particularly some of the plays of Shakespeare (Merriam 2002); and of some important political texts, like the *Federalist Papers*, a set of eighteenth-century essays about the US Constitution (Mosteller and Wallace 1964).

The first language-based proposal to solve questions of authorship by attempting to access assumed individual linguistic regularities was made by the mathematician de Morgan in 1851. In a letter replying to a biblical scholar, who had asked him to devise a way of deciding on the authenticity of a corpus of letters traditionally attributed to the evangelist St Paul, de Morgan hypothesized that average word length, measured simply in terms of letters per word, would not only be writer-specific and virtually constant but would also even survive translation (de Morgan 1882).

Mendenhall (1887) was the first person to actually test this hypothesis. He counted by hand and then calculated the average number of letters in hundreds of thousands of words drawn not only from the Pauline letters, but also from works by Shakespeare and from two of the major candidate authors for some of his plays, Marlowe and Bacon. While the measure discounted Bacon as a possible author, the word length scores for

Marlowe's later plays, histories, and tragedies, correlated more closely with those for Shakespeare's histories, tragedies, and Roman plays than did the scores derived from the corpus of Shakespeare's comedies.

Although they were not linguists, the analytic approach used by Mosteller and Wallace (1964) to attribute authorship to some of the *Federalist Papers* employed some basic corpus linguistics techniques. The *Papers* are a set of 85 essays published anonymously in 1787–88 and designed to persuade New Yorkers to ratify the new American Constitution. They are now known to have been written by Alexander Hamilton, James Madison, and John Jay, but Hamilton and Madison both claimed sole authorship of 12 of the essays. In their attempt to resolve the dispute and identify the author, Mosteller and Wallace first assumed that there would be what we would now call idiolectal differences in preferences for the selection of a small set of grammatical items. They began by analyzing the frequencies of grammatical items in two corpora made up of texts known to have been written by Hamilton and Madison and selected those items for which there were significant inter-author differences. They found, for instance, that Hamilton used *upon* some 10 times more frequently than Madison, who in turn used *also* twice as often as Hamilton. Armed with 30 such apparently distinguishing preferences, Mosteller and Wallace then analyzed the frequencies of the items in each of the disputed papers. They ultimately assigned all 12 to Madison, a conclusion that coincides with the prevailing view reached by historians on the basis of other evidence. Since then, the *Federalist Papers* have been a favorite testing ground for researchers developing new stylometric methods.

Such methods are fine when the linguist has a lot of text in both the known and the disputed or questioned corpora, but often in forensic cases the available text in both corpora is very limited and it is not possible to establish statistically reliable usage frequency patterns.

McMenamin (2002), in his book on forensic stylistics, points out that there are two major authorship questions that the analyst may be asked to answer. The first, a task which he labels "looking for *consistency*," is concerned with whether a single text or a *corpus* of texts has one author or several. A second question involves looking for *resemblance*, that is asking whether one or more of a set of known authors might have produced one or more of the texts whose authorship is unknown. Often, as part of the same investigation, the linguist may need to first look for consistency within the corpus of texts of unknown authorship, in order to discover whether it is necessary to look for one or several authors, before going on to examine the resemblances between the questioned text(s) and those produced by the candidate author(s).

When the approach is quantitative rather than qualitative, it employs classic corpus linguistics methodology. To exemplify, McMenamin uses a case in which the questioned and known authors both wrote a Californian zip code as *Ca. 91001* (with two spaces between the letters and the numbers) and the task was to assess the rarity and therefore the significance of this format, by discovering how often these independent choices were co-selected in a corpus of addresses written by other authors. The results showed that the version *Ca.*, as opposed to alternatives like *CA*, *CA.*, *Ca*, *ca*, and *ca.*, occurred in 11 percent of the 686 addresses in the corpus, while the choice of 2 spaces between the letters and the numbers, as opposed to the other options of none, a single space or no numbers at all, occurred in 9 percent of addresses. However, the two independent choices—"Ca." and "two spaces following the letters"—were co-selected very rarely, in fact in only 1 percent of the addresses.

This represents one way forward for forensic linguistics—the collection of specialized corpora to provide population-specific statistics on usage, a task already begun by several linguists for, for example, English mobile phone text messages (see Section 36.4 below).

36.1.1 A corpus-assisted analysis of register

In the famous English case of Derek Bentley, reported in detail in Coulthard and Johnson (2007:173–80), Coulthard was briefed to investigate whether an incriminating statement attributed to Bentley might have been partly authored by police officers as Bentley had claimed. One of the marked features of Derek Bentley's supposedly dictated confession is the frequent use of the word "then" in its temporal meaning—11 occurrences in 588 words. This may not, at first, seem at all remarkable, given that Bentley was reporting a series of sequential events and that one of the obvious requirements of a witness statement is accuracy about time. However, a cursory glance at some contemporary lay witness statements showed that Bentley's use of "then" was at the very least atypical, and thus a potential intrusion of a specific feature of police register, deriving from a professional concern with the accurate recording of temporal sequence.

Two small corpora were used to test this hypothesis, the first composed of three ordinary witness statements, totalling some 930 words of text, the second three statements by police officers, totalling some 2270 words. The comparative results were startling: whereas in the ordinary witness statements there is only one occurrence of "then," it occurs 29 times in the police officers' statements, that is an average of once every 78 words. Thus, Bentley's usage of temporal "then," once every 53 words, groups his statement firmly with those produced by the police officers. In this case it was possible to check the findings from the "ordinary witness" data against a reference corpus, the Corpus of Spoken English—a subset of the much larger COBUILD Bank of English—which, at that time, consisted of some 1.5 million running words collected from many different types of naturally occurring speech. "Then" in all its meanings proved to occur a mere 3,164 times, that is only once every 500 words, which supported the representativeness of the witness data and specialness of the data in the corpus of police statements and the Bentley statement.

What was even more striking about the Bentley statement was the frequent post-positioning of the *then*s, as can be seen in the two examples below, selected from a total of 7:

(36.1) Chris **then** jumped over and I followed.
(36.2) Chris **then** climbed up the drainpipe to the roof and I followed.

The opening phrases have an odd feel, because not only do ordinary speakers as we have seen use "then" much less frequently than policemen, they also use it in a structurally different way. For instance, in the COBUILD spoken data corpus "then I" occurred ten times more frequently than "I then"; indeed the structure "I then" occurred only once every 165,000 words. By contrast this phrase occurs three times in Bentley's short statement, once every 194 words, a frequency almost a thousand times greater. In addition, while the "I then" structure, as one might predict from the COBUILD data, did not occur at all in any of the three lay witness statements, there were nine occurrences in one single 980 word police statement, as many as in the entire 1.5 million word spoken corpus. Taken together, the average occurrence in the three police statements was once every 119 words. Thus, the structure "I then" does appear to be a feature of police officers' written register.

36.1.2 Authorship attribution of text messages

Growingly, forensic linguists are getting involved in cases involving instant and text messaging, typically when there is a suspicion that the named sender was not the actual composer. Although the details and therefore the analytic approaches change from case to case, the basic strategy is the same: the forensic linguist creates a series of corpora, at least two and often more, and sets out to isolate the distinctive/idiolectal/idiosyncratic features of each of the corpora.

To exemplify: Jenny Nicholl disappeared on June 30, 2005 and her mobile phone, normally in frequent use, remained switched off except for two ten-minute periods when the phone sent a total of four text messages. Police suspected that she had not authored them. Coulthard was provided with the four suspect messages and a small corpus of authentic text messages sent by Nicholl (see Grant 2010:516–17 for the actual text messages).

There were of course many identical choices in the two corpora, but analysis showed that certain texting abbreviations used in the authenticated messages like "im," "m not," "ive," "cu," and "fone" were not instantiated at all in the suspect messages, which used the alternatives "I am," "aint," "ave," "cya," and "phone," while for several other items where Jenny had one fixed choice the suspect messages displayed variation. In other words, Jenny had a set of encoding rules that differed from those instantiated in the suspect texts and these systematic differences between the two corpora led Coulthard to conclude that the form of the suspect messages was not compatible with their having been produced by Jenny.

36.2 DISPUTED MEANINGS

Linguistics tells us that people can have different intuitions about the semantic scope of a lexical item, or provide different interpretations of the pragmatic meaning of an utterance. To a teenager, the adjectives "wicked" or "sick" may today be the preferred means of positive evaluation, but have an entirely different meaning to her father. A wife's remark "the washing machine's finished," in pragmatic terms an intended suggestion that the husband empty it and hang out the clothes, may be (mis-)understood literally. Such semantic and interpretative differences are normally relatively inconsequential, at least socially, and, in any case, can be successfully negotiated.

Sometimes, however, disputes may arise over the intended meaning of legislative acts, contracts, evidential transcripts of speech, allegedly defamatory or threatening language, etc. Individuals have taken issue with, and legal action against, being described as "a concubine" (Kniffka 2007), "a sex maniac," or "an idiot" (Kredens 2007). Companies have argued over the meaning of the prefix "Mc-" (Lentine and Shuy 1990), the word "bespoke" (see below), or the phrase "The House of Flavor" (Handelman 2008). Forensic linguists are uniquely placed to help in such cases because they can use corpora to identify the prevailing patterns of meaning for the linguistic item in question as used in a given context by members of a particular speech community.

In post-communist Poland's burgeoning free-market economy of the 1990s, an entrepreneur described the business dealings of the country's then-richest person as *największy przekręt w historii Trzeciej Rzeczypospolitej* ("the greatest monkey business of the Third Republic"). The latter responded with legal action claiming the pronouncement to be libelous. In the course of a lengthy lawsuit the Court commissioned at least four expert witnesses to comment on the semantic load of the term *przekręt* ("monkey business") but their conclusions differed significantly. This was possibly because the experts relied on dictionaries in their interpretations; unfortunately, they could not use a language corpus as none existed. Eventually, the Court found in favor of the plaintiff. Writing from a post-corpus-revolution perspective, Kredens (2008), using a 10-million-word sample of contemporary Polish, found that the word collocated with the adjectives *financial, legal,* and *political,* and referred to contexts of dishonest activity and violations of legal regulations, a discovery supportive of the plaintiff.

Some 15 years later and 1,100 miles away, we find another example of a dictionary being used to solve a dispute over meaning but can also see some light at the end of the tunnel. In an adjudication document issued in June 2008, the UK's Advertising Standards Authority (ASA) addressed a complaint concerning the use of the adjective "bespoke," which refers to custom-made clothing. The complainant, a tailoring firm, objected that a competitor's advertisement was misleading because the suits being advertised were not made entirely by hand. The ASA's response was still partly based on the definition of "bespoke" in the *Oxford English Dictionary,* but it also quoted instances of actual usage of the term by other tailoring firms. Interestingly, these were provided by the respondent to bolster its case, in what we can only describe as a lay application of corpus methodology.[1]

A natural next step should arguably be reliance on corpus-only methods in similar cases in an effort to remove the influence of the lexicographer's subjective judgment. That said, we are aware language corpora cannot be treated as an antidote for interpretative subjectivity. They provide more or less raw data and in the process of making sense of

---

[1] The ASA's response can be found at <http://www.asa.org.uk/ASA-action/Adjudications/2008/6/Sartoriani-London/TF_ADJ_44555.aspx> accessed September 23, 2011.

them linguists do have to make decisions. Still, unlike dictionaries, which only offer a fragmented picture of language, corpora can offer a panoramic perspective. Naturally, we must not dismiss modern, corpus-based dictionaries, which essentially present a lexicographer's version of the panorama. Unfortunately, it will normally be a compressed version owing to typographic, or, in the case of online dictionaries, hypertextual, limitations.

Curious readers are advised to first read Shuy (2008 and 2010) and then undertake their own analyses of the disputed meanings discussed there; the British National Corpus and the American National Corpus can both be accessed online,[2] as can be numerous other English-language corpora.

36.3 CORPORA IN LANGUAGE AND LAW RESEARCH

Advances in digital technology and the ready availability of both data and corpus tools mean that a lot of corpus compilation and exploration projects are nowadays undertaken on a do-it-yourself basis. A significant proportion of recent research into language and law is based on specialized corpora derived from language use in legal settings. Studies differ in the extent to which they rely on corpus-derived information; some use statistical measures to explore textual characteristics quantitatively, while others treat the corpora as essentially collections of homogeneous texts providing, at the click of the mouse, the relevant information on, say, usage patterns. Cross-cutting this distinction is another, corpus-based and corpus-driven approach to data analysis (Tognini-Bonelli 2001). In a corpus-based analysis data are used essentially to back a preformulated theory, whereas in corpus-driven studies generalizations are made inductively, that is following the discovery of recurrent patterns. These two approaches, of course, are not mutually exclusive.

Goźdź-Roszkowski's (2011) study of variability within legal language is a prime example of how the application of corpus methodology can yield results challenging hitherto-held tacit assumptions. His 5.5 million word American Law Corpus consists of seven genre categories: academic journals, briefs, contracts, legislation, opinions, professional articles, and textbooks. The textual characteristics analyzed include vocabulary distribution and use, extended lexical expressions, and lexico-syntactic co-occurrence patterns. Agentless passive structures, for example, turn out to be most characteristic of contracts and textbooks but quite scarce in opinions, briefs, and academic journals. Goźdź-Roszkowski concludes that, rather than being the uniform phenomenon it is often presented as, legal English is in fact a "system of related domain-specific genres, which vary widely in terms of patterning, [i.e.] recurring lexical and lexico-grammatical combinations discernible in large collections of authentic texts by means of quantitative and qualitative analytical techniques" (2011:16).

---

[2] See <http://www.natcorp.ox.ac.uk/> and <http://www.americannationalcorpus.org>, respectively, both accessed September 23, 2011.

In an analysis of the O. J. Simpson trial, Cotterill (2003) uses the concept of semantic prosody to look at the "subtle terms which are used by the prosecution to construct an image of Simpson as a violent man ultimately capable of murdering his wife" (2003:66). She finds evidence in the COBUILD corpus to demonstrate how some of the seemingly neutral words and phrases used by the prosecution in fact carry negative associations. Heffer (2005), in turn, uses a corpus compiled from transcripts of over 100 English criminal jury trials to describe what he calls "legal-lay discourse," that is courtroom interaction between legal professionals and lay participants.

Another judicial setting, police interviews with suspects and witnesses, has also attracted linguists' attention of late. Haworth (2010:8) considers the police interview with suspects as "a multi-purpose, multi-audience and multi-format mode of discourse." She secured 276 interview tapes from a number of different police stations in England and, having transcribed a representative sample, used her corpus to investigate the evidential dimension of police interview discourse in the English criminal justice process. The analysis revealed a number of problems both with regard to the interaction in the interview room itself, and in the treatment of interview material as evidence in the courtroom. Haworth provides some recommendations for dealing with these. MacLeod (2010) used a corpus of police interviews with women reporting rape to look at discursive patterns of interactions between the interviewers and the alleged victims. Having revealed patterns of, inter alia, interactional control and negotiation, she identified some wide-ranging implications for the training of police officers in the UK. Fadden (2007) analyzed six police interviews (three with aboriginal and three with non-aboriginal suspects) and found that the linguistic behavior in those two groups was different on a discourse level. She notes that Canadian Aboriginals' "[p]reference for being short on words...may give police and later on juries, the impression that aboriginal suspects are not defending themselves or that they unwittingly appear untrustworthy, or have information they wish to conceal" (2007:320).

Finally, Solan (2010:72–9) discusses how even the United States Supreme Court has used corpus-based analyses. In one case the Court had to determine the meaning of the word "carry" in a statute that enhanced the punishment of someone who carried a firearm while committing a drug crime. The question was whether a defendant who had a gun in the trunk of his car was "carrying" it. Judges used the Bible, works of Shakespeare, and a computer search of newspapers as informal corpora, with both the majority and the dissent citing examples that supported their interpretations.

36.4 CORPORA FOR FORENSIC APPLICATIONS

If, following the recent growth of forensic linguistics and its successful exploitation of corpus linguistic methods and resources, there is still a cause for concern, it is a fact that we still know relatively little of how language is used in forensic situations, essentially when crimes are committed or accompanied by words. For obvious reasons such data are difficult to obtain. That said, some progress is being made.

Jones and Bennell (2007), for example, used 33 genuine and 33 simulated suicide notes from Schneidman and Farberow (1957) to develop statistical prediction rules to discriminate between the two types. They found that average sentence length (higher for simulated notes) and expression of positive affect (more common in genuine notes) were particularly effective discriminators. Shapero (2011) has succeeded in compiling a corpus of 286 suicide notes, 212 authored by males and 74 by females. Having first analyzed word and keyword lists, she tagged her corpus semantically using Wmatrix, a corpus analysis tool developed at Lancaster University.[3] She found that lexicalization patterns within certain categories—for example liking, negatives, future time, knowledge, and kin—were distinct from those in the written component of the British National Corpus. Both Shapero's and Jones and Bennell's studies have a promising potential in the context of law enforcement as suicide notes from cases of suspicious deaths could be tested against the generic structure and patterns of lexicalization found in genuine notes.

A significant element of the rapid technological developments of recent years has been the increasing use of mobile phones as a means of communication. In 2009 the UK's Mobile Data Association, on the basis of data obtained from the country's mobile network operators, estimated that an average of 11 million messages were sent every hour.[4] Inevitably, as indicated in Section 36.1.2 above, some of them contain linguistic substance which ends up as evidence in criminal investigations (see also, e.g., Coulthard et al. 2010; Grant 2010), and systematic description of texting as a new language variety appears to be one of the most pressing needs in current linguistic scholarship. To be sure, it is already being addressed. Over three years, Tagg (2009) collected an impressive 11,067 text messages totalling 190,516 words. Strictly speaking, hers is not a forensic corpus; rather, the messages all come from everyday interpersonal interactions with no legal consequences. She explores linguistic features which define texting as a language variety and comes up with revealing, data-based conclusions regarding the extent to which texting differs from speech. It is not difficult to imagine that her findings on the role of user agency, awareness, and choice in shaping text messages could one day be exploited by forensic linguists for particular cases where incriminating messages were used. Among other corpora of text messages are Grant's (2010) 10,000-message corpus, Dyer's (2008) 756 messages collected via a web survey from 203 individuals, and the publicly available National University of Singapore's Live Corpus, which, as of February 2011, contains over 10,000 messages.[5]

Another initiative deserving mention is the Communicated Threat Assessment Resource Corpus (CTARC) being developed at the Academy Group Inc. At the time of writing it contains over 500 threatening texts obtained from real-life cases and has approximately 75,000 words (Fitzgerald, personal communication). CTARC is already being used for large-scale research projects. Gales (2010), using a corpus and discourse

---

[3] <http://ucrel.lancs.ac.uk/wmatrix/> accessed September 23, 2011.
[4] <http://www.text.it/mediacentre/press_release_list.cfm?thePublicationID=749C769E-15C5-F4C0-99E6A252A5A98607> accessed September 23, 2011.
[5] <http://wing.comp.nus.edu.sg> accessed September 23, 2011.

analytic approach, looked at 470 threatening letters from the corpus to uncover patterns of epistemic and affective meaning within the genre.

36.5 THE INTERNET AS A CORPUS

Can the internet be treated as a corpus? Purists might (rightly) point to the lack of part-of-speech tagging—and hence limited possibilities of syntactic analysis including colligation patterns in particular. There is also the problem of an acute imbalance between spoken and written language; most of the internet contains the latter. These admittedly serious shortcomings notwithstanding, we believe that in the context of forensic linguistics a more pertinent question to ask is whether the internet and corpus linguistic methodology are mutually exclusive. We do not think this to be the case and in Sections 36.5.1 and 36.5.2 below provide examples of how the internet can actually provide information that may be missing from traditional corpora and how this information can be exploited methodologically.

Google, currently the most popular search engine, offers an array of search options which, with some ingenuity, can be used to emulate traditional corpus searches at least to some extent.[6] For example, the following search syntax

<"a   very   *   increase"   site:publications.parliament.uk   date:3   filetype:pdf
-economy–budget>

will result in Google searching the website of the UK Parliament for the string "a very [one or more words] increase" in pdf documents published online in the last three months; the documents will most likely have nothing to do with the current economic situation.

In February 2011 the search returned 5 hits.

a very sharp increase
a very significant increase (×2)
a very large increase
a very substantial increase

In linguistic terms, these results tell us about the kind of adverbially intensified adjectives preceding the noun "increase." Importantly, contextual and co-textual information is available instantly through hypertext. If we remove the temporal operator "date:3" we get another instance of "a very significant increase" plus a new item, "a very real increase." If we consider the fact that, say, legal acts or court judgments are routinely published online, it suddenly becomes possible to research certain aspects of legal language without the need to compile a specialized corpus. But the web as a corpus can be exploited in other ways as well.

---

[6] For an explanation of the more advanced features of Google Web Search, see <http://www.google.com/support/websearch/bin/answer.py?answer=136861> accessed September 23, 2011.

36.5.1 Co-selection

One of the perennial concerns of academic linguists is unacknowledged textual borrow-ing or *plagiarism*, in particular how much text one needs to demonstrate that a student has plagiarized. Coulthard in Coulthard and Johnson (2007) reports two cases where police officers had created interview records by copying text from pre-existing state-ments. The persuasive task was to show how quickly linguistic encoding becomes unique and therefore how little shared identical text one needs to argue that one text is based on another or both on a third. The technique was to use the internet as searched by Google as a massive corpus and to demonstrate how growingly longer strings became rarer in the corpus until there were no examples at all (Coulthard 2004). One shared clause was "I picked something up like an ornament."

String	Instances
I picked	1,060,000
I picked something	780
I picked something up	362
I picked something up like	1
I picked something up like an	0

On the basis of these results, Coulthard postulated that novel sequences of 10 words or more were very likely to be unique, that is only composed once, though there could be many repetitions or quotings. Six years later Culwin and Child (2010), reporting a much more wide-ranging Google corpus-based study, argued that uniqueness is likely to kick in at around 6 running words. Such search engine based evidence can be very persuasive to judges as they can easily go and check the claims for themselves, though of course jurors are forbidden to do their own research while on jury duty.

36.5.2 Meaning in underrepresented genres

One of the present authors, Kredens, was recently asked to carry out an analysis of an interpreted police interview with an alleged rape victim and provide information on what she actually meant in connection with a specific sexual act.[7] At one point during the interview she said the following words in Polish:

(36.3) *wtedy on włożył mi członka i nie dał mi po prostu nic powiedzieć, nic robić*

---

[7] We are grateful to J P French Associates, who managed the case, for their permission to use this example.

This translates literally as:

(36.4) "then he inserted [me] his penis and simply wouldn't let me say or do anything."

However, the interpreter at the police station came up with the following version:

(36.5) "then he put his penis in my mouth and he told me to shut up."

Later in the investigation it turned out that oral sex had not actually taken place and so the police wanted to know why the interpreter made the mistake, possibly fearing that the defense lawyers might try to undermine the record of the interview as unreliable evidence because of what might have been seen as the interpreter's incompetence.

When one looks at the Polish text and its translation in (36.4), it is obvious the alleged victim did not actually specify the type of penetration—she used the verb "insert" without the prepositional phrase. However, the interpreter provided this additional information, having made the erroneous assumption that oral sex *had* taken place. The most obvious explanation for this mistake is that the interpreter may have assumed that because the alleged victim said she was physically unable to "say anything," this was because the penis had been inserted into her mouth.

In his analysis for the police, Kredens used the linguistic concept of markedness combined with corpus linguistic methodology. In a nutshell, according to markedness theory unmarked items are more common and more natural: for example, in English, when asking someone about their age, it is customary to say "How old are you?" so in the context of normal social interaction the use of "How young are you?" with the stress on "young" would sound odd, or, in linguistic terms, be classified as "marked usage." Similarly, when offered a glass of wine, a teetotal person may respond by saying "Thank you, but I don't drink" (unmarked usage), rather than "Thank you, but I don't drink alcohol" (more marked). In such situations, the verb "drink" does not need an object to be realized because the context makes it clear what the communicative intention is. The question that arose in this case was about the unmarked usage of the Polish phrase *włożyć członka* ("insert one's penis") when no prepositional phrase is present. To provide an answer, Kredens first consulted the largest Polish-language corpus, The National Corpus of the Polish Language, which has about 450 million words. With no relevant information obtained, he then used the internet as a corpus. A Google exact match search for the phrases *włożył mi członka* ("inserted his member") and *włożył mi penisa* ("inserted his penis") yielded 14 and 52 matches, respectively, and some 90 percent of the results came from contexts referring to vaginal penetration. Importantly, *all* of the instances of the two phrases where they were not accompanied by a prepositional phrase complement seemed to refer to vaginal penetration. It then seemed that the use of the phrases "inserted his member/penis" without specifying the orifice normally presupposed vaginal penetration. However, rather than this unmarked use, the interpreter seems to have elected to rely on co-textual information, which may have prompted her to supply what the corpus confirms to be statistically a marked location.

This case illustrates how the internet can provide valuable data where traditional balanced corpora fail. Sexually explicit texts are under-represented in corpora of general English, whereas, from a linguistic perspective, they are *over*-represented on the Internet and this is also true of many other types of texts. An example here comes from forensic linguist Tim Grant's work in a conspiracy-to-murder case (see Coulthard et al. 2010), where the meaning of the verb "duppy" as used within a speech community in East London was crucial to the semantic interpretation of an internet chat. There are only seven instances of "duppy" in the British National Corpus, all of them nouns, and Grant compiled his own corpus from relevant internet sites, including ones where enthusiasts of a genre of urban music known as *grime* exchanged views (the defendants were both aspiring grime artists). On the basis of data obtained this way, he opined that the chat contained a reference to soliciting murder. A similar approach was taken by Kredens, who was asked by the police to provide an interpretation of a sentence allegedly spoken by a member of a North London gang. With no satisfactory information found in the existing corpora of general English, Kredens compiled a corpus largely from data available on the video-sharing website YouTube, relying heavily on lyrics found in rap and hip-hop music videos.

36.6 CONCLUSIONS

We hope we have given a sufficiently wide range of examples to indicate the value of language corpora and corpus techniques across the whole spectrum of forensic linguistics. Over the past 15 years linguists have created many corpora and produced a large number of useful tools; it now seems requisite for forensic linguists to make use of these valuable resources. There is little doubt that corpora can, and often should, serve as both a point of departure and a source of reference in investigations in contexts where legal and linguistic interests converge. Their demonstrative and educational facility has yet to be fully exploited but, as the first sentence of this chapter exemplifies, the potential for social and in particular judicial recognition is certainly there.

CHAPTER 37

DETECTING PLAGIARISM

DAVID WOOLLS

37.1 INTRODUCTION

37.1.1 Plagiarism

In this chapter, plagiarism is understood as copying from a written or published source, fully or partially, without attribution to that source. The need to avoid plagiarism is written into the regulations for the presentation of academic work at all universities, and many colleges and schools, and failure to observe the regulations can lead to the loss of grades (marks in UK English), loss of a degree classification, or expulsion. Outside this specific academic use, in most countries any original work published under the name of an author has automatic copyright protection, resting either with the author, the publisher, or both, which means, subject to doctrines such as fair use, that nobody can copy all or part of the work which is so protected without first obtaining permission to do so from the copyright holder. This does not necessarily have to be paid for but it must be obtained.

37.1.2 Detection

Detection here is used in the sense of an investigation of a set of texts for the presence of apparent plagiarism. It is only since the advent of electronic storage of text and the creation of tools to search and compare the documents in such stores that exploration for the presence of identical or similar material has become viable. This sort of detection is largely a twenty-first-century practice and is also dominated by the commercial sector, with the exception of programs for monitoring the writing of computer programs themselves, which have been developed inside universities and are generally freely available. This commercial emphasis in the text area results partly from the complexity of the task of providing coverage for a wide range of subjects and languages, and partly from the cost of the resources entailed in providing anything approaching comprehensive coverage of the potential electronic sources.

Prior to this, and continuing today, the discovery of material known or believed to come from an unacknowledged and previously published source was the domain of the informed reader. The detection that followed such discovery entailed the location first of a book or paper believed to be a source and then the passage within it, and the assembly of a case from the passages so found. The task of automated detection is to provide the material for the assembly of a case.

37.2 HUMANS AND COMPUTERS

In all the discussion that follows, it is important to bear in mind that there is one very important distinction between how humans and computers process text. Computers "read" text as a stream of characters and recognize "words" by their boundaries: spaces, commas, periods, and the like. Humans presumably do much the same, as in English we read from left to right and utilize the same boundary markers, although we generally appear to read in words rather than characters. However, human readers can *recognize* whole passages from prior reading and knowledge of the subject area, whereas computer programs can only apply rules they are given and can only apply them to the data they have been given. Computer recognition, such as it is, is achieved by pattern matching with stored material. Neither the material nor the rules can cover the same breadth of source knowledge of the human reader nor, in the case of academic writing, supply the expected *standard* of writing of a particular student's essay based on prior examples or the instant recognition of a style change which triggers suspicion in such a reader. The application of well-designed, if restricted, rules is not necessarily a weakness, as such rules will be consistently, exhaustively, and objectively applied. But it is a significant difference that has important consequences for computer program designers; the eventual users will be reading the data output by the program, and they must be able to recognize that what a program suggests as related material is the sort of thing that they would have noticed if they had in fact read all the documents themselves. The limitation to the immediately available or electronically accessible data for comparison is an insurmountable weakness in all cases except those where the dataset is complete or sufficient.

It should be clear from the above that it is prudent for the data produced by electronic detection systems to be subject to review by humans. The primary aims of a computer detection system are to ensure that all documents that need to be examined are identified and that the areas of concern are clearly marked to assist the review process. Except in cases where the documents are identical it is currently difficult to give a computer program a means of evaluating the significance of even extensive shared material, particularly where it has been modified.

37.3 THE DETECTION PRINCIPLE

The primary purpose of electronic plagiarism detection systems is to identify potential problem areas. That is, they function like the prior reading recall for a human reader, by drawing the human reader's attention to areas where a relationship exists between two documents. So a computer program replicates the task of a detective, which is to find clues and gather evidence, rather than to decide on guilt or innocence (Johnson and Woolls 2009).

37.3.1 Detecting plagiarism

The fundamental requirements for anyone bringing a charge of plagiarism are that:

(1) the suspect sections of document under review are recognizably present in a document published earlier; and

(2) the suspected author is known or presumed to have had access to this earlier document; and

(3) such sections have been used in such a way that the reader would not realize that the words do not originate with the author of the suspect document.

The documentary requirement highlights the fact that this sort of accusation can only arise when there is a document which is openly available enough to allow the assessment of the extent of the similarity between two phrases, sentences, or even complete documents. This only became possible with the advent of the dissemination of printed multiple exact copies of an author's work and the collection of these books in libraries. What has happened in the early part of the twenty-first century is that the number of documents known to be available to an author with access to the internet has grown to enormous proportions. What is no longer known to those marking an essay is the number and content of relevant documents which may have been used by the student in writing the essay. The norm until the end of the twentieth century was that the student would make use of the reading list and a small number of relevant journals and other books with which an instructor would expect to be familiar even if not included on the reading list. The consequence of this is that the marker now has a much reduced ability to recognize a source which has been appropriated rather than cited.

37.3.2 Electronic detection

Detecting plagiarism electronically is only possible because of the creativity of the human mind. When given the same question to answer, independently produced essay answers are almost always more unlike than like each other both at vocabulary and sentence levels. This is true even where students read the same material or are required to refer to the same base scenario. The electronic factor is that it is possible to create segments of text at any level from document down, and summarize the data in such a way as to allow comparison for equality or proportional similarity. Because uniqueness is expected, most such comparisons result in no similarity whatsoever, bringing those segments which do appear similar to the surface for evaluation. If sentences were more prone to similarity, such comparisons would generate far too much data to be useful for evaluation.

Without having access to all the sentences ever written, it is not possible to put a figure on the probability of two exact sentences occurring. However, one might expect to find a significant occurrence of identical sentences in the output from the computer program used by the Universities and Colleges Admissions Service (UCAS) in the United Kingdom. This has monitored all personal statements in applications to UK universities since September 2007. Each of these contains around 30 sentences, and comparison is made at sentence level. Including the development phase, over 3 million personal statements have been processed to date, so around 90 million sentences. The criteria are set to looking for much lower levels of matching that will be acted on, to ensure that no false negatives are returned. Using less than 50 percent of matching content between sentences and requiring a minimum of three such sentences to be reported, the reporting rate is less than 5 percent and almost all of these can be traced to a relatively small number of known and regularly used sources, including applicants submitting a very close copy of a prior year's application. That is, even though they are all provided with a base template of what should be included and all with the intent of obtaining a place at university, the vast majority of the sentences the candidates write are different from each other.

37.4 DETECTION IN PRACTICE

Electronic detection requires the collection of material relevant to the particular work being reviewed. There are two broad types of collection: current and previous work from within an organization and generally available content from the internet. Organizations such as UCAS, mentioned above, or universities with electronic submission policies in place, clearly come into the first category, as they have large collections of related material, as do large corporations, law firms, and professional bodies. Search engines fall into the second category, but for them to be useful other than for finding plagiarism already suspected it is necessary to build mechanisms to search their indexes on a large and automated scale, or to build a similar database of such potentially related material and indexes designed for the specific task of detection rather than search. This latter approach is taken by some commercial detection services.

The two methods of collection also produce differences in search potential. Where one has all the data it is possible to build indexes of any depth to allow the level of comparison of new material with what is held already. This is commonly used to check student essays for shared material, and is sometimes referred to as collusion detection, although it can highlight plagiarism from third sources as well, where one essay cites correctly and another does not. Where one is using the whole of the internet, which is growing hourly, the most common method is to base the detection on the occurrence of successive sequences of words, as there are many fewer sequences than there are individual words. Particularly where more than one such sequence is found in the same pair of documents, this can be indicative of copying, even more so if the sequences are themselves close together.

37.4.1 Indexing

To locate any sequence when comparing documents, all systems need some sort of indexing methodology. Probably the most common is the inverted index, the form of index you will find at the end of this book, where words considered of primary interest can be looked up and the pages on which they occur are listed. The major difference between that type of index and a computer index is that most, if not all the words in a document will be contained in a computer index, particularly one looking for plagiarism, because what exactly might have been plagiarized is unknown. Another major difference is that the words are generally recorded in terms of their offset from the beginning of the document rather than with page numbers. This is normally done in terms of individual characters, but is perhaps more easily illustrated in terms of words. Here are the word position offsets for the phrase "*in* terms *of* individual characters" from the front of the document to this point as I write, using just the content words of the phrase.

terms	1834	1854	
individual	1698	1856	
characters	384	428	1857

This means that to this point in the writing only one phrase in the document meets the criteria of having all three terms in close proximity. If this phrase occurs in another document, the same close proximity would be apparent, as for example 2070, 2072, 2073, unless the document was an exact copy. The advantage of using character offsets is that the length of the words can also be taken into account simply by subtracting the distances between the start points and checking whether they fit the pattern being searched. Once a phrase has been identified, the full segment can be retrieved and the exactness of match determined by including the more frequent function words in the comparison.

37.4.2 Fingerprints

The table above also illustrates the general principle that while searching for single words will produce multiple hits, searching for sequences will always produce fewer hits. The minimum length of such sequences is a matter of some debate, but between 6 and 8 words in sequence has been employed to avoid the overmatching of short common sequences while attempting not to miss matches by expecting too much. Once sequence lengths have been decided, it is normal to transform them to a single number. This can be achieved because computers represent all written characters with a unique number This, in turn, provides a natural means of feeding into complex algorithms which guarantee a unique representation of any sequence of the same words wherever they occur. Such algorithms can produce a number of the same length for anything from a full document down to a single word, and particularly at the document level this has given rise to the description of the number as a "digital fingerprint." It is important to realize that such a fingerprint belongs to the document not to the person writing it. That is, it tells us nothing about authorship, only whether this document exists somewhere else in identical form.

The technology for this is related to, if not founded on, the principles behind controlling electronic message transmission. Electronic messages are usually sent in pieces and reassembled at the receiving end. Before sending, the whole message is treated mathematically to give what is called a message digest. At the receiving end, the pieces are put together in the correct order and the message digest recalculated. If it is identical then the message has been received intact, otherwise it has been garbled or bits are missing. The principle used is to apply consistent mathematical transformations to the numerical value of characters to reach a very large number that is almost certain to be unique. Because they are designed to be standards and they only work to encode (the digest summarizes the input but it is impossible to get back to the input from the digest), the code is public.

One such code which has been used in the following calculations is the Secure Hash Standard SHA-1.[1] We are going to use a sentence from earlier in the chapter to illustrate both this and other aspects of plagiarism detection: "Detecting plagiarism electronically is only possible because of the creativity of the human mind."

The SHA-1 number for this entire sequence is

Digest: BE 92 69 25 63 0D 3C A1 5C 92 D5 42 C0 00 94 E4 65 F2 FF 08

This is the hexadecimal format of a 160 digit number. This digest number will always be the same for this exact sequence. The number length will also always be the same whatever the length of the text. For example, here is the number for "Detecting."

Digest: D6 E2 B2 CB 2E 9D B8 5F CB F3 7A 64 B9 07 6A FD 11 4D 46 2C.

When indexing large amounts of text, this ability to compress any document or subsequence of a document into 40 characters is convenient both for calculation and for lookup. Where whole paragraphs are copied from one document to another, and each document is indexed by paragraph, copy-and-paste plagiarism is readily found. The main decision for the use of such an algorithm is the depth at which the indexing will be made and the type of indexing which will be undertaken. While it is possible to use the

---

[1] <http://www.itl.nist.gov/fipspubs/fip180-1.htm> accessed September 23, 2011.

orthographical boundaries of paragraph and sentence, or even clause, it is more common to use set sequence lengths, either as 'tiles' (8 words followed by 8 words followed by 8 words...) or overlapping (words 1–8, followed by words 2–9, followed by words 3–10). The latter format gives the greatest coverage and allows for minor differences, but is a heavyweight solution both in terms of computation and storage.

37.4.3 Limitations

It will be evident that what a machine can do that a human cannot is to check a whole document rapidly, either in its entirety or in componential form against each of a set of other documents. The "detection principle" introduced above is the reason that this is very effective, especially in cases where sections of text are being copied. Finding even one, and certainly a number of such sections in a pair of texts can be an indicator of an unexpected relationship between them.

However, there is one serious disadvantage to the methodology, which is that the change of a single character produces a very different number, which is a deliberate aspect of the security-oriented encoding system which is designed to indicate even a single change. Here is the digest for the previous sentence with "the" omitted from "the change."

Original:

Digest: 9F E8 EB 20 CE FC 92 03 45 48 11 CB 55 3A 2C A6 85 55 98 49

Amendment 1:

Digest: 7B 1F AC 37 39 31 30 1D A9 B0 5D 87 81 DF 41 66 77 95 18 68

And here is the digest with "the change of" replaced by "changing":
Amendment 2:

Digest: CC 10 A5 F1 3D FC 5E EA 40 C3 72 F3 AF 4F 07 DE E4 03 68 DE

As can be seen, there is nothing to indicate that these digests refer to two sentences which are almost identical. Because of the tendency of real plagiarists to make minor changes in the material they borrow, this poses problems for the use of such algorithms to identify this sort of copying. There are additional mathematical approaches to automatic plagiarism detection, well represented by Stein and Meyer zu Eißen (2007), Stein et al. (2011), and Potthast et al. (2011), discussion of which is outside the scope of this chapter.

However, both language and human nature offer some assistance to the problem. From the language perspective, it is not in fact a simple matter to alter every clause and retain the meaning of the sentence. There are some structural elements which simply need to be present or require too much re-writing to make the task worthwhile. So some segments will generally remain untouched. And the human nature element means that if someone is borrowing something substantial from another author, this is because they do not have the time, skill, or inclination to write the section themselves, so much will remain unaltered. As long as the detection process can be applied in segments of some consistent length which is short enough to identify unchanged material, then potential sections can be identified, which is all that is required at the initial phase, as required by the "detection principle."

37.5 MATCHING WITH WORDS

The central problem facing automated detection is the flexibility of language, which allows some local transformation of a text without loss or change of meaning. Anything based on the requirement for the characters to be delivered to an algorithm in the same order, immediately runs into difficulties. To illustrate, we return to our sentence:

> "Detecting plagiarism electronically is only possible because of the creativity of the human mind."

This time we will rewrite it a little:

> "Electronic plagiarism detection is only possible because of human creativity."

These two sentences say much the same thing, although, as we will see, not exactly the same thing. In the light of the above discussion, it is clear that the only preserved sequence is "is only possible because of," a five-word sequence largely formed from function words. The content words have been switched round, with some loss of precision but broadly retaining the meaning of the original. But in addition to being switched round, the parts of speech of the words have also had to be changed. The non-finite nominal clause as subject of the original "Detecting plagiarism electronically," comprising a verb, noun, and adverb, has been replaced with "Electronic plagiarism detection" a simple noun phrase comprising an adjective, noun modifier, and noun. So not only are the words in a different order, two of them are different shapes. In the case of "human creativity," the shapes remain the same, but the order is different and we have lost the word "mind." This has two effects on the requirement for an automated detection system. A decision needs to be taken on how to record the word forms and if possible some degree of flexibility needs to be in place to allow for changes in order.

Before we progress to examining how this can be achieved, it is worth pausing to consider the actual effect of the amendments. It is important to remember that detection systems are just that, they are not *grading (marking)* systems. Grading (marking) is still being undertaken by human readers, who expect what they are reading to be coherent. In our example, the original expression is unambiguous. It is detection that is being done electronically. This is partly because the clause contains clear indicators of the functions: a non-finite verb "detecting" modified by an adverb "electronically" in relation to "plagiarism." The reformulation is ambiguous, because it is not immediately clear whether the modifier of detection is simply plagiarism, in which case it is "plagiarism detection" which is "electronic," or whether "plagiarism" is being modified by "electronic," in which case it is "electronic plagiarism" that is being "detected." The change in meaning when replacing "creativity of the human mind" with "human creativity" is even clearer, in particular a loss of precision. The challenge for any would-be plagiarist is to disguise the borrowing while still making sense. Short illustrations such as these cannot do justice to the difficulty of sustaining this over stretches of borrowed material, which is what makes the less precise methodologies adequate in many cases for the pure detection of plagiarism. But to show the full extent of borrowing, more flexibility is required for comprehensive automated detection.

37.5.1 Fuzziness

In addition to word order changes, only using part of another text, *for example by omitting a clause such as this italicized one*, again disrupts a numerical system, but in this case there may be no loss of communicative meaning.

So what is really required in order to look for change is a concept of "fuzziness." That is, we do not necessarily require the same word or the same form of a word or the same sequence of words to appear in a sentence or some other text segment, but we do expect some lexical similarity in the segment. But as soon as we move away from identity, we encounter the problem of how to divide up the texts for comparison, what words to use and what transformations are needed to do the comparison. That involves consideration of the words which make up phrases, clauses, and sentences.

37.5.2 Stop-lists

We have mentioned that matching between sections of two texts is unexpected, but it is also clear that the simple overlap of some of the individual words is not at all unexpected. "The," "of," "to," "and," "that," "those," "is," "in," "it," and "a" are all words one would be surprised *not* to find in other paragraphs both within this chapter and in the paragraphs of any other document. This is because they belong to the organizational components of the English language, the grammar. Because they do things to the words around them, they are also known as *function words*. "In principle," and "in other paragraphs" are different constructs using "in," for example. Their other distinctive feature is that they are generally much more frequent in texts than the non-grammar words, generally known as *content words*. In many computational linguistic applications this frequency results in their being collected together on what is termed a "stop-list" and discounted altogether for vocabulary comparison purposes. This is certainly helpful in avoiding over-matching but can cause a computer program's discriminatory powers to be something like the telegraphic stage of early child language, for example "Daddy car." To know whether the child saying this actually meant "man" and "van," expressing the concept "There is a man in that van" requires a context often only available to a parent. Such loss of context indicates that we need computers to make as much use of the language as we as humans do to achieve understanding of the flexibility with which we can use language.

37.5.3 Content words

As noted, words other than the function words are generally referred to as content words; despite the contextual difficulty mentioned above, each of the two words "Daddy" and "car" can be said to mean something independently. It is content words that are most often used for initial comparison, and although this can be done at document level, more precision is attainable by dividing a document into segments, frequently sentences but sometimes clauses. This allows the words of the text to be indexed by segment within a document rather than simply by occurrence within a document, as is the norm in information retrieval systems and web search engines. This segment level indexing allows similar segmenting to be applied to the material requiring checking, and the comparison of each segment with every segment in the base collection. Word-based systems compare each segment word by word allowing them to arrive at a measure of how similar each segment is to any others. The central principle is that, when compared with any other sentence, a given sentence is either exactly the same as, completely different from, or on a cline between those extremes in terms of the words used. As pointed out in Woolls (2010) and developed further in Section 37.5.4 below, what actually counts as similar can be quite complex, but once an agreed definition has been reached, or parameter choice provided for users, a computer program can be designed which applies the comparison methodology consistently and objectively. When applied exhaustively this too is computationally expensive and the areas to which it is most likely to be applied are those where the checking is against a discrete complete collection of potentially similar material. For example, UCAS in the UK can use this technology (Woolls 2010) because they have all the personal statements in their possession and control. But the principle can also be applied to any data that can realistically be indexed in this way.

It is important to understand that this form of searching is distinctly different from web-based searching. The document-indexed orientation of web searching is joined with the fact that web search results report on the first match which best matches the search term. This is what forms the "snippet" returned by search engines, although this is not always a continuous section of the text. It can also be a composite of different locations where different words of the search string appear in different locations in the same document. This is indicated by the ellipsis in some of the results. Web searching and web plagiarism detection have to work like this because it would be impossible to produce results at the speeds achieved if exhaustive searching were undertaken. In addition, it is often necessary to select the first or "best" match from a number of repetitions of the source, since documents can be posted on the web multiple times by multiple users in different circumstances. Web detection has to rely on the fact that if sufficient material is found in common, it may not matter whether the exact source used has in fact been identified. The fact that it has been found at all is frequently sufficient. But it is necessarily inexact. This is not the case where all the data are available and there is sufficient computing power to return results within a sensible time period. So, the word-based search described above is more akin to the Find Next feature in word-processors, or on browser pages when reading the individual documents returned by the initial search, with the difference that the exhaustive finding is under programmatic control.

37.5.4 Different word forms

Any agreed definition of similarity needs to take account of the fact that words can change their form or position. "Detecting" and "detection" are clearly related to each other and are to some extent interchangeable, although as we have seen, substituting one for the other does not always preserve the exact meaning. The decision in automated detection is whether to treat *detection* and *detecting* as the same, because they share a root form, or different because they have different suffixes, a potential indicator of change. In this case, an index can be built using either a stem common to both words, "detect" in this case, or the lemma, or the root form of the word, which in this case would also be "detect," but is not necessarily identical; "found" is the past tense of "find" for example. Using such systems, re-writing of "**Detecting plagiarism** electronically" as "The **detection** of **plagiarized** material using a computer" would register as a match with a 50 percent overlap level set if this was a complete phrase. The highlighted words would act as matches although they are not the same shape as the original. Although comprehensive re-writing is difficult to sustain systematically, the challenge for an automated detection system is to identify where such change has been carried out in an attempt to avoid detection.

37.6 PRACTICAL DETECTION

In the arena of academic writing, the majority of plagiarism *detection*, as opposed to identification or discovery, is now done using one or more of the automated detection techniques as described above. And in most of these cases, the task involves comparing an essay on a single subject with other essays within the group or externally available. But this is not always the case, particularly in distance learning, where the institutions provide extensive materials on line. Such cases provide particular difficulties for human markers and electronic systems alike, although electronic systems may encounter more problems, as we discuss below.

One major problem comes from the removal of the principle of uniqueness of sentences both within and between texts. That is, in an essay on a given topic, one would not expect to find substantial similarity between sentences within that essay. As mentioned earlier, the central plank of plagiarism detection of any sort is that it is also true that one would not expect to find substantial similarity between sentences in one essay and those in another independently produced essay on the same subject. This is because the arrangement of ideas, the expression of those ideas, and the conclusions we present from those different arrangements are individual and result in different sentences even where they are expressing the same concepts. However, when using distance learning material as a primary source of learning prior to writing, both these principles can fail to hold. All students answering the questions can be expected to indicate, directly or indirectly, that they have read the relevant material provided and, where the questions are prefaced by a scenario, elements of the scenario can legitimately appear more than once within the body of the answers. If the answer papers are merely compared with each other this will result in an appearance of collusion between students. If the answer papers are compared with the learning materials and question rubric, it would appear to a computer program that plagiarism was present. This is less likely when human readers are involved, given that they will have the question paper available to them and were probably involved in the creation or delivery of the learning materials.

Separating the elements which can be explained from those that might indeed suggest plagiarism or collusion needs special handling in a computerized system. This is particularly important where the percentage of similarity between documents is being used as a primary indicator of potential plagiarism. If this is not taken into account, the proportion of students coming under scrutiny when they have in fact made appropriate use of the source material can increase substantially. One preventative measure used, in particular by the Open University in the UK, is to run the question rubric against all answer papers to identify segments which are common to both and in particular appear in a number of different answer papers. Removal or identification of such passages before a second comparison run assists in locating truly suspect proportions of similarity. This works better with short rubrics than for longer scenarios or the learning materials themselves. In these cases the reliable identification of potential matching with known sources is a requirement.

Within many disciplines the use of tables to present work is encouraged. This too presents a challenge for both human and machine reading. If tabular data or graphs are copied between documents it does not take long for a human reader to recognize identity. Where only some of the data are the same, this becomes more of a challenge, both in terms of finding it and in terms of assessing the significance of the similarity. For machine reading, decisions on whether or how to compare tabular material are frequently dependent on the effectiveness of the extraction mechanism. Extracting text from word processed documents frequently results in a single entry per line, and special functions are required to compare such output. Moreover, students are not obliged to use the same orientation for their tables, so a column by column presentation doesn't look like a row by row presentation when extracted for comparison anyway.

Presenting the results from any system of detection is also not an exact science. It is possible to identify the amount of shared vocabulary, of course, and this can work well when the texts are of roughly the same length and on the same topic, as with many literary essays. But as soon as text lengths become imbalanced or texts are compared with longer or shorter potential sources, the way in which any similarity is expressed needs some consideration. In such cases it is preferable to use the shorter text as the benchmark. This is because the presence of a substantial amount of similarity between the shorter text and the longer will always point to the possibility of a non-accidental relationship between the two. But this means that the relationship can be complex when considering a single document and comparing it with two longer and two shorter sources. Percentages must be clearly expressed and identifiable. Copying an entire five-sentence document into a document with 100 sentences would only show a 5 percent similarity if expressed from the longer document perspective, whereas the author of that document has in fact used 100 percent of the shorter work. If the 100 sentence document also uses 5 sentences from a 1,000 sentence document, this would show as only 0.5 percent of the longer document and 5 percent of the shorter, but would still represent potential misconduct.

Furthermore, if individual sentences are deemed suspect even when not identical, the words which are different will represent different percentages of the whole if both grammar and content words are considered or if the grammar words are excluded. Proportionate measures in terms of sentence counts, segment counts, or other measures are all prone to the same problems as soon as the identity of any section is disrupted. Because a lack of similarity is the expected norm, any automated measurement needs to work from the bottom up to indicate levels of overlap, and it is generally necessary for human readers to assess the significance of any sections highlighted in this way. This sort of problem is not restricted to automated systems, of course. Armed with a highlighter pen, a human has to make the decision whether to highlight a whole sentence which has some measure of similarity with another, or to just identify the similarities or the changes.

This is one of the issues that makes plagiarism cases a source of much anguish in academia because it generates a large amount of work to identify and build a case with no guarantee of success once built.

37.7 CONCLUSION

Automated plagiarism detection is difficult once there is a departure from full copy-and-paste of sections of another document. This is because of the difficulty of modeling the potential uses of language and creating programs that can identify the similarities between segments of texts even after they have undergone grammatical and lexical transformation. It remains the case that some plagiarism is always readily identifiable, and that in many cases this is sufficient to provide an indication that a document is suspect. But there are areas where any use of third party material is disallowed, and the amount may be very small and so frequently modified, that to find such material, only exhaustive and detailed electronic comparison can alert a human reader to the existence of a problem.

PART IX

SPEAKER IDENTIFICATION

CHAPTER 38

LANGUAGE ANALYSIS FOR DETERMINATION OF ORIGIN: OBJECTIVE EVIDENCE FOR REFUGEE STATUS DETERMINATION

PETER L. PATRICK

38.1 WHAT EVIDENCE IS AVAILABLE?

REFUGEES are persons who can show "a well-founded fear of being persecuted for reasons of race, religion, nationality, membership of a particular social group, or political opinion" in their home country (UN 1951, "Geneva Convention"). An asylum seeker who lacks documents presents two main types of evidence:

- Her body, i.e. medical evidence relating to age, torture, injury, etc.
- Her story, i.e. linguistic evidence—including all interviews, recordings, statements, and texts in the Refugee Status Determination (RSD) process, and the possibility of collecting new evidence.

This chapter focuses on the latter. Not all speech and text evidence is commonly used in the processes of linguistic analysis which LADO comprises—indeed, LADO (Language Analysis for Determination of Origin) commonly involves collecting small amounts of speech specifically for linguistic analysis, and ignoring the rest—though linguistic analyses of various types (e.g. discourse or narrative analysis) consider the wider evidence base (Maryns 2005; Blommaert 2009; Jacquemet 2009). Many interviews and statements given by asylum seekers in the RSD process also contain information relevant to assessing their linguistic background, repertoire, and experience more broadly, which is necessary to properly frame and inform the narrower LADO analysis that typically occurs. Within this narrower perspective, relevant questions include:

- How does one assess such linguistic evidence?
- What factors influence its production and use?
- Who is properly qualified to perform assessment?
- Who actually does so in existing LADO regimes?
- What do RSD stakeholders need to know in order to commission, evaluate, and reliably use valid linguistic evidence?
- What role should the linguistic profession have in monitoring LADO analysis and processes of assessment?

38.2 LADO as a field

Language assessment and testing by applied linguists and other language professionals occurs in many contexts: first language acquisition, adult second language learning and acquisition, formal study of "foreign languages," language disorders, speech therapy, and use of vernacular and standard languages in educational contexts. Each of these constitutes a major field of inquiry within linguistics and other disciplines, often with prescribed and accredited courses of study leading to undergraduate and postgraduate degrees, backed up by extensive research programs and thousands of peer-reviewed scholarly publications (e.g. McNamara and Roever 2006, an overview of language testing for adult speakers).

LADO is not such a field. It has been performed only since the 1990s, when the language expertise in Scandinavian government bureaus first became out-sourced to private language firms. It is little-known to most linguists or language professionals; is primarily administered by government bureaus or profit-oriented agencies—which reveal little about their methods even under questioning by the courts and tribunals (and publish less). In practice, there are no minimum credentials which language analysts must meet to perform their work, and it is common for analysts to engage in LADO without any discernible qualifications. Immigration judges are poorly positioned to evaluate LADO reports before them; existing standards for expert evidence in civil or criminal law are frequently not applied in asylum tribunals, and case law is small and haphazard to date.

LADO came into common use in response to governments' need for dependable objective evidence from acknowledged expert fields, in order to help answer questions of identity, origin, and nationality concerning undocumented asylum seekers. It is a field of practice crying out for an evidence base, review of methods and results, and prescription of best-practice by qualified linguistic professionals, and regulation by appropriate authorities to ensure comparable standards across jurisdictions.

At present, fewer than 100 publications specifically on LADO exist, most since 2000, including studies of individual cases (Corcoran 2004; Singler 2004), disciplinary perspectives on method (Broeders 2010; McNamara et al. 2010; Patrick 2010), examinations of linguistic areas (de Rooij 2010) and national regimes from both linguistic (Maryns 2006; Cambier-Langeveld 2010b; ten Thije 2008;) and legal perspectives (Zwaan 2007; Vedsted-Hansen 2010; Vanheule 2010), and experimental or theoretical studies (Fraser 2009; Wilson 2009), as well as recent conference proceedings (Zwaan et al. 2010). Eades (2010) traces the early history of LADO.

38.3 GUIDELINES FOR BEST-PRACTICE IN LADO

A logical reference point for describing LADO practice is the "Guidelines for the use of language analysis in relation to questions of national origin in refugee cases" (hereafter the Guidelines; Language and National Origin Group 2004). Though intended as a starting point in a new, urgent, and rapidly-developing field of linguistic practice, they are frequently cited in tribunal cases in European countries and now constitute the standard reference and guidance document on LADO. This 2,000-word document was drawn up and signed by 19 linguists from Australia, Belgium, the Netherlands, Sweden, the UK, and the USA. They included distinguished experts in applied linguistics, bilingualism, language assessment, discourse analysis, language policy, forensic phonetics, linguistic anthropology, and language contact. Several broad guidelines first address the general limitations of, and requirements for, linguistic expertise; while others specifically address problems that frequently arise in LADO contexts.

The Guidelines were published in the *International Journal of Speech, Language and the Law* in 2004, and in *Applied Linguistics* (Eades 2005). The document is available via UNHCR's RefWorld site of RSD information.[1] The Guidelines have been endorsed worldwide by professional associations of linguists, both theoretical and applied. They are cited by Stygall (2009:26–1) as an exemplar of "codes of ethics for forensic settings," and have been cited and responded to by a host of organizations concerned with the fair treatment of refugees, ranging from the UN High Commission on Refugees, to administrative agencies in various countries. In a recent review article, Diana Eades wrote, "most of the basic information in the Guidelines about investigation of the relationship between the speech of asylum speakers and their claimed origins is at an introductory level of linguistics and remains uncontroversial among linguists" (Eades 2010:39), as their broad endorsement confirms.

---

[1] <www.unhcr.org/refworld> accessed September 23, 2011.

38.4 MIRROR, MIRROR IN THE TONGUE ... BASIC ASSUMPTIONS AND QUESTIONS

The assumption motivating LADO is one that seems plausible to the linguistically untrained: the way a person speaks is intimately related to their place of origin, hence—by a leap of logic about which linguistics has nothing to say—their citizenship. The image of a "linguistic passport" expresses this vividly: evidence of one's (native) tongue today testifies strongly to the place in which one was born and first learned to speak. On this basis, LADO is used as a gate-keeping mechanism to assess claims of origin, weeding out the false and confirming the true.

Linguists, especially sociolinguists, are familiar with language as a gate-keeping mechanism in institutional settings: the workplace, with hiring, promotion, and the exercise of language choices at stake; schools, for admissions, testing, advancement, and evidence of (dis)ability; the courts and policing, where it influences perceptions of probity and credibility of suspects and witnesses. In all these contexts, there are well-documented cases of discrimination and injustice where language has been taken as a neutral, value-free property. Sociolinguists have demonstrated, moreover, that language is highly sensitive to social properties including age, class, gender, region, ethnicity, and race (Chambers 2009; Chambers et al. 2002)—a list familiar to students of equality and anti-discrimination law—as well as attitudes and ideologies. Unlike laypeople, sociolinguists are well aware that relations between language and even such "permanent" aspects of identity are very complex and take a multitude of forms. This is also necessarily true of national origin or citizenship, political properties which have no intrinsic relation to language at all. Thus the basic LADO question is a *sociolinguistic* one:

> How does an applicant's linguistic performance in a LADO context correlate with their history of speech community membership and language socialization?

38.5 LINGUISTIC SOCIALIZATION AND SPEECH COMMUNITIES

One's way of speaking is not simply a matter of where one is born or has lived; language is a social, communal property, and is natively acquired for most people within a family—which may itself be multilingual, shift over time, or be of mixed membership—and a community, whose characteristics may not match those of the family, and which encompasses ways of speaking that are greater and more varied. Common sense suggests that the stress and fragmenting of communities under the conditions of conflict, oppression, and war that often result in large numbers of refugees, further strains the associations between language and place of origin in what are already typically multilingual or diglossic communities. Indeed, what is often required of LADO is not merely tracing a person to a single country, but rather to a region or ethnic group—and obviously regions and ethnic groups range across national boundaries.

While traditional ways of speaking may certainly be long associated with particular groups and specific places, the link to modern nationhood is often a tenuous one, and the tendency for such isomorphic links (Nation = People = Language) to weaken is widespread in our globalizing age. Even where relatively stable or well-described speech communities (Patrick 2002) are relevant to LADO, they are likely to contain a wealth of complexity that requires expert knowledge in order to carefully identify a displaced speaker's relationship to them. However, even stable "contemporary speech communities increasingly comprise translocal, complex, multilayered, polycentric, and socioeconomically stratified semiotic spaces" (Stroud 2009:434), while many refugees have suffered years of displacement from their home regions, often in refugee camps with mixed and shifting populations (Fraser 2011a). Thus there are many asylum seekers for whom mapping language onto social history is difficult or unreliable, and should simply not be attempted. Where it is deemed feasible, Blommaert argues for a sociolinguistics not of languages, but "of speech and repertoires [which] index full histories of people and places, not just institutionally genred origins" (2009:416). For these reasons and others, LADO can be an especially complex form of high-stakes forensic analysis, requiring detailed knowledge of sometimes obscure and understudied linguistic varieties, extensive familiarity with sociolinguistic patterns and findings, considerable expertise in data collection and analysis, awareness of the particular forensic context, and a commitment to careful and objective evaluation and formulation of conclusions.

The principle that linguistic socialization into a speech community lies at the heart of LADO was first given a prominent place in the Guidelines. This principle is now widely accepted by government bureaus (e.g. Norway, UDI 2009; Switzerland, Baltisberger and Hubbuch 2010), academic researchers (Eades 2009; Fraser 2009; Cambier-Langeveld 2010a), and some commercial agencies (de Taalstudio, Verrips 2010).

38.6 INSTITUTIONAL POSITIONS IN LADO

There are several key institutional positions involved with LADO. Immigration and asylum bureaucrats include case owners who administer individual asylum cases, and separate presenting officers who argue cases on appeal. Some bureaus, including the UK Border Authority, do not employ linguists or linguistically trained officers, while others do. The Lingua agency of the Swiss Federal Office of Migration employs a team of academically-qualified linguists to rigorously vet, support, and train the native-speaker interviewers and independent academics who respectively collect and analyse LADO data; their linguistic knowledge informs the process of commissioning and interpreting the latter's linguistic reports (Baltisberger and Hubbuch 2010). Belgium's CEDOCA, the documentation arm of the RSD agency, has linguistic officers who commission and interpret LADO reports on a limited number of languages, using external analysts—not necessarily linguists (Vanheule 2010). One government agency will sometimes perform LADO for another.

Analysis firms are primarily commercial, profit-oriented entities. The two largest, both Swedish, are Verified and Sprakab. In addition to owners and managers, who may not be linguists, they employ a certain number of staff with linguistic credentials (normally BA or MA level), and a much larger number of non-expert analysts. These analysts appear to do the primary analysis, as well as conduct interviews, though they are said to be supervised by the linguists (who often do not claim expertise in the analyzed language). The analysts frequently lack extensive scientific training; their principal qualification is that they are said to be native speakers of the language they are employed to analyze. However, at least in Sprakab linguistic reports (of which I have examined 60 in the UK asylum process since 2008), analysts often do not reveal which is their native language; when they do it is not always the case that they are native speakers of the particular dialect being analyzed—even when that dialect is very distant from the standard variety they do speak, as in the case of Bajuni versus Kenyan or Tanzanian Swahili.

These firms have been employed by Australia, Austria, Belgium, Canada, Denmark, Ireland, Norway, Sweden, and the UK, at least. Some government bureaus which have linguists on staff, for example the Netherlands OCILA, also contract with these analysis firms, either to check their own analysis or in place of providing one themselves. As firms compete for contracts, commercial pressure is necessarily exerted on the detail and quality of reports, which may be as brief as 4 pages, with only 1–2 pages of data and analysis, based on interviews as short as 12 minutes.

Considering these types of LADO performed directly for governments as the primary mode, two other modes also occur. In contra-analysis, new data are collected from the asylum seeker and analysed as part of appealing a decision, and a new LADO report is produced independently of the primary analysis. A distinct place is held by De Taalstudio, an Amsterdam analysis firm headed by Dutch linguist Maaike Verrips, which now works with the Norwegian government, but until 2010 mainly provided contra-expertise in Netherlands appeals. Uniquely among analysis firms, De Taalstudio's staff of qualified (MA, PhD) linguists mediate between lawyers representing asylum seekers and linguistic experts, providing an analytic template which aims to ensure all reports conform with the Guidelines. They also differ from other firms in that all analyses are performed by qualified linguists (Verrips 2010).

A third type of work is independent assessment of LADO reports in appeals cases, in which the primary LADO report is evaluated by a qualified linguist or language expert without producing a new one. This may be done by academic linguists, such as the author, who has submitted around 50 assessment reports in UK cases since 2008—work commissioned directly by lawyers or NGO caseworkers representing asylum seekers and paid by legal services funding. Independent academic research linguists also enter the picture in ways already described: as experts employed by bureaus such as the Swiss, or Germany's BAMF; or by firms such as De Taalstudio. In such cases, the experts generally have independent academic careers and research reputations which serve to qualify them for the tribunals, and against which their LADO work can be evaluated (not generally the case with other firms).

Occasionally, interpreters are also asked to perform LADO functions, either by lawyers on appeal or in tribunal hearings by immigration judges (and quite commonly "on the ground," by police or border guards, as well as asylum commissions, in countries that lack a formal LADO process; see Morgades 2010; Pretto 2010). UK case law recognizes that interpreter training does not constitute proper qualification for linguistic analysis, and that not "every person who speaks a particular language or dialect is to be regarded as an expert," able to "distinguish accurately between different dialects and to be able to attribute dialects to different sources".[2] Thus despite their expertise in other areas of language, court interpreters find themselves in the same position as lawyers, immigration judges, and other workers in the legal system—and indeed government bureau employees who are not linguistically trained—in that they simply have no expertise which qualifies them to perform LADO. The same can be said for another stakeholder, the Country of Origin Information (COI) expert, whose functions of researching and making available to caseworkers and tribunals relevant information on a country or region that asylum seekers come from, may sometimes involve compiling language information (CORI 2010).

38.7 INSTITUTIONAL PRESSURES ON LADO

Stakeholders in all these institutional positions come under a variety of pressures due to such factors as rules of procedure, staffing levels, caseload, costs, profit motive, and government policies. There certainly exist contrasting institutional norms, practices, ideology, and rewards, too, across institutions. It cannot be ignored that the type and specific level of education, professional training, and language attitudes of persons holding these distinct positions may differ crucially. All these factors exert influence on their beliefs, assumptions, and practice with regard not only to issues of language, but to questions of expertise, for example: What constitutes a fact? How important is best-practice?

Certain types of knowledge or expertise are necessary to perform specific functions. Bureau case owners, legal representatives, judges, and analysis firms (if they accept to test claimants' knowledge in this regard) must know how to access relevant COI. Similarly, native-speaker knowledge is generally required for interpreting. And while linguists value native speakers' naive knowledge of their language as a resource in analysis generally, and also in LADO, again, scientific linguistic training is required to qualify one to perform LADO analysis in the view of many linguists. This point is not conceded by some commercial firms or governments—those which allow linguists who have no

[2] AA (Language diagnosis: use of interpreters) Somalia [2008] UKAIT 00029. (=UK Asylum and Immigration Tribunal), paras 10 and 7.

expertise in the relevant language to supervise work by analysts not properly trained to do linguistic analysis—though it is accepted by their colleagues in De Taalstudio and Lingua, and implied in, for example, the AA decision cited above. The Swiss authorities state that "in order to treat [complex] cases adequately, a proper training in linguistics [is] indispensable.... Co-operation with academically-trained linguists clearly improved the quality of Lingua reports...scientific and well-developed argumentation also heightened the credibility of the analyses before the appeal court" (Baltisberger and Hubbuch 2010:13–14).

However, just as minimum basic training in COI is offered to UK Border Authority case owners, one may argue that all parties to commissioning, performing, or evaluating LADO reports ought to possess at least a correct *basic* understanding of the level of complexity involved in relating language use to social experience and identity. The lack of such awareness in some companies and bureaus at present not only constrains the best use of language information as an aid to RSD, but much more seriously, it currently undermines the validity and reliability of LADO in RSD processes. Errors, misinterpretations, and incorrect judgments flowing from such lack of understanding—or, to put it differently, from inadvertently giving folk beliefs and myths about language precedence over expert scientific knowledge—can only contribute to the incidence of miscarriages of justice in RSD decisions.

38.8 WHY SHOULD "LADO ANALYSTS" = "LINGUISTS"?

"Linguist" has both folk and expert senses in English: a person who speaks several languages (regardless of their training), versus a specialist in linguistic science (for which post-graduate training is required). The folk sense is widespread, as witness the title of the Institute of Linguists, a reputable UK institution involved in training and certifying interpreters and translators—few of whose members qualify as scientific linguists, and none of whose training courses and examinations covers linguistic science. It is no wonder if lawyers, judges, and bureaucrats are confused about what linguistics is and why it is necessary in LADO.

Necessary elements of linguistic expertise for LADO include the study of language structure at the levels of phonetics, phonology, the lexicon, syntax, and morphology—all of which are explicitly required as components of most LADO reports. Equally necessary areas which are often not highlighted in reports include semantics, pragmatics, language acquisition and contact, and patterns of language usage, change, and variation. Engagement in research by academically-trained linguists has led to the development of tools, methods, and techniques which define the standards for linguistic analysis, and training in these is a minimum requirement for the post-graduate qualifications that are expected of any linguist. An extensive knowledge of the scientific literature, and the demonstrated ability to contribute to it via presenting research at open conferences and submitting publications for peer review, are also necessary criteria for meeting "the definition of a linguist as a scholar who is highly trained and deeply involved in the scientific study of language" (Shuy 2009:221). It is natural that such criteria are also constitutive of most legal definitions of experts and expertise, and the fact that not only the analysts but even the supervising linguists employed by some bureaus and firms fail to meet them is cause for concern.

Given this standard of expertise, many language professionals with significant skills, training, or experience nevertheless fail to qualify as scientific linguists. Court interpreters may be highly trained and certified, yet have studied little or no linguistics, and rarely if ever conduct analysis or research. People who have studied "foreign" languages at university or elsewhere typically also lack linguistic analytic or comparative training. It is rare to find any formal training in "exotic" unwritten languages—which make up the majority of LADO analyses—hence few or no standards exist for assessing knowledge of such languages. The extensive work of language testing and assessment for distinguishing degrees of knowledge of English (or other prominent international languages often studied at school) is almost entirely lacking for smaller unwritten languages such as Bajuni, Malinke, Sierra Leone Krio, or even languages such as Sorani, Hazargi Dari, or Somali which are written, and whose native speakers number in the millions. Indeed, basic descriptions, grammars, and dictionaries are often lacking, underdeveloped or simply inadequate for LADO purposes.

Sociolinguistic awareness should also be part of the LADO analyst's toolkit. Sociolinguistics is the comparative study of speech communities, linguistic practices, and social ecologies of language. The basic LADO issue is not a phonetic, syntactic, or dialectological one, but a sociolinguistic one: relating ways of speaking to the communities and processes by which they were formed. In addition, LADO frequently needs to make critical reference to such sociolinguistic issues as:

- how unequal power in bureaucratic contexts affects speech;
- how ethnic/racial/class conflict affects cross-cultural communication;
- why people switch codes and mix languages, and what such behavior means; and
- pressures to assimilate to standard/majority speech and language ideology.

Sociolinguists are also typically professionally involved with or knowledgeable of other issues having relevance to LADO, such as:

- regional dialects, social variation, and language change;
- forensic, clinical, and other institution-based linguistics;
- language planning, at academic, government, local, or NGO levels;
- research on multilingualism, often with linguistic minorities;
- bilingual education and other school-centered language issues;
- language endangerment, preservation, and revitalization;
- discourse analysis of talk by powerful/vulnerable speakers; and
- ethnolinguistic research with indigenous peoples.

All these elements frequently occur in LADO interviews and affect results. Failure to command knowledge of the extensive research literature frequently leads to inadequate analysis or misleading claims in LADO reports.

Not all linguists are trained in sociolinguistic perspectives, while some sociolinguists are trained as all-round linguists. There is no competition of specialisms here, but rather a need to draw on a broad range of capabilities suited to understanding the LADO context, of which sociolinguistic research is an essential component.

38.9 STANDARDS OF EXPERTISE

A logical step towards improving the validity, consistency, and robustness of LADO would be to admit only analysis by qualified linguists who satisfy stringent requirements for expertise. This is recommended by the Guidelines (#3, "Language analysis must be done by qualified linguists," Language and National Origin Group (LNOG) 2004:262), and is in effect what the Swiss bureau Lingua's vetting process attempts to do. However, it seems desirable to require it by means more regular, and more integral to the legal systems of asylum-granting states.

An obvious mechanism for this is to count LADO as expert testimony and treat it the same as other areas of law do. A striking feature of LADO is that this is not always the case. As readers will know, one may be subject to legal requirements and standards for expertise in order to give expert linguistic testimony in criminal cases, for example in the USA[3] or the UK.[4] Common or typical features of such requirements include:

- details/limits of an expert's relevant qualifications must be declared openly;
- the expert has a duty to provide independent, unbiased, objective opinion;
- the expert must make explicit all evidence, data, and assumptions relied upon;
- the expert must cite relevant scientific or professional literature in reports;
- expert testimony must be shown to be the product of reliable principles and methods which are generally accepted in the scientific community;
- the expert's methods must have been tested, subjected to peer review, and publication;
- the expert must disclose whether all analyses/tests/measurements were made by the expert;
- the expert must acknowledge a range of opinion, and motivate the choices made;
- the expert must fairly give facts/arguments counter to the opinion expressed.

---

[3] *Daubert v Merrell Dow Pharmaceuticals, Inc.* 509 US 579 (1993), 113 S. Ct. 2786 (the Daubert standard); US Federal Rules of Evidence (1975) 702 *et seq.*

[4] *R v Bowman* [2006] EWCA Crim 417 (March 2, 2006): Clause 177, points 1–7; *National Justice Compania Naviera S.A. v Prudential Assurance Company Limited* [1993], 2 Lloyds Rep. 68, "Ikarian Reefer Guidelines".

All of these are standard expertise requirements in many nations' courts, yet many LADO reports fail to satisfy even one of these criteria. However, since RSD often occupies a special legal niche, they may not apply as one would expect. For example, in the UK, RSD decisions are made by the Home Office and reviewed under civil administrative law. The Asylum and Immigration Tribunal in 2007 issued a set of *Practice Directions* (UKAIT 2007) whose section 8A includes many of the provisions set out above. Yet it has been accepted by the courts that LADO reports rendered on contract to the government need not meet these criteria for expertise, since they are provided to the decision maker (UK Border Authority) rather than the tribunal.[5] On the other hand, when a decision is appealed and the commercial LADO report is reviewed by an independent expert, the latter must satisfy the *Practice Directions* criteria. Similar conditions exist elsewhere in which expertise rendered to the government is viewed in a different light than that rendered in defense of asylum seekers appealing unfavorable decisions (Verrips 2010).

It is difficult to see why expertise should be differentiated, in effect, according to whose purposes it serves. One of the guiding axioms of forensic linguistic work, which surely applies to most experts, is that testimony provided by an expert to a court should be the same, and of the same scientific standard, regardless of which party requested it or to which tribunal it is submitted. Leveling the playing field would unify expert linguistic testimony in LADO cases with other arenas of forensic expert work, and have a beneficial effect on the scientific standard of language analysis across the board. However, it would be likely to create disruption in the legal arena: certainly many commercial analysts would fail to meet such standards, thus casting into doubt thousands of analyses they have co-authored to date which have been accepted by governments around the world. Nevertheless, European governments have striven for years to provide common rules governing many aspects of the asylum process via a Common European Asylum System, in order to make results consistent and predictable across the region, and it has been argued that such harmonization should include procedural safeguards regarding provision of expert evidence (Tax 2010).

38.10 THE ROLE OF NATIVE SPEAKERS IN LADO

Among the many debated aspects of LADO practice, the most controversial—resolution of which might have significant legal consequences—concerns the question of what role should be played by native speakers of relevant languages who lack formal qualifications for linguistic analysis. The problem arises partly because of the volume of cases potentially requiring linguistic expertise. It is exacerbated by the stance of some governments that arguably employ LADO to achieve speedy and desirable outcomes at

---

[5] RB (Linguistic evidence—Sprakab) Somalia [2010] UKUT 329 (IAC). (=UK Upper Tribunal, Immigration and Asylum Cases).

low cost, a need that may be met by commercial agencies who also respond primarily to pressures of cost, efficiency, and profit. The solution adopted by two Swedish agencies and the Dutch Immigration and Naturalisation Service's language analysis bureau, OCILA, involves having non-expert native speakers (NENSs) perform analysis under the supervision of persons with some linguistic qualifications, who may not know the language involved. The former NENS analysts are said to be trained and tested in-house by the latter linguists, but details of this process are not made public, even to the courts.

On one hand, it is clear that linguistic training is required to align analysis with such descriptions as exist for the languages that occur in LADO cases—descriptions which are generally written by linguists for linguists. On the other hand, one might consider that NENS may serve as valuable aids in LADO, given the paucity of materials. Indeed this position is uncontroversial and likely to be accepted by the great majority of linguists. It is widely agreed that native speaker competence is a prime source of information for language description. NENSs who are representative of their speech community can unreflectively produce typical and idiomatic speech. The real question is not *whether*, but *how*, NENS knowledge should be used in LADO.

The 2004 Guidelines caution that "The expertise of native speakers is not the same as the expertise of linguists" (LNOG 2004:263), and thus NENSs should not be asked to perform analysis, as is commonly done by some firms and bureaus. This is not only because they lack the positive expertise that comes with post-graduate training in scientific linguistics: it is also because misleading myths about language need to be neutralized. In order to competently do linguistic analysis, it is necessary to identify the features of folk beliefs, prejudices, and assumptions about language that we are all socialized into in our communities, and be rigorously trained to operate independent of their influence.

Non-expert native speakers who lack such training are likely to possess typical biases toward standard or majority languages or dialects and against vernacular ones; be unaware of linguistic variation and diversity; misunderstand language mixing and contact languages; and accept dominant language attitudes and ideologies as natural or factual. Wilson (2009) demonstrates that NENS and linguists professionally employed by LADO agencies show the highest confidence in their own analysis (regardless of accuracy, see also Fraser 2009), compared to the caution displayed by qualified academic linguists; in her test of accent identification, NENS and academic linguists performed better (with no significant difference between them) than agency linguists.[6]

General higher education credentials do not alleviate this situation for NENS: rather, university education can reinforce bias against linguistic minorities, validate linguistic purism and prescriptivism over a descriptively accurate approach, privilege writing over speech, and support the conflation of Language, People, and Nation. By contrast, linguistic training works to eliminate language prejudice among practitioners, to separate

---

[6] Wilson stresses that her experiment is not to be interpreted as approximating normal LADO testing conditions, "due to the large differences between this task…and a professional asylum seeker language analysis" (2009:10).

normative responses from scientific facts, and to enable analysts to use objective meth-ods (e.g. the International Phonetic Alphabet) to arrive at valid and reliable results.

It is important to recognize that the Guidelines specifically, and academic linguists generally, do not denigrate the abilities or relevance of native speakers (NSs)—rather the Guidelines attempt to warn non-linguists about the distinct nature of NS competence vis-à-vis scientific linguistic expertise. Some misleading statements have been generated about this, with the effect of exploiting controversy, by LADO practitioners working for firms or governments which depend upon NENS to conduct analysis. For example, Dr Tina Cambier-Langeveld, senior linguist of the Dutch Office for Country Information and Language Analysis, claims, "The authors of the *Guidelines*...do not recognise the relevance of *the expertise of native speakers*" (2010a: 31, my emphasis—she echoes the perhaps unfortunate phrase of the Guidelines cited above). A working group of the International Association for Forensic Phonetics and Acoustics, chaired by Cambier-Langeveld, drafted a resolution which IAFPA passed in 2009, which includes: "IAFPA recognizes the contribution to be made by [...] linguists with in-depth research knowledge of the language(s) in question [...] and trained native speakers, with the lat-ter working under the guidance and supervision of the former" (see also Moosmüller 2010). It seems safe to say that most properly qualified linguists are aware of the value of native speaker data for linguistic analysis. Cambier-Langeveld (2010b) compares NENS and academic experts' conclusions in eight cases of false claims where the country of origin was later established with certainty, all pre-Guidelines. Five feature disputed results between government analysis and contra-analysis, in which the latter produced two false positive results. On this basis she claims that the involvement of NSs is crucial. Fraser (2011b) and Verrips (2011) critique her arguments in detail.

Eades comments, "This aspect of the *Guidelines* was uncontroversial among the 19 signatories, so members of the Language and National Origin group which authored the *Guidelines* have been somewhat surprised by the strength of the objection from LADO practitioners" (2010:38), and the discussion above makes clear that in fact some govern-ment and commercial agencies themselves do not permit analysis by unqualified native speakers for reasons of quality assurance and credibility. At the same time, it is equally evident that merely by virtue of being native speakers of a language, NSs do not possess anything that should be recognized either by the linguistic profession or by the legal sys-tem as "expertise." The standard definitions of expertise cited above do not refer to native speaker competence, and it is not covered by the type of experience that is sometimes allowed to substitute for formal qualifications (see also Shuy 2009; Butters 2009; Stygall 2009; and Olsson 2008).

Native speaker competence is simply not a type of explicit, learned knowledge that may be specified, tested, and confirmed as underlying an expert's opinion and setting it apart qualitatively from an ordinary person's. It is not the product of reliable principles and methods generally accepted in the scientific community, and attested via peer review and publication. Rather, it is a type of implicit knowledge acquired in childhood, the nature of which still needs to be clarified by research, that all normal members of a speech community share, and which in fact is emphatically everyday and ordinary.

Linguists are unlikely to confuse the nature and relative value of folk etymologies with lexicographic analysis, or language prejudices with sociolinguistic surveys; nor should they conflate native speaker knowledge with scientific linguistic expertise, especially when the consequences for asylum seekers' welfare are critical.

There are pragmatic reasons for insisting that native speakers play an essential role in performing LADO analyses—the maintenance of working methods which grew up independently of, and preceded by, linguistic inquiry into LADO, as well as cost and workload pressures conspiring to favor compromises that shift the burden of linguistic analysis away from the few qualified linguists and onto the many un- or under-qualified NENSs. However, in light of the fact that the position is disputed in government, commercial, and academic sectors, and regularly challenged in asylum tribunals, the argument now requires clarification and a basis in research—comparing different degrees of linguistic knowledge—which, at present, does not exist.

38.11 CONCLUSION

The Guidelines have established a basic reference point but much further work is urgently required. Several new sources of research exist, a dozen colloquia and conference sessions have occurred since 2003, and the topic of LADO features regularly at meetings of the International Association of Forensic Linguists and the International Association for Forensic Phonetics and Acoustics. The Language and Asylum Research Group (LARG), convened in 2010 by Diana Eades and the author, facilitates and supports research and discussion of LADO—not just among linguists, but also other academics, professionals, and workers concerned with refugee and asylum issues.[7] Such research can help ensure that LADO procedures are accurate and fair to those whose welfare and even lives may depend on them.

---

[7] LARG's website (<http://www.essex.ac.uk/larg/> accessed September 23, 2011) contains a comprehensive bibliography, case law references, and other information.

CHAPTER 39

....

FACTORS AFFECTING LAY PERSONS' IDENTIFICATION OF SPEAKERS

....

A. DANIEL YARMEY

A perpetrator speaking over the telephone or one whose face was obscured or disguised are examples of incidents that might lead to testimony on voice identification. Earwitness identification is part of the general area of person identification but refers specifically to victims' and witnesses' verbal descriptions of voices and speaker identification. The primary purpose of this chapter is to present a scientific overview of factors that affect the accuracy of speaker identification, or what is referred to as aural-perceptual analysis.

39.1 RELIABILITY AND VALIDITY OF SPEAKER RECOGNITION AND IDENTIFICATION

....

What can forensic linguists and research psychologists tell the legal community and potential jurors about those factors that influence the accuracy and completeness of voice descriptions and speaker identifications (see reviews by Bull and Clifford 1999; Hollien 2002; Rose 2002; Solan and Tiersma 2005; Wilding et al. 2000; Yarmey 2005, 2007)? Although many laypersons give significantly more credibility to the identification of speakers than is justified (Yarmey et al. 2001, 2004, but see also Philippon et al. 2007a), experts generally agree that earwitness descriptions and identification should be treated by the criminal justice system with great caution. Aural-perceptual identifications are difficult and error prone: false identifications are common and often exceed the correct identification rate (hits) in both laboratory research and field experiments. However, identification can be highly accurate for some witnesses and for some voices, but not others, for both familiar and unfamiliar speakers (Blatchford and Foulkes 2006;

Rose and Duncan 1995). Given certain witness and suspect characteristics, situational or event qualities, and evidence-gathering procedures, all voice descriptions are not necessarily poor, and identifications are not necessarily erroneous.

In spite of potential problems of speaker distortion arising from system effects (e.g. poor telephone transmission, background noise, etc.) and person effects (e.g. fear, anxiety, health problems, etc.), voice identification is possible given certain factors. For example, identification is facilitated by relatively long speech samples showing an overall consistency in pitch, habits, and other distinctive characteristics in the total configuration of sound factors (Ladefoged and Ladefoged 1980; Yarmey 1991a). Even with relatively short speech samples, the greater the variety in speech sounds, the better the subsequent identification (Roebuck and Wilding 1993). Perceptions of voice quality, such as melody and calmness, facilitate discriminations between positive and negative impressions. These impressions are related to moralistic judgments of good guys and bad guys and influence accuracy of recognition (Philippon et al. 2008; Yarmey 1993). Philippon et al. (2008:75) suggest, "Evolutionary theories could explain the existence of a bad guy stereotype in terms of survival (Petrinovich, 1995). Indeed, one's survival depends on discriminating between good and bad people, which could be inferred from auditory cues (i.e. voices)."

Speaker identification is facilitated when listeners use a pool of voice parameters from which they select subsets for auditory recognition, such as pitch level, pitch patterns, and variability, vocal intensity patterns, dialect, articulation, general voice and speech quality, and prosody (the timing and/or melody of speech) (Hollien 2002). If one parameter lacks usefulness, recognition and identification can still occur if one or more parameters are sufficiently distinctive. It is unlikely that a sole characteristic determines identification of an individual from all other speakers; besides, the critical parameters are not the same for all speakers (Lavner et al. 2000). There is no single way and no unique characteristic that ensures accurate aural-perceptual voice identification.

Although voices are stored as organized acoustic attributes which distinguish one speaker from another (Klatt and Klatt 1990), memory for pitch of speech can be distorted during voice recognition. Listeners have a partiality toward selecting voices lower in pitch than low-pitch targets, and in selecting voices higher in pitch than high-pitch targets (Mullennix et al. in press; Stern et al. 2007).

Finally, speaker recognition is dependent on the ability of listeners to select features for analysis as a function of interspeaker variability being greater than intraspeaker variability. Interspeaker variability is defined as the differences between two or more individuals in speech characteristics. That is, because of physiological differences in the structure of speech mechanisms and use of the voice tract, as well as the influence of geographical, educational, and socioeconomic factors, different speakers have different sounding voices. In contrast, intraspeaker variability refers to the differences in speech within the same speaker spoken over time. A given individual rarely pronounces a given word or phrase in an identical way on different occasions, even if the second utterance is produced in succession (Hollien 1990). Changes in mood, emotion, intentions, thought distractions, situational demands, and health and physical status contribute to intraspeaker variability. Thus, for an earwitness to discriminate features of a perpetrator, the suspect's voice must be remembered as having one or more speech characteristics that differentiate him or her from a set of foils in a voice lineup. The selection of the suspect's voice depends upon the availability of features that maximize interspeaker variability while minimizing intraspeaker variability.

39.2 WITNESS AND PERPETRATOR VARIABLES

The police do not have the luxury of handpicking their witnesses (or culprits) but must interview any and all male and female victims or witnesses, all of whom can differ in age, race, expertise, and other characteristics.

39.2.1 Gender differences

Most speaker identification research has failed to reveal significant differences between male and female witnesses (e.g. Thompson 1985; van Lancker et al. 1985a, 1985b; Yarmey 1986; Yarmey and Matthys 1992; Yarmey et al. 2001). However, women have been found superior to men but only in identifying female speakers (Roebuck and Wilding 1993; Wilding and Cook 2000).When gender differences occur in recognition they are typically attributed to selective attention to female-oriented versus male-oriented interests (Powers et al. 1979).

39.2.2 Listener's age

Voice recognition by 5- and 6-year olds, although inferior to that by adults, is significantly better than chance in recognition of familiar speakers (Bartholomeus 1973; Murray and Cort 1971). All children are more accurate at identifying more familiar speakers than they are at identifying less familiar speakers (Spence et al. 2002). Voice recognition substantially improves between the ages of 6 and 10, with the performance of some 10-year olds equivalent to that of adults. Between the ages of 10 and 13 recognition performance tends to plateau or decline but returns to adult levels by age 14 (Mann et al. 1979).

Children between 3 and 8 years of age show a poor ability to identify a speaker from voice lineups (Peters 1987). Children aged 5–6 years of age also are highly suggestible. Although instructed that the target voice may or may not be present, young children are prone to make a high number of false identifications in target-absent lineups. False identifications, however, decrease with increasing age of witnesses (Clifford and Toplis 1996).

Relatively little research has been conducted on developmental differences in voice identification. Although both children and adults are poor at voice identifications on average (Clifford 1997), participants between the ages of 21 to 40 are superior to those over the age of 40 (Bull and Clifford 1984). The perception of speech is adversely affected with aging especially when listening occurs with background noise, or with distortions resulting from poor acoustics or an amplification system. Older persons, in contrast to young adults, have an attention deficit and perform more poorly on several memory tasks (e.g. Bornstein 1995; Yarmey 2001a). They thus have greater problems in remembering the source of specific vocal information. That is, elders can confuse words they actually said from words they imagined saying, and words one person said from words another person said (Hashtroudi et al. 1989). When older adults are engaged in multitask processing while listening to two speakers and subsequently having to decide who said what, they are less likely to differentiate the source of their information (Johnson et al. 1995).

39.2.3 Ethnicity, other race, and accented voices

Witnesses can accurately recognize the ethnicity or race of someone just from hearing single words or a phoneme's length of speech (Flege 1984; Lass et al. 1978). Speakers' ethnicity is judged through non-standard dialect or racial speech cues for dialects of African American Vernacular English, Chicano English, and Standard American English (Purnell et al. 1999). Courts in both Kentucky and California have affirmed the legality of judged racial identity from speech by a lay witness (Baugh 2000; *Clifford v Kentucky*, 1999).[1] However, judging racial identity from heard speech can lead to misidentifications, prejudice, and stereotyping (Smalls 2004; Wiehl 2002). Giles and Bourhis (1982) found that most (80 percent) third-generation black immigrants in Wales descended from the West Indies were falsely identified as white speakers of the same socio-economic background. Recognition of accents is a function of more than race or ethnicity: it is also dependent upon socio-economic factors, education, historical and political groupings over time, and geographical regions of various sizes.

Witnesses are better at identifying speakers of their own ethnicity than those of other races. Thompson (1987) found that monolingual English-speaking listeners were better at identifying bilingual targets' voices after a 1-week retention interval on spoken English, followed by English spoken with a heavy Spanish accent, and poorest speaking in Spanish. Goggin et al. (1991) found that voice identification improved by nearly 200 percent when the listener was familiar with the language, in contrast to when statements were spoken in a foreign language. Consistent superiority in own-race speaker identification effects exist (see also Doty 1998; Hollien et al. 1982; Köster et al. 1995; Philippon et al. 2007b; Schiller and Köster 1996; Vanags et al. 2005). Witnesses who are most familiar with the languages, dialects, or standard-accented voices of suspects are more accu-

---

[1] *Clifford v Kentucky*, 7 SW 3d 371 Ky1999.

rate in their voice lineup identifications (Kerstholt et al. 2006). Unfortunately, the courts do not have objective standards to determine the credibility and truthfulness of witnesses' voice-identification abilities (Smalls 2004).

39.2.4 Blind listeners

Common sense suggests that blind listeners compensate with enhanced hearing. The blind are superior to the sighted in: sound localization; the ability to identify very short intervals between two consecutive noise bursts; speech discrimination (Muchnik et al. 1991); and the identification of speech at low sound levels especially in the presence of competing environmental noise (Niemeyer and Starlinger 1981). Although one study found blind participants superior to the sighted in recognizing a speaker from a voice lineup, there were no significant differences within the blind participants as a function of level of blindness (e.g. totally blind, blind with perception of light, blind with residual sight, and blind with goodish sight) (Bull et al. 1983). Other studies confirm that blindness does not result in superior voice recognition (Cobb et al. 1979; Winograd et al. 1984) or superior speaker identification (Elaad et al. 1998).

39.2.5 Witness confidence

Jurors are influenced by the confidence expressed by witnesses. However, witness confidence can change over time and is highly malleable (Devenport et al. 1999). Confidence–accuracy correlations of speaker identifications for unfamiliar speakers are non-significant or relatively low; however, they are moderated by voice-sample durations, tone, quality of speech, and familiarity with the speaker's voice (Orchard and Yarmey 1995; Yarmey and Matthys 1992). Olsson et al. (1998) found that identification for unfamiliar speakers is typically made with overconfidence, low accuracy, and little correlation between confidence and accuracy. However, significant confidence–accuracy correlations have been found for highly familiar speakers (e.g. family members, best friends) speaking in normal conversational tone, but not in whispers (Yarmey et al. 2001).

39.2.6 Witness descriptions and identification

On average witnesses provide only four or five voice characteristics of speakers such as pitch, enunciation, and tone of voice despite being repeatedly prompted to describe additional characteristics (Yarmey 2001b, 2003). Accuracy of voice identification is not related to the completeness of descriptions, accuracy in recall of what was said by the perpetrator, recall of specific words stated during the crime, or voice lineups containing only phrases spoken during the crime versus non-identical phrases (Yarmey 2001b). However, identification is significantly superior for witnesses who participate in a conversation with the perpetrator rather than who simply overhear his voice (Hammersley and Read 1985; Nolan and Grabe 1996). Also, in contrast to non-distinctive voices, descriptions of distinctive voices are reliable over a 1-week retention period (Yarmey 1991b).

39.2.7 Emotional arousal and stress

Perpetrator stress and anger increase speaking rate and the number of speech bursts (Hollien et al. 1982, 1993). Yelling and stress-related speech that can occur during crimes are seldom reproduced in the construction of voice lineups. Changes in voice tone from anger to conversation-type speech significantly interfere with subsequent identification (Saslove and Yarmey 1980). If possible, when constructing a lineup, police should tape-record a suspect and foils using the same tone of speech as used by the perpetrator during the commission of the crime. Unfortunately, the emotional state and tone of voice of the perpetrator are seldom given consideration by the courts (Solan and Tiersma 2003). Furthermore, victims and witnesses may experience severe stress or trauma which may be expected to influence attention, memory, and verbal reports (Christianson, 1992).

39.3 VOICE SAMPLES

39.3.1 Familiar speakers

Recognition of familiar speakers can be excellent (Hollien et al. 1983), but familiarity is not a guarantee of accuracy (Read and Craik 1995). Misidentification of familiar voices can occur because of changes in context and expectations (Ladefoged 1978; Ladefoged and Ladefoged 1980). Some familiar speakers are readily identified because of distinctive regional accents, idiosyncratic features, and high or low pitch, but familiar speakers with average pitch values can be consistently misidentified (Foulkes and Baron 2000).

Rose and Duncan (1995) showed that highly familiar speakers are identified at an 85 percent accuracy rate after listening to taped 45-second voice samples. Similarly, Yarmey et al. (2001) found that highly familiar, moderately familiar, and not-so familiar speakers were identified from relatively lengthy voice tapes at 85 percent, 79 percent, and 49 percent accuracy rates, respectively. Most interestingly, unfamiliar speakers elicited a high error rate with 45 percent falsely identified as a familiar person, even though listeners were permitted to state that they did not know who the speaker was. Recently Blatchford and Foulkes (2006) found that listeners correctly identified familiar speakers from two shouted utterances, *get him!* in 52 percent of the cases, and in 81 percent of cases based on hearing shouts of *face down on the ground and hands behind your back now!* Consistent with these findings Yarmey (2004) found that familiar speakers in a closed test using four speakers were correct in 47 percent of cases with the shouted utterance *help me!* compared with 68 percent accuracy for *hello* spoken normally. Yarmey also showed that familiar speakers uttering short linguistic material were significantly more easily recognized than were familiar speakers uttering non-linguistic ones such as laughter, coughing, or moaning which yielded relatively poor identification.

39.3.2 Opportunity to listen

Voices can be recognized from exposure to speech of a duration of 2 seconds or less (Bricker and Pruzansky 1966). Nevertheless, the larger the statistical sampling of a speaker's speech repertoire, the greater the accuracy of identification. However, longer voice-sample durations (18 seconds to 8 minutes) may also increase the false alarm rate (Cook and Wilding 1997; Yarmey and Matthys 1992).

A word of caution: triers-of-fact may believe longer opportunities to observe a perpetrator increase the probability of identification. However, the reported duration of heard speech usually depends upon witnesses' estimations, and such estimations can be faulty. Speech lasting between 15 seconds and 8 minutes is significantly overestimated in duration with women giving substantially greater overestimations than men (Orchard and Yarmey 1995; Yarmey et al. 1994).

39.3.3 Voice disguise

Perpetrators often can avoid identification by degrading the quality of speech through holding a pencil between the front teeth (de Figueiredo and de Souza Britto 1996), whispering (Orchard and Yarmey 1995, Procter and Yarmey 2003), changing voice pitch (Künzel 2000; Manning et al. 2000), or tone (Saslove and Yarmey 1980), and impersonating another speaker (Schichting and Sullivan 1997). Intoxication also shifts most voices to a higher pitch level that could act as a disguise (Hollien and Martin 1996).

39.4 SITUATIONAL AND PROCEDURAL VARIABLES

39.4.1 Telephone effects

Although telephone lines are known to degrade the speech signal, particularly in the loss of high-frequency energy, recent research comparing telephone transmitted speech with face-to-face speech in field situations revealed no significant differences in lineup identifications between the two modes of presentation (Yarmey 2003; see also, Kerstholt et al. 2006; Perfect et al. 2002; Yarmey 1991b).

39.4.2 Retention interval

Clifford (1983) found identification to decline over 1-week, 2-week, and 3-week delays in testing from 50 percent to 43 percent and 9 percent accuracy, respectively. Clifford and Denot (cited in Bull and Clifford 1984) found voice recognition not to decline between delays of 1 and 2 weeks but significant decrements occurred after 3 weeks (see also, Bull and Clifford 1984; Clifford 1980; Clifford et al. 1981; Huss and Weaver 1996; McGehee 1937, 1944 (but see Yarmey et al. 2008); Papcun et al. 1989; Yarmey and Matthys 1992).

In contrast, other research has revealed little loss in accuracy occurring over 24 hours (Legge et al. 1984; Saslove and Yarmey 1980). Broeders and Rietveld (1995) found performance to be similar over 3 weeks, with 84 percent accuracy after 1 week and 80 percent accuracy at 3 weeks. Similarly, Kerstholt et al. (2006) found no significant differences in identification accuracy after 1, 3, or 8 weeks. Accuracy of recognition also did not decline between 2 and 14 days when a witness was involved in a conversation with a target speaker (Hammersley and Read 1985). The failure to find a decline in accuracy of identification has been confirmed in studies by Kerstholt et al. (2004) for 1-week retention; Legge et al. (1984) for 10-days retention; and van Wallendael et al. (1994) for 2-weeks retention.

The effects of delay in testing clearly depend upon more than time passing. A number of moderating factors are involved such as differences in attention, voice distinctiveness, ease of acquisition, the length of the heard voice sample, changes in voice quality between acquisition and test, and so forth.

39.4.3 Multiple perpetrators

Crimes often involve two or more perpetrators who talk to each other and with the victim. Recognition performance significantly decreases as a function of hearing 5 to 20 voices (Legge et al. 1984), and 2, 3, 4, to 8 voices (Carterette and Barneby 1975).

39.5 VOICE LINEUPS

Earwitnesses may be exposed to the voice of the suspect in a single-person confrontation (showup) or in a many-person lineup, where the witness is asked whether the speaker has been heard before (recognition memory), and to identify the person whose voice most resembles the perpetrator (speaker identification).

Choosing a speaker's voice is not the equivalent of making an accurate identification. Choosing and accuracy are dependent first of all on whether the offender is actually present in the lineup and who is chosen (offender, innocent suspect, or foil) (Malpass and Devine 1984). An identification of a suspect only suggests that the individual could be the perpetrator as opposed to proving he/she definitely is the perpetrator. Selection may merely indicate that the chosen voice bears a strong resemblance to the voice of the perpetrator. Similarly, failure to make a selection does not prove that the perpetrator is not present. Instead, a false negative response or miss may occur rather than a correct rejection of the lineup.

39.5.1 SHOWUPS VERSUS LINEUPS

In contrast to voice lineups, single-person confrontations or showups are relatively rare but do occur on occasion (*Stovall v Denno*, 1967;[2] Yarmey in press). Two naturalistic field studies have been conducted comparing the accuracy of speaker identification in showups and lineups (Yarmey et al. 1994; Yarmey 2003). In both experiments accuracy of identification in showups (28 percent and 28 percent, respectively) and in six-person lineups (9 percent and 27 percent, respectively) was poor. Both experiments showed that significantly more false identifications of the "innocent" suspect were found in the showup than in the lineup condition. An innocent "sound-alike" suspect is at significantly more risk of being misidentified in a single-person confrontation than in a many-person voice lineup.

39.6 CONCLUSIONS

Although the criminal justice system actively seeks witness descriptions and identification of suspects, such evidence is recognized as the primary cause of false convictions (Huff et al. 1986). According to the Innocence Project website (May 29, 2009) the application of DNA technology to criminal cases has exonerated 238 convicted individuals in the United States, and of these cases more than 75 percent of the defendants were convicted as a function of mistaken eyewitness identification. What percentage of these cases involved mistaken earwitness identification either in whole or in part is unknown.

Scientific studies indicate that false alarm rates on voice identification often exceed hit rates, and the correct rate of identification is typically at 50 percent or lower, with only a few experiments approaching 85 percent accuracy. Several investigators have replicated these results across many laboratories in different countries. If the results of these scientific investigations can be generalized they probably fall below most, if not all, judicially acceptable levels of decision making (cf. Blatchford and Foulkes 2006; Rose and Duncan 1995; Yarmey et al. 2001).

---

[2] *Stovall v Denno*, 388 U.S. 293, 302 (1967).

In *United States v Duran* (1993),[3] the Ninth Circuit affirmed a conviction for bank robbery in which the primary evidence consisted of voice identification by a bank teller. The Court concluded:

> both tellers had ample opportunity to listen to Duran's voice during the robbery.... As Duran left, he threatened everyone in the bank: "don't move or we'll kill you." Both tellers were likely very attentive during the robbery given Duran's weapon and threats, as evidenced by their accurate descriptions of Duran and his distinctive voice and the fact that neither teller equivocated in her identification of Duran's voice. Moreover, the in-court identifications occurred just three months after the bank robbery. (cited in Solan and Tiersma 2003:383)

Speaker identification is not impossible and may be reliable for some earwitnesses. However, triers-of-fact should be very cautious in drawing conclusions based solely on speaker identification evidence.

---

[3] *United States v Duran*, 4 F.3d 800 (9th Cir. 1993).

CHAPTER 40

....

FORENSIC SPEAKER COMPARISON: A LINGUISTIC–ACOUSTIC PERSPECTIVE

....

PAUL FOULKES
PETER FRENCH

40.1 INTRODUCTION

....

IN the 1994 movie *Clear and Present Danger*, Harrison Ford investigates a murder. His principal clue is a recording of the suspect's voice on the victim's answer machine, consisting of the phrase "the machine is still on, Moira." A voice expert listens (once) to these eight syllables and recognizes the voice as similar to that on another recording that he has recently analyzed. Comparing the two recordings, he rapidly constructs a profile of the speaker: "he's Cuban, aged 35 to 45, educated in the United States... *eastern* United States." The answer machine recording is then uploaded (at high speed) into a giant computer that, in a matter of seconds, generates a 90.1 percent probability of "a match" against a background population of hundreds of thousands of candidates.

It goes without saying that fictional accounts of voice analysis, which abound in recent film and television drama, are in many respects a long way removed from reality in the detail they portray (a phenomenon widely known as the "CSI effect," in reference to the television series; Schweitzer and Saks 2007). However, the example does illustrate two of the tasks undertaken in forensic voice and speech analysis. First, where the voice of a criminal has been recorded but no suspect has yet been apprehended, features of the voice can be examined to ascertain information about the speaker's regional, social, and ethnic background. This task is known as *speaker profiling* (Jessen 2008). Second, comparative analysis can be made against a reference sample known to have been produced by a particular talker. This task is now generally referred to as *speaker* or *voice comparison* (or *speaker/voice identification*). We estimate that around 70 percent of casework undertaken by forensic phoneticians falls into this category.

With the exception of one particular application concerning the use of linguistic analysis to determine the origin of asylum seekers (see Section 40.4), speaker profiling is undertaken relatively infrequently. For example, the laboratory with which the authors are affiliated, J P French Associates, handles around five cases annually. It is usually requested in cases where the police have not yet identified a perpetrator. Typical examples include kidnappings (where the voice of a kidnapper may be heard in a ransom demand) and robberies (in which a masked robber's speech may be captured on a CCTV soundtrack).

The most (in)famous case in which profiling played a crucial role was that of the Yorkshire Ripper hoaxer (Ellis 1994). The Ripper murdered 13 women in Yorkshire. Information gathered during the investigation, including eyewitness accounts from survivors of brutal attacks, suggested that the perpetrator was a local Yorkshireman. After the eleventh murder the police received a tape, apparently from the killer. Ellis, an expert in English dialects, was asked to analyze the voice. He pinpointed the speaker's origin as Sunderland, a city in northeast England. The investigation subsequently changed course, with the hunt targeting a man from the north-east, despite Ellis's warnings that the tape might have been a hoax. Eventually it emerged that the killer, Peter Sutcliffe, was indeed a Yorkshireman. The tape had been a hoax. The hoaxer, John Humble, remained at large for 26 years. Ellis's analysis had been remarkably accurate: Humble had lived all his life in Sunderland, only two miles from the suburb identified by Ellis (see further French et al. 2006).

Speaker comparison is undertaken far more frequently than profiling. The recordings at issue might be abusive or threatening voicemail messages, ransom demands, fraudulent calls to financial institutions, or hoax calls to the emergency services. Increasingly, and especially in cases related to drugs and terrorism, the recordings are the product of covert surveillance by the police or security services. In the UK, where all police interviews have been recorded since the late 1980s, reference samples typically consist of the interview tape.

It is now accepted by all speech scientists that voice alone cannot be used to establish identity with absolute certainty. There are several reasons why. First, there is no indelible feature of any individual's voice, equivalent to a fingerprint or a DNA profile. That is, there are no unchanging, biologically-determined properties of voice, speech, or language. Second, no vocal feature is present in every utterance produced by a speaker. Voices contain many components of different types, some of which are independent of one another, and which are organized on several structural levels. For example, speech sounds are combined into words, which in turn form larger grammatical units. Suprasegmental components such as fundamental frequency and voice quality are overlaid on the string of consonants and vowels. Only a subset of the componential features is present in any given utterance. Third, it is likely that no feature of any voice is invariant. Different voices overlap to some extent in their composition, and all vocal features vary within certain parameters as a result of many different factors. Some of these features are *in part* biologically-determined, such as a speaker's long-term fundamental frequency (f0), which is largely dependent on the anatomy and physiology of the vocal cords. However, many are the product of environmental learning, determined by the speaker's regional and social background. The speaker's general regional accent/dialect is an obvious example. Still other aspects of speech and language are shaped by the situational context in which speech takes place. Many people, for example, instinctively speak more loudly when listening conditions are sub-optimal, as when speaking against background noise (an effect known as the Lombard reflex). Raising the amplitude of speech has various effects on the acoustic signal, including raising the speaker's f0. Fourth, when recorded, vocal features may be further affected by technical aspects of the transmission or circuitry, for example as a result of being passed through a telephone line. As a consequence of such factors, vocal patterns may vary from situation to situation (unlike, say, a person's fingerprints or DNA profile, which are immutable).

Although analysis of vocal features cannot determine a speaker's identity, it can provide a wealth of information about the speaker, albeit to varying degrees of precision and confidence. It is for this reason that the label *speaker comparison* is now preferred to *identification*. The analytic process itself is therefore obviously not as fast or clear-cut as typically presented in fictional accounts. However, analysis of vocal features can certainly yield results that have crucial evidential value, although in most cases such evidence is used in a corroborative role alongside other information. Much research in forensic phonetics is devoted to identifying the features that offer the best potential to distinguish between individuals: features that have small within-speaker variation but large cross-speaker variation.

Globally, speaker comparison is carried out using three general methodologies: (1) "voiceprinting," (2) analysis using automatic systems, and (3) linguistic–acoustic analysis. Voiceprinting is discussed in Section 40.2. We share the view of the great majority of academic linguists that this method is scientifically untenable. Automatic methods involve the application of speech and speaker recognition technology. Discussion of such methods is beyond the scope of this chapter. Campbell (1997) offers an accessible introduction. Automatic methods are increasingly being used in combination with the linguistic–acoustic method, each offering their own advantages (Künzel and Gonzalez-Rodriguez 2003; Jessen 2008). The linguistic–acoustic method is the longest established, and at present the most widely used. In Section 40.3 we elaborate on the general methodology, with illustrations from cases. We end with a critical look at current debates in the field, with an eye on future developments. First, however, we begin with a brief historical review of forensic speaker comparison.

40.2 Historical overview of forensic speaker comparison

Perhaps the first reported legal case involving voice identification is that of William Hulet, who was tried for high treason in 1660 as the executioner who beheaded King Charles I (Hollien 1990). The executioner was masked, but a witness identified Hulet from his voice after hearing him beg the King's forgiveness prior to delivering the fatal blow. In this example, of course, identification was made by a naive listener rather than a trained expert. This type of identification remains relatively frequent in legal cases, and has been the subject of much research to assess, for example, the reliability of listeners in recognizing voices under different conditions (see Chapter 39).

Speaker identification/comparison by experts dates back to the 1960s. In the UK the first known case in which expert evidence was delivered in court was in 1967. This involved Stanley Ellis providing linguistic, phonetic, and acoustic evidence in the defense of a man accused of making a hoax call to the fire service (Ellis 1990). From that time, casework in the UK has been handled almost exclusively by phoneticians. The number of cases using forensic speaker comparison evidence increased from a mere handful in the early 1980s to several hundred a year at present.

In contrast to the position in the UK, forensic speaker comparison methods in the USA were mainly developed by engineers and audiologists rather than by linguists and phoneticians. In the USA, too, the possibility of forensic speaker identification entered public consciousness in the early 1960s, with the development of the *voiceprinting* technique. The label was first used by two of the pioneers of spectrography, Grey and Kopp (1944), and was clearly coined to parallel the more established technique of fingerprinting. In the forensic context, voiceprinting was first discussed in detail by Kersta (1962), although it seems likely that secret research was carried out in the USA during World War II. A similar line of work was developed in the Soviet Union under the epithet *phonoscopy* (Eriksson 2005).

The technique involves the visual inspection of spectrograms, that is, computer-generated displays of the time, frequency, and amplitude components of speech sounds. Kersta (1962:1253) hypothesized that talkers produce utterances containing "unique features," just as fingerprints are thought to be particular to each individual. His hypothesis was based on the notion that no two speakers share the same vocal tract anatomy or habitual articulatory strategies. Thus the speech of any two individuals should, in principle, be distinguishable, and the unique anatomy and physiology of each individual should leave a unique imprint on that person's speech. According to Kersta, these unique features could be identified and compared via physical images of speech (in a method again analogous to fingerprinting). He claimed a high success rate in identifying talkers using the method. A later study by Tosi et al. (1972) attempted to replicate Kersta's findings using various experimental designs. Examiners of spectrographic printouts were trained to compare a small number of key spectral features. Tosi et al. also reported a high identification rate, with between 0.5 percent and 18 percent error, depending on the test structure.

While the method apparently showed promise, it was quickly dismissed by the scientific communities in phonetics and acoustics, and rejected as inadmissible by some jurisdictions. The experimental materials used by Kersta and colleagues were highly controlled and did not reflect the natural variability found in voices (outlined above). It is recognized by phoneticians and linguists that different speakers, when uttering the same words, may cast very similar spectrographic patterns, while the same speaker can produce starkly different patterns under varying conditions. (For further critical discussion of voiceprinting see Bolt et al. 1973; Nolan 1983; Hollien 1990, 2002; Rose 2002; Meuwly 2003a,b; Eriksson 2005.) In 2007 the International Association for Forensic Phonetics and Acoustics (IAFPA) issued a resolution concerning voiceprinting, concluding: "The Association considers this approach to be without scientific foundation, and it should not be used in forensic casework."[1]

Despite widespread rejection of the technique by academics, however, voiceprinting is still practiced to this day by some private voice examiners in the USA. Analysts at the American Federal Bureau of Investigation (FBI) also use voiceprinting in investigative work, although they do not produce their findings in evidence.

Unhelpfully, the term "voiceprinting" is used with different senses. For forensic practitioners it refers to the visual comparison of spectrograms, as in the original sense intended by Kersta. For some non-linguists the term has often been extended to cover any form of acoustic analysis, including the acoustic element of the linguistic–acoustic method discussed in this chapter. This is also how "voiceprinting" appears to have been (mis)understood in some legal cases, with the result that some courts in the USA have rejected all forms of acoustic analysis as inadmissible (Tiersma and Solan 2002). "Voiceprint" is also found in a third sense in the automatic speaker identification literature, as a synonym for a computational model of a voice (e.g. Wang et al. 2004). Confusion over the definition and status of voiceprinting has led to severe inconsistency across American courts in how speaker comparison evidence is handled (thanks also in part to arguments over whether speaker comparison is admissible in courts under the *Daubert* criteria; Tiersma and Solan 2002). A further unfortunate legacy of voiceprinting in the USA is therefore a lack of clear understanding among the judiciary and the general public of how forensic speaker comparison can be performed, and of the probative value of reputable methods of voice comparison. Hollien (1990: 207) describes voiceprinting as "a problem that simply will not go away." It still hasn't.

Failure to understand the strengths and limitations of the science(s) involved in any forensic discipline gives rise to the danger of poor practice, and may open the field to potential charlatanry. Either may result in potential miscarriages of justice. Butters (2010a), for example, cites testimony from a case in which a self-proclaimed language expert was unable to explain the term "alveolar" (a basic phonetic term introduced in first year linguistics courses, applied to sounds such as [t, d, n] that are made with tongue constriction at the ridge behind the upper teeth). Reports can also be found of speaker comparison cases being conducted by dialect enthusiasts with no formal qualifications; engineers; even mineralogists (Braun and Künzel 1998:19).

In recent years significant steps have been taken to regulate and standardize practice in speaker comparison, as well as to provide a sound academic grounding. The IAFPA was established in 1991, supports an annual conference, and has an official publication in the *International Journal of Speech, Language and the Law*. The IAFPA also has a Code of Practice to which all members are bound.[2]

Notwithstanding the predominance of automatic methods in some jurisdictions, the majority of speaker comparison work around the world currently uses linguistic–acoustic methods. In the early literature on speaker comparison there was debate on the relative merits of auditory versus acoustic analysis (Baldwin and French 1990; Nolan 1990; French

---

[1] <http://www.iafpa.net/voiceprintsres.htm> accessed August 23, 2010.
[2] <http://www.iafpa.net/code.htm> accessed August 23, 2010.

1994). Nowadays, however, both auditory and acoustic analysis are generally seen to have advantages and disadvantages. They are regarded as complementary, and most analysts employ both in their casework. We turn now to an overview of these methods.

40.3 THE LINGUISTIC–ACOUSTIC APPROACH

The linguistic–acoustic method of speaker comparison is the principal one used in the UK. It is also standard in Australia, Austria, Finland, Germany, the Netherlands, and Sweden. In the USA it has been espoused by leading academic linguists such as Hollien, Labov, and Ladefoged, and is used routinely by the US Secret Service. It has also been used in at least 20 other countries to our knowledge, including Ghana, Hong Kong, India, Pakistan, Russia, South Africa, and the former Yugoslavia, and it has been employed in courts of all levels including the International Commission of Enquiry and the UN International War Crimes Tribunal. Textbooks by Hollien (1990, 2002) and Rose (2002) offer a thorough critical discussion of the approach.

The method involves the reduction of speech into its component units—consonants, vowels, intonation, lexicon, grammar, etc. A range of analytic techniques is applied as appropriate for each type of unit, established as general methods in a range of fields including phonetics, phonology, acoustics, sociolinguistics, and discourse analysis. To a large extent these methods are uncontroversial within their fields of origin. Features are extracted from and compared across criminal recordings and reference samples of a suspect's voice. Although, as noted earlier, no feature of any voice is indelible or perma- nently present, it is known that some features vary more than others both within the repertoire of individual speakers and in the population as a whole. The most useful fea- tures for analysis are thus those that display relatively little within-speaker variation, but relatively large cross-speaker variation. Much research in the field aims to identify the potential of different features to discriminate between speakers.

In the remainder of the chapter we illustrate the general procedures followed by exam- ples from cases that we have conducted using this method.[3] Detailed case reports follow- ing similar methods are provided by Milroy (1984), Ash (1988), Labov (1988), Baldwin and French (1990), Hollien (1990, 2002), and Rose (2002). The *International Journal of Speech, Language and the Law* also regularly publishes case reports, notably French et al. (2006).

40.3.1 Preparatory work

Before analysis commences, digital clones of exhibits are made (or digital copies in the case of original analogue exhibits). These are then edited to provide working samples of the voices in question, and to eliminate other voices and portions of excessive back-

---

[3] Materials are from authentic cases, but some names and other identifying information have been changed or removed.

ground noise, where possible. At J P French Associates we generally aim to extract working samples containing between 90 seconds and five minutes of speech. We ensure that the mode of speech is as consistent as possible across the samples. That is, if the criminal is engaged in ordinary fluent speech, delivered at a normal speaking level, the working sample from the suspect should be similar in nature. If the criminal sample contains sections of elevated voice, shouting, whisper, or other deviations from normal conversation, these sections are removed, or treated separately if comparable material is available for the suspect.

40.3.2 Analytic framework

Two general types of analysis are undertaken: auditory and acoustic. Auditory analysis is applied on two levels: the segmental level, dealing with the pronunciations of consonant and vowel sounds, and the suprasegmental or prosodic level, pertaining to longer-domain features such as intonation, articulation rate, and voice quality. In some cases there may also be reference to features beyond phonetics and phonology, such as unusual lexical choice, use of non-standard or otherwise unusual syntax or morphology, the presence of pathological features, or distinctive discourse patterns.

40.3.3 Auditory analysis

Analysis usually begins at the suprasegmental level with an assessment of voice quality. The approach taken to the description of voice quality is analytic as opposed to holistic. Using a version of the Edinburgh Vocal Profile Analysis scheme (Laver 1980) specially modified for forensic purposes, the voices in the criminal and reference recordings are evaluated and scored in respect of phonation features, and muscular and articulatory settings. In total, 38 dimensions are considered in the scheme we presently use in our casework. A section of the formal protocol form we use is shown in Figure 40.1.

Continuing at the supresegmental level, patterns of rhythm, tempo, and intonation are investigated across the samples. With regard to rhythm and tempo, for example, one might pay particular attention to the presence of syllables sustained beyond their normal durations, staccato features and departures from the canonical stress-timed patterns associated with most dialects of English. Intonation is examined in respect of both tonicity (the placement of major "sentence stresses") and tonality (the selection of pitch contours—rising, falling, falling–rising, etc). Conventional descriptive frameworks are used to capture features considered to be of significance.

Articulation rate may in some cases also be examined during the auditory analysis. This is calculated in terms of the number of phonological syllables per second the talker produces in each sample. This aspect of the analysis may become particularly important where the data fall towards the margins of normal speaker behavior. Background population statistics indicate that most speakers produce between 4.4 and 5.9 syllables per second (Goldman-Eisler 1968). When one encounters rates of syllable production

	FIRST PASS		SECOND PASS			
	Neutral	Non-Neutral	SETTING	Not. 1	Mark. 2	Extr. 3
C. PHONATION FEATURES						

		Present		Scalar Degree		
	SETTING	Neutral	Non-neutral	Not. 1	Mark. 2	Extr. 3
12. Voicing type	Voice					
	Falsetto					
	Creak					
	Creaky					
13. Laryngeal frication	Whisper					
	Whispery					
	Breathy					
	Murmur					
14. Laryngeal irregularity	Harsh					
	Tremor					

FIGURE 40.1 Section of vocal profile analysis protocol used by J P French Associates

Adapted from Laver (1980).

that fall markedly below or above this range, the patterns found may be considered distinctive.

Phonetic transcription of speech segments also figures highly in the auditory analysis. Salient segments and in some instances extended passages of speech are transcribed using the resources of the International Phonetic Alphabet (IPA). The IPA contains over 80 characters for consonants alone, plus a rich set of diacritics to capture fine-grained aspects of pronunciation.

An example is shown in (40.1). The criminal recording in this case was made through an intercom system at a sheltered housing unit for elderly people in northern England. The caller (who was obviously female) gained access to one home and stole valuables. A suspect, Cooper, was subsequently apprehended. The recording, which was of poor technical quality, consisted of only four seconds of speech—far too little for analysis by automated methods. Yet the transcription, by its focus on the various components of the speech, reveals a rich source of material that could be used for comparison with the suspect's voice.

(40.1) Transcription of disputed sample, R –v– Cooper. Bracketed sections were too distorted for reliable analysis.

Text: *I've come to see the lady at number two.* [operator's turn removed] *(I'm fro)m the Home Care I've come to collect her sheet(s).*

IPA: av ˈkʰʊm tsiː? ˈɫɛɪdjə? nʊmbə ˈ↑\tʰəʉuː [...] (...)m? ˈʌʊm kʰɛːɹ av ˈkʰʊm tʰə ˈkʰɫɛktʰ ə ˈʃɪiː?

From the transcription in (40.1) we can observe at least the following features:

- the diphthong /aɪ/ is reduced to a monophthong [a] (in both instances of *I've*);
- the typical northern English /ʊ/ is used (*come, number*);
- the schwa vowel is fully elided (*to, collect*);
- /t/ is realized as a glottal stop in word-final position (*at, sheet*);
- /l/ is 'dark' in syllable-onset positions (*lady, collect*);
- despite the general northern accent, /eɪ/ and /əʊ/ are pronounced as diphthongs rather than local monophthong forms (*lady, Home*);
- /uː/ and /iː/ are not monophthongal (*two, sheet*);
- the final syllable in each of the two speaking turns is markedly elongated (*two, sheet*);
- the intonational contour on *two* includes an upstep prior to a falling tone;
- the definite article is realized as the local northern form [ʔ];
- /h/ is deleted (*Home, her*);
- the speaker is not rhotic (no syllable-final /r/ is pronounced in *number, her*) but she uses linking /r/ (i.e. /r/ is pronounced when in final position and followed by a vowel, in *Care I've*).

Further comments could be made in respect of other segmental and suprasegmental features. Note that many of the observable features are also robust to the channel mismatch problem that can impede acoustic analysis and which also has a severe impact on automatic speaker identification (Campbell 1997): the poor recording quality is irrelevant when it comes to observing, for example, the use of diphthongs rather than monophthongs, the presence or absence of segments, dialectal pronoun forms, or unusual durational features.

On the basis of patterns revealed by an extended transcription, more extensive analysis might then be carried out with reference to the whole working sample (or indeed the entirety of the evidential material) of any features that the analyst judges to have probative value. In the case of Cooper, the material illustrated in (40.1) comprises the whole disputed sample. However, every one of the features listed above was also observed in Cooper's reference sample.

The features to be analysed auditorily are mainly consonant and vowel realizations, often extracted and compared with reference to phonological criteria. For example, in English /t/ is highly variable in the phonetic forms speakers use, with [tʰ t̚ ɾ ʔ ɹ] all possibilities in British dialects (Wells 1982). However, some of these variants are found only in certain phonological contexts (for example, syllable-initial, syllable-coda, or between vowels). Some variants show very different statistical distributions in line with phonological or other linguistic criteria. For instance, speakers generally delete /h-/ in unstressed pronouns (*her, him*), especially in object position, much more frequently than in nouns and verbs.

In addition to broad segmental realizations we also examine dynamic aspects of speech production. Speakers differ, for example, in whether they allow neighboring sounds to assimilate (e.g. in the realization of *vodka* as [vɒgkə], where the alveolar /d/ assimilates in place of articulation to the following velar /k/), whether they produce epenthetic sounds in particular sequences (e.g. a [t] in *once*), or whether they reduce or delete unstressed vowels or syllables (as shown in the example in (40.1)).

Other features that provide potentially useful idiosyncratic evidence can also be analyzed auditorily. These include lexical choice (e.g. frequent use of a particular term of address, such as *mate, pal, dude, chap*), and grammatical and discourse patterns. For example, potentially distinctive syntactic or morphological features might include non-standard verb forms such as *he were, they was*; use of the generic tag question *innit?* (= *isn't it*, used for all tenses, persons, and numbers); or variability in pronoun placement (*he gave it me* versus *he gave me it*). Discourse level features of interest include the frequency and distribution of discourse markers (*like, sort of, know what I mean? you get me?*), and pausing behavior (silent or filled pauses, length of pauses, location of pauses with respect to discourse or syntactic unit boundaries).

If a given feature appears particularly important we might undertake a formal quantification of variants, following methods routinely used in sociolinguistics (Tagliamonte 2006). In one particular case, for example, we quantified variant types used for /r/. The disputed sample in this case was a set of covert recordings made over many hours in a car, again in northern England. In our view the speech of the suspect, Quilley, differed in several significant ways from that recorded in the covert material, including with respect to /r/. In some northern dialects /r/ is variably realized as a tap, [ɾ] (Wells 1982). The speaker in the disputed recordings regularly used taps, but only in word-medial intervocalic positions (e.g. *very*) and in linking contexts (e.g. *where is*). However, first impressions and an initial auditory analysis suggested Quilley did not use taps. In order to demonstrate the extent of differences such as this across the recordings we quantified pronunciation types used for /r/ in the relevant phonological contexts. Auditory analysis was largely sufficient for this purpose, as the recordings were of relatively good technical quality, and the difference between the tap and other (approximant) variants was generally clear. However, acoustic analysis was also used to confirm auditory impressions. The speaker in the disputed sample produced taps in 64 percent of possible instances, while Quilley failed to produce a tap in over two hours of reference material. Similar stark differences were also found in respect of other variables analyzed.

Finally, certain of the features examined auditorily are non-linguistic. These may concern patterns of audible breathing, throat clearing, or tongue clicking, for example. Whilst such features would undoubtedly be subject to detailed acoustic investigation across the samples, the auditory stage at least serves as the initial platform for their identification and assessment.

40.3.4 Acoustic analysis

Acoustic analysis is undertaken on a subset of the features identified in the auditory phase of the process. Measurements can be made of frequency, duration, and/or amplitude components of the speech sample. For example, the calculation of the speaker's long-term average fundamental frequency is routine. So too is an analysis of the constituent vowel resonances or formants, which can offer detailed information about the speaker's articulatory and phonological patterns.

Note that the use of acoustic analysis should not be confused with the procedure of voiceprinting referred to in Section 40.2. The acoustic record is not used for side-by-side pattern matching through visual impression. Rather, it is the basis for systematic quantitative analysis of the phonetic and phonological features generally accepted as constituent units of speech and language. The essential diagnostic features of each unit are extracted and measured following principles established in phonetics and acoustics. These principles include making justified allowances for variation in the data. It is well known that people tend to speak more loudly when using the telephone, and that this modified behavior results in an epiphenomenal effect of raising the speaker's f0. This has been demonstrated experimentally by, for example, Hirson et al (1995). In measuring and comparing f0 in forensic materials, then, it would be justifiable (all things being equal) to treat measured f0 in phone call data as artificially high.

Measurement of f0 is relatively easy. Average values (mean, mode, median) offer an indicator of whether a speaker has a generally high or low-pitched voice, while measurements of range or variability (such as the standard deviation) indicate whether a voice is monotonous or "lively." F0 is a rare example of a vocal feature for which population statistics are available (e.g. Hudson et al. 2007). However, the majority of individuals fall into a relatively narrow range (c. 100–130 Hz for men in spontaneous speech; Künzel 1989). It is, therefore, only very high or low average f0 values that are likely to offer strong probative value. Moreover, f0 is especially susceptible to within-speaker variation, for example due to ill health, speaking loudly, or speaking when emotional (Braun 1995). Thus, although f0 measures are easily obtained, they are used with particular caution and are rarely significant in arriving at positive conclusions. However, where the differences found across the criminal and known samples are in the reverse direction predicted from the research literature (e.g. f0 is lower in a telephone recording than a direct recording), they can play a stronger role in reaching a negative conclusion, that is, elimination of the suspect.

Vowel formant analysis is also undertaken in most cases. The center frequency values of the first three formants (reflecting the three lowest resonant frequencies of the vocal tract) offer a clear indication of how that vowel was articulated (Stevens 1998). Comparative analysis can thus provide useful information on similarity or difference between speakers. An example of formant data is shown in Figure 40.2. This formant plot shows measured data for two vowels from the Yorkshire Ripper hoax tape compared with John Humble's reading of the same text (French et al. 2006). Note first that there is variability within the data from each recording. This is as expected, and reflects the fact that the "same sound" is pronounced in slightly different ways each time by a given individual (and again confirms the point that, unlike fingerprints, vocal features are not invariant). The distribution of both vowels, however, falls in a similar space for the two recordings, with considerable overlap between the datasets. The conclusion to be drawn is that the speakers' vowel productions are similar in quality. This does not mean that the same speaker must be involved, however, as many other English-speaking

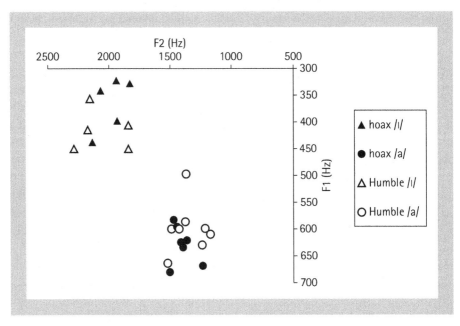

FIGURE 40.2 Formant plot for vowels /ɪ/ (e.g. *did*) and /a/ (e.g. *Jack*), comparing Yorkshire Ripper hoax tape (filled symbols) and John Humble (unfilled symbols)

adult males would produce similar data. On the other hand there is no evidence of inconsistency, such that Humble might have been rejected as a potential candidate.

For all features analyzed we must take account of potential sources of variation in the materials. It is common, for example, for a case to involve comparison of telephone recordings (especially for criminal samples) with directly-recorded materials (such as police interview tapes). Telephone transmission affects acoustic properties, thanks to the limited bandwidth of transmission using current technology. Frequency components outside the range of *c.* 340–3700 Hz are diminished or removed by the transmission. Thus it may not be possible to compare at all those features whose key components are found outside the 340–3700 Hz range (such as sibilant fricatives, which have most energy in the higher frequencies). Other features may be modified by the transmission, and thus differ significantly across the samples. In such cases the difference is artefactual rather than indicating that two different speakers are involved. For example, telephone transmission significantly raises the first formant of vowels (Künzel 2001; Byrne and Foulkes 2004).

Not all measurements taken from a spectrographic analysis relate to the frequency dimension. Time domain features are immune from the deleterious effects of telephone transmission and restricted frequency bandwidth. Such features may relate to the overall durations of consonants in given phonological contexts (e.g. nasals, liquids, or fricatives in intervocalic positions) or the durations of the sub-components of consonants (e.g. the voice onset times or burst lengths of syllable-initial plosives).

40.3.5 Comparison of data and expression of conclusions

Once data have been assembled for both the disputed and known samples, formal comparison is undertaken in order to reach an overall view on the possibility that the suspect is also the speaker in the criminal recording.

Comparison is neither straightforward nor uncontroversial. For some analysts, the task is largely impressionistic, as implied in our example of formant comparison (Section 40.3.4). However, it is also possible in some circumstances to make statistical comparison of case data relative to a reference dataset drawn from the same speech community to which the suspect belongs (see our comments on articulation rate in Section 40.3.3). This approach is championed in forensic phonetics by Rose (2002, 2006) and Rose and Morrison (2009; see also Robertson and Vignaux 1995). It mirrors the process applied in some other forensic disciplines such as DNA analysis. Comparative data are presented in the form of a likelihood ratio (LR). In effect an LR expresses the likelihood of obtaining the measured data from the suspect relative to the likelihood of obtaining it from someone other than the suspect. In strict terms, the LR refers to support for competing hypotheses about speaker identity, namely the prosecution hypothesis that the suspect is the speaker versus the defense hypothesis that someone other than the suspect produced the questioned sample. While we are supportive of this approach in principle, the fact remains that the background population data needed to make such calculations are simply not available for the great majority of the very large set of features that might be analyzed in a given case (French et al. 2010).

Whichever comparative approach is undertaken, there is an asymmetry in terms of the strength of conclusions that are drawn (Nolan 2001). Negative conclusions can, in general, be drawn more robustly than positive ones. This is because it is possible to observe differences between samples that cannot reasonably be explained away with reference to principles of linguistics or phonetics, and thus point to different speakers being involved. For example, we have encountered cases in which the suspect's regional accent of English is totally different from that in the disputed material (e.g. Welsh/Liverpool, African/Caribbean), and with no reason to suspect vocal disguise. In another case the suspect was a middle-aged heroin addict with pathological voice features (including very low pitch, and harsh and creaky phonation) but the disputed sample was spoken by her 5-year old daughter. These are extreme cases, but similar negative conclusions may also be drawn on the basis of inexplicable inconsistencies in vowel or consonant patterns, for instance. By contrast, consistency between samples does not indicate speaker identity, since all vocal features overlap between individuals. The strongest positive conclusions might include features that indicate some sort of speech pathology (e.g. stutter) combined with an unusual accent, and extreme f0 measurements or unusual voice quality. Even in such cases, however, it cannot be established for certain that no other speaker exhibits such a combination of features.

For the majority of forensic phoneticians, the outcome of a speaker comparison analysis is an expression of opinion ranged on a scale of confidence. This principle is stated in the IAFPA Code of Practice. Categorical statements that the suspect is or is not the culprit are possible, but rare, and generally restricted to closed-set comparison tasks. These are cases where it can be established independently that the voice in question must belong to a small set of possible candidates. For example, if a covert recording is made in a vehicle, video surveillance may prove that only two or three individuals were present in the car at the time of the recording. In such cases it may be possible to establish beyond reasonable doubt that some candidates could not have uttered the material in question because of marked differences in vocal pitch, voice quality, or general dialect type, for example.

Conclusions expressed via likelihood ratios indicate the strength of the conclusion through the numerical values of the LR. By contrast, impressionistic statements are made with reference to an explicit scale of confidence. In the UK, a framework for expressing conclusions was agreed upon by almost all practitioners in 2006 (French and Harrison 2007). Potentially, this involves making two decisions: the first concerning consistency and the second concerning distinctiveness. The consistency decision has three possible outcomes:

- Consistent—the samples are consistent with having come from the same speaker;
- Not consistent—the samples are not consistent with having come from the same speaker;
- Neutral—in some cases, where for example there are insufficient data or conflicting indications, it may not be possible to arrive at a decision.

If the decision regarding consistency is a positive one, it might be expressed as follows: "I have found no differences between the known and questioned samples of a kind that would cause me to argue that the questioned speaker in the criminal recording is not Mr A. On the contrary, the voice and speech features that are present in that recording are consistent with those found in the interview recording of Mr A in all relevant respects."

In cases where there is a positive outcome in respect of consistency, the analyst takes the further step of assessing how distinctive or unusual the features common to the recordings may be. This assessment has a bearing on whether, and to what extent, the features found could be shared by other speakers. At present, UK practitioners express distinctiveness with reference to the following five-point scale:

(5) exceptionally distinctive—the possibility of this combination of features being shared by other speakers is considered to be remote;
(4) highly distinctive;
(3) distinctive;
(2) moderately distinctive;
(1) not distinctive.

In cases where the questioned samples are found to be inconsistent with having been produced by the suspect, eliminations may be expressed either categorically or as a matter of likelihood.

The issue of how conclusions should be expressed is a matter of continuing debate and we do not see the framework set out here as set in stone. Indeed, developments are in progress and it may well be that we shall presently move to the use of an LR approach, albeit a verbal impressionistic, rather than a numerical, one.

40.4 SUMMARY AND OUTLOOK

In this chapter we have attempted to provide a brief overview of the most widely used approach to speaker comparison. The field of forensic speech science is, however, a rapidly changing one. Methods advance in line with technological developments, and must also be tailored to particular judicial systems and to changes in legal precedent. We end by outlining a number of issues that we consider vital for the advancement of the field and which we anticipate will shape research in the coming years.

First, it remains to be seen to what extent a fully quantifiable LR approach can be established, especially for dialectally diverse languages like English (French et al. 2010). For such an approach to be forensically viable, adequate reference populations need to be assembled. This is no trivial matter given the range of features that might need to be analyzed in a given case, and the array of factors that need to be controlled in constructing a reference dataset. It is common practice at present to delimit reference populations via a small set of very broad demographic criteria such as general regional accent and speaker sex. It is well known in sociolinguistics, however, that some features of speech may vary in complex ways according to many other social and stylistic factors. The list is long, but includes age (defined in both social and biological terms), gender (as a social construct distinct from the biological property of sex), ethnicity, community of practice, speaking style, addressee, and conversational function (Foulkes 2010). Moreover, in languages with high dialectal diversity, like English, there may be dramatic differences in the distribution of (especially) consonant and vowel pronunciations, even in narrowly circumscribed locations. Reference data might also be controlled for factors other than social and stylistic ones. These include effects of the recording environment (e.g. use of various types of telephone, internet telephony, Lombard speech, the specific transmission medium) and short-term or long-term speaker effects (e.g. as a result of health problems, smoking, or use of intoxicants). It must also be borne in mind that reference data are likely to have a limited "shelf-life," since all languages undergo constant change. Key diagnostic features might not be adequately represented in an outdated dataset (Loakes 2006). More generally there is debate as to how, or indeed whether, reference populations can be tailored to particular cases.

Indeed, further research will continue to extend our understanding of the range of factors that exert significant effects on speech, voice, and language. We are only just beginning to conceptualize and model the full range of sources and parameters of variation, especially in the context of rapid changes in technology. Recent and ongoing work that explores some of these factors includes studies of distance from and orientation to microphones (Vermeulen 2009), technical effects of recording hardware (Gold 2009), effects of software types and settings on acoustic analysis (Harrison 2008), and the vocal effects of intoxicants such as heroin (Papp 2008).

An area likely to see significant development in the coming years is LADO—Language Analysis for the Determination of Origin (see Chapter 38). LADO is used as a component of asylum seeker cases, and can be considered a type of speaker profiling exercise. There has been considerable controversy about LADO in academic circles, among government agencies, and in the media (e.g. Fraser 2009; Cambier-Langeveld 2010b; Swiss Federal Office for Migration 2010; Travis 2003). At present, methods of analysis differ across LADO agencies, with no standard testing methods yet established. There is considerable dispute over who is most suitable to carry out this work, what professional qualifications and training are required, and the value of including trained native speakers in the process (e.g. Eriksson 2008). More generally there are calls for empirical investigation of both currently practiced methods, and also more generally into aspects of speech perception and speaker/dialect analysis that underpin identification of linguistic features (e.g. Fraser 2009). Phoneticians have only recently entered the LADO debate, but experimental work demonstrates the importance of phonetic/phonological analysis as a step in the analysis procedure (Foulkes and Wilson 2011).

The future will undoubtedly see further integration of automatic systems and traditional approaches. Here, though, it is unclear how to balance the relative contributions from speech technology and from phonetics/linguistics. It also appears that automatic systems are still some way from reaching the reliability required to handle typical forensic materials.

Finally, we should not forget that an essential part of a forensic analyst's job involves public relations work—articulating to courts, police forces, and the general public not just the analytical conclusions of casework but also the limitations of our methods and findings. As recorded speech becomes ever more frequently encountered as evidence, it is vital for the sake of justice that we counter the "CSI effect."[4]

[4] Thanks to Louisa Cawley, Natalie Fecher, Michael Jessen, Christin Kirchhübel, Richard Rhodes, Lisa Roberts, and Dominic Watt for helpful comments and discussions.

References

Abramovitch, Rona, Michele Peterson-Badali, and Meg Rohan (1995) Young People's Understanding and Assertion of their Rights to Silence and Legal Counsel, *Canadian Journal of Criminology* 37:1–18.

Adams, Karen L., and Daniel T. Brink (1990) *Perspectives on Official English: The Campaign for English as the Official Language of the USA*. Berlin: Mouton de Gruyter.

Adegbija, Efurosibina (1994) *Language Attitudes in Sub-Saharan Africa: A Sociolinguistic Overview*. Clevendon, Philadelphia, and Adelaide: Multilingual Matters.

Adekunle, Mobolaji A. (1990) Language in a Multicultural Context, in E. Nolue Emenanjo (ed.), *Multilingualism, Minority Languages and Language Policy in Nigeria*. Bendel State: Central Books, 239–47.

Adelsward, Viveka, Karin Arosson, and Linda Joensson (1987) The Unequal Distribution of Interactional Space: Dominance and Control in Courtroom Interaction, *Text* 7(4):313–46.

Adler, Mark (1991) Bamboozling the Public, *New Law Journal* 26 July. <www.adler.demon.co.uk/pub.htm> accessed August 25, 2011.

—— (1993) British Lawyers' Attitudes to Plain English, *Clarity* 28:29–41. <www.adler.demon.co.uk/pub.htm> accessed August 25, 2011.

—— (2007) *Clarity for Lawyers* (2nd edn). London: The Law Society.

—— (2008) In Support of Plain Law: An Answer to Francis Bennion, *The Loophole* August:15–35. <www.adler.demon.co.uk/pub.htm> accessed August 25, 2011.

—— (2010) Legalese and Plain Language, *The Loophole* January 2010:74 <www.opc.gov.au/calc/loophole.htm> accessed October 3, 2011.

—— (2011a). What is Plain Language (When There's More Than One Egg on the Wall)?, <www.adler.demon.co.uk/comment.htm> accessed October 3, 2011.

—— (2011b). Professionalizing Plain Language, <www.adler.demon.co.uk/comment.htm> accessed October 3, 2011.

—— (2013) Full Disclosure: The Truth, the Whole Truth, and Nothing but the Truth?, <www.adler.demon.co.uk/disclosure.htm> accessed January 31, 2015.

Adrey, Jean-Bernard (2005) Minority Language Rights Before and After the 2004 EU Enlargement: The Copenhagen Criteria in the Baltic States, *Journal of Multilingual and Multicultural Development* 26(5):453–68.

Ahmad, Khurshid (2005) Checking up and Looking in: Self-Plagiarism in Science and Technology. Unpublished Plenary Lecture, Language and the Law 2005: East Meets West, University of Lodz, September.

Ainsworth, Janet E. (1993) In a Different Register: The Pragmatics of Powerlessness in Police Interrogation, *Yale Law Journal* 103:259–322.

—— (2008) "You Have the Right to Remain Silent... But Only if You Ask for it Just So": The Role of Linguistic Ideology in American Police Interrogation Law, *International Journal of Speech, Language, and Law* 15:1–21.

Alba, Richard and Victor Nee (2003) *Remaking the American Mainstream: Assimilation and Contemporary Immigration*. Cambridge, MA: Harvard University Press.

Alcaraz Varó, Enrique and Brian Hughes (2002) *Legal Translation Explained*. Manchester: St. Jerome Publishing.

—— and —— (2007) *Diccionario de Términos Jurídicos Inglés-Español—A Dictionary of Legal Terms Spanish–English* (10th edn). Barcelona: Editorial Ariel.

Algra, Nikolaas Egbert (2000) *Oudfries Recht 800–1256*. Ljouwert: Fryske Akademy.

Allard, France (2005) Entre le droit civil et la common law: la propriété en quête de sens, in Jean-Claude Gémar and Nicholas Kasirer (eds), *Jurilinguistique: entre langues et droits [Jurilinguistics: Between Law and Language]*. Montreal and Brussels: Éditions Thémis, Bruylant, 217–18.

Alschuler, Albert W. (1996) A Peculiar Privilege in Historical Perspective: The Right to Remain Silent, *Michigan Law Review* 94:2625–67.

Alston, William P. (1967) Vagueness, in Paul Edwards (ed.), *The Encyclopedia of Philosophy*. New York: Macmillan, 218–21.

—— (2000) *Illocutionary Acts and Sentence Meaning*. Ithaca, NY: Cornell University Press.

Amano, N. and K. Kondo (eds) (1999) *Tango-Sinmitu-do [Familiarity of Words]*, NTT Database Series, Tokyo: Sanseido.

American Law Institute (1981) *Restatement of the Law: Contracts* (2nd edn). St. Paul, MN: American Law Institute Publishers.

Amsterdam, Anthony G. (1960) Void-for-Vagueness Doctrine in the Supreme Court, *University of Pennsylvania Law Review* 109:67–116.

Anderson, J. (2008) Just Semantics: The Lost Readings of the Americans with Disabilities Act, *Yale Law Journal* 117:992–1069.

Angermeyer, Philipp Sebastian (2006) "Speaking English or What?": Codeswitching and Interpreter Use in New York Small Claims Court. PhD dissertation, New York University.

Annis, Peter (1985) *Le bilinguisme judiciaire en Ontario: théorie et réalité*. Ottawa: Association des juristes d'expression française, 49–50.

Ansre, G. L. (1976) National Development and Language, Prologue to Language Policy Formulation and Implementation. 12th West African Language Congress, University of Ife, Ile-Ife.

Argamon, Shlomo, Casey Whitelaw, Paul Chase, Sobhan Raj Hota, Navendu Garg, and Shlomo Levitan (2007) Stylistic Text Classification Using Functional Lexical Features, *Journal of the American Society for Information Science and Technology* 58(6):802–21.

Armstrong, Sharon Lee, Lila Gleitman, and Henry Gleitman (1983) What Some Concepts Might Not Be, *Cognition* 13:263–308.

Arzoz, Xabier (2008) Introduction, in Xabier Arzoz (ed.), *Respecting Linguistic Diversity in the European Union*. Amsterdam: John Benjamins, 1–13.

Ash, Sharon (1988) Speaker Identification in Sociolinguistics and Criminal Law, in Kathleen Ferrara et al. (eds), *Linguistic Change and Contact. Proceedings of the 16th Annual Conference on New Ways of Analyzing Variation*. Austin, TX: University of Texas, 25–33.

Asmara Declaration (2000) *Against All Odds: African Languages and Literatures into the 21st Century*. Asmara, Eritrea (quoted in Ndhlovu 2008:142).

Asprey, Michèle M. (2003) *Plain Language for Lawyers* (3rd edn). NSW: The Federation Press.

Astington, Janet W. and David R. Olson (1987) Literacy and Schooling: Learning to Talk about Thought. Paper presented at the Annual Meeting of the American Educational Research Association, Washington, DC.

Atkinson, John M. and Paul Drew (1979) *Order in Court: The Organization of Verbal Interaction in Judicial Settings*. London: Macmillan.

Austin, John L. (1962) *How To Do Things with Words*. New York and London: Oxford University Press; Cambridge, MA: Harvard University Press.

—— (1971) Performative-Constative, in John Searle (ed.), *The Philosophy of Language*. Oxford: Oxford University Press.

Awonusi, Victor O. (2004) Cycles of Linguistic History: The Development of English in Nigeria, in A. B. K. Dadzie and S. Awonusi (eds), *Nigerian English: Influences and Characteristics*. Lagos: Concept Publications, 46–65.

Ayer, A. J. (1936) *Language, Truth, and Logic*. London: Gallancz.

Ayres, Ian (2008) Racial Profiling in L.A.: The Numbers Don't Lie, *Los Angeles Times*, October 23, A27.

Azar, Moshe (2007) Transforming Ambiguity into Vagueness in Legal Interpretation, in A. Wagner, D. Cao, and W. Werner (eds), *Interpretation, Law and the Construction of Meaning. Collected Papers on Legal Interpretation in Theory, Adjudication and Political Practice*. Dordrecht: Springer, 141–67.

Baayen, R. H. (2008) *Analyzing Linguistic Data: A Practical Introduction to Statistics Using R*. New York: Cambridge University Press.

Baird, Abigail A. and Jonathan A. Fugelsang (2004) The Emergence of Consequential Thought: Evidence from Neuroscience, *The Royal Society* 359:1797–804.

Baker, Gordon (1997) Preface, in F. Waismann, *The Principles of Linguistic Philosophy* (2nd edn, Rom Harré, ed.) London: Macmillan.

Baker, John Hamilton (1990) *Manual of Law French* (2nd edn). Aldershot: Scolar Press.

Baker, Tom, Alon Harel, and Tamar Kugler (2004) The Virtues of Uncertainty in Law: An Experimental Approach, *Iowa Law Review* 89:433–94.

Baldwin, John and J. Peter French (1990) *Forensic Phonetics*. London: Pinter.

Balkin, Jack M. (2007) Abortion and Original Meaning, *Constitutional Commentary* 24.

Balteiro, Isabel and Miguel Angel Campos-Pardillos (2010) A Comparative Study of Latinisms in Court Opinions in the United States and Spain, *International Journal of Speech Language and the Law* 17:95–118.

Baltisberger, Eric and Priska Hubbuch (2010) LADO with Specialized Linguists: The Development of Lingua's Working Method, in K. Zwaan, P. Muysken, and M. Verrips (eds), *Language and Origin. The Role of Language in European Asylum Procedures: A Linguistic and Legal Survey*. Nijmegen: Wolf Legal Publishers, 9–19.

Bamgbose, Ayọ (1991) *Language and the Nation: The Language Question in Sub-Saharan Africa*. Edinburgh: Edinburgh University Press.

—— (2000) *Language and Exclusion: The Consequences of Language Policies in Africa*. Hamburg, London: LIT VERLAG Münster.

Bar, Christian von, Eric Clive, Hans Schulte-Nölke, et al. (eds) (2009) *Principles, Definitions and Model Rules of European Private Law. Draft Common Frame of Reference (DCFR) Interim Outline Edition*. Munich: Sellier.

Barbour, Stephen (1998) Reflections on Nationalism and Language, *Current Issues in Language & Society* 5(3):194–8.

Barnes, Annette (1988) *On Interpretation: A Critical Analysis*. Oxford: Basil Blackwell.

Baron, Dennis (1990) *The English-Only Question: An Official Language for Americans?* New Haven: Yale University Press.

Baron, Irene (2003) Diversité linguistique et cultures juridiques: les langues constituent-elles un obstacle à l'integration européenne?, *Copenhagen Studies in Language* 29:153–66.

Barsky, Robert F. (1994) *Constructing a Productive Other: Discourse Theory and the Convention Refugee Hearing.* Amsterdam/Philadelphia: John Benjamins.

——(2000) *Arguing and Justifying: Assessing the Convention Refugees' Choice of Moment, Motive and Host Country.* Aldershot, UK; Burlington, VT: Ashgate.

Bartholomeus, Bonnie (1973) Voice Identification by Nursery School Children, *Canadian Journal of Psychology* 27:464–72.

Bascuas, Ricardo J. (2007) Fourth Amendment Lessons from the Highway and the Subway: A Principled Approach to Suspicionless Searches, *Rutgers Law Journal* 38:719–91.

Bastarache, Michel (ed.) (2004) *Language Rights in Canada* (2nd edn). Cowansville, Québec: Éditions Yvon Blais.

——and Andrée Boudreau Ouellet (1993) Droits linguistiques et culturels des Acadiens et des Acadiennes de 1713 à nos jours, in J. Daigle (ed.), *L'Acadie des Maritimes.* Moncton: Chaire d'études acadiennes, 386–7.

——et al. (2008) *The Law of Bilingual Interpretation.* Markham, Ontario: LexisNexis Canada.

Baugh, John (2000) Racial Identification by Speech, *American Speech* 75:362–4.

Beardsmore, H. Baetens (1980) Bilingualism in Belgium, *Journal of Multilingual and Multicultural Development* 1(2):145–54.

Beaupré, Michael (1986) *Interpreting Bilingual Legislation.* Toronto: Carswell.

Beebe, Barton (2006) A Defense of the New Federal Trademark Antidilution Law, *Fordham Intellectual Property Media & Entertainment Law Journal* 16:1143–74.

Bellamy, Richard (1999) *Liberalism and Pluralism: Towards a Politics of Compromise.* London: Routledge.

Benedikter, Thomas (2006) *Legal Instruments of Minority Protection in Europe—An Overview.* Bolzano/Bozen: EURAC <www.gfbv.it/3dossier/eu-min/autonomy-eu.html> accessed August 25, 2009.

——(ed.) (2008) *Europe's Ethnic Mosaic: A Short Guide to Minority Rights in Europe.* Bozen/ Bolzano: EURAC Research. Online at: <www.eurac.edu/NR/rdonlyres/51B280EF-2EA8-4DFA-AC78-85AA5705244F/0/EuropesEthnicMosaic_FINAL_ for_website.pdf> accessed October 12, 2009.

Bengoetxea, Joxerramon (1993) *The Legal Reasoning of the European Court of Justice: Towards a European Jurisprudence.* Oxford: Clarendon Press; New York: Oxford University Press.

—— Neil MacCormick, and Leonor Moral Soriano (2001) Integration and Integrity in the Legal Reasoning of the European Court of Justice, in Gráomme De Búrca and J. H. H. Weiler (eds), *The European Court of Justice.* Oxford: Oxford University Press.

Benmaman, Virginia (1997) Legal Interpreting by Any Other Name is Still Legal Interpreting, in Silvana E. Carr, Rhoda Roberts, Aideen Dufour, and Dini Steyn (eds), *The Critical Link: Interpreters in the Community.* Amsterdam/Philadelphia: John Benjamins, 179–90.

Bennett, Robert W. (2003) *Talking It Through: Puzzles of American Democracy.* Ithaca, NY: Cornell University Press.

——(2006) *Taming the Electoral College.* Stanford, CA: Stanford University Press.

Bennion, Francis (2007) Confusion Over Plain Language Law, *The Commonwealth Lawyer* 16:63–8.

Bentham, Jeremy (1988) *A Fragment on Government: The New Authoritative Edition by J. H. Burns and H. L. A. Hart.* Cambridge: Cambridge University Press.

Berger, Raoul (1977) *Government by Judiciary*. Cambridge, MA: Harvard University Press.

Berk-Seligson, Susan (1990, 2002) *The Bilingual Courtroom: Court Interpreters in the Judicial Process*. Chicago: The University of Chicago Press.

—— (1999) The Impact of Court Interpreting on the Coerciveness of Leading Questions, *Forensic Linguistics: The International Journal of Speech, Language and the Law* 6:30–56.

—— (2000) Interpreting for the Police: Issues in Pre-trial Phases of the Judicial Process, *Forensic Linguistics* 7(2):212–37.

—— (2005) Language and the Law: Court Interpretation, in Dennis Kurzon and John Gibbons (eds), issue on Language and the Law, in the *Encyclopedia of Language and Linguistics* (2nd edn). Oxford: Elsevier.

—— (2009) *Coerced Confessions: The Discourse of Bilingual Police Interrogations*. Berlin/New York: Mouton de Gruyter.

Berry, Brewton (1968) *The Education of the American Indians: A Survey of the Literature*. Columbus, OH: Ohio State University Press.

Beswick, Jaine E. (2007) *Regional Nationalism in Spain: Language Use and Ethnic Identity in Galicia*. Clevedon: Multilingual Matters.

Beveridge, Barbara (2002) Legal English—How it Developed and Why It is Not Appropriate for International Commercial Contracts, in H. Mattila (ed.), *The Development of Legal Language*. Helsinki: Talentum Media, 55–79.

Bhatia, Vijay K. (1983) *An Applied Discourse Analysis of English Legislative Writing*. Birmingham: University of Aston.

—— (1987) Textual-mapping in British Legislative Writing, *World Englishes* 6(1):1–10.

—— (1993) *Analysing Genre: Language Use in Professional Settings*. New York: Longman.

Biber, Douglas, Stig Johansson, Geoffrey Leech, Susan Conrad, and Edward Finegan (1999) *Longman Grammar of Spoken and Written English*. Harlow: Pearson Education Ltd.

Bird, Stephanie J. (2002) Self-Plagiarism and Dual Redundant Publications: What is the Problem? Commentary on "Seven Ways to Plagiarize: Handling Real Allegations of Research Misconduct", *Science and Engineering Ethics* 8:543–4.

Bix, Brian H. (1993) *Law, Language and Legal Determinacy*. Oxford: Clarendon Press.

—— (2003) Can Theories of Meaning and Reference Solve the Problem of Legal Determinacy?, *Ratio Juris* 16:281–95.

—— (2005) Cautions and Caveats for the Application of Wittgenstein to Legal Theory, in J. K. Campbell, M. O'Rourke, and D. Shier (eds), *Topics in Contemporary Philosophy*. Cambridge, MA: MIT Press.

—— (2010) Defeasibility and Open Texture, in J. Ferrer Beltran and G. Ratti (eds), *Essays on Legal Defeasibility*. Oxford: Oxford University Press.

Black's Law Dictionary (2014) (10th edn). ed. Brian A. Garner. St. Paul, MN: West Publishing Company. (Page numbers in Chapter 3 relate to 1999 edition.)

Blackett, Tom (1998) *Trademarks*. London: Macmillan.

Blatchford, H. and P. Foulkes (2006) Identification of Voices in Shouting, *International Journal of Speech, Language and the Law* 13:241–54.

Blommaert, Jan (2009) Language, Asylum and the National Order, *Current Anthropology* 50(4):415–41.

Bobbitt, Philip (1991) *Constitutional Interpretation*. Oxford: Basil Blackwell.

Bolt, Richard H., Franklin S. Cooper, Edward E. David, Peter B. Denes, James M. Pickett, and Kenneth N. Stevens (1973) Speaker Identification by Speech Spectrograms: Some Further Observations, *Journal of the Acoustical Society of America* 54:531–4.

Borgsmidt, Kirsten (1988) The Advocate General at the European ECL: A Comparative Study, *European Law Review* 3:106–19.

Bork, Robert H. (1971) Neutral Principles and Some First Amendment Problems, *Indiana Law Journal* 47:1–35.

Bornstein, Brian H. (1995) Memory Processes in Elderly Eyewitnesses: What We Know and What We Don't Know, *Behavioral Sciences and the Law* 13:337–48.

Borris, Christian (1994) Common Law and Civil Law: Fundamental Differences and their Impact on Arbitration, *Arbitration* 60(2):78–85.

Boudreau, Cheryl, Arthur Lupia, Mathew D. McCubbins, and Daniel B. Rodriguez (2007) What Statutes Mean: Interpretive Lessons from Positive Theories of Communication and Legislation, *San Diego Law Review* 44: 957–92.

Brannigan, Augustine and Michael Lynch (1987) On Bearing False Witness: Credibility as an Interactional Accomplishment, *Journal of Contemporary Ethnography* 16:115–46.

Braselmann, Petra D. E. (1991) Der Richter als Linguist. Linguistische Überlegungen zu Sprachproblemen in Urteilen des Europäischen Gerichtshofes, *Sprache und Literatur in Wissenschaft und Unterricht* 22(2):68–85.

Braun, Angelika (1995) Fundamental Frequency: How Speaker-Specific is It? *Studies in Forensic Phonetics* (BEIPHOL 64):9–23.

—— and Hermann Künzel (1998) Is Forensic Speaker Identification Unethical—Or Can It Be Unethical *Not* To Do It? *Forensic Linguistics* 5:10–21.

Brazil, Jeff and Steve Berry (1992) Color of Driver is Key to Stops in 1-95 Video, *Orlando Sentinel Tribune* August 23:Al.

Bredimas, Anna (1978) *Methods of Interpretation and Community Law.* Amsterdam, New York, Oxford: North-Holland Publishing Company.

Brennan, Mary and Richard Brown (2004) *Equality before the Law: Deaf People's Access to Justice.* Durham: Deaf Studies Research Unit, University of Durham.

Brennan, Michael and Rachel Greenstadt (2009) Practical Attacks against Author Recognition Techniques. Paper at IAAI, Pasadena, CA.

Breyer, Stephen (2005) *Active Liberty: Interpreting our Democratic Constitution.* New York: Knopf.

Bricker, Peter D. and Sandra Pruzansky (1966) Effects of Stimulus Content and Duration on Talker Identification, *Journal of the Acoustical Society of America* 40:1441–9.

Brière, Eugène J. (1978) Limited English Speakers and the *Miranda* Rights. *TESOL Quarterly* 12(3):235–45.

Brink, David O. (1988) Legal Theory, Legal Interpretation, and Judicial Review, *Philosophy & Public Affairs* 17:105–48.

—— (1989a) Legal Positivism and Natural Law Theory Reconsidered, Again, *Canadian Journal of Law and Jurisprudence* 2:171–4.

—— (1989b) Semantics and Legal Interpretation (Further Thoughts), *Canadian Journal of Law and Jurisprudence* 2:181–91.

—— (2001) Legal Interpretation, Objectivity, and Morality, in Brian Leiter (ed.), *Objectivity in Law and Morals.* Cambridge: Cambridge University Press.

Broeders, A. P. A. (2010) Decision-Making in LADO: A View from the Forensic Arena, in Karin Zwaan, Pieter Muysken, and Maaike Verrips (eds), *Language and Origin. The Role of Language in European Asylum Procedures: A Linguistic and Legal Survey.* Nijmegen: Wolf Legal Publishers.

Broeders, T. and T. Rietveld (1995) Speaker Identification by Earwitnesses, in Angi Braun and
    J.-P. Köster (eds), *Studies in Forensic Linguistics*. Trier: Wissenschaftlicher Verlag.

Brown, Gillian and George Yule (1983) *Discourse Analysis*. Cambridge: Cambridge University
    Press.

Brown, L. Neville and Tom Kennedy (2000) *The Court of Justice of the European Communities*
    (5th edn). London: Sweet & Maxwell.

Brown, Penelope and Stephen Levinson (1978a) *Politeness*. Cambridge: Cambridge
    University Press.

—— and —— (1978b) Universals in Language Usage: Politeness Phenomena, in Esther
    N. Goody (eds), *Questions and Politeness: Strategies in Social Interaction*. Cambridge:
    Cambridge University Press.

Brown-Blake, Celia Nadine and Paul Chambers (2007) The Jamaican Creole Speaker in the
    UK Criminal Justice System, *The International Journal of Speech, Language and the Law*
    14:269–94.

Buccieri, M. Elaine (2004) Cause of Action for Trademark Infringement under the Lanham
    Act, *Causes of Action Second Series* 10, 501 (electronically distributed by Thomason Reuteus/
    Westlaw without subsequent page references).

Bull, Ray and Brian R. Clifford (1984) Earwitness Voice Recognition Accuracy, in G. L. Wells
    and E. F. Loftus (eds), *Eyewitness Testimony: Psychological Perspectives*. New York: Cambridge
    University Press.

—— and —— (1999) Earwitness Testimony, in Anthony Heaton-Armstrong, Eric Shepherd,
    and David Wolchover (eds), *Analysing Witness Testimony*. London: Blackstone Press.

——, Harriet Rathborn, and Brian R. Clifford (1983) The Voice Recognition Accuracy of Blind
    Listeners, *Perception* 12:223–6.

Burge, Tyler (1979) Individualism and the Mental, *Midwest Studies in Philosophy* 4: 73–122.

Burgins, Scott (1995) Jurors Ignore, Misunderstand Instructions, *American Bar Association
    Journal* May: 30, 31.

Burr, Isolde and Tito Gallas (2004) Zur Textproduktion im Gemeinschaftsrecht, in Friedrich Müller
    and Isolde Burr (eds), *Rechtssprache Europas. Reflexionen der Praxis von Sprache und
    Mehrsprachigkeit im supranationalen Recht*. Berlin: Duncker & Humblot, 195–242.

Butt, Peter and Richard Castle (2006) *Modern Legal Drafting* (2nd edn). Cambridge: Cambridge
    University Press.

Butters, Ronald R. (2008a) A Linguistic Look at Trademark Dilution, *Santa Clara Computer
    and High-Technology Law Journal* 24:101–13.

—— (2008b) Trademarks and Other Proprietary Terms, in John Gibbons and Teresa Turrell
    (eds), *Dimensions of Forensic Linguistics*. Amsterdam: John Benjamins, 231–47.

—— (2009) The Forensic Linguist's Professional Credentials, *International Journal of Speech,
    Language and the Law* 16(2):237–52.

—— (2010) Trademarks: Language that One Owns, in Malcolm Coulthard and Alison Johnson
    (eds), *The Routledge Handbook of Forensic Linguistics*. London: Routledge.

Byrne, Catherine and Paul Foulkes (2004) The Mobile Phone Effect on Vowel Formants.
    International Journal of Speech, Language and the Law 11:83–102.

Cabanellas, Guillermo and Luis Alcalá-Zamora y Castillo (2003) *Diccionario enciclopédico de
    derecho usual* (28th edn). Buenos Aires: Editorial Heliasta.

Calabresi, Guido (1982) *A Common Law for the Age of Statutes*. Cambridge, MA: Harvard
    University Press.

Calster, Geert van (1997) The EU's Tower of Babel—The Interpretation by the European Court of Justice of Equally Authentic Texts Drafted in More Than One Official Language, *Yearbook of European Law* 17:363–93.

Camayd-Freixas, Erik (2008) Statement at the U.S. District Court for the Northern District of Iowa Regarding a Hearing on "Arrest, Prosecution, and Conviction of 297 Undocumented Workers in Postville, Iowa, from May 12 to 22, 2008" before the Subcommittee on Immigration, Citizenship, Refugees, Border Security and International Law; <http://judiciary.house.gov/hearings/pdf/Camayd-Freixas080724.pdf> accessed August 20, 2011.

Cambier-Langeveld, Tina (2010a) The Validity of Language Analysis in the Netherlands, in Karin Zwaan, Pieter Muysken, and Maaike Verrips (eds), *Language and Origin. The Role of Language in European Asylum Procedures: A Linguistic and Legal Survey.* Nijmegen: Wolf Legal Publishers, 21–33.

—— (2010b) The Role of Linguists and Native Speakers in Language Analysis for the Determination of Speaker Origin, *International Journal of Speech, Language and the Law* 17:67–93.

Cameron, Deborah (2000) Styling the Worker: Gender and the Commodification of Language in the Globalised Service Economy, *Journal of Sociolinguistics* 4:323–47.

Campbell, Joseph P. (1997) Speaker Recognition: A Tutorial, *Proceedings of the IEEE* 85:1437–62.

Cao, Deborah (2004) *Chinese Law: A Language Perspective.* Aldershot: Ashgate Publishing.

—— (2007a) Inter-lingual Uncertainty in Bilingual and Multilingual Law, *Journal of Pragmatics* 39:69–83.

—— (2007b) *Translating Law.* Clevedon: Multilingual Matters.

—— and Xingmin Zhao (2008) Translation at the United Nations as Specialised Translation, *JoSTrans*:39–54.

Capotorti, Francesco (1979, 1991) *Study of the Rights of Persons Belonging to Ethnic, Religious and Linguistic Minorities.* New York: United Nations.

Cardozo, B. N. (1921) *The Nature of the Judicial Process.* New Haven, CT: Yale University Press.

Carlen, Pat (1976) *Magistrates' Justice.* London: Martin Robertson.

Carterette, E. C. and A. Barneby (1975) Recognition Memory for Voices, in E. Cohen and G. Nottebohn (eds), *Structure and Processes in Speech Perception.* New York: Springer.

Cassell, Paul G. (1996) *Miranda's* Social Costs: An Empirical Reassessment, *Northwestern University Law Review* 90:387–499.

Cate, Fred H. and Newton N. Minow (1993) Communicating with Juries, *Indiana Law Journal* 68:1101–18.

Cauffman, Elizabeth and Laurence Steinberg (2000) (Im)maturity of Judgment in Adolescence: Why Adolescents May Be Less Culpable than Adults, *Behavioral Sciences and the Law* 18:741–60.

CCH Macquarie Dictionary of Law (1996) North Ryde (NSW, Australia): CCH.

Chafe, Wallace L. (1985) Some Reasons for Hesitating, in Deborah Tannen and Muriel Saville-Troike (eds), *Perspectives on Silence.* Norwood, NJ: Ablex Publishing.

Chambers, J. K. (2009) *Sociolinguistic Theory.* Oxford: Blackwell.

——, P. Trudgill, and N. Schilling-Estes (eds) (2002) *The Handbook of Language Variation and Change.* Oxford: Blackwell.

Chaski, Carole E. (1997) Who Wrote It? Steps Toward a Science of Authorship Identification, *National Institute of Justice Journal* September. Also available through

National Criminal Justice Reference Service; <http://www.ncjrs.org NCJ 184604> accessed August 20, 2011.

—— (1998) *A Daubert-Inspired Assessment of Current Techniques for Language-Based Author Identification.* ILE Technical Report 1098. Also available through National Criminal Justice Reference Service; <http://www.ncjrs.org NCJ 172234> accessed August 20, 2011.

—— (2001) Empirical Evaluation of Language-Based Author Identification Techniques, *International Journal of Speech, Language and the Law* 8(1):1–65.

—— (2005) Who's at the Keyboard? Authorship Attribution in Digital Evidence Investigations, *International Journal of Digital Evidence* 4(1); <http://www.ijde.org> accessed August 25, 2011.

—— (2007a) Multilingual Forensic Author Identification Through N-Gram Analysis, International Association of Forensic Linguists 8, Seattle, WA, July.

—— (2007b) Empirically Testing the Uniqueness of Aggregated Stylemarkers, Panel on Authorship Attribution. International Association of Forensic Linguists 8, Seattle, WA, July.

—— (2007c) The Keyboard Dilemma and Author Identification, in Sujeet Shinoi and Philip Craiger (eds), *Advances in Digital Forensics III.* New York: Springer.

—— (2008) The Computational-Linguistic Approach to Forensic Authorship Attribution, in Frances Olsen, Alexander Lorz, and Dieter Stein (eds), *Law and Language: Theory and Practice.* Düsseldorf: Düsseldorf University Press.

—— (2009) Validation Testing for FLASH ID on the Chaski Writer Sample Database, with Mark A. Walch. Questioned Documents Section. American Academy of Forensic Sciences Annual Meeting, Denver, CO.

—— (2012) *Language As Evidence: Computational Forensic Linguistic Methods* (forthcoming). Lanham, MD: University Press of America.

Chomsky, Carol (2000) Unlocking the Mysteries of Holy Trinity: Spirit, Letter, and History in Statutory Interpretation. *Columbia Law Review* 100:901–56.

Chomsky, Noam (1965) *Aspects of the Theory of Syntax.* Cambridge, MA: MIT Press.

Chon, Margaret (1995) On the Need for Asian American Narratives in Law: Ethnic Specimens, Native Informants, Storytelling, and Silences, *Asian Pacific American Law Journal* 3:4–32.

Christensen, Ralph and Michael Sokolowski (2002) Wie normativ ist Sprache? Der Richter zwischen Sprechautomat und Sprachgesetzgeber, in U. Haß-Zumkehr (ed.), *Sprache und Recht.* Berlin, New York: de Gruyter, 64–79.

Christianson, Sven-Åke (1992) Emotional Stress and Eyewitness Memory: A Critical Review, *Psychological Bulletin* 112:284–309.

Churchill, Ward (1997) *A Little Matter of Genocide. Holocaust and the Denial in the Americas 1492 to the Present.* San Francisco: City Lights Books.

Cialdini, Robert A. (2008) *Influence: Science and Practice* (5th edn). Upper Saddle River, NJ: Pearson.

Clair, Nancy (1994) Informed Choices: Articulating Assumptions Behind Programs for Language Minority Students, *ERIC/CLL News Bulletin* 18:1.

Clare, Isobel C. H., Gisli H. Gudjonsson, and Philippe Harari (1998) Understanding of the Current Police Caution (England and Wales), *Journal of Community and Applied Social Psychology* 8:323–9.

Clayman, Steven E. (1992) Footing in the Achievement of Neutrality: The Case of News-Interview Discourse, in P. Drew and J. Heritage (eds), *Talk at Work: Interaction in Institutional Settings.* Cambridge: Cambridge University Press, 163–98.

Clifford, B. R. (1980) Voice Identification by Human Listeners: On Earwitness Reliability, *Law and Human Behavior* 4:373–94.

—— (1983) Memory for Voices: The Feasibility and Quality of Earwitness Evidence, in S. M. A. Lloyd-Bostock and B. R. Clifford (eds), *Evaluating Witness Evidence*. Chichester: Wiley.

—— (1997) A Comparison of Adults' and Children's Face and Voice Identification. Paper Presented at the 5th European Congress of Psychology, July 6–11. Dublin, Ireland (cited in Bull and Clifford (1999)).

—— and R. Toplis (1996) A Comparison of Adults' and Children's Witnessing Abilities, in N. Clark and G. Stephenson (eds), *Investigative and Forensic Decision Making: Issues in Criminological and Legal Psychology*. Leicester: British Psychological Society.

—— Harriet Rathborn, and Ray Bull (1981) The Effects of Delay on Voice Recognition Accuracy, *Law and Human Behavior* 5:201–08.

Cobarrubias, J. (1983) Ethical in Status Planning, in J. Cobarrubias and J. A. Fishman (eds), *Progress in Language Planning: International Perspectives*. The Hague: Mouton Press.

Cobb, Nancy J., David N. Lawrence, and Nancy D. Nelson (1979) Report on Blind Subjects' Tactile and Auditory Recognition for Environmental Stimuli, *Perceptual and Motor Skills* 48:363–6.

Cocozza, Joseph J. and Kathleen Skowyra (2000) Youth with Mental Health Disorders: Issues and Emerging Responses, *Juvenile Justice* 7:3–13.

Colin, Joan and Ruth Morris (1996) *Interpreters and the Legal Process*. Winchester: Waterside Press.

Colwell, Lori H., Keith R. Cruise, Laura S. Guy, Wendy K. McCoy, Krissie Fernandez, and Heather H. Ross (2005) The Influence of Psychological Maturity on Male Juvenile Offenders' Comprehension and Understanding of the *Miranda* Warning, *Journal of the American Academy of Psychiatry and Law* 33:444–54.

Conklin, Nancy Faires and Margaret A. Lourie (1983) *A Host of Tongues: Language Communities in the United States*. New York: Free Press.

Conley, John M. and William M. O'Barr (1990) *Rules versus Relationships: The Ethnography of Legal Discourse*. Chicago and London: University of Chicago Press.

—— and —— (1998) *Just Words: Law, Language, and Power*. Chicago: University of Chicago Press.

Connolly, Andrew C., Jerry A. Fodor, Lila R. Gleitman, and Henry Gleitman (2007) Why Stereotypes Don't Even Make Good Defaults, *Cognition* 103:1–22.

Connor, Jacqueline (2004) Jurors Need to Have Their Own Copies of Instructions, *Los Angeles Daily Journal*, February 25, p. 7.

Constantinesco, Léontin-Jean (1974) *Traité de Droit Comparé*. Paris: Librairie générale.

Coode, George (1845) *On Legislative Expression, or the Language of Written Law*. London: William Benning and Co.; also <http://books.google.com/books>.

Cook, Susan and John Wilding (1997) Earwitness Testimony: Never Mind the Variety, Hear the Length, *Applied Cognitive Psychology* 92:617–29.

Cooke, David J. and Lorraine Philip (1998) Comprehending the Scottish Caution: Do Offenders Understand Their Right to Remain Silent?, *Legal and Criminological Psychology* 3:13–27.

Cooke, Michael (1996) A Different Story: Narrative versus "Question and Answer" in Aboriginal Evidence, *Forensic Linguistics* 3(2):273–88.

Cooper, Virginia G. and Patricia A. Zapf (2007) Psychiatric Patients' Comprehension of *Miranda* Rights, *Law and Human Behavior* 32:390–405.

Corbin, Arthur (1952) *Corbin on Contracts.* St. Paul, MN: West Publishing Co.

Corcoran, Christine (2004) A Critical Examination of the Use of Language Analysis Interviews in Asylum Proceedings: A Case Study of a West African Seeking Asylum in the Netherlands, *International Journal of Speech, Language & the Law* 11(2):200–21.

CORI (Country of Origin Research and Information) (2010) Challenges and Commonalities in Providing Objective Evidence for Refugee Status Determination. University of Westminster, 10–11 June 2010. Conference programme and report. <www.cori.org.uk> accessed October 5, 2011.

Cornu, Gérard (2005) *Linguistique juridique* (3rd edn). Paris: Montchrestien (2nd edn 2000).

—— (2007) *Vocabulaire juridique* (8th edn). Paris: PUF.

Côté, Pierre-André (2000) *The Interpretation of Legislation in Canada* (3rd ed). Scarborough, Ontario: Carswell.

—— (2005) La tension entre l'intelligibilité et l'uniformité dans l'interprétation des lois plurilingues, in Jean-Claude Gémar and Nicholas Kasirer (eds), *Jurilinguistique: entre langues et droits [Jurilinguistics: Between Law and Language]*, Montreal and Brussels, Édition Thémis, Bruylant, 129.

Cotterill, Janet (2000) Reading the Rights: A Cautionary Tale of Comprehension and Comprehensibility, *Forensic Linguistics* 7(1):4–25.

—— (2003) *Language and Power in Court: A Linguistic Analysis of the O.J. Simpson Trial,* Houndmills and New York: Palgrave Macmillan.

—— (2005) "You Do Not Have to Say Anything..." Instructing the Jury on the Defendant's Right to Silence in the English Criminal Justice System, *Multilingua* 24:7–24.

Coulthard, Malcolm (1994) Forensic Discourse Analysis, in Malcolm Coulthard (ed.), *Advances in Written Text Analysis.* London: Routledge, 242–58.

—— (2004) Author Identification, Idiolect and Linguistic Uniqueness, *Applied Linguistics* 25:431–47.

—— and Alison Johnson (2007) *An Introduction to Forensic Linguistics: Language in Evidence.* London/New York: Routledge.

—— and —— (2010) *Routledge Handbook of Forensic Linguistics.* London/New York: Routledge.

—— Tim Grant, and Krzysztof Kredens (2010) Forensic Linguistics, in Ruth Wodak, B. Johnstone, and P. Kerswill (eds), *Handbook of Applied Linguistics.* Thousand Oaks, CA and London: SAGE Publications, 529–44.

Council of Europe (1992) *European Charter for Regional or Minority Languages.* Strasbourg: Council of Europe. ETS 148. <www.coe.int/t/dg4/education/minlang/default_en.asp> accessed August 18, 2009.

—— (1995) *Framework Convention for the Protection of National Minorities.* Strasbourg: Council of Europe, ETS 157. <www.coe.int/minorities> accessed August 18, 2009.

Covington, Martin V. and Carol L. Omelich (1987) "I Knew It Cold before the Exam": A Test of the Anxiety-Blockage Hypothesis, *Journal of Educational Psychology* 79:393–400.

Craith, M. N. (2003) Facilitating or Generating Linguistic Diversity. The European Charter for Regional or Minority Languages, in Gabrielle Hogan-Brun and Stefan Wolff (eds), *Minority Languages in Europe. Frameworks, Status, Prospects.* Hampshire: Palgrave Macmillan, 56–72.

Crawford, James (1992) *Hold Your Tongue: Bilingualism and the Politics of "English Only."* Reading, MA: Addison Wesley Publishing Co.

—— (1995) *Bilingual Education: History, Politics, Theory, and Practice* (3rd edn). Los Angeles: Bilingual Educational Services, Inc.

Creifelds, Carl (2014) *Rechtswörterbuch*. 21. Aufl. München: Beck.

Crooker, Constance Emerson (1996) *The Art of Legal Interpretation: A Guide for Court Interpreters*. Portland, OR: Continuing Education Press, Portland State University.

Crystal, David and Derek Davy (1969) *Investigating English Style*. London: Longman.

Culwin, Fintan and Mike Child (2010) Optimising and Automating the Choice of Search Strings when Investigating Possible Plagiarism, *Proceedings of the 4th International Plagiarism Conference, Newcastle UK, 21–23 June 2010*; <http://www.plagiarismadvice.org/conference/previous-plagiarism-conferences/4th-plagiarism-conference-2010> accessed August 25, 2011.

Cutler, Anne (1982) The Reliability of Speech Error Data, in Anne Cutler (ed.), *Slips of the Tongue and Language Production*. The Hague: Mouton, 561–82.

Cutts, Martin (1996) *The Plain English Guide*. Oxford: Oxford University Press.

Damaška, Mirian R. (1997) *Evidence Law Adrift*. New Haven, CT: Yale University Press.

Danet, Brenda (1980) Language in the Legal Process, *Law and Society* 14(3):445–564.

Dann, B. Michael and George Logan III (1996) Jury Reform: The Arizona Experience, *Judicature* 79:280–86.

Das Gupta, Jyotirindra (1968) Language Diversity and National Development, in Fishman et al. (eds), *Language Problems of Developing Nations*. London: Wiley and Sons, 17–26.

Dattu, Firoz (1998) Illustrated Jury Instructions: A Proposal, *Law & Psychology Review* 22:67–102.

David, René and Brierley, John (1985) *Major Legal Systems in the World Today* (3rd edn). London: Stevens (1st edn 1978).

Davidson, Ronald A. (2005) Analysis of the Complexity of Writing Used in Accounting Textbooks over the Past 100 Years, *Accounting Education: An International Journal* 14:53–74.

Davies, Patricia L. and James D. Rose (1999) Assessment of Cognitive Development in Adolescents by Means of Neuropsychological Tasks, *Developmental Neuropsychology* 15:227–48.

Davis, Abbe D., Dixie D. Sanger, and Mary Morris-Friehe (1991) Language Skills of Delinquent and Nondelinquent Adolescent Males, *Journal of Communication Disorders* 24:251–66.

Davis, Deborah (2008) Selling Confession: The Interrogator, the Con Man, and Their Weapons of Influence. *Wisconsin Defender* 16(1):1–16.

—— (2010) Lies, *Damned* Lies, and the Path from Police Interrogation to Wrongful Conviction. In M. H. Gonzales, C. Tavris, and J. Aronson (eds), *The Scientist and the Humanist: A Festschrift in Honor of Elliot Aronson*. New York: Psychology Press, 211–47.

—— William C. Follette, and Richard A. Leo (2007) Effects of Interrogation Tactics on Recommendation of False Confession for the Innocent. Paper presented at The Interrogations and Confessions, El Paso, TX, September.

—— and Richard Leo (2006) Strategies for Prevention of False Confessions, in Mark R. Kebbell and Graham M. Davies (eds), *Practical Psychology for Forensic Investigations and Prosecutions*. New York: John Wiley, 121–50.

—— Richard A. Leo, and W. C. Follette (2008) Recommending False Confession for the Innocent. Paper presented at the American Psychology-Law Society.

—— Richard A. Leo, D. Knaack, and D. A. Bailey (2006) Sympathetic Detectives with Time Limited Offers: Effects on Perceived Consequences of Confession. Paper presented at the Association for Psychological Science.

—— and William T. O'Donohue (2004) The Road to Perdition: Extreme Influence Tactics in the Interrogation Room. In William T. O'Donohue and Eric R. Levensky (eds), *Handbook of Forensic Psychology*. New York: Elsevier, Academic Press, 897–996).

—— T. Weaver, and Richard A. Leo (2007) Effects of Failed Polygraph Results on Perceived Wisdom of True and False Confessions. Paper presented at the American Psychological Association, San Francisco, August.

Davis, Daniel (1996) The Reliability of Speech Error Data. Trademark Law: Linguistic Issues, *Language and Communication* 16(3):255–62.

Davis, Tom (1996) Clues and Opinions: Ways of Looking at Evidence, in Hannes Kniffka, Malcolm Coulthard, and Susan Blackwell (eds), *Recent Developments in Forensic Linguistics*, Frankfurt: Peter Lang, 53–73.

de Figueiredo, Ricardo Molina and Helena de Souza Britto (1996) A Report on the Acoustic Effects of One Type of Disguise, *Forensic Linguistics* 3:168.

de Groot, Gerard-René (1992) Recht, Rechtssprache und Rechtssystem, *Terminologie et traduction*, 3:279–316.

—— (1999) Das Übersetzen juristischer Terminologie, in Gerard-René de Groot and Reiner Schulze (Hrsg), *Recht und Übersetzen*. Baden-Baden: Nomos, 11–47.

—— (2006) Legal Translation, in Jan M. Smits (ed.), *Elgar Encyclopedia of Comparative Law*. Cheltenham, UK and Northampton, MA: Edward Elgar, 423–33.

—— and Conrad van Laer (2008) The Quality of Legal Dictionaries: An Assessment, *Maastricht Working Papers. Faculty of Law* 2008/6 (available online).

de Groot-van Leeuwen, Leny E. (2006) Merit Selection and Diversity in the Dutch Judiciary, in Kate Malleson and Peter H. Russell (eds), *Appointing Judges in an Age of Judicial Power: Critical Perspectives from around the World*. Toronto: University of Toronto Press, 145–58.

de Morgan, Sophia Elizabeth (ed.) (1882) *Memoir of Augustus de Morgan by His Wife Sophia Elizabeth de Morgan with Selections from His Letters*. London: Longman's Green and Co.

De Pablo, M. (2001) City Police to Provide Custody Suites Copies for Blind and Partially Sighted; <http://www.cityoflondon.police.uk/CityPolice/Media/News/NewsArchive/2001/ blindprisoners.htm>, accessed March 21, 2010.

de Varennes, Fernand (1996) *Language, Minorities and Human Rights*. The Hague, Boston, London: Martinus Nijhoff.

—— (1997) *To Speak or Not to Speak: The Rights of Persons Belonging to Linguistic Minorities*; <http://www.unesco.org/most/ln2pol3.htm> accessed August 25, 2011.

—— (2000) Tolerance and Inclusion: The Convergence of Human Rights and the Work of Tove Skutnabb-Kangas, in Robert Phillipson (ed.), *Rights to Language. Equity, Power and Education*. Mahwah, NJ and London: Lawrence Erlbaum Associates, 67–71.

—— (2008) International Law and Education in a Minority Language, in Stephen May and Nancy Hornberger (eds), *Language Policy and Political Issues in Education*, Volume 1, *Encyclopedia of Language and Education* (2nd edn). New York: Springer, 121–35.

—— (2009) Language Rights Standards in Europe: The Impact of the Council of Europe's Human Rights and Treaty Obligations, in Susanna Pertot, Tom M. S. Priestly, and Colin H. Williams (eds), *Rights, Promotion and Integration Issues for Minority Languages in Europe*. Basingstoke: Palgrave Macmillan, 23–31.

Del Valle, Sandra (2003) *Language Rights and the Law in the United States. Finding Our Voices*. Clevedon: Multilingual Matters.

Delvaux, Louis (1956) *La Cour de Justice de la Communauté Européenne du Charbon et de l'Acier*. Gembloux: J. Duculot.

Derlén, Mattias (2009) *Multilingual Interpretation of European Union Law*. Austin, Boston, Chicago, New York; The Netherlands: Wolters Kluwer.

Devenport, Jennifer L., Christina A. Studebaker, and Steven D. Penrod (1999) Perspectives on Jury Decision-Making, in Francis T. Durso (ed.), *Handbook of Applied Cognition*. Chichester: Wiley.

Devine, Dennis J., Laura D. Clayton, Bejamin B. Dunford, Rasmy Seying, and Jennifer Pryce (2001) Jury Decision Making: 45 Years of Empirical Research on Deliberating Groups, *Psychology, Public Policy, and Law* 7(5):622–727.

Dickerson, F. Reed (1965) *The Fundamentals of Legal Drafting*. Boston: Little Brown.

Domijan-Arneri, Michaela (2009) Problems in Multilingual Litigation—A Practical Perspective, in S. Šarčević (ed.), *Legal Language in Action: Translation, Terminology, Drafting and Procedural Issues*. Zagreb: Globus, 345–60.

Donahue, John J. III (1998) Did *Miranda* Diminish Police Effectiveness?, *Stanford Law Review* 50:147–80.

Doty, Nathan Daniel (1998) The Influence of Nationality on the Accuracy of Face and Voice Recognition, *American Journal of Psychology* 111:191–214.

Drew, Paul (1992) Contested Evidence in Courtroom Cross-examination: The Case of a Trial for Rape, in Paul Drew and John Heritage (eds), *Talk at Work: Interaction in Institutional Settings*. Cambridge: Cambridge University Press, 470–520.

——(1985) Analyzing the Use of Language in Courtroom Interaction, in T. Van Dijk (ed.), *Handbook of Discourse Analysis, Vol. 3*. Amsterdam: North-Holland, 133–48.

Driedger, E. A. (1982) Legislative Drafting Style: Civil Law versus Common Law, in Jean-Claude Gémar (ed.), *Langage du droit et traduction/The Language of the Law and Translation*, Montreal: Linguatech/Conseil de la Langue Française, 63–81.

DuBay, William H. (2004) The Principles of Readability. Costa Mesa, CA: Impact Information; <http://www.impactinformation.com/impactinfo/readability02.pdf> accessed June 1, 2009.

Dunbar, Robert (2001) Minority Language Rights in International Law, *International and Comparative Law Quarterly* 50:90–120.

——(2008) Definitively Interpreting the European Charter for Regional or Minority Languages: The Legal Challenges, in Robert Dunbar, G. Parry, and S. Klinge (eds), *The European Charter for Regional or Minority Languages: Legal Challenges and Opportunities*. Strasbourg: Council of Europe Publishing, 37–61.

——and Tove Skutnabb-Kangas (2008) Forms of Education of Indigenous Children as Crimes Against Humanity? Expert paper written for the United Nations Permanent Forum on Indigenous Issues (PFII). New York: PFII. In the PFII system: Presented by Lars-Anders Baer, in collaboration with Robert Dunbar, Tove Skutnabb-Kangas, and Ole Henrik Magga; <http://www.un.org/esa/socdev/unpfii/documents/E_C19_2008_7.pdf> accessed August 25, 2011.

Dunivant, Noel (1982) *The Relationship between Learning Disabilities and Juvenile Delinquency*. Williamsburg, VA: National Center for State Courts.

Dunstan, R. (1980) Context for Coercion: Analyzing Properties of Courtroom Questions, *British Journal of Law and Society* 7:61–7.

Dworkin, Ronald (1977) *Taking Rights Seriously*. Cambridge, MA: Harvard University Press.

——(1985a) Is There Really No Right Answer in Hard Cases?, in Ronald Dworkin (ed.), *A Matter of Principle*. Cambridge, MA: Harvard University Press, 119–45.

——(ed.) (1985b) *A Matter of Principle*. Cambridge, MA: Harvard University Press.

—— (1986) *Law's Empire*. Cambridge, MA: Harvard University Press.

—— (2006) *Justice in Robes*. Cambridge, MA: Harvard University Press.

Dyer, Wynde (2008) Just Text Me: The Preliminary Results of a Text Message Corpus Compilation Pilot Project. Paper presented at the Fourth International Conference on Technology, Knowledge and Society 2008, Northeastern University, Boston.

Eades, Diana (1997) Language in Court: The Acceptance of Linguistic Evidence about Indigenous Australians in the Criminal Justice System, *Australian Aboriginal Studies* 1:15–27.

—— (2005) Applied Linguistics and Language Analysis in Asylum Seeker Cases, *Applied Linguistics* 26(4):503–26.

—— (2009) Testing the Claims of Asylum Seekers: The Role of Language Analysis, *Language Assessment Quarterly* 6:30–40.

—— (2010) Guidelines from Linguists for LADO, in Karin Zwaan, Pieter Muysken, and Maaike Verrips (eds), *Language and Origin. The Role of Language in European Asylum Procedures: A Linguistic and Legal Survey*. Nijmegen: Wolf Legal Publishers, 35–41.

Eagleson, Robert (1985/1987) Article in the *Sydney Morning Herald* 20 January 1985, quoted in *Plain English and the Law*: A Report by the Law Reform Commission of Victoria (Australia).

Easton, Susan (1998) *The Case for the Right to Silence*. Aldershot: Ashgate Publishing.

Eckert, Penelope and Sally McConnell-Ginet (2003) *Language and Gender*. Cambridge: Cambridge University Press.

Ehrlich, Susan (2001) *Representing Rape*. London: Routledge.

Eisenberg, Theodore and Martin T. Wells (1993) Deadly Confusion: Juror Instructions in Capital Cases, *Cornell Law Review* 79:1–17.

Elaad, Eitan, Sima Segev, and Yishai Tobin (1998) Long-Term Working Memory in Voice Identification, *Psychology, Crime & Law* 4:73–88.

Elias, Penelope K., Merrill F. Elias, Ralph B. D'Agostino, Halit Silbershatz, and Philip A. Wolf (1999) Alcohol Consumption and Cognitive Performance in the Framingham Heart Study, *American Journal of Epidemiology* 150:580–89.

Elias, Stephen and Richard Stim (2004) *Patent, Copyright, and Trademark: An Intellectual Property Desk Reference* (7th edn). Berkeley, CA: Nolo.

Ellis, Stanley (1990) "It's Rather Serious…" Early Speaker Identification, in Hannes Kniffka (ed.), *Texte zu Theorie und Praxis Forensischer Linguistik*. Tübingen: Max Niemeyer Verlag, 515–21.

—— (1994) The Yorkshire Ripper Enquiry: Part 1, *Forensic Linguistics* 1:197–206.

Elwork, Amiram, Bruce D. Sales, and James J. Alfini (1977) Juridic Decisions: In Ignorance of the Law or in Light of It?, *Law & Human Behavior* 1:163–89.

Emenanjo, E. Nolue (ed.) (1990) *Multilingualism Minority Languages and Language Policy in Nigeria*. Agbor: Central Books Ltd.

Emery, Erin (2002) The Jury That Couldn't: Scenes from a Mistrial in Teller County, *Denver Post*, July 3:1A.

Endicott, Timothy (2000) *Vagueness in Law*. Oxford and New York: Oxford University Press.

—— (2002) *Law and Language: The Stanford Encyclopaedia of Philosophy*. (Winter Edition) <http://plato.stanford.edu/archives/fall2010/entries/law-language> accessed October 11, 2011.

—— (2005) The Value of Vagueness, in Vijay K. Bhatia (ed.), *Vagueness in Normative Texts*. Bern: Lang.

Engberg, Jan (2004) Statutory Texts as Instances of Language(s): Consequences and Limitations on Interpretation, *Brooklyn Journal of International Law* 29(3):1135–66.

—— (2009) Individual Conceptual Structure and Legal Experts' Efficient Communication, *International Journal for the Semiotics of Law* 22(2):223–43.

Ephratt, Michael (2008) The Functions of Silence, *Journal of Pragmatics* 40:1909–38.

Eriksson, Anders (2005) Forensic Phonetics. Paper presented at Interspeech (9th European Conference on Speech Communication and Technology), Lisbon, Portugal; <http://www.ling.gu.se/~jonas/forensic/Eriksson_tutorial_paper.pdf> accessed August 23, 2010.

—— (2008) Guidelines? What Guidelines? Paper presented at the IAFPA Conference, Lausanne, Switzerland.

Eskridge, William N. (1990) The New Textualism, *UCLA Law Review* 37:621–91.

—— (1994) *Dynamic Statutory Interpretation.* Cambridge, MA: Harvard University Press.

Eskridge, William N., Jr., Philip P. Frickey, and Elizabeth Garrett (2006) *Legislation and Statutory Interpretation* (2nd edn). New York: Foundation Press.

Eurobarometer (2005) Europeans and Languages, Special Eurobarometer 237—Wave 63.4. European Commission; <http://ec.europa.eu/public_opinion/archives/ebs/ebs_237.en.pdf> accessed August 24, 2011.

European Commission (2008) Communication from the Commission to the European Parliament, the Council, the European Economic and Social Committee and the Committee of the Regions. Multilingualism: An Asset for Europe and a Shared Commitment. Brussel 18.09.2008 COM(2008) 566 final; <http://ec.europa.eu/education/languages/pdf/com/2008_0566_en.pdf> accessed September 1, 2009.

Extra, Guus and Durk Gorter (2008) The Constellation of Languages in Europe, in Guus Extra and Durk Gorter (eds), *Multilingual Europe: Facts and Policies.* Berlin: Mouton de Gruyter, 3–61.

Fadden, Lorna (2007) Quantitative and Qualitative Analyses of Police Interviews with Canadian Aborginal and Non-Aboriginal Suspects, in Krzysztof Kredens, Stanisław Goźdź-Roszkowski (eds), *Language and the Law: International Outlooks.* Frankfurt am Main: Peter Lang, 305–22.

Feeney, Floyd (2000) Police Clearances: A Poor Way to Measure the Impact of *Miranda* on the Police, *Rutgers Law Review* 32:1–114.

Fenner, Susanne, Isable C. H. Clare, and Gisli Gudjonsson (2002) Understanding of the Current Police Caution (England and Wales) among Suspects in Police Detention, *Journal of Community and Applied Social Psychology* 12:83–93.

Ferguson, Bruce A. and Alan C. Douglas (1970) A Study of Juvenile Waiver, *San Diego Law Review* 7:39–54.

Ferreri, Silvia (2006) Communicating in an International Context, in Barbara Pozzo and Valentina Jacometti (eds), *Multilingualism and the Harmonisation of European Law.* Alphen aan den Rijn: Kluwer Law International, 33–44.

Finegan, Edward (1982) Form and Function in Testament Language, in Robert J. DiPietro (ed.), *Linguistics and the Professions.* Norwood, NJ: Ablex, 113–20.

Fishman, Joshua A. (1991) *Reversing Language Shift. Theoretical and Empirical Assistance to Threatened Languages.* Clevedon: Multilingual Matters.

Flege, James Emil (1984) The Detection of French Accent by American Listeners, *Journal of the Acoustical Society of America* 76:692–707.

Flesch, Rudolf (1950) Measuring the Level of Abstraction, *Journal of Applied Psychology* 32:221–33.

Foley, Regina M. (2001) Academic Characteristics of Incarcerated Youth and Correctional Educational Programs, *Journal of Emotional and Behavioral Disorders* 9:248–59.

Follette, William C., Deborah Davis, Richard A. Leo (2007) Mental Health Status and Vulnerability to Interrogative Influence, *Criminal Justice* 22:42–9.

Forston, Robert F. (1975) Sense and Non-Sense: Jury Trial Communication, *Brigham Young University Law Review* 1975:601–37.

Foulkes, Paul (2010) Exploring Social-Indexical Knowledge: A Long Past but a Short History, *Laboratory Phonology* 1:5–39.

——— and Anthony Baron (2000) Telephone Speaker Recognition Amongst Members of a Close Social Network, *Forensic Linguistics* 7:181–98.

——— and Kim Wilson (2011) Language Analysis for the Determination of Origin: An Empirical Study, in *Proceedings of the 17th International Congress of Phonetic Sciences*. Hong Kong, 691–4. <http://www.icphs2011.hk/resources/OnlineProceedings/RegularSession/Foulkes/Foulkes.pdf>

Fraassen, Bas van (1970) Rejoinder: On a Kantian Conception of Language, in Robert M. Martin (ed.), *The Paradox of the Liar*. New Haven, CT: Yale University Press, 59–66.

Franklin, Benjamin (1753) Letter to Peter Collinson (May 9, 1753), in Leonard W. Labaree and Whitfield J. Bell (eds), *The Papers of Benjamin Franklin*, vol. 4. New Haven, CT: Yale University Press (1961).

Fraser, Bruce (1998) Threatening Revisited, *Forensic Linguistics* 5:159–73.

Fraser, Helen (2009) The Role of "Educated Native Speakers" in Providing Language Analysis for the Determination of the Origin of Asylum Seekers, *International Journal of Speech, Language and the Law* 16:113–38.

——— (2011a, in press) Language Analysis for the Determination of Origin (LADO), in C. A. Chapelle (ed.), *Encyclopedia of Applied Linguistics*. Wiley-Blackwell.

——— (2011b) The role of Linguists and Native Speakers in Language Analysis for the Determination of Origin. A Response to Tina Cambier-Langeveld. To appear in *International Journal of Speech, Language and the Law* 18.

Frege, Gottlob (1964) *The Basic Laws of Arithmetic. Exposition of the System*. Berkeley, CA: University of California Press.

French, J. Peter (1994) An Overview of Forensic Phonetics with Particular Reference to Speaker Identification, *Forensic Linguistics* 1:169–81.

——— and Philip Harrison (2007) Position Statement Concerning Use of Impressionistic Likelihood Terms in Forensic Speaker Comparison Cases, *International Journal of Speech, Language and the Law* 14:137–44.

——— ——— and Jack Windsor Lewis (2006) R -v- John Samuel Humble: The Yorkshire Ripper Hoaxer Trial, *International Journal of Speech, Language and the Law* 13:255–73.

——— Francis Nolan, Paul Foulkes, Philip Harrison, and Kirsty McDougall (2010) The UK Position Statement on Forensic Speaker Comparison: A Rejoinder to Rose and Morrison, *International Journal of Speech, Language and the Law* 17:143–52.

Fromme, Kim, Elizabeth Katz, and Elizabeth D'Amico (1997) Effects of Alcohol Intoxication on the Perceived Consequence of Risk Taking, *Experimental and Clinical Psychopharmacology* 5:14–23.

Frowein, Jochen Abr., Rainer Hofmann, and Stefan Oeter (eds) (1994/1995) *Das Minderheitenrecht europäischer Staaten*. Teil 1. Teil 2. Beiträge zum ausländischem öffentlichem Recht und Völkerrecht. Band 108/109. Berlin: Springer-Verlag.

Gadamer, Hans-Georg (1960) *Wahrheit und Methode. Grundzüge einer wissenschaftlichen Hermeneutik*. Tübingen: Mohr.

Gaines, Jane M. (1991) *Contested Culture: The Image, the Voice, and the Law*. Chapel Hil, NC: University of North Carolina Press.

Gaines, Philip (2002) Negotiating Power at the Bench: Informal Talk in Sidebar Sessions, *Forensic Linguistics: The International Journal of Speech, Language, and the Law* 9(2):213–34.

Gal, Kinga (2000) The Council of Europe Framework Convention for the Protection of National Minorities and its Impact on Central and Eastern Europe, *JEMIE—Journal of Ethnopolitics and Minority Issues in Europe* Winter:1–17.

Gal, Susan (1991) Between Speech and Silence: The Problematics of Research on Gender and Language, in Micaela Di Leonardo (ed.), *Gender at the Crossroads of Knowledge: Feminist Anthropology in the Postmodern Era*. Berkeley, CA: University of California Press.

—— (2001) Language, Gender, and Power: An Anthropological Review, in Alessandro Duranti (ed.), *Linguistic Anthropology: A Reader*. Malden, MA: Blackwell.

Gales, T. (2010) Threat Level High: A Corpus-driven Approach to Authorial Intent in Threatening Communications, Unpublished PhD dissertation, University of California, Davis.

Gallie, Walter B. (1956) Essentially Contested Concepts, *Proceedings of the Aristotellian Society* 56:167–98.

Garcia, Monique and Ray Long (2008) Study Sees Racial Bias in Traffic-Stop Searches, *Chicago Tribune*, July 25:1.

García, Ofelia, Tove Skutnabb-Kangas, and María Torres-Guzmán (eds) (2006) *Imagining Multilingual Schools. Languages in Education and Globalization*. Clevedon, Buffalo, and Toronto: Multilingual Matters.

Garner, Bryan (2011) *A Dictionary of Modern Legal Usage* (3rd edn). New York: Oxford University Press.

Gémar, Jean-Claude (ed.) (1982) *Langage du droit et traduction*. Montréal: Linguatech et Conseil de la langue française.

—— (1995) *Traduire ou l'art d'interpréter, Langue, droit et société: éléments de jurilinguistique*, vol. 2: *Application—Traduire le texte juridique*. Sainte-Foy: Presses de l'Université du Québec.

—— (2006) What Legal Translation Is and Is Not—Within or Outside the EU, in Barbara Pozzo and Valentina Jacometti (eds), *Multilingualism and the Harmonisation of European Law*. Alphen aan den Rijn: Kluwer Law International, 69–77.

Gerven, W. van (2004). The ECJ Case-Law as a Means of Unification of Private Law?, in Arthur Hartkamp, Martijn Hesselink, Ewoud Hondius, Carla Joustra, Edgar du Perron, and Muriel Veldman (eds), *Towards a European Civil Code* (3rd edn). The Hague: Kluwer Law International, 101–24.

Gibbons, John (1990) Applied Linguistics in Court, *Applied Linguistics* 11:229–37.

—— (2001) Revising the Language of New South Wales Police Procedures: Applied Linguistics in Action, *Applied Linguistics* 22:439–69.

—— (2003) *Forensic Linguistics: An Introduction to Language in the Justice System*. Oxford: Blackwell.

—— (ed.) (1994) *Language and the Law*. Harlow: Longman.

Giedd, Jay N., Jonathan Blumenthal, Neal O. Jeffries, F. X. Castellanos, Liu Hong, Alex Zijdenbos, Tomas Paus, Alan C. Evans, and Judith L. Rapoport (1999) Brain Development During Childhood and Adolescence: A Longitudinal MRI Study, *Nature* 2:861–3.

Giles, S. Howard and Richard Y. Bourhis (1982) A Reply to a Note on Voice and Racial Categorization in Britain, *Social Behavior and Personality* 10:249–51.

Gilson, Jerome and Ann Gilson Lalonde (1999) *Trademark Protection and Practice*. Cumulative Supplement Vols. 1 and 3. New York: Matthew Bender.

Godsey, M. A. (2006) Reformulating the *Miranda* Warnings in Light of Contemporary Law and Understandings, *Minnesota Law Review* 90:781–825.

Goffman, Erving (1979) *Forms of Talk*. Philadelphia: University of Pennsylvania Press.

—— (1981) Footing, in Erving Goffman, *Forms of Talk*. Oxford: Basil Blackwell, 124–59.

Goggin, Judith P., Charles P. Thompson, Gerhard Strube, and Liza R. Simental (1991) The Role of Language Familiarity in Voice Identification, *Memory and Cognition* 19:448–58.

Gogtay, Nitin, Alexandra Sporn, and Liv S. Clasen (2004) Comparison of Progressive Cortical Gray Matter Loss in Childhood-onset Schizophrenia with That in Childhood-onset Atypical Psychoses, *Archives of General Psychiatry* 61:17–22.

Gold, Erica (2009) The Effects of Video and Voice Recorders in Cellular Phones on Vowel Formants and Fundamental Frequency. MSc dissertation, University of York.

Gold, James M. and Philip D. Harvey (1993) Cognitive Deficits in Schizophrenia, *Psychiatric Clinics of North America* 16:295–312.

Goldman-Eisler, Frieda (1968) *Psycholinguistics*. London: Academic Press.

Goldstein, Alan M. and Naomi E. Sevin Goldstein (2010) *Best Practices in Evaluating Capacity to Waive Miranda Rights: Volume in Best Practices in Forensic Mental Health Assessment*. New York: Oxford University Press.

Goldstein, Naomi E. Sevin, Lois Oberlander Condie, Rachel Kalbeitzer, Douglas Osman, and Jessica L. Geier (2003) Juvenile Offenders' *Miranda* Rights Comprehension and Self-reported Likelihood of Offering False Confessions, *Assessment* 10:359–69.

——, Oluseyi Olubadewo, Richard E. Redding, and Frances J. Lexcen (2005) *Mental Health Disorders: The Neglected Risk Factor in Juvenile Delinquency*. New York: Oxford University Press.

——, Christina L. Riggs Romaine, Heather Zelle, R. Kalbeitzer, J. Serico, and L. Wrazien (2008) Juveniles' Comprehension of the *Miranda* Warnings in the 21st Century. Paper presented at the annual conference of the *American Psychology—Law Society*, Jacksonville, FL.

——, Heather Zelle, and Thomas Grisso (2010) *The Miranda Rights Comprehension Instruments—II*. Sarasota, FL: Professional Resource Press.

González, Roseann, Vicky Vásquez, and Holly Mikkelson (1991) *Fundamentals of Court Interpretation*. Durham, NC: Carolina Academic Press.

Good, Anthony (2004) "Undoubtedly an Expert"? Anthropologists in British Asylum Courts, *Journal of the Royal Anthropological Institute* 10:113–33.

Goodwin, Charles (1996) Professional Vision, *American Anthropologist* 96(3):606–33.

Gorter, Durk (2006) Minorities and Language, in Keith Brown (ed. in chief), *Encyclopedia of Language and Linguistics* (2nd edn) (ELL2). London: Elsevier, 156–9.

Gotti, Maurizio (2008) *Investigating Specialized Discourse*. Bern: Peter Lang.

—— (2009) Globalizing Trends in Legal Discourse, in Frances Olsen, Alexander Lorz, and Dieter Stein (eds), *Translation Issues in Language and Law*. Düsseldorf: Düsseldorf University Press.

Gotti, Maurizio and Šarčević, Susan (eds) (2006) *Insights into Specialized Translation*. Bern: Peter Lang.

Goźdź-Roszkowski, Stanisław (2011) *Patterns of Linguistic Variation in Legal English. A Corpus-based Study*, Frankfurt am Main: Peter Lang.

Grant, Tim (2010) Txt 4n6: Idiolect Free Authorship Analysis, in Malcolm Coulthard and Alison Johnson (eds), *Routledge Handbook of Forensic Linguistics*, London/New York: Routledge, 508–22.

Grant, Tim and Kevin Baker (2001) Identifying Reliable, Valid Markers of Authorship: A Response to Chaski, *International Journal of Speech Language and the Law* 8(1): 66–79.

Greenawalt, R. Kent (1992) The Right to Silence and Human Dignity, in Michael J. Meyer and William A. Parent (eds), *The Constitution of Rights: Human Dignity and American Values*. Ithaca, NY: Cornell University Press.

Grey, G. and G. A. Kopp (1944) Voiceprint Identification, *Bell Telephone Laboratories Report*:1–14.

Grice, H. P. (1969) Utterer's Meaning and Intention, *Philosophical Review* 78:147–77.

—— (1975) Logic and Conversation, in Peter Cole and Jerry L. Morgan (eds), *Syntax and Semantics 3: Speech Acts*. New York: Academic Press, 41–58.

—— (1989) *Studies in the Way of Words*. Cambridge, MA: Harvard University Press.

—— (1999) Logic and Conversation, in Adam Jaworski and Nikolas Coupland (eds), *The Discourse Reader*. London and New York: Routledge.

Grieve, Jack (2007) Quantitative Authorship Attribution: An Evaluation of Techniques, *Literary and Linguistic Computing* 22(3):251–70.

Grin, François (2003) *Language Policy Evaluation and the European Charter for Regional or Minority Languages*. London: Palgrave Macmillan.

—— (2008) The Economics of Language Education, in Stephen May and Nancy H. Hornberger (eds), *Language Policy and Political Issues in Education*, Volume 1. *Encyclopedia of Language and Education* (2nd edn). New York: Springer, 83–94.

—— and Tom Moring (2002) *Final Report: Support for Minority Languages in Europe*. Brussels: European Commission; <http://europa.eu.int/comm/education/policies/lang/languages/langmin/files/support.pdf> accessed April 3, 2009.

Grisso, Thomas (1981) *Juveniles' Waiver of Rights: Legal and Psychological Competence*. New York: Plenum Press.

—— (1997) The Competence of Adolescents as Trial Defendants, *Psychology, Public Policy, and Law* 3:3–32.

—— (1998) *Instruments for Assessing Understanding and Appreciation of Miranda Rights*. Sarasota, FL: Professional Resource Press.

—— (2002) *Evaluating Competencies: Forensic Assessment and Instruments* (2nd edn). New York: Springer.

—— Laurence Steinberg, Jennifer Wooldard, Elizabeth Cauffman, Elizabeth Scott, Sandra Graham, Fran Lexcen, N. Dickon Repucci, and Robert Schwartz (2003) Juveniles' Competence to Stand Trial: A Comparison of Adolescents' and Adults' Capacities as Trial Defendants, *Law and Human Behavior* 27:333–63.

Gudjonsson, G. and I. Clare (1994) The Proposed New Police Caution (England and Wales): How Easy Is It to Understand?, *Expert Evidence* 3:109–12.

Gudjonsson, Gisli H. and Krishna K. Singh (1984) Interrogative Suggestibility and Delinquent Boys: An Empirical Validation Study, *Personality and Individual Differences* 5:425–30.

Guo Chengwei (2001) *The Spirit of Chinese Legal Genealogy*. The Publishing House of China University of Political Sciences and Law.

Gustafsson, Marita (1975) *Some Syntactic Properties of English Law Language*. Publications of the Department of English, No. 4. Turku: University of Turku.

Habermas, Jürgen (1981) *Theorie des kommunikativen Handelns*. Frankfurt a.M.: Suhrkamp.

Hale, Sandra (2004) *The Discourse of Court Interpreting: Discourse Practices of the Law, the Witness and the Interpreter*. Amsterdam/Philadelphia: John Benjamins.

Hale, Sandra and John Gibbons (1999) Varying Realities: Patterned Changes in the Interpreter's Representation of Courtroom and External Realities, *Applied Linguistics* 20:203–20.

Hall, Jerome (1937) Nulla Poena Sine Lege, *Yale Law Journal* 47:165–93.

Haller, William and Godfrey Davies (1944) *The Leveller Tracts 1647–1653*. New York: Columbia University Press.

Halliday, Michael (1994) *Introduction to Functional Grammar* (2nd edn). London: Edward Arnold.

—— and Ruqaiya Hasan (1976) *Cohesion in English*. London: Longman.

Hammersley, Richard and J. Don Read (1985) The Effect of Participation in a Conversation on Recognition and Identification of the Speakers' Voices, *Law and Human Behavior* 9:71–81.

Hancher, Michael (1979) The Classification of Cooperative Illocutionary Acts, *Language in Society* 5.

Handelman, Jeffery A. (2008) *Guide to TTAB Practice*, Vol. 1. New York: Aspen Publishers.

Haney, Craig and Mona Lynch (1994) Comprehending Life and Death Matters: A Preliminary Study of California's Capital Penalty Instructions, *Law & Human Behavior* 18:411–36.

Hannaford-Agor, Paula L. and Stephanie N. Lassiter (2008) Contemporary Pattern Jury Instruction Committees: A Snapshot of Current Operations and Possible Future Directions 1. Paper prepared for National Pattern Jury Instructions Conference, April 17–18, 2008, Columbus, OH (unpublished paper, on file with author).

Hansen, Mark (2003) Learn How They Learn: Knowing Modes of Adult Education Helps Lawyers Create Successful Presentations, *American Bar Association Journal*: August 26.

Hare, Victoria C. and Denise A. Devine (1993) Topical Knowledge and Topical Interest Predictors of Listening Comprehension, *Journal of Educational Research* 76:157–60.

Harris, Richard. J. (1973) Answering Questions Containing Marked and Unmarked Adjectives and Adverbs, *Journal of Experimental Psychology* 97:399–401.

Harris, Sandra (1984) Questions as a Mode of Control in Magistrates' Courts, *International Journal of the Sociology of Language* 49:5–27.

—— (2001) Fragmented Narratives and Multiple Tellers: Witness and Defendant Accounts in Trials, *Discourse Studies* 3(1):53–74.

Harrison, Philip (2008) Formant Measurement Errors from Synthetic Speech, *Proceedings of the Institute of Acoustics* 30:638–45.

Hart, H. L. A. (1958) Positivism and the Separation of Law and Morals, *Harvard Law Review* 71:593–629.

—— (1994) *The Concept of Law* (2nd edn). Oxford: Clarendon Press.

Harvey, Malcolm (2005) Pardon My French: The Influence of French on Legal English, in Jean-Claude Gémar and Nicholas Kasirer (eds), *Jurilinguistique: entre langues et droits— Jurilinguistics: Between Law and Language*. Bruxelles & Montréal: Bruylant & Les Éditions Thémis, 261–75.

Hashtroudi, Shahin, Marcia K. Johnson, and Linda D. Chrosniak (1989) Aging and Source Monitoring, *Psychology and Aging* 4:106–12.

Haworth, Kate (2010) An Analysis of Police Interview Discourse and its Role(s) in the Judicial Process, Unpublished PhD dissertation, The University of Nottingham.

Heath, Shirley Brice (1981) English in Our Language Heritage, in Charles A. Ferguson and Shirley Brice Heath (eds), *Language in the USA*. Cambridge: Cambridge University Press.

Heffer, Chris (2005) *The Language of Jury Trial: A Corpus-aided Analysis of Legal-lay Discourse*. Basingstoke: Palgrave Macmillan.

Heijenoort, Jean van (1986) Frege and Vagueness, in Leila Haaparanta and Jaakko Hintikka (eds), *Frege Synthesized. Essays on the Philosophical and Foundational Work of Gottlob Frege*. Dordrecht; Boston, Hingham, MA: D. Reidel and Kluwer Academic Publishers, 31–45.

Heinrichs, R. Walter and Konstantine K. Zakzanis (1998) Neurocognitive Deficit in Schizophrenia: A Quantitative Review of the Evidence, *Neuropsychology* 12:426–45.

Helms, Jeffrey L. (2007) Analysis of the Components of the *Miranda* Warnings, *Journal of Forensic Psychology Practice* 7:59–76.

Hennes, Marc Scott (2007) Manipulating *Miranda*: *United States v. Frazier* and the Case-in-Chief Use of Post-Arrest, Pre-*Miranda* Silence, *Cornell Law Review* 92:1013–41.

Henrard, Kristin (2000) *Devising an Adequate System of Minority Protection: Individual Human Rights, Minority Rights and the Right to Self-Determination*. The Hague, Boston, London: Martinus Nijhoff Publishers.

—— and R. Dunbar (2008) *Synergies in Minority Protection: European and International Law Perspectives*. Cambridge: Cambridge University Press.

Hepworth, Mike and Brian S. Turner (1982) *Confession*. London: Routledge.

Herbst, Robert (2002) *Dictionary of Commercial, Financial and Legal Terms* (6th edn). Thun: Translegal.

Herget, James E. and Stephen Wallace (1987) The German Free Law Movement as the Source of American Legal Realism, *Virginia Law Review* 73:399–455.

Herrmann, Frank L. and Brownlow Speer (2007) Standing Mute at Arrest as Evidence of Guilt: The "Right to Silence" Under Attack, *American Journal of Criminal Law* 35:1–21.

Hesselink, Martijn W. (2001) *The New European Legal Culture*. Deventer: Kluwer.

Heuer, Larry and Steven D. Penrod (1989) Instructing Jurors: A Field Experiment with Written and Preliminary Instructions, *Law & Human Behavior* 13:409–30.

Heugh, Kathleen and Tove Skutnabb-Kangas (eds) (2010) *Multilingual Education Works*. Delhi: Orient BlackSwan.

Hewitt, William E. (1995) *Court Interpretation: Model Guides for Policy and Practice in the State Courts*. Williamsburg, VA: National Center for State Courts.

Heydon, Georgina (2007) When Silence Means Acceptance: Understanding the Right to Silence as a Linguistic Phenomenon, *Alternative Law Journal* 32:147–51.

Hill, Claire and Christopher King (2004) How Do German Contracts Do as Much with Fewer Words?, *Chicago-Kent Law Review* 79:889–926.

Hill, Kyall (2005) Legal English in Japan: A Translator's Perspective, *Clarity* 53(May):48–50.

Hiltunen, Risto (1984) The Type and Structure of Clausal Embedding in English, *Text* 4:107–21.

—— (2001) "Some Syntactic Properties of English Law Language": Twenty-five Years after Gustafsson (1975), in Risto Hiltunen, K. Battarbee, M. Peikola, and S.-K. Tanskanen (eds), *English in Zigs and Zags*. Anglicana Turkuensia 23:53–66. Turku: University of Turku.

Hinton, Leanne, Matt Vera, and Nancy Steele (2002) *How to Keep Your Language Alive: A Commonsense Approach to One-On-One Language Learning*. Berkeley, CA: Heyday Books.

Hirsch, Eric D., Jr. (1973) *Validity in Interpretation*. New Haven, CT: Yale University Press.

Hirson, Allen, J. Peter French, and David Howard (1995) Speech Fundamental Frequency over the Telephone and Face-to-Face: Some Implications for Forensic Phonetics, in J. Windsor Lewis (ed.), *Studies in General and English Phonetics*. London: Routledge, 230–40.

Hirst, Graeme and Olga Feiguina (2007) Bigrams of Syntactic Labels for Authorship Discrimination of Short Texts, *Literary and Linguistic Computing* 22(4):405–17.

Hjelmslev, Louis (1953) *Prolegomena to a Theory of Language*, translated by Francis Whitfield. Indiana University Publications in Anthropology and Linguistics, Memoir 7. Baltimore: Waverly Press.

Hoecke, Mark van (2002) *Law as Communication*. Oxford and Portland, OR: Hart.

Hoekstra, Ruth and Marijke Malsch (2003) The Principle of Open Justice in the Netherlands, in Peter. J. van Koppen and Steven D. Penrod (eds), *Adversarial versus Inquisitorial Justice: Psychological Perspectives on Criminal Justice Systems*. New York: Kluwer/Plenum, 333–46.

Hofstadter, Richard (1969) *The Idea of a Party System*. Berkeley, CA: University of California Press.

Hollien, Harry F. (1990) *The Acoustics of Crime*. New York: Plenum.

—— (2002) *Forensic Voice Identification*. New York: Academic Press.

—— and C. A. Martin (1996) Conducting Research on the Effects of Intoxication on Speech, *Forensic Linguistics* 3:107–28.

——, Wojciech Majewski, and E. Thomas Doherty (1982) Perceptual Identification of Voices Under Normal, Stress and Disguise Speaking Conditions, *Journal of Phonetics* 10:139–48.

—— J. A. Saletto, and S. K. Miller (1993) Psychological Stress in Voice: A New Approach, *Studia Phonetica Posnaniensia* 4:5–17.

Holtgraves, T. M. (2002) *Language as Social Action*. Mahwah, NJ: Erlbaum.

Home Office (1991) *Police and Criminal Evidence Act 1984 (s. 66) Codes of Practice*, (rev edn). London: HMSO.

—— (2008) *Police and Criminal Evidence Act Codes of Practice—Code C: Detention, Treatment and Questioning of Persons by Police Officers*. London: HMSO.

—— (2011) *Notice of Rights and Entitlements*. <http://www.homeoffice.gov.uk/police/rights-entitlements-foreign-la1> accessed October 9, 2011.

Hooker, Michael B. (1978) *Adat Law in Modern Indonesia*. Kuala Lumpur: Oxford University Press.

Hoopes, Rob (2003) Trampling *Miranda*: Interrogating Deaf Suspects, in C. Lucas (ed.), *Language and the Law in Deaf Communities*. Washington, DC: Gallaudet University Press, 21–59.

Hotta, Syûgo (2006) A Linguistic Exploration of Foreign Terms in Trademarks, in Ysolde Gendreau (ed.), *Intellectual Property: Bridging Aesthetics and Economics—Propriete intellectuelle: Entre l'art et l'argent*. Montreal: Editions Themis, 207–31.

—— (2007a) A Linguistic Exploration of Trademark Dilution, in M. Teresa Turell, Maria Spassova, and Jordi Cicres (eds), *Proceedings of the 2nd European IAFL Conference on Forensic Linguistics / Language and the Law*. Barcelona: Institut Universitari De Linguistica Aplicada, Universitat Pompeu Fabra.

—— (2007b) Morphosyntactic Structure of Japanese Trademarks and Their Distinctiveness: A New Model for Linguistic Analysis of Trademarks, *Language and the Law: International Outlooks*. The Lodz Studies in Language Series. Frankfurt am Main, Berlin, Bern, Bruxelles, New York, Oxford, Wien: Peter Lang Publishing Group, 379–92.

—— (2009) *Saiban to Kotoba no Chikara (Trials and Language Power)*. Tokyo: Hitsuji Shobo.

—— and Masahiro Fujita (2007) The Psycholinguistic Foundation of Trademarks: An Experimental Study, in M. Teresa Turell, Maria Spassova, and J. Cicres (eds), *Proceedings of the 2nd European IAFL Conference on Forensic Linguistics / Language and the Law*. Barcelona: Institut Universitari De Linguistica Aplicada, Universitat Pompeu Fabra, 173–8.

Hotta, Shûgo and Sachiko Shudo (2009) Hyougi ni okeru Saiban-kan ni yoru Gengo Koui (Speech Acts of Professional Judges in Deliberations). Paper read at the 11th Annual Meeting of the Pragmatics Society of Japan.

—— Takeshi Hashiuchi, and Masahiro Fujita (2008) Mogi Hyougi no Gengogakuteki Bunseki: Hasuwa no Chikara kara Mita Mogi Hyougi (Linguistic Analysis of Mock Trials: Mock Trial Viewed through Power of Utterances). Paper read at the 10th Annual Meeting of the Pragmatics Society of Japan.

Houck, Noel and Susan M. Gass (1997) Cross-cultural Backchannels in English Refusals: A Source of Trouble, in Adam Jaworski (ed.), *Silence: Interdisciplinary Perspectives*. Berlin: Mouton de Gruyter.

Hountondji, Paulin J. (2002) Knowledge Appropriation in a Post-Colonial Context, in Catherine A. Odora Hoppers (ed.), *Indigenous Knowledge and the Integration of Knowledge Systems. Towards a Philosophy of Articulation*. Claremont: New Africa Books, 23–38.

Howald, Blake Stephen (2008) Authorship Attribution Under the Rules of Evidence: Empirical Approaches—A Layperson's Legal System, *International Journal of Speech, Language, and the Law* 15(2):219–47.

Hudson, Toby, Gea de Jong, Kirsty McDougall, Philip Harrison, and Francis Nolan (2007) F0 Statistics for 100 Young Male Speakers of Standard Southern British English, *Proceedings of the 16th International Congress of Phonetic Sciences*, Saarbrücken 1809–12.

Huff, Ronald, Ayre Rattner, and Edward Sagarin (1986) Guilty Until Proven Innocent, *Crime and Delinquency* 32:518–44.

Human Rights Committee (2005) *Human Rights Fact Sheet* No. 15 (Rev. 1) *Civil and Political Rights*. Geneva: United Nations.

Humber, Eugénie and Pamela C. Snow (2001) The Oral Language Skills of Young Offenders: A Pilot Investigation, *Psychiatry, Psychology, and Law* 8:1–11.

Huss, Matthew T. and Kenneth A. Weaver (1996) Effect of Modality in Earwitness Identification: Memory for Verbal and Nonverbal Auditory Stimuli Presented in Two Contexts, *Journal of General Psychology* 123:277–87.

Hutton, Chris (2009) *Language, Meaning and the Law*. Edinburgh: Edinburgh University Press.

Hyde, Dominic (2008) *Vagueness, Logic and Ontology*. Aldershot: Ashgate.

Ilboudo, Paul Taryam and Norbert Nikièma (2010) Implementing a Multilingual Model of Education in Burkina Faso: Successes, Issues and Challenges, in Kathleen Heugh and Tove Skutnabb-Kangas (eds), *Multilingual Education Works*. Delhi: Orient BlackSwan.

Inbau, Fred Edward, John E. Reid, Joseph P. Buckley, and Brian C. Jayne (2001) *Criminal Interrogations and Confessions* (4th edn). Gaithersburg, MD: Aspen.

International Association for Forensic Phonetics and Acoustics (2009). Resolution: "Language and Determination of National Identity cases". <http://www.iafpa.net/langidres.htm> accessed 16 April 2013.

Jacquemet, Marco (2009) Transcribing Refugees: The Entextualization of Asylum Seekers' Hearings in a Transidiomatic Environment, *Text and Talk* 29(5):525–46.

Jakobson, Roman (1959) On Linguistic Aspects of Translation, in Reuben Arthur Brower (ed.), *On Translation*. Cambridge, MA: Harvard University Press, 232–39.

James, Neil (2009a) Defining the Profession: Placing Plain Language in the Field of Communication, *Clarity* 61(May):33–7.

—— (ed.) (2009b) *Professionalising Plain Language*. Sydney: Plain English Foundation.

Jaworski, Adam (1993) *The Power of Silence: Social and Pragmatic Perspectives*. Newbury Park, CA: Sage.

Jayne, Brian C. and Joseph Buckley (eds) (1999) *The Investigator Anthology: A Compilation of Articles and Essays about the Reid Technique of Interviewing and Interrogation.* Chicago: John E. Reid & Associates.

Jessen, Michael (2008) Forensic Phonetics, *Language and Linguistics Compass* 2:671–711.

Johannesen, Richard L. (1974) The Functions of Silence: A Plea for Communication Research, *Western Speech* 38:25–35.

Johnson, Alison and D. Woolls (2009) Who Wrote This: The Linguist as Detective, in Susan Hunston and David Oakey (eds), *Introducing Applied Linguistics.* London: Routledge, 111–18.

Johnson, Keith (1998) Readability; <http://www.timetabler.com> accessed June 1, 2009.

Johnson, Marcia K., Doreen M. De Leonardis, Shahim Hashtroudi, and Susan A. Ferguson (1995) Aging and Single Versus Multiple Cues in Source Monitoring, *Psychology and Aging* 10:507–17.

Jones, Natalie J. and Craig Bennell (2007) The Development and Validation of Statistical Prediction Rules for Discriminating between Genuine and Simulated Suicide Notes, *Archives of Suicide Research* 11:1–15.

Jónsson, Ólafur Páll (2009) Vagueness, Interpretation, and the Law, *Legal Theory* 15:193–214.

Joos, Martin (1961) *The Five Clocks.* New York: Harcourt, Brace and World.

Jörg, Nico, Stewart Field, and Chrisje Brandts (1995) Are Inquisitorial and Adversarial Systems Converging?, in Christopher Harding et al. (eds), *Criminal Justice in Europe. A Comparative Study.* Oxford: Clarendon Press, 41–56.

Judge, Anne (2000) France: "One State, one Nation, one Language?", in Stephen Barbour and Cathie Carmichael (eds), *Language and Nationalism in Europe.* Oxford: Oxford University Press, 44–82.

Juola, Patrick (2008) *Authorship Attribution* (Foundations and Trends in Information Retrieval). Delft: Now Publishers Inc.

—— (2009) JGAAP: A System for Comparative Evaluation of Authorship Attribution, *Journal of the Chicago DHCS Colloquium* (*JDHCS*) 1:1. Chicago: University of Chicago Division of Humanities.

—— and Shlomo Argoman (2008–11) NSF Award 0751087.

—— and R. H. Baayen (2005) A Controlled-Corpus Experiment in Authorship Identification by Cross-Entropy, *Literary and Linguistic Computing* 20(Suppl 1):59–67.

Kahn, Rachel, Patricia A. Zapf, and Virginia G. Cooper (2006) Readability of *Miranda* Warnings and Waivers: Implications for Evaluating *Miranda* Comprehension, *Law and Psychology Review* 30:119–42.

Kakuta, Masayoshi and Tatsumi Naohiko (2000) *Chiteki Zaisanho* (Intellectual Property Law). Tokyo: Yuhikaku Aruma.

Kalven, Harry, Jr. and Hans Zeisel (1966) *The American Jury.* Boston: Little Brown & Co.

Kambam, Praveen and Christopher Thompson (2009) The Development of Decision-Making Capacities in Children and Adolescents: Psychological and Neurological Perspectives and Their Implications for Juvenile Defendants, *Behavioral Sciences and the Law* 27:173–90.

Kamwendo, Gregory Hankoki (2006) No Easy Walk to Linguistic Freedom: A Critique of Language Planning During South Africa's Decade of Democracy, *Nordic Journal of African Studies* 15:53–70; also <http://www.njas.helsinki.fi/pdf-files/vol15num1/kamwendo3.pdf> accessed July 17, 2008.

Kaplan, Robert B. (ed.) (2002) *The Oxford Handbook of Applied Linguistics.* Oxford: Oxford University Press.

Karlsson, Fred (2007) Constraints on Multiple Center-Embedding of Clauses, *Journal of Linguistics* 43:365–92.

Kassin, Saul M., Richard A. Leo, Christian A. Meissner, Kimberly D. Richman, Amy-May Leach, and Dana La Fon (2007) Police Interviewing and Interrogation: A Self Report Survey of Police Practices and Beliefs, *Law and Human Behavior* 31:381–400.

Kassin, Saul M., Steven A. Drizin, Thomas Grisso, G. H. Gudjonsson, Richard A. Leo, and Allison D. Redlich (2010) Police-Induced Confessions: Risk Factors and Recommendations. *Law and Human Behavior* 34:3–38.

Kawagoe, Naoko (2003) *Hosoku no Setsuzokushi "tada" "tadashi" ni tsuite* (On Supplementary Discourse Connectives *"tada"* and *"tadashi"*), Ningen Bunka Gakubu Kenkyuu Nenpou (Tezukayama Gakuin University, Faculty of Human and Cultural Studies) 5:82–101.

Keefe, Rosanna (2000) *Theories of Vagueness*. Cambridge: Cambridge University Press.

Kelman, Mark (1987) *A Guide to Critical Legal Studies*. Cambridge, MA: Harvard University Press.

Kelsen, Hans (1979) *Allgemeine Theorie der Normen*, K. Ringhofer and R. Walter (eds), Vienna: Manz.

Kennedy, Duncan (1997) *A Critique of Adjudication*. Cambridge, MA: Harvard University Press.

Kenny, Sally J. (2000) Beyond Principals and Agents: Seeing Courts as Organisations by Comparing *Référendaires* at the European ECJ and Law Clerks at the U.S. Supreme Court, *Comparative Political Studies* 33:593–625.

Kersta, Lawrence G. (1962) Voiceprint Identification, *Nature* 196:1253–7.

Kerstholt, José H., Noortje J. M. Jansen, Adri G. van Amelsvoort, and A. P. A. Broeders (2004) Earwitnesses: Effects of Speech Duration, Retention Interval and Acoustic Environment, *Applied Cognitive Psychology* 18:327–36.

——, ——, ——, and —— (2006) Earwitnesses: Effects of Accent, Retention and Telephone, *Applied Cognitive Psychology* 20:187–97.

Kesavan, Vasan and Michael Stokes Paulsen (2002) Is West Virginia Unconstitutional?, *California Law Review* 90:293–301.

Keselj, Vlado, Fuchum Peng, Nick Cercone, and Calvin Thomas (2003) N-Gram-Based Author Profiles for Authorship Attribution, *Proceedings of PACLing'03*, Halifax, Canada, 255–64.

Kessler, David K. (2009) Free to Leave? An Empirical Look at the Fourth Amendment's Seizure Standard, *Journal of Criminal Law & Criminology* 99:51–88.

Kevelson, Roberta (1982) Language and Legal Speech Acts: Decisions, in Robert J. DiPietro (ed.), *Linguistics and the Professions*. Norwood, NJ: Ablex Publishing Co.

Kimble, Joseph (1994–95) Answering the Critics of Plain Language, *The Scribes Journal of Legal Writing* 5:51–85.

—— (1996–97) Writing for Dollars, Writing to Please, *The Scribes Journal of Legal Writing*, 6:1–38.

—— (2005) *Lifting the Fog of Legalese*, Durham, NC: Carolina Academic Press.

—— (2007) Lessons in Drafting from the New Federal Rules of Civil Procedure (Part 5), *Michigan Bar Journal*: December 50, 51.

King, Robert D. (1997) Should English be the Law?, available at <www.theatlantic.com/issues/97apr/english.htm> accessed September 1, 2011.

Kinoshita, Yuko, Shunichi Ishihara, and Philip Rose (2009) Exploring the Discriminatory Potential of F0 Distribution Parameters in Traditional Forensic Speaker Recognition, *International Journal of Speech, Language and the Law* 16:91–111.

Kjær, Anne Lise (2003) Convergence of European Legal Systems: The Role of Language, *Copenhagen Studies in Language* 29:125–37.

—— (2004) A Common Legal Language in Europe?, in Mark van Hoecke (ed.), *Epistemology and Methodology of Comparative Law in the Light of European Integration*. Oxford: Hont.

—— (2007) Legal Translation in the European Union: A Research Field in Need of a New Approach, in Stanislaw K. G.-R. Kredens (ed.), *Language and the Law: International Outlooks*. Frankfurt a.M.: Lang, 69–95.

—— (2008a) The Every-Day Miracle of Legal Translation (review of Deborah Cao, *Translating Law*), *International Journal of Semiotics and Law* 21:67–72.

—— (2008b) Introduction: Language as Barrier and Carrier of European Legal Integration, in Hanne Petersen et al. (eds), *Paradoxes of European Legal Integration*. Aldershot: Ashgate, 149–56.

Klarman, Michael J. (1991) An Interpretive History of Modern Equal Protection, *Michigan Law Review* 90:252.

Klatt, Dennis H. and Laura C. Klatt (1990) Analysis, Synthesis, and Perception of Voice Quality Variations Among Female and Male Talkers, *Journal of the Acoustical Society of America* 87:820–57.

Klinge, Valerie and John Dorsey (1993) Correlates of the Woodcock–Johnson Reading Comprehension and Kauffman Brief Intelligence Test in a Forensic Psychiatric Population, *Journal of Clinical Psychology* 49:593–8.

Kloss, Heinz (1966) German-American Language Maintenance Efforts, in Joshua A. Fishman et al. (eds), *Language Loyalty in the United States: The Maintenance and Perpetuation of Non-English Mother Tongues by American Ethnic and Religious Groups*. The Hague: Mouton.

—— (1977) *The American Bilingual Tradition*. Boston: Newbury House.

—— and H. Haarmann (1984) The Languages of Europe and Soviet Asia, in Heinz Kloss and Grant D. McConnell (eds.) *Linguistic Composition of the Nations of the World: 5. Europe and the USSR*. Quebec: Les Presses de l'université Laval, 11–75.

Kniffka, Hannes (2007) *Working in Language and Law: A German Perspective*. Basingstoke: Palgrave Macmillan.

Koller, Werner (1989) Equivalence in Translation Theory, in A. Chesterman (ed.), *Readings in Translation Theory*. Helsinki: Finn Lectura.

—— (1995) The Concept of Equivalence and the Object of Translation Studies, *Target* 7:191–222.

Komter, Martha L. (1998) *Dilemmas in the Courtroom: A Study of Trials of Violent Crime in the Netherlands*. Hillsdale, NJ: Lawrence Erlbaum Associates.

—— (2002) The Suspect's Own Words: The Treatment of Written Statements in Dutch Courtrooms, *Forensic Linguistics. The International Journal of Speech, Language and the Law* 9(2):168–92.

—— (2006) From Talk to Text: The Interactional Construction of a Police Record, *Research on Language and Social Interaction* 39(3):201–28.

Kontra, Miklós (2009) Language-based Educational Discrimination in the Carpathian Basin. The Seventh Annual Lecture on Language and Human Rights, University of Essex, UK.

—— Robert Phillipson, Tove Skutnabb-Kangas, and Tibor Várady (eds) (1999) *Language: a Right and a Resource. Approaching Linguistic Human Rights*. Budapest: Central European University Press.

Koppel, Moshe and Jonathan Schler (2003) Exploiting Stylistic Idiosyncrasies for Authorship Attribution, in *Proceedings of IJCAI'03 Workshop on Computational Approaches to Style Analysis and Synthesis*, Acapulco, Mexico; <http://citeseer.ist.psu.edu/article/koppelo3exploiting.html> accessed September 1, 2011 (requires registration).

——, —— and Shlomo Argamon (2009) Computational Methods in Authorship Attribution, *Journal of the American Society for Information Science and Technology (JASIST)* 60(1):9–26.

Koppel, Moshe, Jonathon Schler, and Shlomo Argamon (2011) Authorship Attribution in the Wild, *Language Resources and Evaluation* 45(1) (special issue on Plagiarism and Authorship Analysis).

Koppen, Peter van and Steven D. Penrod (eds) (2003) *Adversarial versus Inquisitorial Justice: Psychological Perspectives on Criminal Justice Systems*. New York: Kluwer Academic.

Köster, O., N. O. Schiller, and H. J. Künzel (1995) The Influence of Native-Language Background on Speaker Recognition, in K. Elenius and P. Branderud (eds), *Proceedings of the Thirteenth International Congress of Phonetic Sciences*. Stockholm 4:306–9.

Krausneker, Verena (1998) Sign Languages in the Minority Languages Policy of the European Union. MA thesis, Vienna: University of Vienna.

Krauss, Michael (1992) The World's Languages in Crisis, *Language* 68:4–10.

Kredens, Krzysztof (2007) Linguistic Expert Evidence in Polish Courts. Paper presented at the 8th biennial meeting of the International Association of Forensic Linguists, 12–15 July 2007, Seattle, University of Washington.

—— (2008) Korpusy językowe w językoznawstwie sądowym (Language Corpora in Forensic Linguistics), in Barbara Lewandowska-Tomaszczyk (ed.), *Podstawy językoznawstwa korpusowego* (Foundations of Corpus Linguistics), Łódź University Press, 270–9.

—— (2009) "I Never Said That!" The Problem of Translated Records of Interpreted Police Interviews with Suspects. Paper presented at the 9th Biennial Conference on Forensic Linguistics/Language and Law, July 6–9, Amsterdam.

Kripke, Saul (1972) *Naming and Necessity*. Cambridge, MA: Harvard University Press.

—— (1982) *Wittgenstein on Rules and Private Language*. Cambridge, MA: Harvard University Press.

Kučera, Henry and W. Nelson Francis (1967) *Computational Analysis of Present-Day American English*. Providence, RI: Brown University Press.

Kuner, Christopher (1991) The Interpretation of Multilingual Treaties: Comparison of Texts versus the Presumption of Similar Meaning, *Comparative Law Quarterly* 40:953–64.

Künzel, Hermann J. (1989) How Well Does Average Fundamental Frequency Correlate with Speaker Height and Weight?, *Phonetica* 46: 117–25.

—— (2000) Effects of Voice Disguise on Speaking Fundamental Frequency, *Forensic Linguistics* 7:149–79.

—— (2001) Beware of the "Telephone Effect": The Influence of Telephone Transmission on the Measurement of Formant Frequencies, *Forensic Linguistics* 8:80–99.

Künzel, Hermann J. and Joaquín Gonzalez-Rodriguez (2003) Combining Automatic and Phonetic–Acoustic Speaker Recognition Techniques for Forensic Applications, *Proceedings of the 15th International Congress of Phonetic Sciences*, Barcelona, 1619–22.

Kurzon, Dennis (1985) Clarity and Word Order in Legislation, *Oxford Journal of Legal Studies* 5:269–75.

—— (1986) *"It is Hereby Performed...". Explorations in Legal Speech Acts*. Amsterdam: John Benjamins.

—— (1987) Latin for Lawyers: Degrees of Textual Integration, *Applied Linguistics* 1987:233–40.

—— (1992) When Silence May Mean Power, *Journal of Pragmatics* 18:92–5.

—— (1994a) Linguistics and Legal Discourse: An Introduction, *International Journal for the Semiotics of Law* 7:5–12.

—— (1994b) Silence in the Legal Process: A Socio-Pragmatic Model, in Bernard S. Jackson (ed.), *Legal Semiotics and the Sociology of Law*. Oñati, Spain: Oñati Proceedings.

—— (1995) The Right of Silence: A Socio-Pragmatic Model of Interpretation, *Journal of Pragmatics* 23:55–69.

—— (1996) "To Speak or Not to Speak": The Comprehensibility of the Revised Police Caution (PACE), *International Journal for the Semiotics of Law* 9:3–16.

—— (1997) "Legal Language": Varieties, Genres, Registers, Discourses, *International Journal of Applied Linguistics* 7:119–39.

Labelle, Andrée (2000) La corédaction des lois fédérales au Canada vingt ans après: quelques réflexions, *Legal Translation, History, Theory/ies and Practice*; <http://www.tradulex.org/Actes2000/LABELLE.pdf> at 8, accessed September 1, 2011.

Labov, William (1988) The Judicial Testing of Linguistic Theory, in Deborah Tannen (ed.), *Linguistics in Context: Connecting Observation and Understanding*. Norwood, NJ: Ablex, 159–82.

—— and Joshua Waletsky (1989) Narrative Analysis, in June Helm (ed.), *Essays on the Verbal and Visual Arts*. Seattle: University of Washington Press.

Ladas, Stephen P. (1995) *Patents, Trademarks, and Related Rights: National and International Protection*, Vol. II. Cambridge, MA: Harvard University Press.

Ladefoged, Peter (1978) Expectation Affects Identification by Listening, *UCLA–Working Papers in Phonetics* 41:41–2.

—— and Jenny Ladefoged (1980) The Ability of Listeners to Identify Voices, *UCLA–Working Papers in Phonetics*, 49:43–51.

Lakoff, Robin (1995) Cries and Whispers: The Shattering of the Silence, in Kira Hall and Mary Bucholtz (eds), *Gender Articulated: Language and the Socially Constructed Self*. New York: Routledge.

Lancker, D. van, J. Kreiman, and K. Emmorey (1985a) Familiar Voice Recognition: Patterns and Parameters. Part 1: Recognition of Backward Voices, *Journal of Phonetics* 13:19–38.

——, —— and T. D. Wickens (1985b) Familiar Voice Recognition: Patterns and Parameters. Part 2: Recognition of Rate-Altered Voices, *Journal of Phonetics* 13:39–52.

Langille, Brian (1988) Revolution Without Foundation: The Grammar of Scepticism and Law, *McGill Law Journal* 33:451–505.

Language and Asylum Research Group (LARG) (2011) <www.essex.ac.uk/larg/> accessed September 1, 2011.

Language and National Origin Group (LNOG) (2004) Guidelines for the Use of Language Analysis in Relation to Questions of National Origin in Refugee Cases, *International Journal of Speech, Language & the Law* 11(2):261–6.

Lass, Norman J., Pamela J. Mertz, and Karen L. Kimmel (1978) The Effect of Temporal Speech Alterations on Speaker Race and Sex Identifications, *Language and Speech* 21:279–90.

Laver, John (1980) *The Phonetic Description of Voice Quality*. Cambridge: Cambridge University Press.

Lawson, Gary and Guy Seidman (2006) The Jeffersonian Treaty Clause, *Illinois Law Review* 2006:7.

Leckey, R. (2007) Prescribed by Law/Une règle de droit, *Osgoode Hall Law Journal* 45:571.

Leech, Geoffrey (1983) *Principles of Pragmatics*. Harlow: Longman.

Legge, Gordon E., Carla Grossmann, and Christina M. Pieper (1984) Learning Unfamiliar Voices, *Journal of Experimental Psychology: Learning, Memory, and Cognition* 10:298–303.

Legrand, Pierre (2005) Issues in the Translatability of Law, in Sandra Bergmann and Michael Wood (eds), *Nation, Language, and the Ethics of Translation*. Princeton, NJ: Princeton University Press, 30–50.

Legrand, Pierre (2008) Word/World (of Primordial Issues for Comparative Legal Studies), in Hanne Petersen et al. (eds), *Paradoxes of European Legal Integration*. Aldershot: Ashgate, 185–233.

Leibowitz, Arnold H. (1969) English Literacy: Legal Sanction for Discrimination, *Notre Dame Lawyer* 45:7–67.

Leiter, Brian (2007) *Explaining Theoretical Disagreement*; <http://ssrn.com/abstract=1004768> accessed September 29, 2009.

Lentine, Genine and Roger W. Shuy (1990) Mc-. Meaning in the marketplace, *American Speech* 65(4):349–66.

Leo, Richard A. (1996) *Miranda*'s Revenge: Police Interrogation as a Confidence Game, *Law and Society Review* 30:259–88.

—— (2001) Questioning the Relevance of *Miranda* in the Twenty-first Century, *The Michigan Law Review* 99(5):1000–29.

—— (2004) The Third Degree and the Origins of Psychological Interrogation in the United States, in G. D. Lassiter (ed.), *Interrogations, Confessions, and Entrapment*. New York: Kluwer Academic/Plenum Publishers, 37–85.

—— (2008) *Police Interrogation and American Justice*. Cambridge, MA: Harvard University Press.

—— and Deborah Davis (2010) From False Confession to Wrongful Conviction: Seven Psychological Processes, *Journal of Psychiatry and the Law* 38:9–56.

—— and Welsh S. White (1999) Adapting to *Miranda*: Modern Interrogators' Strategies for Dealing with the Obstacles Posed by *Miranda*, *Minnesota Law Review* 84:397–472.

Levi, Judith N. (1990) *Language in the Judicial Process*. New York: Plenum Press.

Levin, Harvey S., Kathleen A. Culhane, Joel Hartmann, Karen Evankovich, et al. (1991) Developmental Changes in Performance on Tests of Purported Frontal Lobe Functioning, *Developmental Neuropsychology* 7:377–95.

Lewis, M. Paul (ed.) (2009) *Ethnologue: Languages of the World* (16th edn). Dallas, TX: SIL International; <http://www.ethnologue.com/> accessed August 10, 2009.

Lewis, M. Paul, Gary F. Simons, and Charles D. Fennig (2014). *Ethnologue: Languages of the World* (17th edn). Dallas, TX: SIL International; <http://ethnologue.com>.

Lezak, Murial D. (1983) *Neuropsychological Assessment* (2nd edn). New York: Oxford University Press.

Li, Jiexun, Rand Zheng, and Hsinchen Chen (2006). From Fingerprint to Writeprint, *Communications of the ACM* 49(4):76–82.

Liao, Meizhen (2002) The Status-quo of Chinese Courtroom Trial from the Perspective of Questioning, *Yuyan Wenzi Yingyong (Applied Linguistics)* 4:25–36.

—— (2003) *A Study on Courtroom Questions, Responses and their Interaction*. Beijing: Law Press.

—— (2004) The Principle of Goal and Goal Analysis of Chinese Courtroom Cooperation, *Journal of Foreign Languages* 5.

—— (2005a) The Principle of Goal and Goal Analysis: A New Way of Doing Pragmatics, *Rhetorical Learning* 3:1–10.

—— (2005b) Principle of Goal and Goal Analysis: A New Way of Doing Pragmatics, *Rhetorical Learning* 4:5–11.

—— (2009a) A Study of Interruption in Chinese Criminal Courtroom Discourse. *Text & Talk* 29(2):175–99.

—— (2009b) *Trial Communication Strategies*. Beijing: Law Press.

Lichtenberg, Illya D. (1999) Voluntary Consent or Obedience to Authority: An Inquiry into the "Consensual" Police-Citizen Encounter. Unpublished doctoral dissertation.

——(2001) *Miranda* in Ohio: The Effects of Robinette on the "Voluntary" Waiver of Fourth Amendment Rights, *Howard Law Journal* 44:349–74.

Loakes, Deborah (2006) A Forensic Phonetic Investigation into the Speech Patterns of Identical and Non-Identical Twins. PhD Dissertation, University of Melbourne.

Loftus, Elizabeth (1975) Leading Questions and Eyewitness Report, *Cognitive Psychology* 7:560–72.

López-Rodríguez, Ana M. (2004) Towards a European Civil Code without a Common European Legal Culture? The Link between Law, Language and Culture, *Brooklyn Journal of International Law* 29(3):1195–220.

Love, Harold (2002) *Attributing Authorship: An Introduction*, Cambridge: Cambridge University Press.

Lowenstein, Daniel Hays (1985) Political Bribery and the Intermediate Theory of Politics, *UCLA Law Review* 32:784.

Lucci, Eugene A. (2005) The Case for Allowing Jurors to Submit Written Questions, *Judicature* 89:16–19.

Luhmann, Niklas (1993) *Das Recht der Gesellschaft*. Frankfurt a.M.: Suhrkamp.

Luttermann, Karin (2009) Multilingualism in the European Union Status Quo and Perspectives: The Reference Language Model, in Günther Grewendorf and Monika Rathert (eds): *Formal Linguistics and Law*. Berlin/New York: Mouton de Gruyter, 315–38.

Lynch, Michael and David Bogen (1996) *The Spectacle of History. Speech, Text, and Memory at the Iran-Contra Hearings*. Durham, NC/London: Duke University Press.

Mac Aodha, Máirtín (2009) The Bilingual Legal Dictionary and the Translator, in S. Šarčević (ed.), *Legal Language in Action: Translation, Terminology, Drafting and Procedural Issues*. Zagreb: Globus, 261–73.

McAuliffe, Karen (2006) Law in Translation: The Production of a Multilingual Jurisprudence by the ECJ of the European Communities. PhD Thesis, The Queen's University of Belfast.

——(2008) Enlargement at the ECJ of the European Communities: Law, Language and Translation, *European Law Journal* 14:6.

——(2009) Translation at the ECJ of the European Communities, in D. Stein, Frances E. Olsen, Ralph Alexander Lorz, and Dieter Stein (eds), *Translation Issues in Language and Law*. Basingstoke: Palgrave Macmillan.

McBarnet, Doreen (1981) The Royal Commission and the Judges' Rules, *British Journal of Law and Society* 8(1):109–17.

McCarthy, J. Thomas (1984) *Trademarks and Unfair Competition* (2nd edn). San Francisco: Bancroft-Whitney Co.

McCawley, James D. (1979) Verbs of Bitching, in James D. McCawley (ed.), *Adverbs, Vowels, and Other Objects of Wonder*. Chicago: University of Chicago Press.

——(1985) Kuhnian Paradigms as Systems of Markedness Conventions. In A. Makkai and A. Melby (eds), *Linguistics and Philosophy: Studies in Honor of Rulon S. Wells*. Amsterdam: Benjamins, 23–43.

Macchiaroli, Christopher (2009) To Speak or Not to Speak: Can Pre-*Miranda* Silence Be Used as Substantive Evidence of Guilt?, *Champion* 33:14–17.

McCormick, Charles T. et al. (1999) *McCormick on Evidence* (5th edn). St. Paul, MN: West Publishing.

McEnery, Tony and Andrew Wilson (1996) *Corpus Linguistics*. Edinburgh: Edinburgh University Press.

McGehee, Frances (1937) The Reliability of the Identification of the Human Voice, *Journal of General Psychology* 17:249–71.

McGehee, Frances (1944) An Experimental Study of Voice Recognition, *Journal of General Psychology* 31:53–65.

Mackay, A. J. G. (1887) Introduction to an Essay on the Art of Legal Composition Commonly Called Drafting, *Law Quarterly Review* 3:326.

McKay, Kathleen E., Jeffrey M. Halperin, Susan T. Schwartz, and Vanshdeep Sharma (1994) Developmental Analysis of Three Aspects of Information Processing: Sustained Attention, Selective Attention, and Response Organization, *Developmental Neuropsychology* 10:121–32.

Macleod, Peter R. (1997) Latin in Legal Writing: An Inquiry into the Use of Latin in the Modern Legal World, *Boston College Law Review* 1997:238.

MacLeod, Nicola J. (2010) Police Interviews with Women Reporting Rape: A Critical Discourse Analysis. Unpublished PhD dissertation, Birmingham: Aston University.

McManus, Michael, Norman E. Alessi, W. Lexington Grapentine, and Arthur S. Brickman (1984) Psychiatric Disturbance in Serious Delinquents, *Journal of the American Academy of Child Psychiatry* 23:602–15.

McMenamin, Gerald R. (1993) *Forensic Stylistics.* Amsterdam: Elsevier.

—— (2002) *Forensic Linguistics: Advances in Forensic Stylistics.* London: CRC Press.

—— (2004) Disputed Authorship in US Law, *The International Journal of Speech Language and the Law* 11(1):73–82.

McNamara, Tim and Carsten Roever 2006. *Language Testing: The Social Dimension.* Oxford: Blackwell.

——, Carolien van den Hazelkamp, and Maaike Verrips (2010) Language Testing, Validity and LADO, in Karin Zwaan, Pieter Muysken, and Maaike Verrips (eds), *Language and Origin. The Role of Language in European Asylum Procedures: A Linguistic and Legal Survey.* Nijmegen: Wolf Legal Publishers, 61–71.

Maeda, Masahide (ed.) (2006) *Saiban-in no tame no Yoku Wakaru Houritsu Yougo Kaisetus (Guide to Legal Terms for Lay Judges).* Tokyo: Tachibana Shobo.

Magga, Ole Henrik, Ida Nicolaisen, Mililani Trask, Robert Dunbar, and Tove Skutnabb-Kangas (2005) Indigenous Children's Education and Indigenous Languages. Expert paper written for the United Nations Permanent Forum on Indigenous Issues. New York: United Nations.

Mahmood, Tahir (1986) *Hindu Law* (2nd edn). Allahabad: The Law Book Company.

Malpass, Roy S. and Patricia G. Devine (1984) Research on Suggestion in Lineups and Photospreads, in Gary L. Wells and Elizabeth F. Loftus (eds), *Eyewitness Testimony: Psychological Perspectives.* New York: Cambridge University Press.

—— (2009) *Democracy in the Courts. Lay Participation in European Criminal Justice Systems.* Aldershot: Ashgate.

Malsch, Marijke and Ian Freckelton (2005) Expert Evidence in the Netherlands and Australia. *Psychology, Public Policy & the Law* 11(1):42–61.

—— and —— (2009) The Evaluation of Evidence: Differences between Legal Systems, in H. Kaptein, H. Prakken, and B. Verheij (eds), *Legal Evidence and Proof: Statistics, Stories, Logic.* Aldershot: Ashgate.

—— and Johannes F. Nijboer (eds) (1999) *Complex Cases: Perspectives on the Netherlands Criminal Justice System.* Amsterdam: Thela Thesis.

Mancini, G. Frederico (1991) The Making of a Constitution for Europe, in Robert O. Keohane and Stanley Hoffmann (eds), *The New European Community: Decisionmaking and Institutional Change.* Boulder; San Francisco; Oxford: Westview Press.

Mancini, Susanna and Bruno de Witte (2008) Language Rights as Cultural Rights—a European Perspective, in Francesco Francioni and Martin Scheinin (eds), *Cultural Human Rights.* Leiden and Boston: Martinus Nijhoff Publishers, 247–84.

Mankiewicz, René H. (1962) Die Anwendung des Warschauer Abkommens, *Rabels Zeitschrift* 27:456–77.

Mann, V., R. Diamond, and S. Carey (1979) Development of Voice Recognition: Parallels With Face Recognition, *Journal of Experimental Child Psychology* 27:153–65.

Manning, John F. (2003) The Absurdity Doctrine, *Harvard Law Review* 116:2387–486.

Manning, R. K., D. Fucci, and R. Dean (2000) College-Age Males' Ability to Produce the Acoustic Properties of an Aging Voice, *Perceptual and Motor Skills* 94:767–71.

Marder, Nancy S. (2005) *The Jury Process.* New York: Foundation Press.

—— (2006) Bringing Jury Instructions into the Twenty-First Century, *Notre Dame Law Review* 81:449–511.

Martínes Bargueño, Manuel (1992) Pasado y presente del lenguaje administrativo castellano, *Revista de llengua i dret* 1992:7–23.

Maryns, Katrijn (2005) Monolingual Language Ideologies and Code Choice in the Belgian Asylum Procedure, *Language & Communication* 25:299–314.

—— (2006) *The Asylum Speaker: Language in the Belgian Asylum Procedure.* Manchester: St. Jerome.

Matoesian, Gregory (2005) Nailing Down an Answer: Participations of Power in Trial Talk, *Discourse Studies* 7(6):733–59.

Mattila, Heikki E. S. (2002) De Æqualitate Latinitatis Jurisperitorum: Le Latin Juridique dans les Grandes Familles de Droit Contemporaines à la Lumière des Dictionnaires Spécialisés, *Revue internationale de droit comparé* 3:717–58.

—— (2005) Jurilinguistique et latin juridique, in J.-C. Gémar and N. Kasirer (eds), *Jurilinguistique: entre langues et droits—Jurilinguistics: Between Law and Language.* Brussels and Montreal: Bruylant & Les Éditions Thémis, 71–89.

—— (2007) Multilingual Term Banks of Criminal Law, in P. Laitinen (ed.), *Nordisk Workshop för straffrätt* 23–25.3.2007. Juridiska Fakulteten. Lapplands Universitet (Rovaniemi), C 50.

—— (2008a) European Integration and Legal Communication, in H. Petersen, A. L. Kjær, H. Krunke, and M. R. Madsen (eds), *Paradoxes of European Legal Integration.* Aldershot: Ashgate, 253–76.

—— (2008b) Les abréviations juridiques. Méthode de recherche jurilinguistique, *International Journal for the Semiotics of Law—Journal international de sémiotique juridique* 21(4):347–61.

—— (2009) Los cambios del lenguaje administrativo en el mundo de hoy. Un balance comparativo de los últimos 25 años, *Revista de llengua i dret* 51:17–37; also <http://www10. gencat.net/eapc_rld/darrer_numero> accessed September 7, 2011.

—— (2013) *Comparative Legal Linguistics: Language of Law, Latin and Modern Lingua Francas.* (2nd edn) (trans Christopher Goddard). Aldershot: Ashgate.

May, Stephen (1999) Language and Education Rights for Indigenous Peoples, in Stephen May (ed.), *Indigenous Community-based Education.* Clevedon: Multilingual Matters, 42–66.

—— (2001) *Language and Minority Rights: Ethnicity, Nationalism and the Politics of Language.* Harlow: Pearson Education Ltd.

Maynard, Douglas W. (1990) Narratives and Narrative Structure in Plea Bargaining, in Judith Levi and Anne Graffam Walker (eds), *Language in the Judicial Process.* New York: Plenum.

Megale, Fabrizio (2008) *Teorie della traduzione giuridica. Fra diritto comparato e "translation studies".* Napoli: Editoriale Scientifica.

Mellinkoff, David (1963) *The Language of the Law*. Boston and Toronto: Little, Brown and Co.

—— (1992) *Dictionary of American Legal Usage*. St. Paul, MN: West Publishing Company.

Mendenhall, Thomas C. (1887) The Characteristic Curves of Composition, *Science* 11:237–49.

Merlini, Raffaela (2009) Seeking Asylum and Seeking Identity in a Mediated Encounter, *Interpreting: International Journal of Research and Practice in Interpreting* 11:57–92.

Merriam, Thomas (2002) *Marlowe in Henry V: A Crisis of Shakespearian Identity?* Oxford: Oxquarry Books.

Merritt, Marilyn (1976) On Question Following Question in Service Encounters, *Language in Society* 5:315–57.

Merryman, John Henry (1985) *The Civil Law Tradition* (2nd edn). Stanford, CA: Stanford University Press.

Messenheimer, Sharon, Christina L. Riggs Romaine, Melinda Wolbransky, Heather Zelle, Jennifer M. Serico, Lindsay Wrazien, Naomi E. Sevin Goldstein (2009) Readability and Comprehension: A Comparison of the Two Versions of the *Miranda* Rights Assessment Instruments. Paper presented at the annual conference of the American Psychology-Law Society, San Antonio, TX, March.

Meuwly, Didier (2003a) Le mythe de "L'empreinte vocale" (I), *Revue Internationale de Criminologie et de Police Technique et Scientifique* 56:219–36.

—— (2003b) Le mythe de "L'empreinte vocale" (II), *Revue Internationale de Criminologie et de Police Technique et Scientifique* 61:361–74.

Meyer, Bonnie J. F. and Roy O. Freedle (1984) Effects of Discourse Type on Recall, *American Educational Research Journal* 21:121–43.

Miller, George A. (1956) The Magical Number Seven, Plus or Minus Two: Some Limits on Our Capacity for Processing Information, *Psychological Review* 63:81–97.

Milroy, James (1984) Sociolinguistic Methodology and the Identification of Speakers' Voices in Legal Proceedings, in Peter Trudgill (ed.), *Applied Sociolinguistics*. London: Academic Press, 51–72.

Mineka, Susan, Eshkol Rafaeli, and Iftah Yovel (2003) *Cognitive Biases in Emotional Disorders: Information Processing and Social-Cognitive Perspectives*. New York: Oxford University Press.

Ministry of Justice (2008) *Arrests for Recorded Crime (Notifiable Offences) and the Operation of Certain Police Powers under PACE England and Wales 2006/07*. London: HMSO.

Mirfield, Peter (1997) *Silence, Confessions and Improperly Obtained Evidence*. Oxford: Clarendon Press.

Mitchell, John B. (2000) Why Should the Prosecutor Get the Last Word? *American Journal of Criminal Law* 27(2):139–216.

Mithun, Marianne (1999) *The Languages of Native North America*. Cambridge: Cambridge University Press.

Mohanty, Ajit K. (2000) Perpetuating Inequality: The Disadvantage of Language, Minority Mother Tongues and Related Issues, in Ajit K. Mohanty and Girishwar Misra (eds), *Psychology of Poverty and Disadvantage*. New Delhi: Concept Publishing Company, 104–17.

Molot, J. (2006) The Rise and Fall of Textualism, *Columbia Law Review* 106:1–69.

Monaghan, Henry (1981) Our Perfect Constitution, *New York University Law Review* 56:383–4.

Moore, Michael S. (1981) The Semantics of Judging, *Cardozo Law Review* 54:151–294.

—— (1982a) Moral Reality, *Wisconsin Law Review* 1982:1016–56.

—— (1982b) The Semantic of Judging, *Southern California Law Review* 54:151–294.

—— (1985) A Natural Law Theory of Interpretation, *Southern California Law Review* 58:277–398.

—— (1987) Metaphysics, Epistemology, and Legal Theory, *Southern California Law Review* 60:453–506.

—— (1989) The Interpretive Turn in Modern Theory: A Turn for the Worse?, *Stanford Law Review* 41:871–957.

—— (1992a) Law as a Functional Kind, in R. P. George (ed.), *Natural Law Theory: New Essays*. Oxford: Clarendon Press.

—— (1992b) Moral Reality Revisited, *Michigan Law Review* 90:2424–533.

—— (2002) Legal Reality. A Naturalist Approach to Legal Ontology, *Law and Philosophy* 21:619–705.

Moosmüller, Sylvia (2010) IAFA Position on Language Analysis in asylum procedures, in Karin Zwaan, Pieter Muysken, and Maaike Verrips (eds) *Language and Origin. The Role of Language in European Asylum Procedures: A Legal and Linguistic Survey*. Nijmegen: Wolf Legal Publishers, 43–47.

Moréteau, Olivier (1999) L'anglais pourrait-il devenir la langue juridique commune en Europe?, in R. Sacco and L. Castellani (eds), *Les multiples langues du droit européen uniforme*. Torino: ISAIDAT—Editrice L'Harmattan Italia, 151–61.

Morgades, Silvia. (2010) The Asylum Procedure in Spain: The Role of Language in Determining the Origin of Asylum Seekers, in Karin Zwaan, Pieter Muysken, and Maaike Verrips (eds), *Language and Origin. The Role of Language in European Asylum Procedures: A Linguistic and Legal Survey*. Nijmegen: Wolf Legal Publishers, 159–75.

Morita, Yoshiyuki (1980) *Kiso Nihongo 2* (Basic Japanese). Tokyo: Kadokawa Shoten.

Morris, Ruth (1999) The Gum Syndrome: Predicaments in Court Interpreting, *Forensic Linguistics: The International Journal of Speech, Language and the Law* 6:6–29.

Morton, A. Q. and James McLeman (1964) *Christianity and the Computer*. London: Hodder and Stoughton.

—— and —— (1980) *The Genesis of John*. Edinburgh: St Andrew Press.

Moseley, Christopher (ed.) (2009) *Unesco Interactive Atlas of the World's Languages in Danger*, <http://www.unesco.org/culture/languages-atlas/en/atlasmap.html> accessed September 29, 2011.

Mosteller, Federick and David L. Wallace (1964) *Inference and Disputed Authorship: The Federalist*. New York: Springer-Verlag.

Mott, Nicole L. (2003) The Current Debate on Juror Questions: "To Ask or Not To Ask, That Is the Question", *Chicago-Kent Law Review* 78:1099–125.

Muchnik, Chava, Michal Efrati, Esther Nemeth, Michal Malin, and Minka Hildesscheimer (1991) Central Auditory Skills in Blind and Sighted Subjects, *Scandinavian Audiology* 20:12–23.

Muhammad, Bushar (1995) *Pokok-pokok Hukum Adat* (Basics of Customary Law). Jakarta: Pt Pradnya Paramita.

Mulla, Dinshah Fardunji and Sunderlal Trikamlal Desai (1986) *Principles of Hindu Law*. Bombay: N. M Tripathi Private Limited.

Mullennix, John W., Steven E. Stern, Benjamin Grounds, R. Kalas, Mary Flaherty, Sara Kowalok, Eric May, and Brian Tessmer (2010) Earwitness Memory: Distortions for Voice Pitch and Speaking Rate, *Applied Cognitive Psychology* 24(4):513–26.

Munday, Roderick (2009) *Evidence*. Oxford: Oxford University Press.

Munsterman, G. Thomas, Paula L. Hannaford-Agor, G. Marc Whitehead (eds) (2006) *Jury Trial Innovations*. Williamsburg, VA: National Center for State Courts.

Murphy, Gregory L. (2002) *The Big Book of Concepts*. Cambridge, MA: MIT Press.

Murray, T. and S. Cort (1971) Aural Identification of Children's Voices, *Journal of Auditory Research* 11:260–2.

Myers, Wade C., Roger C. Burket, Beverly Lyles, L. Stone, and John P. Kemph (1990) DSM-III Diagnoses and Offenses in Committed Female Juvenile Delinquents, *Bulletin of the American Academy of Psychiatry and Law* 18:47–54.

Nadler, Janice (2003) No Need to Shout: Bus Sweeps and the Psychology of Coercion, *Supreme Court Review* 2002:15–222.

—— (2005) Flouting the Law, *Texas Law Review* 83:1399–441.

NAJIT (National Association of Judiciary Interpreters and Translators) (2004) Code *of Ethics and Professional Responsibilities.* <http://www.najit.org/about/NAJITCodeofEthicsFINAL.pdf> acccessed October 4, 2011.

Nakane, Ikuko (2007) Problems in Communicating the Suspect's Rights in Interpreted Police Interviews, *Applied Linguistics* 281:87–112.

National Academies of Sciences (2009) *Strengthening Forensic Science in the United States: A Path Forward.* Washington, DC: National Academies Press.

Ndhlovu, F. (2008) Language and African Development: Theoretical Reflections on the Place of Languages in African Studies, *Nordic Journal of African Studies* 17:137–51.

Ndoye, M. (undated) Bilingualism, Language Policies and Educational Strategies in Africa, <www.unesco.org/education/africa/Bilingualism_IIEP.doc> accessed July 18, 2008.

Nelson, Caleb (2005) What is Textualism? *Virginia Law Review* 95:347–418.

New Zealand Law Commission (2008) *Presentation of New Zealand Statute Law.* Wellington: Law Commission available from <http://www.lawcom.govt.nz/sites/default/files/projectAvailable Formats/NZLC%20IP2.pdf> accessed January 31, 2015.

Newman, Paul (2007) Copyright Essentials for Linguists, *Language Documentation and Conservation* 1(1):28–43; <https://scholarspace.manoa.hawaii.edu/handle/10125/1724> accessed September 2, 2011.

Ngcobo, Mtholeni N. (2007) Language Planning, Policy and Implementation in South Africa, *An Ambilingual Journal* 2(2):June.

Ngũgĩ, wa Thiong'o (1987) *Decolonising the Mind. The Politics of Language in African Literature.* London: James Currey Ltd.

Nic Shuibhne, Niamh (2002) *EC Law and Minority Language Protection.* The Hague: Kluwer Law International.

Niemeyer, W. and I. Starlinger (1981) Do the Blind Hear Better? Investigations on Auditory Processing in Congenital or Early Blindness, *Audiology* 20:2–23.

Nihon Bengoshi Rengoukai (2008a) *Saiban-in Jidai no Houtei Yougo (Courtroom Language in the Era of the Mixed Court)*, A. Goto, (ed.). Tokyo: Sanseido.

—— (2008b) *Saiban-in no tame no Houtei Yougo Handbook (A Handbook for Lay People).* Tokyo: Sanseido.

Nikièma, Norbert and Paul Taryam Ilboudo (2011) Setting a Tradition of Mother Tongue-Medium Education in "Francophone" Africa. The Case of Burkina Faso, in Tove Skutnabb-Kangas and Kathleen Heugh (eds), *Multilingual Education and Sustainable Diversity Work: From Periphery to Center.* New York: Routledge, 197–215.

Nimmer, Melville B. and David Nimmer (2010) *Nimmer on Copyright.* New York: Matthew Bender.

Nippold, Marilyn A. (1993) Developmental Markers in Adolescent Language: Syntax, Semantics, and Pragmatics, *Language, Speech, and Hearing Services in Schools* 24:21–28.

Nolan, Francis J. (1983) *The Phonetic Bases of Speaker Recognition.* Cambridge: Cambridge University Press.

—— (1990) The Limitations of Auditory-Phonetic Speaker Identification. In H. Kniffka (ed.), *Texte zu Theorie und Praxis Forensischer Linguistik*. Tübingen: Max Niemeyer, 457–79.

—— (2001) Speaker Identification Evidence: Its Forms, Limitations, and Roles. *Proceedings of the Conference "Law and Language: Prospect and Retrospect"*, Levi, Finland; <http://www.ling.cam.ac.uk/francis/LawLang.doc> accessed August 23, 2010.

—— (2005) Forensic Speaker Identification and the Phonetic Description of Voice Quality, in William J. Hardcastle and Janet Mackenzie Beck (eds), *A Figure of Speech: A Festschrift for John Laver*. Mahwah, NJ: Lawrence Erlbaum, 385–411.

Nolan, Francis J. and Esther Grabe (1996) Preparing a Voice Lineup, *Forensic Linguistics* 7:74–94.

O'Barr, William M. (1982) *Linguistic Evidence: Language, Power, and Strategy in the Courtroom*. New York: Academic Press.

—— and Bowman K. Atkins (1980) "Women's Language" or "Powerless Language"? in Sally McConnell-Ginet, Ruth Borker, and Nelly Furman (eds), *Women and Language in Literature and Society*. New York: Praeger.

Oberlander, Lois B. and Naomi E. Goldstein (2001) A Review and Update on the Practice of Evaluating *Miranda* Comprehension, *Behavioral Sciences and the Law* 19:453–71.

—— ——, and Caleb N. Ho (2001) Preadolescent Adjudicative Competence: Methodological Considerations and Recommendations for Practice Standards, *Behavioral Sciences and Law* 19:545–63.

Okawara, Mami Hiraike (2006a) Shihou Gengo no Barrier Free (Lifting the Language Barrier between Legal Experts and Lay People), *Gekkan Gengo (Monthly Language)* 35(7): 40–5.

—— (2006b) Saiban-in Saiban ni okeru Wakari yasui Shiho no Ronri to Kouzou (Towards Plain Legal Reasoning for the Lay Judge System), *Jiyuuto Seigi (Freedom and Justice)* 57(6):22–32.

—— (2006c) Saiban-in no Shiko Taikei (Thought Process of Lay Judges), *Kikan Keiji Bengo (Quarterly Defence Lawyering)* 46:66–8.

—— (2006d) A Linguistic Analysis of some Japanese Trademark Cases, *International Journal of Speech, Language and the Law* 15:101–4.

—— (2007) Saiban-in Seido no Kinouka: Shimin Sanka no tame no Gengo Bunseki (Linguistic Analysis for the Enhancement of Lay Judge System), in T. Tanase (ed.), *Shimin Shakai to Hou (Civil Society and Law)*. Kyoto: Mineruva Shobo.

—— (2008a) *Shimin kara Mita Saiban-In-Saiban (The Mixed Court as Viewed by Lay People)*. Tokyo: Akashi Shoten.

—— (2008b) Saiban-in no Mesen ni Tatta Saishu Benron (Closing Arguments from the Viewpoints of Lay Judges), *Hanrei Times* 1260:95–101.

—— (2009a) Settoku no Gengogaku (Persuasion of Linguistics), in Sadato Goto, Satoshi Shinomiya, Takashi Takano, and Takafumi Hayano (eds), *Saiban-in Saiban: Keiji Bengo Manual (Lay Judge Courts: Manual for Criminal Defense)*. Tokyo: Daichi Hoki.

—— (2009b) *Houritsuka no Kotoba to Shimin no Kotoba no Kousaku (A Complicated Mixture of Legal Words and Lay Words)*. A Paper presented at the Japanese Association of Sociology of Law.

—— (2009c) *Saiban Omoshiro Kotoba Gaku (Peculiar Courtroom Language Studies)*. Tokyo: Taishukan Shoten.

Olsson, John (2004) *Forensic Linguistics: An Introduction to Language, Crime, and Law*. London: Continuum.

—— (2008) *Forensic Linguistics* (2nd edn). London: Continuum.

Olsson, Nils, Peter Juslin, and Anders Winman (1998) Realism of Confidence in Earwitness Versus Eyewitness Identification, *Journal of Experimental Psychology: Applied* 4:101–18.

Olvera, Rene L., Margaret Semrud-Clikeman, Steven R. Pliszka, and Louise O'Donnell (2005) Neuropsychological Deficits in Adolescents with Conduct Disorder and Comorbid Bipolar Disorder: A Pilot Study, *Bipolar Disorders* 7:57–67.

Ono, Ichitaro (1992) Satsui (Intent to Murder), in M. Kobayashi and T. Kashiro (eds), *Keiji Jijitsu Nintei—Jou (Fact-Finding in Criminal Cases—1st volume)*. Tokyo: Hanrei Times Sha, reprinted 2006.

Opeibi, Olusola Babatunde (2000) One Language Model in Ethnic and Inter-Group Relations: A Bridge Across Cultures, *Journal of Cultural Studies, Ethnicity and African Development* 2:187–97.

—— (2002) The Sociolinguistics of the English Language. Department of English, University of Lagos, Nigeria (unpublished).

—— (forthcoming) *A Discourse Study of Legal Communication in Nigeria*.

Opitz, Kurt (1983) The Properties of Contractual Language: Selected Features of English Documentary Texts in the Merchant Marine Field, *Fachsprache* 4:161–70.

Orchard, Tara L. and A. Daniel Yarmey (1995) The Effects of Whispers, Voice-Sample Durations, and Voice Distinctiveness on Criminal Speaker Identification, *Applied Cognitive Psychology* 9:249–60.

Ó Riagáin, Dónall (2002) Gàidhlig and Other Lesser Used Languages: What Future in the New Europe? Paper, Department of Celtic and Scottish Studies, University of Edinburgh. Online at <www.arts.ed.ac.uk/celtic/poileasaidh/gaelic&other.html> accessed August 14, 2009.

OSCE (1996) The Hague Recommendations Regarding the Education Rights of National Minorities; <www.osce.org/documents/hcnm/1996/10/2700_en.pdf> accessed August 12, 2009.

—— (1998) The Oslo Recommendations Regarding the Linguistic Rights of National Minorities; <www.osce.org/documents/hcnm/1998/02/2699_en.pdf> accessed August 12, 2009.

—— (1999) The Lund Recommendations on Effective Participation of National Minorities in Public Life. The Hague: Foundation for Inter-Ethnic Relations; <www.osce.org/publications/hcnm/1999/09/31545_1151_en.pdf> accessed August 12, 2009.

—— (2001) Warsaw Guidelines on Minority Participation in the Electoral Process. Warsaw: OSCE Office for Democratic Institutions and Human Rights; <www.osce.org/publications/hcnm/2001/01/31627_1162_en.pdf> accessed August 12, 2009.

—— (2003) Guidelines on the Use of Minority Languages in the Broadcast Media. The Hague: Office of the High Commissioner on National Minorities; <www.osce.org/publications/hcnm/2003/10/31598_1160_en.pdf> accessed August 12, 2009.

—— (2008) The Bolzano/Bozen Recommendations on National Minorities in Inter-State Relations;   <www.osce.org/publications/hcnm/2008/10/33388_1189_en.pdf>   accessed August 12, 2009.

Oviedo, Gonzalo and Luisa Maffi (2000) *Indigenous and Traditional Peoples of the World and Ecoregion Conservation. An Integrated Approach to Conserving the World's Biological and Cultural Diversity*. Gland, Switzerland: WWF International & Terralingua.

Owen, Charles (1996) Readability Theory and the Rights of Detained Persons, in H. Kniffka (ed.), *Recent Developments in Forensic Linguistics*. Frankfurt: Peter Lang, 279–95.

Oyetade, Oluwole S. (2003) Language Planning in a Multi-ethnic State: The Majority/Minority Dichotomy in Nigeria, *Nordic Journal of African Studies* 12:105–17.

Pan, Christoph (2009) Die Minderheitenfrage in der Europäischen Union, *Europäisches Journal für Minderheitenfragen* 1:20–31.

Papcun, George, Jody Kreiman, and Anthony Davis (1989) Long-Term Memory for Unfamiliar Voices, *Journal of the Acoustical Society of America* 85:913–25.

Papp, Viktória (2008) The Effects of Heroin on Speech and Voice Quality. MSc dissertation, University of York.

Parker, Anthony (1964) *Modern Conveyancing Precedents*. London: Butterworths.

—— (1969) *Modern Will Precedents*. London: Butterworths.

Patrick, Peter L. (2002) The Speech Community, in J. K. Chambers, P. Trudgill, and N. Schilling-Estes (eds), *Handbook of Language Variation and Change*. Oxford: Blackwell, 573–97.

—— (2010) Language Variation and LADO (Language Analysis for Determination of Origin), in Karin Zwaan, Pieter Muysken, and Maaike Verrips (eds), *Language and Origin. The Role of Language in European Asylum Procedures: A Linguistic and Legal Survey*. Nijmegen: Wolf Legal Publishers, 73–87.

Patten, Alan (2001) Political Theory and Language Policy, *Political Theory* 29:691–715.

Patterson, Dennis (1996) *Law and Truth*. Oxford: Oxford University Press.

Paunio, Elina and Susanna Lindroos-Hovinheimo (2010) Taking Language Seriously: An Analysis of Linguistic Reasoning and Its Implications in EU Law, *European Law Journal* 16(4):395–416.

Pavlenko, Aneta (2008) "I'm Very Not about the Law Part": Nonnative Speakers of English and the *Miranda* Warnings, *TESOL Quarterly* 42:1–30.

Peirce Edition Project (eds) (1998) *The Essential Peirce*. Vol. 2. Bloomington, IN: Indiana University Press.

Peng, Fuchun, Dale Schuurmans, and Shaojun Wang (2003) Language and Task Independent Text Categorization with Simple Language Models, in *Proceedings of HLT-NAACL*, Edmonton, 110–17.

Pentassuglia, Gaetano (2002) *Minorities in International Law*. Strasbourg Cedex: Council of Europe Publishing.

Perfect, Timothy J., Laura J. Hunt, and Chrisopher M. Harris (2002) Verbal Overshadowing in Voice Recognition, *Applied Cognitive Psychology* 16:973–80.

Peters, D. P. (1987) The Impact of Naturally Occurring Stress on Children's Memory, in Stephen J. Ceci, Michael P. Toglia, and David F. Ross (eds), *Children's Eyewitness Memory*. New York: Springer-Verlag.

Peters, Marybeth (2005) Statement of Marybeth Peters, The Register of Copyrights, before the Subcommittee on Intellectual Property, Committee on the Judiciary, United States Senate, 109th Congress, 1st Session, May 25, 2005; <http://www.copyright.gov/docs/regstat052505.html> accessed February 6, 2010.

Petrinovich, Lewis (1995) *Human Evolution, Reproduction, and Morality*. London: Plenum Press.

Peyró, Francisco (1999) Le "qui-dit-quoi" de l'acquis communautaire, *Terminologie et traduction* 2: 52–69.

Philippon, Axelle C., Julie Cherryman, Ray Bull, and Aldert Vrij (2007a) Lay People's and Police Officers' Attitudes Towards the Usefulness of Perpetrator Voice Identification, *Applied Cognitive Psychology* 21:103–15.

——, ——, ——, and —— (2007b) Earwitness Identification Performance: The Effect of Language, Target, Deliberate Strategies and Indirect Measures, *Applied Cognitive Psychology* 21:539–50.

——, Julie Cherryman, Aldert Vrij, and Ray Bull (2008) Why is My Voice So Easily Recognized in Identity Parades? Influence of First Impressions on Voice Identification, *Psychiatry, Psychology and Law* 15:70–7.

Philips, Susan U. (1985) Interaction Structured through Talk and Interaction Structured through "Silence", in Deborah Tannen and Muriel Saville-Troike (eds), *Perspectives on Silence*. Norwood, NJ: Ablex Publishing.

Philips, Susan U. (1987) The Social Organization of Questions and Answers in Courtroom Discourse, in Leah Kedar (ed.), *Power through Discourse*. Norwood, NJ: Ablex, 83–111.

—— (1998) *Ideology in the Language of Judges: How Judges Practice Law, Politics, and Courtroom Control*. Oxford: Oxford University Press.

Phillipson, Robert (1999) International Languages and International Human Rights, in Miklós Kontra et al. (eds), *Language: A Right and a Resource*. Budapest: Central European University Press.

—— (2009) *Linguistic Imperialism Continued*. New York: Routledge/Taylor & Francis.

Philp, Kenneth R. (1977) *John Collier's Crusade for Indian Reform, 1920–1954*. Tucson, AZ: University of Arizona Press.

Piatt, Bill (1990) *Only English? Law and Language Policy in the United States*. Albuquerque, NM: University of New Mexico Press.

Pigeon, Louis-Philippe (1982) La traduction juridique—L'équivalence fonctionnelle, in J.-Cl. Gémar (ed.) (1982) *Langage du droit et traduction*. Montréal: Linguatech et Conseil de la langue française.

Pigolkin, A. S. (ed.) (1990) *Iazyk zakona*. Moscow: Iuridicheskaia literatura.

Pinkal, Manfred (1991) Vagheit und Ambiguität, in Arnim von Stechow, Dieter Wunderlich, A. Burkhardt, G. Ungeheuer, H. E. Wiegand, H. Steger, and K. Brinker (eds), *Semantik. Ein internationales Handbuch der zeitgenössischen Forschung = Semantics*. Berlin: de Gruyter, 250–69.

—— (1995) *Logic and Lexicon. The Semantics of the Indefinite*. Dordrecht, Boston: Kluwer Academic Publishers.

Pöchhacker, Franz (1997) "Is There Anybody Out There?" Community Interpreting in Austria, in S. E. Carr, R. Roberts, A. Dufour, and D. Steyn (eds), *The Critical Link: Interpreters in the Community*. Amsterdam/Philadelphia: John Benjamins.

Polanyi, Livia (1981) Telling the Same Story Twice, *Text* 1:315–16.

Polenz, Peter von (2013) *Deutsche Sprachgeschichte vom Spätmittelalter bis zur Gegenwart* I. II. III. (2nd edn) Berlin: Walter de Gruyter.

Pöllabauer, Sonja (2004) Interpreting in Asylum Hearings: Issues of Role, Responsibility and Power, *Interpreting* 6:143–80.

—— (2006) "Translation Culture" in Interpreted Asylum Hearings, in Anthony Pym, Miriam Shlesinger, and Zuzana Jettmarová (eds), *Sociocultural Aspects of Translating and Interpreting*. Amsterdam/Philadelphia: John Benjamins.

—— (2007) Interpreting in Asylum Hearings: Issues of Saving Face, in Cecilia Wadensjö, Birgitta Englund Dimitrova, and Anna-Lena Nilsson (eds), *The Critical Link 4: Professionalisation of Interpreting in the Community*. Amsterdam/Philadelphia: John Benjamins.

Pollicino, Oreste (2004) Legal Reasoning of the Court of Justice in the Context of the Principle of Equality Between Judicial Activism and Self-Restraint, *German Law Journal* 5(3):283–317.

Pomerantz, Anita (1984) Agreeing and Disagreeing with Assessment: Some Features of Preferred/Dispreferred Turn Shapes, in J. Maxwell Atkinson and John Heritage (eds), *Structure of Social Interaction: Studies in Conversational Analysis*. Cambridge: Cambridge University Press.

Pommer, Sieglinde (2006) *Rechtsübersetzung und Rechtsvergleichung*. Frankfurt am Main: Peter Lang.

Poon Wai-Yee, Emily (2005) The Cultural Transfer in Legal Translation, *International Journal for the Semiotics of Law* 18(3–4):307–23.

Poscher, Ralf (2009) The Hand of Midas: When Concepts Turn Legal, or Deflating the Hart–Dworkin Debate, in Jaap C. Hage and Dietmar von der Pfordten (eds), *Concepts in Law*. Dordrecht, Heidelberg, London, New York: Springer, 99–115.

Posner, R. (1990) *The Problems of Jurisprudence*. Cambridge, MA: Harvard University Press.

Post, Leonard (2004) Spelling It Out in Plain English, *National Law Journal* November 8: 1, 19.

Postema, Gerald J. (2010) Positivism and the Separation of Realists from their Skepticism, in P. Cane (ed.), *The Hart Fuller Debate: 50 Years On*. Oxford: Hart Publishing.

Potthast, Martin, Alberto Barrón-Cedeño, Benno Stein, and Paulo Rosso (2011) Cross-Language Plagiarism Detection. *Language Resources and Evaluation* 45(1):45–63.

Powers, Peter A., Joyce L. Andriks, and Elizabeth F. Loftus (1979) Eyewitness Accounts of Females and Males, *Journal of Applied Psychology* 64:339–47.

Pozzo, Barbara and Valentina Jacometti (eds) (2006) *Multilingualism and the Harmonisation of European Private Law*. Alphen aan den Rijn: Kluwer Law International.

Pretto, Claudia (2010). The Use of Language Analysis in the Italian Asylum Procedure, in Karin Zwaan, Pieter Muysken, and Maaike Verrips (eds), *Language and Origin. The Role of Language in European Asylum Procedures: A Linguistic and Legal Survey*. Nijmegen: Wolf Legal Publishers, 187–97.

Price, Zachary (2004) The Role of Lenity as a Rule of Structure, *Fordham Law Review* 72:885–942.

Proctor, Erica. E. and A. Daniel Yarmey (2003) The Effect of Distributed Learning on the Identification of Normal-Tone and Whispered Voices, *Korean Journal of Thinking & Problem Solving* 13:17–29.

Prucha, Francis Paul (1975) *Documents of United States Indian Policy*. Lincoln, NE: University of Nebraska.

Psathas, George (1995) *Conversation Analysis: The Study of Talk-in-Interaction*. Thousand Oaks, CA: Sage.

Puissochet, Jean-Pierre (1975) *The Enlargement of the European Communities: A Commentary on the Treaty and the Acts Concerning the Accession of Denmark, Ireland and the United Kingdom*. Leyden: A.W. Sijthoff.

Purnell, Thomas, William Idsardi, and John Baugh (1999) Perceptual and Phonetic Experiments on American English Dialect Identification, *Journal of Language and Social Psychology* 18:10–24.

Putnam, Hilary (1975) The Meaning of "Meaning", in *Mind, Language and Reality: Philosophical Papers Vol. 2*. Cambridge: Cambridge University Press.

Quine, Willard O. (1957) Speaking of Objects, *Proceedings and Addresses of the American Philosophical Association* 31:5–22.

—— (1960) *Word and Object*. Cambridge, MA: Technology Press of the Massachusetts Inst. of Technology.

Quirk, Randolph, Sidney Greenbaum, Geoffrey Leech, and Jan Svartvik (1985) *A Comprehensive Grammar of the English Language*. London: Longman.

Rakove, Jack N. (1996) *Original Meanings*. New York: Alfred A. Knopf.

Ramseyer, J. Mark and Minoru Nakazato (1998) *Japanese Law*. Chicago: Chicago University Press.

Rayo, Agustin (2007) Ontological Commitment, *Philosophy Compass* 2:428–44.

Raz, Joseph (2009) *Between Authority and Interpretation*. Oxford: Oxford University Press.

Read, Daniel J. and Fergus I. M. Craik (1995) Earwitness Identification: Some Influences on Voice Recognition, *Journal of Experimental Psychology: Applied* 1:6–18.

Redding, Richard E. (2006) The Brain-disordered Defendant: Neuroscience and Legal Insanity in the Twenty-first Century, *American University Law Review* 56:51–127.

Reifman, Alan, Spencer M. Gusick, and Phoebe C. Ellsworth (1992) Real Jurors' Understanding of the Law in Real Cases, *Law and Human Behavior* 16:539–54.

Reiss, Katharina and Hans Vermeer (1984) *Grundlegung einer allgemeinen Translationstheorie*. Tübingen: Max Niemeyer.

Rich, Lloyd L. (1996) How Much of Someone Else's Work May I Use Without Asking Permission?: The Fair Use Doctrine, Part I; <http://www.publaw.com> accessed September 5, 2011.

Richardson, G., Gisli H. Gudjonsson, and T. P. Kelly (1995) Interrogative suggestibility in an adolescent forensic population, *Journal of Adolescence* 18:211–16.

Riggs Romaine, Christina L., Naomi E. Sevin Goldstein, Heather Zelle, Anna Heilbrun, and Melinda Wolbransky (2008) Then and Now: Comparing Juveniles' Comprehension of the *Miranda* Warning in the 1970s and Today. Part of a symposium: The *Miranda Rights Comprehension Instruments-II*. Presented at the annual conference of the *American Psychology-Law Society*, Jacksonville, FL, March.

Rigney, Azucenz. C. (1999) Questioning in Interpreted Testimony, *Forensic Linguistics* 6:83–108.

Roberts, Rhoda (1997) Community Interpreting Today and Tomorrow, in Silvana E. Carr, Rhoda Roberts, Aiden Dufour, and Dini Steyn (eds), *The Critical Link: Interpreters in the Community*. Amsterdam/Philadelphia: John Benjamins.

Robertson, Bernard and George A. Vignaux, (1995) *Interpreting Evidence*. Chichester: Wiley.

Robinson, O. F., T. D. Fergus, and W. M. Gordon (2000) *European Legal History* (3rd edn). Oxford: Oxford University Press.

Robinson, Paul H., Michael T. Cahill, and Daniel M. Bartels (2010) Competing Theories of Blackmail: An Empirical Research Critique of Criminal Law Theory, *Texas Law Review* 89:291–348.

Rock, Frances (2007) *Communicating Rights: The Language of Arrest and Detention*. Basingstoke: Palgrave Macmillan.

Rodriguez, Cristina M. (2006) Language and Participation, *California Law Review* 94:687–768.

Roebuck, Rebecca and John Wilding (1993) Effects of Vowel Variety and Sample Length on Identification of a Speaker in a Lineup, *Applied Cognitive Psychology* 7:475–81.

Rogers, Richard (2008) A Little Knowledge is a Dangerous Thing…Emerging *Miranda* Research and Professional Roles for Psychologists, *American Psychologist* 63:776–87.

—— Kimberly S. Harrison, Lisa L. Hazelwood, and Kenneth W. Sewell (2007a) Knowing and Intelligent: A Study of *Miranda* Warnings in Mentally Disordered Defendants, *Law and Human Behavior* 31:401–18.

—— ——, Daniel W. Shuman, Kenneth W. Sewell, and Lisa L. Hazelwood (2007b) An Analysis of *Miranda* Warnings and Waivers: Comprehension and Coverage, *Law and Human Behavior* 31:177–92.

——, Lisa L. Hazelwood, Kenneth W. Sewel, Daniel W. Shuman, and Hayley L. Blackwood (2008a) The Comprehensibility and Content of Juvenile *Miranda* Warnings, *Psychology, Public Policy, and Law* 14:63–87.

—— —— ——, K. Harrison, and D. Shuman (2008b) The Language of *Miranda* Warnings in American Jurisdictions: A Replication and Vocabulary Analysis, *Law and Human Behavior* 32:124–36.

Rooij, Vincent A. de (2010) Language Analysis for the Determination of Origin: A Look into Problems Presented by East and Central African Cases, in Karin Zwaan, Pieter Muysken, and Maaike Verrips (eds), *Language and Origin. The Role of Language in European Asylum Procedures: A Linguistic and Legal Survey*. Nijmegen: Wolf Legal Publishers, 133–44.

Rosch, Eleanor (1975) Cognitive Representations of Semantic Categories, *Journal of Experimental Psychology: General* 104:192–233.

Rose, Philip (2002) *Forensic Speaker Identification*. London: Taylor & Francis.

—— (2006) Technical Forensic Speaker Recognition: Evaluation, Types and Testing of Evidence, *Computer Speech and Language* 20:159–91.

—— and S. Duncan (1995) Naïve Auditory Identification and Discrimination of Similar Voices by Familiar Listeners, *Forensic Linguistics* 10:1–17.

—— and Geoffrey S. Morrison (2009) A Response to the UK Position Statement on Forensic Speaker Comparison, *International Journal of Speech, Language and the Law* 16:139–63.

Ross, Lisa B. (2007) Learning the Language: An Examination of the Use of Voter Initiatives to Make Language Education Policy, *New York University Law Review* 82:1510–46.

Ross, William G. (1994) *Forging New Freedoms: Nativism, Education, and the Constitution, 1917–1927*. Lincoln, NE: University of Nebraska Press.

Rubenstein, H., L. Garfield, and J. A. Millikan (1970) Homographic Entries in the Internal Lexicon, *Journal of Verbal Learning and Verbal Behavior* 9:487–94.

Rubio-Marín, Ruth (2003) Language Rights: Exploring the Competing Rationales, in Will Kymlicka and Alan Patten (eds), *Language Rights and Political Theory*. Oxford: Oxford University Press, 52–79.

Ruck, Martin D., Daniel P. Keating, Rona Abramovitch, and Christopher J. Koegl (1998) Adolescents' and Children's Knowledge about Rights: Some Evidence for how Young People View Rights in Their Own Lives, *Journal of Adolescence* 21:275–89.

Rummel, Dieter (2005) An Apology for Terminology, *NordTerm* conference in Reykjavik, June 2005 (PowerPoint slides).

Russano, Melissa B., Christian A. Meissner, Fadia M. Narchet, and Saul M. Dassin (2005) Investigating True and False Confessions within a Novel Experimental Paradigm, *Psychological Science* 16(6):481–86.

Russell, Sonia (2000) "Let Me Put it Simply…": The Case for a Standard Translation of the Police Caution and its Explanation, *Forensic Linguistics* 7(1):26–48.

—— (2002) "Three's a Crowd": Shifting Dynamics in the Interpreted Interview, in Janet Cotterill (ed.), *Language in the Legal Process*. Basingstoke, UK: Palgrave Macmillan.

Ryan, Christopher M. (1990) Age-related Improvement in Short-term Memory Efficiency During Adolescence, *Developmental Neuropsychology* 6:193–205.

Rybnicek, Jan M. (2009) "Damned if You Do, Damned if You Don't?": The Absence of a Constitutional Protection Prohibiting the Admission of Post-arrest, Pre-*Miranda* Silence, *George Mason University Civil Rights Law Journal* 19:405–40.

Sacco, Rodolfo (2005) Language and Law, in B. Pozzo (ed.), *Ordinary Language and Legal Language*. Milano: Giuffrè, 1–21.

Sacks, Harvey, Emanuel Schegloff, and Gail Jefferson (1974) A Simplest Systematics for the Organization of Turn-taking in Conversation, *Language* 50:696–735.

Sainsbury, Richard M. (2001) *Paradoxes*. Cambridge: Cambridge University Press.

Samuelson, Pamela (1994) Self-Plagiarism or Fair Use, *Communications of the ACM* 37:21–5, n. 2.

Sandrini, Peter (1999) Translation zwischen Kultur und Kommunikation: Der Sonderfall Recht, in Peter Sandrini (ed.), *Übersetzen von Rechtstexten*. Tübingen: Gunter Narr, 9–43.

——(2009) Der transkulturelle Vergleich von Rechtsbegriffen, in S. Šarčević (ed.), *Legal Language in Action: Translation, Terminology, Drafting and Procedural Issues*. Zagreb: Globus, 151–65.

Sanou, Fernand (1990) Who's Afraid of National Languages as Instructional Media and Why?, in Unesco/Unicef (eds), *African Thoughts on the Prospects of Education for All*. Dakar: Unesco/Unicef, 75–96.

Šarčević, Susan (1985) Translation of Culture-bound Terms in Laws, *Multilingua* 4: 127–33.

——(1989) Conceptual Dictionaries for Translation in the Field of Law, *International Journal of Lexicography* 2: 277–93.

——(1997) *New Approach to Legal Translation*. The Hague: Kluwer Law International.

——(2000) *New Approach to Legal Translation* (2nd edn; 1st edn 1997). The Hague: Kluwer Law International.

——(2002) Problems of Interpretation in an Enlarged European Union, in Rodolfo Sacco (ed.), *L'interprétation des textes juridiques rédigés dans plus d'une langue*. Torino and Paris: L'Harmattan, 239–72.

——(2004) Creating EU Legal Terms: Internationalisms vs. Localisms, in Miran Humar (ed.) *Terminologija v času globalizacije / Terminology at the Time of Globalization*. Ljubljana: ZRC SAZU, 129–38.

——(2005) The Quest for Legislative Bilingualism and Multiculturalism: Co-drafting in Canada and Switzerland, in Jean-Claude Gémar and Nicholas Kasirer (eds), *Jurilinguistique: entre langues et droits/ Jurilinguistics: Between Law and Language*. Montreal and Brussels: Éditions Thémis, Bruylant, 277–92.

——(ed.) (2009) *Legal Language in Action: Translation, Terminology, Drafting and Procedural Issues*. Zagreb: Globus.

Saslove, Howard and Yarmey, A. Daniel (1980) Long-Term Auditory Memory: Speaker Identification, *Journal of Applied Psychology* 65:111–16.

Savigny, Eike von (1991) Passive Disobedience as Violence. Reflections on German High Decisions, in James B. Brady and Newton Garver (eds), *Justice, Law, and Violence*. Philadelphia: Temple University Press, 53–64.

Saville-Troike, Muriel (1985) The Place of Silence in an Integrated Theory of Communication, in Deborah Tannen and Muriel Saville-Troike (eds), *Perspectives on Silence*. Norwood, NJ: Ablex Publishing.

Scalia, Antonin (1997a) *A Matter of Interpretation*. Princeton, NJ: Princeton University Press.

—— (1997b) "Common" Law Courts in a Civil-Law System: The Role of United States Federal Courts in Interpreting the Constitution and Laws, in Antonin Scalia, *A Matter of Interpretation: Federal Courts and the Law*. Princeton, NJ: Princeton University Press.

Schäffner, Christina (1997) Where is the Source Text?, in Gerd Wotjak and Heide Schmidt (eds), *Modelle der Translation—Models of Translation. Festschrift für Albrecht Neubert*. Frankfurt am Main: Vervuert, 193–211.

Schane, Sanford (1989) A Speech-Act Analysis of Consideration in Contract Law, in Paul Pupier and Jean-Marie Woehrling (eds), *Language and Law*. Montreal: Wilson & Lafleur.

—— (2006) *Language and the Law*. London: Continuum.

Schechter, Frank I. (1927) The Rational Basis of Trademark Protection, *Harvard Law Review* 813.

Schichting, Frank and Kirk P. H. Sullivan (1997) The Imitated Voice—A Problem for Voice Lineups? *Forensic Linguistics* 4:148–65.

Schiller, N. O. and O. Köster (1996) Evaluation of a Foreign Speaker in Forensic Phonetics: A Report, *Forensic Linguistics* 3:176–85.

Schilling, Theodor (2010) Beyond Multilingualism: On Different Approaches to the Handling of Diverging Language Versions of Community Law, *European Law Journal* 16(1):47–66.

Schler, Jonathan, Moshe Koppel, Shlomo Argamon, James Pennebaker (2006) Effects of Age and Gender on Blogging, *Proceedings of AAAI Spring Symposium on Computational Approaches for Analyzing Weblogs*. Menlo Park, CA: Association for the Advancement of Artificial Intelligence (AAAI).

Schlesinger, Rudolf, Hans Baade, and Peter Herzog (1998) *Comparative Law: Cases, Text, Materials* (6th edn). New York: Foundation Press.

Schmitt, Carl (2008) *Constitutional Theory*. Durham, NC: Duke University Press.

Schneidman, Edwin S. and Norman L. Farberow (eds) (1957) *Clues to Suicide*. New York: McGraw-Hill.

Schöpflin, György (2009). The Slovak Language Law is Discriminatory and Restrictive; <http://euobserver.com/9/28440> accessed September 1, 2011.

Schroth, Peter W. (1986) Legal Translation, *American Journal of Comparative Law* 34:47–65.

Schübel-Pfister, Isabel (2004) *Sprache und Gemeinschaftsrecht—Die Auslegung der Mehrsprachig verbindlichen Rechtstexte durch den Europäischen Gerichtshof*. Berlin: Duncker & Humblot.

Schulhofer, Stephen J. (1996) *Miranda*'s Practical Effect: Substantial Benefits and Vanishingly Small Social Costs, *Northwestern University Law Review* 90:500–63.

Schweitzer, Nicholas J. and Michael J. Saks (2007) The *CSI Effect*: Popular Fiction about Forensic Science Affects the Public's Expectations about Real Forensic Science, *Jurimetrics* 47:357–64.

Schwenzer, Ingeborg (2005) Art. 35, in Peter Schlechtriem and Ingeborg Schwenzer (eds), *Commentary on the UN Convention on the International Sale of Goods (CISG)* (2nd edn). Oxford: Oxford University Press.

Scott, Elizabeth S., N. Dickon Reppucci, and Jennifer L. Woolard (1995) Evaluating Adolescent Decision Making in Legal Contexts, *Law and Human Behavior* 19:221–44.

Scotton, Carol M. (1990) Elite Closure as Boundary Maintenance: The Case of Africa, in Brian Weinstein (ed.), *Language Policy and Political Development*. Norwood, NJ: Ablex Publishing Corporation, 25–42.

Searle, John (1969) *Speech Acts: An Essay on the Philosophy of Language*. Cambridge: Cambridge University Press.

—— (1997) *The Construction of Social Reality*. New York: Free Press.

—— and Daniel Vanderveken (1985) *Foundations of Illocutionary Logic*. Cambridge: Cambridge University Press.

Seidman, Louis M. (2007) *Silence and Freedom*. Stanford, CA: Stanford University Press.

Sen, Amartya (2005) *The Argumentative Indian. Writings on Indian Culture, History and Identity*. London: Penguin.

Senese, Louis (2005) *Anatomy of Interrogation Themes: The Reid Technique of Interviewing and Interrogation*. Chicago: John E. Reid & Associates.

Shapero, Jess (2011) The Language of Suicide Notes, unpublished PhD dissertation. The University of Birmingham, <http://etheses.bham.ac.uk/1525/> accessed September 30, 2011.

Shavell, Steven (1993) An Economic Analysis of Threats and Their Illegality: Blackmail, Extortion, and Robbery, *University of Pennsylvania Law Review* 141:1877.

Shuy, Roger W. (1993) *Language Crimes: The Use and Abuse of Language Evidence in the Courtroom*. Oxford: Blackwell.

—— (1997) Ten Unanswered Language Questions about *Miranda*, *Forensic Linguistics* 4(2) 51–73.

—— (2002) *Linguistic Battles in Trademark Disputes*. New York: Palgrave Macmillan.

—— (2003a) Linguistics and Trademark Dilution, *Trademark Dilution Forum*. International Trademark Association 13.1–13.19.

—— (2003b) Plagiarism Once More, Forensic Linguistics List-serv. Posted February 12, 2003; <https://www.jiscmail.ac.uk/cgi-bin/webadmin?A2=ind03&L=FORENSIC-LINGUISTICS &D=0&P=56673&F=P> accessed February 9, 2010.

—— (2008) *Fighting over Words: Language and Civil Law Cases*. New York: Oxford University Press.

—— (2009) Ethical Questions in Forensic Linguistics: Introduction to Papers from a Linguistic Society of America Panel Presentation, San Francisco, California, 9 January 2009, *International Journal of Speech, Language and the Law* 16(2):219–26.

—— (2010) *The Language of Defamation Cases*. New York: Oxford University Press.

Siegel, Jonathan R. (2001) What Statutory Drafting Errors Teach Us about Statutory Interpretation, *George Washington Law Review* 69:309–66.

—— (2009) The Inexorable Radicalization of Textualism, *University of Pennsylvania Law Review* 158:117–78.

Sifianou, Maria (1997) Silence and Politeness, in Adam Jaworski (ed.), *Silence: Interdisciplinary Perspectives*. Berlin: Mouton de Gruyter.

Silver, Richard (2000) The Right to English Health and Social Services in Quebec: A Legal and Political Analysis, *McGill Law Journal* 45:681–92.

Simmons, Ric (2005) Not "Voluntary" But Still Reasonable: A New Paradigm for Understanding the Consent Searches Doctrine, *Indiana Law Journal* 80:773–824.

Sin, King-kui (1998) The Missing Link between Language and Law: Problems of Legislative Translation in Hong Kong, in H. Kjell and J. Turi (eds), *Multilingual Cities and Language Policies*. Vasa: Akademi University Social Science Research Unit, 195–208.

Sinclair, John McHardy (1991) *Corpus, Concordance, Collocation*. Oxford: Oxford University Press.

—— and Malcolm Coulthard (1975) *Towards an Analysis of Discourse: the English Used by Teachers and Pupils*. London, Oxford University Press.

Singler, John Victor (2004) The "Linguistic" Asylum Interview and the Linguist's Evaluation of it, with Special Reference to Applicants for Liberian Political Asylum in Switzerland, *International Journal of Speech, Language and the Law* 11(2):222–39.

Skrapka, Marty (2006) Silence Should be Golden: A Case against the Use of a Defendant's Post-arrest, Pre-*Miranda* Silence as Evidence of Guilt, *Oklahoma Law Review* 59:357–402.

Skutnabb-Kangas, Tove (1984) *Bilingualism or Not—the Education of Minorities*. Clevedon, UK: Multilingual Matters (new edition 2008, Delhi: Orient BlackSwan).

—— (2000) *Linguistic Genocide in Education—or Worldwide Diversity and Human Rights?* Mahwah, NJ and London: Lawrence Erlbaum Associates (South Asian updated edition in 2008, Delhi: Orient BlackSwan).

—— and Ulla Aikio-Puoskari (2003) Exclusion or Inclusion—Linguistic Human Rights for a Linguistic Minority, the Deaf Sign Language Users, and an Indigenous People, the Saami, in Philip Lee (ed.), *Many Voices, One Vision: The Right to Communicate in Practice*. Penang, Malaysia: Southbound; and London: WACC, 59–88.

Skutnabb-Kangas, Tove and Robert Dunbar (2010) *Indigenous Children's Education as Linguistic Genocide and a Crime Against Humanity? A Global View*. Gáldu Čála. Journal of Indigenous People's Rights No 1, 2010. Guovdageaidnu/Kautokeino: Gáldu, Resource Centre for the Rights of Indigenous Peoples (http://www.galdu.org) As an e-book, free of charge, at http://www.e-pages.dk/grusweb/55/.

—— and Kathleen Heugh (eds) (2011) *Multilingual Education and Sustainable Diversity Work: From Periphery to Center*. New York: Routledge.

—— and Teresa McCarty (2008) Key Concepts in Bilingual Education: Ideological, Historical, Epistemological, and Empirical Foundations, in Jim Cummins and Nancy Hornberger (eds), *Language Policy and Political Issues in Education*, Volume 1, *Encyclopedia of Language and Education* (2nd edn). New York: Springer, 3–17.

—— and Robert Phillipson (1994) Linguistic Human Rights, Past and Present, in Tove Skutnabb-Kangas and Robert Phillipson (eds), in collaboration with Mart Rannut, *Linguistic Human Rights. Overcoming Linguistic Discrimination*. Berlin and New York: Mouton de Gruyter, 71–110.

—— ——, Ajit K. Mohanty, and Minati Panda (eds) (2009) *Social Justice Through Multilingual Education*. Bristol, Buffalo, NY, and Toronto: Multilingual Matters.

Smalls, D. (2004) Linguistic Profiling and the Law, *Stanford Law and Policy Review* 15: 579–604.

Smith, Linda Tuhiwai (1999) *Deconstructing Methodologies: Research and Indigenous Peoples*. Dunedin: University of Otago Press; New York: Zed Books.

Smith, Viktor (2003) Linguistic Diversity and the Convergence of European Legal Systems and Cultures: Is Legrand's Pessimism Justified?, *Copenhagen Studies in Language* 29:139–51.

Soames, Scott (2003) Higher-Order Vagueness for Partially Defined Predicates, in J. C. Beall (ed.), *Liars and Heaps. New Essays on Paradox*. Oxford: Clarendon, 128–50.

—— (2009) Interpreting Legal Texts: What Is, and What Is Not Special about Legal Texts, in Scott Soames, *Philosophical Essays*, vol. 1, Princeton, NJ: Princeton University Press, 403–23.

—— (2010) The Possibility of Partial Definition, in Richard Dietz und Sebastiano Moruzzi (eds), *Cuts and Clouds. Vagueness, its Nature, and its Logic*. Oxford, New York: Oxford University Press, 46–62.

—— (2011a) What Vagueness and Inconsistency Tell Us about Interpretation, in Andrei A. Marmor and Scott Soames (eds), *Philosophical Foundations of Language in the Law*. Oxford: Oxford University Press, 31–57.

—— (2011b) Vagueness and the Law, in: Andrei Marmor (ed.), *The Routledge Companion to Philosophy of Law*. New York: Routledge, forthcoming 2012; <http://www.bcf.usc.edu/~soames/forthcoming_papers/> accessed September 30, 2011.

Sobkowiak, Wlodzimierz (1997) Silence and Markedness Theory, in Adam Jaworski (ed.), *Silence: Interdisciplinary Perspectives*. Berlin: Mouton de Gruyter.

Solan, Lawrence M. (1993) *The Language of Judges*. Chicago: The University of Chicago Press.

—— (1997) Learning our Limits: The Decline of Textualism in Statutory Cases, *Wisconsin Law Review* 1997:235–83.

—— (2005) Vagueness and Ambiguity in Legal Interpretation, in Vijay K. Bhatia (ed.), *Vagueness in Normative Texts*. Bern: Lang, 73–96.

—— (2009) The Interpretation of Multilingual Statutes by the European Court of Justice, *Brooklyn Journal of International Law* 34(2):277–301.

Solan, Lawrence M. (2010) *The Language of Statutes: Laws and their Interpretation*. Chicago: University of Chicago Press.

—— and Peter M. Tiersma (2003) Hearing Voices: Speaker Identification in Court, *Hastings Law Journal* 54:373–435.

—— and —— (2005) *Speaking of Crime: The Language of Criminal Justice*. Chicago: University of Chicago Press.

Solum, Lawrence B. (2008) Semantic Originalism; <http://papers.ssrn.com/sol3/papers.cfm?abstract_id=1120244> accessed September 5, 2011.

Sorensen, Roy (1989) The Ambiguity of Vagueness and Precision, *Pacific Philosophical Quarterly* 70:174–83.

—— (2001) Vagueness has No Function in Law, *Legal Theory* 7:387–417.

—— (2004) *Vagueness and Contradiction*. Oxford: Clarendon Press.

—— (2006) *Vagueness*; <http://plato.stanford.edu/entries/vagueness/> accessed September 29, 2009.

—— (2007) Vagueness and the Logic of Ordinary Language, in Dale Jacquette (ed.), *Philosophy of Logic*. Amsterdam: Elsevier, 155–71.

Soriano, Leonor Moral (2003) A Modest Notion of Coherence in Legal Reasoning. A Model for the European Court of Justice, *Ratio Juris* 16(3):296–323.

Sourioux, Jean-Louis and Pierre Lerat (1975) *Le langage du droit*. Paris: Presses Universitaires de France.

Sowell, Elizabeth R., Paul M. Thompson, Colin J. Holmes, Terry L. Jernigan, and Arthur W. Toga (1999) In Vivo Evidence for Post-adolescent Brain Maturation in Frontal and Striatal Regions, *Nature* 2:859–61.

Spassova, Maria (2006) Las Marcas Sintácticas de Atribución Forense de Autoría de Textos Escritos en Español. Master's Thesis, Institut Universitari di Lingüística Aplicada, Universitat Pompeu Fabra, Barcelona.

Spence, Melanie J., Pamela R. Rollins, and Susan Jerger (2002) Children's Recognition of Cartoon Voices, *Journal of Speech, Language, and Hearing Research* 45: 214–22.

Sperber, Dan and Deirdre Wilson (1986) *Relevance: Communication and Cognition*. Oxford: Basil Blackwell.

Spivak, Gayatri Chakravorty (2008) *Other Asias*. Oxford: Blackwell Publishing.

St Vincent, S. and T. Hamilton (nd/post-2001) Author Identification with Simple Statistical Methods. Department of Computer Science, Swarthmore College, Swarthmore, PA; <http://www.linguisticevidence.org> accessed October 10, 2011.

Stahl, Steven A. and William E. Nagy (2006) *Teaching Word Meanings*. New York: Routledge.

Stamatatos, Efstathios (2008) Author Identification: Using Text Sampling to Handle the Class Imbalance Problem, *Information Processing and Management* 44:2.

—— (2009) A Survey of Modern Authorship Attribution Methods, *Journal of the American Society for Information Science and Technology* 60(3):583–56.

Stavropoulos, Nicos (1996) *Objectivity in Law*. Oxford: Clarendon Press.

Stein, Benno and Sven Meyer zu Eißen. (2007) Fingerprint-based Similarity Search and its Applications, in Kurt Kremer and Wolker Macho (eds), *Forschung und wissenschaftliches Rechnen 2006*. Gesellschaft für wissenschaftliche Datenverarbeitung, 85–98.

——, Nedim Lipka, and Peter Prettenhofer (2011) Intrinsic Plagiarism Analysis, *Language Resources and Evaluation* 45(1):63–82.

Steinberg, Laurence (2008) A Social Neuroscience Perspective on Adolescent Risk Taking, *Developmental Review* 28:78–106.

——and Elizabeth Cauffman (1996) Maturity of Judgment in Adolescence: Psychosocial Factors in Adolescent Decision Making, *Law and Human Behavior* 20:249–72.

——and Kathryn C. Monohan (2007) Age Differences in Resistance to Peer Influence, *Developmental Psychology* 43:1531–43.

——and Elizabeth S. Scott (2003) Less Guilty by Reason of Adolescence, *American Psychologist* 58:1009–18.

Steiner, George (1998) *After Babel: Aspects of Language and Translation* (3rd edn). Oxford, New York, Toronto: Oxford University Press.

Stenstrom, Anna-Brita (1984) *Questions and Responses in English Conversation.* Malmo: Liber Forlag.

Stern, Steven E., John W. Mullennix, Olivier Corneille, and Johanne Huart (2007) Distortions in the Memory of the Pitch of Speech, *Experimental Psychology* 54:148–60.

Stevens, Kenneth N. (1998) *Acoustic Phonetics.* Cambridge, MA: MIT Press.

Stoel, Max van der (1999) *Report on the Linguistic Rights of Persons Belonging to National Minorities in the OSCE Area. + Annex. Replies from OSCE Participating States.* The Hague: OSCE High Commissioner on National Minorities.

Stolfo, Marco (2009) Unity in Diversity: The Role of the European Parliament in Promoting Minority Languages in Europe, in Susanna Pertot, Tom M. S. Priestly, and Colin H. Williams (eds), *Rights, Promotion and Integration Issues for Minority Languages in Europe.* Basingstoke: Palgrave Macmillan, 32–43.

Strauss, Marcy (2001) Silence, *Loyola Los Angeles Law Review* 35:101–62.

Stroud, Christopher (2009) Commentary, *Current Anthropology* 50(4):434–5.

Strouhal, Ernst (1986) Rechtssprache und Bürokratismus, in T. Öhlinger (ed.), *Recht und Sprache.* Vienna: Manz.

Stubbs, Michael (2006) Language Corpora, in Alan Davies and Catherine Elder (eds), *The Handbook of Applied Linguistics.* Oxford: Blackwell Publishing Ltd., 106–32.

Stygall, Gail (1994) *Trial Language: Differential Discourse Processing and Discursive Formation.* Amsterdam and Philadelphia: Benjamins.

——(2001) A Different Class of Witnesses: Experts in the Courtroom, *Discourse Studies* 3(3):327–49.

——(2009) Guiding Principles: Forensic Linguistics and Codes of Ethics in Other Fields and Professions, *International Journal of Speech, Language and the Law* 16(2):253–66.

Sullivan, Ruth (2008) *Sullivan on the Construction of Statutes* (5th edn). Markham, Ontario: LexisNexis Canada.

Sundby, Scott E. (2005) *A Life and Death Decision: A Jury Weighs the Death Penalty.* New York: Palgrave Macmillan.

Swales, John M. (1990) *Genre Analysis.* Cambridge: Cambridge University Press.

—— and Vijay K. Bhatia (1983) An Approach to the Linguistic Study of Legal Documents, *Fachsprache* 5(3):98–108.

Swann, Jerre B. Sr. (2003) Dilution Redefined for the Year 2002, *Trademark Review* 92:585–623.

Sweller, John (1988) Cognitive Load During Problem Solving: Effects on Learning, *Cognitive Science* 12:257–85.

Swiss Federal Office for Migration (2010) Analyses of Origin: Reactions from the Academic World and Further Development; <http://www.bfm.admin.ch/bfm/en/home/themen/migration_analysen/sprachanalysen/lingua/reaktionen.html> accessed August 23, 2010.

Szilágyi, N. Sándor [1994] (2003) Törvény az etnikai és nyelvi identitással kapcsolatos jogokról, valamint az etnikai é nyelvi közösségek méltányos és harmonikus együttéléséről (Bill on the Rights Concerning Ethnic and Linguistic Identity, and the Fair and Harmonious Coexistence of Ethnic and Linguistic Communities), in *Mi egy más: Közéleti irások.* Kolozsvár: Kalota Könyvkiadó, 576–664.

Tagg, Caroline (2009) A Corpus Linguistic Study of SMS Text Messaging, unpublished PhD dissertation. The University of Birmingham, <http://etheses.bham.ac.uk/253/> accessed September 30, 2011.

Tagliamonte, Sali (2006) *Analysing Sociolinguistic Variation*. Cambridge: Cambridge University Press.

Tallon, Dennis (1995) Français juridique et science du droit: quelques observations, in Gérard Snow and Jacques Vanderlinden (eds), *Français juridique et science du droit*. Bruxelles: Bruylant, 339–49.

Tannen, Deborah (1985) Silence: Anything But, in Deborah Tannen and Muriel Saville-Troike (eds), *Perspectives on Silence*. Norwood, NJ: Ablex Publishing.

—— and Muriel Saville-Troike (eds) (1985) *Perspectives on Silence*. Norwood, NJ: Ablex.

Tax, Blanche (2010) The Use of Expert Evidence in Asylum Procedures by EU Member States—The Case for Harmonised Procedural Safeguards. In Karin Zwaan, Pieter Muysken, and Maaike Verrips (eds), *Language and Origin. The Role of Language in European Asylum Procedures: A Linguistic and Legal Survey*. Nijmegen: Wolf Legal Publishers, 225–32.

Tebo, Margaret Graham (2006) Flying Under the Radar, *American Bar Association Journal* January: 34, 36.

Teplin, Linda A., Karen M. Abram, Gary M. McClelland, Mina K. Dulcan, and Amy A. Mericle (2002) Psychiatric Disorders in Youth in Juvenile Detention, *Archives of General Psychiatry* 59:1133–43.

Texas Youth Commission (2006) Commitment Profile for New Commitments: Fiscal Years 2002–2006; <http://www.tyc.state.tx.us/research/profile.html> accessed June 1, 2009.

Thije, Jan D. ten (2008) Language Politics at European Borders: The Language Analysis Interview of Asylum Seekers in the Netherlands, in Georges Lüdi, Kurt Seelmann, and Beat Sitter-Liver (eds), *Sprachenvielfalt und Kulturfrieden Sprachminderheit—Einsprachigkeit—Mehrsprachigkeit: Probleme und Chancen sprachlicher Vielfalt*. Fribourg: Paulus-Verlag / Academic Press, and Stuttgart: Kohlhammer Verlag, 227–51.

Thompson, Cecilia (2001) The Protection of Minorities within the United Nations. In Snežana Trifunovska (ed.), *Minority Rights in Europe*, The Hague: Asser Press, 115–38.

Thompson, Charles P. (1985) Voice Identification: Speaker Identifiability and a Correction of the Record Regarding Sex Effects, *Human Learning* 4:19–27.

—— (1987) A Language Effect in Voice Identification, *Applied Cognitive Psychology* 1:121–31.

Thornberry, Patrick (1991) *International Law and the Rights of Minorities*. Oxford: Clarendon Press.

—— (1997) Minority Rights, in Academy of European Law (ed.), *Collected Courses of the Academy of European Law*. Volume VI, Book 2. The Netherlands: Kluwer Law International, 307–90.

—— (2002) *Indigenous Peoples and Human Rights*. Manchester: Manchester University Press.

—— and María Amor Martin Estébanez (eds) (2004) *Minority Rights in Europe (A Review of the Work and Standards of the Council of Europe)*. Strasbourg Cedex: Council of Europe Publishing.

—— and Dianna Gibbons (1997) Education and Minority Rights: A Short Survey of International Standards, *International Journal on Minority and Group Rights. Special Issue on the Education Rights of National Minorities* 4(2):115–52.

Tiersma, Peter M. (1986) The Language of Offer and Acceptance: Speech Acts and the Question of Intent, *California Law Review* 74:189–232.

—— (1987) The Language of Defamation, *Texas Law Review* 66:303–50.

—— (1990) The Language of Perjury: "Literal Truth," Ambiguity, and False Statement Requirement, *Southern California Law Review* 63:373–431.

—— (1992) Reassessing Unilateral Contracts: The Role of Offer, Acceptance and Promise, *UC Davis Law Review* 26:1–86.

—— (1995a) The Language of Silence, *Rutgers Law Review* 48:1–99.

—— (1995b) Dictionaries and Death: Do Capital Jurors Understand Mitigation?, *Utah Law Review* 1995:1–49.

—— (1999) *Legal Language.* Chicago and London: University of Chicago Press.

—— (2001) The Rocky Road to Legal Reform: Improving the Language of Jury Instructions, *Brooklyn Law Review* 66:1081–119.

—— (2002) The Language and Law of Product Warnings, in Janet Cotterill (ed.), *Language in the Legal Process.* Houndmills: Palgrave, 54–71.

—— (2004) Plagiarism vs Copyright; <https://www.jiscmail.ac.uk/cgi-bin/webadmin?A2=ind04&L=FORENSIC-LINGUISTICS&P=R7765>, posted August 19, 2004, accessed February 8, 2010.

—— (2006a) Some Myths About Legal Language, *Law, Culture and the Humanities* 2:29–50.

—— (2006b) Toward More Understandable Jury Instructions: The California Experience, *Criminal Justice* Spring: 5–11.

—— (2010) *Parchment, Paper, Pixels: Law and the Technologies of Communication.* Chicago: University of Chicago Press.

—— and Laurence M. Solan (2002) The Linguist on the Witness Stand: Forensic Linguistics in American Courts, *Language* 78:221–39.

Toggenburg, Gabriel (2008) *The EU's Evolving Policies vis-à-vis Minorities: A Play in Four Parts and an Open End.* Bolzano/Bozen: EURAC.

Tognini-Bonelli, Elena (2001) *Corpus Linguistics at Work.* Amsterdam: John Benjamins.

Tollefson, James W. (1991) *Planning Language, Planning Inequality.* London and New York: Longman.

—— and Amy B. M. Tsui (2003) Contexts of Medium-of-Instruction Policy, in James W. Tollefson and Amy B. M. Tsui (eds), *Medium of Instruction Policies. Which Agenda? Whose Agenda?* Mahwah, NJ: Lawrence Erlbaum, 283–94.

Tomaševski, Katarina (1996) International Prospects for the Future of the Welfare State, in *Reconceptualizing the Welfare State.* Copenhagen: The Danish Centre for Human Rights, 100–17.

—— (2000) *Economic, Social and Cultural Rights. Progress Report of the Special Rapporteur on the Right to Education, Katarina Tomaševski, Submitted in Accordance with Commission on Human Rights resolution 1999/25.* United Nations, Economic and Social Council, E/CN.4/2000/6, February 1, 2000.

Tonkin, Humphrey (2003) *Issues in Global Education: Language and Society.* Occasional Papers from the American Forum for Global Education, Number 178.

Torres Carballal, Pablo de (1988) Trends in Legal Translation: The Focusing of Legal Translation through Comparative Law, in Paul Nekeman (ed.), *Translation, Our Future, XIth World Congress of FIT.* Maastricht: Euroterm, 447–50.

Tosi, Oscar, Herbert Oyer, William Lashbrook, Charles Pedrey, Julie Nicol, and Ernest Nash (1972) Experiment on Voice Identification, *Journal of the Acoustical Society of America* 51:2030–043.

Travis, Alan (2003) Language Tests to Uncover Bogus Iraqi Asylum Seekers, *The Guardian* March 12.

Trinch, Shonna L. (2003) *Latinas' Narratives of Domestic Abuse: Discrepant Versions of Violence*. Amsterdam and Philadelphia: Benjamins.

Troebst, Stefan (1999) Preface and Acknowledgements, in María Amor Martín Estébanez and Kinga Gál, *Implementing the Framework Convention for the Protection of National Minorities*. Flensburg: ECMI, 3.

Troisfontaines, Paul (1981) Le langage judiciaire, *Annales de la Faculté de droit, d'économie et de sciences sociales de Liège* 1981: 153–69.

Trosborg, Anna (1995) Introduction, in Anna Trosborg (ed.), *Laying down the Law—Discourse Analysis of Legal Institutions*. Special issue of *Journal of Pragmatics* 23(1):1–5.

—— (1997a) Contracts as Social Action, in Britt-Louise Gunnarsson, Per Linell, and Bengt Nordberg (eds), *The Construction of Professional Discourse*. London: Longman.

—— (1997b) *Rhetorical Strategies in Legal Language: Discourse Analysis of Statutes and Contracts*. Tübingen: Gunter Narr Verlag.

Turell, M. Teresa (2008) Plagiarism, in John Gibbons and M. Teresa Turell (eds), *Dimensions of Forensic Linguistics*. Amsterdam: Benjamins, 265–99.

——, Maria Spassova, and Jordi Cicres (eds) (2007) *Proceedings of the Second European IAFL Conference on Forensic Linguistics/Language and Law*. Barcelona: Institut Universitari de Lingüística Aplicada.

Turi, Joseph G. (1990) Le droit linguistique et les droits linguistiques, *Cahiers de Droit* 31:642.

Turnbull, William (2003) *Language in Action: Psychological Models of Conversation*. London: Routledge.

Tushnet, Mark (1991) Critical Legal Studies: A Political History, *Yale Law Journal* 100:1515–44.

Tyler, Tom R. (1990) *Why People Obey the Law*. New Haven, CT: Yale University Press.

UDI (2009) *Specified Requirements for Language Analysis for the Norwegian Immigration Administration*. Oslo: Utlendings Direktoratet, July.

UKAIT (2007) *Practice Directions*, sec. 8A. London: Asylum and Immigration Tribunal.

UNESCO (1997) Working Document, Intergovernmental Conference on Language Policies in Africa, Harare, March 17–21.

United Nations (1951) Convention Relating to the Status of Refugees; <http://www.unhcr.org/protect/PROTECTION/3b66c2aa10.pdf> accessed September 7, 2011.

United Nations High Commissioner for Refugees (n.d.) RefWorld Site for RSD Information; <www.unhcr.org/refworld> accessed September 7, 2011.

Usher, J. A. (1981) Language and the European ECJ, *International Contract Law and Finance Review* 3: 227–85.

van Calster, Geert, *see* Calster, Geert van

van Fraassen, Bas, *see* Fraassen, Bas van

van Gerven, W., *see* Gerven, W. van

van Hoecke, Mark, *see* Hoecke, Mark van

van Koppen, Peter, *see* Koppen, Peter van

van Lancker, D., *see* Lancker, D. van

van Wallendael, Lori R., *see* Wallendael, Lori R. van

Vanags, Thea, Marie Carroll, and Timothy J. Perfect (2005) Verbal Overshadowing: A Sound Theory in Voice Recognition, *Applied Cognitive Psychology* 19:1127–44.

Vanheule, Dirk (2010) The Use of Language Analysis in the Belgian Asylum Procedure, in Karin Zwaan, Pieter Muysken, and Maaike Verrips (eds), *Language and Origin. The Role of Language in European Asylum Procedures: A Linguistic and Legal Survey*. Nijmegen: Wolf Legal Publishers, 177–85.

Várady, Tibor (2006) *Language and Translation in International Commercial Arbitration from the Constitution of the Arbitral Tribunal through Recognition and Enforcement Proceedings*. The Hague: T.M.C. Asser Pr., and West Nyack, NY: Cambridge University Press.

Varzi, Achille C. (2007) Supervaluationism and its Logics, *Mind* 116:633–75.

Vedsted-Hansen, Jens (2010) The Use of Language Analysis in the Danish Asylum Procedure, in Karin Zwaan, Pieter Muysken, and Maaike Verrips (eds), *Language and Origin. The Role of Language in European Asylum Procedures: A Linguistic and Legal Survey*. Nijmegen: Wolf Legal Publishers, 199–207.

Verma, Babu Ram (1988) *Islamic Law-Personal Being Commentaries on Mohammedan Law (in India, Pakistan and Bangladesh)* (6th edn by Mirza Hameedullah Beg and Babu Ram Verma). Allahabad: Law Publishers [India] Private Limited.

Vermeule, Adrian (2006) *Judging Under Uncertainty: An Institutional Theory of Legal Interpretation*. Cambridge, MA: Harvard University Press.

Vermeulen, Jos (2009) "Beware of the Distance": Evaluation of Spectral Measurements of Synthetic Vowels Re-recorded at Different Distances. MSc dissertation, University of York.

Verrips, Maaike (2010) Language Analysis and Contra-expertise in the Dutch Asylum Procedure, *International Journal of Speech, Language & the Law* 17(2):279–94.

—— (2011) LADO and the Pressure to Draw Strong Conclusions. A Response to Tina Cambier-Langeveld, *International Journal of Speech, Language and the Law* 18(1):131–43.

Viljoen, Jodi L. and Ronald Roesch (2005) Competence to Waive Interrogation Rights and Adjudicative Competence in Adolescent Defendants: Cognitive Development, Attorney Contact, and Psychological Symptoms, *Law and Human Behavior* 29:723–42.

—— Jessica Klaver, and Ronald Roesch (2005) Legal Decisions of Preadolescent and Adolescent Defendants: Predictors of Confessions, Pleas, Communication with Attorneys, and Appeals, *Law and Human Behavior* 29:253–77.

—— Ronald Roesch, and Patricia A. Zapf (2002) An Examination of the Relationship between Competency to Stand Trial, Competency to Waive Interrogation Rights, and Psychopathology, *Law and Human Behavior* 25:481–506.

—— Patricia A. Zapf, and Ronald Roesch (2007) Adjudicative Competence and Comprehension of *Miranda* Rights in Adolescent Defendants: A Comparison of Legal Standards, *Behavioral Sciences and the Law* 25:1–19.

Vogenauer, Stefan (2005) Eine Gemeineuropäische Methodenlehre des Rechts-Plädoyer und Programm, *Zeitschrift für Europäisches Privatrecht* 2005(2):234–65.

—— (2006) Statutory Interpretation, in Jan M. Smits (ed.), *Elgar Encyclopaedia of Comparative Law*. Northhampton, MA: Edward Elgar Publishing.

von Bar, Christian, *see* Bar, Christian von

von Polenz, Peter, *see* Polenz, Peter von

von Savigny, Eike, *see* Savigny, Eike von

Wadensjö, Cecilia (1998) *Interpreting as Interaction*. New York: Longman.

Waismann, Friedrich (1945) Verifiability, in *Proceedings of the Aristotelian Society, Supplementary Volume* 19:119–50.

—— (1979) *Ludwig Wittgenstein and the Vienna Circle* (ed. B. F. McGuiness). Oxford: Basil Blackwell.

Waldron, Jeremy (1994) Vagueness in Law and Language. Some Philosophical Issues, *California Law Review* 82:509–40.

—— (2011) Vagueness and the Guidance of Action, in Andrei A. Marmor and Scott Soames (eds), *Philosophical Foundations of Language in the Law*. Oxford: Oxford University Press, 58–82.

Walker, Anne Graffam (1985) The Two Faces of Silence: The Effect of Witness Hesitancy on Lawyers' Impressions, in Deborah Tannen and Muriel Saville-Troike (eds), *Perspectives on Silence*. Norwood, NJ: Ablex Publishing.

Wallendael, Lori R. van, Amy Surace, Deborah Hall Parsons, and Melissa Brown (1994) "Earwitness" Voice Recognition: Factors Affecting Accuracy and Impact on Jurors, *Applied Cognitive Psychology* 8:661–77.

Walter, Stephen and Carol Benson (2012) Language Policy and Medium of Instruction in Formal Education. In Bernard Spolsky (ed.), *The Cambridge Handbook of Language Policy*. Cambridge: Cambridge University Press, 278–300.

Wang Guiyuan (2008) *Chinese Characters and Chinese History and Culture*. Renmin: University of China.

Wang, Yuan, Yunhong Wang, and Tieniu Tan (2004) Combining Fingerprint and Voiceprint Biometrics for Identity Verification: An Experimental Comparison. In David Zhang and Amil K. Jain (eds), *International Conference on Biometric Authentication 2004* (LNCS 3072) Berlin: Springer-Verlag, 663–70.

Ward, James D. (2004) Jury Practice: The New Civil Jury Instructions, *California Lawyer* February: 38–40.

Ward-Lonergan, Jeannene M., Betty Z. Liles, and Angela M. Anderson (1998) Listening Comprehension and Recall Abilities in Adolescents with Language-learning Disabilities and without Disabilities for Social Studies Lectures, *Journal of Communication Disorders* 31:1–32.

Wascher, James D. (2005) The Long March Toward Plain English Jury Instructions, *Chicago Bar Association Record* February–March:50–5.

Wei, Li (2000) Dimensions of Bilingualism, in Li Wei (ed.), *The Bilingualism Reader*. London: Routledge, 2–21.

Weigand, Edda (2008) Towards a Common European Legal Thinking: A Dialogic Challenge, in Hanne Petersen, Anne L. Kjær, Helle Krunke, and Mikael Rask Madsen (eds), *Paradoxes of European Legal Integration*. Aldershot: Ashgate, 235–52.

Weinstein, Brian (1982) *The Civic Tongue: Political Consequences of Language Choices*. New York: Longman.

Wells, John C. (1982) *Accents of English* (3 vols). Cambridge: Cambridge University Press.

Westerhaus, Jennifer (2003) Review of Roger Shuy, *Linguistic Battles in Trademark Disputes*, *International Journal of Speech, Language and the Law* 10(2):292–96.

Weston, Martin (1991) *An English Reader's Guide to the French Legal System*. Oxford: Berg.

White, James B. (1994) *Justice as Translation*. Chicago: The University of Chicago Press.

—— (2005) Translation as a Way of Understanding the Language of Law, in B. Pozzo (ed.), *Ordinary Language and Legal Language*. Milan: Giuffrè, 61–81.

Wiehl, Lia (2002) "Sounding Black" in the Courtroom: Court-Sanctioned Racial Stereotyping, *Harvard Blackletter Law Journal* 18:185–210.

Wilding, John and Susan Cook (2000) Sex Differences and Individual Consistency in Voice Identification, *Perceptual and Motor Skills* 91:535–8.

——, —— and Josh Davis (2000) Sound Familiar?, *The Psychologist* 13:558–62.

Williams, J. Robert G. (2008) Ontic Vagueness and Metaphysical Indeterminacy, *Philosophy Compass* 3:763–88.

Willis, Vanessa (2008) The Government's Use of Pre-*Miranda* Silence in its Case-in-Chief: An Alternative Approach under *Schmerber v. California*, *University of Cincinnati Law Review* 77:741–58.

Wilson, Kim (2009) Language Analysis for the Determination of Origin: Native Speakers vs. Trained Linguists. MSc dissertation in Linguistics, University of York.

Winn, Peter A. (1992) Legal Ritual, in Roberta Kevelson (ed.), *Law and Aesthetics*. New York: Peter Lang.

Winograd, E., N. H. Kerr, and M. J. Spence (1984) Voice Recognition: Effects of Orienting Task, and a Test of Blind Versus Sighted Listeners, *American Journal of Psychology* 97:57–70.

Wittgenstein, Ludwig (1968) *Philosophical Investigations* (3rd edn). New York: Macmillan.

—— (1975) *Philosophical Remarks*. Chicago: University of Chicago Press.

—— (1999) *Philosophical Investigations*. The German text, with a revised English translation by G. E. M. Anscombe. Malden, MA: Blackwell Publishing.

Woehrling, Jean-Marie (2005) *The European Charter for Regional or Minority Languages. A Critical Commentary*. Strasbourg: Council of Europe.

Wolff, H. Ekkehard (1998) Multilingualism, Modernisation, and Post-Literacy: Some Central Issues Concerning the Promotion of Indigenous African Languages in a Democratic Society, in M. Ambrose, J. Read, and V. Webb (comp.), *Workshop Papers: The Role of African Languages in Democratic South Africa*. March 5–6, 1998: University of Pretoria, CentRePoL; <www.np.ac.za/academic/libarts/crpl/1998-03-05-wolff.pdf> accessed July 18, 2008.

Woo, Junda (1994) Arizona Panel Suggests Jury Reforms, *Wall Street Journal*: October 25: B5.

Wood, Lee Alexandra (1996) Voir Dire Hardship-Case Requests and Possible Consequences from Patterns of Interaction, *The SECOL Review* 20(2):182–202.

Woolls, David (2010) *Computational Forensic Linguistics—Searching for Similarity in Large Specialised Corpora*, in Malcolm Coulthard and Alan Johnson (eds), *The Routledge Handbook of Forensic Linguistics*. London: Routledge.

World Resources Institute, World Conservation Union, and United Nations Environment Programme (1992) *Global Biodiversity Strategy: Policy-makers' Guide*. Baltimore: WRI Publications.

Wurm, S. A. and Theo Baumann (2001) *Atlas of World Languages in Danger of Disappearing*. Paris: UNESCO Publishing.

www.Reid.com

Xia Zhengnong (1989) *Cihai (A Comprehensive Dictionary of Chinese Characters and Phraseology)*. Shanghai Dictionary Publishing House.

Yablon, Charles (1987) Law and Metaphysics, *Yale Law Journal* 96:613–66.

Yamanaka, Nobuhiko (1995) On Indirect Threats, *International Journal of Semiotics Law* 8:37.

Yan Fu, 1981. *The Spirit of the Laws*. Beijing: Commercial Press.

Yarmey, A. Daniel (1986) Verbal, Visual and Voice Identification of a Rape Suspect Under Different Levels of Illumination, *Journal of Applied Psychology* 71:363–70.

—— (1991a) Descriptions of Distinctive and Non-Distinctive Voices over Time, *Journal of the Forensic Science Society* 31:421–8.

—— (1991b) Voice Identification Over the Telephone, *Journal of Applied Social Psychology* 21:1868–76.

Yarmey, A. Daniel (1993) Stereotypes and Recognition Memory for Faces and Voices of Good Guys and Bad Guys, *Applied Cognitive Psychology* 7:419–31.

—— (1995) Earwitness Speaker Identification, *Psychology, Public Policy, and Law* 1:792–816.

—— (2001a) The Older Eyewitness, in M. B. Rothman, B. D. Dunlop, and P. Entzel (eds), *Elders, Crime and the Criminal Justice System*. New York: Springer.

—— (2001b) Earwitness Descriptions and Speaker Identification, *Forensic Linguistics* 8:113–22.

—— (2003) Earwitness Descriptions Over the Telephone and in Field Settings, *Forensic Linguistics* 10:65–77.

—— (2004) Common-Sense Beliefs, Recognition and the Identification of Familiar and Unfamiliar Speakers from Verbal and Non-Linguistic Vocalizations, *International Journal of Speech, Language and the Law* 11:267–77.

—— (2007) The Psychology of Speaker Identification and Earwitness Memory, in R. C. L. Lindsay, David F. Ross, J. Don Reid, and Michael Toglia (eds), *Handbook of Eyewitness Psychology Vol. 2: Memory for People*. Mahwah, NJ: Lawrence Erlbaum Associates.

—— (2008) Showups, in Brian L. Cutler (ed.), *Encyclopedia of Psychology and Law*. Thousand Oaks, CA: Sage Reference.

—— and Eva Matthys (1992) Voice Identification of an Abductor, *Applied Cognitive Psychology* 6:367–77.

——, A. Linda Yarmey, and Meagan J. Yarmey (1994) Face and Voice Identifications in Show-ups and Lineups, *Applied Cognitive Psychology* 8:453–64.

—— —— ——, and Lisa Parliament (2001) Commonsense Beliefs and the Identification of Familiar Voices, *Applied Cognitive Psychology* 15:283–99.

——, Meagan J. Yarmey, and Leah Todd (2008) Frances McGehee (1912–2004): The First Earwitness Researcher, *Perceptual and Motor Skills* 106:387–94.

Zaichkowsky, Judith Lynne (2006) *The Psychology Behind Trademark Infringement and Counterfeiting*. Hillsdale, NJ: Lawrence Erlbaum Associates, Inc.

Zambrano-Paff, Marjorie (2008) Cortesía y Conversación: de lo Escrito a lo Oral, in Antonio Briz, Antonio Hidalgo, Marta Albelda, Josefa Conteras, and Nieves Hernández Flores (eds), *Proceedings of the 3rd Colloquium of the EDICE Program*. Valencia/Stockholm: Universidad de Valencia/Programa EDICE.

Zhang, Mo (2006) *Chinese Contract Law: Theory and Practice*. Leiden: Martinus Nijhoff Publishers.

Zimmerman, Don H. (1969) Record-Keeping and the Intake Process in a Public Welfare Agency, in Stanton Wheeler (ed.), *On Record: Files and Dossiers in American Life*. New York: Russell Sage, 319–54.

Zwaan, Karin (ed.) (2007) *De taalanalyse in de Nederlandse asielprocedure. Een juridische en linguïstische verkenning*. Nijmegen: Wolf Legal Publishers.

——, Pieter Muysken, and Maaike Verrips (eds) (2010) *Language and Origin. The Role of Language in European Asylum Procedures: A Linguistic and Legal Survey*. Nijmegen: Wolf Legal Publishers.

Index

generic structure 65–6
Geneva Convention 533
genre 60–6
German 251, 260, 262, 264
Germany 16–17, 18, 22, 37, 250, 538
Ghana 279
globalized legal order 25–26; 175–7, 182–5
gratuitous promises 105, 107, 109, 111
Greece 262
Greek 15
Grice, Paul 154, 330, 331, 345, 349–50
Guarantee Clause (US Constitution) 126
Guidelines for the Use of Language
    Analysis 535, 537, 538, 542, 544–46
Guinea 279

Hague Conventions 197–8
Hamer v Sidway 107
Hart, H. L. A. 149–152
Hayakawa, S.I. 253
hearsay 295, 376
hedging 322
heroin 572
Hindu Law 29
homicide 364
    Japanese law of 384, 388–94
homonymy 129–30, 132
human rights 235–7, 280
Hungary 261
hypotaxis 41, 43, 46

IAFPA (International Association for Forensic
    Phonetics and Acoustics) 560, 561, 570
IATE 38
Iceland 18
if-clauses 64
illocutions, types of 102–4, 108
immediacy 409, 411n
immersion, as educational method 258
immigration 253
    and asylum 427–430
indeterminacy 6, 88, 114, 128–9, 132–6, 146–9,
    151–5, 290
indictments 62, 383, 412–3
indigenous/tribal peoples 235–247

in North America 248–50
Indonesia 17
inferences. *See* Cooperative Principle
inquisitorial system of justice 409–10
insurance policies 61, 62, 64
Inter-Active Terminology for Europe 38
interdiscursivity 66
International Commission of Enquiry 562
International Plain Language Working
    Group 67
International Trademark Association 449
interpretation of statutes 87–99, 145–55
    intentionalism 154
    interpretation vs. construction 15–5
    judicial discretion 149–52
    legislative intent 87, 97, 152–154, 155
    linguistics 145
    literary theory 145
    methods of 217–31
    of multilingual texts 197, 199
    purpose 91
    teleological 217, 220–31
    translation errors 229–31
    uniform interpretation and application of
        EU Law 217, 218, 220, 222–3, 231
interpreters, and police caution 324–5
    consecutive 421, 422, 431, 432
    in African courts 282
    in asylum proceedings 539, 540, 541
    simultaneous 421, 422, 432
interrogation 295–8, 312–25, 354–66, 425
    in inquisitorial system 411, 416
    interpreters' role in 423–7
    maximization 363, 365
    minimization 363, 365
    offers made during 361–2
    phases of 360
    promises of leniency, 354, 365–6
    sympathetic detective with a time-limited
        offer 361, 362
    theme development method 363–5
intertextuality 66
intoxicants 326, 571–2
invasion of privacy 465
investigation, documentary method of 411
    interview 312–25
    preliminary 410, 411

OXFORD HANDBOOKS IN LINGUISTICS

Lightning Source UK Ltd.
Milton Keynes UK
UKOW05f0057241215

265299UK00002B/2/P

9 780198 744962